Frommer's®

Bali & L

2nd Edition

by Jen Lin-Liu & Candice Lee

WILEY

John Wiley & Sons, Inc.

Published by:

JOHN WILEY & SONS, INC.

Copyright © 2012 John Wiley & Sons Inc, The Atrium, Southern Gate, Chichester,
West Sussex PO19 8SQ, UK
Telephone (+44) 1243 779777
Email (for orders and customer service enquiries): cs-books@wiley.co.uk. Visit our Home Page on
www.wiley.com

Publisher: Kelly Regan
Production Manager: Daniel Mersey
Editor: Fiona Quinn
Project Editor: Hannah Clement
Cartography: Andrew Murphy
Photo Editor: Cherie Cincilla, Richard H. Fox, Jill Emeny
Front cover photo: Sunrise behind Gunung Agung from the beach in Amed, Bali, Indonesia © Edmund
Lowe / Alamy Images
Back Cover photo: Detail of Yellow crested tucan bird © John Kershaw / Alamy Images

For information on our other products and services or to obtain technical support, please contact our
Customer Care Department within the U.S. at 877/762-2974, outside the U.S. at 317/572-3993 or fax
317/572-4002.

British Library Cataloguing in Publication Data

A catalogue record for this book is available from the British Library
ISBN 978-1-118-09600-0 (pbk), ISBN 978-1-118-22355-0 (ebk), ISBN 978-1-118-23691-8 (ebk),
ISBN 978-1-118-26194-1 (ebk)

Typeset by Wiley Indianapolis Composition Services

Printed and bound in the United States of America

5 4 3 2 1

CONTENTS

LIST OF MAPS

ABOUT THE AUTHORS

After first visiting Bali in 2003, **Jen Lin-Liu** travels to the island frequently and has written about Bali and Lombok for numerous publications including *The New York Times* and *Travel + Leisure*. She is the author of *Serve the People: A Stir-Fried Journey Through China* (Harcourt, 2008) and a forthcoming book about the food of the Silk Road (Riverhead Press). She lives in Beijing, where she lives in the old traditional neighborhoods near the cooking school and restaurant she owns, Black Sesame Kitchen.

Candice Lee has lived in Beijing for the past five years and has worked as a manager and cooking instructor at Black Sesame Kitchen for three years with previous experience working with HIV/AIDS, research, and event managing. She explores, eats, and scrappily finds her way through as many new places as possible (usually by bicycle).

ACKNOWLEDGMENTS

I would like to thank my husband Craig Simons for his hard work in scoping out new gems across Bali and Lombok. I would also like to express my appreciation for Kevin Bell of Bali Eats, Ni Made and the team at the Samaya, and John Halpin of the COMO Shambhala. The team at the Oberoi Lombok was gracious and helped us get out a jam in Lombok — thank you Rudy! Thank you also to editor Fiona Quinn for her input and feedback to make this a better book.

—Jen Lin-Liu

HOW TO CONTACT US

In researching this book, we discovered many wonderful places—hotels, restaurants, shops, and more. We're sure you'll find others. Please tell us about them, so we can share the information with your fellow travelers in upcoming editions. If you were disappointed with a recommendation, we'd love to know that, too. Please write to:

Frommer's Bali & Lombok, 2nd Edition
John Wiley & Sons, Inc. • 111 River St. • Hoboken, NJ 07030-5774

ADVISORY & DISCLAIMER

Travel information can change quickly and unexpectedly, and we strongly advise you to confirm important details locally before traveling, including information on visas, health and safety, traffic and transport, accommodation, shopping and eating out. We also encourage you to stay alert while traveling and to remain aware of your surroundings. Avoid civil disturbances, and keep a close eye on cameras, purses, wallets and other valuables.

While we have endeavored to ensure that the information contained within this guide is accurate and up-to-date at the time of publication, we make no representations or warranties with respect to the accuracy or completeness of the contents of this work and specifically disclaim all warranties, including without limitation warranties of fitness for a particular purpose. We accept no responsibility or liability for any inaccuracy or errors or omissions, or for any inconvenience, loss, damage, costs or expenses of any nature whatsoever incurred or suffered by anyone as a result of any advice or information contained in this guide.

The inclusion of a company, organization or Website in this guide as a service provider and/or potential source of further information does not mean that we endorse them or the information they provide. Be aware that information provided through some Websites may be unreliable and can change without notice. Neither the publisher or author shall be liable for any damages arising herefrom.

FROMMER'S STAR RATINGS, ICONS & ABBREVIATIONS

Every hotel, restaurant, and attraction listing in this guide has been ranked for quality, value, service, amenities, and special features using a **star-rating system.** In country, state, and regional guides, we also rate towns and regions to help you narrow down your choices and budget your time accordingly. Hotels and restaurants are rated on a scale of zero (recommended) to three stars (exceptional). Attractions, shopping, nightlife, towns, and regions are rated according to the following scale: zero stars (recommended), one star (highly recommended), two stars (very highly recommended), and three stars (must-see).

In addition to the star-rating system, we also use **eight feature icons** that point you to the great deals, in-the-know advice, and unique experiences that separate travelers from tourists. Throughout the book, look for:

special finds—those places only insiders know about

fun facts—details that make travelers more informed and their trips more fun

kids—best bets for kids and advice for the whole family

special moments—those experiences that memories are made of

overrated—places or experiences not worth your time or money

insider tips—great ways to save time and money

great values—where to get the best deals

warning—traveler's advisories are usually in effect

The following abbreviations are used for credit cards:

AE	American Express	DISC	Discover	V	Visa
DC	Diners Club	MC	MasterCard		

TRAVEL RESOURCES AT FROMMERS.COM

Frommer's travel resources don't end with this guide. Frommer's website, **www.frommers. com**, has travel information on more than 4,000 destinations. We update features regularly, giving you access to the most current trip-planning information and the best airfare, lodging, and car-rental bargains. You can also listen to podcasts, connect with other Frommers. com members through our active-reader forums, share your travel photos, read blogs from guidebook editors and fellow travelers, and much more.

THE BEST OF
BALI & LOMBOK

Betwen the two Indonesian islands of Bali and Lombok, you can experience it all—from pristine, quiet beaches to a throbbing nightlife scene and more: Culture, world-class surfing, lush rice paddies, volcanic mountain scenery, and fantastic year-round weather. But wait, there's more. The island pair also offers the best-rated resorts at reasonable prices, flawless service, and pampering, cut-rate spa treatments.

A Hindu haven in the Muslim-majority Indonesian archipelago, Bali has for years attracted artists, honeymooners, spiritual seekers, surfers, and those otherwise looking for the "good life," while Lombok attracts more rugged travelers looking for an off-the-beaten-path experience. The Balinese and the people of Lombok have always been accommodating hosts, and their acceptance of different lifestyles has drawn an assortment of "misfit" residents. During your trip, you're destined to meet some real characters, whether they be of the "Kuta cowboy" variety—young Indonesian bachelors trolling the beach for foreign girlfriends—or the cult of New Age, yoga-obsessed foreigners who've settled in the rice paddies of Ubud.

The Balinese practice a unique amalgam of Indian Hindu traditions, Buddhism, ancient Javanese customs, and indigenous, animistic beliefs. The beauty of their faith colors every aspect of life, from fresh flowers strewn everywhere in obeisance to the calm of morning prayer at the temple. During your visit, you're sure to catch the distinctive tones of the gamelan, a xylophone-like instrument, and the gathering of sarong-clad worshipers at the island's ubiquitous temples. Meanwhile, you'll experience a moderate Muslim culture in Lombok. After a decade of ups and downs, Bali's tourism industry is on the upswing. With terrorism fears dwindling, Bali is becoming crowded with more visitors than ever, while Lombok remains the Bali of two decades ago, The movie *Eat, Pray, Love*—disparagingly called Eat, Pay, Leave by some locals—has added to Bali's tourism surge. The rise in the number of tourists has led to overcongested roads, that have doubled travel times around the island, and rampant overdevelopment of bland, indistinguishable-looking villas in the south. But the glut of new villas and developments means that good deals are still available on the island.

You'll likely hear complaints from longtime residents that much of Bali's charm has been lost with its growing villas, strip malls, Western outposts of Starbucks and Dunkin' Donuts, and its sometimes-rowdy nightlife. But get out of south Bali, the center of the island's development, and you'll be rewarded in every direction with quiet villages, pristine scenery, and plenty of time to restore your "inner balance."

THE best UNIQUE BALINESE EXPERIENCES

- **Strolling in a Village in the Morning:** Local color is at its brightest in the mornings in a village in Bali. Take a leisurely stroll and you'll see children in uniform walking hand in hand to school, mothers bringing back the day's provisions from the market, and men and women placing offerings throughout the village and in the temples. It's a stunning start to your day in paradise.

- **Calling on a Balian:** What's a Balian you say? The simplest explanation is a medicine man (or woman) or a spiritual healer. The Balinese visit them for cures to illness, emotional distress, and all manner of problems. Currently, you'll hear the name **Ketut Lyer** bandied about as the healer made famous by Elizabeth Gilbert's book *Eat, Pray, Love*. Eager seekers form lines running round the block of his Ubud home-cum-practice, so don't bother going there. Instead ask a Balinese friend or someone at your hotel where they recommend you go, as every good Balinese has a Balian. Appointments aren't necessary and there are normally no phone calls you can make to find your special healer: It's all about just showing up on a first-come, first-served basis, trying your luck, and leaving a donation. Good Balians don't discuss money with a client. What you leave is what you decide to leave and many Balinese without much spare cash leave rice and simple offerings. Short of scouring the villages for your own healer, the best and most professional healers can be found at **Five Elements,** a retreat in Ubud (see p. 44).

- **Eating with Locals at a Warung:** Warungs (roadside cafes) serve some of the best local food on the island. Pull up a well-worn wooden stool to a group table and pick your food from the buffet. One of the best warungs is in Seminyak, the **Warung Sulawesi** (p. 88), where flavors of Bali are mixed with the piquant offerings of far-flung Indonesian islands. In Ubud, even though it is well discovered, go for the suckling pig at **Ibu Oka** (p. 184). Ask anyone where it is and they'll point you in the right direction.

- **Participating in a Ceremony:** No matter where you're staying in Bali, you can get yourself invited to a ceremony through either a friendly villa staff member or your hotel concierge. Pick up the spiritual vibe, keeping in mind that "ceremony" is often just a word that replaces "celebration." Don't forget your sash and sarong.

- **Watching a Balinese Dance Performance:** Bali's highly stylized traditional dances have evolved from ancient Hindu rites and often take the performer into a trancelike state. The best way to see such a performance is in a temple, but dances at public theaters and even on hotel grounds can be equally entrancing. Don't pass up an opportunity to see the rarely performed *Oleg Tambulilingan:* It's a sexy virtuoso duet depicting a randy male bumblebee courting a coy lady bee.

THE best TEMPLES

Take a guide when visiting temples and you'll understand far more about each one: The layout and style of most temples is the same, and so it's the specific history that brings out the life in them. Always dress appropriately and observe temple rules.

- **Pura Besakih:** This temple makes the "Best of" solely because of its importance and its spectacular ceremonies. It's the largest and the holiest, known as the "Mother Temple," and translates literally as the "Temple of Spiritual Happiness." Go early, avoid the crowds, and take your own guide. See p. 231.
- **Pura Goa Giri Putri:** This is quite an extraordinary experience. You enter the cave, on one side of the mountain, on your hands and knees through a small gap in the rocks, and then pass 450m (1,500 ft.) inside the mountain only to come out the other side on to a beautiful valley. A visit here justifies a day trip to Nusa Penida on its merits alone. See p. 131.
- **Pura Gunung Kawi:** Bali's "Valley of the Kings" is hewn in the cliffs, and on both sides of the river are massive commemorative monuments to 11th-century kings and queens. Strictly speaking, Gunung Kawi isn't a temple, but it's nevertheless considered a holy place. A visit here is an unforgettable experience. See p. 186.
- **Pura Lempuyang:** Only for the fit and willing, it takes some 1,700 winding steps up through the forested slopes of Mount Lempuyang to reach Pura Lempuyang, and the views on to Mount Agung are divine. See p. 242.
- **Pura Luhur Batukaru:** This is one of the six axial temples sacred to all Hindu Balinese and one of the most ancient sacred sites on the island. Majestically nestled in the jungle, at the head of the valley on the slopes of Batukaru, this is a wonderful place to wander round. See p. 218.
- **Pura Luhur Uluwatu:** This is a dramatically perched sea temple on the cliffs above the legendary surf break Uluwatu, and possibly Bali's most spectacular shrine. The best time to visit is at sunset. Be sure to take in the nightly Kecak dance show and mind the gap—the railings are few and far between. See p. 145.
- **Pura Tanah Lot:** Otherwise known as Pura Pakendungan, this temple sits dramatically on a rock, surrounded by black sand and pounding surf, and is possibly the most picturesque and most photographed temple on the island—especially so at sunset. The temple is reachable only during low tide and can get very busy with coach-loads of tourists, so it's best seen in the early morning. See p. 270.
- **Pura Ulan Danu Bratan:** This temple sits on the edge of Lake Bratan and is worth a visit if only for its beautiful surroundings. The part of the temple that gets all the attention is the 11-roof meru (altar), situated on a point of land, jutting out into the lake. Sadly, the lake and the surrounding area can get overrun with litter from visiting tourists. See p. 213.
- **Tirta Empul:** This temple is built around a sacred spring, Tampak Siring, and the Balinese have used its two bathing spots for a millennium. The springs are believed to have magical powers and bring good health and prosperity. Pack your bathing suit, go at sunrise, and experience the springs as the Balinese do. See p. 188.

THE best DIVING & SNORKELING

- **Nusa Penida:** This island is the nearest dive site for those staying in the south of the island. It's a 40-minute boat ride from Sanur and benefits from the main deepwater channel current running down the Lombok Strait. The main draw is from July to November when there's a high chance of swimming with the large Mola mola (oceanic sunfish); around the same time, you might find manta rays. See p. 130.
- **Bloo Lagoon:** This small, white sand bay just outside Padangbai isn't normally a recipe for finding interesting fish, but the treasure-trove of marine life here

includes sharks, stonefish, scorpionfish, and nudibranches. One of the highlights of this dive spot is its night dives. See p. 234.

o **Gili Biaha:** This island is a 25-minute boat ride north of Candidasa and has some of Bali's most stunning diving. Here you'll find a vast diversity of fish, sharks, and frequent pelagic visitors set against a backdrop of chiseled, black walls with beautiful, healthy corals and often superb visibility. Go to the Shark Cove and you're almost guaranteed to see a white tip shark or two. See p. 234.

o **U.S.A.T. Liberty:** Certainly the most famous and popular dive site in Bali, this wreck lies between 3m and 37m (10 ft.–120 ft.) from the surface and can be enjoyed by serious divers and snorkelers alike. It's easy to reach from the shore and hosts more than 300 species of fish. Go for a night dive. See p. 247.

o **Menjangan Island:** Situated in the West Bali National Park, 10km (6 miles) offshore, this deer-inhabited island offers deep coral-reef walls only 45m to 90m (150 ft.–300 ft.) from shore, with a diversity of coral gorgonian fans and plenty of small and medium-size fish on view. The protected island is reached by boats staffed by ex-fishermen from the area. The high visibility coupled with the gentle currents makes this an exceptional place for the whole family. See p. 279.

o **Belongas Bay:** This bay in south Lombok has many excellent dive sites and pristine and as yet unpolluted reefs. There's plentiful macro life and an abundance of mackerel, tuna, barracuda, Napoleon wrasse, and white and black tip reef sharks. You may even see hammerhead sharks. See p. 49.

o **The Gili Islands:** Located off the west coast of Lombok, and with more than 20 accepted sites, this is an ideal location to base yourself if you want to spend the day sub aqua. The Gilis are famous for their turtles, and if you're quick and fortunate, you may even get to swim with them. See chapter 15.

THE best BEACHES

The image of Bali as a beach destination probably derives from its surf-dominated tourist origins back in the 1970s. But although there are many beautiful beaches, they're less typical of the island as a whole. Planning your beach trip requires thought—not least because the rip and swell that lure surfers pose a less hospitable attraction for swimmers.

o **Bingin Beach:** Of all the amazing golden beaches on the Bukit, this remains as charming and original a spot as you can get. Untroubled to date by overzealous developers, and with surfers doing a daily show out front, this is a perfect beachside experience. See p. 146.

o **Ku de Ta:** Although more of a bar than a beach, treat it as the latter and book one of the four-person sun loungers; kick back for the day with top-drawer service on tap. See p. 82.

o **Kuta, Lombok:** Pristine, bright blue bays and expert surfing, flanked by rocky hills, with very few tourists and touts, make the beaches around Kuta one of the best-kept secrets in southeast Asia. See p. 308.

o **Sanur Beach:** Although similar in style to the Nusa Dua resort, Sanur retains an old-world charm and connection to a more authentic Bali, with mile after mile of traditional warungs competing with top-class resorts set on the boardwalk. This is a great spot for sailing, kite surfing, and child-friendly swimming. See p. 101.

o **Pantai Pasir Putih (White Sand Beach):** This idyllic spot, off the tourist trail, is a closely guarded secret. Just beyond Candidasa, it's a perfect crescent beach protected by two high promontories with a dozen picturesque warungs serving cold beer and prawns. This setting is the closest Bali comes to the Caribbean with azure waters and gentle breezes. See p. 239.

o **Private beach between the Banyan Tree and the Semara Resorts, Bukit Peninsula:** Although all beaches are public property in Bali, this span of fine sand and crystal blue water, protected by reef and imposing cliffs, is as private as things get, and it's the perfect place for a swim. Access is through the Banyan Tree and Semara resorts, or the Karma Kandara with its excellent Nammos Beach Club and Restaurant. See p. 150.

o **The Gili Islands:** Here, you'll find near-perfect, soft white sand beaches. Quite how they've managed to retain their innocence for so long is a mystery. Take a 3-day break. See p. 323.

THE best ACTIVITIES FOR KIDS

o **Surfing:** Teenagers can take part in many of the surfing and kite schools on the island, depending on the time of year and prevailing winds. Sanur is the best area for learning to kite surf and Kuta Beach is ideal for wave surfing. See chapter 4 for more on surfing.

o **Waterbom:** Youngsters will love you for taking them to this water park, but be forewarned, once you've visited you'll never hear the end of it. The place is great fun, exhilarating, and well managed with surprisingly good food. The management has rigged it too by offering you a discount card on exit for a repeat visit within 7 days. Your saving grace after this generous day out with the children is that they'll be so knackered they'll hit the sack early. See p. 69.

o **Bali Safari & Marine Park:** Children of all ages will love the zebras, rhinos, and wildebeest roaming as free as they're going to get this side of the savanna. Add in the animal rides and daily shows and this makes a terrific break from the sea and surf for youngsters. See p. 113.

o **Green Camp:** Let your children have their own natural discovery of the wonders of Balinese culture and the great outdoors from planting rice, picking cocoa, and making chocolate to climbing one of the hundreds of coconut trees that dot the landscape of this cool camp. If they like getting dirty (and what child doesn't) this is the place. Parents can exhaust and educate at the same time. The camp is seasonal and courses are weekly or daily—drop-ins are welcome. See p. 194.

o **Bali Bird Park:** Certainly one of the best-managed bird parks and rehabilitation centers in the world, this is an experience that all ages will relish. The Bali starlings, birds of paradise, and Komodo dragons are each worth the trip in their own right, never mind all together. See p. 113.

o **Bali Tree Top Adventure Park:** Tree Top will test the bravery and agility of all ages from 6 to 60. Budding Tarzans are catered for in the wondrous setting of the Bedugul Botanical Garden. The six levels range from brave children to super-hero. A must for the outward bound. See p. 213.

o **Menjangan Resort:** Take the safari jeeps with rooftop seating around the estate to view the deer, monkeys, and wild boar in the hedgerow. There's world-class snorkeling at Menjangan Island, horse riding, trekking, and bird watching to keep any child amused. You can even stay in charming cabins in the mangroves—great for inspiring botanists. See p. 282.

o **Elephant Safari Park:** Children get a kick out of feeding and washing the cute, well-cared-for baby elephants here. If you stay overnight in the park's hotel, you can arrange for an elephant to pick you up at your door and take you on a night safari. See p. 194.

THE best RESORT HOTELS

o **Alila Villas Soori:** Up the coast from busy and crowded Seminyak, these pristine villas sit on a black-sand beach framed by palm trees. Private plunge pools, movies and music on demand via Apple TV, and delicious yet healthy food, make this a must if you're willing to splurge. See p. 272.

o **Amankila:** Perched above a private dark-sand beach, this Aman property, featuring a three-tiered lap pool that mimics the look of the nearby rice paddies, has Moorish-style villas with amazing views of the Lombok Strait. See p. 237.

o **COMO Shambhala:** This resort is so self-confident that it calls itself "The Estate"—and it's a title that's well-earned. With 41 hectares (100 acres) of sculpted grounds and wild jungle, top-notch detox and wellness programs steered by qualified specialists, as well as elegant rooms with antique touches, you may never want to leave. See p. 173.

o **Desa Seni (Canggu):** Although certainly not one of the more costly or extravagant options, this bijou resort will nourish your soul in a way that sometimes money just can't buy. From the incredibly tasteful layout, to the complimentary yoga classes and organic dining sourced right from the resort's own gardens, you'll leave relaxed and restored. See p. 96.

o **Four Seasons, Jimbaran Bay:** The thatched-roof bungalows overlooking a gorgeous bay give you a taste of "old Bali"—with all the luxuries of a five-star resort. See p. 137.

o **The Oberoi Lombok:** The thatched-roof rooms and villas overlook a beautiful strip of beach and the Gili Islands beyond, although most guests enjoy the setting so much they don't set foot away from the resort. What's more, the resort offers diving, snorkeling, and surfing. See p. 316.

THE best VALUE ACCOMMODATIONS

o **Alam Sari (Ubud):** This hotel offers an excellent combination of setting, social responsibility, and low price—and is a delightful find for families, ecowarriors, and those who want to immerse themselves in Balinese culture. See p. 178.

o **Desa Dunia Beda (Gili Islands):** There are plenty of inexpensive places to stay on the Gilis, but this quiet resort, next to one of the best snorkeling spots on the Gilis, features classy, romantic joglo (Javanese-style bungalows). See p. 330.

o **Novotel Kuta (Lombok):** Pristine beachfront, five-star hotel amenities, and a quiet, out-of-the-way location are the benefits of this beautiful—and inexpensive—resort. See p. 310.

o **Pearl Beach Resort (Lombok):** This is one of our favorite places to stay in all of Lombok and Bali—and it's just US$70 per night. The only place to stay on the tiny island of Gili Asahan, this set of new, beachside bungalows offers some of the area's best snorkeling. See p. 307.

THE best DINING

- **La Lucciola:** This is the most elegant beachside dining experience in Bali. Accessed over a charming footbridge and sitting on one of the prettiest stretches of Seminyak Beach, this is a wonderful place for a leisurely meal at any time of the day. Mellow, magical, and memorable. See p. 84.

- **Nutmegs:** Picturesque Nutmegs overlooks a spacious garden filled with frangipani trees and hundreds of candles that twinkle under the stars. The open kitchen remains wondrously calm given the level and variety of cooking on offer. See p. 83.

- **Sardine:** Quite possibly Bali's most charming restaurant. Built entirely of bamboo with a stunning rice paddy view in the posh Petitenget area of Seminyak, the design is as innovative as the daily changing menu. Fresh sardines feature high on the menu. See p. 85.

- **Sarong:** Running the gamut of Asian cuisine, this buzzing Seminyak eatery draws crowds like bees to honey. What makes it great? Superbly decadent decor of chandeliers, soft lighting, plenty of mirrors, and an expansive bar—people-watching nirvana. See p. 85.

- **Sip:** A better French bistro outside of France would be hard to find and with more than 100 wines and champagnes on offer, it's a crowd-puller for the general managers and restaurateurs that run the competition. See p. 85.

- **Minami:** Hardly something you'd expect in the rice paddies of Ubud, the Japanese-owned Minami serves delicious Osaki-style bento boxes with some of the freshest sashimi on the island. The immaculate cuisine complements the airy white dining room. See p. 181.

- **Echo Beach (Canggu):** Sunday nights on the beach here are famous for their seafood barbecue with picnic tables and stools by the waterfront, lots of gregarious groups of friends and families, and live rock and roll. The scene would suit the 1960s but it's still family-friendly. See p. 96.

- **Jimbaran Bay:** A visit to Bali isn't complete without a trip to Jimbaran for seafood. Come at sunset, dip your toes in the sea, watch the local families splashing in the waves, have a beer, and settle down to a seriously delicious seafood barbecue by candlelight. See p. 133.

- **Kayuputi at St. Regis:** Grab a private cabana overlooking the white sand beach, settle into the white overstuffed cushions, and choose from the seasonal selection of Sturia and Prunier caviar and oysters. Enjoy the ocean breeze and ask the award-winning sommelier for his recommendation while you peruse the menu. Make lunch hour a day out and at the end hope the breeze blows your bill away. See p. 159.

- **Mozaic (Ubud):** Chris Salan's restaurant in the heart of Ubud has become the most coveted fine-dining experience on the island. His six-course tasting menus, with optional wine pairing, should be on everyone's Ubud itinerary. Crayfish sourced from Java cooked with curry butter and passionfruit cream is the kind of consistent innovation that makes this place a shining star that gets three stars from us. See p. 180.

- **Warung Bule (Lombok):** Next to Kuta beach, a local chef—who formerly worked for the Novotel and has cooked for presidential visits—cooks some of the best seafood on the island. It's an unassuming little hole-in-the-wall lit by candlelight and often visited by expats in the know. See p. 311.

THE best SPAS

o **Five Elements:** The most authentic Balinese massages on the island can be found at the new Five Elements Healing Center where the owners, an intrepid American and Italian couple, have sought out the best traditional healers from around the island for invigorating massages in a pristine riverside setting. This is the real deal and not for the faint-hearted; expect them to pummel you into putty. See p. 44.

o **Theta Spa:** The best treatment rooms in this hip destination spa in Bali's Kuta have floor-to-ceiling windows overlooking the beach that let you look out while nobody else can see in. All the treatments use natural ingredients with honey being a favorite, and after a bit of pampering you can hang at the spa bar—a magnet for the tanned and trendy. See p. 67.

o **Jari Menari:** The award-winning Jari Menari's name, "Dancing Fingers," immediately gives the wrong impression that a massage here is going to be on the delicate side. With all-male masseurs it couldn't be further from the truth. The "Four Handed" massage has two practitioners working in rhythmic harmony. See p. 90.

o **Thallaso at Ayana:** Seawater is considered holy by the Balinese who use it not only to receive the ashes of their loved ones, but also to cleanse temples and even themselves. You needn't go that far to have a holy experience. In the world's largest aqua-tonic seawater therapy pool at the Ayana, you have a priceless view of the Indian Ocean and experienced hands to lead you. See p. 137.

o **COMO Shambhala:** "The Source" therapy rooms have full-frontal views of the Ayung river gorge. Treat yourself to the Hot River Stone Massage where stones collected on-site are warmed and used gently to massage those aching knots in your body. See p. 173.

o **The Jiwa Spa at the Conrad:** After a day at the beach, book in for the signature treatment "Ocean Flow" that combines elements of flowing strokes with acupressure similar to the movement of ocean waves. See p. 165.

o **The Remede Spa at St. Regis:** The Remede Spa is deliciously indulgent and open to nonresident guests. Make the most of your time by using the Aqua Vitale pool set in the elegant spa courtyard. Be sure to take advantage of the complimentary Jacuzzi, steam, and sauna. Carpe diem. See p. 162.

o **Four Seasons Sayan:** The new Watsu Pool at the Four Seasons was built specifically for the water therapy guru Elisa Senese, who practices Watsu Waterflow therapy and craniosacral balancing. Elisa's mild movements bring you into a weightless state intended to make you feel as cosseted as being back in the womb. See p. 174.

o **Maya Ubud Spa:** Go for the oversize circular baths and outdoor bales (thatched pavilions) that hang serenely over the edge of the river. Listen to the sound of chirping cicadas and birds and relax after your treatment of choice in a jasmine-and frangipani-infused bathtub. See p. 174.

o **Beach Massage:** Sometimes the best things in life are almost free and a US$5 massage on the comfort of your own beach lounger is pretty close to both. At just about any tourist beach in Bali, wizened women with strong hands and hearts will approach you for massages. Chances are you won't be disappointed.

BALI IN DEPTH

Bali measures 153km (95 miles) east to west and 111km (69 miles) from tip to toe. Although small, a rich millennia of history has fostered an artistically diverse population, with virtually every Balinese skilled as artisan, dancer, or artist and living a spiritual life. Bali boasts more temples than houses, and ceremonies can last for days or even weeks. The island also has beaches, volcanoes, rice paddies, mountain treks, arts and crafts, rivers (for rafting), ceremonies and blessings, mountaintop sunrises, and beachside sunsets. Whichever Bali you're looking for, it's waiting to be found. Ask a typical visitor or expat what Bali means to them and you'll get many different answers. Small certainly doesn't mean limited when it comes to Bali.

BALI TODAY

Against a tumultuous historic backdrop, and in an otherwise Muslim-dominated archipelago, Bali has somehow managed to retain its Hindu independence while flourishing as a tourist paradise. The Balinese amalgam of Hindu traditions, Buddhism, and ancient Javanese practices with their acceptance of different lifestyles, has led many outsiders to call this place home—or at the very least to return time and time again. Recent efforts by politicians to impose Muslim Sharia law and far-reaching antipornography measures in Indonesia indicate that support for an Islamic state is still strong in some areas of this vast nation. Thankfully, the Governor of Bali has gone on record as declaring that the law won't be enforced in Bali, although for cultural and historic reasons rather than for the economic benefits that tourism brings. Bali has seen a huge inflow of foreign investment in recent years. Luxury resorts and multimillion-dollar villas are commonplace, even despite the fact that only Indonesian citizens can own land in freehold title. Foreigners investing in Bali adhere to different ownership forms, which all have time limits on the control of the land in question—though it's still possible to own a patch of paradise.

Indonesia as a whole has seen improvements in infrastructure, telecoms, education, and health, and although Bali still lacks many modern facilities, it's well ahead of the pack. That said, the roads remain potholed, with piles of litter, and many locals still use the rivers for all aspects of their daily ablutions. Although this peaceful island has been dealt various blows in recent years, not least the bomb attacks of 2002 and 2005, the government has shown resolve to wipe out local terrorist cells and tighten security. Most locals think that any repeat of the bombings is unlikely, and

BALI'S royal REGENCY PAST

Bali is divided into one municipality, Denpasar, and eight regencies. Each regency has a capital, which further consists of a number of districts, divided into villages and then comprised of a *banjar* (or a series of *banjar*), which are the local, traditional neighborhood organizations.

Today's regencies have historic roots. The south coast at Gelgel was settled by the son of the last Rajah of Majapahit who declared himself the King of Bali or the Dewa Agung in the 14th century. The Dewa, in an attempt at some form of orderly rule, subdivided the island into principalities, which he then gave to his relatives and generals to govern. Over time, these principalities became increasingly independent and their descendants became princelings and then rajahs of smaller kingdoms. Many of the princelings set out to extend their influence and lands beyond their limited principalities and conquered, among others, the neighboring lands of Lombok and Sumbawa.

The arrival of the Dutch in 1596 with their superior weaponry, organized forces, and willingness to trade were fundamental in Bali's development by not allowing any single dynasty to dominate. The local regencies took the somewhat pragmatic approach of recognizing Dutch supremacy and engaging in trade treaties while retaining, or more accurately being allowed to retain, their local autonomy. The Dutch themselves had their eyes on greater prizes, notably the Spice Islands (the Moluccas to the east), and they largely left Bali to its own devices. With the increasing interest of the British in the region, however, Bali became strategically important, given its proximity to the Dutch lands and plantations in nearby Java. The regencies of Buleleng, Jembrana, and then Karangsem, Gianyar, and Bangli all submitted themselves to Dutch control leaving the remaining three of Badung and Tabanan in 1906 and Klungkung in 1908 to fall in the dreadful *puputan* (for more on these mass suicides, see the later section "The Advent of Colonialism").

Ancestors of the royal families still live and work in what is left of their palaces although they now use their old homes as hotels or guesthouses or antiques shops. But the Balinese, with the caste system still relevant if not completely intact, retain their regents as the center of their community.

the island has been rewarded with a resurgence in popularity. At the same time, Bali is increasingly global. Travelers are emerging from Russia and China, competing with the traditional Australian, Japanese, and European markets. The travel industry is struggling to keep up with demand, but dozens of new hotels have kept prices manageable, particularly during the low season from January to July and mid-September to mid-December.

The greatest change has come as many Balinese leave the rice fields to work in the tourism industry; but the island's culture has survived intact, and is perhaps stronger than ever. As with any paradise that isn't so undiscovered anymore, some people say that the little island isn't what it was. Certainly it's not the 1930s island of German artist Walter Spies (who lived here from 1927 until his death in 1942) and Charlie Chaplin (who visited in 1932), but it remains an enchanted isle that—with a little searching—will provide whatever you're looking for.

LOOKING BACK: BALI HISTORY
Early History

Although Bali's recorded history is scant (even in the last 100 years), there's evidence of a Stone Age people dating to around 2,500 B.C. and the arrival of the first migrations of the Austronesian people. These rice-eating travelers of Chinese and Malayan descent arrived via the maritime trade routes of southeast Asia via Taiwan and the Philippines, cultivating rice as they went. They first introduced and developed the complex irrigation system, subak, which survives to this day.

A Bronze Age people of Chinese and Vietnamese descent from the Dong Son area of Vietnam arrived in the 3rd century B.C., bringing bronze, copper, and iron. Their first sites were in the northwest at Cekik near what is now Gilimanuk and inland at Sembiran. Evidence from these sites indicates a population of fishermen, hunters, and farmers. Their graves show evidence of metallurgy and that they had by this stage acquired the skills to cast or smelt copper, bronze, and iron.

The lasting influence for much of Bali came from the Indian traders who arrived around the 1st century A.D. These mainly peaceful merchants also brought Hinduism. By the 5th century, a Hindu kingdom had been founded in Bali.

Bali's history, as a whole, is populated with many different groups of people; many of these diverse communities lived self-sufficiently and independently from each other. Indonesia claims to be a mix of some 250 ethnic groups, and the Balinese have their own special genetic blend of Chinese and Malay, with traces of Polynesian and Melanesian mixed in with Indian and Javanese.

Among the diverse groups that arrived in Bali after the original Chinese settlers, was a group of some 400 who came from the village of Aga, in East Java, around the 8th century. They settled in the remote mountainous area around Gunung Agung and their communities prospered. Bali Aga societies survive intact and to this day decry and resist most forms of outside influence—with little or no contact with the outside world, their arcane ways are still evident in their original colonies of Campuhan, Taro, Tegalalang, and Batur. Their societal structures exist on rigid and ancient rules and visits by outsiders and tourists can still be a daunting and occasionally harrowing experience. They remain a tough and hardened society, far removed from much of the Bali that most visitors know.

The topography of the island therefore gave way to two forms of living: the people of the mountains and the people of the sea. It's the gentrified southern and coastal people, with their civilizing Javanese customs and easy natural resources, that have given Bali its overarching identity.

By the 11th century, the influence of the Javanese, with their then predominately Hindu beliefs, was being felt more and more. Initially they came peacefully and shared reciprocal political and artistic ideals. This union of the two islands, Bali and Java, was cemented under the rule of Javanese King Airlangga, whose mother moved to Bali shortly after his birth. This informal connection allowed Bali to remain semi-autonomous for the next 200 years until King Kertanegara conquered Bali in 1284.

Although his reign was short lived (he was murdered about 8 years later), his son, the great Vijaya, founded the Majapahit dynasty, which lasted from 1293 to 1520. The influence of this dynasty reached as far afield as the Malaysian peninsula and the very eastern extent of what is now the Republic of Indonesia. The Majapahit bequeathed to Bali many of the features of its present-day society, from the style of royal rule to its architecture and the structures of its temples. The Majapahit also brought the principles of the caste system, which are adhered to today.

The ascendancy of Islam and its spread into Java in the late 15th century caused the Hindu Majapahit dynasty to falter and ultimately disintegrate into feuding sultanates. The last Javanese Majapahit king high-tailed it to Bali, taking with him many of the court's intellectuals, artists, and priests. This wave of culture and spirituality formed the basis of Balinese society that we see today as such a rich and cultured heritage.

Included in this exodus was the great priest Nirartha who, it's believed, introduced many of the complexities of Balinese religion and was a founder of many of the major temples on the island. Bali's Hindu influences and the unique way of life have managed to withstand the dominance of Islam for centuries. To this day, Bali remains the only non-Islamic island in the whole of Indonesia.

The Advent of Colonialism

Marco Polo in 1292 and Vasco de Gama around 1512 were known to have reached Indonesia, but the first European to set foot on Bali is credited as the Dutchman Cornelis de Houtman in 1597. He, like many others since, was captivated with the island and when it came time to leave, he's said to have taken almost a year to round up his crew. The Dutch were more driven by financial gain than cultural pleasures and the control of the Spice Islands, the Moluccas, was a higher priority than the beauty and charms of Bali. Therefore, they established trading posts in Bali instead of taking any forceful control.

Dutch colonial control expanded across the Indonesian archipelago in the early part of the 19th century, including an increasing presence in Bali. By then, Bali's independent kingdoms that we know today—Klungkung, Karangasem, Buleleng, Jembrana, Tabanan, Mengwi, Badung, Gianyar, and Bangli—had taken shape. By this time the Dutch were intent on adding the whole of Bali to their colonial ambitions and set about its capture. It took separate and simultaneous wars from 1846 to 1849, and the actions of various Balinese kings using the colonizers to advance their own local ends, for the Dutch to take control of even just the north of the island. And it wasn't until the wars of the rajahs, from 1884 to 1894, that the Dutch finally extended their rule to the east. Karangasem and Lombok fell in 1894 and finally the Rajah of Gianyar, in a ploy where self-interest took precedence over island sovereignty, was convinced by the new Lords of Ubud to make peace with the Dutch.

The south refused to yield to Dutch rule and although some of the older guard preached peace, they were overruled by a group of headstrong young princes who defeated the Dutch in a surprise attack. Needless to say, the Dutch didn't take this lightly and a larger force was dispatched to Bali to make a stand against the stubbornly resistant and proud southern kingdoms of Tabanan, Klungkung, and Badung. And yet, the Dutch were still seeking justification for an all-out assault.

In 1904, a Chinese schooner struck the reef near Sanur. The Dutch government made what were essentially unreasonable demands for compensation, which was refused by the Rajah of Badung, with the support of Tabanan and Klungkung. A dispute over the rights to plunder the cargo ships (traditionally held by the Balinese) presented the Dutch with the reasoning needed to launch a new attack. In 1906 the full force of the Dutch navy rocked up at Sanur, initiating the Badung War. After blockading the southern ports and having various ultimatums ignored, the Dutch mounted large naval and ground assaults and in September they marched on the palace of Badung.

At the palace, the Dutch weren't met by the expected resistance, but instead by a silent procession with the rajah at the lead dressed in white cremation garb, armed only with a kris (a ceremonial dagger), followed by his supporters. His march stopped some 100 paces from the Dutch and then a priest plunged the kris into his chest. The rest of the procession followed suit and proceeded to kill either themselves or others in the procession. Sensing certain defeat at the guns of the heavily armed Dutch, the noble Balinese decided not to suffer the ignominy of defeat or surrender, but instead had their death rites applied and voluntarily entered into the ritual mass suicide rite known as *puputan*. Despite the Dutch pleas for them to surrender, this *puputan* ended in the deaths of an estimated 4,000 Balinese men, women, and children. That same afternoon a similar event took place at the palace of Pemecutan. The Rajah of Tabanan and his son surrendered, but both committed suicide 2 days later in a Dutch prison. The last remaining regency, Klungkung, brokered a peace deal.

Not surprisingly, the atrocity of the *puputan* garnered worldwide condemnation and even a member of the Dutch Upper House of Parliament labeled the scandal the "extermination of a heroic race." The Netherlands' image as a responsible and even-handed colonial power was seriously compromised.

The deal that had been brokered with Klungkung fell apart when the Dutch attempted to take monopoly control of the opium trade. Riots erupted in Gianyar and the Dutch sent the troops back in, forcing the rajah to flee to Klungkung. He attempted an all-out attack, initially by himself, armed only with a ceremonial kris believed to wreak havoc on the enemy. He was brought down by a single bullet. Seeing the death of their beloved, his six wives turned their krises on themselves and committed suicide. They were then followed by the others in the procession coming out of the palace. With this last *puputan*, the Dutch could finally claim victory over the island.

The victory proved to be spiritually and morally empty, however, and the Dutch governors were able to exercise little influence. Local control over religion and culture generally remained intact. For most commoners, life went on whether they were being ruled by their new colonial masters or the previous rajahs.

The advent of tourism and travel after World War I brought new influences and greater worldwide attention to Bali. The island became home to anthropologists Margaret Mead and Gregory Bateson, and artists Miguel Covarrubias and Walter Spies. Musicologist Colin McPhee, in his autobiographical book *A House in Bali*, fostered the Western image of Bali as "an enchanted land of aesthetes at peace with themselves and nature." Celebrity visitors such as Noel Coward and Charlie Chaplin, Barbara Hutton and Doris Duke, helped make Bali synonymous with a latter-day Garden of Eden. It was at about the same time that Pandit Nehru, the reflective and scholarly first Prime Minister of India, described Bali as the "Dawn of the World." Western tourism soon landed on the island.

The Road to Independence

Dutch rule over Bali came later than in other parts of the East Indies, such as Java and Maluku, and it was never as well established. Despite the long road to colonization, the Dutch period lasted only until Imperial Japan occupied Bali in 1942, for the duration of World War II. After Japan's Pacific surrender in August 1945, the Dutch attempted to return to Indonesia, including Bali, and to reinstate their prewar colonial administration. But Indonesia and Bali resisted, this time armed with Japanese weapons. One of the many heroes of the time was the wartime resistance leader Colonel I Gusti Ngurah Rai who spent the war years tormenting the Japanese. His death, in an almost suicidal attack considered the final *puputan*, is another footnote in the heroic history of Bali and its warriors.

The Dutch tried to maintain their colonial rule for another 4 years before finally conceding that they no longer had a role as masters in the East Indies. The Republic of Indonesia that had been originally constituted by Sukarno and Mohammed Hatta, in the immediate aftermath of World War II, now included Bali and the 12 other island states the Dutch had attempted to retain. On December 29, 1949, with the inclusion of these last states in the Republic of the United States of Indonesia, the curtain came down on the Dutch East Indies.

Post-Colonial Indonesia: From 1949 Onward

The tentative federation, led by Sukarno and Mohammed Hatta, attempted to consolidate this 17,000-island nation. The road to peace and prosperity wasn't without its troubles. Sukarno, who had been a revolutionary, moved from democracy to autocracy and on to authoritarianism. Regional and factional problems led him eventually, in July 1959, to dissolve the assembly and assume full dictatorial powers. Increasingly, Sukarno was becoming pro-Communist and received aid from Communist sources. He made little secret of his desire to make amends for centuries of Western colonialism in southeast Asia and he was perhaps driven more by this than any actual Communist sympathies. In 1963, he went as far as to make a stand against the formation of Malaysia, seeing it as a puppet for continued British rule. He was ultimately unsuccessful and failed to bring the disputed, now Malay lands, of northern Borneo into the Indonesian Republic.

The economic cost of this failure on the fledgling economy, coupled with Sukarno's alienation from the West and resulting lack of financial support when it was most needed, created hyperinflation, which lasted throughout the early part of the decade. The resulting social unrest and Sukarno's failing health weakened his iron grip on the country.

Matters came to a head on the night of September 30, 1965, when eight senior generals were taken from their houses, supposedly by a group of Communist renegade army divisions, and were either summarily executed or taken to Halim airport where they met the same fate. The later justification that these actions were taken to prevent an army-led coup didn't convince many people. A certain General Suharto convinced the other surviving generals to plan their own countermove, and in a surprisingly easy manner they regained control of the military faction. Sukarno stayed in power but Suharto had emerged as a major political figure.

The backlash against the Communists in 1965 after the attempted coup is one of the bloodiest in Indonesian history. Bali was the scene of some of the worst atrocities, where mobs rounded up suspected Communists and sometimes just clubbed them to death. As many as 500,000 suspected Communists or ethnic Chinese were massacred in Indonesia, with about 100,000 being killed in Bali alone—at the time, 5% of Bali's population. Sukarno, who had enjoyed unprecedented levels of popularity, was on his way out. Finally in 1966, he fled the presidential palace and remained president for another year only nominally.

Under Suharto, the military gained far-reaching influence over national affairs. For the next 3 decades, until his undoing by the economic crisis of 1997, Indonesia enjoyed a period of sustained prosperity, even despite Suharto's embezzling autocracy and his cronies' horrific graft. Fortunately the economic meltdown had an upside: the resulting riots and protests brought an end to Suharto's military-led rule and in June

1999, Indonesians enjoyed their first free parliamentary election since 1955. They overwhelmingly ousted the incumbent.

Indonesia achieved a tentative peace under a provisional democratic government headed by President Megawati, daughter of Sukarno. Although she inherited political instability and an economy in crisis, she addressed corruption and the military's human rights record. However, her rule only lasted until 2004 when she was defeated by the former military general Susilo Bambang Yudhoyono, otherwise known as SBY. His coalition government, based on his moral code of honesty and anticorruption, also came out on top in the elections of 2009.

ART & CRAFTS

This small island developed its own distinctive arts during "Bali's Golden Age" under the patronage of the Gelgel kings, when the island was largely independent. These arts remain the touchstones of the culture and Balinese psyche and life—arts are so intrinsic that the Balinese language has no word for art or artist.

Under a regency decree, whole villages became dedicated to one craft or artistic discipline. From this we have Ubud and Batuan for paintings, Mas for wood carvings, Celuk for silver and gold markets, and Batubulan for stone carvings. Outside of royalty, the temples were the main patron of the arts. Art has always played an important role for the temples and their ceremonies, which can be entirely given over to one form of artistic expression.

The tradition of art in Bali has largely been one of anonymity, in which individuals created and performed their arts and crafts not for personal aggrandizement but to serve and glorify their village, community, and temple, and class or caste was irrelevant. For example, princes, goldsmiths, and drivers would all perform different parts in the same orchestra or dance.

This lack of posterity permeates many aspects of Balinese life. Although they revere and remember the spirits of the dead, the Balinese don't themselves seek immortality—just as they know that their wood carvings will eventually rot, their soft sandstone sculptures crumble, and termites eat their canvases.

Much of the way art was expressed, certainly in paintings, has changed with the circumstances. The temples and rajahs are no longer the island's biggest art patrons. A new class of customer has arrived with new demands: the tourist. In the mid-1920s, with the arrival of international artists such as Walter Spies and Rudolf Bonnet, a very traditional style of painting (wayang), in which images are depicted as two-dimensional figures, emerged as a new distinctive art movement. What remains today is a combination of traditional artisans using conventional methods and time-honored customs and new and expressive art forms that are increasingly experimental.

Performing Arts

Dance, theater, and music all blend together in Balinese culture, and no Balinese would think of a show that separated each of the component parts. The generic term for this traditional theater, as with the style of painting, is *wayang*, which literally means shadow. Dance, drama, and music also play a central part in ritual ceremonies and temple blessings. Their history is told and passed down through the generations in the many dramatic tales performed on a regular basis. Until the advent of television, this was how history was transmitted.

THEATER

Of the many forms of theater, **Wayang Kulit** is the best known and most often performed. This is a dance with shadow puppets, featuring intricately cut figures, originally made from buffalo parchment, called *kulit,* meaning leather or skin. The puppeteers project the images against a screen and depict tales from the Hindu epics, accompanied by a xylophone-like gamelan ensemble.

Other similar types of theater are **Wayang Arja,** a puppet opera set to music telling romantic stories. In **Wayang Golek,** wooden doll puppets are operated from below by rods. **Wayang Karucil** is somewhere in between Golek and Kucil, and the puppets are made from thin bits of wood. **Wayang Beber** uses illustrations and scrolls along with a narrator who sings and tells the story.

DANCE

As with theater, Balinese dance mainly portrays stories from Hindu epics, the **Ramayana** being the most common. There are more than a dozen differing styles of dance and all can be incredibly powerful with many of the performers entering true trance-like states.

Balinese dancing originated with religious dance, although it has become increasingly theatrical, with characters that were once demons or devils now more for the amusement of the crowd. Each movement in a dance is made up entirely of prescribed gestures. This leaves little room for improvisation, though much can be enhanced by the individual dancer or troupes' interpretation, emotional intensity, and expressiveness of their features. During any dance, watch the dancers' faces, and particularly the eyes. Like many displays of art, there are certain aspects that can't be taught.

Among the many different varieties of Balinese dance, the following are the most important: **Kecak,** or the Ramayana Monkey Dance, is the most famous and most powerful. A circle of up to 150 men, wearing only checked cloths, chant rhythmically "cak cak cak cak cak" while throwing their arms up in the air, dancing round the circle or rocking on the ground, over and over, to and fro. The dance tells the tale of a monkey king and his warriors. Walter Spies worked with the local dancer Wayan Limbak to turn the dance into a more dramatic performance though it comes as no surprise that kecak was originally a trance ritual with its origins in exorcisms. One of the most famous places to see this dance is at sunset at **Pura Luhur Uluwatu** (p. 145) surrounded by real monkeys who are as naughty as some of the characters being portrayed.

Barong and Rangda (or the Barong and Kris dance) has been mainly adapted for tourists and is a fight between good and evil with the King of the Spirits (*barong*) overcoming the demon queen (*rangda*) after the wicked queen has cast a spell on the *barong* and his supporters making them stab themselves with their krises. The *barong* however is able to make the daggers cause no harm and so they stab themselves with no effect, but spectators, especially those in the front row, are usually left feeling as though they've witnessed some form of exorcism—the dance's original purpose.

Among the other dances, **Legong** is a graceful one performed by young girls. **Baris** is a traditional war dance in which a solo dancer depicts the feelings of a young warrior prior to battle. **Topeng** is a masked drama with tales of mythical kings and gods. A narrator, who wears a half mask, tells the story accompanied by the gamelan (see below) with dance, fight, and comedy. **Wayang Wong** is a shadow dance in which the players wear masks and tell an aristocratic love story between Rama and Rawana with soft delicate music. It was originally only ever performed in four royal palaces and has always been considered the most aristocratic of plays.

MUSIC

Bali is renowned for its profusion of musical performances and the variety of its instrumental ensemble, the **gamelan** orchestra: a group of players with xylophone-like instruments, drums, and gongs that can range up to 50 in number. Each gamelan has its own specific tuning and is considered a single entity. All Balinese music is based around the gamelan, which is an integral part of all ceremonies and performing arts. The sound is easily identifiable and identified with Bali.

Musical styles vary regionally: The music of western Bali, for example, uses gamelan instruments made from bamboo (*jegog*), which grows to enormous sizes and means that it can take up to four men to carry one instrument. There are some 25 types of varying sizes of gamelan instruments in metal, bronze, or bamboo. Of the various different styles, the **Gong Keybar,** introduced in the early 1900s, is nowadays the most popular form. If you're curious to see the manufacture and production of gamelan instruments, visit **Tihingan** (p. 225) in east Bali.

Painting

WAYANG STYLE

The classic Balinese painting style is *wayang,* which takes its origins from the shadow puppets of the same name (see "Theater," above). Clear rules determine the shapes, colors, and even the positioning of the characters—noble on the left, evil on the right, just as they are in a performance. Paintings were traditionally on *langse,* which were broad rectangular cloths used as wall hangings in temples or curtains in palaces, or on *ider-ider,* which were similar to scrolls. This style of painting continues to flourish thanks to the drive of **Nyoman Mandara** in the 1960s and his government-sponsored painting school.

Other traditional styles are **Batuan,** which is strongly *wayang*-based and involves hundreds of painted images of Balinese life, and **Keliki,** which is similar to an old Batuan style showing mythical characters engaged in the struggle of good against evil, though the Keliki paintings are rarely larger than 20cm × 15cm (8 in. × 6 in.). The **Pengosekan** style deals with nature, plants, and insects and emerged as recently as the 1960s with influences that could certainly be ascribed to "flower power."

German artist Walter Spies (1895–1942) and Dutch Rudolf Bonnet (1895–1978) helped evolve more abstract terms of expression during the 1920s. Their arrival in Bali coincided with a seismic cultural shift as the increasing Dutch colonial influence removed the power and money from the rajahs and the temples. This meant that the rajahs were no longer the main patrons and financial supporters of artists and as such could no longer dictate the traditional styles. This two-pronged influence led to a huge change and an explosion in the whole artistic movement. No more were artists retained purely for the benefit of the temple or the palace with their constrained and preordained styles; now they had to cut their cloth for a new style of buyer, the tourist. This new freedom of expression brought individual displays of talent leading to fame for the likes of **I Gusti Nyoman Lempod** and **Sudjojono** whose work now commands hundreds of thousands of dollars. I Gusti Nyoman Lempod's paintings are full of energy and characterize everyday life as well as religious themes. Two other Balinese artists of note are **Nyoman Gunarsa** and **Made Wianta** who are considered to be the pioneers of Balinese contemporary art.

PITA MAHA & THE MODERN STYLE

Spies had originally been enticed to Bali from Java at the behest of the royal family. With Bonnet and one of the local princes, Cokorda Gede Agung Surapati, he established the **Pita Maha,** an artists' cooperative that allowed artists to develop their own expressive style and to even sign the canvas. Pita Maha means literally "great vitality," but it also means "ancestor," which resonates particularly well with the Balinese. Here the cooperative sponsored and controlled the quality of work of selected artists and sold pieces through the gallery. In later years many of the sponsored paintings were donated to the **Puri Lukisan** (p. 188), the oldest museum in Ubud. World War II and Spies's incarceration—for his fondness for certain young Balinese boys—disrupted the movement. Bonnet's return in the 1950s never quite reclaimed the past glories, nor did the Ubud Painters group, which replaced Pita Maha. The 1950s saw the further input of **Arie Smit** who developed a Matisse-style of painting with lots of bright colors, fish or frogs on bicycles, and ducks with hats. Many of his paintings now hang in the **Neka Museum** (p. 189).

Crafts

TEXTILES & WEAVING

Prized for their stunning beauty, variety, and role in traditional costume and ceremony, the traditional textiles of Bali and Indonesia are woven, twined, batiked, tie-dyed, embroidered, and embellished works of art and are among the best treasures to acquire while visiting anywhere in Indonesia. Fine, authentic, handmade textiles are available in antiques shops, boutiques, galleries, and markets. Religious paraphernalia, shrines, dancers, priests, masks, and offerings are all wrapped, bound, draped, or ornamented with specifically prescribed textiles, redolent with symbolic meaning. Bali is by no means unique in this regard. Throughout Indonesia, traditional textiles are ritual objects, stored wealth, trade goods, bride wealth, and tokens of prestige.

Bali itself is extraordinarily rich in textile traditions. Ikat cloths have patterns dyed into the individual threads before they're woven, with the design only appearing on the loom. The effect creates jagged borders between one color and the next and bold

 BUYING textiles

If you want to purchase textiles in Bali, develop an eye for the kind of cloth you like and then shop around. When you look at textiles, in general, it's best to start at the high end (and perhaps come back to it). First, try the galleries at five-star hotels and reputable antiques shops in Ubud and Seminyak for antique textiles, and then visit markets and boutiques for contemporary pieces. You may well return to the high-end shops, and obtain good value there, because their owners know the world market and are adept at sourcing the very finest examples. They're also more likely to

identify textiles correctly as to origin, age, and quality. Expect reputable galleries to offer literature and anecdotal information about collectible textiles. They're your best source of accurate information.

Use your eyes and judge for yourself: After all, you're choosing a work of art. Ultimately, your feeling is the best guide. Whatever type of Indonesian textile you choose to acquire, choose well, and then rest assured that you've acquired an object of lasting value, for both its visible and spiritual attributes.

BALI'S craft VILLAGES AT A GLANCE

As with art, crafts are also specific to individual villages. Be careful where and from whom you buy because many artifacts are now imported and may be machine- rather than handmade. And again, as with art, some of these are very hard to tell from original works. The following crafts are matched with their villages.

Basketware & Painting: Batuan
Carving: Penarukan
Coconut & Bone Carving: Bangli; Tampaksiring

Gamelan Instruments & Gongs: Blahbatu; Sawan; Tihingan
Jewelry: Tampaksiring; Ubud
Masks: Mas; Puaya
Pottery: Pataen; Pejaten; Ubung
Puppets: Puaya
Silver & Gold: Budakeling; Celuk
Stone Carving: Batubulan
Temple Decorations (umbrellas, wind chimes, and so on): Sukawati
Weaving: Belayu; Beratan; Gianyar; Mengwi; Sidemen; Tenganan
Wood carving: Jati; Mas; Pujung; Tegallalang; Ubud

patterns in a wide range of color palettes. Most ikat is now made in Gianyar regency and around Klungkung (p. 225). Traditional markets in large towns are a good place to shop, or go directly to ikat workshops to buy ready stock and watch the weaving process first hand.

Songket is fashioned with threads of cotton, silk, gold, or silver that float on the base cloth in a variety of patterns. Again, east Bali, especially Klungkung (p. 225) and Sidemen (p. 227), are among the best places to find good contemporary songket.

Geringsing textiles are woven only in Tenganan (p. 236), using a painstaking double-ikat technique, in which both the warp and weft threads are patterned prior to weaving. The quality of antique pieces has never been matched by contemporary weavers, although a revival is underway. Antique and high-quality new pieces fetch thousands of dollars.

WOOD

Wood carvings and craft is a particular specialization of the Balinese. Historically, wood carvings were for ornamentation in palaces, temples, and houses of high caste. With increasing tourist demand, attention has lately been turned to the more portable, less ghoulish, and less antidemonic items. There are plenty of carved Buddha heads and garudas (mythical birds) as well as traditional styles of furniture, all mainly in local woods such as belalu, suar, or even teak (be on the lookout for sandalwood, for its delightful and lasting fragrance). Such pieces tend to be small and detailed, with a propensity for elephants, and are slightly more pricey than other carvings. A lot of the intricate doorways that you see in many villas these days are imported from Java, the local ones having been snatched up a long time ago.

BALINESE ARCHITECTURE

Balinese architecture has developed characteristic gorgeous gates, airy pavilions, mystical statues, and romantic gardens. This holds true even in the 21st century, where we find Bali at an architectural crossroads between Mannerist splendor and minimalism, and ever at the cutting edge of international tropical design.

The buildings, tropical gardens, and temple umbrellas that leapt off the travel posters in the last days of the 20th century are still to be found, albeit beneath a thick veneer of other new and differing styles. The "New Look," for which Bali is now equally famous, is a result of decades of experimentation with modernism and the notion of "New Asia."

Bali's many looks derive from the island's architectural traditions of outdoor living, pavilions in all shapes and sizes, and walled compounds. "Bali style" is essentially a courtyard architectural style, inherited no doubt from the Chinese, with indigenous and Hindu-Javanese influence. The original architectural style of Bali, which can still be found in the mountain villages of Belantih, Songan, and Trunyan (p. 209) near Danau Batur (Lake Batur), was simple and almost severe: low-eaved, high-pitched-roof, single-unit dwellings made of bamboo and timber sitting on packed mud or stone plinths. The dwellings are arranged on terraces, according to clans and castes, and set in rows, aligned with the mountain-to-sea axis. Similarly the temples of this mountain Bali culture (called Bali Aga) were almost Zen-like in their austerity (the old temple of Pura Puseh at Bayung Gede (p. 204) is one example).

As classical Javanese Hinduism was introduced into Bali in waves, starting as early as the 10th century, and as people started to populate the flatter coastal regions, the rows of simple, single-hut dwellings grew into courtyards of multipurpose pavilions—following the South Indian model—which eventually grew walls and gates in the Chinese or Javanese style. Chinese influence had been strong along Bali's north coast through trade since the beginning of the first millennium, and that region's architecture retains a strong Chinese character. The terraced sanctuaries and worshiping grounds of the animistic ancients slowly became Hindu temples, but retained much of their original nature; shrines remained oriented toward the mountains, the abode of the pre-Hindu gods, even as they grew towers, gates, and shrines, modeled on Hindu-Javanese prototypes.

At the beginning of the 20th century, when many Balinese palaces were razed after the series of horrific *puputan* of 1906 and 1908, Dutch colonial architectural styles started to take hold. Influence in the north, with neoclassical bungalows, is still visible in Singaraja and the mountain village of Munduk; other examples are in Denpasar in the south. The building of the Art Deco Hotel Denpasar in 1935 could be seen as the start of the modern era of Balinese architecture. From then on, all the island's princes—always keen to adopt, absorb, and adapt—wanted colonial-style pavilions, and little pensiones, modeled on the Hotel Denpasar, sprung up across the island.

Other "princes" had started arriving in Bali by the 1930s: a colony of foreign artists and scholars who wanted to live like the Balinese, but in a palatial manner. Many settled near Ubud, where local prince Tjokorda Agung Sukawati proved a great patron and mentor (he was a cofounder of the Pita Maha Art Foundation). Walter Spies invented the modified wantilan, the traditional cock-fighting pavilion found in every town square, during this time, in an attempt to get his baby grand piano between the columns of his home. The **Balinese Dream Home movement** started during this Happy Valley-esque prewar era. The Le Mayeur home (p. 113) is now a museum, and Spies's home in Ubud is now the Hotel Tjampuhan (p. 176). Musicologist Colin McPhee's home is now the Taman Bebek Villas (p. 177) in Sayan, and the Hotel Denpasar still stands, largely untouched.

Within a brief period of time Bali began exporting ideas for tropical resorts to the entire world. Even the brutalist Bali Hyatt in Sanur, completed in 1973, provided a platform for the next generation of tropical hotel design stars, who went on to create

The legend of Bali as a spiritual, idyllic Hindu haven began with the artist Walter Spies, who arrived on the island in the 1920s upon the invitation of Ubud's royalty. Certain books also perpetuated that image, including Colin McPhee's chronicle *A House in Bali*. But things really heated up in the last couple of years, spurred by the publication of Elizabeth Gilbert's *Eat, Pray, Love*, a memoir that describes the author's meetings with a local healer and ends with her finding love on the island. The book was turned into a movie in 2010, starring Julia Roberts.

culturally referenced resorts highlighting local architecture and materials around the globe. The main lobby of the Bali Hyatt (p. 105) remains today as the largest single pavilion on the island, a masterpiece in coconut and bamboo.

Since the 1930s, a trend to do better than the Balinese at creating glamorous architecture and interiors was embraced by dream-home owners, hotel developers, and architects—both foreign and Indonesian. Hotels became the new temples of Bali, just as the Balinese were deserting their traditional architecture in favor of more Western home designs. Balinese villages and south Bali suburbs today are littered with examples of Hindu wedding cake, Ghost Train Gothique, and Imelda Marcos Modern interspersed with pure Hindu-Balinese temples, and the occasional Majapahit palace and traditional courtyard home.

EATING & DRINKING

The rich array of food found in the rest of Asia is, to many, sadly lacking in Bali. But then again, many who come to Bali don't experience authentic Balinese cuisine. Food plays a central role in Balinese ceremonies and offerings, and it's seen more as a staple of life than a luxury. This is reflected in the manner in which the daily ration is served, usually portable and often without too much experimentation and choice. Balinese meals tend to be eaten quickly and without fanfare. People simply eat when they're hungry, and dining out or in groups isn't a normal social convention. Festivals are the major exception, when food is prepared in an elaborate and decorative manner and eaten communally, marking the occasion as something out of the ordinary.

Most of the daily staples include rice, accompanied by vegetables and a small amount of either fish or meat, with a range of spices and chilies, usually cooked in the early morning, and consumed whenever the need arises. Coconut remains central to Balinese cooking and can be grated or squeezed to produce cream, or the oil is used for frying. The husks can be used for cooking in an open fire which, when barbecuing fish, can sometimes be an overpowering flavor. Other spices and herbs common to Balinese cooking are ginger, galangal, turmeric, lemongrass, chili, and lime, with palm sugar and tamarind to sweeten it all up.

Owing to Hindu origins, the Balinese rarely eat beef although this is also partly due to the inability to keep meat fresh, given limited refrigeration.

Local Dishes

Warungs (roadside cafes) in Bali and Indonesia are best described in Balinese culture as the equivalent of a French cafe. Almost all locals will buy at least one meal a day at their local warung—you should at some stage consider eating at one. The obvious dish to choose is **nasi campur,** rice with a mix of whatever else has been cooked that day. You go to the counter, where the dishes are on display behind a glass screen, armed with a pointing finger (about the only time pointing is acceptable in Bali), and indicate the dishes you want. The options usually include roasted and/or curried chicken, *tempeh,* sweet and sour pork, fried fish, various steamed greens, and **urap,** a pungent, warm salad of steamed vegetables with coconut and spices.

A similar way of serving an array of food is **padang** style, which originated in Sumatra, where all the dishes for the day are laid out on a table and you help yourself. Hygiene can be an issue here as many customers take from the communal dishes using only their hands. You'll see the same array of food with side dishes of sambal, but in general the dishes tend to be very spicy. A favorite **padang** dish is **rendang,** a spicy stew, usually beef or mutton, slow cooked in coconut and spices until the sauce is almost fully absorbed by the meat.

For more freshly cooked foods, **bakso** is a soup of noodles and meatballs, served as an anytime snack; **bakwan** has spicy wontons; **soto ayam** is chicken soup with noodles, topped off with egg, tomatoes, and spices typically for lunch.

The perennial favorite, for when you can't think of what to eat or just want something simple, is **nasi goreng,** which is fried rice with vegetables and chicken and/or prawns. Alternatively, *mie goreng* has noodles rather than rice as the base. **Gado gado** is a vegetable salad served with a spicy peanut sauce dressing and usually crispy prawn crackers.

For a snack, you have plenty of choice: tempeh is crunchy, shelled soy beans mixed with a special strain of yeast to form a small flat cake, and then fried; **lumpia** (spring rolls) are large crispy pastry skins filled with meats and/or vegetables with mild spices and then deep fried; satay is ubiquitous on the island and makes a great snack. It's made of chicken, beef, goat (*kambing*), or fish, which is threaded on bamboo skewers and grilled over coconut husk coals, and then usually served with *saus kacang* (a spicy peanut sauce). Sate lilit is minced meat or fish with spices on lemongrass skewers—possibly the most delicious way of serving satay.

 A Dish You Might Want to Avoid

Beware of *sate anjing,* which is made from dog.

Palm sugar and coconut are the anchors on the sweet side. You'll find *bubuh injun* (black sticky rice) served in a hot sticky sauce of palm sugar and coconut cream. Rice flour cakes are popular and at breakfast you may also see Balinese pancakes, which are coconut pancakes dipped in palm sugar. Other dishes use bananas such as godoh or *pisang rai,* which are fried or steamed bananas, respectively, coated in coconut.

The menu and preparation changes for ceremonies. Much care and attention is given not only to the preparation of food, but also the choice of dishes appropriate to serve as offerings to show commitment to communal social obligations. Among those traditionally served are *babi guling, bebek betutu,* and *lawar* because they require much preparation; they're usually undertaken by the whole community. At large festivals, you can see whole teams working through the day making the ceremonial dishes.

Babi guling is a spit-roasted, whole, stuffed baby pig presented intact on the table for feasts or banquets. The spicy filling is made of, among other things, chili, turmeric, ginger, galangal, onions, and garlic all basted in coconut oil and a bit more

EATING AT THE kaki LIMA

Kaki lima are small carts along the road-side and in busy areas around towns and markets that turn out a variety of quick, inexpensive meals.

Martabak is a deep-fried chicken or duck-egg omelet with spices and ground meat. Carts selling *martabak* usually also sell *putu*, a small green-colored roll like a pancake, filled with palm sugar, and *terang bulan*, larger pancakes with sweet chocolate-flavored condensed milk, nuts, and other toppings.

Kaki lima also sell fried rice or noodles (*nasi* or *mie goreng*). *Bakso* is a spicy and delicious soup with noodles, meatballs, and other local snacks such as *gorengan*, a selection of deep-fried tofu, tempeh, and savory pastries.

Use caution when eating at the *kaki lima*, because quality and hygiene can vary: The owners have little access to running water to wash their plates properly.

turmeric. Duck (*bebek*) is best served as **bebek betutu,** covered in a spicy paste, wrapped in banana leaf, and slow-cooked in a pit of embers. **Lawar** remains one of Bali's most famous local dishes and, as it must be consumed immediately, isn't found in restaurants. Made from pig's blood and spices, together with an assortment of other goodies, *lawar* can be found in every village in Bali. The meat distinguishes the type of *lawar*—chicken, duck, beef, pork, turtle, or even dragonfly, but thankfully turtles are now rarely used.

Drinks

Fresh, young **coconut milk** is refreshing and healthy. Drill a hole, drink the juice, and scrape the juicy coconut flesh from the inside of the shell. A variety of drinks are based on young coconut (*kelapa muda*). **Es campur** is somewhere between a drink and a dessert—shaved ice topped with sweet condensed milk and a variety of agar-agar-based jellies. Similar is *es buah,* which has chopped fresh fruit. *Es rumput laut* adds locally harvested seaweed.

Fresh **juices** (*jus aneka buah*) are available everywhere. Fresh lime juice (*jus jeruk nipis*) is a good thirst quencher, as is fresh watermelon (*semangka*) or orange juice (*jus jeruk*), sometimes confusingly made from tangerines, but which tastes even better. When ordering, make sure you ask for any sugar to be served on the side. Often you ask for a fresh fruit juice only for it to be loaded with extra sugar.

You'll find many places selling Bali **kopi** (coffee) and it's normally wonderful. Generally, Balinese coffee is processed using the wet method, which results in a sweet, soft coffee with good consistency. However, although the coffee is good, the way it's served and presented can leave a little to be desired. For some reason, the Balinese seem to overpower and then underfilter the coffee, leaving large dollops of ground coffee in your mug.

BEER, WINE & MOONSHINE

Bali sits outside the normal ways of the rest of the Muslim-dominated country and therefore alcohol, though expensive, is readily available. Imported wines and spirits tend to be expensive, as import duties are on a value basis that was raised to 300% in 2008.

The locally produced wines are Hatten and Wine of the Gods, with white, red, and rosé varieties, from grapes grown in Bali. There's also Two Islands—red and white

The Rijsttafel

Rijsttafel is an Indonesian feast, described as the "Crown Jewel of Indonesian Cuisine" and is translated from the Dutch as "rice table." Up to 40 dishes are served in small proportions and accompanied by rice. It originated in colonial times when the Dutch felt they needed a banquet that represented the multiethnic nature of the East Indies archipelago. Popular dishes include egg rolls, *gado gado,* sambal, and pickles, satay of all types, fish, fruit, vegetables, and nuts enhanced by coriander, basil, bay leaves, cardamom, galangal, and lemongrass. You can try this feast at the excellent **Bumbu Bali** (see p. 166) in Tanjung Benoa, **Warung Enak** (see p. 185) in Ubud (see p. 168), or either of the **Oberoi** hotels on Bali and Lombok (see p. 79 and p. 316).

wines—made from Australian grapes imported as grape juice and then fermented and bottled here. The rosés with plenty of ice are perfectly drinkable; the rest are more an acquired taste.

One shining bright light—literally, as its name means "star"—is the local beer, **Bintang,** served ice cold everywhere. The other locally produced beer, by a Western-owned firm, is **Storm Beer,** both dark and light.

Home brews *arak, brem,* and *tuak* are popular among the locals but are basically moonshine. **Arak** is an extremely alcoholic brew made from rice, and distilled and fermented until it becomes a clear white spirit. Alcohol content varies greatly but it's usually just strong and not particularly tasty. It can be served with ice, mixed with local honey and fresh limes, or added to cocktails to disguise the taste. In any case, the whole *arak* production was completely closed down in June 2009 because one rogue manufacturer added methanol to his batch, which resulted in at least 27 deaths (among them four foreigners) and the blindness of many others.

Brem is a rice wine and hasn't been affected by methanol; white rice produces the white *brem* and black rice is used for red *brem.* Usually sold while still "young," the white tends to be slightly sour and the red, quite sweet, similar to a light port wine.

Tuak is made from juice extracted from the aren palm. When fresh, it's a light pink color and not alcoholic; the sweet drink with a strange odor is popular with locals, especially at feasts and parties. The alcoholic variety is made from *tuak* that has been mixed with palm sugar, poured into earthenware containers, and buried. Once fermented, the *tuak* turns a lighter color and has varying degrees of alcoholic content, depending on the strength of the original brew and the length of time underground. The smell and flavor are quite pungent and vaguely rotten. Along with *arak,* it's definitely an acquired taste.

WHEN TO GO

Weatherwise, there's generally no unpleasant time to visit to Bali—you'll almost always have plenty of warm, sunny weather. High season is roughly from April to October, when Bali is dryer and slightly cooler. Peak season is the month of August and early September; the 2 weeks surrounding Christmas and New Year; the week beginning with Chinese New Year (usually in January or February); and Easter week. Low season is roughly mid-January to June. December and January are characterized by sudden and short thunderstorms in the afternoon, though sometimes it can rain for days, flooding all the rivers and roads. The best time to go for discounted hotel rates is mid-September to mid-December and mid-January to June (excepting the Chinese New Year and Easter weeks), when you'll find rates slashed to half of what you'd pay during high and peak seasons.

Weather

Bali lies between latitude 08 45S and longitude 115 10E, which places it firmly in the tropics. Accordingly, average year-round temperatures are a balmy 26°C to 29°C (80°F–85°F) varying only with altitude. The average temperatures in the central mountains are 18°C to 24°C (64°F–75°F). Days are generally 12 hours long year-round. In general, Bali and Lombok have similar weather, though Lombok is dry and receives less rain than Bali. There are basically two seasons in Bali: rainy season and dry season. The hot and sticky **rainy season** lasts October to March with occasional downpours that can obscure all visibility. The popular **dry season,** from April to October, referred to as "summer" by the locals even though it's the southern hemisphere, is cooler and much more pleasant. From June to August, the temperature drops slightly and there's usually a refreshing cool breeze in the air.

Average Bali Temperatures, Rainfall & Humidity

MONTH	LOW (C/F)	HIGH (C/F)	RAINFALL MM/IN	HUMIDITY (%)	SEASON
January	26/79	32/90	300/12	85	Wet
February	26/79	32/90	280/11	75	Wet
March	25/77	32/90	215/8½	70	Wet
April	25/77	33/91	100/4	65	Dry
May	25/77	32/90	85/4	60	Dry
June	23/73	31/88	75/3	60	Dry
July	21/70	31/88	55/2	60	Dry
August	23/73	31/88	40/1½	60	Dry
September	24/75	32/90	90/3½	65	Dry
October	25/77	33/91	100/4	75	Wet
November	26/79	32/90	150/6	80	Wet
December	26/79	32/90	295/12	85	Wet

Holidays

PUBLIC HOLIDAYS

Most of the major Christian, Muslim, Hindu, and Buddhist holidays are celebrated in Bali. The government also sets a few additional days every year during the year, though Islamic holiday dates change year to year. The following dates pertain to 2012. **January:** 1 New Year; 23 Chinese New Year; **February:** 5 Maulid (Birth of the Prophet); **March:** 23 Nyepi (Balinese New Year); **April:** 6 Good Friday, 28 Waisak Day (Buddha's birthday); **May:** 6 Waisak Day (Buddha's birthday); 17 Ascension Day; **August:** 17 Indonesia Independence Day; 19 and 20 Eid-ul-Fitr Muslim festival to end Ramadan; **October:** 26 Idul Adha, cattle sacrifice and hajj pilgrimage; **November:** 15 Islamic New Year (1432); **December:** 25 Christmas.

Major Religious Events & Festivals

ON BALI

Festivals and religious events are important features in the social landscape of Bali, and are also permanent fixtures in Balinese daily life. Celebrations in Bali follow a lunar calendar rather than the Western calendar. Thus many major festivals fall on different dates over the years.

Although the temple festivals (see below) are pretty to witness, a village festival is a rare treat. Most villages have their own annual festivals generally exclusive to their village. They can be enormous spectacles and worth a visit. Take a guide to explain the traditions, and help with translations, as most people who attend don't speak English. Look out for the **Med-medan** in Denpasar (see below), **Ngerebeg Ceremony** in Tegalalang, **Usaba Sambah festival,** which includes the *makare kare* and *maayunan* in Tenganan (p. 236).

Galungan, the most prestigious festival (similar to Christmas on the Western calendar), occurs every 210 days and lasts for 10 days (Aug 29, 2012; Mar 27, 2013; Oct 23, 2013; May 21, 2014). The festival celebrates the coming of the gods and ancestral spirits to earth to dwell again in the homes of their descendents. Festivities are characterized by offerings, dances, new clothes, plenty of feasting, and visits to family and friends. On the 10th day, the celebrations end with **Kuningan** (Sept 8, 2012; April 6, 2013; Nov 2, 2013; May 31 2014) where the families bid their farewells to the gods and spirits.

Every village in Bali celebrates Galungan and Kuningan by adorning the outside of their houses with a *penjor,* a decorative tall bamboo pole, about 8m (26 ft.) high, with palm leaves, rice stems, coconuts, and corn. At the end of each of the poles hangs a *sampian,* a beautiful plaited palm leaf creation. Some poles are decorated with lights similar to a Christmas tree. The poles are usually installed on the Tuesday before Galungan: They should be removed and the ornaments burned after 42 days.

Tawur Kesanga, or **Ogoh-Ogoh day,** occurs the day before Nyepi (see dates below). Villagers hold a large exorcism-celebration at the main village crossroad. Throughout the month of March, you'll see villages making large ogoh-ogoh, fantastic 4½m to 6m (15 ft.–20 ft.) papier-mâché effigies. Neighboring villages compete to build the scariest and largest *ogoh-ogoh* imaginable. After sunset, the villages carry their *ogoh-ogoh* on a bamboo platform through the streets to the sound of gamelan. When they arrive at the crossroad, the *ogoh-ogoh* are held aloft to a crescendo of noise from drums, gongs, cymbals, and voices. In order to start the new year with a clean slate, tradition demands that evil spirits are woken up and driven away from the island by loud clashing noise. The carnival ends with the *ogoh-ogoh* being led to the beach where they're burned (though more recently, given the cost of manufacture, they're sold on to collectors).

Nyepi (Mar 23, 2012; Mar 12, 2013; Mar 31, 2014; Mar 21, 2015), the day following the dark moon of the spring equinox, opens a new year of the Saka calendar. It's the Balinese equivalent of New Year's Eve in the Western calendar. It's celebrated by "a day of silence," fasting, and meditation, which begins at 6am and ends the

---

Etiquette for Visiting Temples & Ceremonies

You may be allowed to enter certain temples, even at ceremony time, but be sure to respect temple etiquette: Wear a sarong and sash and observe all signs regarding temple rules. Women aren't allowed to enter if they're menstruating, are pregnant, or have given birth within the past 6 weeks.

You can enter some ceremonies but don't just go charging in—ask one of the *pecalang* (those dressed in checked black and white sarongs) if you can go in first. *Note:* Don't stand higher than a priest during a ceremony because this is disrespectful.

ONLINE traveler's TOOLBOX

www.agoda.com: Discount hotel bookings; excellent cut-rate prices offered, often cheaper than Orbitz and Travelocity

www.asiawebdirect.com: A guide to booking hotel rooms in Bali

www.baliblog.com: Blog about Bali, powered by Whygo.com with deals on flights to and accommodations in Indonesia

www.bali.com: The best online guide to Bali with an excellent blog

www.balidiscovery.com: Award-winning website with up-to-date information on everything you need to know about Bali for your holiday

www.baliguide.com: An insider's guide to Bali

www.bali-paradise.com: Complete online travel guide to Bali

www.baliplus.com: Bali's biggest little guide book online, with up-to-date information on exhibitions, festivals, and just about everything

www.balistarisland.com: A one-stop travel agency to Bali

www.balitourismboard.org: The official tourist board website

www.gili-paradise.com: The best online resource for the Gili Islands

www.i-escape.com: All the details on the best hip hideaways

www.indo.com: Comprehensive travel guide to Indonesia

www.istylemagazine.com: I Style Magazine's website for great fashion and home decor shops

www.kecak.com: Booking portal for Bali and Lombok hotels

www.thelombokguide.com: The definitive guide to Lombok

www.theyakmag.com: Bali's most fashionable rag with the latest in fashion, food, and accommodations

following day at 6am. During the day, people respect strict rules set centuries ago: no working, no entertainment (even love-making), no traveling, no talking, no TV and radio, no eating, and no lights—most *banjar* cut off power to the area, though they will give electricity to families who have babies or young children. People aren't allowed to leave their houses and security guards, called *pecaleng*, patrol the streets to ensure no one disobeys the rules. The airport is closed and no flights are allowed to land or take off during the day. Hotels are allowed electricity to feed their guests but aren't allowed to let their guests leave the property. The traditional "fear" is that evil spirits may still have not left the island and any sound will draw them to your house. By being silent, the evil spirits will leave in search of noise.

Saraswati, the fifth day of the Indian month Magh (Jan–Feb), is a day devoted to the goddess of knowledge, arts, and literature, Dewi Saraswati. To mark the occasion, offerings are placed on books and shrines. Students and teachers attend special ceremonies in schools and universities.

ON LOMBOK

The main religious event on Lombok is the **Bau Nyale Festival** (Feb or Mar; p. 310). The Lingsar Temple is the site of a mock war in October for **Perang Topat** (p. 295).

Calendar of Events

For an exhaustive list of events beyond those listed here check http://events.frommers.com, where you'll find a searchable, up-to-the-minute roster of what's happening in cities all over the world.

Bali Spirit Festival (www.balispiritfestival. com): A yoga festival based in Ubud over a week in March or April.

Bali Arts Festival (www.baliartsfestival.com; **Taman Werdhi Budaya Arts Center,** Jl. Nusa Indah, Denpasar; ℂ 0361/227176; www. artifoundation.org): A month-long (typically June–July) festival in Denpasar. Dancers from all over Bali gather for the opening grand parade. Events include traditional dances, music, and night markets. Special foreign groups are also invited to perform.

Senggigi Festival: A week-long cultural festival in July in Lombok's tourism central.

Sanur Kite Festival: Typically held over 3 days during July or August, depending on the wind, in Kesiman, near Sanur. Daily competitions are attended by thousands of locals and teams from overseas keen to win a prize.

Negara Bull Races (Bali Tourism Board in Denpasar ℂ **0361/235600):** Traditional bull races occur every other Sunday from July through October in Parancak.

Nusa Dua Festival: A week-long festival in August offering an insight into Balinese culture and customs with art, cultural, and sporting events.

Sanur Village Festival (www.gotosanur. com): A weekend festival in August that celebrates Sanur with music and dance.

Kuta Karnival (www.kutakarnival.com): A week in September of surfing competitions, games, music, and food in Kuta.

Ubud Writers Festival (www.ubudwriters festival.com): A festival to exchange ideas and celebrate writing in Bali and the world; 1 week in October.

LAY OF THE LAND

Only 37km (23 miles) separates Bali from Lombok, although there's some 1,300m (4,265 ft.) of vertical drop in the Lombok Strait. This almost trivial distance belies an evolutionary lifetime in the development of plants and animals. The deep ridge forms part of the fabled **Wallace's line,** the imaginary boundary drawn in 1859 by Alfred Russel Wallace, which runs between the far west coast of Australasia through to southeast Asia and separates the natural world in two parts. On one side, you find only those animals and fauna similar to Australia, such as marsupials or cockatoos, and on the other, Bali side are monkeys and woodpeckers. Wallace's observations provided Darwin with information that accelerated his thesis on the *Origin of the Species.* Quite bizarrely, even birds observe this line.

Bali's place at the edge of the Indo-Australian and northern Eurasian tectonic plates is indeed explosive, and little wonder that the island is dominated by volcanoes. A volcanic mountain range stretches all the way across the island; northern and southern plains surround this mountain range, with the northern being narrower and hillier, making rice-growing more difficult, while the southern plain is rich and intensively cultivated, with terraced rice fields dominating the landscape.

Gunung Batur remains a very active volcano and erupted three times in the 20th century, in 1905, 1926, and 1963, and continued spouting until 1974. The highest mountain, **Gunung Agung,** was quiet for almost 150 years, but erupted quite spectacularly with little warning in 1963, killing some 2,000 people and destroying much of the local vegetation and surrounding villages. It also lowered itself by some 200m (656 ft.).

Although Bali was made famous by its surf, the images of a golden sand playground are often wide of the mark, because the majority of the popular coastline of the west is dominated by rocks or black volcanic sand. Golden beaches and coral reefs are rarer than the pervading tourism image of Bali suggests, and are the exception rather than the rule. The north coast has much coarser sand and the east has mainly stones and pebbles, although there are some hidden gems.

Flora & Fauna

Huge banyan trees grow majestically in the grounds of temples or other holy places. Tamarind trees are typically found on the north coast, and in the highlands acres of clove trees planted by Suharto to make local cigarettes, still smoked today, grow in abundance.

Some 15 varieties of bamboo grow on Bali alone, which are used in anything from baskets, satay sticks, and furniture to great 3,000-sq.-m (32,291-sq.-ft.) buildings. Mangrove trees hug the shores near Sanur and farther south toward Tanjung Benoa. On the Bukit, where the land is arid, flame and acacia trees create a shrubland.

The most important of all crops on Bali is rice. It has shaped the culture and the landscape, and it's no coincidence that the word for rice, *nasi*, also means meal. Rice is the main crop of the island and is grown in such abundance that even as the cornerstone of the staple diet for all, there's sufficient left over for export. In the last part of the 20th century, attempts were made to increase the number of crops per year from two to three using artificial nutrients and fertilizers. What was overlooked however was the complex system of irrigation, *subak*, developed over hundreds of years, and the interdependence of each *sawah*, or rice field. The disturbance of this shared irrigation between farmers, who themselves have not been fully aware of just how developed and interdependent they were, has had in some cases crippling results.

The west of the island has coconut plantations. Most of the original taller coconut varieties are now being replaced with the dwarf hybrids that have higher yields. Coconut trees are extremely valuable to the community, not only for the coconuts, but also for their many byproducts. Other crops include fruit and vegetables around Bedugul. With heights of around 1,200m (3,937 ft.), the cool temperatures together with the nutrient-rich soil are ideal conditions for most vegetable growing. These cool temperatures are also ideal for coffee and Indonesia is the fourth largest producer of coffee globally. Although most of the coffee grown is in Java and Sumatra, Bali also plays a small part in the export. Coffee plantations are in the central mountains around Munduk, Batukaru, and even Kintamani.

On the western side of Wallace's line, Bali is the natural home to mammals associated with the Indo-Asian continent, although the last tiger seen here was apparently shot dead in 1937. However, Bali is still rich with the likes of deer, civets, wild buffalo, and more monkeys than you'd care to shake a stick at—not least because they'd likely take it from you and shake it right back. Furthermore, Bali has more than 300 species of birds such as swallows, starlings, and sea eagles. The underwater world, especially around Nusa Lembongan and Penida, contains some of the greatest varieties of fish and shellfish in the world, such as the Mola mola, sea horses, manta rays, dolphins, and sharks.

RESPONSIBLE TRAVEL

With its exceptional natural sites and indigenous cultures, Indonesia could become one of the world leaders in ecotourism, with Bali playing a key role. But ecotourism development in Bali is still far from its potential, even though increasing awareness and more educated travelers have made this sector the most interesting growth segment of tourism in Bali today.

Historically, Bali attracted the rich, the cultured, and the bohemian seeking the idyllic island life. Yet this paradise situation eventually gave way to the advent of cheaper travel brought on by a new wave of tourists, many initially seeking the surf of Kuta. Low-end hotels and guesthouses quickly sprang up to cater to this new market.

To counter this tourist insurgency, the government of the day had a plan: containment. The maxim was that tourist revenues were good, but tourism on the whole was bad. The government attempted to keep this growing wave within the confines of a government-sponsored tourist enclave, Nusa Dua, but this strategy proved to be short-lived. Not only did tourism persist beyond the artificial boundaries, but also it soon became clear that focusing tourism in one area at the expense of all others created an imbalance in tourist revenues and led to an uneven and unsustainable demand for water, waste-disposal, and road use, not to mention negative ecological impact and coastal erosion.

Rolling forward to today when one would hope that some lessons had been learned, the demand for basic utilities and the need to dispose of the waste and effluence of the millions of tourists still leads many of the grand hotels of Seminyak and Kuta to pollute the immediate seas and beaches on which their revenues rely.

The effects on the social strata and structure of Bali has been, to date, much contained, due in many parts to the self-policing and self-appointed village council, the banjar. They rule over social laws and are a necessary ally for any hotel, villa, or other business. Woe betide any who challenges their authority without just cause.

Tourists, too, have reacted against their irresponsible past. The noisy few that pollute the streets and bars of Kuta are slowly being outnumbered by a responsible and growing majority seeking the peace and natural charms of the original Bali. This is evidenced by the increasing number of eco- and socially responsible semi-educational resorts. The **Aman hotel group** is possibly the most high profile, tourist-dependent business that prides itself on bringing more to a community than it can take away.

Bali is now seeing a huge development in ecotourism resorts, but although some are extremely good, others make promises they don't keep. While in no way an exclusive list, we recommend the following accommodations, which are all trying to do something positive for the local environment: **The Menjangan** (p. 282), **Munduk Moding Plantation** (p. 216), **The Oberoi Lombok** (p. 316), **Puri Lumbung Cottages** (p. 216), **Sarinbuana Eco Lodge** (p. 219), and **Udayana Eco Lodge** (p. 152). Some newer resorts are fully off the grid, powered by solar or wind and even charging separately for air-conditioning, such as **Gili Eco Villas** (p. 330).

Among the more dedicated offerings is **C Bali** (p. 210) and the village ecotourism network **JED** (p. 40) with their four initiatives in Sibetan, Kiadan Pelaga, Tenganan, and Nusa Ceningan.

The waters around Bali and Lombok offer some of the best diving in the world, however the coral reefs and the marine ecosystems face increased pressures from sedimentation, pollution, overfishing, reef bombing, cyanide fishing, and exploitative recreational activities. Various initiatives and teams of dive schools are working together to help promote the rejuvenation of damaged reefs, educate fishermen about safe fishing practices, and protect the reefs from any further erosion. The **Gili Eco Trust** (p. 337) works with all seven of the dive schools in the Gili Islands with outstanding success. In Permuteran, **Reef Seen Aquatics** (p. 264) has built the largest "Biorock" installation in the world while working with the local community to create other successful restoration projects. The World Wildlife Federation in Indonesia is

JOHN hardy's BALI

John Hardy, founder of the Green School (p. 194), is a bon vivant, visionary, and Canadian-gone-Balinese. Here are his principles for living and exploring Bali:

Walk   You can walk safely everywhere; you could walk across Bali and never walk on the road. So, get off the road and walk. There's always a path down to the river; there's always a path across the river up the other side.

Bike   Get on a bicycle. If you're too hot or tired to ride uphill, take a bus up the hill and ride downhill—any hill. You really can't get lost if you ride downhill; eventually you'll end up at the ocean. Take any road down from Kintamani. If you can say the word Ubud, you can get there.

Get a Guide   If you can afford a ticket to get here, you can afford a guide.

Nothing fancy, just someone you've convinced to show you Bali—the sister, cousin, uncle of the person that's running your hotel. Go to temple; go to the mountains; go anywhere, such is the magic of the guide.

Get Dressed   When the Balinese called the gods down, they called them to bless all souls on the planet. This is magic, so get dressed for it. Ask a Balinese person to help you get the proper temple attire. Every Balinese person, rich or poor, has it and goes to temple. And so should you.

Eat Temple Food   The food in the temple is amazing and made as an offering—you won't taste this anywhere else. If there's any way you can talk your guide into getting you temple food, it's worth the effort.

working with Friends of the Reef to help protect the reef in the **West Bali National Park** (p. 279).

In addition to the resources for Bali listed above, see frommers.com/planning for more tips on responsible travel.

BALI & LOMBOK REGIONS & SUGGESTED ITINERARIES

3

Y ou'll never tire of temples to visit, beaches to discover, and trails to hike in Bali and Lombok. In truth, there's so much here for the visitor to do that a week or even two may not seem enough time to enjoy island life—just ask any of the expats who now call the islands home. But you can certainly cram in a lot of activity, thanks to Bali's extensive tourism infrastructure and an endless array of people and companies ready to take you wherever you want to go.

Physically, Bali is divided in half, east to west, by a volcanic mountain chain, and north to south by deep river gorges. **Black volcanic sand** is the norm, but white sand beaches periodically dot the coast, with some of the most spectacular either on the Bukit Peninsula or hidden in the remote east, with its crystal clear seas that are perfect for **diving and snorkeling.** Two active **volcanoes** dominate the island: Gunung Agung, the apex of Balinese religious and cultural belief, and Gunung Batur, with its twin calderas and shimmering lake, Danau Batur. The northwest is given over mainly to the **national park** and the central mountains to coffee and crops.

Most tourists spend their time in the southern areas of Bali (the Bukit Peninsula, Kuta, and Seminyak) with a side trip to Ubud, but if you have more time, you'll be rewarded with plenty of off-the-beaten-track experiences.

THE REGIONS IN BRIEF

Bali

SOUTH BALI   You'll find the most developed area of Bali on this triangular wedge of tropical lowlands south of Ubud, next to the surfing hotspot of the Bukit Peninsula. The tourist hub of Seminyak-Legian-Kuta is next door to the international airport and provides a convenient first stop and a good base for day trips. **Kuta** is perhaps the most developed, with the cheapest digs on the island. The tourist influx makes this the place to come for nightlife, which attracts a younger, backpacking crowd, but you'll find much better fine-dining options in Seminyak. Unfortunately, Kuta Beach has a very strong current, which makes swimming difficult and dangerous, but it's a surfer's paradise with rip curls and challenging waves. **Seminyak** is certainly Bali's chicest "village," home to the majority of the island's expats and upscale hotels. See chapters 5 and 6.

Denpasar is Bali's capital, with a population of more than a half-million. Although most visitors completely bypass the city for more idyllic surrounds, it's home to the Bali Museum (p. 99), one of the island's best for a general overview of Balinese history and culture.

Although **Sanur** has a history of hosting international visitors that dates to the beginning of the 20th century, it maintains a level of tranquility near impossible to find in the tourist mania of Seminyak-Legian-Kuta. Surfing, windsurfing, scuba diving, and snorkeling are the main attractions here. Just off shore are the islands of **Nusa Penida, Nusa Lembongan,** and **Nusa Ceningan,** which provide some of Bali's finest scuba diving and are an easy boat ride from the mainland. See chapter 7.

BUKIT PENINSULA   Globetrotting surfers head to this dollop of land just to the south of the airport, and it's now hot on the lists of hotel and resort developers. **Jimbaran Bay,** just past the airport, is famous for its beach lined with seafood restaurants. **Nusa Dua** is a government-sponsored-and-built, walled, high-end resort that sits above the eastern cliffs and is soon to be joined by a similar new development, Pecatu Indah, on the west. In the meantime, the surf still rages at **Uluwatu,** providing one of Bali's, and indeed the world's, most famous waves. See chapter 8.

UBUD   Simply put, Ubud's raison d'être is to be Balinese. The island's rich culture—with traditions, artistry, and spirituality that encompass seemingly every aspect of daily life—thrives here in a multitude of temples, museums, art galleries, and artisan villages. Money and development in Ubud is funneled toward preserving traditions and encouraging cultural innovations; international chain companies are kept at bay. You really can't visit Bali without seeing Ubud! See chapter 9.

CENTRAL MOUNTAINS   Volcanic **Gunung Batur,** with its double caldera, is the biggest draw for visitors to the central mountains. Although your experience of the mountain may be compromised by overly aggressive touts and busloads of tourists, the view from the top at sunrise is certainly worth it. Don't overlook the other highland charms hidden in villages on the volcano's slopes. Bring your hiking shoes and warm clothes—it's a different world up here. See chapter 10.

EAST   The volcanic chain of mountains that dominates Bali's landscape is home to the center of the Balinese world: **Gunung Agung.** On the drive up to the mountain and **Pura Besakih,** Bali's largest and holiest temple, you'll pass through one of Bali's most scenic areas, the **Sidemen Valley.** East Bali also has its fair share of gorgeous coastline and some of Bali's greatest scuba diving and snorkeling is right off the shore of **Tulamben** and **Amed.** See chapter 11.

NORTH   North Bali's seaside villages and resorts are charming and quiet, made remote by the central mountains that divide the island. See chapter 12.

WEST   The western half of Bali is dominated by the **West Bali National Park,** with its hiking and bird-watching, and supreme diving off **Menjangan Island.** See chapter 13.

Lombok

WEST   The west coast is Lombok's most developed area and the home of the majority of islanders. The cities of **Ampenan, Mataram,** and **Cakranegara** serve as the main jumping off point to the rest of the island. Both the port and airport are here. See p. 293. **Senggigi,** just north of the cities, is Lombok's main tourist hub, with the most hotels and resorts on the island, and is the home base for many of the island's tour providers. See p. 298.

SOUTHWEST This peninsula remains Lombok's least developed area in terms of tourism and thus provides a unique opportunity to explore hidden bays and deserted beaches. See p. 305.

SOUTH A new megaresort near Lombok's **Kuta** has been proposed for south Lombok, which has possibly some of the finest beaches in all Indonesia. The surf here is also internationally renowned. See p. 308.

CENTRAL The cooler central region of Lombok presents your best opportunity for shopping. Small artisan villages that produce ikat cloth, baskets, and pottery are scattered among the hills here. See p. 302.

NORTH This is the seat of **Gunung Rinjani,** Lombok's sacred volcano and destination for many of the island's tourists. See p. 313.

EAST To see the least developed and least visited area of Lombok, come to the east. The villages here are home to a very traditional society of Sasak people. You can also catch a ferry to the islands of Komodo and Flores from here. See p. 319.

The Gili Islands

These three tiny islands (**Gili Air, Gili Meno,** and **Gili Trawangan**) have no cars, scant electricity and running water, and little connection to the outside world. Therefore, they're very popular among backpackers, surfers, and anyone looking to go off the grid for a while. Aside from scuba diving, the main draw here is the potential to spend all your time with your feet in the sand. See chapter 15.

THE BEST OF BALI IN 1 WEEK

The two most popular places to base your visit are the **Seminyak/Canggu** area (chapter 6) and **Ubud** (chapter 9). Seminyak offers great surfing, beaches, shopping, restaurants, and nightlife while Ubud will take you into the heart of Bali's cultural life and its lush green rice paddies.

Day 1: Beach & Shopping

From low price to high, we recommend checking into the following accommodations in the Kuta/Seminyak/Canggu area: **Three Brothers Inn** (p. 60), **Desa Seni** (p. 96), or the **Samaya** (p. 79). After breakfast, head to **Ku de Ta** (p. 82) and grab one of the sun loungers. Spend the morning soaking up the sun and scanning the surfers. For some retail therapy, head down Jalan Laksmana and Jalan Raya Seminyak where there are plenty of places to pick up gifts to take home and threads for the beach. Catch the sunset at **Woo Bar** (p. 95), on the beachfront at the new **W Resort** (p. 80). For dinner, take in an Italian meal at **La Lucciola** (p. 84) or **EVO** (p. 84), or delve into some spicy Indian dishes at **Sarong** (p. 85).

Day 2: Pamper Yourself

Head to **Desa Seni** (p. 98) and start your day with a Pilates or yoga class. Enjoy a healthy light lunch of ingredients from the organic garden. Enjoy a spa treatment

Suggested Bali & Lombok Itineraries

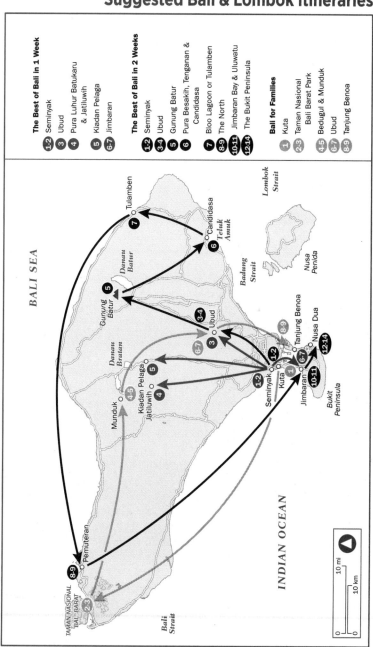

The Best of Bali in 1 Week
1-2 Seminyak
3 Ubud
4 Pura Luhur Batukaru & Jatiluwih
5 Kiadan Pelaga
6-7 Jimbaran

The Best of Bali in 2 Weeks
1-2 Seminyak
3-4 Ubud
5 Gunung Batur
6 Pura Besakih, Tenganan & Candidasa
7 Bloo Lagoon or Tulamben
8-9 The North
10-11 Jimbaran Bay & Uluwatu
12-14 The Bukit Peninsula

Bali for Families
1 Kuta
2-3 Taman Nasional Bali Barat Park
4-5 Bedugul & Munduk
6-7 Ubud
8-9 Tanjung Benoa

at **Jari Menari** (p. 90) or the **Theta Spa** (p. 67), followed by tea at **Biku** (p. 86) or cocktails at the whimsical **Sea Circus** (p. 87), followed by a sunset visit to **Tanah Lot** (p. 270), one of Bali's most magical temples. For dinner, head to **Hotel Tugu in Canggu** (p. 97) or back to **Seminyak** for an assortment of restaurants to choose from.

Day 3: Downtown Ubud

Transfer to one of Ubud's fantastic resorts set in the rice paddies. Our favorites include, from low price to high, **Alam Sari** (p. 178), the **Uma Ubud** (p. 175), and the **COMO Shambhala** (p. 173). Take the day to absorb the bustle of downtown Ubud, stopping at the **Neka** (p. 189) and the **ARMA** (p. 188) museums. Pause at **Sari Organic** (p. 185) or **Clear Café** (p. 183) for a healthy lunch and coffee, and afterwards bargain for woodwork and sarongs along Monkey Forest Road. Finish your day with world-class dining at **Minami** (p. 181) or **Mozaic** (p. 180), followed by martinis at rollicking **Naughty Nuri's** (p. 184).

Day 4: Rice Paddies & Adventure

Start with an early visit to **Pura Luhur Batukaru** (p. 218) and soak in the spirits and the cool jungle air. Then head for a trek around the mystical rice paddy fields of **Jatiluwih** (p. 217). The cool western uplands, overlooking half the island, offer magnificent views. In the afternoon, go on an adventurous white-water rafting trip with **Bali Adventure Tours** (p. 52), or visit the **Bali Bird Park** (p. 113) or the **Elephant Safari Park** (p. 194). End the day back in central Ubud with a European meal at the romantic **Bridges** (p. 180) or a traditional rijsttafel feast at **Warung Enak** (p. 185).

Day 5: Give Back to Bali

Spend the day with JED (a local ecotourism mini-network) at the traditional village **Kiadan Pelaga** (p. 214) in the central mountains. You'll learn about the process of growing and making coffee, see dry rice paddy fields, and meet the members of a small community. The villagers will prepare a traditional Balinese feast for you. All proceeds go right back to the village.

Day 6: Beach Bliss

Transfer to a luxurious splurge spa resort on the Bukit Peninsula for your final two days; recommendations include the **Ayana** (p. 138), the **Four Seasons Jimbaran Bay** (p. 137), and the new **Banyan Tree** (p. 150). Take in a swim at your respective resort's pristine beach, or head to the **Nammos Beach Club** at the Karma Kandara (p. 150) to swim in the safe shallow waters and for delicious Mediterranean plates. Take in a spa treatment at any of the recommended resorts above or visit the gorgeous cliffside temple **Uluwatu** (p. 145) at sunset. For supper, head to **Jimbaran Bay** (p. 133) beach for the festive holiday-like atmosphere—complete with mariachis.

Day 7: Last Minute Sun, Shopping & Spa

Take it easy on your last day. Soak up that last bit of sun, do some shopping, and splash out on a spa treatment before reluctantly making your way back to the airport.

THE BEST OF BALI IN 2 WEEKS

If you have 2 weeks to spare, you can take a more leisurely and complete tour of the island.

Days 1 & 2: Seminyak

Lounge at the oceanfront pool at the luxurious **Legian** (p. 78), followed by a sunset visit to the temple **Pura Tanah Lot** (p. 270). The next day, take a surf lesson at the **Rip Curl School of Surf** (p. 68), followed by a sunset cocktail and dinner at **Ku de Ta** (p. 82).

Days 3 & 4: Ubud

After the 1-hour drive to **Ubud** (chapter 9), base yourself at either the **COMO Shambhala** (p. 173) or the **Chedi Club** (p. 173)—worth every rupiah. Take a morning trek through the rice paddies and then check into one of the many local spas. Tuck into a gourmet French meal at **Mozaic** (p. 180) for dinner. The next day, peruse the numerous shops on Monkey Forest Road and take a break at the **Monkey Forest** (p. 195), where you can feed the monkeys a few bananas. Late in the afternoon, take the 1-hour drive to Penelokan, a town that sits on the outer crater's edge of **Gunung Batur** (**Mount Batur**) (p. 209). The best of the local accommodations is the brand new **Ayu Resort** (p. 211).

Day 5: Gunung Batur

Make the 2-hour ascent of Gunung Batur, an active volcano. At the top, you can boil eggs in pockets of erupting steam and walk along one of the volcano's ridges. In the afternoon, rent a car for the 2-hour trip to check-in to **Candidasa** (p. 238) on Bali's east shore. The boutique **Alila Manggis** (p. 237) has good value accommodations, beachside massage pavilions, and one of the area's best restaurants, **Sea Salt** (p. 237).

Days 6 & 7: The East

Take a day trip to **Pura Besakih** (p. 231), Bali's most important temple, and spend the afternoon wandering around Tenganan village, followed by dinner at **Vincent's** (p. 241) in Candidasa. The next day, go diving or snorkeling at the **Bloo Lagoon**. If you're an advanced diver, sign up for the famed wreck dive at **Tulamben** (p. 247).

Days 8 & 9: The North or Lombok

To truly get away from it all, head to either Bali's northern (chapter 12) beaches by car or the neighboring island of **Lombok** (chapter 14) via plane or boat. In the north, stay at the **Matahari Beach Resort** (p. 265), which provides bungalows with traditional Balinese facades and a Michelin star-worthy restaurant. On Lombok, the most luxurious (and good value) option is the **Oberoi** (p. 316), with a gorgeous swimming pool and secluded beach.

Days 10 & 11: Jimbaran Bay

Rent a car to the romantic yet local area of **Jimbaran Bay** (p. 133), home to a number of the world's top resorts. The cream of the crop are the **Karma Kandara**

(p. 150) and the **Four Seasons Resort at Jimbaran Bay** (p. 137). Visit the cliffside temple **Uluwatu** (p. 145) at sunset, followed by a grilled lobster and shrimp dinner at **Menega Café** (p. 143), the best seafood hut on Jimbaran beach.

Days 12–14: The Bukit Peninsula

End your holiday by winding down beachside or poolside at any number of the resorts near **Uluwatu** (p. 145). Visit **Bumbu Bali** (p. 166), one of the island's top restaurants, which offers authentic Balinese cuisine and cooking classes.

BALI FOR FAMILIES

Bali is an excellent choice for family holidays; with so much on offer, you're spoiled for choice. To top this, the Balinese love youngsters and often slather them in attention. Your children will be enchanted by the local color that surrounds them from the picturesque underwater world to the noisy ceremonies. Most resorts cater to children with clubs, programs, and classes such as kite making and Balinese mask painting and you can often get discounted interconnecting rooms and children's meals.

Day 1: Kuta

Start your children's trip off with a rip and sign them up for a half-day surfing lesson at **Rip Curl School of Surf** (p. 68) or with **Marcy** (p. 68). Either way, you can lounge on a beach chair while they have their lessons.

For the afternoon, head to the water park **Waterbom** (p. 69). Have dinner at **Papa's** (p. 64) and order an explosive volcano pizza—lit at your table, it burns for 2 minutes before youngsters get to blow it out.

Days 2 & 3: Taman Nasional Bali Barat Park (West Bali National Park) in Menjangan

It's a 3-hour drive from Seminyak, but be a good troop leader and lead your pack on a 2-day adventure to the 1,000-hectare (2,471-acre) **Taman Nasional Bali Barat Park** (**West Bali National Park**) (p. 279). It's worth it. Stay at the family-friendly **Menjangan Jungle and Beach Resort** (p. 282) in a hut in the mangroves. Snorkel off the coral reef walls of Menjangan Island. After lunch, take a jeep tour of the park where wildlife, including deer, monkeys, wild chickens, and wild boar, gather at the watering holes.

Fill your second day with an early morning bird-watching tour, kayaking at high tide, horseback riding, and trekking. Your hotel will help you organize all your activities.

Days 4 & 5: Bedugul & Munduk

Your drive to Bedugul and the beautiful **Botanical Garden** (p. 213) will take you through bamboo forests. After the gardens, head to the **Bali Tree Top Adventure Park** (p. 213), where the whole family can try their hands at a variety of adventure circuits and all sorts of active play. In the afternoon check into the **Puri Lumbung Cottages** (p. 216), which has stunning panoramas of the rice fields and coast.

SUGGESTED LOMBOK itineraries

It's a 25-minute flight or 2-hour boat ride to Lombok, which means that this neighboring island demands several days of your time.

Spend at least 2 days on Lombok. Base yourself in **Senggigi** (p. 298), the tourism hub, and take scuba-diving trips along the coast. Rent a driver to take you on a shopping tour through the island interior. If you're really ambitious, you can make it to the **Gili Islands** (chapter 15) to spend the night, but these dots of sand are best enjoyed over a few days and without a rush.

With a little more time you can scale sacred **Gunung Rinjani** (p. 317)—treks last from 2 to 4 days. Or head the opposite direction and go to the south coast, perhaps the most beautiful strip of sand and rock in all of Indonesia. Use **Kuta** (p. 54) as a base for exploring the beaches, surf, and back roads, and to witness the sunset.

Lombok is also a key transportation point for travel to islands east, such as Komodo and Flores. Lombok-based **Sunda Trails** (p. 294) can take you there.

Days 6 & 7: Ubud & Surrounding Area

There are three options for the day here and even if you're running a democracy, it's going to be hard to choose given the names alone: the **Elephant Park** (p. 194), the **Bali Bird Park** (p. 113), or the **Bali Safari & Marine Park** (p. 113). Check in to the luxurious **Chedi Club** (p. 173) in time for their scrumptious afternoon tea (included in the price) or the **Alam Sari** (p. 178), with activities for youngsters such as painting, kite making, mountain biking, and swimming.

In the morning, either go to the **Monkey Forest** (p. 195) and spend some time with those pesky relatives or go **rafting** (p. 193). In the afternoon stroll the streets for some shopping or just enjoy the hotel pool and relax.

Days 8 & 9: Tanjung Benoa

Spend your final family time in the relaxed setting of the **Conrad** (p. 165). Heaps of activities here for children include water-skiing, windsurfing, snorkeling, banana boating, and jet-skiing. Check your young ones into the all-day children's club while you grab a *bale* (thatched pavilion) and catch up on some reading. The resort even has spa treatments specifically for children so that the entire family can pamper themselves simultaneously. On one of your nights here, hire an in-house babysitter and dine at **Rin** (p. 167) or **Spice** (p. 167), afterwards taking a romantic moonlit walk along the promenade.

ACTIVE TRIP PLANNER

Bali and Lombok offer travelers a fantastic opportunity to combine lazy luxury with heart-pounding adventure and even a bit of personal spiritual enrichment. The azure seas of the Indian Ocean that frame the islands provide the coral reefs and world-famous waves sought by professional divers and hardened surfers alike, and the climate encourages lush green jungles that climb up a picturesque volcanic mountain range ideal for hikers and trekkers. If you seek artistic adventure or personal and spiritual growth, the many varied communities centered around Ubud will help you learn about the island's artistic heritage and, should you wish, let you seek introspection. You may also find your peace on a yoga mat.

ORGANIZED TRIPS & TOURS

Indonesia- & Bali-Based Tour Operators

Independent travelers tend to view organized tours as antithetical to the joy of discovery, but the truth is that there aren't many undiscovered places left in Bali. Besides, leaving the details to an expert frees up substantial time to concentrate on something else—like your vacation. Most tours include local guides, all land transportation, hotels, meals, and any gear that may be required. Guides are particularly useful in Lombok, which compared to Bali is still largely "undiscovered" and where few locals speak English.

Organizing a specialized tour in Bali from your hotel or villa is as easy as calling your concierge or villa manager. Nearly all tourism businesses, from restaurants and car rental companies to hotels, can arrange virtually any trip you dream of. These are small islands with a very tight-knit tourism infrastructure and community. If your point of contact can't arrange the trip personally, chances are they'll know exactly who to call—such is the Balinese sense of hospitality.

BALI **Bali Discovery Tours ★★** (© 0361/286283; www.bali discovery.com) is one of the island's largest and most established tour operators and offers customized and off-the-shelf tours. With 20 years of experience, these guys really know their stuff. The website has up-to-date news on what's happening on the island and a comprehensive list of practical tips and advice to make your holiday a success.

JED ★ (**Jaringan Ekowisata Desa**; © 0361/737447; www.jed.or.id) is an ecotourism, nongovernmental organization that works with four traditional Balinese villages (Pelaga Kiadan, Sibetan, Tenganan, and Cenigan). It organizes day visits to experience village life as well as overnight stays with a village family. This is a very local affair with local guides, local food, and all profits going to the local communities.

Sobek ★★ (© 0361/768050; www.balisobek.com) is a well-established and ethical adventure tour company that arranges and runs white-water rafting, cycling, and trekking all over Bali. Sobek invests heavily in providing the highest safety standards of all companies on the island. All staff receive on-going safety training and language courses to ensure the highest of standards are met.

ABL Tours and Travel (© 0361/731520; www.baliwww.com) is one of the busiest leading tour operators. It can assist with organizing custom-made tours, villa and hotel accommodations, and even weddings.

Bali Adventure Tours (© 0361/721480; www.baliadventuretours.com) can arrange fun day and overnight itineraries to volcanoes, the jungle, and rural villages, and organize rafting and biking.

Bali Trail Blazers ★ (© 0361/842-7181; www.bali-trailblazers.com) offers long bike adventures complete with guides who once rode for "Team Bali."

Dive Around Bali (© 081/237549845; www.divearoundbali.com) specializes in custom dive trips throughout Bali and Lombok.

LOMBOK & THE GILI ISLANDS **Island Promotions** (© 0361/753241; www.gili-paradise.com) provides accurate and up-to-date information on transport, hotels, and activities for the Gili islands. It has a reliable booking service to plan activities before you arrive.

Sunda Trails (© 0370/647390; www.sundatrails.com) offers off-the-beaten-track tours to remote villages on Lombok and the nearby islands. It specializes in creating tailor-made programs for those looking for something a little bit different from the usual packages available.

International Tour Operators

Asia Transpacific Journeys (2995 Center Green Court, Boulder, CO 80301, U.S.A.; © **303/443-6789** or 800/642-2742; fax 303/443-7078; www.asiatranspacific.com) deals with small groups and custom programs that include luxury accommodations. Tours to Bali can take in the island of Komodo on a traditional Indonesian schooner or trekking in the central mountains.

Backroads (801 Cedar St., Berkeley, CA 94710, U.S.A.; © **510/527-1555** or 800/462-2848; fax 510/527-1444; www.backroads.com) is a cycling and hiking specialist that organizes trips round the island taking in the village communities, the fantastically rich underwater world, and the beaches and scenery of Bali.

Carrier (No. 1 Lakeside, Cheadle, Cheshire SK8 3GW, U.K.; © **0161/491-7630;** www.carrier.co.uk) was voted by Condé Nast Traveler readers as the number-one favorite tour operator. Their service is second to none. Based in the U.K., Carrier can organize luxury stays in villas and hotels throughout Bali and Lombok.

Elegant Resorts (The Old Palace, Chester CH1 1RB, U.K. © **01244/897551;** www.elegantresorts.co.uk) is a renowned luxury resort tour operator that arranges accommodations and packages staying in all the best resorts in Bali and Lombok.

G Adventures (19 Charlotte St., Toronto, Ontario M5V 2H5, Canada; © **888/800-4100** in the U.S. and Canada; © **0844/272-0000** in the U.K.; www.gadventures.com) is a sustainable adventure travel organization with agents all over the world (check the website for a detailed list). It specializes in holidays for independent travelers looking for something unique and organizes trips on both Bali and Lombok.

Intrepid Travel (11 Spring St., Fitzroy, Victoria 3065, Australia ☎ **613/9473-2626** or 613/9473-2673 (in Australia); fax 613/9419-4426; ☎ **0800/781-1660** (in U.K.); ☎ **800/970-7299** (in U.S.); www.intrepidtravel.com) is probably the best choice for an off-the-beaten-track tour on both Bali and Lombok. Intrepid caters its trips to the culturally discerning, those with humanitarian goals, those in search of comfort and adventure, those on a budget, or those looking for a looser structure and lots of options. Its name is its motto, and with some of the best guides in Asia, these folks will take you to the back of beyond safely and in style.

i-to-i (☎ **0113/205-4620** in the U.K. or **800/985-4852** in the U.S.; www.i-to-i.com) is a globally recognized travel organization that places volunteers in overseas projects that assist local communities. Packages include surfing and teaching English or working with orphans and the disabled in Bali.

Kuoni (Kuoni House, Dorking, Surrey RH5 4AZ, U.K.; ☎ **0844/488-0468** (in U.K.); www.kuoni.co.uk), a well-established firm, specializes in long-haul trips with tours to Bali, Lombok, and the Gilis.

Responsible Travel (☎ **01273/600-030;** www.responsibletravel.com) is the leading ethical travel agent and a joint initiative with Conservation International. It works with local communities to create authentic experiences throughout Bali and Lombok.

Trailfinders (48 Earls Court Rd., London W8 6FT, U.K.; ☎ **020/7368-1200;** www.trailfinders.com) is undoubtedly the leading travel agent in the U.K. and Ireland for holidays to Bali and Lombok, and specializes in honeymoons.

ACTIVITIES A TO Z
Performing Arts & Crafts Schools

Ever since the days of Walter Spies in Ubud, Western artists have discovered profound inspiration in Bali's landscape. Of course, the Balinese were doing it long before the Westerners caught on.

The Suly Resort & Spa, Jl. Cok. Rai Pudak, Br. Yangloni, Peliatan (☎ 0361/976185; www.sulyresort.com; Rp100,000 per person per hour), has joined with Bali Global Ashram Foundation to create an education platform where visitors can take classes in pottery, painting, dance, wood carving, kite making, and cooking to name a few. Classes are run by professional and well-known Balinese instructors.

PERFORMING ARTS   The multicultural center **Pondok Pekak,** Jl. Monkey Forest, Ubud (☎ **0361/976194**), essentially a library, is a resource center that brings locals and Westerners together. It offers a wide range of community activities for children and adults largely focused on the Sanggar (traditional music and dance organization). Programs include gamelan and dance (legong and Frog dance) lessons. There is also a selection of traditional Balinese workshops, which allow visitors to learn about fruit carving, Indonesian language, and mask carving.

The **Mekar Bhuana Conservatory,** Jl. Gandapura III, no. 501X, Depasar (☎ **0361/464201** or 081/999191104; www.balimusicanddance.com), runs a selection of courses on gamelan and Balinese dance.

Tjokorda Raka Swastika, Puri Saren, Ubud (☎ **0361/975753**), an accomplished musician who has played with and taught many of the best orchestras in Bali, is now running courses on gamelan and any other musical instruments that form part of the *gong kebyar*. **Pak Tjokorda Raka** is an excellent teacher for all levels. Classes are held in his house on the grounds of Puri Saren, Ubud's Palace.

POTTERY   Italians Marcello and Michela Massoni head **Gaya Ceramic and Design ★★**, Jl. Raya Sayan, Ubud (✆ **0361/7451413;** www.gayafusion.com), which produces pottery for famous brands such as Armani and Bulgari. It offers a selection of courses and a residency program with instructors from all over the globe.

The **Sari Api Ceramic Studio,** Jl. Suweta 176, Ubud (✆ **0361/977917** or 081/24660919; www.sariapi.com), allows guests to explore their creativity using clay. Beginners classes for both children and adults give an introduction to throwing clay on a wheel as well as hand building. Studio space can be rented out to skilled potters.

SILVERSMITHING & JEWELRY   **Studio Perak,** Jl. Hanoman, Ubud (✆ **081/23651809;** www.studioperak.com), employs traditional Balinese silversmithing. Husband and wife Ketut and Joanna have developed their own courses for visitors to try their hands at making Balinese-styled jewelry. Opt for their 3-hour course and make a ring or pendant. Children from 8 years are also welcome.

TEXTILES   **Threads of Life**'s ★, Jl. Kajeng 24, Ubud (✆ **0361/972187;** www.threadsoflife.com), courses explore the history, weaving, dyeing techniques as well as the traditions of ikat and batik using handspun threads and natural dyes. The money goes to support local communities. Classes cost between Rp50,000 and Rp150,000.

The best place to learn about the rich history of batik and the techniques of the trade is with Bali's own batik artist **Ketut Sujana** (✆ **0361/979097** or 081/23762280). Ketut offers hands-on courses for individuals or groups. His workshop is behind his studio in Lungsiakan, on the main road opposite Fly Café outside Ubud. Ketut charges Rp50,000 an hour. Allow about 3 hours for your first course.

Biking ★★

Bali seen from a bike is far more engaging than when seen from a speeding car. You won't see one village where the children don't stop what they're doing to wave and cheer you on. With 1 week in Bali and a good guide, you may be able to circumnavigate the island's full distance of 410km (255 miles). Stick to the back roads as much as you can, and avoid the main road north up the west coast, the main artery for tired lorry drivers going in and out of Java.

A full-day biking tour with a reputable company costs from about Rp500,000 and will generally include bike, lunch, and a local English-speaking guide. Multiday tours either circumvent the island completely or pass through the mainly uncluttered, less traveled roads of the mountainous center and flats of the east.

For those looking for multiday bike tours, Sanur-based **Bali Trail Blazers** ★ (✆ **0361/842-7181;** www.bali-trailblazers.com) specializes in off-road adventures and long trips led by professional Balinese riders. A 10-day trip around the entire island including a guide, bikes, and overnight stay costs about US$1,200 per person and can be adjusted for individual tastes. Highly experienced mountain-bike riders looking for an off-road adventure can book single-track riding through tiny, remote villages. Prices are US$100 per person per day including transport, bike, and lunch. U.S.-based **Pedaler's Pub & Grille** (✆ **877/998-0008;** www.pedalerspubandgrille.com) does a 7-day tour called the "Bali Paradise Ride," which takes you from Ubud, down to Candidasa, and up round the east coast on fairly empty roads and back via Kintamani for US$1,595 including your guide, accommodations, meals, and van support en route.

For relaxed road riding that's more focused on culture than on burning calories, Wayan, the energetic and enthusiastic owner of **Balibike.com ★** (✆ **0361/978052;** www.balibike.com) offers a day trip from Kintamani back down to Ubud on "only his

ALTERNATIVE health & WELLNESS A TO Z

Bali was recently voted the "Asian Spa Capital of the Year" by Asia Spa. Bali hosts numerous alternative therapies for wellness and spiritual enlightenment. Here are some of the most unique offerings on the island.

Ayurveda Uma Inder (℡ 081/236206136; uma_inder@hotmail.com; www.yoga withuma.com), in Ubud, is an Ayurvedic Practitioner and Panchakarma Specialist in women's health. Uma offers consultation, treatments, and self-care educational programs. She's also an ayurvedic doula with experience in fertility awareness, conscious conception, lactation support, and pre-/post-natal wellness programs.

Balian A *Balian* (p. 2) is a traditional Balinese healer. Two favorites are: **Cokorda Rai** (℡ 081/805477388), in Ubud, who reads auras and energy; and **Pak Ketut Arsana,** the founder of Ashram Munivara, dedicated to the teachings of Shiva. Contact him through Ubud Bodyworks Healing Centre, Jl. Hanoman 25, Ubud (℡ 0361/975720; www.ubud bodyworkscentre.com). Also visit **Five**

Elements (℡ 0361/469206; www. fiveelements.org), a healing center in Ubud. The most famous Balians at the moment are **Wayan** and **Ketut Liyer** from the book *Eat, Pray, Love*. You can visit them but with so many Western tourists calling on them, they've somehow lost their charm. Wayan is based in her shop Traditional Balinese Healing in Ubud on Jalan Jembawan; Ketut still practices from his house in Pengosekan. Ask any hotel or villa for directions as the street doesn't have a name.

Herbs & Medicinal Plants Lilir and **Westi** (℡ 081/23816024 or 081/ 23816020; www.baliherbalwalk.com), in Ubud, are a Balinese couple whose families go back nine generations as medicinal plant healers. Both do early morning herb walks through the rice fields, drinking tea, and teaching about the medicinal plants found along the way.

Holistic & Intuitive Healing Frederique Nault (℡ 081/23920615; healing@ indosat.net.id), in Kuta, is a qualified naturopath whose innovative treatments

known secret roads." He will collect you from as far afield as Kuta and take you to Kintamani for breakfast with a view over Lake Batur. You then head mainly downhill back to Ubud for the most delicious lunch, home cooked by his wife, before he returns you to your hotel. Groups reach up to 20 but feature a couple of guides, with one at the back to encourage stragglers. The cost is Rp400,000 from Kuta and Rp350,000 from Ubud including bikes, helmets, breakfast, lunch, and transfers.

Bali-based **Archipelago Adventures** (℡ **0361/844-4624;** www.archipelago-adventure.com) will do 1-day trips on the back roads. It charges US$65 per person if there are only two of you, but less for larger groups.

Lombok has a similar terrain to Bali but there are far fewer accommodations options and once you leave the established tourist west coast, you may well have to rely on your own canvas, or homestays. However, although there are extra hardships and a whole heap of extra planning required, the rewards can be greater. The roads are a lot less clustered and you'll encounter little traffic when north of Senggigi. If you're planning on cycling on Lombok, a guide is a good idea. One word of warning: The coastal areas aren't as flat as they are in Bali.

With a little bit of initiative, some research, and armed with a detailed map, you can head out on your own and explore Lombok. You'll find basic accommodations are drawn from a comprehensive range of powerful methods, such as craniosacral therapy and energy psychology, personally tailored to suit the individual's needs. **Dr. Susan Spillman** (✆ 081/337812502; www.baliartsandtours.com), in Ubud, starts sessions with an in-depth discussion of your concerns and then employs energy work and/or Quantum-Touch—primarily used for pain relief or reduction.

Meditation   Frank Wilson (Brahma Kumaris World Spiritual University, the Meditation Shop; ✆ 081/805398000; www.themeditationshop.org) offers rajah yoga meditation for relaxing, refreshing, and clearing the mind and heart. **Pak Kadek Suambara** (✆ 08/5237131444) in Ubud offers meditation and laughter yoga. The **Bali Usada Meditation Foundation** can be reached at ✆ 0361/289209; www.balimeditation.com (Ngurah Rai 328, Bypass Sanur, Denpasar).

Natural & Raw Food Counseling   Mark Ament (✆ 0361/972033) www.healing vibes.com), in Ubud, is a specialist in healing through living foods and internal cleansing and offers powerful techniques designed to help you lose weight and overcome severe allergies and chronic depression.

Oils   Gabrielle Souczek (✆ 0361/972033) in Ubud at the Healing Vibes Studio performs Raindrop Technique essential oil massages designed to push toxins out of your tissue, oxygenate your cells, repair DNA, eliminate viruses, bacteria, and inflammation, release emotional issues, and leave you feeling vibrant.

Sound Healing   Swami Bodhi Arun (✆ 08/5935174112), in Ubud, accompanies meditation with the vibration and sound of crystal quartz bells.

Tarot Readings   Jan Merrills (✆ 081/999334188; www.janmerrills.com), in Ubud, is an experienced tarot reader, who advises on your current and future life. Or learn to read the cards yourself in an intimate full-day course.

along your route without having to book in advance and there are plenty of places to buy water. You will, however, miss out on some of the history and local knowledge that a local guide usually provides. Look to do no more than 80km (50 miles) in a day.

A reliable company in Lombok is **Mountain Bike Lombok** (✆ 081/999097126; mountainbikelombok@gmail.com), on the main street in Senggigi next to Bumbu Café. Tours are designed for the fit and unfit alike. A 2-hour guided tour costs Rp100,000 per person.

In both Bali and Lombok, roads are narrow and heavily used. Avoid main routes and always wear a helmet. It's possible to rent or borrow bikes from many hotels and ride on your own, at your own pace.

Bird-Watching

Bali and the surrounding islands are a haven for casual bird-watchers and avid twitchers alike. With the successful reintroduction of what was once the world's most endangered species—the eponymous Bali starling is now back and flying free—the island can hold its head up high.

The most well-known and idiosyncratic tours are with Victor Mason who runs **Bali Bird Walks** ★ (✆ 0361/975009; www.balibirdwalk.com), along with his partner

Su and her brother Pink. They've been the best birding guides for the past 15 years. Depending on conditions and demand, they'll take you on a tour of the rice fields around Ubud (for US$33 per person including lunch). They also do walks around Batukaru or if you want they'll head for the sea and wetlands.

Friends of the National Park Foundation (FNPF; ℰ 0361/977978; www.fnpf.org), is a nonprofit organization that works with local communities to assist with the preservation of wildlife in Indonesia. It owns over 20,000 hectares (49,421 acres) on Nusa Penida where they've set up a bird sanctuary. It's currently working on two recovery programs for the Bali starling and the lesser sulphur-crested cockatoo with some success. Come for a day of bird-watching with a dedicated guide or stay the night on the island.

Boating & Sailing ★★★

Several smaller islands are easily accessible from Bali and Lombok, making these two a wonderful base for exploration. The sailing season for many traditional Indonesian boats is May to September. Although a lot of the more established boats are booked almost a year in advance, an increasing number of charter and sail companies are sprouting up. A lot of the shorter trips, typically 5 days, give or take, will focus on the Komodo islands while the longer ones venture out in to the Banda Sea.

The **Royal Bali Yacht Club** (www.royalbaliyachtclub.com) is all dinghies and lasers on Serangan Island, a reclaimed bit of scrubland on the road to Sanur. It has a small facility in Sanur in front of the Mercure hotel on the beach. Visitor membership is only Rp250,000; the club has various boats for rent and will provide lessons at pretty low rates (Rp50,000 per hour per person). If you want to sail, or take the children for the day, it's fun, safe, and low key.

Some of the larger hotels in **Sanur and Nusa Dua** have their own accompaniment of lasers, dinghies, and catamarans for you to use. If your hotel doesn't, you'll easily find various places along the beach that rent them. However, you'll find no sailing nor boats for rent anywhere on the west coast of Bukit peninsula because there are few places to land them safely.

In a different league from many other boats, with prices to match, are the offerings of **Silolona** (ℰ 0361/287326; www.silolona.com), **Ombak Putih** (ℰ 0361/283358; www.ombakputih.com), **Raja Laut** (ℰ 060/88228599; www.rajalaut.com), and newcomer **El Aleph** (info@eastmonsoon.com; www.elalephcruising.com). These are luxury cruises in traditional Phinisi-styled boats, offering educational adventures that take you to some of the most beautiful, and, other than by boat, inaccessible spots in the archipelago. If you've managed to tuck any money away, pretend this is your rainy day and take a trip on one of these before your number's called!

Pitched somewhere in between the high-end charter boats and the mass-market day trips is a journey on what's affectionately known as the Pirate Ship or the Bulan **Purnama** ★★★ (www.bulan-purnama.com). It does both charters and individual cabins and you can rent it out for somewhere in the region of 1,000€ a day, with diving and on-board staff included. This traditional Phinisi wooden boat runs dive and surf charters through the eastern islands, including Komodo to Moyo and then Lombok, or even Labuan Bajo to Komodo. Home anchorage is Gili Trawangan, and the company also organizes Gili Island cruises, starting in Bali. For the less ambitious, try a day trip on a large charter yacht: **Sail Sensations** (ℰ 0361/725864; www.sailsensations.com) will take you to Lembongan for the day; the **Waka** (ℰ 0361/723629; www.the-waka.com) will do the same on a catamaran.

Websites www.baliintaran.com/bali-cruises and www.balicruises.com are useful, though they're ultimately booking agents. They have new and updated information on available boats and may be able to fit your individual dates and requirements.

Cooking ★

Several half- and full-day cooking courses are on offer in Bali. The day typically starts with a visit to a local fresh food market to learn about all the ingredients that go into creating a Balinese dish. The chef will then explain the techniques that are used to put together your dish and once cooking is over, you're rewarded with eating your creation. Look into the following schools: **Alila Manggis** resort in Manggis (℡ 0363/41044; www.alilahotels.com); **Bambu Bali** in Nusa Dua (℡ 0361/774502; www.balifoods.com); and in Ubud, **Casa Luna** (℡ 0361/973282; www.casalunabali.com) and **Mozaic** (℡ 0361/975768; www.mozaic-bali.com). Hotels may also arrange classes on request. **Hanging Gardens** (p. 175) is one of note.

Fishing

Although you can have much fun going out at 5am on a jukung (fishing boat) with a local fisherman, the fishing consists of throwing a simple baited line out the back of a boat and trolling the current or alternatively using a hand line. It's not exactly adrenalin-filled and your time will be spent either puttering out and back at about 4 knots or sitting watching your local friend doing all the fishing (though you'll be fascinated by just how many fish they catch using this method).

Given the amount of marine life and the virtually guaranteed chance of success, it's somewhat surprising that there are so few game fishing boats. If you do find someone to take you out, make sure that the boat has a covered area, looks shipshape, and you have plenty of sunscreen and liquids. Most boats will leave from either Benoa or Padangbai harbors; costs range from US$80 to US$200 per person for 4 hours and boats usually take no more than four people, although some can take as many as eight. Species you're likely to find include Spanish mackerel, wahoo, mahimahi, all sizes of tuna, sail fish, and barracuda.

Established operators are **Bali Fishing** (www.bali-fishing.com) and **Ena Fishing,** Jl. Tirta Ening 1, Sanur (℡ 0361/288829; www.enafishing.com). Ena also runs a night trip leaving at sundown and returning 4 hours later. It's also recently added a freshwater fishing trip to Lake Buyan although the fish here are smaller than those in Lake Batur.

Bali Sports Online

To find out what's happening in the sports world of Bali at any time, check out the Sanur-based Bali sports online magazine at www.stiffchilli.com.

Another option, and labeled as "fishing at its finest," is **Yos Dive** (℡ 0361/773774, 0361/775440, or 0361/775438; www.yosdive.com), based out of Tanjung Benoa. Trolling for 4 hours from a power boat for between two and four people at a time costs US$200 per person. You can also charter a covered power boat for the day, with driver for US$625, including fuel and lunch.

Possibly the best boat is operated by **Blue Water Express** (℡ 0361/895-1082 or 0361/841-3421; www.bwsbali.com). You can charter the whole boat for Rp5,500,000 for 4 hours or Rp8,000,000 for 8 hours. The boat uses GPS and fish-finding technology to locate the shoals. A half-decent picnic lunch is included. The boat carries up to 10 passengers, but only four lines can be used at a time.

Although Lombok has many fishermen, fishing is simply a necessary fact of life. Most fishermen or boat owners are, however, only too delighted to take you out. Prices for a few hours should be about Rp400,000 depending on fuel usage. **Lombok Marine** (© 0370/692225; www.lombokmarine.com), in Mataram, will take you to Desert Point or possibly to deep water spots beyond the Gilis. This is on a traditional jukung and not a speedboat with any facilities other than an awning. In the north, the Oberoi hotel (p. 316) takes up to 5 people for morning fishing trips for $225; outside guests can also book. Trips leave at 6:30am and return at 11am. Hotel chefs are happy to cook the catch.

Golfing ★★★

You could make golf the sole reason for a trip to Bali. The island has several world-class 18-hole courses and a charming 9-hole course. They're all different in style; one in the cool of the mountains, three others fringed by the sea, and the **Bali Beach** 9-hole course (© 0361/287-7333; www.balibeachgolfcourse.com) in the flatlands of Sanur.

The Indonesian Open, the first PGA tour event to visit Bali, was played (with much success) in 2009 at the newest of the courses, **New Kuta Golf** (© 0361/848-1333; www.newkutagolf.com) at Pecatu.

The longest admired of Bali's courses is the Greg Norman–designed **Nirwana** (© 0361/815960; www.nirwanabaligolf.com) at Le Méridien, facing Pura Tanah Lot. This course has won many accolades over the years, among them Best Golf Course in Asia 2005 by *Asian Golf Monthly.* The **Bali Golf and Country Club** (© 0361/771791; www.baligolfandcountryclub.com) is located near many of Bali's top hotels in Nusa Dua.

The **Bali Handara Kosaido** 18-hole course (© 362/342-2646; www.balihandara kosaido.com; US$150 for 18 holes with cart and caddy) bills itself as the highest course in Indonesia. Set next to a lake amid low mountains at the center of Bali, it offers cool and quiet, as well as a tennis court, spa, and hotel.

Prices reflect the high quality of the courses, but check with your hotel, as many have discounted arrangements. Book ahead. Pro shops mainly sell only golf accessories and clothing although they often rent very good golf clubs (and sometimes shoes) at differing levels and price points.

Somewhat surprisingly given the level of tourism on the island, Lombok has two 18-hole courses. The **Lombok Golf Kosaido Country Club** (© 0370/640137; www.99bali.com/golf/lombokkosaido) close to the Oberoi Hotel was designed and is owned by the same people who brought you the Bali Handara Kosaido course. The other, the **Rinjani Country Club Golf & Resort** (© 0370/633839; www.lombok-golf.com), is actually on the side of Mount Rinjani, only 20 minutes from Mataram. Both thankfully are priced far more competitively than their Bali counterparts, with prices ranging from US$65 to US$85 including greens fee and caddy, although a buggy is extra and costs US$25 at Kosaido. You have to walk at Rinjani. Both will rent you clubs and even shoes.

Hiking & Trekking ★★

The year-round temperate climate, the challenging but not daunting terrain, the fascinating culture, and the layers of history at every turn make Bali and Lombok wonderful places to explore on foot. The islands are also small enough that you'll never feel like you're in the middle of nowhere and the prospects of getting totally lost are pretty limited. Hiking is best (and safest) during the dry season (Apr–Oct).

Most peaks, if they're your goal, are scale-able in less than 8 hours, and many can be done in less than 4. The one great trek that takes you farthest from regular habitation and requires careful preparation is **Mount Rinjani** (p. 317) on Lombok. This challenging excursion will take 2 to 4 days, and most definitely requires a guide.

The majority of other mountain treks also necessitate a guide because you'll want to be at the summit by sunrise and so need to head out in darkness at any time from 2am onward. You should be provided with both a head and hand torch. Sunrise, when you get there, is quite a magical and a sublime experience—weather permitting. It's no wonder that the Balinese consider the peak of **Mount Agung** (p. 231) the island's most sacred spot. So much so that you're not allowed to climb at certain times of the Balinese year. Climbing Mount Agung is a pilgrimage for all Balinese and most undertake it at least once during their lifetime.

Trekking agents for Bali include **Bali Adventure Tours** (© 0361/721480; www.baliadventuretours.com); **Clipper** (© 0361/256245; www.clipperdiscovery.com); **Sobek** (© 0361/287059; www.balisobek.com); and Gede from **Bali Sunrise Tours** (© 081/8552669; www.balisunrisetours.com).

For Lombok, many tour agents and trekking offices are based in Senggigi, Senaru, Sembalun Lawang, and Sembalun Bumbung. **Lombok Rinjani Trekking** (© 0370/668-6625; www.lombokrinjanitrekking.com) and **Rinjani Trekking Club** (© 081/75730415; www.info2lombok.com) offer fully equipped treks. Ensure you check in with the official **Rinjani Trek Management Board** (© 0370/641124 or 081/1390047; www.lombokrinjanitrek.org) for all aspects of trekking and guides on Mount Rinjani.

Scuba Diving & Snorkeling ★★★

Bali and Lombok are situated in the heart of the Indo-Pacific, the world's richest marine bio-geographic zone. Due to the Indonesian throughflow, both islands receive plankton-rich waters that foster a diverse underwater ecosystem.

Pelagics (open-ocean marine life) include manta rays, whalesharks, and during July to mid-November Mola molas (the weird-but-wonderful ocean sunfish). The reefs are ideal for snorkeling with profuse hard and soft corals, gorgonian and other seafans, coral bushes, and sponges including some massive barrel sponges. Altogether more than 2,000 species of reef fish thrive in Bali's waters, and then you'll find eels, crabs, lobsters, turtles, starfish, and shrimp, as well as nudibranches, mimic octopus and wonderpus, ambon scorpionfish, rhinopias, and ghost pipefish. Truly, the list goes on.

The best diving in Bali is along the east coast and in the island's northwest corner. **Secret Bay** (p. 280) provides the best "muck dive" with plenty of small, colorful life including seahorses and batfish. In the east, **Tulamben** (p. 247) has a U.S. Army transport ship that sank during World War II and is filled with an extraordinary variety of marine life (and, during the high season, divers). The waters around Nusa Penida hold larger fish—sharks, turtles, and from July to mid-November Mola mola—but because currents can be strong these are for more advanced divers.

Lombok has only just begun to develop as a dive destination and the reefs are healthier, with many that have hardly ever seen a diver. The best current sites are in the island's southwest: **Sunken Island** and **Secret Garden** near Sekotong (p. 305) both have healthy coral and large fish and turtles. Sunken Island is also ideal for snorkeling. **Belongas Bay** has two sea spires where large fish including hammerhead sharks, mackerel, barracuda, and eagle rays are common. During the dry season, there are often reports of more than 100 hammerhead sharks in the area around a spire called Magnet, but because of strong currents, it's for divers holding advanced certification only. Downcurrents have pulled divers to the ocean bottom at around 50 or 60m (160–210 ft.).

Diving at Gili Trawangan, Gili Meno, and Gili Air is quick, fun, and easy, and these are the best places to get certified. Nearly a dozen shops offer courses, and once you're finished, Bali and Lombok are next door for more exciting dives.

OUTFITTERS   Most scuba outfitters on the islands can arrange trips to any of the dive sites. The most popular, one-stop local outfitters are:

Aqua Marine Diving, Jl. Raya Petitenget, Seminyak (📞 **0361/473-8020;** www. aquamarinediving.com), combining British ownership with the expertise of local dive staff, makes for an unbeatable combination. Aqua Marine runs day trips and fully inclusive intensive underwater safaris to the island's best sites. **Skubaskool,** Jl. Dyanapura/Abimanyu 9, Seminyak (📞 **0361/733845;** www.skubaskool.com) is a well-run French operation (although everyone speaks great English) with packages (13 days/12 nights and 22 dives) that enable you to circumnavigate the island.

Other PADI (Professional Association of Diving Instructors— the most reputable international diving organization) dive centers, include: **Abyss Adventures,** Jl. Danau Poso 36b, Sanur (📞 **0361/271317** or 0361/288610; www.abyssadventures. com); **Bali Crystal Divers,** Jl. Tamblingan 168, Sanur (📞 **0361/286737;** www. crystal-divers.com); **Eurodive,** Lipah Bunutan, Amed (📞 **0363/23605;** eurodive bali.com); **Menjangan Resort,** West Bali National Park (📞 **0362/94700;** www. menjanganresort.com); **Mimpi Resort Menjangan,** Banyuwedang (📞 **0362/94497;** www.mimpi.com); **Paradise Palm Beach Bungalows** in Tulamben (📞 **0362/22918;** www.paradise-tulamben.com); **Scuba Seraya Resort,** Desa Tukad Dabu, Tulamben (📞 **0361/282594;** www.scubaseraya.com); and **World Diving Lembongan,** Pondok Baruna, Jungutbatu (📞 **081/23900686;** www.world-diving.com).

In south Lombok, the only dive company is **Dive Zone,** Senggigi (📞 **081/ 916001426;** www.divezone-lombok.com).

The Gili islands, by contrast, are chock full of options. Three of the best are **Blue Marlin Dive** (📞 **0370/634387;** www.bluemarlindive.com), **Dream Divers** (📞 **0370/634547;** www.dreamdivers.com), and **Manta Dive** (📞 **0370/643649;** www.manta-dive.com).

INSURANCE   Most holiday insurance policies don't cover scuba diving; some don't cover snorkeling either. The best idea is to have **DAN** (Divers' Alert Network; www.diversalertnetwork.org) membership and coverage which provides evacuation for diving- and nondiving-related incidents, and dive-related medical treatment. You get peace of mind and an expert in diving-related injuries/problems at the end of the phone, no matter where in the world you find yourself.

WHEN TO DIVE   In Bali, the rainy season runs from October to March. The monsoon patterns, lunar calendar, and seasonal upwelling of rich, cold water in the Lombok Strait (between Bali and Lombok) generally means that April to June and September to November offer the best seasons for diving. July to August and December to January are very good, while February to March usually has the least to offer. Although you can see manta rays year-round, the best season is April to May and for Mola mola it's August to October.

Surfing ★★★

Bali shot to surfing prominence on the back of Albert Falzon's 1972 epic Morning of the Earth. The opening shots of this now infamous surf movie feature the trademark cave of Uluwatu (but the wave itself was actually Australia's Winki-Pop, contrary to popular belief). Now, after years of adventure, exploration, and intrepid traveling against nature and all odds, Indonesia is one of the most sought-after and cherished surfing destinations on earth, with Bali its base station and beating heart.

Sitting roughly in the middle of the Indonesian archipelago's 17,000-plus islands, Bali lies 8 degrees south of the equator and enjoys two distinct seasons. The shorter, hotter wet season runs from December through to the end of March while the more popular and longer season runs from April through to the end of November. Bali has breaks on both the east and west coasts, and so hungry wave seekers can find offshore conditions on this world-famous surfing island every single day of the year. Now that the east coast waves of the wet season are becoming more popular and well known, surfing tourists are starting to visit in larger numbers at this time of year, too. With the quality and consistency of waves in Bali it's possible to escape the masses by venturing farther away from the more famous spots.

THE BREAKS As far as surfing real estate goes, pound for pound, mile for mile, Bali's **Bukit Peninsula** (p. 133) is only perhaps equaled by the meccalike North Shore of Oahu, in Hawaii. Uluwatu (p. 145) lies on the southwest corner of Bali and is the home to one of the most sacred Hindu temples on Bali. **Padang Padang** (p. 147) is one of the country's heaviest and most dangerous waves. Just north is **Bingin** (p. 147), a short and hollow ride, suited to tube-riding and the flamboyant trickery displayed by the cunning local surfers who govern the place. On the east coast, **Sanur** (p. 101) is a high-quality surfing area in the most picturesque of settings. **Sri Lanka** (p. 163) is another highlight to this surfing wonderland. The beach is immaculate, a rarity in these parts, and carries the polished persona of a private resort-style beach. **Nusa Dua** (p. 163) can get big—really big. With a take-off zone the size of an American football field, the heaving chunks of ocean swell provide aquatic thrills to the willing and can deliver the uninitiated into a world of unforeseen pain. Join the throngs of tourists and locals at **Kuta Reef** (p. 68), easily spotted from your plane window to the north of the ocean-intruding runway.

Lombok is home to the infamous **Desert Point** (p. 306), voted by Australian surf bible, *Tracks* magazine, as the best wave on earth. Notoriously fickle and affected by the strong currents ripping through the Lombok trench (the world's second-deepest stretch of ocean), many surfers camp out here for months on end waiting for magic to happen. Now within easy striking distance from Bali, particularly if you own a helicopter, when the waves get good here the word spreads pretty quickly. In stark contrast to Desert Point, **Ekas** (p. 309) has a variety of waves for beginners all the way through to advanced surfers.

OUTFITTERS & INFORMATION Most of the surfing outfitters on the islands will be able to set you up with a full surfing itinerary. Some of the best equipped are: **Tropicsurf** (© **07/54554129 in** Australia or 081/916666607 in Bali; www.tropic surf.net), headed by Jack Chisholm (ask for Jack), offering private guided and personalized coaching services. The only surf school worldwide to be inducted into Australia's surfing hall of fame, Tropicsurf is the global leader in surf coaching, for beginners to world champions, and is the best upmarket service in Bali. **Marcy's Surf Coaching** (© **081/23859454**; www.teachsurf.com) is a true original and Marcy (a suntanned New Zealander with 20 years' coaching experience in Bali alone) will get you on your feet in no time. Best training is one on one, but he'll also do groups. **Girls Surf Retreats** (© **081/916666607**; www.girlssurfretreat.com) offers surf, fitness, yoga, and spa pampering retreats with a maximum of six guests; women only. **Surf Goddess Retreats** (www.surfgoddessretreats.com) is run by girls for girls. The company organizes all inclusive, "surfari" packages, including yoga and spa treatments. Special care is also placed on the accommodations and food, which are second to none. The **Rip Curl School of Surf** (© 0361/735858; www.schoolofsurf. com) is an internationally respected surf company that organizes surf and paddle boarding—the latest craze to hit the shores—courses for beginners and experienced surfers.

Surf Travel Online (© 0361/737056; www.surftravelonline.com) features up-to-date information on surf packages, boat charters, and surf camps in Bali, Lombok, and throughout Indonesia.

Tennis

Tennis is new to Bali and, especially, Lombok, where there are only a handful of courts, most of them in hotels. But locals are increasingly interested and if you want to spend part of your vacation on a court, most areas—particularly around the resorts—have options. Because many resorts don't have good equipment, you should bring your own rackets and balls.

In Kuta, **Bali Clay Court Tennis,** Jalan Petitenget, Gang Cendrah Wasih #25 (© 08/2144155116) has a single, lit court and offers coaching. North of Seminyak, the **Canggu Club Tennis Center,** Jl. Pantai Berawa Banjar Tegal Gundul (© 0361/844-6385; www.cangguclub.com/tennis) has two outdoor and two indoor courts, as well as two hitting walls; coaching is available. Many of Bali's courts are in Nusa Dua. **The Nikko Bali Resort and Spa** (© 0361/773377; www.nikkobali.com) has three covered, lit courts.

Bali Tennis Magazine (www.balitennis.com) has information about courts and tournaments and can arrange coaching and tennis holidays. **Pure Tennis** (www.pure tennis.asia) cooperates with a number of top resorts with tennis courts and can arrange trips and coaching. The Nikko, Westin, and Conrad hotels in Nusa Dua participate in the group.

White-Water Rafting

Bali has two main rivers for rafting that are both category III: the Ayung, just outside Ubud, and the **Telaga Waja** in the foothills of Mount Agung, which is only a category III due to its distance from help. And although these aren't going to challenge the most intrepid of rafters, the scenery, backdrop, and occasional adrenalin rush, especially in the rainy season, justifies their position as the number-one organized adventure tour on the island. Remarkably, something like 10% of all visitors to the island go white-water rafting—that makes some 250,000 of you.

There are only some five or so fully licensed, properly registered and insured rafting companies. Three of them are **Bali Adventure Tours** (© 0361/721480; www.bali adventuretours.com), **Bali View Rafting** (© 0361/793-4980; www.baliviewrafting. com), and the original—and still the most popular—**Sobek** (© 0361/768050; www. balisobek.com). Increasingly more companies are getting licensed as the authorities start to enforce and police slightly better, so others will become legitimate too.

Each raft journey takes about 2 hours and is suitable for ages 6 and up. Some companies have their own lunch place at the end with warm showers and fresh towels. Be prepared for a long walk down many, many steps (we stopped counting at 450) and then up again (thankfully not quite as many, most people have stopped counting by then).

Prices vary between the rafting companies; generally expect to pay between US$50 and US$72 for adults and US$30 and US$52 for children. Family packages range from US$150 to US$200 depending on what promotions companies are running at the time. Sometimes, it's better to book through an agent. **Bali Discovery Tours** ★★★ (✆ 0361/286283; www.balidiscovery.com) often runs Internet promotions where you can make large savings off the published price, but do book through one of the established, accredited companies.

Yoga & Spiritual Journeys ★

Muslims are barred from practicing yoga due to its connection to Hinduism, even though yoga itself isn't a religion. As Bali doesn't have a Muslim majority, yoga is openly practiced and advertised. With such a large expat community, you'll see ads for private yoga classes posted up on community boards in coffee shops and local hangouts. A majority of the resorts, hotels, and villas on Bali offer some form of yoga, either from an in-house teacher or as host to yoga retreats. Don't expect to find much by way of yoga offerings on Lombok, which is an island of Muslim majority.

In the Seminyak/Canggu area, the **Desa Seni** (✆ 0361/844-6392; www.desaseni.com), a hippie-boutique resort in lush green grounds, allows outside guests. It's one of the best places on the island to practice your breathing and stretching. In southern Bali, try **Bikram Yoga Kuta** (✆ 0361/769040; www.bikramyoga.com) or **Jiwa Yoga** (✆ 0361/841-3689; www.jiwayogabali.com))in Petitenget.

The **Yoga Barn** (✆ 0361/970992; www.theyogabarn.com) is a rustic, spiritual space, set amid terraced rice paddies, in the middle of Ubud. It's an inspiring and beautiful environment for the nourishment of body, mind, and soul.

Throughout the island you'll find small and large retreats, some dedicated to holistic practices and others offering a broad spectrum of related activities. One of the most prominent services is **Bali Spirit** (✆ 0361/970992; www.balispirit.com). Contact it directly to discuss extended holistic practice; yoga and meditation retreats; and detox centers. The extensive list of practitioners and retreats makes this place the one-stop shop for the best services on the island.

One World Retreats (✆ 0361/289752; www.oneworldretreats.com) is a travel service that specializes in tracking down retreats and workshops led by world-renowned yoga and Pilates teachers.

In the north, **Zen Bali** (✆ 0361/289752; www.zenbali.com) combines ayurveda, pranayama (breathing practices), yoga, and meditation with beauty treatments. Leading practitioners are on hand to provide assistance; this retreat offers unique and specialist programs for beginners and the advanced.

Bali is home to several spiritual communities that welcome visitors. The **Gandhi Ashram,** in Candidasa (✆ 0363/41108; www.ashramgandhi.com), is a community of followers of Mahatma Gandhi. Members practice their founder's beliefs through prayer, meditation, and yoga. Visitors and volunteers are welcome to join the community.

The **Nirarta Centre** (✆ 0366/530-0636; www.awareness-bali.com) is tucked up in the hills of the Sidemen Valley. This center focuses on one-to-one self-guided or guided seminars to assist with personal development.

KUTA & LEGIAN

Just a 10-minute drive from the airport, Kuta and the adjoining area of Legian are popular destinations for budget travelers and Aussies who hop over to Bali for long weekends or holidays. By no stretch of the imagination is Kuta the "real" Bali. Indeed, some might say that the area is a den of iniquity, with all the bars, drag queen shows, and Kuta cowboys waiting to find a foreign woman who'll give them a taste of the good life. Over the years, Kuta and Legian have fallen victim to rampant commercialization, which has drastically changed the environment from a small fishing village lining a pristine beach to a hopping city with blaring disco music, while Legian has followed suit. Kuta is for the younger crowd looking for action, and so if that describes you by all means stay awhile.

5

In 1936, Bob Koke, a young Hollywood photographer and the first professional surfer in Bali, arrived with his future wife, Louise Garret. Their original plan was to paint and photograph Bali's wild natural scenery, but they became so enchanted that they decided to stay and open a small bamboo and thatch roof hotel.

The real action in Kuta began after World War II, when Westerners and Balinese became intoxicated by the idea that Kuta could become a popular tourist destination yielding great profits for both local and foreign investors. By the late 1960s, Kuta had become a favorite for hippies and other intrepid travelers from Australia and Europe. By the 1970s, surfers began arriving in earnest. Development continued at a slow pace until the 1980s, when numerous restaurants and hotels started going up. And by the 1990s, the environmental impact of the proliferation of businesses generated bad traffic jams, illegal immigrants from other Indonesian islands, hawkers, and serious waste management problems. The development in Kuta spilled north into Legian, and in the 2000s the urban sprawl has pushed even farther upward into Seminyak and Canggu (see chapter 6). The biggest burden fell on the farmers who were forced to sell their fields due to the construction of buildings that ultimately resulted in the cut-off of their water supply. Those who refused to sell could no longer cultivate their crops. It was the end of an agrarian era for Kuta, which is now one of the most developed areas in Bali.

ESSENTIALS
Getting There & Getting Around

Kuta is near the airport, and most hotels offer free airport pickup. If hiring a cab, go to the airport's official taxi counter, where you'll pay a set fare to any destination in Kuta and Legian, typically Rp60,000.

Walking aside, as a means of getting around taxis are the best means of transportation in Kuta. Be sure to request that they use a meter. **Blue Bird** and **Komotra** taxis are the most reliable; beware of the white taxis who often try to scam naive tourists. Avoid the ridiculously priced horse and buggies (cidomo), which charge up to Rp150,000 to get from one end of Kuta to the other.

Visitor Information

The Bali Department of Tourism operates a **visitor information** center at Jalan Benasari 36B (✆ **0361/754090** or 081/23928098).

Layout

Kuta and Legian form a big rectangle. To the west are the beaches; Legian beach is north of Kuta beach. North of Legian is Seminyak while south of Kuta is Tuban (or South Kuta Beach).

The two main north–south streets are **Jalan Pantai Kuta** and **Jalan Legian.** They're connected east–west by **Jalan Benesari, Poppies Gang I,** and many quaint gang (alleys). To make things extra confusing, some streets have two names. These include Jalan Pura Bagus Taruna, which is also Jalan Werkudara; Jalan Segara is also Jalan Jenggala; Jalan Kartika Plaza is also Jalan Dewi Sartika; Poppies Gang II is also Jalan Batu Bolong; Jalan Stria is also Jalan Kediri; Jalan Pantai Kuta is also Jalan Pantai Banjar Pande Mas; and Jalan Padma is also Jalan Yudistra. Locals, business owners, and maps use a combination of these names.

[FastFACTS] KUTA

ATMs ATMs are on nearly every corner in Kuta.

Currency Exchange Storefront exchange services line most streets and offer the best rates. **Central Kuta Money Changer** on Jalan Pantai Kuta, Suci Arc Street 19 (✆ **0361/762866**), generally offers good rates.

Hospitals Try the **Bali International Medical Centre (BIMC),** Jl. Bypass Ngurah Rai 100X (✆ **0361/761263**), open daily from 8am to midnight; sometimes this center will send someone to your hotel. Another option is the **International SOS Bali,** Jl. Bypass Ngurah Rai (✆ **0361/710505**).

Internet Access Many restaurants and cafes have free Wi-Fi for customers. Internet cafes generally charge between Rp10,000 and Rp37,000 per hour.

Pharmacies Of the many options available in Kuta, **Kimia**, Jl. Raya Tuban 15 (✆ **0361/757483;** 24 hr), is the biggest and usually offers more foreign brand medications than smaller pharmacies.

Police The Tourist Police (✆ **0361/763753**) are on Jalan Pantai Kuta. Open 24 hours.

Safety Pedestrians must watch for **reckless motorbike drivers** who use the sidewalks to avoid traffic on Jalan Legian. You'll also be harangued by some of the most **aggressive touts** on the island, and the beaches are crowded with so-called masseurs. Kuta is known for some unsavory folks who are adept at **picking pockets** or **snatching purses** off shoulders. The **Kuta Cowboys** are the young men who hang out on the beach all day surfing and at night look for girls. For the most part they want to practice their English, flirt, and have fun. However if drugs become apparent or if you feel threatened in any way whatsoever, leave the scene immediately and head back to your hotel. It can't be emphasized enough that drugs are illegal in Bali and the consequences are dire.

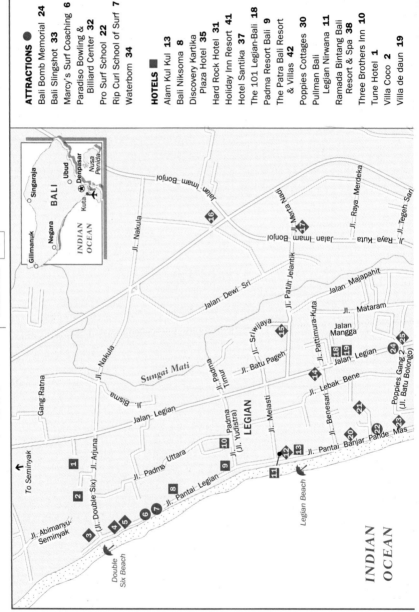

ATTRACTIONS ●

Bali Bomb Memorial **24**
Bali Slingshot **33**
Marcy's Surf Coaching **6**
Paradiso Bowling &
  Billiard Center **32**
Pro Surf School **22**
Rip Curl School of Surf **7**
Waterbom **34**

HOTELS ■

Alam Kul Kul **13**
Bali Niksoma **8**
Discovery Kartika
  Plaza Hotel **35**
Hard Rock Hotel **31**
Holiday Inn Resort **41**
Hotel Santika **37**
The 101 Legian-Bali **18**
Padma Resort Bali **9**
The Patra Bali Resort
  & Villas **42**
Poppies Cottages **30**
Pullman Bali
  Legian Nirwana **11**
Ramada Bintang Bali
  Resort & Spa **38**
Three Brothers Inn **10**
Tune Hotel **1**
Villa Coco **2**
Villa de daun **19**

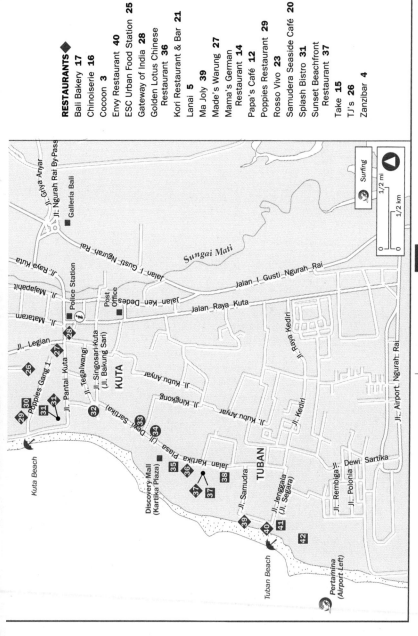

RESTAURANTS ◆

Bali Bakery **17**
Chinoiserie **16**
Cocoon **3**
Envy Restaurant **40**
ESC Urban Food Station **25**
Gateway of India **28**
Golden Lotus Chinese
  Restaurant **36**
Kori Restaurant & Bar **21**
Lanai **5**
Ma Joly **39**
Made's Warung **27**
Mama's German
  Restaurant **14**
Papa's Café **12**
Poppies Restaurant **29**
Rosso Vivo **23**
Samudera Seaside Café **20**
Splash Bistro **31**
Sunset Beachfront
  Restaurant **37**
Take **15**
TJ's **26**
Zanzibar **4**

5

KUTA & LEGIAN | Essentials

57

WHERE TO STAY

Kuta, Legian, and Tuban (or South Kuta Beach as it was renamed in 2009) offer hotels ranging from five-star fabulous to the fringes of ferocity within one door or two of each other. On Jalan Raya Kuta, along the stretch of beach north from Tuban through to Legian, you'll predominantly hit large beach resorts for families, several stylish and secluded boutique digs, and loads of simple garden hotels that present great value. Snake around the nearby alleyways and you'll discover some hidden treasures, as well as the most basic of bed-and-breakfasts and party-style pads reserved for insomniacs. Traffic around Kuta is terrible; plan your check-in and -out so that they aren't anywhere near rush hour (mid-morning and late afternoon).

Kuta

EXPENSIVE

Bali Niksoma ★   Perfectly positioned between Legian and Seminyak, this boutique resort has a superb two-tiered pool and minimalist cottage-style rooms. Super-size bathrooms have separate his and her vanities. Resort facilities are limited to a restaurant and small spa. Comparatively, this resort is a little pricey for what you get, but the beachfront location (with amazing pool) and proximity to shops, nightlife, and restaurants is what this place is really all about.

Jl. Padma Utara Legian Kaja, Legian. www.baliniksoma.com. ✆ **0361/751946.** Fax 0361/735587. 57 units. Peak season US$236–US$840, 4-bedroom villa US$1,150; high season US$454–US$810, 4-bedroom villa US$1,130; low season US$186–US$424, 4-bedroom villa US$1,100. Rates include buffet breakfast. AE, MC, V. **Amenities:** Restaurant; bar; gym; Jacuzzi; 2 outdoor pools; room service; sauna; spa; Wi-Fi (for a fee). *In room:* A/C, TV/DVD, CD, hair dryer, minibar.

Discovery Kartika Plaza Hotel   This is one of Kuta's long-time hotels right on the main strip. The classic oceanfront rooms feature dark varnished furnishings and spectacular views of Kuta Beach, which is just steps away. The style is a complementary blend of modern-minimalist with ethnic accents—adorned with beautiful Balinese carvings. A private outdoor veranda has daybeds for enjoying the intoxicating environment. The "Ocean suites" have beautiful rattan furnishings, state-of-the-art equipment, and great views of the massive pool. The spacious marble bathrooms with large bathtubs invite you to totally unwind in absolute luxury.

Jl. Kartika Plaza, Kuta. www.discoverykartikaplaza.com. ✆ **0361/751067.** Fax 0361/753988. 318 units. High season US$245–US$995; low season US$220–US$975. AE, DC, MC, V. **Amenities:** 3 restaurants; pool bar; babysitting; children's club; concierge; gym; Jacuzzi; 2 outdoor pools; room service; sauna; tennis and squash court; watersports. *In room:* A/C, TV, stereo or CD, hair dryer, minibar, Wi-Fi (free).

Hard Rock Hotel ☺   No doubt an American icon and the only one of its kind in Indonesia. Take a walk down memory lane with Mick Jagger, Janis Joplin, and other rockers whose photographs decorate the walls of this beachfront hotel. The rooms have an Art Deco style in soft pastels and include great rock memorabilia. Check out the loft rooms, which have a deluxe master bedroom and an additional bedroom on the second floor. The facilities include Bali's largest freeform pool with a real sand island at the center, water slides for children, a recording studio, and a climbing wall.

Jl. Pantai, Banjar Pande Mas, Kuta. www.hardrockhotels.net. ✆ **0361/761869.** Fax 0361/761868. 418 units. US$260–US$410 double; US$450–US$600 suite. AE, DC, MC, V. **Amenities:** 4 restaurants; 3 bars; children's club; concierge; health club; outdoor pool (w/swim-up bar); spa; room service; rock library; Wi-Fi. *In room:* A/C, TV, minibar, Wi-Fi.

Padma Resort Bali ★ ☺ You'll have everything you need at the Padma, a pleasant beachside compound just the right distance from the fray for peace and quiet, but close enough to go play and shop. There's something for the whole family here, including a good kids' club, daily activities, a roster of day trips, the fine Mandara Spa, and cultural classes such as egg painting and musical demonstrations. Garden rooms have parquet floors and Balinese furnishings. Standard rooms all have balconies and great views. Family rooms open onto a patio and central garden. There's a quiet, tout-free grassy spot between the pool and the beach where children can frolic.

Jl. Padma 1, Legian. www.hotelpadma.com. ☏ **0361/752111.** Fax 0361/752140. 405 units. US$285–US$423 double; US$465 chalet. AE, DC, MC, V. **Amenities:** 3 restaurants; 4 bars; outdoor pool; tennis court; game area w/Internet and PlayStation; tour desk; car rental; business center; 24-hr. room service; babysitting; laundry service; club-level rooms; meeting rooms. *In room:* A/C, satellite TV, minibar, fridge, safe, IDD phone.

Pullman Bali Legian Nirwana ★ 🗡 Set in the heart of the Kuta nightlife scene but in a compound large enough for peace and quiet, this new hotel provides good value and is certain to become popular in the coming years. Rooms are mid-sized and modern and feature wood floors and spacious bathtubs. For an extra US$20 a day, upgrade to a beach view room. For a quieter experience, opt for building two on a higher floor. Several pools—including one with beach view from the rooftop—grace the property. Yoga classes are complimentary on weekends.

Jl. Melasti 1, Legian. www.pullmanbalilegiannirwana.com. ☏ **0361/762500.** Fax 0361/762400. 387 units. High season US$250–US$520; low season US$250–US$485. AE, MC, V. **Amenities:** 2 restaurants; 2 bars; babysitting; children's club; concierge; health club, outdoor pool; rooftop pool. *In room:* TV, DVD, hair dryer, minibar, Wi-Fi.

Villa de daun ★★ 🛍 Among the chaos of high-octane Kuta sits this exclusive retreat of 12 luxuriously appointed villas. Owners Michelle and Jimmy have captured the vibe of the island with stylish live-in pads with indulgent bathrooms, and private swimming pools and gazebos. Add 40-inch plasma TVs with knockout Bose sound systems, gourmet kitchens complete with fridges that stock the iciest drinks on the planet, and lavish king-size beds perfect after a day out bargaining with the locals. You're breaths away from the bevy of shops, restaurants, and local nightlife but a good 500m (1,640 ft.) walk to the beach. Get in if you can.

Jl. Raya Legian, Kuta. www.villadedaun.com. ☏ **0361/756276.** Fax 0361/750643. 12 villas. High season US$351–US$451 1-bedroom, US$651 2-bedroom, US$751 3-bedroom; low season US$301–US$401 1-bedroom, US$601 2-bedroom, US$701 3-bedroom. AE, MC, V. **Amenities:** Restaurant; babysitting; concierge; room service; spa (p. 67). *In villa:* A/C, TV/DVD, CD, hair dryer, minibar, Wi-Fi (free).

MODERATE

The 101 Legian-Bali For a cheap, no-frills room in the heart of Kuta's nightlife, this is a top option. The hotel, which opened in 2011, offers small but colorful and clean rooms; make sure you ask for one with windows. The property is geared toward the young, partying set: during the day, the small rooftop pool draws a crowd of young people, many sleeping off hangovers.

Jl. Raya Legian 117, Kula. www.the101bali.com. ☏ **0361/300-1101.** Fax 0361/300-2101. 198 units. US$215–US$300 w/breakfast. MC, V. Amenities: restaurant; bar; pool; spa. *In room:* A/C, TV; minibar; Wi-Fi (free).

Alam Kul Kul First opened in 1989, this popular beachfront resort is best known for its excellent Italian restaurant Papa's, which was probably one of the first pizzerias in the area. The resort has since undergone a massive renovation; the modern and comfortable rooms are perfect for families and while pristinely clean and modern, still offer a relaxed and casual ambience. The resort fronts Legian beach, though you have to cross a very busy road before you hit the sand.

Jl. Pantai Kuta, Legian. www.alamkulkul.com. ☎ **0361/752520**. Fax 0361/766861. 80 units. High season US$170–US$235; low season US$120–US$185. AE, DC, MC, V. **Amenities:** 2 restaurants, including Papa's Café (p. 64); bar; babysitting; concierge; outdoor pool; room service; spa (p. 67); Wi-Fi (for a fee). *In room:* A/C, TV, hair dryer, minibar.

Ramada Bintang Bali Resort & Spa ★ ☺

This resort is set on more than 6 hectares (15 acres) of tropical gardens extending down to the beachfront of South Kuta. The "Romantic" rooms are ideal for honeymooners or any couple seeking something out of the ordinary. The cozy rooms have elegant netting over the bed, parquet floors, and ethnic accents throughout. Bathrooms feature marble floors and a nice bathtub. The excellent activity program includes yoga, aqua aerobics, beach volleyball, and water pillow fights. Kids have their own special program to keep them busy so parents can have a relaxing holiday in paradise.

Jl. Kartika Plaza, Kuta. www.bintang-bali-hotel.com. ☎ **0361/753292**. Fax 0361/752015. 402 units. High season US$155–US$685 standard, US$1,435 suite; low season US$120–US$650 standard, US$1,400 suite; extra bed US$35. AE, DC, MC, V. **Amenities:** 2 restaurants; coffee shop; lounge; 2 bars; babysitting; children's club and play group; concierge; gym; health club; Jacuzzi; outdoor pool; room service; sauna; spa (p. 67); tennis court; Wi-Fi (for a fee). *In room:* A/C, TV, hair dryer, Internet (for a fee), minibar.

Villa Coco ★ ☺

This place is ideal for families, couples, or groups who want to be beachfront near a patrolled surfing beach, restaurants, and nightlife. The property has direct access to Legian beach and also backs onto the famous Jalan Double Six shopping street. The affordable one- and two-bedroom garden and pool villas have their own entrances and small gardens and lawns. Although there's no restaurant, you do have 24-hour room service and breakfast, lunch, or dinner can be served poolside. Individual barbecues, cooked at your villa, are good value and reflect the no-nonsense style of the Australian owners.

Jl. Double Six, Gang Villa Coco, Legian. www.villacoco.com. ☎ **0361/730736.** Fax 0361/734828. 15 units. Peak season US$160–US$730; high season US$125–US$640; low season US$100–US$580; extra bed US$35. 7-night minimum stay. AE, MC, V. Amenities: Restaurant; pool bar; babysitting; outdoor pool; room service; Wi-Fi. In *villa:* A/C, TV/DVD, movie library; CD, kitchenette, minibar.

INEXPENSIVE

Poppies Cottages 🛍

These renovated cottages were originally built in 1980. The beautiful wooden interior and marble open-air bathrooms with sunken tubs make this a wonderful find. The rooms are a bit small for the price, but everything is very clean and comfortable. The small central pool resembles a natural pond, surrounded by verdant garden nooks perfect for lounging. The cozy poolside bar is a great place for lunch or a refreshing cocktail. Guests can also conveniently dine at Poppies Restaurant (p. 64), just across the alley.

Poppies Lane I, Kuta. www.poppiesbali.com. ☎ **0361/751059.** Fax 0361/752364. 20 units. US$79–US$93 double (seasonal rates available) plus 21% service fee. AE, DC, MC, V. **Amenities:** Restaurant; bar; outdoor pool; room service. *In room:* A/C, TV, Wi-Fi (free).

Three Brothers Inn ★ 🍴 🛍

This place is often booked out for its rock-bottom rates—you simply can't do better than this sprawling compound of traditional Balinese architecture set around gardens and a large pool. Rooms and bathrooms are clean and spacious, though a little dark. Be sure to book an upper-floor room with

A/C unless you don't mind the heat. The property is located in a mess of alleys behind the Padma Hotel so make sure to keep a map handy.

Jl. Legian, Legian. www.threebrothersbungalows.com. ☏ **0361/751566.** 50 units. Rp33,000–Rp85,000. MC, V. Amenities: Restaurant; bar; pool; spa. *In room:* A/C (in some), fans (in some), TV, fridge.

Tune Hotel This new property has applied the discount airline carrier model of its parent company, Air Asia, to the motel business. Bizarrely, one of the property's few amenities is a prominently located mini-mart, which sets the tone for the entire place. Clean, efficient rooms are just large enough to fit a double bed and come with a very cramped bathroom. Request a room with a window facing the outside of the property or you may develop a severe case of claustrophobia. Rates fluctuate between Rp50,000 and Rp350,000—the lower the occupancy, the cheaper the rooms. You'll pay extra for things such as air-conditioning, towels (Rp16,500 for rental), and hair dryers. If all you're looking for is a room to sleep in and you can get a rate on the lower end, this may fit the bill. The hotel runs a second location in Kuta with a mix of single and double beds while the Legian location only features double beds.

Jl. Arjuna (Double Six off Jl. Pantai Legian), Legian. www.tunehotels.com. ☏ **03/79625888** (Malaysian Booking Center). 169 units. From Rp129,000. MC, V. Amenities: Restaurant. *In room:* A/C (from Rp40,000/12 hr); Wi-Fi (Rp40,000/24 hr).

Tuban (South Kuta Beach)

Holiday Inn Resort ★ ☺ Don't let the motel name of this newly refurbished resort deter you. Ultra-contemporary in style and set on sun-kissed Segara beach, this hip hotel delivers the latest in all things "concept." This resort is as fabulous for families as it is for fashionistas with its range of facilities. The five Family and six Kids Suites have beds shaped like sail boats with captains' wheels, circus tent wardrobes, bean bags, and giant plasma TVs with Wii and Xbox, plus super stylish interconnecting rooms for the grown-ups. The resort's Baruna Suites and split-level villa-esque Arjuna suites (most of which face the ocean) are sleek, modern, and super-spacious in design. While the kids are reveling in the Teen-Zone or Rascals underwater club, adults can enjoy the spa or lounge at one of the restaurants.

Jl. Wana Segara 33, Tuban. www.bali.holidayinn.com. ☏ **0361/755577.** Fax 0361/754549. 195 units. High season US$175–US$244; low season US$134–US$329. AE, MC, V. **Amenities:** 2 restaurants, including Envy (p. 66); coffee shop; lounge; pool bar; babysitting; children's club; concierge; gym; outdoor pool; room service; spa (p. 67); Wi-Fi (for a fee). *In room:* A/C, TV/DVD, hair dryer, minibar, MP3 docking station.

Hotel Santika ⚑ All the rooms at this charming boutique-style hotel are decorated with natural stone and wood, including attractive granite bathroom counters with marble floors. The overall effect is a warm and cozy environment—a refreshing change from other area hotels. The Garden bungalow features four-poster beds, an outdoor shower, terrazzo floors, and serene garden views. All bungalows have Kamasan paintings hanging above the beds or on the walls. The Ocean Front Suites are secluded from the rest of the property and have private swimming pools and lovely ocean views. It's certainly very good value for money.

Jl. Kartika Plaza, Tuban. www.santikabali.com. ☏ **0361/751267.** Fax 0361/751260. 171 units. Year-round US$175–US$350; extra bed US$50. Peak season US$225 deluxe, US$325–US$375 bungalow, villa US$475; high season US$190–US$200 deluxe, US$290–US$340 bungalow, US$440 villa; low season US$175–US$185 deluxe, US$275–US$325 bungalow, US$425 villa. AE, DC, MC, V. **Amenities:** 3 restaurants, including Sunset Beachfront Restaurant (p. 66); 2 bars; lounge; babysitting; children's club; 3 outdoor pools; room service; spa; tennis court; Wi-Fi (for a fee). *In room:* A/C, TV, hair dryer, minibar.

The Patra Bali Resort & Villas ★   This hidden treasure has become a prime luxury getaway for the elite. A long list of kings, queens, and heads of state have stayed here. Situated right next to the airport, you might wrongly assume that the noise would be unbearable, but in truth, it's quite peaceful here. The rooms are attractively decorated in traditional Balinese style with exquisite wood furnishings, marble bathrooms with huge bathtubs, and private balconies overlooking a tropical landscape. The luxurious private villas are ideal for families or couples seeking solitude. Many of the villas have private plunge pools and 24-hour butler service. There's also a large seaside swimming pool and a private club exclusive to guests.

Jl. Ir. H. Juanda, Tuban. www.patrabali.com.☏ **0361/751161.** Fax 0361/752030. 228 units. Peak season US$316–US$620 standard, US$430–US$1,855 villa; high season US$306–US$610 standard, US$420–US$1,845 villa; low season US$266–US$570 standard, US$380–US$1,805 villa; extra bed US$40. AE, DC, MC, V. Amenities: 2 restaurants; coffee shop; 2 lounges; pub; babysitting; children's club; concierge; gym; outdoor pool; room service; spa; tennis court; Wi-Fi (for a fee). *In room:* A/C, TV, hair dryer, minibar.

WHERE TO EAT

Kuta & Legian
MODERATE

Bali Bakery ★   Cafe   Locally owned Bali Bakery has a huge selection of bakery items and a full menu. The air-conditioned comfort makes it a prime destination for escaping the heat on Jalan Raya Kuta; locals head here for everything from a simple milkshake to a three-course dinner.

Jl. Imam Bonjol, Kuta.☏ **0361/755149.** Main courses Rp35,000–Rp100,000. MC, V. Daily 7:30am–10:30pm.

Chinoiserie ★ 🍴 CHINESE   For out-of-the-ordinary Chinese food with a modern twist you can't beat this newcomer—or its striking red frontage. Young Singaporean owner, hotelier, and restaurateur Bernard Foo has put panache and loads of chi-chi into Chinoiserie with a stunning decor (no surprise, he also has an interior decorating business). The cuisine is really more authentic Singaporean fare, better known as Peranakan, which is a combination of cooking styles—think Chinese, Malay, Indian, and Thai with a smattering of Indonesian and Western influences. Thankfully, MSG (monosodium glutamate) is missing here with sauces that are light and fragrant and dishes that range from dim sum to duck pancakes to feast on.

Jl. Sunset 7, Kuta.☏ **0361/808-8777.** www.chinoiseriebali.com. Main dishes Rp40,000–Rp118,000. MC, V. Daily 11am–11pm.

Cocoon ★ INTERNATIONAL   Set right across the street from Legian Beach and right in the heart of the Double Six nightclub area, this new restaurant-cum-beach club offers tapas by its pool or a more formal dining area indoors. The menu features extensive cocktails and reasonably priced wines while dishes hail from Europe, the Middle East, and Asia. You can order massages and manicures too. The venue often hosts parties into the late evening and attracts a mix of locals, tourists, and expats, making it a day and night destination.

Jl. Double Six, Blue Ocean Boulevard, Seminyak. ☏ **0361/731266.** www.cocoon-beach.com. Main courses Rp40,000–Rp270,000. AE, MC, V. Daily 8am–3am.

ESC Urban Food Station BISTRO   There's not much you won't find at this eatery with some 200-plus items on its nearly 24/7 urban fare menu. You can Wi-Fi over breakfast waffles and New York City bagels with a steaming Driscoll coffee, nosh on salads and pastas, or tuck into the Longhorns Texas BBQ to revive you after a bout of shopping or a night on the town. Portions are massive.

Jl. Legian 61, Legian. ☏ **0361/756362.** www.escbali.com. Main courses Rp45,000–Rp152,000. MC, V. Daily 24 hr. Grill available after 6pm only.

Gateway of India INDIAN   This superb, family-run, Indian restaurant is always busy. Customers can sit at the front and watch the activity on the street while relishing their Madras fish or tikka masala. The restaurant has an a la carte menu of more than 200 dishes. Favorites include mixed vegetable pakora, tandoori chicken Madras, vegetable biryani, and other meat, fish, and vegetable specialties. This successful little restaurant also has outlets in Seminyak, Nusa Dua, and on Jalan Sunset.

Jl. Pantai Kuta 11, 3rd floor. ☏ **0361/754463.** Reservations recommended. Main courses Rp64,000–Rp125,000. MC, V. Daily 11am–11pm.

Golden Lotus Chinese Restaurant ★ 🍴 CHINESE   Kuta's best-kept secret. Inside the Bali Dynasty Hotel, this elegant restaurant serves some of the finest Cantonese and Szechuan cuisine in Bali. Many guests also frequently stop in for all-you-can-eat dim sum, which include 60 varieties for only Rp85,000 (Sun 10am–2:30pm). The stir-fried beef and the fried prawns with yellow bean curd sauce are absolutely scrumptious.

In the Bali Dynasty Hotel, Jl. Kartika Plaza, Kuta. ☏ **0361/752403.** www.balidynasty.com. Reservations recommended. About Rp300,000 for 2 people; set menu Rp125,000–Rp227,500 for up to 6 dishes. AE, MC, V, DC. Daily 11:30am–2pm; 6–9:45pm.

Kori Restaurant & Bar ★ INTERNATIONAL/STEAKHOUSE   Valet parking in the narrow and chaotic Poppies Gang II? Finery uncharacteristic of Bali abounds at this chic venue. Sit in the dining room, replete with linen and silver, or on one of the more romantic cushioned bamboo platforms that bridge the narrow garden oasis. The light lunch menu features malai köfte (spicy vegetarian fritters in a curry sauce) or the mouth-burning Bali chili burger (if you dare). The dinner menu successfully mimics a Western steakhouse. Try the mixed grill of U.S. beef loin, spare ribs, pork cutlet, and Nuernberger sausages; or order the Singapore chili crab, savory and spicy fresh black Bali crabs served with a bib. At the high end of the menu is the giant seafood grill, cooked and served on a hot lava stone.

Poppies Gang II, Kuta. ☏ **0361/758605.** www.korirestaurant.co.id. Reservations recommended. Main courses Rp30,000–Rp140,000. AE, DC, MC, V. Daily noon–11pm.

Lanai INTERNATIONAL   This beachside hangout has a sushi bar and panini menu. This is where the crowds converge at sunset for a beer, or take a break from the beach for a fresh fruit juice over a game of backgammon. The menu has a good choice of snacks, Indonesian food, sandwiches, pizzas, and pasta. Particularly recommended is the sesame-crusted ahi tuna with wasabi mayo, lamb shawarma pita wrap, Lanai burger, and blueberry cheesecake.

Jl. Double Six, Kuta. ☏ **0361/731305.** Reservations recommended. Main courses Rp26,000–Rp95,000. MC, V. Daily 7am–11pm.

Mama's German Restaurant ★ 🍴 GERMAN   Mama's opened in 1985. By offering substantial German home cooking at low prices, it has proved to be a popular hangout with travelers and become a Kuta institution. In addition to hot dogs, burgers, French fries, and ice cold beer, the menu bursts with authentic German dishes including roast pork (schweinebraten), Vienna schnitzel (Wienerschnitzel), rolled beef (roulade) with cabbage and dumplings, German sausages, German meat balls (frikadellen), spit-roasted chicken, pork roast, and huge pork knuckles. Mama's also has a beer garden and a separate Dining Club with a cocktail bar, a large billiards table, and live music in the evenings. It serves imported draft beer and German schnapps, along with a limited but well-priced wine list.

Jl. Legian, Kuta. ✆ **0361/761151.** www.bali-mamas.com. Reservations recommended. Main courses Rp82,500–Rp150,000. AE, MC, V. Daily 24 hr.

Papa's Café ★ ☺ ITALIAN   The sound of crashing waves mixes easily with the grinding espresso machine at Papa's beachfront restaurant. The standards here are above-average with the vegetables sourced from Bedugul and the meats all imported from Australia. A favorite dish is the Kintamani Volcano Pizza, stuffed with beef, ham, spicy sausage, pepperoni, and salami, and pumped with air until it resembles a mountain and arrives flaming at the table. Top it off with the award-winning chocolate cake with peanut brittle. Each night features live in-house music.

In the Alam Kul Kul (p. 59), Jl. Pantai Kuta, Legian. ✆ **0361/755055.** www.papascafe.com. Reservations recommended. Volcano pizza Rp125,000; pasta Rp89,000–Rp199,000; steak Rp145,000–Rp175,000; seafood platter for 2 Rp499,000. AE, MC, V. Daily 10am–midnight.

Poppies Restaurant ASIAN/INTERNATIONAL   Poppies Restaurant is so famous it even has two lanes named after it. Established around 1973, it serves Asian and Western dishes of fresh fish and seafood, soups, curries, lobster, steaks, and vegetarian dishes such as a delicious veggie curry with brown rice. Poppies gets its veggies from Organic Nature, one of Bali's pioneers in organic farming.

Poppies Cottages, Poppies Lane I, Kuta. ✆ **0361/751059.** www.poppiesbali.com. Reservations recommended. Men must wear shirts. Main courses (Indonesian) Rp47,000–Rp66,000. AE, MC, V. Daily 8am–11pm.

Rosso Vivo ★ ITALIAN   Wandering sophisticates will home in on the brilliant red umbrellas lining this small oasis beachfront eatery. Fresh salads, seafood, homemade pasta, Milanese-inspired meat dishes, and delectable desserts are a brilliant entree to poolside cocktails and a ringside view as the sun says "ciao." Ideal for afternoon tea, tapas, and romantic dinners accompanied by nightly jazz with local musicians from sunset onward.

In the Kuta Seaview Hotel, Jl. Pantai Legian, Legian. ✆ **0361/751961.** www.kutaseaviewhotel.com. Reservations recommended. Main courses Rp65,000–Rp240,000; set menus US$35–US$75. MC, V. Sun–Thurs 7am–1am; Fri–Sat 7am–2am.

Samudera Seaside Café 🍴 INTERNATIONAL/INDONESIAN   Although this place offers a good variety of Western food, the specialty is Indonesian cuisine so if you want to try nasi goreng (fried rice with veggies and egg), satay campur (chicken, beef, seafood, and fish with peanut sauce on skewers), or any other local delicacy, this is the place. The Western food is just okay. Every Tuesday it offers a set menu and Thursdays has a big Italian buffet. There are great views of Kuta Beach across the road, so you can watch a fabulous sunset while you dine.

Grand Istana Rama hotel, Jl. Panta, Kuta, Kuta. ✆ **0361/752208.** www.grandistanarama.com. Reservations recommended. Main courses Rp65,000–Rp135,000; Fri and Mon set menu Rp175,000; Thurs buffet Rp175,000. AE, MC, V. Daily 24 hr.

Splash Bistro ☺ INTERNATIONAL/INDONESIAN   You can have it all here, served poolside, from nachos to grilled sirloin to burgers. There are also some excellent Indonesian dishes on the menu such as traditional oxtail soup. The huge wood-fired pizzas come with an assortment of toppings. Children can play in the massive swimming pool while you rock out to old and new songs, sip cool cocktails, and enjoy the great food. It's an all-American dream.

In the Hard Rock Hotel (p. 58), Jl. Pantai Kuta, Kuta. ☏ **0361/761869.** Main courses Rp69,000–Rp139,000. AE, MC, V. Daily 11am–10pm.

Take ★★ 🏠 JAPANESE This authentic Japanese restaurant serves up just about the finest Japanese food on the island. Every evening, from 6pm onward, the place is packed with Koreans and Japanese who come to dine on the freshest fish and daily imported seasonal food. The owner is often on hand to give advice on what's good. There's loads to choose from, and the picture menu will steer anyone unfamiliar with Japanese food in the right direction.

Jl. Patih Jelantik, Legian. ☏ **0361/759745.** www.rama-restaurants-bali.com. Reservations recommended. Main courses Rp55,000–Rp400,000. AE, MC, V. Daily 11am–midnight. Also on Jl. Padma, Legian, ☏ **0361/750760.**

INEXPENSIVE

Made's Warung ★★ 🏠 INDONESIAN This is a longtime Bali favorite, and for good reason. If it's busy, and it often is, don't be surprised if you end up sharing a table. Gado gado, satay, and curries are all recommended. Fun surprises on the menu include a bagel with smoked marlin, tofu burgers, and Caesar salad. Don't pass up the daily specials, particularly the fresh fish. Beverages range from iced coffee and juice to very potent booze concoctions (be warned).

Br. Pando Mas, Kuta (☏ **0361/755297**), also in Seminyak (p. 86). www.madeswarung.com. Main courses Rp30,000–Rp300,000. AE, MC, V. Daily 10am–11:30pm.

TJ's ★★ MEXICAN TJ's is one of Kuta's legends, open since 1984. TJ's famous margaritas were the first in Bali and many say that they're still the best. Some of the loyal staff members have been at TJ's from the very beginning, and the customers are a mix of tourists, regulars, and old friends; people come back year after year. If you want a taste of Kuta history, you might just find it wrapped in an enchilada, served with a spicy salsa, and toasted with a margarita. The food is excellent, with a wide range of delicious starters and main courses including dips, nachos, buffalo wings, quesadillas, tacos, enchiladas, tostadas, fajitas, salads, and baked potatoes followed by some truly wicked deserts such as the delectable mango cheesecake with raspberry sauce.

Poppies Lane 1/24, Kuta. ☏ **0361/751093.** www.tjsbali.com. Main courses Rp35,000–Rp65,000 (limit Rp100,000). MC, V. Daily 8:30am–11pm.

Zanzibar ★ 🏠 ☺ INTERNATIONAL Zanzibar is a funky and fun restaurant with tables on a raised terrace and second-floor balcony overlooking the beach. This is a good place to do lunch, or to enjoy a snack, a cappuccino, or an ice-cold beer, and is also the perfect choice for a meeting place, a game of pool, or to check your e-mail. From 5pm on, Zanzibar fills up with punters wanting to pay homage to the setting sun. You won't go hungry either, with a wide choice of the best real Italian pizzas in town, a fine selection of pasta, sandwiches, Indonesian food, vegetarian food, meat and fish, and a superb mezze platter. A bit more upmarket than the other beachside restaurants on the strip, Zanzibar serves chilled sounds from the DJ box and free snacks from the bar on Sundays from 5pm until 8pm.

Jl. Double Six, Legian. ☏ **0361/733528.** www.zanzibarbali.com. Main courses Rp66,000–Rp92,000. MC, V. Daily 7am–midnight.

5

KUTA & LEGIAN

Where to Eat

Tuban

Envy Restaurant ★ ITALIAN   Envy is a fabulous destination for sunset cocktails and late-night lounging. The brilliant, Italian-inspired menu covers the spectrum of delicious beachside flavors, such as poached jumbo prawns with a tropical citrus dressing, squid ink spaghetti, Australian Wagyu beef, and the most sensational pizzas from the stone hearth oven. Special mention goes to the lethal tiramisu. The lava-lamp-like bar top morphs in color as the sun sets and you'll insist on trying as many fashionable cocktails as you can muster. Watch the envious parade of locals and tourists on the esplanade that fronts the restaurant as you listen to chilled and sensual grooves by the resident DJ.

In the Holiday Inn Resort (p. 61), Jl. Wana Segara 33, Tuban. ✆ **0361/752527.** www.envy-bali.com. Reservations recommended. Pizza Rp68,000–Rp95,000; pasta Rp49,000–Rp98,000; small plates Rp78,000–Rp98,000; grill Rp320,000–Rp90,000. AE, DC, MC, V. Daily 11am–midnight.

Ma Joly ★★★ 🎖️📷 FRENCH/INTERNATIONAL   Ma Joly is bargain, five-star dining—you'd pay double the price for food not nearly as good elsewhere. This superb beachfront restaurant is hidden away at the end of a quiet road in Tuban and is well worth navigating to no matter where you're staying in Bali. The refined and uncomplicated menu appeals with rabbit and langoustine with fennel and walnuts; the must-try grilled entrecote of Angus beef served with salty caramel, star anis, and mint; a selection of fine wines; and sensational desserts. Tip: This is a perfect place to be seduced by the Segara beach sunset.

In the Kupu Kupu Barong, Jl. Segara, Tuban. ✆ **0361/753708.** www.ma-joly.com. Reservations recommended. Lunch Rp70,000–185,000; dinner Rp150,000–Rp195,000; set menu Rp425,000 and up for 4 courses and coffee. AE, MC, V. Daily noon–3pm, dinner 5:30–10:30pm.

Sunset Beachfront Restaurant INDONESIAN/INTERNATIONAL   This restaurant has excellent food, which you can enjoy while watching one of Kuta's fabulous sunsets. Try one of their special stone dishes with your choice of fish, lamb chops, or steak served on a piping hot stone. You cook your meal yourself. Other options include wood-fired oven pizzas, delicious salads, and exceptional Indonesian dishes such as nasi goreng.

In the Hotel Santika (p. 61), Jl. Kartika Plaza, Tuban. ✆ **0361/751267.** Main courses Rp85,000–Rp180,000. AE, MC, V. Daily 7am–11pm.

EXPLORING KUTA & LEGIAN

Apart from surfing and sunbathing on Kuta Beach ★ and shopping, there isn't a great deal to do in Kuta, so book tours to destinations across the island using Kuta as a hub.

The **Bali Bomb Memorial,** on the site of the original Paddys on Jalan Legian, commemorates the 202 lives taken during the tragic bombing that occurred on Bali on October 12, 2002. At the center of the memorial are the names of all the people who were killed. The attack was the deadliest act of terrorism in the history of Indonesia.

BOWLING & SNOOKER **Paradiso Bowling & Billiard Center** (✆ 0361/758882), on Jalan Kartika Plaza, has an 18-lane bowling alley and a spacious billiard center with 38 snooker tables.

SLINGSHOT "Get in, sit down, shut up, and hang on" is the catchphrase of the **Bali Slingshot.** Situated beside Kuta Centre in Tuban (✆ **0361/736151;** admission including T-shirt US$25; package for two persons including T-shirts and video

US$59), the slingshot is a bit like a reverse bungy. A capsule that accommodates up to two people is lifted to two huge vertical towers by gigantic bungy cords. The cords are stretched to capacity before the capsule is released and catapulted 50m (164 ft.) skyward in less than 2 seconds, spinning on its own axis at its maximum height before decelerating into a series of bounces and being lowered back down to its launch pad.

SPAS Kuta has plenty of spas and massage outlets, most in the resorts and hotels. Spas are open daily. **Cozy** ★, Jl. Sunset, Block A3 (© **0361/766762;** foot reflexology Rp76,000, body massage Rp86,000; MC, V; daily 11am–10pm), is popular for cheap massages and has a bar for freshly made juice and tea. The few massage tables are partitioned by curtains only—but with these prices who's complaining.

In Villa de daun (p. 59), the **DaLa Spa** (www.dalaspa.com; single treatment US$32–US$65, package for single US$86–US$210, package for couple US$159–US$389; AE, MC, V; daily 9am–10pm) is a seductive boudoir-cum-spa parlor. Delicious treatments include a chai bath, Balinese coffee, and chocolate scrub.

In Kupu Kupu Barong, the beachfront **Gaya Spa** (www.gaya-spa.com; single treatment US$40–US$60, package US$105–US$158; AE, DC, MC, V; daily 9am–10pm) is unpretentious but seriously good. Expert therapists know exactly how to unhinge those niggling knots and knead your body with great precision. They do fantastic massages such as the deeply therapeutic stone massage with Reiki.

The **Jamu Traditional Spa** ★★ (© 0361/704581; www.jamutraditionalspa.com; body treatments US$65–US$80, massage US$25–US$65, package US$80–US$160; AE, MC, V; daily 9am–9pm) in Alam Kul Kul (p. 59) draws inspiration from age-old healing practices found across the Indonesian archipelago. *Jamu* refers to the herbal elixirs that local women consume in their pursuit of natural health and beauty and is still widely used to this day. Using only natural ingredients such as fresh fruit, flower blossoms, and indigenous herbs and spices, Jamu offers such exclusive treatments as the Papaya Kemiri Mint Body Wrap and the Fruit and Nut Facial. It also runs the Jamu Spa School with 1-week certificate courses so you can take home the artful massage and indulge your family and friends.

Treatments at **Patra Bali Resort** (p. 62; single treatment US$15–US$45, package US$85–US$150; AE, DC, MC, V; daily 9am–9pm) include complimentary use of the spa's Jacuzzi. If you really want to unwind, be sure to try one of their treatment packages such as the Refreshing Mind Package—2 hours and 15 minutes of pure bliss—or the Sunset Package—4 hours of total pampering from head to toe.

The new beachfront **Tea Tree Spa** (single treatment Rp460,000–Rp730,000, signature Rp1,060,000; AE, MC, V; daily 9am–9pm) in the Holiday Inn Resort (p. 51) has a range of aptly titled therapies such as "Because You Deserve It," "Hold My Calls," and "Out for Lunch."

The **Theta Spa** ★★★, on the beach of Ramada Bintang Bali Resort, Jl. Kartika Plaza (© **0361/755726;** www.thetaspa.com; single treatment US$27–US$92, package US$122; AE, MC, V; daily 10am–11pm, last booking 8pm) is a tucked-away destination spa worth making a special effort to experience. All massages and treatments use natural products. If you're a couple, try Theta Honey Love, a chocolate and almond scrub. Afterwards you're wrapped in Borneo honey and left to soak in a bath of milk and flower petals.

SURFING ★ Surfers from all over the world are drawn to Kuta's breakers, which are at their best between May and September. Kuta beach can be an ideal place to learn with its soft sandy beaches, consistent rip, and its normally friendly breaks.

Swimming on Kuta Beach at Double Six

Unfortunately, the Kuta surf makes recreational swimming virtually impossible. Even past the breakers, the current can be too strong. Pay close attention to swimming warnings and restrictions, and be very careful if you do swim. Only swim in between the flags on Kuta beach. Sometimes lifeguards will be on duty but don't rely on them. Several people die every year in the water.

Rentals & Schools   Plenty of surf shops line the main drag and will help with board rental or tide information. Your hotel can arrange a private or group lesson, but we suggest the following schools and teachers:

The **Rip Curl School of Surf,** Jl. Arjuna (© **0361/735858;** www.schoolofsurf. com; from US$49 for an hour lesson, board rental US$5 for 4 hr. or US$10 for 8 hr.) was established in 1998 and has an international reputation for offering great service. The professional, predominately Indonesian team provides courses for children, novices, and day trips for the more advanced. They'll also teach you paddle boarding if you can balance long enough and stand the abuse from the surfing contingent.

Learn to surf with one of the top surf schools in Bali, voted "Best Surf School in Bali" for 3 consecutive years by *Magic Wave Surf Community Magazine.* **Pro Surf School,** Jl. Pantai Kuta (© **0361/744-1466;** www.prosurfschool.com; lessons start from €45), offers comprehensive surfing lessons for beginning, intermediate, and advanced surfers, as well as surf trips around Bali.

For those looking for their own surf guru, you can experience the thrill of surfing taught by professional surfers who know all the ins and outs of each break—and they may even share some secret locations if you promise not to tell. **Marcy's Surf Coaching ★★★**, Jl. Arjuna (© **081/23859454;** www.teachsurf.com; lessons start at Rp400,000 per hr.), is the name of the outfit run by a New Zealander who has been living and surfing in Bali for the last 20 years. Marcy (arguably also a life coach) will get you up on a surfboard on day one. For advanced surfers, he'll work out a program, and for the proficient, he'll take you to some of the best, uncrowded surfing areas in Bali. Marcy specializes in one-to-one coaching. You may recognize him in the water—he's the one shouting "Paddle, paddle, paddle!"

Jack Chisholm ★★★ (© **081/916766607;** jack@tropicsurf.net; prices upon inquiry) spends his time between the Maldives and Bali and manages Tropicsurf (p. 51) in Bali, specializing in a variety of surfing holidays. Jack is also an enthusiastic photographer and filmmaker who captures his idea of the very essence of beauty when a wave and a surfer are in natural unison. Jack runs all-girl surf retreats and attempts, very badly (sadly), to play the guitar.

The Waves   Kuta Reef (*best swell:* west or southwest; **best size:** 3–5 ft.; **best winds:** southeast) is an easy short boat ride out from the beach at Tuban. This is a fantastic wave, best a couple of hours after low tide on the incoming. Many local and international surfers cut their teeth on this wave early in their trips before heading to more advanced reef break options. Kuta Reef is a really fun wave when it's on; patience and good manners are the key to surfing happiness out here. This wave can be spotted from the beach and the short boat ride (easily negotiated with boatmen from shore) adds an element of Indo adventure to your daily surf.

Exploring Kuta & Legian

KUTA & LEGIAN

If the swell is up, head around to the north of the runway and you'll find **Airport Rights** (**best swell:** west or southwest; **best size:** 3–6 ft.; **best winds:** southeast), a long right breaking for over 100m (328 ft.). It's really good at 3 to 5 feet and is a lonely right on a coast of infamous lefts. Take the same boat as you would for Airport and Kuta Reef waves, but buckle down for a longer ride to this take-off zone. This wave is best surfed on higher tides with a strong swell running.

Airport Left (**best swell:** south; **best size:** 4–5 ft.; **best winds:** southeast) is a short wave running out in front of the airport runway at Tuban. It's often packed with Japanese surfers seeking a mellow, less threatening and competitive surfing experience for their annual holidays. Despite the short length of ride and the crowd factor, it can still be a fun place to surf.

Waterbom ★★ ☺ If the children aren't getting enough of a kick out of the busy beach at Kuta, take them to this water park. Right in the heart of Kuta is a tropical adventure park that caters to children and adults. The 3.8-hectare (9½-acre) site is designed around a tropical garden and includes exhilarating water rides, slides, and trails. For those who prefer to keep themselves dry, there are plenty of other options: A spa, a climbing wall, shops, and a poolside bar. The food court has good Italian, French, Indonesian, and American outlets.

Jl. Kartika Plaza, Kuta. ✆ **0361/755676.** www.waterbom.com. Adults US$26 1-day pass, US$42 2-day pass, children 2–12 years old US$16 1-day pass; US$26 2-day pass. Daily 9am–6pm.

SHOPPING

Shopping in Kuta isn't nearly as swank as in Seminyak (see chapter 6). What you will find is surfer gear, cheap sarongs and printed batik shirts and shorts, beaded belts, designer knock-offs, and tourist knickknacks. Don't be fooled by the first price offered, because prices are generally three times what they should be, and so be prepared to bargain hard. On **Poppies Gang II** you'll find everything from tie-dyed sarongs, shorts, swimsuits, knock-off cologne, hats, and wristwatches. Traffic-jammed **Jalan Legian** also has a large selection of shops and restaurants. **Jalan Pantai Kuta** has a few good fashion and accessories shops. **Kuta Square** has international brand knock-off stores including Nike and Armani—don't get suckered into paying high prices.

The **Discovery Mall** (✆ 0361/755522; www.discoveryshoppingmall.com) on Jalan Kartika Plaza has a multitude of high-end shops, along with a good selection of international restaurants, cafes, and banks. The **DFS Galleria Bali** on Jalan Bypass Ngurah Rai, Kuta (✆ **0361/761945;** www.dfsgalleria.com) is the oldest luxury shopping mall in Bali but is currently undergoing renovations. You can find duty-free goods such as Chanel, Coach, and other big brands (designer labels here are the real deal). **Galleria Bali** has a variety of affordable restaurants that serve both international and Indonesian food. Free shuttle service is offered from many Kuta hotels. Istana Kuta Galleria, in a strategic area between Kuta and Legian, consists of 250 shops and many good Indonesian and Western restaurants.

Most stores are open daily from 9am to 9pm.

Books

For books, stop by **Periplus,** with locations in Discovery Mall (✆ **0361/769757**), **Kuta Square** (✆ **0361/763988**), **Carrefour** (✆ **0361/847-7336**) in Seminyak, and even at the airport.

Clothing

On Jalan Legian, you'll find a mix of classier stores such as **Uluwatu** (✆ 0361/751933), which produces handmade lace clothing called krawang. Its product line includes women's clothing, nightwear, and bed and table linens. **Body & Soul** (✆ 0361/767169) is another good shop with trendy Hong Kong-inspired clothing for women. The styles are youthful and fresh with smaller sizes but there are a few items for fuller-figured women. Their Bambini line offers a good selection of really cute fashions for children 3 to 8 years old with an emphasis on girlie clothes and a few styles for boys, too. For handbags, funky shoes, accessories, and hip clothing, visit the **Decollage** (✆ 0361/758510) boutique.

On Jalan Pantai Kuta, **Emily the Strange** (no phone) offers a variety of T-shirts, tanks, hoodies, sweatshirts, dresses, bizarre collectible toys, and fun accessories; **Skin** (✆ 0361/765020) is for those seeking unisex clothing in cotton, silk, and linen.

In Kuta Square, **Milo's** ★★ (✆ 0361/754081; www.milos-bali.com) is the one exception that's worth checking out for beautiful designer clothing for men and women. Milo, an Italian born designer, finds great inspiration for his exclusive designs from orchids and other flowers indigenous to Bali. Dresses, blouses, and skirts come in a mix of elegant floral motifs in satin and silk. This is high-end couture, so be prepared to pay up to US$400 for designs. A great shoe store for big-size men's and women's shoes is **Maju Jaya** (✆ 0361/751184). Women's sizes go up to European 45 and men's to 46. Most of their shoes are leather with a good selection of sandals, closed shoes, dress shoes, and children's shoes. Prices go from Rp75,000 on up.

Paul Ropp ★★ Paul Ropp is a name that you'll see on every fashion street in Bali. Instantly recognizable in Bali, Paul Ropp designs for people who want to stand out in a crowd. Accordingly, bright yellows, burnt oranges, fiery reds, and shocking pinks are categorized within a Fire theme; turquoises, sapphires, aquamarines, violets, and sea-grass represent Water; and so on. The garments, for men and women, include long flowing appliqué skirts, baggy embroidered cotton pants, camisoles in sheer silk, loosely woven country-cotton shirts, graceful beaded evening dresses, silk crepe sarongs, and slippers garnished with jewels. Kuta Galleria, Jl.Patih Jelantik, Kuta.✆ 0361/769359. www.paulropp.com.

Groceries & Wine

J Cuvee, Jl. Kartika Plaza 20, Kuta (✆ 0361/761888), offers a wide selection of international wines, but with recent government crack-downs on illegal wine imports, prices have escalated and so be prepared to pay more than what you'd pay at home.

An outlet of the French supermarket **Carrefour** is on Jalan Sunset, Kuta (✆ 0361/847-7222), and stocks everything from fridges, art material, and cheap clothing to Western and local food and produce. It has an excellent fish counter and the bread is the best on the island.

Dijon ★★ 🏠 This delightful deli offers a fantastic selection of hams, cured meat, cheeses, and antipasti; imported meats from Australia and New Zealand; and a daily selection of fish and shellfish. If you're pining for familiar foods from back home, this is the place that's likely to stock it. Their small cafe, **the Corner,** next door, is the perfect place to grab a coffee, a quick lunch, or an early supper. A bulletin board here is filled with local news and information on all sorts of services such as private yoga lessons, swimming classes for children, and so on Jl. Setiabudi, Kuta.✆ 0361/759636. www. dijon-bali.com.

Housewares & Furniture

Farah's Oriental Rugs & Carpets, Jl. Bypass Ngurah Rai 5, Kuta (✆ **0361/766-9012**), offers an exclusive collection of more than 2,500 handmade rugs, carpets, and *kilim* (Turkish non-pile rugs). **Vinoti Living,** in Galleria Bali, Kuta (✆ **0361/752723** or 752720), has an excellent selection of high-end contemporary furniture skillfully crafted from ash and nyatoh woods. Their furniture designs are sleek with clean lines. You can also find an impressive collection of artwork, including antique look-alike objects from more remote regions of Indonesia. **Lightcom,** Jl. Patih Jelantk, Kuta inside Komplek Pertokoan Kuta Gallery (✆ **0361/769246**), offers a wide array of stunning indoor and outdoor lighting imported from the U.S., Europe, Australia, and China. The designs are simple and very contemporary.

The name says it all: the **Why Not Shop,** Jl. Nakula, corner of Imam Bonjol, Kuta (✆ **0361/499001;** www.whynot-shop.com), offers a surplus of Asian home decor items such as paintings, furniture, and lighting as well as some nice jewelry and clothing. There are some unusual finds here and everything is handmade and reasonably priced. The **Zire,** Jl. Dewi Sri 21, Kuta (✆ **0361/755431;** www.thezire.com), specializes in synthetic rattan furniture, which is both attractive and highly durable. You can choose from a variety of color schemes and contemporary designs for indoor and outdoor furnishings. It also has some attractive wooden furniture, kitchen accessories, and housewares. Another great one-stop place is **Serba Antik,** Istana Kuta Galleria (✆ **0361/769400;** www.serbaantik.com), which has everything under the sun: curtains, wallpaper, carpets, rugs, furniture, bed covers, upholstery, and more. The furnishings are simple yet elegant, and are beautifully crafted from fine woods and other natural materials.

Cempaka ★ Located along Bali's main thoroughfare in the heart of Kuta, adjacent to Galleria Bali, Cempaka is a stunning, high quality, modern and classic furniture and housewares shop. The staff can help with designing your interior and delivering the goods wherever you live. For those just looking for a gift, there's also plenty to choose from. The specially designed housewares are second to none and you're bound to find something worth hauling back home. Open Monday to Saturday, 9am to 8pm. Jl. Bypass Ngurah Rai 8, Simpang Siur, Kuta. ✆ **0361/766555.**

Surf Shops

Internationally recognized surf clothing and lifestyle brands have their anchor stores in Kuta. The massive two-storey **Rip Curl,** Jl. Legian (✆ **0361/765889;** www.asia.ripcurl.com), is one of three outlets in Kuta. **Quiksilver** is in the Discovery Mall, Kuta (✆ **0361/757838**).

Bali Barrel This surf cult store stocks garments, accessories, and sports gear by numerous manufacturers, including Island Style, O'Neill, Quiksilver, Ocean Earth and Honey Ocean Earth, Spyderbilt, Rizt, and Volcom. The music is upbeat and loud and the central focus is a V-shaped mezzanine, displaying a selection of surfboards. The girly wear upstairs includes sandals with high heels (not exactly beach wear) and a colorful collection of children's stuff. This is also a good outlet for purchasing high-quality eyewear. Jl. Raya Legian, Kuta. ✆ **0361/767237.**

Jungle Surf The first Jungle Surf shop opened on Jalan Legian (near Peanuts Club) in 1993 and was Bali's first big modern surf shop. Its roots go back to the late 1970s when its founder, Ketut Kasih, a surfing legend and one of the very first Balinese surfers, started making and selling Bali's original board shorts. Kuta now has three of these stores to satisfy all your surfing needs. Discounted items are upstairs in the Jalan Legian and Kuta Suci Arcade stores. Jl. Pantai Kuta. ℘ **0361/750097.** www.junglesurfworld.com.

Surfer Girl   Surfer Girl is much more than just an all-girls surf store. This is a one-stop shopping destination where young women can purchase the clothing, board shorts, sandals, accessories, jewelry, and perfume that makes it easier for them to convey the personality and spirit behind their active lifestyles. Most of the popular lines of colorful beach wear and casual wear are imported from Australia. There's a collection of sandals and footwear by Reef, and a range of genuine surf wear from well-known brands designed for, and purchased by, serious surfers and surfer wannabes. Kuta Square, Discovery Mall, Kuta. ℘ **0361/752693.** www.surfer-girl.com.

KUTA & LEGIAN ENTERTAINMENT & NIGHTLIFE

Kuta is the place to be if you want to party late into the night. The action begins roughly at 10pm but really gets going around 11pm and lasts until dawn every night. Don't forget your sunglasses, you'll probably need them. Plenty of clubs and bars have their own unique style, although many are more alike than not.

Balinese Theater

One of the highlights of being in Kuta is the multitude of cultural performances on offer at many of the four-star hotels and restaurants. The **Kuta Paradiso Hotel,** Jl. Kartika Plaza, Tuban-Kuta (℘ **0361/761414;** www.kutaparadisohotel.com), features a nice variety of traditional dance performances with their theme night buffets, on Monday, Wednesday, and Saturday. The **Legian Beach Hotel,** Jl. Melasti (℘ **0361/751711;** www.legianbeachbali.com), presents a gamelan orchestra with elegant Balinese dancers. Performances are also held at **Banjar Tegal,** Jl. Raya Legian (no phone; Rp50,000), every Saturday and Tuesday night at 8pm. Puppet performances (wayang kulit) can be seen in Banjar Buni, Jl. Raya Kuta (no phone; Rp50,000), Monday and Thursday night at 8pm.

Bars & Pubs

Peanuts' Pub Crawl, Jl. Legian and Jl. Melasti (℘ **0361/754226**), is a great way to visit a few of Kuta's infamous watering holes. The crawl begins at Peanuts II, every Tuesday and Saturday. You get to ride in the historic Peanuts' car while barhopping. Peanuts also has a "Welcome to Bali" party every Thursday.

The sports bar at the **Stadium Café,** Jl. Kartika Plaza (℘ **0361/763100**), ensures you always know the score of your favorite team while you're on holiday.

Down in **Poppies Gang I,** you'll find a myriad of small cheap bars, always full with crowds looking for less expensive food and drinks. The **Nusa Indah** (no phone) has been around since the heady days of the 1970s, and nothing much has changed. You can still get super-cheap drinks, and you never quite know who you'll meet at the long bamboo bar.

Vibrant **Bali Joe,** Jl. Caplak Tanduk (℘ **0361/847-5771**), throbs with DJ music, live drag shows, and an enthusiastic patronage of trendy gay men. It has a dance floor, a stage, and bar-top dancing. Regular late-night live entertainment includes themed parties, drag shows, and fashion shows. Shows usually begin around 11pm, but it's best to arrive early. Mizwell (no phone) and **Face Bar** (no phone) next door are also popular gay bars with shows and dancing.

Jalan Melasti   The aging **Aussie Pub** (© 0361/751910) is famous for its icy cold beer and is subsequently full of beer-loving Australians, and then some. The walls are covered in graffiti, so while you're here you can leave your mark. **Bali Rock** (© 0361/754466), opposite the Aussie pub, keeps the live music rocking to appreciative crowds. Easy to find, it's the loudest bar on the street. If "Sweet Child of Mine" gets your blood pumping, do drop in.

Jalan Double Six   The stylish bar of **De Ja Vu** (© 0361/732777; www. myspace.com/dejavubeach) is best for a sunset cocktail. Later in the night things start getting funky and spunky. The small **La Vida Loca** (no phone) club packs them in for vodka drinks, with a great live band nightly, playing mostly Latino grooves. The crowds don't really get here till after 2am. Bring your sunglasses as well as your salsa moves because La Vida Loca parties till sunrise.

Poppies Gang II   The **Bagus Pub** (no phone) is busy day and night serving up ice-cold beers to the holiday brigade. Close to the night spots on Jalan Legian, it's great for meeting other holiday-makers. **Tubes** (no phone) was established in 1986, at a time when surfers had very few places to hang out. No one anticipated just how fast the word would spread about this place by the constantly traveling surfers as they rode the waves to all the corners of the globe. Tubes is popular for playing pool and watching the feature and surf movies shown daily on a big screen. While here, enjoy some good food with a choice from two kitchens: Buffet style *nasi campur* (mixed rice) from the traditional Indonesian kitchen or "No Noodles . . . Western food for when you're all noodled out," offering pasta, pizzas, burgers, and baked potatoes.

Jalan Legian   **Paddy's Bar** (© 0361/758555) packs the crowds to the rafters nightly as DJs play the latest sounds to fired-up backpackers. Buy-two-get-one-free specials keep the party moving in the right direction—or not. Opposite Paddy's and Bounty (see below) is the **Espresso Bar & Pizzeria** (© 0361/752576), a tiny, older bar so crowded that the band stands out on the street to play. Cold beers flow and ensure any would-be rock stars are well oiled enough to brave belting out a number—like "Mustang Sally" in c-very-flat. The first club along the strip to go five floors high, **Sky Garden** (© 0361/756362), is still one of the most popular any night of the week. The street-level base camp serves food all night long, while upstairs DJs crank out different styles of music depending on what floor you want your party plans elevated to. This is a great place to meet old friends and find some new ones if you're anywhere under your 30s.

Jalan Padma   The **Legian Pub** (no phone) is another raucous night spot that starts early in the evening (some folks in there appear to have started a lot earlier). There's live music or karaoke most nights, and a super-friendly bar staff that also like to jump up and sing. Be sure to try the green starfish cocktails, but only with caution. It's hard to know whether it's the clientele or the passing parade who are doing the posing at **Posers** (no phone), an English-style corner pub that makes a fine meeting place over a nice cold ale. On Jalan Sahadewa, the small road linking Jalan Padma and Jalan Melasti, **Legends** (© 0361/755376) is busy every night with the holiday crowd looking for good value drinks and food. There's a live band most nights, so if you can find your way to Jalan Sahadewa keep an ear out for the party noise—you'll be sure to find it.

Clubs

Kama Sutra (© 0361/761999) has become a local teenager hangout, at the north end of Kuta. Nightly shows feature local bands that love to do tried-and-true cover songs; you won't find much (or any) original music in Kuta's clubs. The one exception is Hard Rock Hotel's **Centerstage,** Jl. Pantai Kuta (© 0361/761869), which occasionally features some good live acts, but it can get pretty crowded. **Deejay Café,** Jl. Pantai Kuta (© 0361/755661; www.deejaycafe.com), is the only after-hours club in Kuta, located just behind Stars Surf Café. Their professional DJs and state-of-the-art sound system will get you in the mood to pump and grind on their huge dance floor.

Bounty   It looks like an old boat, but inside the crowd is young and intent on showing off their drinking and dancing skills. After midnight, it's standing room only and every dance podium is packed with revelers usually doused from the regular foam parties. Although the Bounty has a Captain's wheel, no one seems to be at the helm when it sails off into the long dizzy night. Jl. Legian. (© 0361/752529).

Club Double Six ★   Next door to Bacio is the daddy of nightclubs—this one is legendary. On the beach at the far end of Jalan Double Six, this huge club includes a swimming pool and bungy jump. After 3am, it's the hotspot to go to after everyone's been everywhere else. Local and international DJs play the best house and techno around, with a truly impressive sound system that'll have you out on the floor or hanging off the end of a bungy string. Jl. Double Six, Legian. © 0361/756666 during office hours. www.doublesixclub.com.

M-Bar-Go   M-Bar-Go started out as one of Kuta's first stylish nightclubs. This is the hangout for people on gap years and returning expat students—it's a young crowd. Resident and guest DJs play booming house music. Efficient staff members serve a wide variety of drinks and cocktails, and the massive floor space is punctuated by long bars, comfortable sofas, and snug corners. Jl. Legian, Kuta. © 0361/756280.

Rendezvous   Rendezvous provides three floors of live entertainment, pumping house beats, and some of the friendliest bar staff around. Although not a big club, it's big on fun and all manner of madness and mischief. Jl. Padma Utara, Legian. No phone.

SEMINYAK

t's hard to know the boundaries of where Kuta, Legian, and Seminyak begin and end because the three villages have been slowly melding into one another for the past several decades. Today one thing is clear: Seminyak is certainly in a class all its own—and the sunsets are splendid.

Seminyak is Bali's Notting Hill or Soho in London, or Miami Beach, Florida, and has even been compared to Spain's Ibiza. If you come here in August and early September, you'll see why. Chock-a-block with high-octane parties and "ump humph" music, Seminyak's social beat reverberates from Jalan Laksmana all the way to the beach, pulsing along with the rhythm of the waves. The vibe is mixed with royalty, trendy Europeans, financiers that haven't failed, and Jakarta glitterati.

As Seminyak reaches maximum capacity, **Petitenget,** one village over, has become the next even more upmarket locale. After that is **Batu Belig** and then **Canggu,** which is becoming a bit of an expat ghetto. Lack of planning throughout all of this explosive growth is a story in itself.

In the 1960s and 1970s, when foreign tourists first began arriving in Bali in large numbers, the chosen path was always via Kuta. In the 1970s, Sanur (see chapter 7) became the darling of daring travelers on the South Sea's circuit. But it wasn't long before wealthy American Charles Osborn bought 15 hectares (37 acres) of land on the beach in a sleepy little area 5km (3 miles) north of Kuta. At the time, Seminyak was a dozy dream of sea, surf, sand, and green. Osborn hired Australian architect Peter Muller to design a private residence, but the project spun out of control and morphed into a 75-room hotel. In 1974 it was christened the Kayu Aya Hotel. A bad partnership agreement saw the hotel taken possession of by the Balinese partner and fall into disrepair. Overseas investors eventually repossessed the property from the Balinese owner in 1977 and it was bought again by local Balinese (supported by the Oberoi Group). Their hope was that their new property was far enough away that they would thrive in solitary splendor forever. They were mistaken.

ESSENTIALS
Getting There & Getting Around

Seminyak is about 30 to 45 minutes away from Bali Ngurah Rai International Airport, depending on congestion levels. Almost all villas and hotels here offer complimentary pick-up from the airport. If you're taking a cab from the airport, pay for your trip at the official taxi counter located outside the arrival hall before you travel. The approximate cost is about Rp100,000 and prices are fixed.

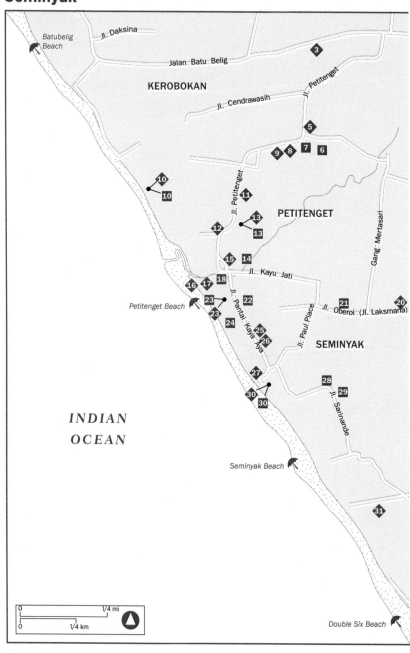

KEROBOKAN

Jl. Daksina

Jalan Batu Belig

Batubelig Beach

Jl. Cendrawasih

Petitenget

PETITENGET

Jl. Petitenget

Jl. Kayu Jati

Gang. Mertasari

Petitenget Beach

Jl. Pantai Kaya Aya

Jl. Paul Place

Jl. Oberoi (Jl. Laksmana)

SEMINYAK

INDIAN OCEAN

Jl. Sarinande

Seminyak Beach

0   1/4 mi
0   1/4 km

Double Six Beach

To Canggu
Jl. Gunung Tangbukan Perahu

Jalan Raya Kerbokan

Jalan Mertanadi

("Eat Street")

Jalan Drupadi

Jalan Sunset

Jalan Dewi

Saraswati 3

Jl. Kunti

Jl. Drupadi
Jl. Raya Seminyak
Jl. Drupadi 1

Jl. Dhyana Pura (Jl. Abimanyu)

Jl. Plawa

Gang Ratna

(Jl. Raya Basangkasa)

Gang Ratna

Jalan Sunset

(Jl. Double Six) Jl. Arjuna

Jalan Nakula

To Kuta,
Legian

HOTELS ■

The Amala **36**
Bali Ayu Hotel & Villas **18**
Casa Artista **28**
The Colony Hotel **22**
The Dusun **14**
The Elysian Boutique
  Villa Hotel **29**
Hotel Vila Lumbung **7**
Kunja **6**
The Legian **24**
Mutiara Bali Boutique
  Resort & Villas **21**
The Oberoi Bali **30**
The Samaya **23**
Sentosa Private Villas
  & Spa **13**
The Villas Bali Hotel
  & Spa **35**
W Retreat & Spa Bali **10**

RESTAURANTS ◆

Baku Dapa **32**
Biku **11**
Breeze **23**
Café Bali **20**
Callego Massage
  & Warung **16**
Chez Gado Gado **31**
Dewi Warung **15**
EVO **13**
Ku de Ta **27**
Kura Kura Restaurant **30**
La Lucciola **17**
La Sal **33**
Made's Warung **34**
Mama San **19**
Métis **2**
Naughty Nuri's **3**
Nutmegs **12**
Ryoshi **38**
Sardine **1**
Sarong **8**
Sea Circus **25**
Sip **37**
Starfish Bloo **10**
Wah Wah **26**
Warisan **4**
Warung Bonita **9**
Warung Sulawesi **5**

Gilimanuk   Singaraja
Negara   BALI
  Ubud
Canggu   Denpasar
Seminyak   Nusa
  Penida

Safety

Note that Seminyak's **sidewalks** are a hazard to your health, with so many gaps and holes that the odd partygoer and shopper has gone missing a time or two.

Be extra cautious if you're going to swim. Every year new tales of tourists being taken down permanently by the **undertow** spread throughout the community. Warning flags with skull and crossbones or cautionary red flags mark some of the worst areas and are put up in front of well-known places such as the Legian Hotel. The farther north you go, the stronger the current and the fewer warning flags. This undertow stretches from Kuta beach, through Seminyak, all the way to Gilimanuk.

Although Seminyak has no public transport, on whatever main street you're walking on hailing a taxi is always easy (**Blue Bird** is the best company). Avoid hotel cars, which run at a premium of Rp300,000 per hour—nearly as much as the cost for a local car and driver for the whole day.

Finding an Address

Every major Seminyak thoroughfare has both an official and unofficial name. Also, gang (small alleyways) often don't even bother with names at all, even though they're used as roads and have shops and restaurants that you'll want to visit. As a general rule, go with the old unofficial street names that everyone can understand with the exception of **Jalan Oberoi** now **Jalan Laksmana,** which seems to be understood no matter which name you use. Here are the unofficial names and their corresponding new official names: Jalan Oberoi is now called Jalan Laksmana; Jalan Raya Seminyak is now called Jalan Raya Basangkasa; Jalan Dhyana Pura or Jalan Gado Gado is now called Jalan Abimanyu; Jalan Double Six is now called Jalan Arjuna.

[FastFACTS] SEMINYAK

ATM   The best ATMs to withdraw money from are **Permata Bank** ATMs. They allow you to withdraw at least two lots of Rp3,000,000 in Rp100,000 notes. **Circle K** on Jalan Laksmana has one as well as several other ATMs.

Pharmacy   **Apotek Taiga Farma,** Jl. Raya Seminyak (✆ **0361/730977**), is open 24 hours.

WHERE TO STAY

Very Expensive

The Legian ★★   If budget isn't a problem, go for broke. The beautiful people from Asia, Europe, and North America flock to the Legian and everyone seems just that much more gorgeous in the stunning surrounds. As an all-suite hotel built like a private beachfront estate, every guest room features a comfortable living room, dining area, spacious bedrooms, and a balcony. The decor is on the masculine side with rich woods and cool marbles, but the whole place is nicely appointed with Indonesian artifacts. Gardens envelop a split-level swimming pool, and refined dining is available at the oceanview, simply named Restaurant, or in the privacy of your suite. The on-site villa complex is also worth your attention.

Jl. Kayu Aya, Seminyak Beach. www.thelegianbali.com. ℰ **0361/730622.** Fax 0361/730623. 66 units. High season US$650 and up; low season US$550 and up. Rates include breakfast. AE, MC, V. **Amenities:** Restaurant; 2 bars; babysitting; bikes; concierge; gym; outdoor pool; room service; spa (p. 90); water-sports; Wi-Fi. *In room:* A/C, TV/DVD, movie library, CD, hair dryer, Internet, minibar, Wi-Fi.

The Oberoi Bali ★★
Even decades after opening, the Oberoi remains at the top of its game and attracts a good share of British travelers. The Oberoi hotel was one of the first luxury hotels on Bali, and it feels like a well-worn leather shoe. The native bungalows of coral stone with wood beams and thatched roofs have become the benchmark for tropical Bali style. Cozy rooms strike a great balance between high-end comforts and local style. Amenities are first class: marble bathrooms with sunken tubs facing private gardens, and goodies such as slippers, robes, and flip-flops for the beach. Private pool villas are luxurious beyond belief. The beach here has a nice expanse of sand with few touts to harass you. Service is genuinely warm and helpful without being fawning, and you can feel at ease here without forgetting that you're in Bali.

Jl. Kayu Aya, Seminyak Beach. www.oberoihotels.com. ℰ **0361/730361.** Fax 0361/730791. 74 units. High season US$355–US$616; low season US$320–US$560. Rates include breakfast. AE, DC, MC, V. **Amenities:** 2 restaurants; bar; babysitting; concierge; gym; outdoor pool; room service; spa; tennis court; Wi-Fi (for a fee). *In room:* A/C, TV/DVD, movie library, CD, hair dryer, Internet, minibar, MP3 docking station.

The Samaya ★★
Close to half of all Samaya's guests are repeat clientele—which comes as no surprise. With a renovation nearly complete, the Samaya will feature luxuriously upgraded villas on the beachfront, in addition to its complex of villas across the street down a residential alley. Sublime sunsets show nightly and an evening at Breeze restaurant overlooking the beach is perfect. Named "Best for Romance" by TripAdvisor, each villa comes with wooden gazebos housing daybeds that make an ideal perch for private dining or a double daybed for a massage for two.

Jl. Laksamana, Seminyak Beach. www.thesamayabali.com. ℰ **0361/731149.** Fax 0361/731203. 60 units. High season US$695 and up; low season US$515 and up. Rates include breakfast. AE, DC, MC, V. **Amenities:** 3 restaurants, including Breeze (p. 83); 2 bars; babysitting; bikes; concierge; gym; outdoor pool; room service; spa; Wi-Fi. *In room:* A/C, TV/DVD, movie library, CD, hair dryer, minibar, MP3 docking station, Wi-Fi (free).

Sentosa Private Villas & Spa ★★
Fashionistas flock to this trendy complex, with its exclusive ensemble of 42 luxury villas. The main pool is surrounded by a top-of-the-line gym, spa, and excellent restaurant and bar, EVO. Every room has the standard amenities—such as flatscreen televisions, integrated music system, and stylish marble bathrooms with sunken bathtubs—and most feature a Jacuzzi and outdoor bamboo showers. The larger villas have kitchens with full-size refrigerators. The boat available for rent would be at home in St. Tropez. Spoil yourself and make a point of booking in advance for a day trip to one of the islands.

Jl. Pura Telaga Waja, Petitenget. www.balisentosa.com. ℰ **0361/730333.** 42 villas. High season US$847 and up; low season US$726 and up but there are almost always special rates offered. Rates include breakfast. AE, MC, V. **Amenities:** Restaurant (Evo, p. 84); bar; babysitting; children's club; concierge; gym; outdoor pool; room service; spa; Wi-Fi. *In villa:* A/C, TV/DVD, hair dryer, minibar.

Expensive

The Amala ★
The Amala has done a good job of creating a relaxing atmosphere in the middle of Seminyak's bustle. You'll hear the occasional hum of motorcycles but

no noise from children, because those 12 and under aren't allowed. A sister resort to the pristine Balé (p. 156) in Nusa Dua, the Amala's emphasis is on its professional spa and central location—a stone's throw from the restaurant and bar scene and a 15-minute walk to the beach. Each spa villa features its own steam shower room and an outdoor bathtub and Jacuzzi, while the more opulent and cozy pool villas each feature an open-air living room and kitchen set around a plunge pool.

Jl. Kunti 108, Seminyak. www.theamala.com. ☏ **0361/738866.** Fax 0361/734299. 12 units. High season US$275 spa villa, US$325 pool villa, US$610 Amala residence; low season US$245 spa villa, US$295 pool villa, US$580 Amala residence. Rates include breakfast. AE, DC, MC, V. **Amenities:** Restaurant; health club & spa, outdoor pool; room service; massage. *In room:* A/C, TV, DVD, fridge, hair dryer, minibar, MP3 docking station, Wi-Fi (free).

The Dusun ★ 🌶 This spacious complex was the second to hit Seminyak's shores and still offers great value for its location and service. The grounds have a mature garden and roomy villas with deep pools. Service is top-notch and the whole place is blissfully quiet. The owners also have a sister property, the boutique all-villa Kunja (☏ **0361/733130;** www.thekunja.com) in Kerobokan.

Jl. Kayu Jati 8, Seminyak. www.the-dusun.com. ☏ **0361/734000.** Fax 0361/734100. 14 villas. High season US$505 1-bedroom, US$910 3-bedroom; low season US$430 1-bedroom, US$825 3-bedroom; extra person US$20. Rates include breakfast. AE, MC, V. **Amenities:** Babysitting; bikes; concierge; outdoor pool; room service; spa; Wi-Fi. *In villa:* A/C, TV/DVD, movie library, stereo or CD, hair dryer, kitchen, minibar, MP3 docking station.

The Elysian Boutique Villa Hotel ★ An open-air restaurant overlooks a swimming pool flanked by intimate cabanas in traditional black-and-white check. Sliding glass doors in the guest rooms open onto the little garden and pool. Base yourself here to party with a groovy wet bar, iPod dock with iPods you can check out for the beach, and a coffee table with a built-in champagne bucket.

Jl. Saridewi 18, Seminyak. www.theelysian.com. ☏ **0361/730999.** Fax 0361/737509. 26 villas. High season US$650; low season US$450. Rates include breakfast. AE, DC, MC, V. **Amenities:** Restaurant; bar; babysitting; bikes; concierge; outdoor pool; room service; spa; watersports. *In villa:* A/C, fan, TV/DVD, movie library, hair dryer, minibar, Wi-Fi (free).

The Villas Bali Hotel & Spa The well-known Villas Bali Hotel and Spa is a better choice than some of the new complexes in the neighborhood. One-, two-, and three-bedroom villas each have their own entrance, pool, and kitchen and are ideal for those who want to enjoy their own surroundings rather than eat out every day. The Prana Spa (p. 89) offers yoga retreats and fabulous treatments; Chill (p. 89) offers natural healing and reflexology for all your aches and pains. If you're on a spa vacation, this is the place to stay.

Jl. Kunti 118X, Seminyak. www.thevillas.net. ☏ **0361/730840.** Fax 0361/733751. 50 villas. High season US$350 and up; low season US$315 and up. Rates include breakfast. AE, DC, MC, V. **Amenities:** Restaurant; babysitting; outdoor pool; room service; 2 spas; Wi-Fi. *In villa:* A/C, TV, stereo or CD, hair dryer, Internet, kitchenette.

W Retreat & Spa Bali ★★ ☺ A sign of the changing times, the W—and its brash, flamboyant style—has arrived. With a prime beachfront spot in northern Seminyak, a lagoon-like swimming pool that snakes across the resort, and playful artsy touches throughout, the W aims to please the hipster, jet-setting crowd. Although the resort offers villas, save your money and go for an ocean-facing room decorated with gray wood tones, greens, and browns—it'll have all the comforts you need. Thoughtful touches grace the resort, including a library with the latest magazines and recent paperbacks, a 24-hour spa, and Bliss products in the bathrooms.

Though the property doesn't specifically cater to children, young parents with tots feel right at home here.

Jl. Petitenget, Seminyak. www.starwoodhotels.com. ☎ **0361/473-8106.** Fax 0361/300-2223. 237 units. High season US$650-US$4,600 rooms, US$700-US$2,550 villa. Low season US$425-US$4,400 rooms, US$800-US$2,250 villa. Rates include breakfast. AE, DC, MC, V. **Amenities:** 2 restaurants; 2 bars; state-of-the-art gym; outdoor pool & children's pool; room service, spa. *In room:* A/C, TV/DVD, CD, hair dryer, minibar, movie library, MP3 docking station, Wi-Fi (free).

Moderate

The Colony Hotel ★ 👜　Next to the Oberoi and Samaya hotels, this new property evokes Bali's Dutch colonial heritage with its white wraparound balcony that decorates the hotel's inner courtyard. Rooms are fitted with dark wood, white wicker furniture, and black-and-white photos of the Colonial era. An 8-m (25-ft.) long pool and a small spa provide in-house relaxation and the beach and Ku De Ta bar (p. 82) are both just across the street.

Jl. Laksmana 22, Seminyak. www.thecolonyhotelbali.com. ☎ **0361/736160.** Fax 0361/736319. 20 units. High season US$175-US$210; low season US$155-US$190. Rates include breakfast. AE, MC, V. **Amenities:** Restaurant; pool; massage room. *In room:* A/C, TV, DVD, minibar, Wi-Fi.

Hotel Vila Lumbung ★　Just a few minutes' walk from the beach in northern Seminyak, this old but regal hotel is popular with Australians and Europeans. Double rooms have recently been renovated and provide all the necessary amenities. For an extra US$50 per night, you can upgrade to a deluxe room with an outdoor shower, stone floors, bathtubs, and antique-looking furniture. The grounds are lush green and there's a large pool with a jungle gym and waterfall. Walk 10 minutes to the W Resort or Potato Head Beach Club for access to the shore.

Jl. Raya Petitenget 1000X, Seminyak. www.hotellumbung.com. ☎ **0361/473-0204.** Fax 0361/473-1106. units. High season US$145 superior room, US$200-US$220 bungalow, US$450 villa; low season US$120 superior room, US$175-US$195 bungalow, US$400 villa. Rates include buffet breakfast. Minimum 3-night stay during peak and high seasons. AE, MC, V. **Amenities:** Restaurant; bar; babysitting; gym; outdoor pool; spa. *In room:* A/C, TV, minibar.

Inexpensive

Baku Dapa INDONESIAN　If you're wondering where to go late at night when you need a good food fix among the bars of Dhyana Pura, check out Baku Dapa. This authentic little warung (roadside cafe) has been serving consistently good Indonesian food at low, low prices for many years. Baku Dapa is renowned for its sop buntut (oxtail soup), probably the best in town. Typical Indonesian dishes on offer include nasi goreng, chicken satay, gado gado (vegetable salad with peanut sauce), tempe goreng (fried soybean), and piping hot tahu goreng (fried tofu), accompanied by a selection of fresh and fiery homemade chili sambal, and followed by pisang goreng (fried banana with honey).

Jl. Dhyana Pura, Seminyak. ☎ **0361/731148.** Main dishes Rp15,000. No credit cards. Daily 24 hr.

Bali Ayu Hotel & Villas ★ 🔔　This relaxing, quiet, and affordable property features a prime location and clean, comfortable rooms and villas. Rooms are spacious, albeit a little characterless, while bathrooms feature large bathtubs and showers with stone walls. There's a welcoming pool and bar area, the beach is just a 15-minute walk away, and restaurants and bars are a few steps from the property.

Jl. Petitenget 99, Seminyak. www.baliayuhotel.com. ☎ **0361/473-1263.** Fax 0361/473-1264. High season US$80-US$125 hotel rooms, US$175-US$415 pool villas; low season US$55-US$100 hotel rooms,

US$150–US$390 pool villas. Rates include breakfast. MC, V. **Amenities:** Restaurant; bar; outdoor pool; Wi-Fi in lobby. *In room:* A/C, TV, fridge.

Casa Artista ★ 🏨 ✦   This funky boutique hotel is themed around tango dancing and has a Spanish feel, from the black-and-white tile floors to the soft guitar music. Eight simple rooms are set around a large common area with a small pool and lounge chairs. Down a quiet alley, the hotel plays movies on a large outdoor screen at night and offers tango lessons from Tuesday to Thursday. A wide, white sand beach is a 5-minute walk. No children under 12 are allowed. Book an upstairs room for more peace and quiet.

Jl. Sari Dewi 17, Seminyak. www.casaartistabali.com. ℂ **0361/736749.** Fax 0361/732847. 8 units. High season US$120–US$150, low season US$100–US$120. Rates include breakfast. AE, MC, V. **Amenities:** Restaurant; outdoor pool; massage. *In room:* A/C, TV, minibar, Wi-Fi (free).

Mutiara Bali Boutique Resort & Villas ★ ✦ 🏨 ☺   "Boutique" is a bit of a stretch, but the rooms and villas at this no-frills resort are definitely a bargain. Opt for the newly renovated upper-floor standard rooms, which come with airy bathrooms and little balconies. A long pool stretches across the grounds and there's even a small open-air gym. Each two-story villa, with traditional Balinese straw roofs, contains two bedrooms, a well-kept garden, and a private pool—they're a steal at around US$200 per night during low season. The property is located on a quiet residential street a 15-minute walk from the beach.

Jl. Braban 77, Br. Taman, Seminyak. www.mutiarabali.com. ℂ **0361/734966.** Fax 0361/735375. 46 units. High season US$135–US$164 rooms, US$385–US$746 villas; low season US$115–US$164 rooms, US$365–US$726 villas. Rates include breakfast. Discount prices on website. AE, DC, MC, V. **Amenities:** Restaurant; pool; airport transfers; gym; room service, spa. *In room:* A/C, TV; Internet (free), minibar.

WHERE TO EAT

Seminyak is teeming with restaurants of every variety and price range. The majority are individual enterprises, although some of the best, such as Blossom and Kura Kura, are part of villa complexes and hotels. The truly international community lends the international restaurants their authentic base.

Expensive

Ku de Ta ★★ 📷 INTERNATIONAL/MEDITERRANEAN   Everyone who's anyone makes their way to Ku de Ta when they're in Bali. It's fabulous fun and you can't beat the awe-inspiring sunsets and beachfront. The indoor and alfresco dining surrounds a plunge pool and grassy courtyard, three bars, and a rooftop lounge. Mediterranean menus are available for lunch and dinner and grazing food is served from noon until 10pm, including Asian tapas, sashimi and sushi, and oysters. August, or "high season" here is high voltage and you can't be too overdressed or underdressed for the annual "Bikini" and "White Party." A DJ spins day and night.

Jl. Laksmana 9, Seminyak. ℂ **0361/736969.** www.kudeta.net. Reservations recommended. Lunch for 2 Rp500,000–Rp700,000; dinner for 2 Rp700,000–Rp1,000,000. AE, DC, MC, V. Daily 8am–1am.

Kura Kura Restaurant ★★ 🏨 📷 EUROPEAN/INDONESIAN   This gem is a favorite for romantic celebrations. The breezy Balinese thatched pavilion—encased in folding glass panels and surrounded by lotus ponds with the sounds of the *angklung* music and crashing waves—makes for a true island experience. Modern European cuisine is served on fine bone china with a white linen silver service. Order the home-cured smoked salmon with anything, especially the signature blinis. Royal Indonesian cuisine and some excellent Indian dishes give a nod of appreciation to the owners of Oberoi. The not-so-gentle reminder on your bill in capital letters that says "No Tipping, Please" means the service you just enjoyed was genuine.

In the Oberoi (p. 79), Jl. Kayu Aya, Seminyak. ☎ **0361/730361.** www.oberoihotels.com. Reservations recommended. Indonesian Rp277,000–Rp410,000; continental Rp350,000–Rp600,000; seafood Rp277,000–Rp1,000,000; set menu Rp400,000. AE, DC, MC, V. Daily 7–10pm.

Nutmegs ★★ 🍴 PAN-ASIAN   This new restaurant at the famous dance bar Hu'u is sleek and stylish. The tables are decked out in crisp white linen, white flowers, and candles. Service is perfect. Exuberant and enthusiastic Chef Philip Mimbimi is a graduate of the Culinary Institute of America with a five-star resume and he makes sure that your experience is charmed. Go with his recommendations of the night and you won't go amiss. The key to his cooking is the freshest ingredients that can be found that day. The club **Hu'u** (p. 95) turns into party central on the weekends so time your meal carefully if you want a quiet night. Otherwise get up and party. Nutmegs is a great alternative to Ku de Ta, with Lychee Martinis that kick. Live music plays every Thursday night.

Jl. Oberoi, Petitenget. ☎ **0361/736443.** www.nutmegs-restaurant.com. Reservations recommended. Main courses Rp128,000–Rp528,000. AE, MC, V. Daily 11:30am–11:45pm.

Starfish Bloo ★ PAN-ASIAN   Led by American chef Jack Yoss—who once worked under Wolfgang Puck—this beachside restaurant at the hip W Retreat aims to impress with an innovative raw bar and dishes than span Asia. Although the interior certainly impresses with giant wooden birdcage-like banquettes, the main attraction is the outdoor dining, next to the crashing waves. The innovative rolls—featuring combinations such as spicy peanut sauce and shrimp tempura—and the delicately presented sashimi are highlights.

In the W Resort and Spa, Jl. Petitenget, Seminyak. ☎ **0361/473-8106.** Reservations recommended. Main courses Rp210,000–Rp240,000. Set menu Rp550,000. AE, DC, MC, V. Lunch noon–3pm; dinner 6–11pm; Sunday brunch 11:30am–3pm.

Moderate

Breeze ★★ EUROPEAN/AMERICAN   Hold on to your tipple with all your strength because this chic open bar sits virtually on the beach and is prone to windy weather. Chef Michael Shaheen showcases Euro-American cuisine that blends the best of the environment with his own vision. Using many indigenous ingredients, the menus are dictated by the local harvest in a "Simple, Seasonal, and Uncomplicated approach." Our favorites include black pepper, sesame tuna (*tataki*), and marinated hamachi (rare yellowtail) with wakame and seaweed salad, tempura nori rice cake, ponzu, and pan-seared diver scallops. The Peking duck—pan-seared confit—is delectable.

In the Samaya (p. 79), Jl. Laksmana, Seminyak. ☎ **0361/731149.** www.thesamayabali.com. Reservations recommended. Sandwiches Rp90,000–Rp105,000; pasta Rp170,000–Rp210,000; main courses Rp110,000–320,000. AE, DC, MC, V. Daily 11am–4pm and 5:30–11pm.

Chez Gado Gado ★★ 🍴 INTERNATIONAL   A recent renovation keeps this beachside institution at the top of its game. Relax at one of the tables on the timber deck above the white-sand beach and enjoy a leisurely lunch or romantic dinner. The menu offers modern European food, such as seared tuna in spice crust and grilled rouleau of chicken; the seafood and Wagyu beef tenderloin are also highlights.

Jl. Abimanyu (Jl. Dhyana Pura), Seminyak. ☎ **0361/736966.** www.gadogadorestaurant.com. Reservations recommended. Main courses Rp200,000. MC, V. Daily 11am–3:30pm, 6–11pm.

EVO ★ ITALIAN   Authentic Italian and Mediterranean dishes are offered at this swanky new restaurant. Though it's set in one of Seminyak's most exclusive villa hotels, the mood is casual, with outdoor seating near the pool on offer. Delicious pizzas come from the wood-fired oven and are complemented by an extensive list of signature cocktails and wines by the glass. The half-priced happy hour from 5pm to 6:30pm daily draws a regular crowd and cooking classes are offered on Friday afternoons.

In Sentosa Private Villas and Spa (p. 79), Jl. Pura Telaga Waja, Petitenget. ☎ **0361/730333.** www.balisentosa.com. Reservations recommended. Main courses Rp70,000–Rp220,000, pizza Rp70,000–Rp120,000, meat Rp110,000–Rp220,000; set menu Rp490,000. AE, MC, V. Daily 7am–10:30pm.

La Lucciola ★★★ MEDITERRANEAN   This happening beachside restaurant—a Seminyak pioneer—is lovingly referred to as "La Looch" and looks out onto one of the prettiest stretches of Seminyak beach. The new Italian chef offers classic Mediterranean fare with a touch of Asian spice. The pan-seared fillet of coral trout with pancetta, marinated artichokes, and preserved lemon dressing is a firm favorite. Finish with a lemon and vanilla bean soufflé and a bracing expresso. The only way to get to the restaurant is through the parking lot of the famous Petitenget Temple (see p. 89) next door—the laughter will lead the way.

Jl. Petitenget, Seminyak. ☎ **0361/730838.** Reservations recommended. Main courses Rp150,000–Rp200,000. AE, MC, V. Daily 9am–11pm.

La Sal SPANISH   Finding La Sal can be hard—it's on a small back lane that connects Jalan Laksmana and Jalan Abimanyu—but on the menu you'll easily find a good choice of tapas such as delicious (imported and expensive) Iberico Bellota ham from acorn-fed, black, free-range pigs, calamari with squid cooked in its own ink, grilled chorizo sausages, crunchy mushrooms, and a delicious veal carpaccio with foie gras and Manchego cheese. The list also includes a clam casserole, garlic prawns in truffle oil, grilled king prawns, crispy pork belly with lentils and mango, twice-cooked lamb shoulder, and paella. You could select from a small but good range of wines, but why not go for sangria instead? Sunday evenings is Argentinian Churrasco night.

Jl. Drupadi II 100, Seminyak. ☎ **0361/738321.** www.lasalbali.com. Reservations recommended. Main courses Rp85,000–Rp895,000. AE, MC, V. Daily 11am–3pm and 6:30pm–midnight.

Mama San ★ ASIAN   The latest venture of Sarong's (see p. 85) Will Meyrick is likely to be a big hit, given his track record. Mama San offers casual pan-Asian street food such as Cambodian baguette sandwiches, Vietnamese soups, and Indonesian takeaway rice dishes. The industrial interior features vintage-retro touches and communal tables that seat up to 20. The restaurant offers daytime cooking classes and a convivial nightclub atmosphere in the evenings, making it a good choice nearly any hour of the day.

Jl. Raya Kerobokan 135. ☎ **0361/733072.** www.mamasanbali.com. Main courses Rp50,000–Rp100,000. AE, MC, V. Daily noon–11pm.

Métis ★★ FRENCH/MEDITERRANEAN   This open-air, 350-seat emporium houses a patisserie, bars, event space, an arts and interior shop, a jewelry boutique, and a women's fashion boutique. The French cuisine focuses on foie gras and seasonal truffles, white asparagus, and mushrooms. Vegetarians also have plenty of options.

Jl. Petitenget 6, Petitenget. ☎ **0361/473-7888.** www.metisbali.com. Reservations recommended. Lunch Rp100,000–Rp160,000; dinner Rp400,000–Rp500,000. AE, MC, V. Daily 11am–4pm and 6–11pm.

Sardine ★★ SEAFOOD   Strikingly housed in a sprawling bamboo structure overlooking rice paddies, Sardines is equally inviting for a drink or a meal. A comfortable lounge area sits next to a pond, home to a school of very rare white koi carp—the chef assures us that they won't end up on your table. The menu is made of predominately fish and organic greens. The owners have taken a tip from the locals and serve surprisingly delicious arak cocktails—no mean feat. Sardines of course are the house specialty on the daily-changing menu.

Jl. Petitenget, Kerobokan. ⓒ **0361/473-8202.** www.sardinebali.com. Main courses Rp110,000–Rp235,000. MC, V. Tues–Sun 11:30am–4pm and 6–11pm.

Sarong ★★ PAN-ASIAN   Chef Will Meyrick takes minimalism out of the equation for both his food and decor at Sarong. The appealing airy *joglo*-style pavilion is draped in gold with gilded mirrors and enormous chandeliers completing the romantic sheen. In contrast, the menu draws on the traditions of hawker or street food from India, Indonesia, China, and Thailand. Merrick elevates pedestrian favorites to sophistication. A must is the betel nut leaf starters with either salmon shrimp galangal coriander or raw tuna betel leaf with lemongrass shallots and lemon basil. Betel nut (the leaf from the arcadia palm) is a known stimulant that causes a sense of heightened alertness, similar to a cup of coffee. If you fancy tandoori, try the Zafferrani Paneer, cheese stuffed with succulent and tangy North Indian chutney. Sarong also has an excellent bar worthy of a visit on its own accord.

Jl. Petitenget 19X, Kerobokan. ⓒ **0361/473-7809.** www.sarongbali.com. Reservations recommended. Main courses Rp170,000 and up. AE, MC, V. Daily 6:30pm–midnight.

Sip ★ FRENCH   Sip is a winner despite its unlikely location across from the Bintang supermarket. Owner Christian Vannequé was France's youngest Head Sommelier at La Tour d'Argent in Paris in the 1970s and has created a wine list for wine novices and wine aficionados alike—no easy task on an Indonesian island. His Wine Climax features outstanding and rare bottles from the Old and the New World. The kitchen is run by Chef Patrick Chauchereau who worked in several two-Michelin-star restaurants in Paris before coming to Bali. Sip offers French home cooking at reasonable prices: escargots in garlic butter, homemade pâtés, traditional cassoulet (our favorite), and *tete de veau ravigotte* (boiled calf's head and tongue in ravigotte sauce). Meals finish with a variety of French cheeses and mouthwatering sweets. The restaurant recently opened a second location in Seminyak called **Sip Grill** (Sunset Road 88x, ⓒ **0361/847-5830;** www.sip-bali.com), with a lively atmosphere suitable for larger groups.

Jl. Raya Seminyak 16A, Seminyak. ⓒ **0361/730810.** www.sip-bali.com. Reservations recommended. Main courses Rp125,000–Rp265,000. AE, MC, V. Tues–Sun noon–11pm; closed for lunch on Sun.

Warisan ★ INTERNATIONAL   After a tumultuous period—during which a management split resulted in the creation of rival Metis (see above)—this Seminyak fine-dining institution is back on the mark, serving a new menu of Mediterranean dishes by a recently hired Belgian chef. The restaurant offers a cozy ambience, both indoors and outdoors, for a romantic meal, and dining is a better value here than at many other Seminyak establishments of the same quality. The grilled Australian rib eye steak and the duo of pan-fried duck breast are highly recommended.

Jl. Raya Kerobokan 38, Br. Taman, Kerobokan. ⓒ **0361/731175.** www.warisanrestaurant.com. Main courses Rp210,000–Rp265,000. MC, V, AE. Daily noon–4pm and 7:30–11pm.

Balinese High Tea

Biku ★★★, Jl. Petitenget (☏ 0361/ 857-0888; www.bikubali.com; main courses Rp50,000–Rp100,000; MC, V; daily 8am–11pm), is an enchanting 150-year-old Javanese *joglo* as regal as its owner, Princess Asri Kerthyasi, and her son, Tjok Gde Kerthyasa, a tea master. High tea is the main draw but don't miss out on breakfast and lunch. Start with a cup of limited edition Javanese tea. A must is the three-tiered presentation of sweets and tea sandwiches and scones with homemade jam and cream. Everything here is baked fresh daily, including the rose petal cupcakes. Don't miss Friday to Sunday, from 1 to 5pm, when you can have a mystical afternoon tea-leaf reading by some of the island's leading psychics. Questions are answered and futures (perhaps) revealed.

Inexpensive

Café Bali ★ INTERNATIONAL   You might accidentally drive right past this tremendously stylish, white clapboard building on Jalan Laksmana, but don't. Dutch and French design maximize giant chandeliers, pretty table tops, comfy sofas, and classic bistro chairs to make you almost forget you're on a tropical island. The cuisine is French-meets-East, with steak frites, dim sum, sashimi, and spring rolls.

Jl. Laksmana, Seminyak. ☏ **0361/736484.** Main courses Rp38,000–Rp89,000. MC, V. Daily 7am–11:30pm.

Callego Massage & Warung [image] INDONESIAN   This warung is the daytime hangout for the gay community in Bali on Petitenget beach. The vibe is ultra casual with scattered plastic chairs and tables with sun loungers available for rent in front of the warung. Expect to see many minute Speedos as well as the occasional tourists wondering where they landed. The food is Indonesian fare with a few uninspired sandwiches but the Bintang is cold and the atmosphere extremely chilled.

Jl. Taman Ganesha 9, Petitenget. ☏ **0361/730370.** Main courses Rp25,000–Rp45,000; pasta Rp15,000–Rp30,000; Indonesian Rp20,000–Rp30,000. No credit cards. Daily 10am–9pm.

Dewi Warung [image] JAVANESE   Across from the Petitenget Temple (see p. 89) is a row of warungs. Facing this row, head for the farthest on the left. Here, the cook, Ibu Dewi, serves fresh soto *ayam* (chicken soup) that's as delicious as it is good for you. The sambal that accompanies the other perfect Javanese specialties has just the right amount of spice and, like all Javanese cuisine, isn't spiced hot like Balinese cuisine. After following my close friend's advice and discovering this jewel, you can now catch me here several days a week on my favorite pink plastic stool.

Jl. Petitenget, Petitenget. No phone. Main courses Rp10,000–Rp20,000. No credit cards. Daily 6:30am–9pm.

Made's Warung ★★ [image] INTERNATIONAL   This is the cream of the warung crop and, having started from humble origins in Kuta beach, Made and Peter's place has since become a landmark at both locations. If it's busy (and it often is) don't be surprised if you end up sharing a table. Made's is a must for first-time tourists and families, who will love their popular Indonesian offerings, such as the recommended *gado gado*, satay, and curries. Go for the infamous Japanese dish of *shabu shabu*, available for a minimum of four people (*shabu shabu* means "swish swish"). The dish is prepared by submerging meat, seafood, or vegetables into a pot of boiling broth. There's also a bagel with smoked marlin, tofu burgers, and Caesar salad. Don't pass up the daily specials, particularly the fresh fish. Choose from beverages ranging from iced coffee and juices to some very potent booze concoctions. Paintings, memorabilia, and nostalgic posters lend a warm and cozy feel and the tables spill out in the courtyard where tango aficionados occasionally tap their toes. Friday and Saturday nights include a live Balinese dance performance.

Jl. Raya Seminyak. ℂ **0361/732130.** www.madeswarung.com. Reservations recommended. Balinese Rp40,000–Rp50,000; Indonesian Rp25,000–Rp60,000; *shabu shabu* Rp90,000–Rp100,000. AE, MC, V. Daily 9am–midnight.

Naughty Nuri's ★ BARBECUE/INDONESIAN   This popular picnic-style Ubud institution recently opened up closer to the beach and serves its trademark ribs, steaks, and a range of Indonesian dishes. The martinis are rumored to the best on the island. The only thing that might be missing here is Brian, the chatty amiable owner who's usually stationed at a table in front of his Ubud location.

Jl. Batubelig 41, Kerobokan. ℂ **0361/847-6722.** www.naughtynurisbali.com. Main courses Rp50,000–Rp100,000. AE, MC, V. Daily 11am–11pm.

Ryoshi ★ JAPANESE   The prices are reasonable for sushi at Ryoshi, and all kinds of other Japanese fare is done just right, too (simply ask the many Japanese guests). Try the butterfish sashimi, a deepwater whitefish with a rich texture and savory flavor. There are locations all over the island, but the Seminyak outlet is by far the best.

Jl. Raya Seminyak. ℂ **0361/731152.** www.ryoshibali.com. Reservations recommended. Wagyu steak Rp150,000–Rp300,000; sushi and sashimi set Rp28,000–Rp86,000; a la carte Rp12,000–27,000. AE, MC, V. Daily 11am–11pm.

Sea Circus ★ INTERNATIONAL   The whimsical name of this colorful roadside cafe and bar is fitting, since it defies categorization and appeals at all hours of the day. The chipper morning types will be drawn to its breakfast standards such as eggs Benedict while the hard-drinking crowd will appreciate its hangover happy meals that come with a 15-minute massage for an extra Rp30,000. Lunch and dinner gravitates toward light fare with an Asian bent; highlights include salt and pepper squid and the fish burger. Stop in anytime for coffee, fresh juices, and granitas, and there's also an extensive list of cocktails.

Jl. Kayu Aya (Oberoi Rd) 22, Seminyak. ℂ **0361/738667.** Seacircus-bali.com. Rp55,000–Rp145,000. AE, MC, V. Daily 8am–midnight.

Wah Wah ★★★ BURGERS   Just a few steps south of Sea Circus, Wah Wah, like its Shanghainese owner of the same name, is frankly bizarre. Its proprietor is an artist and a self-taught culinary genius who has dabbled in just about everything. His idea for his pre-club/lounge/restaurant/bar/gallery/souvenir shop is to make the best hamburgers in the world in bite-size portions and keep the drink prices reasonable. His finger food is made with Wagyu beef, fois gras, blue cheese, and other rich ingredients. He also has veggie burgers. Wah's art adorns the walls: His paintings in deep reds and greens with simple brush strokes on primarily black backgrounds exude a certain degree of sexuality. It's brazen and brash and decidedly unique.

Jl. Laksmana 11A, Seminyak. ℂ **081/8349809.** www.wahwahburger.com. Reservations recommended. Main courses US$13–US$35; 6-course tasting menu US$30. AE, MC, V. Daily 8am–1am.

Warung Bonita ★★ INDONESIAN   This warung is an institution of a different sort. On the odd night you can catch Bonita in top form, dolled up, hat on, and scarf billowing under the fans. Bonita often leads an impromptu cabaret giving diners a fabulous floor show—maybe not Tony-award-worthy, but certainly enjoyable. Warung

THE BEST OF eat STREET

Dozens of restaurants line **Jalan Laksmana,** aka Eat Street. Establishments pop up and close like shutters during a storm. Prices are competitive at all these establishments; part of the fun is strolling down the street before deciding where to dine. Below are a few standout selections; reservations are recommended at all these busy places, and all open daily.

Chandi ★★★ (© 0361/731060; www.chandibali.com; burgers Rp80,000–Rp500,000, vegetarian Rp26,000–Rp42,000, fish Rp78,000–Rp240,000; AE, DC, MC, V; Mon–Thurs 5pm–midnight) serves a "gastronomic twist on Pan-Asian cuisine" with organically grown greens and spices from local farmers.

Centuries of tension between Korea and Japan seem to dissipate at **Kaizan** (© 0361/747-2324; main courses Rp35,000–Rp250,000, set menu Rp70,000–Rp250,000; AE, DC, MC, V; daily 9am–1am)—upstairs is Korean barbecue; downstairs is Japanese. Next door is the little brother restaurant **K2,** a traditional inn-style Japanese restaurant serving Japanese tapas.

Owned by Moroccan locals, **Khaima** (© 0361/742-3925; www.khaimabali.com; main courses Rp49,000–Rp95,000; MC, V; 11am–11:30pm) has excellent appetizers that include filo pastry filled with vegetables, minced lamb, tuna, chicken, or goat cheese;

salads of tomatoes and bell peppers, cinnamon and carrots, or eggplant; and lamb tagines with couscous. Friday and Saturday nights feature belly-dancing performances that see even the most staid customers shaking their booties.

Rumours (© 0361/738720; www.balinesia.co.id; pasta Rp28,000–Rp85,000, steak Rp50,000–Rp120,000, pizza Rp27,500–Rp50,00; AE, MC, V; daily 6pm–midnight) is a bit of a dive, but having a quality Australian T-bone or sirloin for about US$8 is hard to beat. Rumours only accepts reservations until 7:30pm, which should give you an idea of this buzzing bistro's popularity.

Trattoria ★ (© 0361/737082; www.trattoriabali.com; pasta Rp49,000–Rp63,000, fish Rp46,000–Rp75,000; AE, DC, MC, V; daily 11:30am–midnight) has a simple recipe: mix delicious Italian food with reasonable prices with the emphasis on steady clientele rather than haute cuisine. The plentiful, modest food stays true to the roots of the ever-present owner and his brother from southern Italy.

Last but not least, classy Italian dishes at very affordable prices make **Ultimo** (© 0361/738720; www.balinesia.co.id; pizza Rp36,000–Rp58,000, main courses Rp29,000–Rp358,000; AE, MC, V; daily 5pm–midnight) one of the most crowded Eat Street restaurants. Go before 7pm to avoid the crowd or you may wait for up to 30 minutes to be served.

Bonita offers authentic home cooking from the islands and some Western fair as well. Try the Indonesian buffet lunch, which has attracted a loyal following among local and expat residents alike. Every Friday night features a live Balinese performance.

Jl. Petitenget, Petitenget © **0361/473-1918.** www.bonitabali.com. Reservations recommended. Main courses Rp20,000–Rp65,000. MC, V. Daily 8am–11pm.

Warung Sulawesi ★★ INDONESIAN   This little gem is run by an American and his Indonesian partner who serve up some very good Indonesian food. The warung has good food at good prices and provides housing for the staff.

Jl. Petitenget, Petitenget. ℂ **0361/746-3052.** Rice and vegetables Rp3,000–Rp4,000; fish Rp9,000; meat Rp7,000–Rp12,000. No credit cards. Daily 9am–8pm.

EXPLORING SEMINYAK

The main activities in Seminyak are lolling on the beach, shopping till you literally drop (into a hole in the street), or just enjoying your well-earned rest. Remember, the rip currents here make swimming a risky prospect. Many visitors use Seminyak as a base for day trips to explore the rest of the island.

BUNGY JUMPING   A. J. Hackett, Jl. Arjuna, beside Club 66 (ℂ **0361/731144;** www.ajhackett.com/bali; daily noon–8pm, Fri–Sat 2pm–4am; US$79 for one jump, certificate, and T-shirt), jumped into the Guinness Book of World Records in 1987 by being the first and only person to bungy jump 110m (361 ft.) from the Eiffel Tower. Since then he has built a global business for all those thrill-seekers out there. Try your hand at bungy jumping off the Kuta tower (on your own, with a bicycle, or even a motorbike). The sky's the limit.

HORSEBACK RIDING ★★★ 🄾   Sabina, the owner of **Umalas Equestrian,** Jl. Lestari 9X, Banjar Umalas Kauh–Kerobokan (ℂ **0361/731402;** www.balion horse.com; ½-hour rice field tour US$25, 2-hour beach tour US$72, 3-hour beach tour US$102; daily, by reservation, from 7am–9pm), fell in love with Bali 14 years ago. Sabina explains, "I came to Bali and everything was here, beautiful countryside, beaches, and people but I missed my horses so I came up with a plan." Umalas includes 35 stables, indoor and outdoor arenas, paddocks, a swimming pool, a restaurant, and even accommodations for those looking to book a riding holiday.

PETITENGET TEMPLE ★★   As one of the directional temples on the island, Petitenget (along Jl. Petitenget) is a beautiful and busy site on the beach and a beehive of activity. Several *banjar* (village councils) are attached to the temple and the best time to see it is during Melasti (held once a year 3–4 days before Nyepi; Nyepi dates are Mar 23, 2012, March 12, 2013, and March 31, 2014), when thousands of villagers arrive marching in unison toward the temple and through to the beach to cleanse their souls.

SPAS   Body Works, Jl. Kayu Jati 2 (ℂ **0361/733317;** www.bodyworksbali.com; massage Rp107,000–Rp245,000, infrared sauna Rp155,000–Rp320,000, facial Rp175,000–Rp385,000; MC, V; daily 9am–10pm), was the first spa in Seminyak in 1994 and now looks rather dated with its Moroccan-inspired design and girls dressed in blue kebaya (traditional Indonesian blouse-dress) and sarongs. Body Works enjoys much popularity simply because of its location—across the street and diagonally from the Petitenget Temple. Blow dries, crème baths, and manicures and pedicures are the mainstays here as are Balinese massage, *lulur* exfoliating scrubs, and the ever-popular aloe vera facials. The infrared sauna has people booking in for a miracle cure.

One of the spas in the Villas Bali Hotel and Spa (p. 80), **Chill** (Classic US$13, Ultimate Chill US$18, Chill Out US$15, Holistic Chill US$23; AE, MC, V; daily 10am–10pm), has built a fine reputation for reflexology. The Ultimate Chill is a 90-minute indulgence concentrating on the feet, ankles, neck, and shoulders in a combination of reflexology and acupressure. Advance booking is recommended. Also in the Villas Bali Hotel and Spa, the Prana Spa (ayurveda US$84–US$263, massage US$82–US$165; AE, DC, MC, V; daily 9am–10pm) sets itself apart simply by its totally incongruous Mogul-inspired architecture with turrets, towers, look-out posts to nowhere, and ornate hand-painted frescoes. Some of the treatments get their inspiration from the Majapahit royal courts and others hail from ayurvedic medicine. The hotel affiliation offers excellent spa packages and spa cuisine at the attached cafe.

When Glo ★★★, Jl. Kunti 119 (℗ **0361/738689;** www.glogarage.com; mani/pedi Rp175,000–Rp410,000, brows and lashes Rp120,000–Rp160,000, wax Rp115,000–Rp215,000, facial Rp199,000–Rp750,000; MC, V; daily 10am–10pm), opened in Seminyak women from around the island breathed a sigh of relief as finally there was a place to get European-quality manicures and pedicures and not just a foot rub and a splash of paint. The facials are some of the best on the island.

Treatments at **Jari Menari** ★★★, Jl. Raya Seminyak (℗ **0361/736740;** www.jari menari.com; four hand massage Rp495,000; MC, V; daily 9am–10pm), are some of the best worldwide not to mention in Bali. Male masseuses give the infamous "Four Handed Massage," which gives you the pleasure of four palms applying perfect pressure rather than just two. Tuesday massage classes teach a nine-step, 25-minute massage sequence. The session starts with a 40-minute yoga class. Students watch demonstrations and then give and receive treatments. You'll be the best souvenir to give to a loved one back home.

The **Spa at The Samaya** (p. 79; massage US$45–US$90, ayurveda US$99, hot stone US$55–US$75, Balinese Eternal Bliss package US$120–US$210; AE, DC, MC, V; daily 9am–10pm) has a standout location on the beach—it doesn't get any more calming than this. If you're traveling as a couple, book into a beachfront treatment room and enjoy the Balinese Eternal Bliss couples' treatment that lasts 2½ hours. Book this package at sunset and enjoy the view—of the sunset and each other.

Overlooking the rolling surf of the Indian Ocean, **The Spa at The Legian** (p. 78; massage US$65–US$120, beauty treatment US$20–US$120; AE, MC, V; daily 10am–9pm) is famous for its totally self-contained single and double treatment suites, each with a private bathroom and steam room. The treatments are diverse: Choose from ayurvedic shiro dhara, warm stone massage, and reflexology. Excellent couples' massages are available as well as the exotic royal Javanese lulur and Balinese borah body wrap.

Spa Venus ★ (Balinese massage Rp160,000–Rp290,000, reflexology Rp160,000, detox, up to 11 days, US$550–US$950; AE, MC, V; daily 10am–10pm), in the Villa Kubu, offers treatments for longer-lasting results. Massage is by blind therapists who miraculously find those spots that need the most attention. Therapies also include acupuncture, naturopathy, craniosacral therapy, and energy healing.

SHOPPING

Shopping in Seminyak is rife with possibilities, if you can just forgive the bumps and grinds of making your way to your destination by car, motorbike, or on foot—a slightly more hazardous prospect. The goods in Seminyak display local creativity and originality, as opposed to the mid-range labels and surfing duds in Kuta (see chapter 5). The

Periplus Books

The best place for maps, books, and magazines is Periplus. The number-one publisher of books on Asia has a chain of 15 bookshops around Bali. Handy stores are outside Bali Deli on Jalan Kunti; in Seminyak Square; next door to Made's Warung on Jalan Raya Seminyak; and in Kuta's Discovery Mall.

Shipping the Goods Home

From a small lamp to a large 6-m (20-ft.) Buddha, the following shippers will arrange pick up, packing, and delivery of your goods: **Limajari**, Jl. Raya Kerobokan 100x (✆ 0361/730024; www.limajaricargo.com), and **Rim Cargo**, Jl. Laksmana 32 (✆ 0361/737670; www.rimcargo.com). **Sourcing Bali**, Jl. Gunung Salak 31A, Kerobokan (✆ 0361/744-8025; www.sourcing-bali.com; Mon–Fri 9am–5pm, Sat till 3pm), will take care of all your shipping needs and has "personal shopping helpers" who assist with negotiations, product selections, order placement, and payment.

junky jewelry that was once commonplace has given way to high-end gems of immense creativity and originality at a fraction of the cost at home. Housewares are another great deal and Balinese home accessories are found in shops literally around the world from Harrods to Home Depot. Shops are typically open daily 9am to 9pm.

Seminyak has a new shopping mall at Seminyak Square, on Jalan Laksmana, that stocks a selection of the bigger brand names such as Body & Soul (p. 70 in Kuta), Periplus, Quiksilver, and the food shop Casa Gourmet (see p. 95).

Jalan Raya Seminyak

Jalan Raya Seminyak starts at the junction of Jalan Raya Kerobokan and stretches all the way down to Kuta where it turns into Jalan Legian. The street is littered with small boutiques, clothing and craft shops, and houseware stores. Here are some of our favorites, starting at the top of the road nearest to Jalan Raya Kerobokan:

G and V ★★   G and V is the vision of Giuseppe Verdacchi, an Italian architect known on the island as Beppe. It's almost impossible to describe Beppe's style because his acute eye for beauty ranges from textiles, ceramics, woven fabrics, retro-style '40s furniture and decorations, to Art Nouveau wall tiles from the Dutch colonial period. His tabletop accessories combine stone, silver, wood, and semiprecious gems such as turquoise, coral, and black lapis. ✆ **0361/731916.** www.gvbali.com.

Dandelion   Adorable is the word for this bambini boutique that dresses little girls in poppy red trench coats and boys in suitably striped sailor tops and shorts appropriate for boating in the Mediterranean. ✆ **0361/730375.**

Haveli   Situated opposite each other are two Haveli home accessories showrooms. The collection takes inspiration from the many travels of the owners in Southeast Asia and Europe. The rich fabrics include taffeta, silks, satins, Indian saris, and fine French linens. ✆ **0361/737160.** www.havelishop.com.

Word of Mouth   Down a side street, Jalan Kunti, this new design emporium, co-owned by an architect, features a collection of art installation pieces, edgy furnishings, clothing, jewelry, and ceramics. The cafe/bar is the perfect place for a cocktail or a light meal. ✆ **0361/847-5797.** www.wordofmouthbali.com.

By the Sea   Recalling visions of family seaside holidays at their best, this delightful collection of family clothing is produced in 100% cotton in fruity hues with stripes, polka dots, floral motifs, and paisley silk screen prints. ✆ **0361/732198.**

Disini   The owner here is clearly French as everything is appropriately chic. Quilted bedcovers, cushions, and table linens all come with mix-and-match accessories. All

If you're looking to furnish your home with treasure from Indonesia, head to Jalan Mertanadi, better known as Jail House Road. The road has large warehouse-size buildings interspersed with smaller specialist shops selling an assortment of items for the home. There's a billiard specialist, large teak furniture manufacturers, model ship makers, French repro furnishing companies, as well as Indonesian antique furnishings and artifacts.

the natural fabrics are from southeast Asia. Clever designs such as canvas striped beach bags with matching towels are a hit. © **0361/731037.**

Innuendo ★   The silk, chiffon, and cotton separates sold here would sell worldwide at triple the price. Count on finding superb, eclectic outfits pretty and perfect for weddings and special occasions, often with matching wraps and accessories to complete the ensemble. The cuts are irresistible and some of the silks are bias cut. Many are delicately garnished with sequins, Japanese glass beads, and Swarovski crystals. © **0361/742-8814.** www.innuendofashion.com.

Dinda Rella ★★★   It feels like Cinderella's walk-in closet here with embellished evening gowns and cocktail frocks that go from understated beige to over-the-top fuchsia. Evening wear is a fraction of the cost of back home, but sizes are decidedly small. Have a dress made to order in 5 working days. © **0361/734228.** www.dindarella.com.

Papillon   Find good-quality shoes and sandals with lots of embellishment at gratifying prices here. Although it exports around the world, the largest size for women is US 8½/European 39/UK 6. © **0361/734967.**

Biasa ★★   Everybody shops at Biasa, so you know it's good value and good quality. The easy, at-home entertaining wear is comfortable, cool, and suitable for Bali's tropical climate. Colorful, classy, and romantic fabrics include soft cottons, muslins, silks, and linens. The lovely scarves and accessories such as sequined handbags make great gifts. Upstairs is a floor devoted entirely to menswear. © **0361/730308.** www.biasabali.com.

ET Club   Glam yourself up with the large selection of brightly colored bags, belts, and shoes bejeweled in beads and stones that are so popular with the Euro jet-set. Order one in every color. © **0361/734795.**

Jalan Laksmana

This is the best shopping street in Bali. Shop after shop of designer goods, to suit all tastes and budgets, are crammed into one street that stretches from outside the Legian Hotel all the way up to Jalan Raya Kerobokan. Designers from round the world, who now call Bali home, have retail spaces and showrooms selling their wares for less than you'll find in your own country.

Appropriately located on the corner of a busy thoroughfare, the **Tuckshop/Corner Store ★** (no. 10A, © **0361/732115**) is the expat hangout for breakfast, lunch, and coffee and also a clothing shop with men's, women's, and children's clothing by trendy Bali-based designers. Opposite the Tuckshop/Corner Store is a tiny shoe box of a shop called **I Love Bali** (no. 13)—filled with brightly colored casual beachwear. Next door is **Buddha Wear** (no. 15X) for knitted jersey outfits in an assortment of colors. Up the steps from Buddha Wear, **Sabia** (no. 44B; © **0361/733995**) has just the sort of things you need in Bali, St. Tropez, or St. Barts: nifty espadrilles, oversize woven straw beach bags, stylish floppy sun hats, and cool cotton kaftans. A few doors down is **Joy Jewellery** ★★ (no. 40; ✆ 0361/791-4893; www.joy.com.sg), by Dutch owner Jenny, a longtime Bali resident. She told us that Beyoncé had just placed a large order and she was rushing to get the delivery on time. Lots of celebrities find her silver and gold jewelry addictive, but mere mortals can purchase them too at about a quarter of what they would cost in other countries.

For the latest in funky designs and an eclectic mix of accessories, nearby **Prisoners of St. Petersburg** (no. 942) and **Rock 'n' Royalty** (no. 20) are hard to beat, while **Hikari** (no. 36B; ✆ 0361/730888; www.hikari.com) over the road, is for those with a more subdued taste in clothes.

Farther down the road, for fashionistas, are **Lulu Yasmine** (no. 100X; ✆ 0361/736763; www.luluyasmine.com), **Lily Jean** (no. 102x; ✆ 0361/7435715; www.lily-jean.com), and **Magali Pascal** (Jl. Kayu Aya Oberoi 177x; ✆ 0361/736147; www.magalipascal.com). Choose from elegant silk dresses, cut-off shorts, and funky accessories.

Religion This hot underground label presents retro punk designer clothing for men and women—mainly T-shirts, jeans, stretch cotton dresses, and skirts. The sexy, carefree, appliqué patchwork and cutwork, distressed textures, and overcooked screen prints and washes are bold and to some beautiful. Styles are off the shoulder, backless, painted, tied, rushed, and customized. Jl. Laksmana 4A. ✆ **0361/731916.**

Bamboo Blonde Women flock to this large and airy boutique for sundresses, separates, and accessories. The clothes are as cheery as the designer Louise, who can usually be found laughing up a storm as the punters raid her boutique for good quality bargains. This is Bali's answer to Top Shop. Jl. Laksmana 61. ✆ **0361/742-5290.**

Simple Konsep Store ★★ The owners of this Italian boutique have worked with Prada, Armani, and other prestigious labels. This two-level shop would be right at home in Milan with an outstanding assortment of his and hers clothing and Vivienne Westwood accessories. Jl. Laksmana 40. ✆ **0361/730393.** www.sksbali.com.

Maru Gallery ★★ Situated opposite the Legian Hotel, the concept here is "Body–Art–Space," according to American owner Marina Urbas. Currently, Maru has eight international jewelry designers under its wings from Bali, Canada, France, and Italy. Maru has always carried the designs of Nohan, an Indonesian designer who found success in the international and local market with his own distinctive style and fantastic craftsmanship. Aside from the owner's stunning work, one of the signature labels is Mal, designed by a Canadian woman who makes those "must have and will

---

 Icon Asian Arts

This innovative gallery of iconic Asian arts, hence the name (Jl. Oberoi 17; ✆ 0361/733875; www.iconasianarts.com; daily 11am–8:30pm), is run by Bruno Piazza and his partner Susi Johnston, two seasoned figures in art, art history, Asian tribal art, textiles, design, and photography. They bring decades of experience, conscientious collection, and insight into the world of collecting Indonesian tribal art, ethnographica, excavated jewelry, animist art, tribal sculpture, and fine textiles. Their client list reads like the Forbes Magazine top 500 American companies but they'd never drop names—it's not their style. The gallery, with rotating exhibits throughout the year, adheres to the creed: Discussion, Debate, Discovery, and Authenticity.

find any way to get" pieces in gold with luscious Lombok pearls. Prices range from US$15 to US$2,500. Jl. Kayu Aya 7A. ℰ **0361/734102.** www.marubali.com.

FOR MEN

Jl. Oberoi 1 (ℰ **0361/738776**) is a hideaway gem by the former head designer from Biasa (p. 92), an old Bali institution, and a favorite of wealthy Italians in town. Classic linens and cottons fill the racks in subtle tones of taupe and gray. The pashmina scarves complete the Euro look in colors to die for and prices to match.

Much farther down the road is **Deefusion** (see below). In the corner of this furniture emporium is **Nico Perez,** another designer who dresses men effortlessly in linen. Choose from a selection of classic pastel and muted-colored casual ware.

FOR KIDS

Start at the **Corner Store** (see above) for funky T-shirts and separates and then head to **Clara Mia's** (no. 43) for sweet, flowery dresses and shirts too cute for words. **Kiki's Closet** (no. 45a), with kitsch children's wear in bright colors with plenty of fun patterns including polka dots, animal prints, and stripes, is popular with Versace-dressed mothers. For those with more subdued taste, plenty of beautiful embroidered and batik clothing is available at **Kids A Go Go** (Jl. Kayu Aya 29; www.kidsagogo. com) for babies and young children.

INTERIORS

The furniture emporium of **Deefusion** (Jl. Laksmana 117X; ℰ **0361/738308;** www. deefusion.com) sells a selection of modern furnishings from well-known Filipino designers. The showroom will ship directly to your home from their factory in the Philippines.

Jalan Petitenget

Studio 13 ★★★ New Sumatran designer Johnny Rimali got caught on the way from Indonesia to Paris and decided to try his luck in Bali. Success has come quickly and Johnny now sells his jewelry and bags to places such as Barneys in New York and other high-end boutiques. One of his specialties is canvas and nylon tote bags that have become coveted items with the in-crowd. ℰ **0361/307-4113.**

Jemme Jewellery This jewelry shop is glittering with gemstones and just the right mix of extravagance and understated elegance. Luke, the English designer, mixes gemstones, cubic zirconia, silver, semiprecious stones, precious gems such as emeralds and rubies, and 18-carat and white gold. ℰ **0361/473-3508.**

Jalan Kerobokan

Ni Luh Djelantik ★★ This large and imposing shop on the intersection of Jalan Raya Seminyak and Jalan Raya Kerobokan sells ready-to-wear and custom-made shoes and bags in quality leather. Platforms and heels are a specialty and the Indonesian designer is gaining international recognition with Giselle, Kate Moss, and Elle Macpherson all having a pair or two. Shouldn't you, too? ℰ **0361/744-6068.**

Raya Antiques ★★★ With one of the most eclectic collections of antiques on the island, Raya Antiques sells everything from apothecary jars and Dutch colonial pottery to Chinese blue-and-white porcelain. Everything is stylish, including the owner who runs around town in one of the few vintage cars on the island. ℰ **0361/732312.**

Andy's Gallery A fun Aladdin's den of Indonesian artifacts, antique instruments, and pottery. Take your time and really explore because there are some treasures to be found for sure. ℰ **0361/742-9361.**

Groceries

Local products are about a tenth of the cost of the same imported ones. The **produce market** near Seminyak, on the corner of Jalan Raya Kerobokan and Jalan Gunung Tangkuban Perahu, has a wide range of seasonal fruits and vegetables as well as snacks—especially peanuts—available in a dozen different ways.

Bintang, Jl. Raya Seminyak 17 (✆ **0361/730552;** Sat–Thurs 7:30am–11pm, Fri from 8am), has all the basics: noodles and rice, fresh fruit and vegetables, toiletries, a limited selection of wines, and imported cheese and dairy. There's also a film-processing counter, a small pharmacy, and a magazine and book stand. Upstairs is a stationery and household section that sells goods such as light bulbs and plastic glasses.

Bali Deli, Jl. Kunti 117X (✆ **0361/738686;** www.balideli.net; daily 7am–11pm), is astronomically expensive. A box of Cheerios breakfast cereal goes for US$10. Still, it has a huge range of deli products including meat, fish, and a wonderful range of cheeses and other dairy produce, plus fresh fruit, veggies, and baked goods. The courtyard restaurant has an international menu with surprisingly good sushi, salads, pastas, "design your own" sandwiches, desserts, fresh juices, and gourmet coffee.

With good fresh produce, a decent deli counter, and some imported items that won't totally break the bank, the new **Casa Gourmet,** Seminyak Square (✆ **0361/738026;** www.casa-gourmet.blogspot.com; 8am–10pm), is giving Bali Deli a run for its money. The excellent ice cream stand will keep youngsters entertained while you do the shopping.

Grocer & Grind, Jl. Kayu Jati 3X (✆ **0361/737321;** www.grocerandgrind.com; 8am–10pm), is equally good for a gourmet fix. You'll find homemade cakes, quiches, sandwiches, panini, house-smoked salamis, and a deli section with meat and cheese.

SEMINYAK ENTERTAINMENT & NIGHTLIFE

Late-night clubbing in Bali happens in Kuta—which isn't to say that Seminyak doesn't have its fair share of revelry. The party in Kuta is very different from the one in Seminyak, though, which draws a much more high-end crowd. **Hu'u,** Jl. Petitenget (✆ **0361/736443;** www.huubali.com), rocks on the weekends with the high life from Jakarta as well as some older clubbers who enjoy music that isn't all thump and pump. **Ku de Ta,** Jl. Laksmana 9 (✆ **0361/736969;** www.kudeta.net), is a perennial favorite and a mandatory stop of the Bali nightlife circuit and the **Living Room,** Jl. Petitenget 2000X (✆ **0361/735735;** www.thelivingroom-bali.com), is a happening spot on the weekends for European expats and wealthy tourists who come to Bali in high season like bees to honey. The latest addition is the **Red Carpet Champagne Bar,** Jl. Laksmana 42 (✆ **0361/737889;** www.redcarpetbali.com)—the gals in red hot pants on the red carpet out front lure in the punters. You can sit on the outdoor patio bar directly on Jalan Laskmana and watch the roving circus outside.

Woo Bar, Jl. Petitenget (✆ **0361/473-8106**) is the newest addition. The W Hotel's beachside bar offers beautiful sunset views and beanbag chairs and serves trendy mixed drinks and funky music. Friday nights from 10pm there are guest DJs (Mon–Thurs 6–7pm drinks are 2 for 1 and snacks are free). If it slows down, head next door to Potato Head (www.ptthead.com), with its pool, frequent shows and guest DJs. At night there's often a waiting list for tables, which can be reserved ahead. **Maria Magdalena,** Jl. Dhyana Pura 6 (✆ **0361/731622**), is the place to head when other bars close down. Open all night, it gets busy around midnight, attracts a mixed crowd, and frequently has live bands.

CANGGU

Canggu is Seminyak's suburbia. First discovered by surfers looking for new waves outside of Kuta, Canggu's appearance has changed from rolling rice paddies and cattle farms to rows of luxury villas. However, it still retains much of its village community feel—a refreshing change from the car-laden streets of Seminyak. It's a 10-minute hop in a taxi from Seminyak and there's no public transportation here. Plenty of surfers head to the waves with their boards on bikes.

All activities in Canggu are based around surfing; this beach isn't for the idle as there are a lot of rocky outcrops. Of the several surf breaks, Canggu (better known as Tugu; best swell: south/southwest; best size: 3–5 ft.; best winds: east and no wind days) is a popular spot, best during the dry season, April to October. This wave offers punchy, rippable, and super-fun right and left beach break peaks for the masses, all punctuated by a few submarine rocks and marine visitors. This is an early morning wave as lunch-time winds are too strong. On lighter wind days you can surf it until dusk. Canggu is often crowded at dawn during the dry season. Look for windless days in the wet season for some off-season respite.

Echo Beach ★ is just north of the surf break and makes for an easy laid-back day in the sand or on a sun lounger. Sunday nights light up with families and live music.

Where to Stay

Most people in Canggu stay in luxury villas. The older properties tend to have large rolling gardens while the numerous newer ones can be on small plots of land, suitable for those on a budget.

Desa Seni ★★   Set up by a Canadian pair, this eco-friendly resort just north of Seminyak has a Wizard-of-Oz-meets-Balinese-countryside feel. Whimsical cottages with curved eaves and brightly colored umbrellas decorate the grounds, along with several friendly dogs. The individually designed wood bungalows with rustic touches are more luxurious at second glance, with amenities such as air-conditioning, rain-shower-heads, and DVD players and stereos hidden away in the cabinetry. Yoga sessions are held twice daily in an open-air studio, while a saltwater lap pool is the perfect lounging spot. A good surfing beach is just a short walk away, and you're no more than a 15-minute drive away from Seminyak.

Jl. Kayu Putih 13, Canggu. www.desaseni.com. ✆ **0361/844-6392.** 10 units. Year-round US$150 standard; US$290 suite; US$360 villa. AE, MC, V. **Amenities:** Restaurant (p. 98); bar; babysitting; bikes; concierge; outdoor pool; room service; spa. *In bungalow:* A/C, TV/DVD, stereo or CD.

Legong Keraton Beach Hotel ★ ✇   This no-frills property—right on a peaceful beach and boasting a lap-worthy pool—is ideal for price-conscious travelers who want clean, comfortable rooms but aren't so concerned with style. You're 15 minutes away from the center of Seminyak. Every Wednesday night, the hotel hosts a barbecue with traditional Balinese dance.

Jl. Pantai Berawa, Canggu. www.legongkeratonhotel.com. ✆ **0361/473-0280.** Fax 0361/473-0285. 40 units. High season US$105–US$155 standard, US$185 cottage; low season US$80–US$130 standard, US$160 cottage. AE, MC, V. **Amenities:** Restaurant; bistro; bar; pool; Internet; parking; spa; laundry. In room: A/C; TV; IDD phone; minibar; safe.

Oazia Spa Villas ★★ At Oazia you have your own villa with a spa that would be more at home in a five-star resort. A dedicated personal assistant picks you up from the airport and hands you your own mobile phone with their number plugged in—for the rest of your stay your personal assistant is on call for you. A popular program is the "Women's Goddess Workshop," which includes moon cycle awareness, ritual goddess mythology, and tantra beliefs. A gourmet spa menu offers dishes such as poached lobster in a dill lemon sauce and other tempting items that won't put on the pounds.

Jl. Sahadewa, Banjar Anyar, Kerobokan. www.oaziaspavillas.com. ✆ **0361/844-6105.** 3 villas. Peak season US$295–US$890; high season US$270–US$790; low season US$245–US$690. AE, MC, V. **Amenities:** Restaurant; outdoor pool; room service; spa. In villa: A/C, hair dryer, Wi-Fi.

Pantai Lima ★★ The villas here all face Pererenan black beach. Their modern design mixes Balinese style with the quirky yet sophisticated tastes of the young French owner—très chic. The kitchens are overseen by no less than Sebastian Robuchon, nephew of Joel, who needs no introduction.

Jl. Srikandi, Subak Munggu, Tegallantang, Desa Pererenan, Mengwi. www.pantailima.com. ✆ **0361/844-4555.** Fax 0361/844-9555. 3 villas. Peak season US$2,500; high season US$1,750; low season US$1,350. AE, DC, MC, V. **Amenities:** Babysitting; gym; room service; tennis court; Wi-Fi. In villa: A/C, fan, TV/DVD, movie library, stereo or CD, kitchenette.

Tugu Hotel ★★★ 🛎 Owned by a successful philanthropic Indonesian family, this hotel could easily reopen as a living museum. Astounding antiques and art, most notably by Walter Spies and Rudolf Bonnet, from all over Bali and Java are lovingly placed throughout and in the guest rooms. As a member of the Relais & Châteaux hotel collection, this hotel is a magnet for those in the know. Book the Walter Spies suite and get into the melancholy mood of the artist who passionately loved Indonesia—much like the owners of Tugu.

Jl. Pantai Batu Bolong, Canggu. www.tuguhotels.com. ✆ **0361/473-1701.** 21 units. High season US$330 suite, US$600 villa; low season US$285 suite, US$525 villa. AE, MC, V. **Amenities:** 2 restaurants, Waroeng Tugu and Bale Sutra (see p. 98); bar; babysitting; bicycles; gym; outdoor pool; room service; spa; watersports; Wi-Fi (for a fee). In room: A/C, TV/DVD, movie library, hair dryer, minibar.

Villa Ixora 🌿 Hidden away down a dirt road is this small cluster of villas and hotel rooms with a homey French countryside feel. The six hotel rooms are decorated with hardwood floors and Balinese furniture, and nearby is a large swimming pool next to a shaded patio, where breakfast is served. The two villas, featuring two- and three-bedrooms, are rented to families and given their size and the large garden areas surrounding them, are also good value. A small footpath leads to an uncrowded beach with good waves. Although it feels like it's in the middle of nowhere, set next to rice paddies and private homes, the property is just a short drive away from Seminyak.

Jl. Petitenget, Gang Cendrawasih, Kerobokan. www.ixorabali.com. ✆ **0361/739390.** Fax 0361/739394. 8 units. US$77–US$99 double; US$210–US$275 2-bedroom villa; US$275–US$360 3-bedroom villa. MC, V. **Amenities:** Restaurant; pool bar; outdoor pool; airport transfer; room service; Internet access, movie library. In room: A/C, TV, DVD, fridge, minibar, kitchen, Wi-Fi (free).

Vivalavi ★ 🌿 ☺ This French-owned villa hotel is perfect for families or groups of friends seeking an alternative from the usual hotel and resort scene. Each of the private villas comes with its own private yard, daybed pavilion, and Jacuzzi. The villas' two bedrooms, each the same size and decorated with modern furniture, connect to their own bathrooms decorated with greenery and a skylight. In between the bedrooms is a partially outdoor kitchen and living area that opens up to the yard. The common area includes a restaurant, a large swimming pool, and a games area with billiards and a small driving range, and the beach is a short drive away. Another draw is that the hotel is set in a typical Balinese neighborhood with warungs, away from anything remotely touristy.

Jl. Mertasari, Puri Prisklia 31x, Kerobokan. www.vivalavibali.com. (C) **0361/847-6028.** Fax 0361/847-6039. 6 units. US$225–US$286 2-bedroom villas. AE, MC, V. Amenities: Restaurant; bar; outdoor pool; fitness center; spa; sauna; room service; massage; babysitting. In room: A/C, TV, fridge, hair dryer, minibar, Wi-Fi.

Where to Eat

The Beach House ★★ INTERNATIONAL   The Beach House will bring the 1960s back for you. Sunday barbecues draw large groups of friends and family while a live band belts out classics. An excellent seafood buffet is served nightly on picnic tables and benches set up on the deck and at the water's edge. The blackboard above the bar notes "Honest & Tasty Staff, No Happy Hour Just Happy Endings."

Echo Beach, Canggu. (C) **0361/747-4604.** Main courses Rp40,000–Rp80,000. MC, V. Daily 8am–11pm.

Desa Seni Restaurant INTERNATIONAL   The food matches the hippie, organic atmosphere of the resort it's located in. Most of their produce comes from their own organic gardens on the grounds. Salads use exotic fruits and veggies and main courses stick true to simple tropical classics, with pastas, grilled fish, chicken, and vegetables all accented with local herbs and spices.

In Desa Seni village resort (p. 96), Jl. Kayu Putih 13, Canggu. (C) **0361/844-6392.** www.desaseni.com. Lunch Rp45,000–Rp65,000; dinner Rp50,000–Rp85,000. AE, MC, V. Daily 6am–11pm.

Sukerti's ★ 🎒 EUROPEAN   This little gem is tucked behind the Legong Keraton Hotel. Despite its unimposing decor and surroundings, it serves up fantastic European fare such as a duck liver parfait with mango salsa and consommé jelly. Jazz music is live every Wednesday to Friday night.

Jl. Pantai Berawa, Canggu. (C) **0361/855-0056.** Main courses Rp21,000–Rp42,000. No credit cards. Daily 6–11pm.

Waroeng Tugu and Bale Sutra ★★★ 📷 CHINESE/INDONESIAN   Hotel Tugu's two restaurants are the ultimate in intimate dining. Waroeng Tugu, an open-air, traditional Balinese kitchen, has authentic pots on display and antique rustic tables and chairs. Meals are cooked in front of you on a wood-burning stove. An excellent choice is the rijsttafel, with chicken curry, chicken satay, beef in coconut sauce, a prawn croquet, egg in a spicy sauce, shredded beef, bean cake, fried grated

---

Bali Buddha & Cafe Moka

The sister restaurant to the Ubud cafe and grocer, **Bali Buddha**, Jl. Raya Banjar Anyar 25 ((C) **0361/844-5935;** main courses Rp22,000–Rp65,000; no credit cards; daily 7am–10pm), serves up healthy, primarily organic fare, with a large selection of vegetarian dishes. The small grocer has fresh hummus and yogurt, fresh breads and muffins, and dried and fresh fruits.

A branch of Cafe Moka, Jl. Raya Banjar Semer ((C) 0361/844-5933; main courses Rp20,000–Rp58,000; no credit cards; daily 7am–8:30pm), has freshly baked baguettes, quiche, and very good croissants. A small deli counter serves a limited choice of sliced meats and cheeses, milk, and yogurt.

coconut, yellow pickles, a shrimp cracker—and a banana. The Bale Sutra dates back to 1706 when it was used by the Indonesian and Chinese Peranakan family. The stunning red dining room houses a 300-year-old Kang XI Chinese temple. Here you can dine on Chinese cuisine fit for an emperor.

In Tugu Hotel (p. 97), Jl. Pantai Batu Bolong, Canggu. ✆ **0361/473-1701.** www.tuguhotels.com. Set menus Rp275,000–Rp550,000; beach dining Rp660,000. AE, MC, V. Daily 7am–10pm.

DENPASAR

Denpasar, the capital of Bali since 1960, was once an important trading center and the home of the rajahs of Badung before the colonial era. You'll likely pass through from the south on your way to the mountains, rather than stopping, because few tourists stay here. The core of the city is a crisscross of streets extending from Jalan Gajah Mada where the Catur Muka sculpture commemorates the Badung War. This space of land has since been turned into a peaceful park called Puputan Badung Square.

Essentials

GETTING THERE

Denpasar is reached from the bypass from Sanur or from Legian and Seminyak through Jalan Imam Bonjol within a half-hour, although roads are very congested 8 to 9am and 4 to 6pm. From the airport to Denpasar in a taxi should cost approximately Rp50,000.

VISITOR INFORMATION

The main tourist office for Denpasar is Denpasar Government Tourism Office, Jl. Surapati 7 (Puputan Badung Square; ✆ **0361/223602;** Mon–Thurs 8am–3pm, Fri 8am–1pm, closed Sat and Sun). You can pick up a free city map here.

Exploring Denpasar

You can easily see Denpasar's center and many sights on a self-guided walking tour. The best time for this walk is a weekend morning when you'll face much less traffic: It takes you from 9am until about 3:30pm, including museum, temple, and dining stops. Start from Puputan Badung Square where your taxi driver can wait for you. Take in the Jagatnata Temple, Jl. Mayor Wisnu, dedicated to Sanghyang Widi, the supreme god, built in 1953. The white coral shrine (Padmasana) symbolizes the foundation of the world. Next door is the Bali Museum ★★ (✆ **0361/222680;** Rp2,000; daily 8am–3pm), constructed in 1910 in traditional Balinese style. The fascinating exhibits have explanations in clear English on textiles, sacred objects, the Balinese calendar, rituals, masks, costumes, puppets, and prehistoric stone sarcophagi, bronze, and other artifacts.

After the museum, go toward the Arab area to hunt for textiles and gold around Jalan Sulawesi. Head toward Jalan Thamrin to visit the Puri Pemecutan palace, and then the Pura Maospahit temple on Jalan Sutomo, north of the roundabout. A small side lane leads to this peaceful 14th-century temple. The oldest section was likely brought to Bali from the Majapahit Kingdom—though it has been rebuilt since being badly damaged in 1917 by an earthquake. After the temple, go down on to Jalan Gajah Mada to see the Badung and Kumbasari markets (corner of Jl. Gajah Mada and Jl. Sulawesi), selling fresh produce, meat, fruit, flowers, and vegetables. The second floor of Badung has textiles, temple elements, and dance costumes. Eating stalls are on the fourth floor. Kumbasari is the handicraft, textile, and souvenir market. The bird and animal markets and Satria temple are on Jalan Veteran. After the markets, you can easily head back down again toward Puputan Square.

You can watch the traditional kecak (p. 16) dance at Catur Eka Budi, Jl. Waribang, Kesiman (✆ **0361/238935**), every day at 9:30am.

Where to Stay

Although most visitors do a 1-day visit to the city, if you decide to stay, check out: The new Fave Hotel, Jl. Teuku Umar 175 (www.favehotels.com; ✆ **0361/842-2299**); the Adinda Hotel, Jl. Karna 8 (✆ **0361/240435;** fax 0361/235997; high season Rp350,000, low season Rp250,000; AE, MC, V), with air-conditioned rooms; Hotel Puri Ayu, Jl. Jendral Sudirman 14A (www.hotelpuriayu.com; ✆ **0361/245312;** fax 0361/228851; high season Rp652,000, low season Rp544,000; MC, V), near the main business area, or the Inna Bali, Jl. Veteran 3 (www.innabali.com; ✆ **0361/ 225681;** fax 0361/235347; high season Rp700,000, low season Rp500,000; AE, DC, MC, V), the island's oldest hotel, known for serving cruise passengers in the 1930s. The Nakula Familiar Inn, Jl. Nakula 4 (✆ **0361/226446;** Rp150,000 without A/C, Rp200,000 with A/C; no credit cards), is a family losmen (homestay).

Where to Eat

Visiting Denpasar provides the perfect opportunity to try authentic Balinese cuisine. Due to few tourists in the city, tastes are geared toward locals. Most restaurants and warungs can be found on Jalan Sumatra, Jalan Veteran, and Jalan Teuku Umar.

For the best babi guling (roasted baby pig) in Denpasar, keep your eyes peeled for low tables and the tell-tale pork with crispy skin—there's no sign for this gem—on Jalan Sutomo, beside the Maospahit Temple (no phone; about Rp15,000 a plate; no credit cards; daily mid-morning to about 10pm).

The Amsterdam Café & Bakery, Jl. Diponegoro 140 (✆ **0361/235035;** main courses Rp27,000–Rp100,000, MC, V; bakery daily 7am–11pm, restaurant from 6pm) has veal cordon bleu, steaks, and great orange cheesecakes. Hong Kong, Jl. Gajah Mada 99 (✆ **0361/434845** or 420320; main courses Rp18,000–Rp100,000; MC, V; daily 10am–9pm), has a huge menu including sliced beef with black pepper, sapo tahu (bean curd) seafood in clay pot, and, for the bold, braised sea cucumber. The Tiara Dewata Food Center, Jl. Mayjen Sutoyo 55 (✆ **0361/235733**), is a cheap and clean food court offering dishes from many regions.

The following are on Jala Teuku Umar: Baker's Corner (✆ **0361/243861** or 243863; main courses from Rp20,000; AE, MC, V; daily 9am–11pm), a reliable bakery-restaurant-lounge with a vast menu of international dishes; Kak Man (✆ **0361/227188;** main courses Rp20,000–Rp80,000; no credit cards; daily 11am– 11pm), with bebek tutu (steamed duck with Balinese spices); Raya Sayang (✆ **0361/ 262006;** main courses Rp25,000–Rp65,000; MC, V; daily 11am–11pm), the best Chinese restaurant in Denpasar.

Of the warungs, try Warung Sari Boga, Jl. Sutomo 29C (✆ **081/353260759;** nasi campur (mixed rice) Rp8,000; no credit cards; daily 6am–9pm), for its unbeliev- ably varied textures of tofu and tempeh that look and taste like meat. Warung Satria, Jl. Kedondong 11A (✆ **0361/235993;** around Rp15,000; no credit cards; daily 8 or 9am–10pm), is famous for ayam betutu (chicken), betutu bebek (duck), satay lilit (fish), and sambal goreng pedas (hot sambal). Warung Wardani, Jl. Yudistra 2 (✆ **0361/224398;** main courses Rp25,000; no credit cards; daily 8:30am–4pm), specializes in nasi campur. You might also want to try the beef satay, dendeng sapi (beef cooked crisp and spicy), hati sapi (beef heart), and chendol (made of thick coconut milk, palm sugar, and red beans).

SANUR & THE NUSA ISLANDS

The tranquil shores of Sanur are fringed by a series of coral reefs that for centuries have given safe haven to sailing boats and protected the golden-sand shores from storms. One of the oldest archaeological remains on the island can be found here, in Pura Belanjong, a temple built by the Buddhist king Adhipatih Sri Kesari Varmma—the first in the sequence of kings and queens of the Varmadeva Dynasty—in A.D. 914. Within this temple is a stone column crowned by a lotus cushion that bears ancient inscriptions in both old Balinese script and Kawi (similar to Sanskrit). Only partly deciphered, it's thought to refer to a military expedition against enemies in neighboring islands (perhaps Nusa Penida or even some more distant part of the Indonesian archipelago), commemorating victory in battle. Two other similar pillar edicts have been discovered farther inland near Tampaksiring and Bangli, documenting other conquests.

Twenty kilometers (12 miles) off the southeast coast near Sanur, **Nusa Lembongan, Nusa Ceningan,** and **Nusa Penida** make up a group of three islands that offer a sedate and peaceful alternative to the "mainland."

ESSENTIALS

Getting There & Getting Around

Sanur is just 18km (11 miles) from the airport. Taxis from the airport to town charge around Rp100,000, and **Blue Bird taxis** can be called (© **0361/701111**) for the round-trip for about Rp75,000. The journey takes around 20 to 30 minutes. Plenty of Blue Bird taxis patrol the main Sanur strip until about 10pm and so it's easy to hail a cab. If you're going a long distance, it's best to fix a return journey cost. Don't be afraid to ask a taxi to wait for a few hours, because most drivers are happy to. *Bemo* (vans operating as minibuses) prowl the streets, operating on a hop on/hop off basis and are an economic way to tour the strip.

Your hotel or villa can arrange a car (or car and driver) rental. However, if you don't want to pay the commission, you can easily arrange your own from any of the rental car businesses on Jalan Danau Tamblingan, the main street. Expect to pay from Rp220,000 to Rp550,000 a day for a rental. Some companies also offer insurance packages. Be sure to take one, because it's worth the extra money.

Sanur

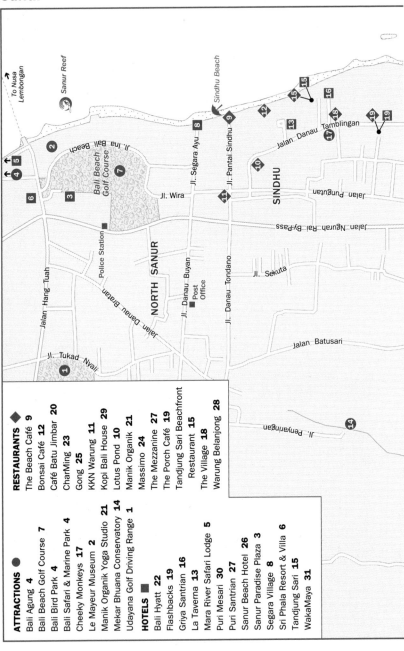

ATTRACTIONS ●

Bali Agung **4**
Bali Beach Golf Course **7**
Bali Bird Park **4**
Bali Safari & Marine Park **4**
Cheeky Monkeys **17**
Le Mayeur Museum **2**
Manik Organik Yoga Studio **21**
Mekar Bhuana Conservatory **14**
Udayana Golf Driving Range **1**

HOTELS ■

Bali Hyatt **22**
Flashbacks **19**
Griya Santrian **16**
La Taverna **13**
Mara River Safari Lodge **5**
Puri Mesari **30**
Puri Santrian **27**
Sanur Beach Hotel **26**
Sanur Paradise Plaza **3**
Segara Village **8**
Sri Phala Resort & Villa **6**
Tandjung Sari **15**
WakaMaya **31**

RESTAURANTS ◆

The Beach Café **9**
Bonsai Café **12**
Café Batu Jimbar **20**
CharMing **23**
Gong **25**
KKN Warung **11**
Kopi Bali House **29**
Lotus Pond **10**
Manik Organik **21**
Massimo **24**
The Mezzanine **27**
The Porch Café **19**
Tandjung Sari Beachfront
  Restaurant **15**
The Village **18**
Warung Belanjong **28**

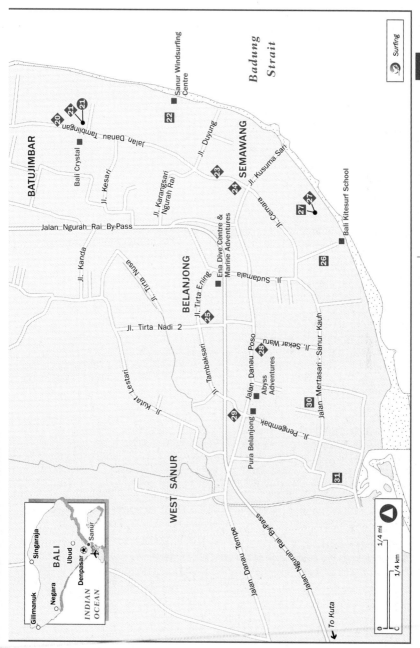

SANUR & THE NUSA ISLANDS | Essentials

7

Surfing

Badung Strait

BATUJIMBAR

SEMAWANG

BELANJONG

WEST SANUR

Sanur Windsurfing Centre

Bali Crystal

Jalan Danau Tamblingan

Jl. Duyung

Jl. Kesari

Jl. Karangsari
Ngurah Rai

Jl. Kusuma Sari

Jalan Ngurah Rai By-Pass

Jl. Cemara

Bali Kitesurf School

Jl. Kanda

Jl. Tirta Nusa

Ena Dive Centre & Marine Adventures

Jl. Sudamala

Jl. Tirta Ening

Jl. Tirta Nadi 2

Tambaksari

Jl. Kutat Lestari

Jalan Danau Poso

Jl. Sekar Waru

Jalan Mertasari - Sanur Kauh

Abyss Adventures

Pura Belanjong

Jl. Pengembak

Jl.

Jalan Danau Tempe

Jalan Ngurah Rai By-Pass

To Kuta

1/4 mi
1/4 km

BALI

Singaraja

Gilimanuk

Negara

Ubud

Denpasar

Sanur

INDIAN OCEAN

103

A BRIEF history OF TOURISM IN SANUR

In many ways, Sanur's history is a microcosm of Bali's modern history, particularly in regards to tourism. After initial European visitors began arriving in the 1920s, Sanur attracted a number of European artists who established homes here—among them Belgian Le Mayeur, Swiss Theo Meier, and Mexican Miguel Covarrubias. Sanur also attracted Walter Spies and Beryl De Zootes who collaborated and recorded their discoveries in a book, *Dance & Drama in Bali*. Much of the research for the anthropological tome *Balinese Character* (compiled by Margaret Mead and her third husband Gregory Bateson) was completed in Sanur during the mid-1930s.

The **Sindhu Beach Hotel** and the **Narmada Hotel,** built in the 1950s, were Sanur's first flirtation with large-scale tourism. Early travelers were delighted with the secluded seaside village, and Sanur began to attract a steady flow of international elite. The **Hotel Bali Beach** was built towards the end of the Soekarno era, with war compensation funds from the Japanese. The construction of this luxurious building, Bali's first ever high-rise, attracted both positive and negative attention: Local sightseers came to Sanur on holiday to view the symbol of Bali's entrance into the world of modernity, while travelers expressed their regret at this blot on the traditional village landscape. In response to the negative reactions a law was passed preventing further construction of any buildings in Bali to a height taller than the coconut palms. This law remains in effect today.

Balinese traditional architecture and decor derived from local arts and crafts became more popular. The **Tandjung Sari Hotel** ★★ (p. 105) and **La Taverna** ★★ (p. 106) set this trend to some extent. Favored by the early jet-setters of the 1960s, these became the haunt of celebrities, artists, and musicians. By the end of the decade, tourism was booming.

The Bali that met Australian artist Donald Friend in 1967 was dealing with the aftermath of immense social unrest, natural disasters, and rampant inflation, conditions that worked in favor for him and his friend Wija Wawo-Runtu in their acquisition of property and antiquities. These were times when the land by the sea still had little value in the eyes of the Balinese and was used only for grazing cattle or growing coconuts. The beach was also considered a dangerous place to spend time, as not only do demons inhabit the sea but also Sanur beach looks to Nusa Penida, where the most evil spirit in Balinese cosmology, Jero Gede Mecaling, is believed to dwell.

By the end of the 1960s, Sanur became a focus for a new international set of expatriates and artists seeking their own piece of paradise and Friend's house was an integral part of the expatriate social scene. The fame and notoriety of his **Villa Batu Jimbar,** built in 1975, soon spread to a new generation of Australian artists. As the Tandjung Sari Hotel grew and new developments were built, Friend had considerable influence in evolving what became the "Sanur Style" of low-rise dwellings inter-relating with meticulously designed gardens.

Locals take good advantage of the **seaside path** for morning constitutionals, and it's fun to join them and their dogs, shortly after sunrise or just before sunset, and stroll from one end to the other in the vibrant tropical glow.

[FastFACTS] SANUR

ATMs The McDonald's, Circle K, Makro, and Hardy all have ATMs, as do the Gazebo Beach Hotel, Grand Bali Beach Hotel, Bali Sanur Besakih Hotel, and Penjor Restaurant.

Banks The following hotels have bank branches on-site: Sanur Paradise Hotel, Grand Bali Beach Hotel, and Sanur Beach Hotel. Individual bank branches are: **Bank Danamon,** Jl. Danau Tamblingan 67; **Lippo Bank,** Kompleks Ruko Sanur Raya 29–30 (✆ **0361/285250**); **Bank Mandiri,** Jl. Danau Tamblingan 27 (✆ **0361/282663**); **BNI,** Jl. Danau Tamblingan 19 (✆ **0361/282590**); **Permata Bank,** Jl. Danau Tamblingan 77 (✆ **0361/270050**).

Currency Exchange Money changers are located along Jalan Danau Tamblingan, the main drag, and in the hotels.

Hospitals & Clinics **Sanur Hospital,** Jl. Bypass Ngurah Rai (✆ **0361/289076**); **Surya Husada,** Jl. Danau Buyan 47 (✆ **0361/285236**); **Dharma Yadnya Private Hospital,** Jl. W.R. Supratman, Tohpati (✆ **0361/224729**); **Clinic Laboratorium Sanur,** Jl. Bypass Ngurah Rai (✆ **0361/289078**); **Clinic Blanjong,** Jl. Sri Kesari 15 (✆ **0361/287250**).

Internet Access Many hotels and villas offer free Wi-Fi. You can buy a Wi-Fi voucher at **Batu Jimbar** (p. 111) and enjoy a coffee and food while surfing in an outdoor setting. Other Internet cafes are on Jalan Danau Tamblingan or Jalan Hang Tuah.

Pharmacies **Guardian Pharmacy,** Jl. Danau Tamblingan 134 (✆ **0361/284343**); **Kimia Farma,** Jl. Bypass Ngurah Rai 232 (✆ **0361/283397**); **Apotik Sanur,** Jl. Danau Buyan 10 (✆ **0361/289312**).

Police The police station is on Jalan Bypass Ngurah Rai (✆ **0361/288597**).

Post Office The post office is on Jalan Danau Buyan and opens Monday to Saturday 8am to 7pm.

Supermarkets **Hardy,** Jl. Danau Tamblingan 136; along the Ngurah Rai Bypass are **Makro, Sarinah Supermarket & Giftshop,** and **Yudistira Supermarket.**

WHERE TO STAY

Expensive

Bali Hyatt 🛍 With its distinctive architecture of traditional materials such as bamboo, thatch, and natural stone, Bali Hyatt captures the best of Balinese outdoor living. This oasis of vast tropical gardens, secluded lily ponds, and picturesque walkways has been melded seamlessly into the serene village life of Sanur. A vast pool connects the resort and garden to the beach. Upgrade to the Regency Club, Hyatt's "hotel within a hotel," for preferential treatment and daily continental breakfast. Many expats in Asia look at this as their preferred vacation home away from home.

Jl. Danau Tamblingan 89, Sanur. www.bali.resort.hyatt.com. ✆ **0361/281234.** Fax 0361/287693. 386 units. Peak season US$180–US$570; high season based on available rate per the day. Rates include breakfast. AE, DC, MC, V. **Amenities:** 5 restaurants; cafe; 5 bars; babysitting; bikes; children's club; concierge; gym; Jacuzzi; outdoor pool; room service; spa; tennis court; watersports; Wi-Fi (public areas for a fee). *In room:* A/C, TV/DVD, hair dryer, Internet, minibar, MP3 docking station (suites only).

Tandjung Sari ★★ 🛍 The name of this hotel comes from a small temple on the beach whose name translates as "Cape of Flowers," referring to this frangipani-clad headland. The original hotel opened in 1962 as a four-bungalow extension to the family home of Wija Wawo-Runtu and has today expanded to a 26-bungalow retreat.

Set amid lush gardens on the beachfront, the individual bungalows have evolved from traditional Balinese architecture and have every comfort you may desire. Guests are given the kind of service that only personal friends could expect, including invitations to cultural events. This is one of the best-kept secrets in Sanur.

Jl. Danau Tamblingan 41, Sanur. www.tandjungsarihotel.com. ✆ **0361/288441.** Fax 0361/287930. 26 units. Year-round US$205–US$345; extra bed US$30. Rates include breakfast. AE, DC, MC, V. **Amenities:** Restaurant (p. 110); bar; concierge; outdoor pool; room service; spa therapy; Wi-Fi. *In room:* A/C, TV/DVD, movie library, stereo or CD, hair dryer, minibar, MP3 docking station.

WakaMaya   Hidden in southern Sanur where coconut groves shade the walkways to the white sand beach, this compound of Balinese-style dwellings has been thoughtfully crafted for both comfort and inspiration. Elements of traditional and rustic art add to the feeling of seclusion, making it the ideal place to unwind, rediscover the serenity of life, and soak up Bali's special atmosphere. A massage center and spa pampers you with a combination of Balinese and Indonesian herbal spices. Relax by a pool designed along the proportions of an ancient Balinese bathing palace. Garden lovers will delight in the mysterious carved statues that peep through lush tropical plantings, ponds, and water features teeming with lilies, lotus, and fish. ***Tip:*** The Waka Resort is now the location for Kokolulu cancer retreats, which are based out of Hawaii. For more information go to **www.cancer-retreats.org**.

Jl. Tandjung Pingging Pantai, Sanur. www.wakamayasanur.com. ✆ **0361/289912.** Fax 0361/270761. 13 villas. High season US$210–US$435; low season US$185–US$410. Rates include breakfast. AE, DC, MC, V. **Amenities:** Restaurant; outdoor pool; room service; spa; Wi-Fi (for a fee). *In villa:* A/C, hair dryer (on request), minibar.

Moderate

Flashbacks ★ 👫   This welcoming, Australian-owned place right in the middle of Sanur has nine rooms that vary from very modest to spacious and fully equipped. The design is reminiscent of traditional Balinese style in the early days of tourism. Bathrooms are worked in natural stone. This is the kind of place where you immediately feel comfortable and there's always great conversation around the main dining table. Australian barbies and long chats infused with laughter long into the night are a common occurrence.

Jl. Danau Tamblingan 110, Sanur. www.flashbacks-chb.com. ✆ **0361/281682.** Fax 0361/281966. 9 units. Year-round Rp160,000–Rp515,000. Rates include breakfast. No credit cards. **Amenities:** The Porch Café (p. 111); saltwater pool; room service. *In room:* A/C, TV, Wi-Fi (free).

Griya Santrian   Owned and operated by the same family as the Puri Santrian (see p. 107), this resort is an easy walk to restaurants and shops along the main Sanur street. The rooms and the furnishings are a mish-mash of styles, with some simply decorated and others with floral bedcovers and rattan furnishings. The proximity to the beach with its *jukung* boats enables guests to enjoy the tempo of village life and the local fishermen's daily routine. A gallery has regular exhibitions of art by local artists, photographers, and sculptors.

Jl. Danau Tamblingan 47, Sanur. www.santrian.com. ✆ **0361/288181.** Fax 0361/288185. 98 units. Peak season US$140–US$210; high season US$130–US$190; low season US$110–US$170; extra bed US$30. Rates include breakfast. AE, DC, MC, V. **Amenities:** Restaurant; bar; lounge; Jacuzzi; 2 outdoor pools; room service; spa; watersports; Wi-Fi (for a fee). *In room:* A/C, TV, hair dryer, minibar.

La Taverna ★★   La Taverna was one of the first beachside hotels in Sanur. The rooms are a harmonious blend of Italian and Balinese styles, featuring thatched roofs, handcrafted antiques, and terrazzo bathrooms. A wide variety of rooms is available, from economy rooms to the private bungalow-style duplex or a two-story suite with large daybeds overlooking its own private garden courtyard. La Taverna is famous for its stone-fire pizza oven, the first on the island, and all pasta and breads are made on-site. Tourists from throughout Southeast Asia hold many fond memories of this place and what it lacks in modern facilities it makes up for in its shabby-chic charm.

Jl. Danau Tamblingan 29, Sanur. www.latavernahotel.com. ℂ **0361/288497.** Fax 0361/287126. 45 units. High season US$100–US$140 standard, US$200–US$600 suite; low season US$80–US$120 standard, US$150–US$600 suite. Rates include breakfast. AE, MC, V. **Amenities:** Restaurant; babysitting; bikes; outdoor pool; room service; spa; Wi-Fi (for a fee). *In room:* A/C, hair dryer, minibar.

Mara River Safari Lodge ★

Directly "Out of Africa," this themed resort is a delightful surprise, located within the **Bali Safari & Marine Park** (p. 113). Rustic wooden boardwalks bleached by the tropical sun lead to a cluster of thatched adobe cottages; behind is a re-created tiny African oasis. Each well-appointed room looks out over this picture-perfect view of zebras and onyx grazing on savanna-like pastures. A 15-minute drive from Sanur, the lodge features 39 suites from deluxe to family rooms, and directly adjoins the Tsavo Lion restaurant and Simba Bar & Lounge, where plate-glass windows separate guests from the lions outside.

In Bali Safari & Marine Park, Jl. Bypass Prof. Ida Bagus Mantra Km. 19, Gianyar. www.mararriversafari lodge.com. ℂ **0361/747-5000.** Fax 0361/950555. 38 units. High season US$220–US$245; low season US$200–US$225. Rates include breakfast. MC, V. **Amenities:** Restaurant; cafe; bar; bikes; concierge; outdoor pool; room service; spa; Wi-Fi. *In room:* A/C, TV, hair dryer, minibar.

Puri Santrian ★

The Puri Santrian is owned and operated by a local family. Balinese traditions of warmth and generosity of spirit shine through the service of the courteous and attentive staff. The spacious Garden Wing rooms overlook lush gardens, with large balconies or terraces. The Beach Wing rooms, with either garden or pool views, are favored by those who want to be close to the water. The bungalows have two rooms in a traditional Balinese-style building, ideal for those who want the privacy of their own home away from home. Eastern and Western influences converge at the spa offering a wide range of treatments—from Balinese body massage, detoxifying seaweed, and volcanic mud body masks to Phytomer's exclusive European marine-elements based products.

The **Santrian Club** is a vast hotel within a complex of 60 terraced suites overlooking manicured tropical gardens and an expansive swimming pool featuring a cascading waterfall, a pulsating whirlpool, and spacious lounging pavilions. Using quality local woods and rattan, these spacious suites have all the modern amenities including marble bathrooms. Specially assigned staff members pay attention to the guests' every need and service includes a complimentary American breakfast, daily fruit platter, and afternoon tea. Children and babies aren't allowed in the clubrooms.

Jl. Cemara 35, Sanur. www.santrian.com. ℂ **0361/288009.** Fax 0361/287101. 183 units. Peak season US$115–US$175; high season US$100–US$160; low season US$85–US$145; extra bed US$30. Rates include buffet breakfast. AE, DC, MC, V. **Amenities:** 2 restaurants, including Mezzanine (p. 110); pool bar; lounge bar; bikes; 2 outdoor pools; room service; spa; watersports; Wi-Fi (for a fee). *In room:* A/C, TV, hair dryer, minibar.

Sanur Beach Hotel

Set on one of the most pristine stretches of the beach in Sanur, this five-star resort has been hosting guests for more than 20 years. The endless facilities are tailored to families with children as much as to businesses wanting to use their conference facilities. There are two tennis courts, what seems like an acre of swimming pool (with a yummy bar), a gym, spa, and just about every watersport you can think of. Rooms are well appointed but dated. You checkin here for the facilities and the view rather than for a luxurious room. Food and drinks cater to large groups with portions to match, but you do get a choice of buffet or a la carte. Many people who come to this resort don't wander—it's that kind of place.

Jl. Danau Tamblingan, Sanur. www.sanurbeachhotelbali.com. ✆ **0361/288011.** Fax 0361/287566. 426 units. High season US$150–US$325; low season US$125–US$300; extra bed US$30. Rates include breakfast. AE, MC, V. **Amenities:** 4 restaurants; 2 bars; bikes; children's club; gym; 2 outdoor pools; room service; spa; 2 tennis courts; watersports; Wi-Fi (free in lobby). *In room:* A/C, TV, minibar.

Sanur Paradise Plaza   The Sanur Paradise Plaza caters to the needs of both business and leisure travelers, with a vast adjoining convention center. The hotel is on the crossroads at the north end of the village, and the suites are in a separate area 10 minutes away. All rooms surround the tropical poolside gardens and have easy access to restaurants and bars, a fully equipped fitness center, and a traditional spa. Camp Splash! features a 30-m (98-ft.) water slide and all-day activities for youngsters. The resort is an easy walk to the nearest beach, but most prefer to take the shuttle to a more secluded spot.

Jl. Hang Tuah 46, Sanur. www.sanurparadise.com. ✆ **0361/281781.** Fax 0361/281782. 329 units. High season US$130–US$260; low season US$110–US$230; extra bed US$20. Rates include breakfast. AE, MC, V. **Amenities:** 2 restaurants; cafe; bar; children's club; gym; Jacuzzi; outdoor pool; room service; spa; tennis court. *In room:* A/C, TV, hair dryer, minibar, Wi-Fi (free).

Segara Village   Parklike garden scenery and stunning ocean outlooks gracefully endow this resort, which follows a unique Balinese village concept. There are five distinct village areas, each seamlessly wrapped in tropical gardens. The newly renovated guest rooms offer warm patches of color, clean lines, and luxurious simplicity. The deluxe rooms feature a state-of-the-art entertainment facility. Three swimming pools and the pristine beach form the foundation for the resort's "fun in the sun" philosophy. The Beach restaurant and bar provides a menu of both Indonesian and international selections. An innovative Jacuzzi bar encourages guests to sip tropical cocktails while enjoying the jets of refreshingly cool water.

Jl. Segara Ayu, Sanur. www.segaravillage.com. ✆ **0361/288407.** Fax 0361/287242. 120 units. Peak season US$205–US$280; high season US$200–US$275; low season US$175–US$250; extra bed US$30. Rates include breakfast. AE, DC, MC, V. **Amenities:** Restaurant; bar; lounge; babysitting; bikes; children's club; concierge; 3 outdoor pools; room service; floodlit tennis court; watersports; Wi-Fi (free in public areas). *In room:* A/C, TV, DVD and movie library (bungalows only), hair dryer, minibar.

Inexpensive

Puri Mesari   This small private hotel at the secluded southern end of Sanur is perfect for guests seeking a peaceful environment and is only a short stroll from Mertasari beach. There's an open-air sitting area, a library, and a restaurant with a large selection of Indonesian and international cuisine. At the heart of the property is the swimming pool, with a sunken bar, the ideal place to cool off with refreshments, plus a children's pool and play area. The simply elegant rooms are decorated with polished natural stone and bathrooms are made of terrazzo. The warm and friendly service is of a level that could only be provided by a family-run hotel.

Jl. Mertasari 66, Sanur. www.purimesari.com. ✆ **0361/281578.** Fax 0361/285738. 21 units. High season US$80–US$115; low season US$70–US$100; extra bed US$25. Rates include breakfast. MC, V. **Amenities:** Restaurant; babysitting; bikes; outdoor pool; room service; Wi-Fi (for a fee). *In room:* A/C, minibar.

Sri Phala Resort & Villa   A great little hidden gem in a quiet part of Sanur, this recently built property comprises 12 spacious deluxe bungalows each with its own private balcony and swimming pool, with lounge and cocktail bar. Guest rooms with natural wood paneling and carved four-poster beds look out over the swimming pool

What to do if you have a late flight departure?

The Gangsa has a special afternoon in store for everyone who has to check out of their hotel early, with flights that don't depart till evening or late at night. The staff will store your bags so that you can spend the afternoon at the spa. Afternoon tea is provided, and guests are free to lounge away by the pool, before joining in a Balinese rijsttafel dinner and being escorted to the airport.

and lounge area tucked into tropical gardens near the welcoming shade of a pavilion. The large bathrooms are complete with sunken tub and marble basin.

Jl. Hang Tuah III-5, Sanur. www.sriphala.com. ✆ **0361/286479.** Fax 0361/289868. 27 units. Peak season US$120–US$320; high season US$100–US$300; low season US$55–US$145; extra bed US$20. Rates include breakfast. AE, DC, MC, V. **Amenities:** Restaurant; bar; Jacuzzi (in Garden villa only); outdoor pool; room service; spa; Wi-Fi (for a fee). *In room:* A/C, TV, minibar.

WHERE TO EAT
Expensive

CharMing ★★ ASIAN FUSION/FRENCH   Brought to you by the owners of Resto Ming, down the road, this charming restaurant is newer and in our opinion better than its counterpart. The creative menu has splendid traditional French and Asian fusion dishes. Snails with garlic butter are always a popular choice, as is the onion soup. Plenty of meat and seafood dishes are on offer for your main course. The beef bourguignon is so tender, it melts in your mouth; the prawns with Balinese spices are another good choice.

Jl. Danau Tamblingan 97, Sanur. ✆ **0361/288029.** www.charming-bali.com. Reservations recommended. Main courses Rp55,000–Rp380,000. AE, MC, V. Daily from 6pm.

Gong ★ BALINESE/INTERNATIONAL   Access this hideaway through the traditional Balinese door that leads into the Gangsa private villas in the depths of Sanur village. The chef of the day takes the time to explain his cooking traditions, why offerings are made before the rice is served, how the spices are crushed, the multiple uses of cinnamon, and all the fascinating little points and tips that will become the memorabilia of a holiday in Bali. He may even invite you back for a cooking lesson. Two menus are offered—one Balinese and the other international. Even for those already familiar with Balinese cuisine this is a menu full of rare treasures. *Sup labu don bayem,* a pumpkin and mixed seafood soup with wild spinach and coconut milk, warming, light, and tasty, makes a terrific starter. Their rijsttafel offers a perfect introduction to Balinese food. A daunting dessert menu of traditional sweets will tempt the glutton in you. Call for directions or ask to be picked up.

In the Gangsa, Jl. Tirta Akasa 28, Sanur. ✆ **0361/270260.** www.thegangsa.com. Reservations recommended. Main courses Rp100,000–Rp150,000; rijsttafel Rp250,000 per person (10 dishes). AE, MC, V. Daily 7am–11pm.

Lotus Pond ☺ ASIAN/ITALIAN   The Asian menu here highlights noodle specialties and the Italian menu serves up a seafood spaghetti to die for. For regional delicacies try the green mango Thai salad and Indian samosa. For the best of Bali you can't go wrong with the rijsttafel. Bring the family—there's plenty of room and when the

Balinese Dance Lessons

On Friday and Sunday afternoons, the local children come to the Tandjung Sari beach *wantilan* (adjoining the pool and restaurant) for lessons in traditional Balinese dance by some of the most famous classical *legong* dancers on the island. This regular gathering is organized by the **Tandjung Sari** **Foundation** (www.tandjungsarihotel.com/news.html), to foster the preservation of the arts for the future generations. Take a moment and watch the future artisans of Bali perfect their form. They'll be delighted that you're taking an interest.

children get bored they can relax or lie down in the comfy chairs of the adjoining lounge. *Tip:* The owner is an avid ceramics collector and he's set up a mini-museum here. Free Wi-Fi hotspot.

Jl. Danau Tamblingan 30, Sanur. ☎ **0361/289398.** www.lotus-restaurants.com. Reservations recommended. Main courses Rp50,000–Rp105,000; *bebek betutu* (duck in a spicy paste, wrapped in banana leaf, order 24 hr. in advance) Rp95,000; 3-course menu Rp110,000. MC, V. Daily 8am–11pm.

The Mezzanine ★ PAN-ASIAN   A special chef is assigned to each cuisine at Mezzanine—Thai, Japanese, Chinese, and Western—and you could come every night for a month without getting bored. Choose from the small sushi bar, or watch the action at the teppanyaki grill. If you like traditional hot food, ask the staff to make it in original spicy style, as the standard here is rather subtle in order to please the sensitive Western pallet. The Thai chef suggested we try the *yam neua yang* (Thai beef salad) and the tofu curry and pad Thai. *Salmon yang tar-si* (salmon in black-bean sauce) is a delicious fusion, and the *gaeng phat ed yang* (duck curry) is very flavorful. The Japanese and Chinese menus offer an equal array of choice, with the standard fresh sushi, California rolls, and tofu salad. Ask for the Japanese chef's special creation. The Chinese king prawn in garlic aioli sauce and the chicken teppanyaki are divine, as is the beef tenderloin. Talk about being spoiled for choice—this is the place.

In the Puri Santrian (p. 107), Jl. Cemara 35, Sanur. ☎ **0361/288009.** www.santrian.com. Reservations recommended. Main courses Rp70,000–Rp300,000. MC, V. Daily 6–10pm.

Tandjung Sari Beachfront Restaurant ★★ INDONESIAN   This legendary restaurant doesn't change. The favorite spot in its heyday for hosting the who's who visiting the island, it's still retained its exquisite simplicity. There were nights when Mick Jagger and friends gathered around the bar, and nobody took any notice. The signature rijsttafel is painstakingly prepared with hand-ground roots and spices, and the *pepes ikan* snapper with Indonesian spices in banana leaf is a testament to the subtle flavors that once made Indonesia a favored destination of the spice-trading ships. Try a dessert reminiscent of colonial days: the *klappertart* coconut pie or Balinese crepes, *dadar unti.*

In the Tandjung Sari (p. 105), Jl. Danau Tamblingan, Sanur. ☎ **0361/288441.** www.tandjungsarihotel.com. Reservations recommended. Main courses Rp80,000–Rp150,000. AE, MC, V. Daily 6:30am–11pm.

Moderate

The Beach Café INTERNATIONAL   This is one of the best places to grab a bite to eat on the beach. The frittatas are an excellent alternative breakfast dish and seafood pasta is especially good, but order half the portion.

Sidhu Beach, Sanur. ☎ **0361/282875.** Main courses Rp70,000–Rp99,000. MC, V. Daily 7am–11pm.

Bonsai Café ★ INDONESIAN/SEAFOOD   Plenty of similar restaurants line this strip, but this one's slightly different because of its unique bonsai garden. The oldest bonsai tree here is apparently 500 years old but most of the others range from 15 to 50 years old. The cafe serves excellent seafood and always has a selection of freshly caught fish and seafood on display.

Jl. Danau Tamblingan 27, Sanur. ✆ **0361/282908.** Main courses Rp64,000-Rp150,000. MC, V. Daily 8am-11pm.

Café Batu Jimbar ★★ CAFE   Known as the best place for wholesome organic salads, and a popular haunt for the rich and famous, this upmarket cafe is generally bustling for breakfast, lunch, and dinner. If the sign of a good restaurant is its return clientele, all the familiar happy faces sitting on the teak deck watching the world go by shows that Café Batu Jimbar has accomplished this with flying colors. The Batu Jimbar salad is legendary: a huge plate of green salad, asparagus, eggplant (aubergine), beetroot, sweet corn, and beans served with raspberry vinaigrette. And for those needing a protein fix there's the Australian tenderloin, Angus strip loin, and lamb. The Indonesian dishes are spicily authentic, and fresh cakes are baked daily. Sunday is market day, when the local organic farmers and artisans bring their fresh wares to sell, and benches are set up with all kinds of Indonesian traditional cakes and snacks—there are even some quality handcrafted clothes, bags, and jewelry.

Jl. Danau Tamblingan 75a, Sanur. ✆ **0361/287374.** www.cafebatujimbar.com. Reservations recommended. Main courses Rp45,000-Rp225,000. AE, MC, V. Daily 7:30am-11pm.

Massimo ★★ ITALIAN   If you're seeking to spend an evening in a warm family atmosphere and enjoy some fine Italian dining at an affordable price, Massimo's is the place. You can't miss it because you're welcomed by a huge array of tempting gelatos on the street in front and Massimo himself is usually around to greet you. He makes his own gelato, pasta and ravioli, mozzarella, and bread. The pasta with ricotta, pachino tomatoes, olives, chili, and mint, and the white and green fettuccine with four cheeses and prosciutto ham are amazing. The wood-fired pizzas have a crispy crust. Try the house's specialty, Pizza Roll, or order some calzone. Children love the dramatic Pizza Volcano. Very quaffable Spanish and Australian wines are also available.

Jl. Danau Tamblingan 228, Sanur. ✆ **0361/288942.** www.massimobali.com. Reservations recommended. Main courses Rp49,000-Rp120,000. MC, V. Daily noon-10:30pm.

The Porch Café INTERNATIONAL   This is a groovy place for breakfast and lunch. Lots of delicious Aussie fare here includes homemade pies, burgers, dory fish filets, and bangers and mash. You can also choose from a selection of excellent tapas and gourmet sandwiches.

In Flashbacks (p. 106), Jl. Danau Tamblingan 110, Sanur. ✆ **0361/281682.** Main courses Rp45,000-Rp65,000. No credit cards. Daily 6:30am-10:30pm.

The Village ITALIAN   This stylish restaurant with pristine white tablecloths and comfortable expansive lounges seems to beckon you in off the street. It's a rare privilege even in these times in Bali to be able to enter a walk-in, climate-controlled wine cellar and choose a wine to accompany your meal. The Venetian scallops in white wine sauce and the portobello mushrooms topped with baked cheese are hard to resist, and the memory lingers on with the crisp white wine.

Jl. Danau Tamblingan 47, Sanur. ✆ **0361/285025.** Main courses Rp60,000-Rp245,000. AE, MC, V. Daily 11am-11pm.

Inexpensive

KKN Warung WARUNG   This warung used to be across the road from where it now stands and during the day it was a garage (at night, staff moved the cars out and the tables in). If you go in the evening it's best to arrive around 6pm. It does a very good stir-fried water spinach and grilled fish. Staff members speak only a little English, but don't let this put you off. The sambal will get your motor running, so to speak.

Jl. Tandakan 5 Sindhu, Sanur. ✆ **0361/282424.** Main courses Rp12,000–Rp30,000; grilled fish Rp7,000 per kilo. No credit cards. Daily 11am–11pm.

Kopi Lubak

Famous for having the best Bali coffee on the island (the Arabica beans grown in the mountainous region of Kintamani), the Kopi Bali House is also one of the few places on the island where the infamous *kopi lubak* civet coffee from Sumatra is served. The coffee cherries are eaten by and passed through the digestive tract of the Asian palm civet *(Paradoxurus hermaphroditus),* collected, and processed hygienically, before being given a medium roast so as not to destroy the complex flavors that develop during the process. Jack Nicholson favored *kopi lubak* in the recent film *The Bucket List,* which has given the coffee a new-found popularity in the West—bringing smiles to many farmers in Kintamani.

Kopi Bali House INTERNATIONAL   With its striking signage stretching up over three floors of shops, it's pretty difficult to miss Kopi Bali House. The range of coffee, imported and local, absolutely dazzles. The menu is eclectic and well executed. First prize goes to the *sop buntut* (spicy oxtail soup) and smoky *ayam panggang* (chicken grilled with Balinese spices). Expats missing home can settle for classic fish and chips. The desserts are too good to be missed and include almond dacquoise and blueberry cheesecake. End with the full-bodied aftertaste of a perfectly prepared Bali coffee and the palate is replete.

Jl. Bypass Ngurah Rai 405E, Sanur. ✆ **0361/270990.** Main courses Rp39,500–Rp110,000. AE, MC, V. Daily 8am–11pm.

Manik Organik ★ VEGETARIAN   This great little vegetarian health food restaurant serves up predominately organic, light meals, salads, sandwiches, soups, snacks, and fresh juices, as well as great coffee and teas. The home-cooked food has no use for preservatives or additives, and the staff are serious about the quality of food they produce. Try the delicious pumpkin soup and Tiny Tofu salad: roasted tofu with tamarind sauce served on a bed of mixed salad.

Jl. Danau Tamblingan 85, Sanur. ✆ **0361/855-3380.** www.manikorganikbali.com. Main courses Rp30,000–Rp41,000. AE, MC, V. 9am–9pm.

Warung Belanjong ★ BALINESE   For a delicious selection of Balinese food in a clean and ordered environment, this is the place to go for lunch. The *siap betutu* (chicken roasted in banana leaves) is a must-try—tender and succulent with a deliciously spiced stuffing, it has a subtle smoky flavor of wood fire. Or go for the *tum siap* (minced chicken cooked in banana leaves) or *pepes be pasih* (fresh fish grilled with spices also in banana leaves). *Nasi campur* (mixed rice) is the most popular dish here. (The menu has no pork.) The Indonesian and European food is excellent and there's plenty of choice for vegetarians. The secret ingredient in the hamburgers, served Australian style, is beetroot.

Jl. Danau Poso 78, Sanur. ✆ **0361/285613.** Main courses Rp51,000–Rp69,000. No credit cards. 9am–10pm.

EXPLORING SANUR

Bali Agung ★ This new cultural performance, shown at the Bali Safari & Marine Park (see below), tells the story of the marriage between a Balinese king and a Chinese princess. The afternoon show involves 180 dancers and singers, puppets, elaborate costumes, and dozens of live animals including elephants and tigers. The ticket price includes admission to the Bali Safari & Marine Park.

Jl. Bypass Prof. Dr. Ida Bagus Mantra, Km 19.8, Sanur. ✆ **0361/950000.** www.balitheatre.com. Performance US$39, including admission to the Bali Safari & Marine Park. Performances Thurs–Sun 2:30pm.

Bali Bird Park ★★★ 📷 Just 15 minutes north and slightly east of Sanur is the Bali Bird Park. The main priority of the park, other than breeding, is that all birds taken in are given the opportunity to return to the wild. The birds have their own, well-tended environment, sympathetic to their natural habitat with different species mixed together. There are some 2,000 varieties of plants alone, and 250 different species of birds with over 1,000 birds in total. Among the rarer species are six varieties of the famed bird of paradise, which until recently were only found in a few remote islands in Papua. Other wildlife include some of the world's most endangered species, the Bali starling, along with the Javan hawk, the cassowary, various types of eagle, and even a few komodo dragons. Don't forget to catch at least one of the free spectacular bird shows that run through the day. The cafe has Western and Indonesian food, and sells some of the tastiest ice cream, all made on the island; the juices are also worth every penny.

Jl. Serma Cok Ngurah Gambir, Singapadu, Batubulan, Gianyar. ✆ **0361/299352.** www.bali-bird-park. com. Adults US$24, children ages 2–12 US$12. Daily 9am–5:30pm.

Bali Safari & Marine Park ★★ Set on 40 hectares (99 acres) of splendid natural habitat, the Bali Safari & Marine Park has 400 animals from regions including Indonesia, India, and Africa. The many sensational highlights include a traditional Balinese purifying sacred bath, the story of man-eating lions in Tsavo of Kenya, and the majestic white tigers of India. This park is the latest establishment of the world-renowned Taman Safari Indonesia, a name made famous for more than 20 years for efforts in nature conservation and recreational business. Bali Safari & Marine Park is tremendously active in protecting endemic and endangered species, as well as orchestrating educational campaigns to save the animals. Shows run throughout the day and, compared to Western prices, this place is a bargain. A Jungle Hopper Package for about US$35 includes the entrance fee, Safari Tram Tour, free entry to the Water Park, and unlimited access to the Theme Park Rides as well as one photo with an animal. While having lunch you can watch white tigers at play in their natural habitat. You can also stay overnight in the park (p. 107), for more animal viewing time.

Jl. Bypass Prof. Dr. Ida Bagus Mantra, Km 19.8, Sanur. ✆ **0361/950000.** www.balisafarimarinepark. com. Admission Rp135,000; free children 2 and under. Mon–Fri 9am–5pm. Pickup can be arranged.

Le Mayeur Museum ★★ The Belgian artist Adrien-Jean Le Mayeur (1880–1958) came to Bali in 1932. His original plan was to stay for 8 months. However, he was deeply impressed by the temple rituals and dances, and further entranced by a young *legong* dancer called Ni Pollok. Bali had worked its magic, and in 1933 he returned, settled in Sanur, and ultimately married Ni Pollok, who became the main subject of his paintings. Le Mayeur's studio is now a museum and gallery. Although time and the damp seaside salt sprays have taken their toll on the art works, the museum is well worth a visit. Due to his Belgian nationality, Le Mayeur wasn't sent

Cheeky Monkeys

Situated down a little alley, off the main drag, **Cheeky Monkeys ★**, Jl. Danau Tamblingan 82 (© **0361/282420**; www. cheekymonkeysbali.com; registration Rp100,000; daily care Rp150,000 for 8:30am–11:30am, Rp35,000 per hour after; daily 8am–4pm), is a children's drop-in center that's also a kindergarten and preschool. It has plenty of toys, a sweet little garden with playhouses, a trampoline, a restaurant serving organic food, and indoor rooms. The lovely staff ensure that your children have lots of fun and meet other children their own age. Activities throughout the day keep your little ones entertained: art classes, cooking, storytelling, and games. The nursery can provide short-term care for visiting families with children under 6 years old; drop-ins are available from 8:15am until 4pm daily. This is the favored nursery in Sanur among the local expats.

---

to prison camp during World War II, but placed under house arrest by the Japanese, and so he was able to continue his work. His place was ransacked, but fortunately he managed to keep his paintings. Wartime shortages meant he had to use rice sackcloth called *bagor* instead of canvas. Unfortunately, these works haven't aged well.

Jl. Hang Tuah, Sanur. © **0361/286201.** Admission Rp10,000 both adults & children. Sun–Thurs 8am–4pm; Fri 8am–1pm.

Mekar Bhuana Conservatory ★★   A recent addition to Sanur's cultural preservation efforts is the Mekar Bhuana Conservatory. After more than 11 years of intensive research in villages across the island, New Zealand ethnomusicologist Vaughan Hatch and his wife, *legong* dancer Putu Evie Suyadnyani, began to realize their mission of cultural preservation by opening a center where people can appreciate and learn about the endangered performing art-forms in Bali. The center has five sets of antique gamelan, a performance space, as well as an archive, and has recently released its first audio recording. Private and group courses are available. Special tours visit workshops where traditional instruments are made, and presentations of the rich array of traditional dance and ceremonial costumes can be arranged.

Jl. Gandapura III 501X, Banjar Kesiman Kerthalangu, Sanur. © **0361/464201** or 081/999191104; www. balimusicanddance.com. Call for more information on lessons and workshops.

CYCLING   All big hotels have rental bikes, and Sanur is the ideal place to cycle around, especially when you keep to the back roads. It's best to set out early morning or late evening, when the weather's cooler and the roads are not too busy.

The best place to cycle is down the promenade. The 5-km (3-mile) stretch takes you from one end of Sanur all the way to the other, passing cafes, restaurants, and fishing boats along the way. The early evening is the best time to ride the beach as you get to mix with the friendly locals enjoying the sea and sedate atmosphere. The ride itself is easy and suitable for the whole family.

There are a few places to rent bikes on Jalan Danau Tamblingan and also along the promenade itself. Prices can vary according to season. Off season the prices will be less but with the arrival of high season the prices shoot up. Don't pay more than Rp50,000 per day. If you want to join a tour, the **Segara Village** hotel (p. 108) runs regular bicycle tours of Sanur.

DIVING & SNORKELING At least 50% of Bali's dive companies are in Sanur even though the diving here isn't great. Instead, Sanur makes a great base for diving expeditions farther afield. The coral reef that follows the coastline is less than 1km (less than 1 mile) off the beach of Sanur. Although the waters here are okay for snorkeling, those learning to dive, and those looking for refresher courses, it's not recommended for experienced divers. There's very little coral, few fish, and often very low visibility. Another consideration is the strong current and the shallow waters at low tide.

For **snorkeling,** many boats are available for rent to go out to the reef at high tide, including glass-bottom boats if you don't want to get wet. There's usually a surface current but the boat will follow you. Don't allow the boatman to drop anchor, which is highly damaging to the reef. He should use the moorings available.

The following dive operators are reliable and always maintain their dive equipment. They also offer valid insurance cover. Be wary of people approaching you offering cheap courses. Costs generally run US$90 to US$125 for a day trip; US$525 for 3 days, 2 nights; and US$935 for 7 days, 6 nights.

Abyss Adventures, 36B Jl. Danau Poso (© **0361/288610;** www.abyssadventures. com), offers technical diving (and tech dive training) and recreational diving if requested. **Crystal Divers Bali,** Jl. Tamblingan 168 (© **0361/286737;** www.crystal-divers.com), specializes in Instructor Development Courses (IDC) and will provide recreational diving if requested. **Enadive Centre & Marine Adventures,** Jl. Tirta Ening 1 (© **0361/288829;** www.enadive.co.id), a five-star Gold Palm PADI dive school, can arrange introduction lessons, PADI courses, and diving throughout Bali.

GOLF The **Bali Beach Golf Course,** Jl. Hang Tuah 58 (© **0361/287733;** www. balibeachgolfcourse.com; 9 holes US$65; 18 holes US$81, prices include green and caddy fees and government tax; driving range Rp45,000 for 50 balls; caddies available at no extra charge but a discretionary tip of approximately Rp30,000 is welcome; club rental Rp25,000 per club or Rp180,000 to Rp220,000 for the set; call © **081/23899166** for lessons with a pro; 1-hour lesson Rp230,000, including 100 balls; AE MC, V), is a 9-hole course in front of the Grand Bali Beach Hotel among mature, tall trees, sculptured gently rolling fairways, and water features. Subtle breaks keep the golfer guessing and are wellbunkered, leaving little room for errant shots. They also have a **floodlit driving range,** the only one in Bali, open daily from 7 until 11pm.

Udayana Golf Driving Range (© **0361/289603;** Rp24,000 morning; Rp255,000 afternoon for 50 balls; club rental Rp25,000 per club, Rp150,000 for set; trainer Rp100,000 for 1 hour, excludes balls and clubs; daily 7am–7pm) is another option for practice, just a few kilometers down the road west of the Grand Bali Beach Golf Course on Jalan Hang Tuah.

KITE- & WINDSURFING Sanur has ideal conditions for windsurfing with its sheltered 5-km (3-mile) long lagoon. Sanur's protective reef creates flat-water cruising conditions inside the lagoon with waves on the reef varying from small to mast height, and the Serangan Island channel is good for speed—the wind's always a few knots stronger than elsewhere. Rental boards are available along the beach in Sanur and generally hotels can provide information on the most convenient supplier. For wind and wave information around Sanur call © **0361/288011** and ask for Blue Oasis.

Bali Kitesurf School, Jl. Cemara 72 (© **0361/284260;** www.bali-kitesurfing. org; 2-hr. level one Rp900,000; 60-min. level two Rp600,000; 60-min. level three Rp600,000), was the pioneering International Kiteboarding Organization center in Indonesia in 2004. Just in front of the club is a good kitesurfing spot in both seasons, during medium-low to high tide.

The **Blue Oasis Beach Club** (www.blueoasisbeachclub.com) at Sanur Beach Hotel, Jl. Danau Tamblingan (© **0361/288011;** kitesurfing US$95–$145, board rental US$20–US$50, kite rental US$35–US$70; windsurfing US$65–US$85, rental US$25–US$80; AE, MC, V), rents Hobie Cats, lasers, and windsurfing boards. Courses are also available.

SAILING The **Royal Bali Yacht Club** aims to encourage and promote the sport of sailing in Bali by providing a forum where both experienced and beginner sailors can meet to learn or practice their skills. Boat ownership isn't necessary to join the club—you can join a boat-owning member for sailing. Laser races are held on several Sundays each month at times suitable to the tide and wind. Tall boats are moored at a clubhouse at Serangan. Regardless of whether you're a novice or an old salt, the club makes a special dispensation to tourists to try out the club. For the latest event calendar check **www.royalbaliyachtclub.com**. This is such a small club that if you want to speak to someone, it's best to call the Commodore directly (© **081/353026067**).

SPAS Spas are open daily. The stunning **Spa at Bali Hyatt** (p. 105; Anom Rejuvenating Massage US$60, avocado scrub US$40; AE, DC, MC, V; daily 9am–10pm) has an Anom Rejuvenating Massage that starts with a therapeutic scrub of copra, dried coconut flesh, pine, and lavender flowers to gently remove dead skin before a combined Swedish and acupressure massage. The avocado body scrub is great for rehydrating the body, and is ideal for anybody suffering jet lag.

The **Jamu Traditional Spa** in the Tandjung Sari (p. 105; © **0361/704581;** www.jamutraditionalspa.com; traditional treatment Rp620,000–Rp760,000, contemporary treatment Rp620,000–Rp760,000, massage Rp235,000–Rp620,000; AE, MC, V; daily 9am–9pm) honors traditional local therapies. Scrubs are a favorite choice here and employ natural ingredients such as candlenuts, coconut, tea leaves, as well as the blended spice mixtures of *boreh* and *lulur*—time-honored ingredients that have superb results. Two very local treatments are the Kerokan Massage, which uses a small coin-size seed to massage your back and neck, and the Selendang, a body wrap used by Indonesian women post-childbirth to help regain elasticity.

Rebab in the Gangsa (single treatment US$35–US$75, package US$80–US$100; MC, V; daily 9am–6pm) isn't to be confused with a rehab spa. Instead, you'll find a holistic spa with a menu of traditional Balinese healing and beauty rituals using indigenous herbs, spices, and plants. The spa's mantra of wellness is based on the Hindu belief that balance is the essence to overall physical and spiritual wellness.

The spa in the **WakaMaya** (p. 106; treatments US$25-US$80; AE, DC, MC, V; daily 8am–9pm) has aromatherapy. Try the Sutra massage: A full-body massage combining pressure points, deep-tissue massage, and long strokes to relieve tension. You can choose your own scent such as Crystal Breeze, a blend of bergamot, lemon, and musk meant to clear the mind and stimulate and uplift while restoring a sense of balance.

SURFING The best time to surf the Sanur coast is the rainy season (Sept–Mar).

Sanur Reef **Best swell:** south; **best size:** 4 to 6 feet; **best winds:** west-southwest. Turn right at the lights at Sanur and you find yourself staring at a magically long surfing set-up (once you manage to park the car). The wave itself is very long and very fun and is a favorite with the crowds on wet season big days.

Serengan **Best swell:** south; **best size:** 4 to 6 feet; **best winds:** west-southwest. This wave is in an area protected from turtle poachers; you can only get access with identification and so please remember to bring it. Turn right, heading toward Sanur from Kuta opposite the Makro, and weave your way along a confusing split road. Look out for oncoming traffic, too. Pass through the village of Serangan and head out onto the reclaimed Turtle Island through the boom gates and drive through the weird, desertlike ambience toward a series of shoreline warungs. A left and right break here are an easy paddle from the beach. Leave your keys and gear with a warung and be sure to buy a thank you *Bintang* beer on the way out. Check out the karaoke-style beach discos in the village of Serengan on the way home. Wear booties if you can or surf the higher tide. A secret spot just a few years ago, Serengan now attracts the masses.

SWIMMING & BEACHES   The Sanur reef makes the ocean here ideal for surfers and also people with young children along the shore side. Sanur doesn't get a strong beach break like Kuta or Seminyak. Swimming is only possible at high tide because low tide exposes the reef. Swimming outside the reef is not recommended.

YOGA   Balispirit runs yoga classes at **Manik Organik Yoga Studio ★★**, Jl. Danau Tamblingan 85 (✆ **0361/855-3380**), daily. Classes are drop in and open level and cost Rp90,000 (buy 10, get 2 free). Yoga mats and blocks are provided. Private classes can be arranged, see Balispirit's Private Tuition/Personal Training page. Schedules are at **www.manikorganikbali.com**.

SHOPPING

Shops are typically open daily, 9am to 9pm.

Clothing

Ibisa   Owned by a former fashion retailer from Sydney's trendy suburb of Paddington, this boutique is a study in cool. Lovely linen and cotton pieces in both plain and prints are perfectly lined on rails and shelves, creating a story for a more classic dresser. Jl. Danau Tamblingan, opposite Griya Santrian Sanur. No phone.

Nogo ★   This is one of Bali's best fabric and textile retailers and is a destination in itself for lovers of local textiles. A good selection of ikat and *endek* fabrics is available. Prepare to bargain. Jl. Danau Tamblingan 104. ✆ **0361/288765**. www.nogobali.com.

Groceries

The Pantry   This delightful deli next door to Café Batu Jimbar (p. 111) stocks a selection of imported foods, including cheese, cold meats, chutneys, pastas, and a small and decent selection of wines. There's a good confectionery section and freshly baked breads that come from the cafe. Jl. Danau Tamblingan. ✆ **0361/281048**.

Sanur Deli & Annie Salon   Pop by here in the morning for fresh Australian-style deli foods, snacks, and salads, and whopping great loaves of freshly baked German rye bread. Stock up on the deli's latest range of delicious tropical jams, pickles, and chutney, and order a cake. If you have extra time on your hands, get your hair colored and cut and have a manicure and pedicure at Annie's Salon next door. Jl. Danau Poso 67. ✆ **0361/270544**.

Housewares

A-Krea ★★   This is a lovely place to browse and pick up gifts. It has a beautiful selection of housewares and some stylish clothes and accessories. The store also stocks traditional batiks, some bamboo baskets, and seashell items. Jl. Danau Tamblingan 51. ✆ **0361/286101**.

Griya Santrian Art Shop Across the road from Nogo (see p. 117), in what's fast becoming the pocket of luxury shopping in Sanur, is the newly opened Griya Santrian Art Shop, beside the Village Italian restaurant (p. 111). The large shop features a boutique section, upmarket handicrafts, designer jewelry, a selection of textiles, and home furnishings. Jl. Danau Tamblingan. ✆ **0361/288181.** www.santrian.com.

Gudang Keramic ★ Samples and seconds from the Jenggala range are piled high here, making this a popular haunt for bargain hunters. A ceramics facility is attached for those who want to try their hand at creating their own designs. Also, part of the complex is an interesting selection of glass sculpture, some of which is available for sale. Jl. Danau Tamblingan. ✆ **0361/289363.**

Hug A Bug On the main street, this is one of the few places catering to young children. Hug a Bug stocks books in a variety of languages as well as toys and hand-made furniture, some clothing, and fancy dress. Jl. Danau Tamblingan 71. ✆ **0361/288445.**

Uluwatu This two-story shop features beautiful handmade Balinese lace and a wonderful assortment of bedding, tablecloths, and a line of classic clothing: White predominates. Jl. Danau Tamblingan. ✆ **0361/288037.** www.uluwatu.co.id.

Markets

Pasar Sindhu (Jl. Danau Tamblingan) is a bustling traditional morning market for fruit and vegetables that turns into a food market in the evenings. On the west side of the Bypass, the original **Pasar Delod Peken,** at Intaran, is even more extensive and stretches along the entire length of the road, starting at dawn every day of the week. At **Café Batu Jimbar** (p. 111) on Sunday mornings is a market that offers organic vegetables, plants, local foods, and fun stalls with a range of local produce and trendy designer articles. The nearby **Manik Organic Restaurant,** at Jl. Danau Tamblingan 85, also offers a regular organic farmers' market on Thursday afternoons and evenings, from 2 to 8pm.

SANUR ENTERTAINMENT & NIGHTLIFE

Sanur is truly magical after sunset. The last light of the day burns with a soft brilliance, and in the afterglow the clouds and the sea often reflect the rosy glow that promises good weather on the following day. Gamelan music echoes on the sea breeze from groups honing their skills. Traditional dance performances are to be seen in a number of restaurants and hotels. The Hyatt's (see p. 105) **Piano Bar** is a cozy enclave. Elegant nightspots such as the **Bali Hai Supper Club** on the rooftop of

The Traditional Dances of Sanur: Ask for Them by Name

Among the more famous dances found in Sanur are the *barong* of Taman with its *telek* or *sandaran* imps; the kris dance of the Black Barong of Singgi; the *baris gede* trance dance of spear-bearing warriors of Banjar Belong; the *topeng* mask dance of Banjar Puseh; and the classical *legong* dance, which is practiced by several different groups. Ask at any hotel for details and they'll be happy to investigate what's on in the region and arrange the whole trip for you.

the Bali Beach Hotel and the sumptuous **Matahari** discotheque at the Bali Hyatt (see p. 105) offer dancing and entertainment till the wee hours.

The Beatles Bar ★★   The owner, Percy Burlace, is obviously a Beatles fan, the story being that he was the promoter of the Beatles Australian tour in the 1960s. The whole place is packed with Beatles memorabilia, posters, books, and trivia. There's even a life-size model of the group. Percy owns the only gold record ("Strawberry Fields Forever") of the Beatles that Michael Jackson didn't own, a replica of which is hanging up in the bar—at least we think it's a copy. When you first go there, you have to pay Rp20,000 to join the "club." For that money, you become a life member and get a free drink. Jl. Sekuta, off Jl. Bypass Ngurah Rai 284. ℂ **0361/289032.**

Tandjung Sari   Come here for cocktails on the beach as the day draws to a close. Although the martinis aren't cheap and this old lady of Sanur might be beginning to show her age, the old-world charm and class is still worth the trip. The service itself is worth it—some of the staff members seem like they've been here since it opened. Sit back and watch the world go by. Jl. Danau Tamblingan 41. ℂ **0361/288441.**

NUSA LEMBONGAN, CENINGAN & PENIDA

Of the three islands near Sanur, **Nusa Lembongan** is geographically closest and remains to date the only real tourist destination. It's famed for its surf breaks and laid-back style. Both **Nusa Ceningan** and **Nusa Penida** are largely unspoiled and for the most part unaware of the majority of developments of the 21st century and are known for their nature, pristine landscapes, and traditional local life and culture. All three islands are famous for their world-class diving and snorkeling.

Day Trips

Day trips are a popular option for the hurried, and a 1-day cruise will bring you to Nusa Lembongan (boats leave from Tanjung Benoa, half an hour away from Sanur) with possibly 100 other similar-minded folk where you're offered snorkeling, banana boat rides, glass-bottom boat trips, sea kayaking, and maybe even a trip to the mangrove forest or a cultural village tour. A buffet lunch and later some form of water slide will also be thrown in. The approximate price is US$90. The following are the main cruise operators serving Nusa Lembongan:

Bali Hai ★, Benoa Harbour (ℂ **0361/720331;** fax 0361/720334; www.balihai cruises.com; cruises 9:15am–4:15pm US$95, sunset dinner cruise 5:45–8:45pm US$45, overnight US$125–US$145 per night; MC, V), the most popular of the day cruises, offers as many options as you can think of, with sailboats, diving, and sunset dinners. This is a one-stop shop.

Bounty, Benoa Harbour (ℂ **0361/726666;** fax 0361/726688; www.balibounty cruises.com; one-way US$35, round-trip US$70, day cruise 10am–4pm US$95, dinner cruise 6–8:30pm US$49; MC, V), runs day trips to Nusa Lembongan.

Waka Louka Cruise ★, Jl. Pulau Moyo 25x (ℂ **0361/723629;** fax 0361/722077; www.wakaexperience.com; catamaran 9am–5:30pm US$108, dinner cruise and sailing, charter only; MC, V), a delightful catamaran, is more stylish than anything else on the market, and organizes day trips and dinner cruises on board.

Sail Sensations ★, Benoa Harbour (ℂ **0361/725864;** fax 0361/725866; www. sailsensations.com; day cruise 9am–5pm US$85, twilight cruise 6:30–9pm US$60, overnight US$380–US$427; MC, V), part of Nusa Lembongan Resort (see p. 125), organizes day trips for US$95, which includes high-speed ferry, village tour, buffet lunch, snorkeling, a 5-minute banana boat ride, and for those wishing to part with another US$17, a bicycle and car mangrove tour.

Island Explorer Cruises, Jl. Bypass Ngurah Rai 622, Suwung (© **0361/728088;** fax 0361/728089; www.bali-cruise.com; day cruises 9am–5pm US$69–US$79; MC, V), part of Coconuts Beach Resort (see p. 126) on Nusa Lembongan, does cruise and stay packages, or even transfer only from Benoa Harbour at US$35 round-trip. The day cruise includes lunch and activities, such as a village and seaweed tour, banana boats, kayaking, fish feeding, or just leisurely sailing a yacht to the island if you prefer a slower pace. Both the Fun Ship and the Sail Boat depart Benoa at 9am, but the yacht takes 2 hours while the fast boat only takes 1 hour. And, yes, the Fun Ship comes complete with its own water slide.

Nusa Lembongan

Nusa Lembongan is surrounded by a beautiful marine park; the magnificent scenery includes white sandy beaches or limestone cliffs dropping vertically into azure seas with the most incredible view back to Bali and Mount Agung. At only 4km (2½ miles) long and 2km (just over 1 mile) wide, you can walk round the island in less than 4 hours. *Note:* Of the three islands detailed in this chapter, Nusa Lembongan has the most extensive facilities for scuba diving.

GETTING THERE

FROM BENOA HARBOUR, BALI INTERNATIONAL MARINA BlueWater Express (© **0361/723479** or 081/338418988; www.bwsbali.com; one-way Rp325,000, round-trip Rp550,000; 10% discount when booking online) has speed boats that whisk you across the water in 30 minutes. The boat departs Benoa at 10am for Gili Trawangan making a quick stop at Nusa Lembongan. Return journeys leave at 1:30pm from Gili T to Benoa, stopping at Nusa Lembongan at 3:30pm. Most people who catch boats from Benoa Harbour to Nusa Lembongan have arranged a day cruise with one of the many luxury cruising companies. You can still buy a travel ticket only without having to take part in all their leisurely activities. See also Island Explorer Cruises, under "Day Trips," above.

FROM SANUR BEACH The fast boats of **Scoot** (Lembongan Island Cruise, Jl. Hangtuah 27; © **0361/285522** or 081/338488088; fax 0361/286913; www. lembonganislandfastcruises.com or www.scootcruise.com; three trips daily) will take you to either Mushroom Bay or Jungutbatu for US$58 round-trip (US$35 one-way). Local hotel transfers on Bali are included in the fee. Scoot's office is next to Dunkin' Donuts opposite the Sanur Paradise Hotel or on the beach near the departure point beside the Grand Bali Beach hotel.

So-called **public boats,** very basic affairs aimed at the local trade, from Sanur beach, leave daily at 8am and 10am (90 min. one-way; Rp35,000). Coming back, the boats leave at 7:30am from Jungutbatu.

A **faster public boat** (© **0361/743-2344;** Rp200,000), costs more but should get you there in about 45 minutes; daily departure from Sanur beach is at 8am in front of the Ananda Hotel. Departures from Nusa Lembongan are at 10:30am, 1, and 3pm.

The **Tanis Lembongan Express** (© **081/338737344;** one-way US$27, round-trip US$45; price includes hotel pickup) takes 25 to 35 minutes from Sanur beach near the Grand Bali Beach hotel; it departs at noon and 4:30pm, returning to Bali at

Nusa Lembongan, Nusa Ceningan & Nusa Penida

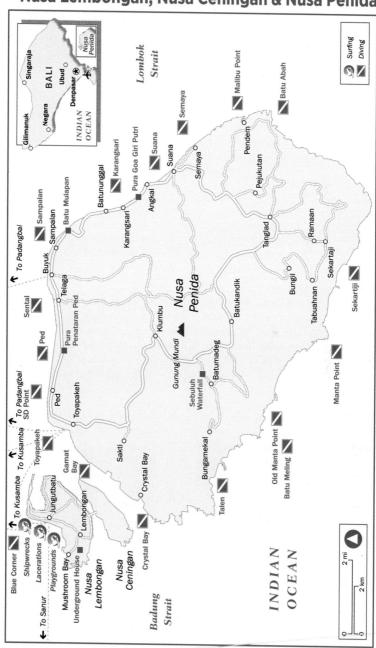

Surfing
Diving

BALI

Singaraja

Ubud

Gilimanuk

Negara

Denpasar

INDIAN OCEAN

Nusa Penida

Lombok Strait

Malibu Point

Batu Abah

Semaya

Suana

Pura Goa Giri Putri

Karangsari

Batununggal

Batu Mulapan

Angkal

Semaya

Semaya

Pendem

Pejukutan

Sampalan

Sampalan

Buyuk

Karangsari

Tanglad

Ramaan

Sekartaji

Telaga

Sental

Pura Penataran Ped

Klumbu

Nusa Penida

Batukandik

Bungil

Tabuahnan

Sekartaji

Ped

Ped

Gunung Mundi

Batumadeg

Sebuluh Waterfall

Manta Point

Toyapakeh

Sakti

Bungamekal

Old Manta Point

Batu Meling

Toyapakeh

Gamat Bay

Crystal Bay

Talen

Jungutbatu

Lembongan

Nusa Lembongan

Nusa Ceningan

Crystal Bay

To Padangbai

To Padangbai SD Point

To Kusamba

To Kusamba

To Sanur

Blue Corner

Shipwrecks

Lacerations

Playgrounds

Mushroom Bay

Underground House

Nusa Lembongan

Badung Strait

INDIAN OCEAN

2 mi

2 km

10:30am and 3pm. The company also arranges fishing trips, surf safaris, and a day cruise, which includes lunch, hotel transfers, and activities.

FROM KUTA   If you're in Kuta, **Perama Tours,** Jl. Legian 39 (✆ **0361/751551;** one-way Rp125,000, round-trip Rp230,000; www.peramatour.com), has a shuttle and boat service. A shuttle bus leaves from Kuta at 10am; the boat leaves from Sanur Beach at 10:30am taking about 40 minutes. Boats return at 8:30am the following day. Catch boats opposite Jalan Hang Tua. The office of Perama Sanur can be found at friendly Warung Pojok in Jalan Hang Tua.

ORIENTATION

The two main Nusa Lembongan beach areas are **Jungutbatu** to the northeast—the original surf destination with backpacker accommodations, chilled bars, and *nasi goreng* (fried rice) or pizza restaurants—and **Mushroom Bay** in the southwest. Mushroom Bay and nearby Tamarind Bay have a more upmarket feel and cater to vaguely well-heeled families wanting to veer from the beaten track or couples wanting a romantic break. However, times change and the hotels of Mushroom Bay now seem slightly dated in comparison to the more recent additions on the hillside above Jungutbatu or the upscale villas just completed on the sunset side of the island. Mushroom Bay also has the added pollution of day-trippers; nonetheless, it's still a very pleasant spot with a great white sandy beach and various beachside restaurants. Dream and Sunset Beach are on the south side of the island.

[FastFACTS] NUSA LEMBONGAN

ATM/Banks   Bring plenty of cash because the island has **no ATMs. Perama Tours** and **Bank Pembangunan Daerah Bali** can change currency and travelers checks. You'll also be charged between 3% and 5% for use of your credit card.

Doctor   A local **doctor** in Jungutbatu will charge you Rp300,000 for a consultation. A small nurse's clinic in Jungutbatu is slightly cheaper.

Internet   Expect to pay about Rp1,000 per minute in Jungutbatu. Typical speeds are much slower than advertised. **GTNET** near the western end of Jungutbatu is a good bet with seven PCs and an on-site technician, open from 10am to 10pm. A wartel phone office at the Mainski Inn has Internet access.

EXPLORING NUSA LEMBONGAN

You can easily rent a bicycle (typically from your hotel) and spend the day pottering round the island. End your day watching a game of competitive inter-village beach volleyball or head to the Mangrove bar at the northern end of the island with a floating pontoon in the middle of the mangroves (though this can be slightly disappointing at low tide). Discover natural springs, learn about seaweed farming, or take an organized trip into the mangroves by canoe.

Many of the day-trip boats do special trips to either the **mangrove forests** or the **seaweed farms**. These are both educational and beneficial to the locals as they receive money directly. You can make your own way to the mangrove forests and seaweed farms but as most of the locals don't speak any English and there's little to see unless you're in the know, it can be a rather unentertaining visit.

Alternatively, on the road out of Mushroom Bay toward Jungutbatu is the **Gala Gala Underground House** built by what can only be described as an eccentric, Made Byasa. It took him some 15 years to fashion this labyrinth by hand. It's well

WALKING FROM TAMARIND TO mushroom BEACH

Make a day of a stroll from Tamarind to Mushroom Beach, stopping for lunch, sunbathing, and a dip en route. Start from Lembongan Island Beach Resort and head toward Coconut Beach. Once there you'll find a small shop behind which is a path that takes you over the headland for views of the sea and coastline. Stop to watch the seaweeders at work. At the end of the headland is an ideal place to swim in the clear waters. Stop off for a beer or coffee at the legendary **Blackie's Warung ★★** and have a chat with the owner himself, who's happy to share his stories of island living on Nusa Lembongan. If you want to spend the day at the beach, this is a perfect place to base yourself, on a sun lounger under the trees. Continue past Ketut's Bungalows and over the hill toward Mushroom Bay. This is one of the safest places to swim on the island because the waters are calm. Choose from any of the restaurants here if you didn't stop at Blackie's and enjoy a long leisurely lunch—beer obligatory. **Bali Beach Café** has a good reputation for food and if you're feeling too lazy to walk back, the staff will happily give you a lift home on the back of a motorbike at no extra cost.

worth stopping at and donating a small amount of money to the upkeep. You can actually climb down inside the house and take your own personal tour through this cold and dank home and wonder how anyone could spend a night in here—never mind 15 years.

Walk, or moped, the yellow **suspension bridge** between Nusa Lembongan and Nusa Ceningan (p. 128) and continue on with a tour of untouched Nusa Ceningan (see p. 128).

The **Lulur Spa** at Batu Karang Lembongan Resort (p. 126) is Nusa Lembongan's first complete spa with facials, massages, pedicures, manicures, and hair treatments. Call ✆ **0366/559-6376** and ask for Lulur Spa for more information.

DIVING   The many dive academies based on Nusa Lembongan serve the dive sites all round the three islands. The ones below are particularly noteworthy, although most offer a similar package at about the same price. A single dive, including all equipment, snacks, and drinks, is US$40 to US$45 and two dives US$70 to US$75. Discounts are available if you book online or are a walk-in. Due to the cool water, you may wish to rent a wetsuit. Stick to accredited dive schools and if you're in the least concerned after having chatted with them, simply move on to the next place. Although Nusa Lembongan has several dive sites around it, the majority of the better-known ones are at Nusa Penida (p. 129). Nusa Lembongan's **Blue Corner,** although deep, is a very popular drift dive, the highlight being a wall that's usually full of fish, sharks, big Napoleon wrasse, sometimes eagle rays, and Mola mola.

World Diving (✆ **081/23900686;** www.world-diving.com) is renowned by many as one of the best dive schools in Indonesia. It's located at Pondok Baruna guesthouse in Jungutbatu. It offers introductory courses all the way through to Assistant Instructor level. This is the only dive school in Nusa Lembongan with a purpose-built training pool. **Bali Lembongan Scuba** (✆ **081/337951181;** www.balilembonganscuba.com) is in Jungutbatu. **Bali Diving Academy Lembongan** (✆ **0361/270252;**

Snorkel, Bicycle & Motorbike Rental

There's no shortage of places offering snorkeling equipment, mountain bikes, and motorbikes for rent. Typical prices are, per day, Rp20,000 to Rp30,000 for snorkeling gear, Rp40,000 for a bicycle, and up to Rp100,000 for a motorbike. No need to lock up your bike or moped—they can't be taken anywhere!

www.scubali.com) is on Jungutbatu beach, within the grounds of Bungalow No 7. In Mushroom Bay, **Pro Dive** (© **0361/726823** or 0361/726823; www.prodivebali. com) has been operating on Nusa Lembongan for just over 2 years, although it's been in Bali since 1992.

FISHING   Most hotels or villas can arrange a fishing trip. The price should be around Rp500,000 for 3 hours, leaving at about 6am and returning at 9am. Most trips are in traditional *jukung,* with a hand line out the back to trawl the current. You'll be amazed at just how many fish they catch on a good day. One of the local characters is **Captain Nemo** on the beach near Playgrounds. Alternatively ask any of the boats on the beach, negotiate, and most will offer an authentic line-fishing experience.

SNORKELING   Many operators on Jungutbatu Beach will take you out in their *jukung* with some form of sun shade. Alternatively, you can join an organized snorkeling trip with one of the diving schools; they also rent you decent gear. Most boat operators charge in the region of Rp400,000 for up to four people for a 2- or 3-hour trip and may take you to places such as Crystal Bay off Nusa Penida or one of the other less busy options. Most *jukung* avoid Manta Point as the sea and currents can become too strong for these boats and novice divers. Plenty of good snorkeling is to be had all round the island and even just off Jungutbatu beach itself. Sometimes you don't have to go that far.

SURFING   The best time to surf around these islands is the dry season (Apr–Oct).

Shipwrecks   Best swell: south-southwest; **best size:** 3 to 6 feet; **best winds:** east-southeast. This superb right-hand wave is at the far northern end on the Nusa Lembongan beach. It offers a relatively easy take-off, a nice barrel section, and a fun "wally" section as the wave wraps around the headland toward the beach and much shallower end section. It's best (and safer) on higher tides. This wave can get crowded depending on how many surf charter boats are passing by. You can also find it with smaller numbers if you're willing to hang around for a while. Beware of a protective element, courtesy of a few local surfers and expatriate residents who like to keep the waves to themselves.

Lacerations   Best swell: southwest; **best size:** 5 to 8 feet; **best winds:** east-southeast. This is the heaviest wave of the three main waves on Nusa Lembongan and is for the most accomplished tube-riders only. If this isn't you, please don't paddle out. Only surfable on the higher tides, Lacerations serves up fast and relentless barrels, over sharp and shallow reef. Further hazards include the wire fish-traps and strong currents. It's not called Lacerations for nothing! The wave can get crowded with a hungry bunch of capable and skilled wave-riders. Show respect and charge when your number is called. No second chances out here.

Playgrounds   Best swell: southwest; **best size:** 3 to 5 feet; **best winds:** east-southeast. This wave gets its name from the floating playground located just beside the break, but it could also have earned the name from the playful nature it possesses. This wave breaks both left and right and can be good from mid- to higher-tides; it's the best bet for the less proficient surfer or the one chasing a mellower experience, sans crowd. The crowds out here are generally smaller than at Lacerations and Shipwrecks.

WHERE TO STAY

Nusa Lembongan hasn't quite turned its back on its surfing roots, though there are now options for surfers who want to return with their families. The island isn't so unrecognizable from its early surfer days.

Mushroom Bay

Hai Tide Huts ☺   This is a favorite place for families. The 15 traditional two-story *lumbung* (former rice) huts, with simple but orderly bedrooms reached by a ladder on the upper floor, are charmingly done and in a great condition belying their 1993 construction. Bathrooms aren't attached but aren't too far away and are kept very clean. The large swimming pool has areas for the whole family. A relaxed lawn fronts the sea with two-person hammocks and plenty of deckchairs to take in the view. Food is buffet style with freshly barbecued seafood, prawns, chicken, and sweetcorn and a la carte pizza (starting at Rp40,000) and steak (starting at Rp65,000). Snorkeling, kayaking, and banana boat trips are available for residents, as well as a unique Semi Submersible Submarine, where you sit in a glass cabin below the waves.

www.balihaicruises.com. ✆ **0361/720331.** 15 units. Year-round 1-night package US$125 per room; 2-bedroom villas US$125 per person, including cruise transfer, activities, and breakfast; additional nights US$90 per room. **Amenities:** Restaurant; bar; outdoor pool; watersports. *In room:* A/C, fan.

Nusa Lembongan Resort   On a manicured peninsula facing north, west, and east in Mushroom Bay, this was until recently the most expensive resort on the island. Twelve well-appointed, air-conditioned villas (two with an extra bedroom) have either a direct view of the sea or a garden view from a private terrace. A terrific swimming pool anchors the lounging area and staff are attentive although possibly more enthusiastic than proficient. A bar and restaurant sit on a lovely terrace overlooking the beach, although the menu is a bit confused and heavy for such a tropical setting. Included in your price is snorkeling and use of canoes and a glass-bottom boat trip. Being at the western point, the resort also has a private sunset viewing deck that drops down from the garden 20m (60ft.) to the sea.

www.nusalembonganresort.com. ✆ **0361/725864.** Fax 0361/725866. 12 villas. High season US$300–US$400; low season US$280–US$300. Rates include breakfast and activities. AE, MC, V. **Amenities:** Restaurant; lounge bar; babysitting; bikes; outdoor pool; room service; spa; watersports. *In villa:* A/C, stereo, minibar.

Waka Nusa Resort   On a hectare (2½ acres) of beachfront, these thatched bungalows have plenty of space and rustic charm. The overall feeling is one of barefoot chic. Plenty of beachfront *bales* are available for lounging and the cloverleaf swimming pool is surrounded by natural stone. Rooms have air-conditioning and hot water. As part of the Waka group, the standard of service is good although the resort also caters to day-trippers, which might annoy overnighters. Eating is semi-communal on long bench tables. The usual fare has starters averaging Rp40,000 and main courses up to Rp80,000. With your booking, you also get kayaking, bicycles, snorkeling, table tennis, badminton, and a trip in a glass-bottom boat. (The size of the glass in the bottom of the boat is about the size of an ice cooler—bring your magnifying glass.)

www.wakaexperience.com. ☎ **0361/723629.** Fax 0361/484695. 10 units. High season US$168; low season US$135. Rates include breakfast and activities. AE, MC, V. **Amenities:** Restaurant; bar; babysitting; bikes; outdoor pool; room service; spa; watersports. *In room:* A/C, minibar.

Jungutbatu

Batu Karang Resort & Day Spa ★   This boutique offering, with its own dedicated spa, is setting new standards on the island. Australian father and son Troy and Alan Sinclair spent 4 years building this classical yet modern stone offering set on the hillside facing the surf breaks. Golf buggies take you up the hill to your suite or villa at the end of the day. All rooms have air-conditioning, Internet, satellite TV, 220-thread cotton sheets, and king-size beds. The outdoor stone baths and showers have views over the spectacular surf breaks. The resort has its own water and sewage treatment plants making it by far the most eco-friendly place to stay. A very decent open plan restaurant and bar are on the lower levels, while farther up is a bar, a beautiful day spa, a 25-m (82-ft.) two-lane lap pool, a smaller swimming pool with a swim-up bar, and an infinity edge pool down below.

www.batukaranglembongan.com. ☎ **0366/559-6376.** Fax 0366/599-6378. 23 units. High season US$230–US$840, minimum stay 3 nights; low season US$225–US$800, minimum stay 2 nights. Rates include breakfast. AE, DC, MC, V. **Amenities:** Muntigs Bar and Restaurant (p. 128); bar; lounge; babysitting; bikes; gym; Jacuzzi; 2 outdoor pools; room service; spa; watersports; Wi-Fi (for a fee). *In room:* A/C, TV, hair dryer, minibar.

Coconuts Beach Resort   This is a very charming option at which each of the traditional stone bungalows rises up the hillside with wondrous views to Playgrounds and Lacerations waves and Mount Agung. The style is simple but handsome: the air-conditioned bungalows have stone floors and bathrooms beautifully tiled in greens and aquamarines; up the hill are a further eight bungalows open to the elements with floor-to-ceiling blinds and curtains rather than windows that let in the sea breeze. Plus, they all get hot water. The pool is pleasant enough and the Sea Breeze restaurant has snapper filets at Rp55,000 and hamburgers at Rp35,000. The better views are higher up the hillside, which makes for a longer walk—so you have to earn it.

www.coconutbeachresorts.com. ☎ **0361/728088.** Fax 0361/728089. 18 units. Year-round US$64 standard. Rates include breakfast. MC, V. **Amenities:** Restaurant; bikes; outdoor pool; room service; watersports. *In room:* A/C, ceiling fan.

Playgrounds   At the southern end of Jungutbatu beach overlooking the surf break, these five rooms in a large house have a choice of fans or air-conditioning. Although these clean and basic rooms with satellite TV have only cold water in the showers, you still get wonderful views from the balconies on the top floor.

www.playgroundslembongan.com. ☎/fax **0366/24524** or 081/74748427. 10 units. High season US$78–US$220. No credit cards. **Amenities:** Restaurant; bar; babysitting; bikes; gym; outdoor pool; room service; watersports. *In room:* A/C (in some), fan.

Shipwrecks Beach Villa   A minute's walk from the beach opposite Shipwreck's surf break, this timber-constructed villa offers three bedrooms overlooking a tropical garden. Each bedroom has a beautiful four-posted bed with an outside bathroom. The property doesn't allow children under 5 years old but it's an ideal property for older families or a collection of surfers. The villa can be rented whole or by the room.

www.nusalembongan.com.au. ☎ **081/338032900.** 3 bedrooms. High season Rp600,000 standard, Rp750,000 master suite; low season Rp560,000 standard, Rp700,000 master suite; extra person Rp130,000. Rates include breakfast. 2 night minimum stay. MC, V. *In room:* A/C, fan.

Sunset & the Rest of the Island

Dream Beach Bungalows   This is a quiet spot with a beautiful white-sand beach on the southwestern part of the island. Of the 11 rooms, seven are single story *lumbung* style with fans and cold water showers. It's basic, erring on budget, but it has great atmosphere. The lovely restaurant serves Thai curries for Rp45,000 and usually fresh tuna every day. Music is mainly reggae on the great upstairs deck where you can have a drink or a bite, and "Don't worry about a thing."

www.dreambeachlembongan.com. ☏ **0361/743-2344.** Fax 0361/292441. 11 units. High season US$85–US$155; low season US$75–US$145. Rates include breakfast. MC, V. **Amenities:** Restaurant; cafe; bar; bikes; outdoor pool; watersports. *In room:* Fan.

Lembongan Island Beach Villas ★★ 🎁   This group of luxury villas is perched on 2 hectares (5 acres) of manicured peninsula. The villas, set in their own landscaped grounds facing either west to the sunset or east to Mount Agung, are environmentally low impact: solar panels heat fresh water collected by the resort; waste water is treated; and wind power is planned for the future. The beautifully styled houses are a mix of three- and four-bedrooms all with floor-to-ceiling sliding windows, kitchens, and a modern feel with their use of limed coconut wood. Café Waru, the stylish bar and restaurant, serves island dishes such as fresh grilled fish and their own home-grown salads. Five shaded *bales* with hanging chairs overlook the ocean near the 18-m (36-ft.) lap pool. Truly Nusa Lembongan has arrived.

www.lembonganbeachvillas.com. ☏ **0366/559-6402** or 081/338561208. 8 villas. High season US$300–US$700; low season US$250–US$600. Rates include breakfast. MC, V. **Amenities:** Cafe; bar; outdoor pool; tennis court; watersports. *In villa:* Fan, kitchen.

WHERE TO EAT

Restaurants are typically open daily, from 7 or 8am to 9 or 10pm.

Mushroom Bay, Sunset Beach & Dream Beach

Café Bali (no phone; main courses Rp35000–Rp60000; no credit cards), in the middle of Mushroom Bay, is the beach's focal point, outside of the hotels, and a great place to hang out. The simple specialties are fresh whole snapper, prawn tempura, and an assortment of decent pizzas. If you can't make it for lunch at **Warung Sunset** (☏ 081/23621633; main courses Rp20,000–Rp30,000; no credit cards), on Sunset Beach, just go for sunset drinks. Fresh, local fish is usually the daily special; choose from plenty of cold drinks, cocktails, and mocktails. Staff will also arrange transport home if you can't quite make it on your own. On Dream Beach is **Café Pandan** (☏ 081/338737344; main courses Rp70,000–Rp100,000; no credit cards), another local favorite. Fresh tuna is the order of the day and Thai curries go for Rp45,000.

Jungutbatu

Most places on this strip cater to the surf crowd. The restaurant at Coconuts Beach Resort (see p. 126), **Sea Breeze** (☏ 0361/7443936 or 0361/728088; www.bali-activities.com; main courses Rp22,000–Rp150,000; no credit cards), serves Indonesian and Western food at reasonable prices with friendly service and an oceanfront bar.

The fun, if predictable, sports bar **Scooby Doo Bar & Restaurant** overlooks the bay. Enjoy a cold beer while watching the sun go down over Bali. The **Mainski Lembongan Resort** (☏ 0361/9237322; www.mainski-lembongan-resort.com; main courses Rp25,000–Rp105,000; MC, V) has a poolside bar that shows music DVDs on the giant screen every night and serves ice cold beers, local and international wines, and a range of fun tropical cocktails. Happy Hour is daily from 5 to 7pm. They also have a pool table, table tennis, and Wi-Fi.

NUSA CENINGAN

This tiny island is untouched by any form of tourism. Access other than by sea is via a 100-m- (328-ft.-) long, bright yellow bridge from the southeastern side of Nusa Lembongan, wide enough only for a bicycle or moped. This beautiful little place has no official accommodations other than homestays, nor indeed is there any litter. What it does have is neat and well-tended stone walls, trees, and shades of old coconut plantations. It makes a very pleasant trip and you're unlikely to meet any other tourists. The locals are friendly and it's virtually impossible to get lost.

In the channel between Nusa Lembongan and Nusa Ceningan, no more than 500m (1,640 ft.) apart, are the **seaweed farms** that support the livelihoods of many of the islanders. Guided tours teach you about seaweed farming, ultimately drawing the conclusion that it's a lot of hard work for not a huge amount of financial gain. Seaweed farmers earn between Rp3,000 and Rp8,000 per kilo (2.2 pounds) of seaweed harvested. Still, it's a living, with a fresh harvest every 4 to 6 weeks.

The **Jaringan Ekowisata Desa (JED)** ★★ (© **0361/737447;** www.jed. or.id), translated as the Village Ecotourism Network, offers educational trips with a farmer who shows you how the locals harvest seaweed. You also learn how to make food from seaweed, including cakes. A trip for two to four people is US$130 per person; five or more people US$105 per person. Price includes all transfers, overnight accommodation in a home-stay, meals, and an all-day guide. JED can also arrange trips if you don't want to stay the night.

The **surf break** here is called simply Ceningan, off the coast between Nusa Lembongan and Nusa Ceningan. It works when the breaks on the other side of Nusa Lembongan don't. This is also known as the Secret Spot.

Bunga Bungalows Restaurant (no phone; main courses Rp35,000–Rp50,000; no credit cards) has various tables and loungers looking out to the surf. The high point is the wood-fired pizzas from Rp35,000 to Rp50,000. Food stops at about 9pm. **Ware Ware** (© **081/23970572;** main courses Rp50,000–Rp95,000; no credit cards) offers grilled catch of the day, *nasi goreng,* and Italian and Indonesian dishes. This place is rightly popular not just for its location on a terrace overlooking the surf. For the catch of the day, try **Lembongan Reef** (© **08/2145393419;** www.lembongan reef.com; main courses Rp30,000–Rp120,000; MC, V), perched on a platform on the hillside overlooking the surf breaks.

Ketut Warung 🍴 THAI Without a doubt a local treasure, not just for Madam Ketut's improbably delicious Thai curries and soups, but also for Ketut himself—a proclaimed healer and generous host. Try the Tom Yum soup, in the simple venue with plain wooden tables and rickety chairs, followed by reflexology and a genuine healing massage by the local master: back pains, knee joints, whatever's ailing you. The warung is just behind the Mainski resort, but ask when you get close and persevere in finding this gem. If lost, ask for Ketut Malom. Definitely recommended, but don't play the grandson at Connect 4!

No phone. Main courses Rp15,000–Rp25,000. No credit cards. Daily 8am–9pm.

Muntigs Bar and Restaurant INTERNATIONAL As with the hotel (Batu Karang Resort, p. 126), this is a notch up from the other island restaurants, although not as romantically set at night as most others that actually front the sea. Come here for good food and drink without busting your budget. The menu makes a refreshing change from the typical options of the rest (don't forget to try the chocolate mousse). The restaurant stocks a wide variety of imported wines—almost as rare as hen's teeth on Nusa Lembongan—and imported beers, and the staff members make great cocktails.

© **0366/248805.** www.batukaranglembongan.com. Main courses Rp80,000–Rp150,000. AE, MC, V. Daily 7:30am–11pm.

Nusa Penida

Nusa Penida is the Bali, or even the Nusa Lembongan, that time left behind. It's a mainly dry and somewhat desolate landscape where nature and wildlife have been left to their own devices. Known to the outside world for being a formal penal colony, it's known to Bali believers as the home of Jero Gede Mecaling, the evil spirit with his horde of devils that's warded off by the Barong Landung dance around Galungang.

Nusa Penida's main attraction is the incredible flora and fauna found scuba diving the crystal clear waters, or exploring the cliffs that drop deep into the sea. The island straddles Wallace's line and its northeastern shores have the most incredible view up the Lombok Strait. Birdlife has remained left alone and many endangered species have prospered.

Rich in many of the simple things, this is a charming island of natural beauty and not even the increasing number of day-trippers (whether those who come for the diving or the Quicksilver clients in their floating pavilion) can detract from its charms.

A daily **market** in Sampalan is open in the early morning from about 5 to 10am selling local and imported (from Bali) fruit and vegetables.

GETTING THERE

Most people arrive on Nusa Penida at Toyapakeh beach from Nusa Lembongan or, if arriving on the **public boat** from Padangbai, at the main port in the administrative capital of Sampalan. Boats should leave Padangbai for Sampalan at 7am and 2pm (Rp30,000 one-way) from the ferry terminal but aren't always reliable. They return from Nusa Penida at 9am and 4pm. Small boat owners will also take you to the island for the right price: Prepare to bargain. If you're only staying a night, you can even negotiate a round-trip fare as the boatman can usually find some cheap accommodations for the night.

Public boats depart daily from Yellow Bridge (Nusa Lembongan) at 6am in front of Nusa Ceningan. They can be a bit sketchy at times and are usually very crowded. There's no same-day round-trip. The ride across is approximately 90 minutes and boats only leave when full.

The fare is Rp300,000 for charter boat transfers (**Scoot Boat** © **00361/285522;** www.scootcruise.com). You can always rent your own boat: Ask any fisherman or inquire at any of the big hotels on Nusa Lembongan.

[Fast FACTS] NUSA PENIDA

ATMs/Banks   The two main banks, Bank Bri and Bank LPD, are on the main street near the hospital. Neither have an ATM although they'll change money for you. Both are open Monday to Friday from 8am to 3pm. A Western Union (© **0366/31880**) in Sampalan should give credit card advances.

Emergencies   The police station, hospital (© **0366/23582**), are in Sampalan.

Internet Access   The island has little or no Internet service.

EXPLORING NUSA PENIDA

Arrange a guide in advance through your hotel or villa, or alternatively rent a bike and guide when you arrive on the beach at Toyapakeh. You'll easily encounter people offering to take you on an escorted motorbike ride round the island or snorkeling. Typically, they charge in the region of Rp150,000 to Rp200,0000 for a full day, which should include your bike and petrol. A trip on the back of a bike to the Bat Cave (see p. 131) alone will cost up to Rp100,000 per person per bike and guide/driver. If you want to rent your own bike for your own tour of the island, a bike costs around Rp80,000 for the day. A local chap who takes regular tours and is knowledgeable and friendly is **Rod** (✆ 081/805333747).

Other trips on the island are to **Telaga,** which is the center for weaving, or to the temples at Semaya or the top of Mount Mundi. Alternatively, you can swim in a beautiful waterfall fed by a natural spring just a 2-km (1¼-mile) walk from Batumadeg, although you'll have to get a guide to lead you.

BIRD-WATCHING   The interior of Nusa Penida has been mainly left alone and nature allowed to keep hold. This is a place for professional twitchers. The **Nusa Penida Bird Sanctuary** ★ (✆ 0361/977978; www.fnpf.org), part of the Friends of the National Parks Foundation (FNPF) and also now sponsored by the Begawan Giri Foundation, is on the road east of Sampalan and has possibly the most Bali starlings found in any one place. The Bali starling was at one stage the most endangered bird in the world, with only seven in the wild. The biggest challenge to rearing birds in the wild, other than poaching, is the proper water and trees to provide the right habitat. Since its inception in 2002, the Nusa Penida Bird Sanctuary has planted some 115,000 trees. The foundation has also managed to get all the villages of Nusa Penida to sign an agreement stating that they'll help preserve the wildlife on the island—indeed the whole island is now a bird sanctuary. Contact the Bird Sanctuary at the Bali Bird Park (p. 113) just north of Sanur for more information on organizing a birding tour.

DIVING   Although Nusa Penida is best known as a diving destination, most of the best-known dive schools are based on Nusa Lembongan (p. 120). The whole Nusa Penida and Nusa Lembongan area offers drift-diving in mild to strong currents. The water can be chilly but is often startlingly clear (with visibility between 15–40m/49–131 ft.), with gorgeous corals and prolific fish, some turtles, sharks, and, July to mid-November, Mola mola (the weird and wonderful-looking ocean sunfish). If you're staying on mainland Bali, you may find it easier and less hassle with boat-transport to also book diving at Nusa Penida/Nusa Lembongan with a mainland operator (p. 115).

The three main north-coast sites—**SD, Ped,** and **Sental**—have many soft corals and fish, such as sweetlips, lionfish, moray eels, scorpionfish and reef sharks, plus turtles, nudis, and crabs.

Toyapakeh, Nusa Penida's most popular dive site, has good visibility and rich, impressive coral formations with big bommies and a profusion of colorful soft corals that provide excellent hiding places for Ribbon eels, banded sea snakes, and nudibranches. If you're here late afternoon, you may see Mandarin fish.

Although a small area, **Gamat Bay** has soft corals, gorgonians, and hard corals (including table corals) and is thus full of reef fish (some quite rare), commensals, and nudibranches. On the outside slope are big bommies, overhangs, and small caves that provide resting places for larger fish. This is also a cleaning station for the ever-popular Mola mola.

Dive Schools on Nusa Penida

The dive school outside of Sampalan branded **Quicksilver** (www.quicksilver-bali.com) shows no evidence of PADI certification. The Quicksilver website states quite proudly that it has insurance coverage up to US$100 per person. An introductory dive is advertised at US$115 against US$45 for an accredited school such as **World Diving** on Nusa Lembongan (a short boat ride from Nusa Penida), where many accredited dive schools are based. See, "Diving," p. 123.

Crystal Bay ★★ is best known for sightings of Mola mola in the July to mid-November season, when water temperature can reach 19°C (66°F). The bay itself is quite beautiful, with good numbers and variety of fish plus gorgeous corals, and also has a **Bat Cave.** You enter from underwater and then surface inside the cave, which is open to the sky, and watch the bats overhead. On the deep wall after the Bat Cave you can often see eagle rays and (if you're lucky) the wobbegong shark, only found in Bali.

Manta Point on Nusa Penida's southwest coast has dramatic limestone cliffs that descend straight into the ocean. The swell and surge however can be strong. The mantas seen here are 2 to 4m (6½–13 ft.) in size at an average depth of 5 to 10m (16–33 ft.); you may see other big fish such as Mola mola, bamboo sharks, shark rays, tuna, tiger mackerel, and dolphins, while the smaller fish include other rays and unicornfish.

As well as seeing the resident manta rays from the sea, you can also do so directly from the cliffs at Manta Point. Your best bet is to get here about 8:30 to 9:30am. It takes you up to 2 hours to get there by bike from Toyabunkah. **Malibu Point,** on southeast Nusa Penida, lies on a very steep slope, with table corals and big bommies. There are huge schools of rainbow runners, big trevallies, and rays. Malibu Point is Nusa Penida's best location to see a variety of sharks.

Batu Abah, on the far side of Nusa Penida, is known for mantas and Mola mola. You need a fast and sturdy boat to reach Batu Abah within a reasonable time. **SNORKELING** For snorkeling, most people head straight for **Crystal Bay,** making it feel a little crowded, particularly given the island's remote location and the number of other bays close at hand. Although you should be observant of currents and not simply head off on your own, you may find it more rewarding to pull in to some of the other bays and snorkel there.

TEMPLES Although known as the **Bat Cave**, to be honest, **Pura Goa Giri Putri** ★★ only has so many bats. Regardless, this is quite extraordinary and justifies a day trip to Nusa Penida. About 45 minutes by bike from Toyabungkah, you arrive at a fairly featureless point and start climbing the 100 or so steep carved stone steps. At the top is a temple where you make a small donation and then you're taken into the cave. You wriggle through the entrance, no bigger than a manhole. The cave then starts opening up and continues on for about 250m (820 ft.) rising to some 100m (328 ft.) in height in the middle. A series of temples in the cave are partially lit. At the far end, you arrive at the other side of the mountain and peer out to a verdant green tree-lined valley that's almost Provençal. You have literally walked through the mountain.

Back at the start, you have a **view** up the Lombok Strait, with Bali to the west and Lombok to the east. You're effectively straddling Wallace's line. On a clear morning, as the sun is still climbing, the view from here is breathtaking.

The main temple on the island is **Pura Penaturan Ped,** an extensive and charming temple on the road out of Sampalan with lots of carvings. Various other temples line the road, such as **Batu Mulapan,** many of them similarly carved in limestone.

WHERE TO STAY & EAT

You have little choice when staying on Nusa Penida. For those comfortable with braving the elements, here are your options: **Made Homestay** (✆ **08/5238814998;** Rp100,000 standard, Rp120,000 twin; rates include coffee for breakfast; no credit cards) is four basic but clean bungalows of Balinese carved stone in a delightful garden. Cold water and fans are the order of the day. The beachside **Mutiara Mas Bungalows** (✆ **081/337077590;** Rp120,000 no A/C, Rp150,000 with A/C; no credit cards) features 10 twin rooms, with either air-conditioning or a fan. Facilities include a couple of *bales* and even a volleyball court. It's a beautiful spot, though the dodgy (and not in the least bit artistic) Art Market is just next door as is the charmless Quicksilver Dive Operation.

For dining, there are various local warungs but none of real note, and so just pick a busy one and hope for the best.

THE BUKIT PENINSULA

The Bukit Peninsula dangles from the southern tip of Bali like a locket on a chain. Bukit means "hill" and encapsulates the whole of the teardrop-shaped area south of the airport starting at Jimbaran Bay ★ on the west side, down through the beaches of Pecatu and the cliffs of Uluwatu ★★, to the southern tip and all the way round to the east side and the government-sponsored five-star tourist enclave of Nusa Dua, continuing up to the strip of Tanjung Benoa.

With its dramatic, craggy coastline and vegetation, or lack thereof, the Bukit is in stark contrast to the rest of Bali with its verdant rice paddies and lush tropical jungle. And whereas rice farming is the staple crop on the rest of Bali, here there are only seaweed farms and limestone quarries, the scars of which are visible from as far afield as Ubud. Thus, the government has aggressively encouraged the development of tourism, giving incentives such as special tax breaks and government funds to established international hotel chains to sweeten the deal.

Historically, the Bukit was a fairly scary place where great herds of banteng (wild Indonesian cattle) and water buffalo roamed free, and where the occasional sighting of Kebo Iwa, the legendary Balinese giant and master builder, sent shivers through the collective Balinese imagination. The Dutch colonials followed the lead of the rajahs and continued the tradition of hunting. The Dutch also banished criminals and undesirables to the Bukit. All this trivia leads you to laugh because the Bukit is nowadays referred to by eager developers as "The Beverly Hills of Bali." Instead of sighting wild boar along these dusty roads, you're more likely to be stuck behind water-truck tanks plodding up the hills in low gear as they carry this scant resource to the villas and resorts.

JIMBARAN BAY ★

The bustling beach town and idyllic getaway of Jimbaran is just south of the Ngurah Rai International Airport, on the neck of the Bukit Peninsula, 20 minutes from Kuta and Seminyak. As this is still predominately a working fishing village, a charming diversion here is simply watching the traditional *jukung* (fishing) boats bring in their catch. Jimbaran has one of the best sandy beaches in south Bali, with clear, calm water great for swimming. Developers were quick to realize this, and Jimbaran now has some of the finest high-end resorts on the island. Despite development, the

The Bukit Peninsula

ATTRACTIONS ●
Garuda Vishnu Kencara
  Cultural Park **32**
Jimbaran fish market **2**
New Kuta Green Park **22**
Paintball Bali **34**
Produce market **1**
Pura Luhur Uluwatu **25**
Puru Ulun Siwi **5**

HOTELS ■
Abi Bali **18**
Alila Villas Uluwatu **28**

Ayana Resort & Spa **17**
Banyan Tree Resort & Spa **31**
Four Seasons Resort
  at Jimbaran Bay **16**
Gending Kedis Luxury
  Villas & Spa **15**
Hotel InterContinental **9**
Jimbaran Puri Bali **7**
Karang Kambar Estate **36**
Karang Putih Villa **35**
Karma Kandara Villas **30**
Kayumanis Jimbaran **6**

Khayangan Estate **26**
The Long House **33**
Mick's Place **19**
Mu Uluwatu **20**
Puri Bambu **3**
Semara Luxury Villa
  Resort Uluwatu **29**
Udayana Kingfisher
  Eco Lodge **4**
Villa Balquisse **12**
Villa Bulan Putih **21**
Villa Shaba **13**

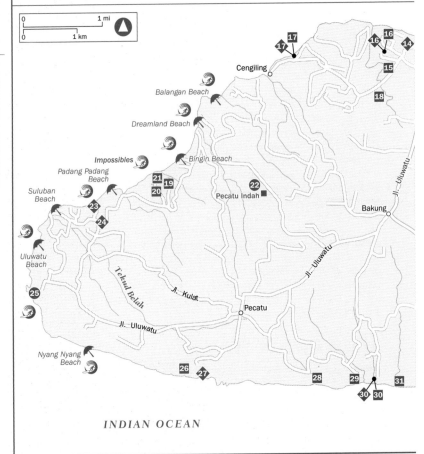

INDIAN OCEAN

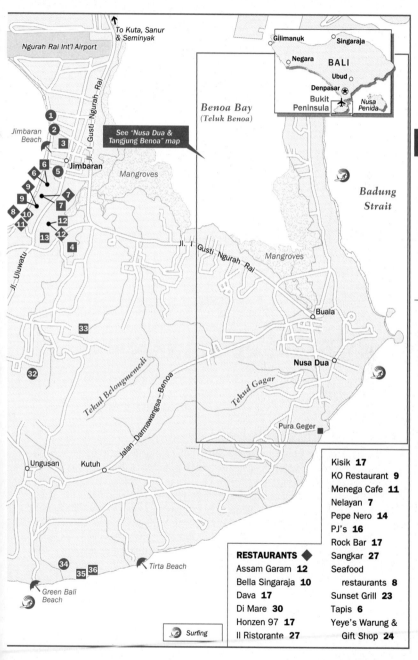

THE BUKIT PENINSULA | Jimbaran Bay

8

To Kuta, Sanur & Seminyak

Ngurah Rai Int'l Airport

Jimbaran Beach

Jimbaran

Benoa Bay *(Teluk Benoa)*

See "Nusa Dua & Tangjung Benoa" map

Mangroves

Jl. I Gusti Ngurah Rai

Badung Strait

Mangroves

Buala

Nusa Dua

Tekud Gagar

Pura Geger

Tekud Belongmemedi

Jalan Darmawangsa - Benoa

Jl. Uluwatu

Ungusan   Kutuh

Tirta Beach

Green Bali Beach

Surfing

BALI

Gilimanuk   Singaraja

Negara

Ubud

Denpasar

Bukit Peninsula

Nusa Penida

RESTAURANTS ◆
Assam Garam **12**
Bella Singaraja **10**
Dava **17**
Di Mare **30**
Honzen 97 **17**
Il Ristorante **27**

Kisik **17**
KO Restaurant **9**
Menega Cafe **11**
Nelayan **7**
Pepe Nero **14**
PJ's **16**
Rock Bar **17**
Sangkar **27**
Seafood
   restaurants **8**
Sunset Grill **23**
Tapis **6**
Yeye's Warung &
   Gift Shop **24**

135

Taxis aren't easy to find on the Bukit peninsula, and though you can walk between a few of the villages, you'll need some form of motorized transport to get around most of the time. Hotels, villas, and restaurants can order a taxi for you when required. If you find yourself without a taxi, call one. Ask how long it will take for the cab to get you because they're notoriously slow. Once you've got a taxi and reached your destination, have your driver wait for you for about Rp12,000 an hour. Check the price with your driver before you depart. For Blue Bird Taxi ✆ 0361/70111.

town still looks like a fishing village, with small seafood shacks serving up some of the best fish dishes on the island—a worthy day trip for good eats alone. The best time to visit is just before sunset, although don't be overly hungry when you arrive as the food can sometimes take a while.

Essentials

GETTING THERE & GETTING AROUND

Jimbaran is on the road to Nusa Dua, 1.5km (less than 1 mile) south of Kuta. **Cabs** are plentiful and cost Rp110,000. *Bemo* (vans operating as minibuses) aren't available here. **Walking** is the best way to get a feel for life in Jimbaran village. The morning provides the opportunity to see offerings placed in every nook and cranny, children in their uniforms heading to school, and mothers going to and from the market.

[FastFACTS] JIMBARAN BAY

Doctor   A doctor is on-site at the following pharmacy daily from 4 to 10pm to consult for any minor ailments.

Pharmacy   Kimia Farmacy, Jl. Gunung Batur A-3 (✆ **0361/847-9785**).

Exploring Jimbaran Bay

The **Puru Ulun Siwi** temple, at the village's main crossroads, dates from the 18th century and is one of the few temples that faces east, rather than north to Mount Gunung Agung as is the usual practice. This is because the temple, once a primitive shrine, became a Hindu-Balinese temple fairly early in the 11th century. At this time, the holy man Mpu Kuturan still followed the custom of his native Java in orienting his temple toward holy Mount Semura in East Java. You might just catch a farmer, from the market across the street, collecting water from the temple to bless his fields for good harvests—and to keep rodents at bay. The **produce market** across the street isn't one of Bali's largest but it is one of the best. Because of its proximity to the seafood market, many of the island's chefs and their staff shop here. As a result, farmers know to bring their best and brightest produce.

SPAS   Spas are open daily. Whatever treatment you choose at the **Four Seasons spa ★★** (p. 137; single treatment US$55–US$380; AE, MC, V; daily 9am–9pm), you won't be disappointed. After your treatment your gracious therapists leave you to bathe in a frangipani-and-rose-petal-filled tub—something best shared between two people.

The Ayana resort (p. 138) has two knock-out spas to splurge on (single treatment US$40–US$190, package US$125–US$700; AE, MC, V; daily 9am–11pm): **Ayana Thallaso ★★★** and **Spa on the Rocks ★★★**. At the Thallaso spa, you bathe in a warmed seawater-fed pool and are pummeled within an inch of your life. This treatment is meant to be invigorating, making it perfect before a night on the tiles. The next day, book into the Spa on the Rocks, which hangs on a cliff top. Pass 2 hours of your time with the "Amazing Jade" massage with warm and cold stones, a 24-point foot reflexology massage, a facial, and a Swedish deep-tissue massage.

Being one of the preferred hotels for conferences in Nusa Dua, the InterContinental (p. 138) has the **Uluwatu spa ★★★** (single treatment Rp250,000–Rp1,000,000, package Rp900,000–Rp2,100,000; AE, MC, V; daily 8am–11pm) that caters to gentlemen with "Jet-setter Stress Relief," sport manicures and pedicures, and "Out to Lunch: Conference Delegates Delight," a 2-hour vigorous massage using steaming hot towels and specialized oils. The package deals are good value in this expensive neck of the woods.

Ornate rooms, with chandeliers and dark moody colors, at **Henna Spa ★** (single treatment Rp115,000–Rp300,000, package Rp300,000–Rp520,000; AE, MC, V; daily 8am–9pm) in Villa Balquisse (p. 139) make for an opulent spa experience. The "Javanese Lulur Royal Ritual" is inspired by the prenuptial treatments of the Royal court of Yogyakarta. The 2-hour treatment includes a massage with handmade frangipani massage oil, followed by 45 minutes of the invigorating Lulur skin scrub with turmeric, rice, and jasmine, followed by the yogurt splash treatment. The smells are so overpowering you'll get hungry. Fortunately the spa also has delicious tapas and a wonderful fresh ginger tea.

SURFING **Airport Right** and **Airport Left** (p. 69), two waves near Kuta, are also easily accessible from Jimbaran Bay. Rent a boat from shore.

Where to Stay

VERY EXPENSIVE

Four Seasons Resort at Jimbaran Bay ★★★ The very picture of luxury, the Four Seasons is on a stunning hillside overlooking the bay. Each thatched villa has a large bedroom and marble bathroom with an oversize tub. The little things stand out: thick towels and fancy bathroom amenities, two sinks, garden showers, a library with Internet access, and snap-to service. Other facilities include a top-notch spa and a cooking school. The horizon pool blends seamlessly with the ocean blue and other small pools invite you to relax and escape from it all. Walk or be driven in a golf cart down to the beach. The beach club has surfing, kayaking, and catamarans.

Jimbaran. www.fourseasons.com. ✆ **0361/701010.** Fax 0361/701020. 147 units. Peak season US$880 and up 1-bedroom, US$2,200 2-bedroom; high season US$780 1-bedroom, US$1,900 2-bedroom; low season US$680 1-bedroom, US$1,700 2-bedroom. Rates may or may not include breakfast. AE, DC, MC, V. **Amenities:** 3 restaurants, including PJ's (p. 140); 2 bars; babysitting; concierge; health club; Jacuzzi; 2 outdoor pools; room service; sauna; spa; 2 synthetic grass floodlit tennis courts; watersports. *In villa:* A/C, satellite TV, DVD, stereo w/CD player, fridge, minibar, Wi-Fi (free).

Gending Kedis Luxury Villas & Spa The name of this ridge-top villa complex translates to "bird song," in deference to the continually chirping birds nestled in the wooded ravine below. Although not directly on the beach, a shuttle service is on standby to Bali's golden mile within minutes. Each villa has a spacious pool and kitchen. You can stock your own wine refrigerator in the bar at your pool, which is a nice touch. The restaurant provides good food for good value.

Jl. Karang Mas Sejahtera 100V, Jimbaran Bay. www.gendingkedis.com. ☎ **0361/708906.** Fax 0361/848-2188. 85 villas. High season US$800 and up; low season US$725 and up. Rates include breakfast and taxes. AE, MC, V. **Amenities:** Restaurant; lounge; bar; babysitting; children's club; gym; room service; spa. *In villa:* A/C, TV/DVD, hair dryer, minibar, pool, Wi-Fi (free).

Jimbaran Puri Bali ★★ 📶 The pioneer resort on Jimbaran beach, the Puri Bali, originally the Pansea, has stylish, self-contained garden cottages scattered among lily ponds, coconut trees, and statuary, set back from the beautiful beach. Despite its top location, this isn't a big resort and you won't have to fight for sun loungers or crawl your way through the crowd to get to the breakfast area. All cottages have terraces, shaded by umbrellas, with privacy-providing screens and outdoor deck showers. Rooms are done in carved teak under thatched roofing, with mosquito netting and natural linen touches. Bathrooms have sunken tubs and all the goodies. The resort is a haven of privacy and calm, a good choice for getting away from it all.

Jl. Uluwatu, Jimbaran. www.jimbaranpuribali.com. ☎ **0361/701605.** Fax 0361/701320. 62 units. Peak season US$495 cottage, US$940 pool villa; high season US$425 cottage, US$835 pool villa; low season US$395 cottage, US$660 pool villa. Rates include breakfast and taxes. AE, MC, V. **Amenities:** 2 restaurants, including Nelayan (p. 142); bar; babysitting; outdoor pool; room service. *In room:* A/C, satellite TV, DVD player, fridge, hair dryer, minibar, Wi-Fi (free).

Kayumanis Jimbaran Set back from a fishing beach beneath a canopy of coconut palms, Kayumanis Jimbaran's spacious, yet rustic, thatch-roofed villas are excellent examples of indoor-outdoor tropical living. Your villa opens onto your private pool where a waft of sea air is mixed with the sweet smell of the frangipani trees. Your personal butler is on-call 24 hours a day to appease your every whim.

Jl. Yoga Perkanthi, Jimbaran. www.kayumanis.com. ☎ **0361/705777.** Fax 0361/705101. 20 villas. Peak season US$590–US$630; high season US$558 1-bedroom, US$688 2-bedroom; low season US$474 1-bedroom, US$585 2-bedroom, plus 21% taxes. Rates include breakfast. AE, MC, V. No children 15 years old and under. **Amenities:** Restaurant (Tapis, p. 142); Jacuzzi; outdoor pool; room service; spa; tennis court. *In villa:* A/C, TV/DVD, hair dryer, kitchen, minibar, MP3 docking station, Wi-Fi.

EXPENSIVE

Ayana Resort & Spa ★★ Although the property cast off its Ritz-Carlton brand name a couple of years ago, it lives up to, and even surpasses, expectations set by its former namesake. You can still expect the same anticipatory service chasing you around the gigantic 77 hectares (190 acres) grounds suspended on a cliff over Jimbaran Bay. Each room is decorated in muted colors with a touch of sea blue to match. The resort has its own private beach. Facilities include five swimming pools, six wedding venues, renowned restaurants, private villas, and more. Don't miss treating yourself to a rejuvenating water treatment session at the **Spa on the Rocks** (p. 137). The new **Rock Bar** (p. 140) has to be one of the best beach bars on the island.

Jl. Karang Mas Sejahtera, Jimbaran. www.ayanaresort.com. ☎ **0361/702222.** Fax 0361/701555. 368 units. Peak season US$385 and up; high season US$269 and up; low season US$219 and up; extra charge for children 4–11 years old US$15, plus 21% taxes. Rates do not include breakfast. AE, MC, V. **Amenities:** 3 restaurants (Kisik, Dava, and Honzen 97; p. 140, p. 141, and p. 141); bar; babysitting; children's club; gym; Jacuzzi; outdoor pool; room service; spa; tennis court. *In room:* A/C, TV/DVD, iPod, hair dryer, minibar, Wi-Fi (free).

Hotel InterContinental ★ ☺ The InterContinental hotel chain knows what savvy travelers want: great service and value. The InterContinental Club (Priority Club Member: free; Ambassador Club Member: US$150 in addition to room rate) here fulfills both requirements. Club members are given priority immigration clearance and delivered to check-in on the Club Floor, where the first matter of business is what you want to drink. Guests who pay for Club-class rooms enjoy evening complimentary cocktails and canapés, all day tea, coffee, and snacks, and an especially lavish spread for breakfast. The Club rooms are oversize and contemporary with elegant bathrooms, spacious living rooms overlooking the Club pool, and gardens. All this is a 2-minute walk to the private beach and the other top-notch facilities. The excellent children's club (Star Trekkers) has superb programs that leave everyone else in peace. The hotel even has its own turtle release program.

Jl. Uluwatu 45, Jimbaran. www.bali-intercontinental.com. 𝄐 **0361/701888.** Fax 0361/701777. 418 units. Peak season US$310 and up; high season US$280 and up; low season US$270 and up. Rates may or may not include breakfast. AE, MC, V. **Amenities:** 2 restaurants (KO Restaurant and Bella Singaraja, p. 141 and p. 141); bar; lounge; babysitting; bikes; children's club; gym; Jacuzzi; outdoor pool; room service; spa; tennis court; watersports. *In room:* A/C, TV/DVD, hair dryer, minibar, Wi-Fi (US$10/24 hr.).

Villa Shaba ★★ 🏷 🛏 This Moroccan-inspired villa is reminiscent of a more genteel age. The five bedrooms surround a central courtyard with flowing fountain. The smart, open-plan kitchen and an elegant drawing room face a generous span of French doors that open to the pool sheltered by mangroves. The suites and bedrooms can be booked individually or you can take over the entire villa. A vintage convertible Volkswagen Safari is on-call to take you to the beach. Beach picnics can be prepared at a moment's notice—complete with chilled champagne and wine.

Jl. Uluwatu, Gang Gigit Sari, Jimbaran. www.shaba-bali.com. 𝄐 **0361/701695.** Fax 0361/703087. 5 bedrooms. Peak season US$300–US$366; high season US$330–US$390; low season US$190–US$330 plus 20% taxes. Rates include breakfast. AE, MC, V. **Amenities:** Restaurant; bar; free airport transfer; babysitting; bikes; outdoor pool; room service; spa. *In room:* A/C, fan, TV/DVD, hair dryer, minibar, MP3 docking station, Wi-Fi.

MODERATE

Abi Bali ☺ Situated on the road between the Ayana and the Four Seasons, this brand-new, mid-priced option offers clean, cheery, and comfortable rooms and villas decorated with Balinese accents. Each villa has an open-air kitchen with a stove and burners (a rarity in most villa hotels), decent-sized pools, and gardens. An on-site spa offers affordable treatments. The family-friendly resort is a little randomly positioned and there's no beach on the premises, but the staff will drop you off at Jimbaran Bay and you're right in the enclave of many five-star resorts.

Jl. Karang Mas Sejahtera 89, Jimbaran. www.abibalivilla.com. 𝄐 **0361/708889.** Fax 0361/888-7877. 32 units. High season US$175–US$195 rooms, US$280–US$410 villas; low season US$150–US$170 rooms; US$250–US$360 villas. Rates include breakfast. AE, MC, V. **Amenities:** Restaurant; lounge; airport transfer; gym; room service. *In room:* A/C, TV/DVD, Internet access (free), minibar; private pool.

Villa Balquisse ★★ 🛏 🏷 "If paradise existed, it can't be far from this" is what one guest wrote in the guest book here, and how right he is. It's hard to find fault with the lavishly decorated bedrooms in warm, earthy tones filled with artifacts, furniture, and pictures lovingly collected by the owner from her world travels. The adjoining spa is an ideal place to shake off the stresses of life in the most luxurious way possible. With additional personal touches such as free sarongs, free drop-offs to the beach in an old Volkswagen convertible, daily afternoon tea, and fruit sticks at 11am wherever you are, this little gem is hard to leave.

Jl. Uluwatu 18X, Jimbaran. www.balquisse.com. 𝄐 **0361/701695.** Fax 0361/703087. 9 units. High season US$180–US$240; low season US$150–US$210. Rates include breakfast. AE, MC, V. **Amenities:** Restaurant (Assam Garam, p. 141); babysitting; bikes; outdoor pool; spa. *In room:* A/C, hair dryer, minibar, Wi-Fi (free).

A Night out on the Rocks

Don't miss the Rock Bar ★★★ (5pm–1am) at the Ayana Resort & Spa (p. 138): It has one of the most stunning locations in Bali. Sitting at the base of sea cliffs, it's so close to the water's edge that the lovely salty sea mist of the crashing waves inspires romance—and a bit of fear. Choose from a long list of cocktails (starting at Rp95,000). Tables are also set in a special section you access via a cable car. DJs perform regularly. This is the sort of spot where expats bring visitors to experience the decadence of living large on the edge.

INEXPENSIVE

Puri Bambu 🛏 Although Puri Bambu has no beachfront, it's in Kedonganan, a peaceful traditional village near Jimbaran, and the beach is only 5 minutes walk away. The large rooms frame lovely garden courtyards, one of which holds a decent-size pool. Be sure to take an early morning or early evening walk around the village to get a feel for the age-old traditions that make Bali so beautiful.

Jl. Pengeracikan, Kedonganan. www.puribambu.com. ✆ **0361/701468.** 48 units. High season US$65–US$95; low season US$50–US$80; extra bed US$12. Rates include taxes and breakfast. MC, V. **Amenities:** Cafe; bar; airport transfer; babysitting; concierge; outdoor pool; room service. *In room:* A/C, TV, hair dryer (on request), minibar, Wi-Fi.

Where to Eat

VERY EXPENSIVE

Kisik ★ SEAFOOD *Kisik* is Balinese for "cliff rising out of the ocean," and is an apt name for this location. The restaurant sits on the shore at the foot of the cliff, a superb sunset spot. At night hundreds of twinkling lights from local fishing boats bob out at sea. The idea here is a copy of the typical Balinese warung with superb service and five-star prices. The menu is determined by the catch of the day. Your catch is grilled in the open kitchen as you like. When the swell is large you can actually feel the mist from the surf. Ask for the corner table with killer views.

In the Ayana Resort & Spa (p. 138), Jl. Karang Mas Sejahtera, Jimbaran. ✆ **0361/702222.** www.ayanaresort.com. Reservations recommended. Fresh seafood Rp250,000–Rp600,000; lobster Rp800,000. AE, DC, MC, V. Daily 5:30–10pm.

PJ's ★★★ MEDITERRANEAN PJ's (Pantai Jimbaran) is a favorite with expats in Bali. Mediterranean-inspired dishes, seafood specialties, and crisp, thin-crust pizza from a wood-burning oven are all served in a breezy seaside pavilion where the palm-fringed bay lies at your feet. The restaurant, attached to the Four Seasons, is planning to upgrade by 2012 with a new poolside bar and a lounge feel. Don't miss the specialty starter of crispy crab cakes with cucumber mint salad, lime, and spicy tomato chutney. The snapper is cooked any way you like it, and, perhaps due to its proximity to the ocean, is the freshest you'll have on the island. The service is attentive but unobtrusive and the general vibe is one of relaxed indulgence. Finish off with the molten chocolate fondant with sour cherries and homemade vanilla ice cream or the chilled passion fruit cheesecake. Or have both.

In the Four Seasons Resort Bali (p. 137), Jimbaran Bay. ✆ **0361/701010.** www.fourseasons.com/jimbaran bay. Reservations recommended. Main courses Rp250,000–Rp715,000; set menu upon request. AE, MC, V. Daily 11am–10pm.

EXPENSIVE

Bella Singaraja ITALIAN You wouldn't expect good Italian food at a resort in Jimbaran Bay, but Bella Singaraja surprises even the most jaded expats. The decor is, unfortunately, a bad attempt at creating a grand dining room, but the food and service more than make up for the copper chiffon curtains. It's always a good start to have a superb antipasto of Italian prosciutto, ham, and mortadella. The veal parmigiana is a fine choice, and the grilled prawns and salad are hard to resist.

In the Hotel InterContinental (p. 138), Jl. Uluwatu 45, Jimbaran. ℂ **0361/701888.** www.bali-intercontinental. com. Reservations recommended. Main courses Rp220,000–Rp460,000; AE, DC, MC, V. Daily 6:30–10:30pm.

Dava ★★★ INTERNATIONAL One of this restaurant's best attributes—other than the martini bar—is its design. The entrance features an open-air reception island, seemingly floating above a free-form pool, which in turn hovers above the Indian Ocean. The setting doesn't detract from the excellent food. The chef says, like most places in Jimbaran, that he serves international cuisine with, "fresh flavors predominately from the sea." A good example of this would be the Five Flavors of the Sea starter: "Lobster, bacon, vinaigrette, orange, sprouts, salmon, lime, black bean, mint, wasabi sorbet, pearl meat, vine ripened tomato, sesame, wakame, yellowfin tuna, Chinese olive praline, caper vinaigrette, chives, Morton Bay bug tail tempura, squid ink, and lemon peel." What a mouthful! There's a great "Martini Club Assiette" where you choose three mini-martinis, out of the selection of 50 on offer, for the price of one.

In the Ayana Resort & Spa (p. 138), Jl. Karang Mas Sejahtera, Jimbaran. ℂ **0361/702222.** www. ayanaresort.com. Reservations recommended. Main courses Rp260,000–Rp580,000 a couple; set menu Rp390,000–Rp500,000. AE, DC, MC, V. Daily 7-10:30am and 6:30-10:30pm.

Honzen 97 ★★ JAPANESE/KOREAN Honzen ("wonderful food") is a traditional Japanese/Korean restaurant for top-quality dining. Choose between *tatami* (Japanese mat) or traditional seating; downstairs is sushi and sashimi and upstairs is Korean. Honzen's sashimi is off the charts compared to the rest of the island.

In the Ayana Resort & Spa (p. 138), Jl. Karang Mas Sejahtera, Jimbaran. ℂ **0361/702222.** www. ayanaresort.com. Reservations recommended. Main courses Rp100,000–Rp1,800,000; set menu teppanyaki Rp700,000–Rp1,200,000; *yakiniku* Rp450,00–Rp800,000. AE, DC, MC, V. Daily noon-2:30pm and 5:30-11pm.

KO Restaurant ★★ JAPANESE Before dinner at one of the island's best Japanese restaurants, enjoy live entertainment, drinks in the sushi lounge, and light snacks of sushi or delicious *robatayaki* skewers, and tempura. Dine in a separate sushi lounge and bar, in a private dining room, or a teppanyaki area where guests watch the culinary flair of Chef Wayan Badra, trained in Kyoto with a Japanese master. Smiling, delicate girls in brightly colored kimonos show you to your table. It's only when you notice their slightly uncomfortable walk in their *tabi* (white socks) with flip flops that you recognize their Balinese origins.

In the Hotel InterContinental (p. 138), Jl. Uluwatu 45, Jimbaran. ℂ **0361/701888.** www.bali-intercontinental. com. Reservations recommended. Main courses Rp290,000–Rp360,000; AE, MC, V. Daily 6:30-11pm.

MODERATE

Assam Garam ★ 🍴 INDONESIAN/MIDDLE EASTERN This charming restaurant opens onto the fertile gardens of the Villa Balquisse. This isn't haute cuisine; it's honest from the heart cooking. For appetizers, it can be hard to choose from a selection of dishes such as light and fresh scallop carpaccio with lime and olive oil marinade; New Zealand lamb and mint rolls; and Moroccan salad, a blend of vegetables, olives, feta, and herbs. Two pages of main courses offer Balinese delights such as roasted duck with spinach, star anise chicken on ginger risotto, and the popular lamb kebab with couscous and vegetables. For dessert, it's hard to resist the almond pear tart and the delicious selection of homemade ice cream.

In Villa Balquisse (p. 139), Jl. Uluwatu, Jimbaran. ✆ **0361/701695.** www.balquisse.com. Reservations recommended. Main courses Rp40,000–Rp90,000; children's menu Rp35,000. AE, MC, V. Daily 7am–10pm.

Nelayan ★★ ☺ FRENCH/MEDITERRANEAN   The Nelayan is all about the chef, and its stunning setting is the icing on the cake. French Executive Chef Lionel Auvray has an impressive track record of five-star cooking around the globe. Children get their own menu and plenty of beachfront to run wild on while you enjoy the *fruits de mer*. The Lobster Extravaganza is an indulgent and delicious five courses, starting with a cocktail, followed by the *amuse-bouche* of thinly sliced lobster and avocado in a raspberry sauce. This is followed by lobster ravioli and lobster medallions in vanilla sauce. Your little banquet ends with a fresh strawberry soup with lemon sorbet.

In the Jimbaran Puri Bali (p. 138), Jl. Uluwatu, Jimbaran. ✆ **0361/701605.** www.jimbaranpuribali.com. Reservations recommended. Main courses Rp210,000–Rp634,000. AE, MC, V. Daily noon–5pm and 7–10:30pm.

Tapis ★   INDONESIAN/WESTERN   This simple and chic restaurant serves inventive Indonesian cuisine and a rijsttafel. The open-air kitchen is on view in a thatched pavilion. Western dishes include all the usual pastas and seafood.

In the Kayumanis Jimbaran (p. 138), Jl. Yoga Perkanthi, Jimbaran. ✆ **0361/705777.** www.kayumanis.com. Reservations recommended. Main courses Rp60,000–Rp265,000; set menus Rp500,000. AE, MC, V. Daily 7am–10pm.

INEXPENSIVE

Jimbaran is a mecca for seafood, with more than two dozen **seafood restaurants** ★★ located right on the beach. The restaurants are quiet at lunchtime but as the sun goes down, crowds arrive to admire the beautiful sunsets and paddle in the sea. Once dark, torches and candles create a wonderfully romantic atmosphere. Diners seat themselves at tables on the beach. The restaurants essentially serve the same fresh catches with a few offering some choice of cooking style.

There are now three distinct sections of seafood shacks. Those at the far end of the bay are the originals—these are locally owned and therefore have a stake in the future and reputation of the area. The newer places are near the Four Seasons and have better toilets and furniture; some also have a full bar service. Check all prices as they tend to get better the farther you go toward the end of the bay. The original strip is better than the newer one between the Four Seasons and InterContinental. The third strip, closest to the airport, is best avoided: They're the greatest rip-offs and possibly unlicensed by the local authorities.

Options are crab, clams, fish, lobster, prawns, and squid laid out at the restaurant entrance on beds of ice and, given the turnover, all guaranteed fresh that day. You can either leave the staff to select the items or go directly to the barbecue area and choose yourself. It's better to pick your own, although actually identifying it after it has been cooked is trickier. Agreeing on a price (see box, "Weighing up the Seafood") up front ensures no surprises later on and don't be afraid to try to haggle—it's expected. The restaurants are rarely expensive and aren't known for ripping anyone off, so be kind. Some places suggest that they don't haggle, but the majority price it in. Keep your ears open to what the local expats are paying per kilo. You'll be amazed by the difference.

Weighing up the Seafood

You pay only for the seafood you select and your drinks in Jimbaran seafood restaurants. The peanuts, vegetables, and platter of fruit at the end should be included. Seafood is sold by the "kilo," although many of the scales are questionable and the restaurateurs expect you to bargain—it's part of the fun. But if you want to be precise, check the scales with a liter of water, which equals 1 kilo. Then you know that they aren't inflating the price.

Prices are reasonable with dinner for two with beer or soft drinks approximately R150,000 to Rp250,000. Wine is available but usually only local Balinese Hatten wine, which is best drunk very cold or very quickly. Feel free to bring your own wine and ask whether corkage applies.

Menega Cafe ★★ SEAFOOD   This place stands out from a row of restaurants that basically offer the same thing for its more unique grilling approach: Most places grill on coconut shells, but here some secret ingredient is added. Though you can certainly enjoy some pleasant conversation and a few Bintang beers with the manager, you'll never get him to tell you the secret.

Jl. Four Seasons Muaya Beach, Jimbaran. ℂ**0361/705888.** www.menega.com. Rp20,000–Rp420,000. MC, V. Daily 8am–midnight.

Pepe Nero ITALIAN ✦   If you're tired of all the hotel fare around Jimbaran and have already been to the seafood stalls (see above), this casual Italian restaurant with a view of Jimbaran Bay is a decent choice for pastas and pizzas. Although the dishes certainly aren't award-winning, it's wildly popular with expats and tourists and is easy on your wallet.

Jl. Wanagiri 18, Jimbaran. ℂ**0361/702111.** Fax 0361/704677. Pepenerobali.com. Rp29,000–Rp190,000. MC, V. Daily 11am–11pm.

Shopping

An increasing number of higher-end retail outlets are on the main access stretch, Jalan Raya Uluwatu. Shops here are spread out, and so map where you're going beforehand. Stores are open daily, typically from 9am to 6 or 7pm.

Cocoon Home   Cocoon is for your home and yourself. Attractive jewelry on sale is from Italy, Mali, and a selection of well-known Bali designers and a Canadian designer working mainly with pearls. Shop for silk scarves with batik designs, cotton sarongs, hats, and bags. For the home, you'll find salad servers and spoons made from horn and silver, and a super selection of picture frames. Jl. Uluwatu 91, Jimbaran. ℂ**0361/705054.**

Ganesha Gallery ★★   This small gallery has a big heart and attracts a flow of dealers, buyers, and admirers. The Ganesha Gallery exhibits a different local or international artist four times a year. Works by both international and local artists always emphasize a connection between the East and West, with a definite eye toward the beauty of Bali. In Four Seasons Resort, Jimbaran. (p. 137). ℂ**0361/701010.**

Jenggala Ceramics ★★★   From humble beginnings in a small crowded workshop on Sanur Beach, Jenggala Ceramics has grown into a multimillion-dollar business that exports around the world. The studio was founded by two, now deceased, Balinese legends: Brent Hesselyn, a New Zealand designer and potter, and Wija

Waroruntu, an Indonesian hotelier. Wija's daughter, Ade, has since taken over the business. You'll encounter ceramics all over Bali—from the markets to your breakfast table—but the best ones are Jenggala. The inspiration comes from natural forms such as frangipani, bamboo, and banana and lotus leaves. The tableware collections in a variety of colors and custom-made sets can be ordered and shipped around the world. An impressive client list includes Chef Jean-Georges Vongerichten who orders sets for his high-profile restaurants in New York, London, and Paris. Monthly exhibits include private collections as well as work of artist-in-residence, Anne van Borselen, a sculptor and a painter from Holland. Visiting and local artists also present ceramics shows here. Jl. Uluwatu II, Jimbaran. ✆ **0361/703311.** www.jenggala.com.

Paul Ropp ★★   Paul Ropp started his career selling marijuana-rolling papers with the U.S. flag on them in New York. He made so much money from this venture that he funded his world travels and wound up in Bali in the 1970s. He and his wife started buying and selling clothes between India and Bali. Now Ropp has dozens of shops on Bali and franchises around the world. All his fabrics originate from over 5,000 Indian workers who operate in home industries to produce intricate, colorful silks, cottons, and wool. Each piece is a bit of bohemian Versace; embrace the company slogan: "Clothes for people who prefer to be naked." Jl. Uluwatu 80, Jimbaran. ✆ **0361/701202.** www.paulropp.com.

Tiempo   This wonderful shop sells decorative art, antiques, and furniture from Java and China and some simply marvelous pieces from Sulawesi, Timor, and Nusa Tenggara. This is a place where you can find something really special to bring home from your Indonesia travels. Jl. Raya Uluwatu I 102, Jimbaran. ✆ **0361/745-0919.**

Warisan Casa   The eclectic and fusion furniture designs here utilize durable timber such as plantation teak, mahogany, and recycled teak with other materials, such as leather, fabrics, glass, and metals. Warisan strives for every product to "last for generations" while reflecting the meaning of *warisan*—Indonesian for "heritage." Jl. Raya Bypass Ngurah Rai Kedonganan. ✆ **0361/701081.** www.warisan.com.

MARKET

Go early to the **Jimbaran fish market ★★★** (also known as Kedonganan Fish Market), on the northeast corner of the main crossroads in the village, just across the street from Pura Ulun Siwi temple. The market opens at 4am and sells the highest quality and freshest seafood in all south Bali. The market and adjacent beach at Jimbaran Bay are hives of morning activity. Colorful wooden boats with their high prows, decorated masts, and ropes covered in bright flags provide a bright burst of color. These elaborately dressed boats come from Java, Sulawesi, and Flores, and stop on every island to sell their catch. The waters nearest to Bali are often overfished, and so most of the seafood comes from other nearby waters. Young boys rush to the boats to help pull them onto shore for the market stall owners to inspect the catch.

 Paint-a-Pot & Make-a-Pot at Jenggala Ceramics

At Jenggala Ceramics, children of all ages can explore their inner Picasso by painting raw, glazed ceramic. If you want to handle your own clay, 2- and 4-hour sessions are priced according to the kilos of clay used. Make a reservation for a group visit of more than two people. Hours for Paint-a-Pot are 9am to 5pm; Paint-a-Pot is US$6 to US$20 depending on the size of pot, Make-a-Pot is US$12 (plus cost of clay).

Buying Fresh Fish

Most villas and even hotels will be happy to have you bring back a fish and cook it for you any way you'd like. Hotels might charge a small fee but the chef at your villa won't. Follow these four steps when buying fish:

- Be prepared. Bring some ice in a cooler or waterproof container so you can transport your fish home. This is crucial no matter how long or short the drive.

- Use your nose. If fish smells fishy, it's not fresh. Fresh fish shouldn't smell bad.
- Use your hands and eyes. When picking your fish, be sure that it has clear eyes and a firm feel. When fish start to go off, their eyes get misty and their flesh gets limp.
- Get it gutted. Tell the seller to gut your fish for you; if you want it scaled, ask.

ULUWATU ★★

On the southwestern tip of the Bukit, Uluwatu is perched high on a cliff overlooking the Indian Ocean. Down below are stretches of secluded beaches, few accessible by road—the only way down is by foot (not for the fainthearted). This also happens to be one of the most famous surf breaks in the world. The views from the cliffs overlooking the break are stupendous and satisfying enough for most visitors.

Getting There & Getting Around

A **taxi** from Kuta to Uluwatu takes 1 hour (in light traffic) up and down winding and dusty, unpaved limestone roads; cost is about Rp150,000 one-way. Make sure you have the contact number of your destination because many taxi drivers will get lost.

Taxis within Uluwatu range in price from Rp50,000-Rp100,000.

Exploring Uluwatu

Garuda Vishnu Kencara Cultural Park ⚑ We'd be remiss if we didn't mention this monstrosity. The park sits above Jimbaran Bay, and was intended to be the greatest cultural park in Indonesia with an enormous statue of the Hindu god Vishnu. If it's ever completed it will be taller than the Statue of Liberty in New York City. The very park's essence is widely debated in Bali among the local population, with some saying it was intended to serve as a "Welcome to Bali" landmark for passengers arriving by plane, while others state simply that it makes a mockery of the Hindu religion.

Jl. Raya Uluwatu, Ungasan Kuta Selatan. ✆ **0361/703603.** www.gwk-culturalpark.com. Admission Rp50,000 adults & children. Daily 8am-9pm.

Pura Luhur Uluwatu ★★ Dramatically perched on a high promontory overlooking the surf at Uluwatu, this is possibly Bali's most visually spectacular shrine. Its name literally translates as "the one on the top." Like most other temples in Bali, the origin is obscure, however inscriptions signed during the reign of King Marakata date the temple to at least 1025. The temple is well known for its walet birds, which can be seen floating and darting in the breeze and perching on the sacred temple. Their nests are an important ingredient in Chinese birds' nest soup.

Dedicated to the spirits of the sea, the temple is an architectural wonder in black coral rock, and despite its age and exposure to the elements, features well-preserved stone carvings. This is one of the six directional temples on the island and is the

Every evening at sunset (6pm) at Pura Luhur Uluwatu dancers present a thrilling performance of kecak, arguably Bali's most famous and dramatic dance. It will cost about Rp5,000 to enter the temple and an additional Rp70,000 to view the dance. Both men and women need to rent sarongs and sashes at the entrance if you're not already traditionally dressed.

southwest guardian against evil spirits. It's also purportedly the dwelling place of almighty deity Bhatana Ruda, god of the elements and cosmic forces. Although the temple complex is open to all, only Hindus are allowed to enter the inner temple. Jl. Labuan Sait, Pantai Suluban, Uluwatu. Admission Rp25,000 adults & children. Daily 8am–6pm.

BEACHES 🏠 Although strong rip currents and shallow waters make the beaches less than ideal for swimming, they're still great for getting wet and enjoying the stunning scenery. Uluwatu is all about the **views. Balangan,** an idyllic, white-sand beach fringed by cliffs, is relatively quiet and is spared the annoying trinket hawkers and too many tourists. A few cafes sit near the tree line, and the water here is safe for swimming, as the waves break over the reef 200m (656 ft.) from the shore. **Bingin ★★★** beach is pockmarked with rock and reef, forming intriguing tide pools at low tide. **Impossibles** beach is another great setting for a seaside walk at low tide, but is more well-known as a prime surf break. **Padang Padang ★★** is archetypically enchanting, being nestled into a pocket of lava rocks; the beach entrance is through a cave crevice. This area is great at low tide for children.

PAINTBALLING ☺ **Paintball Bali,** Jl. Karang Putih 1 (✆ **0361/770300;** www.paintballbali.com; US$65 includes pickup and drop-off, 150 bullets, three waters, one soft drink, and a hot dog; value package US$40 includes 100 bullets, three waters, one soft drink, and fries; daily 9am–5pm), occupies about 3 hectares (7½ acres) of playing fields. Facilities include individual changing rooms and lockers. Have lunch off-site as the offerings here are of the hot-dogs-and-fries variety, even though some food is included in the price. Better yet, bring your own picnic.

PARAGLIDING Take the opportunity to fly over the glittering Indian Ocean, shimmering green rice terraces, and those crazy surfers. Seeing Bali from the sky is a vibrant reminder why this island was earmarked "Island of the Gods." You don't want to go with a paragliding service that isn't up to scratch, so make sure your chosen company has certification from the Bali branch of the Indonesian Aerosport Federation. We recommend tandem flights with **Exo-Fly ★**, Jl. Toyaning 24, Kedonganan (✆ **0361/705517** or 081/1393919; www.exofly.com; US$69 per person, but if you book as a family they charge US$59 per person).

SPA The **Bulgari spa ★★**, Jl. Goa Lempeh, Br. Dinas Kangin, Uluwatu (✆ **0361/ 847-1000;** www.bulgarihotels.com; daily 9am–9pm) is worth a day's indulgence. This is probably one of the finest spas on Bali, housed in an antique, hand-carved teak *joglo* (Javanese house) that was dismantled in Kudos on Java, and authentically re-created on-site. Go for broke with the aptly named "Unforgettable Double Bulgari Royal Lulur" for two people, which lasts 3 hours and includes two therapists per person. Prices are steep (US$93–US$975; AE, DC, MC, V) and so plan on making a full day out of your pampering and use the pool and the relaxation area.

SURFING Some of the best surfing spots in Bali and indeed the world, can be found in the sea surrounding the west coast of the Bukit. These breaks are for experienced surfers only—they're definitely not to be tackled by novices. If the size of the waves doesn't get you, the razor sharp shallow reef will. The best time to surf here is during the dry season (Apr–Oct).

Uluwatu **Best swell:** south; **best size:** 3 to 10 feet; **best winds:** southeast. Home to the famous Uluwatu temple and its colony of crazy monkeys, a casual visitor could be forgiven for overlooking the other zoo down the cliff and in the water at **Saluban Beach,** break point for Bali's most famous waves. This beach has four distinct sections. The farthest out is **Temples,** which likes a mid to high tide and offers long, hollow rides toward the **Peak,** a second take-off spot directly out from Wayan Gondry's famous Green Iguana warung. The third section breaks furiously over a shallow reef and is aptly named **Race Track:** Speed is the key to survival here. Beyond that, toward Padang Padang, is **Outside Corner,** which comes into its own on only the biggest days but provides some of the most incredible heart-in-mouth surfing available on the planet. If you get it wrong here you're washed toward the dangerously jagged rocks of the cliff-line and face a tediously long and treacherous swim back to safety. Sound like fun?

Padang Padang **Best swell:** south; **best size:** 5 to 8 feet; **best winds:** southeast. Just north of Uluwatu is not only one of Bali's premier surf locations, but also one of Bali's nicest beaches. At Padang Padang, an easy paddle out from the lagoon-like shoreline delivers you into the gaping jaws of one of the world's most celebrated left-handers. Best on bigger swells, Padang Padang is a true proving-ground for local and international surfers alike. Be sure to pop into the **Sunset Grill** (p. 153) on the road linking Padang Padang with Bingin.

Impossibles **Best swell:** south; **best size:** 4 to 8 feet; **best winds:** southeast. This long stretch of reef runs north from Padang Padang down to Bingin and owes its name to the incredibly fast and long waves that explode along the "picture perfect" reef. Though widely heralded as an oasis of sorts, given the right swell period and direction Impossibles can still deliver unbelievable waves that will be etched forever in salt across a surfer's memory. It's rare that surfers actually make it, and so expect an absolute beating if you're outrun by the watery freight train and left to battle with the coming wider, wilder sets. Surf it on the mid-tides and on larger swells.

Bingin **Best swell:** south; **best size:** 3 to 5 feet; **best winds:** southeast trade winds. This is one of the best, albeit shortest, left-hand barrels available in Bali. A short, hollow, and punchy ride, Bingin is fondly followed by hordes of local and international surfers looking for an easy bit of tube time.

 Resident Monkeys

Watch out for the local monkeys at Pura Luhur Uluwatu that like to help themselves to hats, handbags, cameras, and even your glasses. They're usually happy to exchange your valuables for some fruit, but try to avoid this tedious and potentially dangerous negotiation.

Locals also standby and act as go-betweens, though you're expected to give them a tip if they help you get your possessions back; some visitors suspect a racket . . . or do we mean "monkey" business?

Sand Fleas

Depending on the time of year and the flow of certain currents you may encounter sand fleas on Uluwatu beach. They seem to be particular to Uluwatu and nobody knows why. It could be because the water here is a bit cooler due to its depth and sand fleas migrate with the flow of currents and in cooler climes. They're invisible at first but once you start feeling the bite, and take a closer look, you'll see that they look like sand. They're perfectly harmless but can be very annoying. Repel them with heavy-duty mosquito repellent or very strong citronella.

Dreamland   **Best swell:** south-southwest; **best size:** 3 to 5 feet; **best winds:** southeast trade winds. This used to be one of the most beautiful and picturesque beaches on all Bali—fully deserving of the apt name. Now the charming, old warungs are gone and the once pristine landscape has been butchered for a monstrosity of a hotel structure to be implanted on the previously amazing cliff-face (p. 149). The golf course hosted the 2008 Indonesian Cup Tournament, for those surfers who like a bit of golf trivia.

Wavewise, Dreamland is a mellow option surrounded by more serious waves, and thus attracts hordes of less skilled surfers. This is still a good option for a cruise session and is best on lower tides. Keep your eyes on everyone and don't forget your mouth guard because collisions are common here.

Balangan   **Best swell:** south; **best size:** 4 to 8 feet; **best winds:** southeast. Balangan is a left-hand wave breaking off the headland to the north of Dreamland. It can be found easily these days owing to the signs and newly sealed roads delivering you straight to this once semi-secret location. As a fast and hollow wave, Balangan has the habit of catching surfers unaware as the bigger sets loom much farther out than where the pack normally assembles. Sitting farther out can pay dividends: As the big sets come, your new friends will watch with jealousy as you take off free from trouble as they contemplate their own imminent smashing. Surf here on the mid- to higher tides.

Surf Board Repairs

If you ding your board, "Cookie the Legend" will fix it for you. From the bottom of the stairs to Uluwatu Surfing Beach, go left. He's the last one in a string of warungs before you reach the cave. You can't miss it.

If you're walking around the cliff tops here, look out for the craggy rocks and be sure not to stub your toes while watching the waves. Also look out for the green pit viper snakes; while rare, they are dangerous (but not deadly). If bitten, allow your wound to bleed for a few minutes, bandage it, and seek medical attention immediately.

Green Balls   Best swell: south; best size: 4 to 6 feet; best winds: west-northwest. Located just near the Bali Cliff Resort (on the peninsula's southern face), the main wave at Green Balls is the right-hander at the bottom of the stairs. On the other side of the channel the left-hander can get good too, with lighter winds or days when there's some north in the breeze. You can check the wave from the cliff top, which is a blessing given the 500 or so steps down to the sand. Hire a local to help you with your gear and take plenty of water. It's a long way down and in this case, what goes down must come back up.

WATERPARK ☺ The **New Kuta Green Park** (Jl. Raya Uluwatu; ✆ **0361 848-4777;** www.newkutagreenpark.com) is located in the massive development in Pecatu. This new waterpark promises fun for the whole family, with waterslides, inner tubes that coast down an artificial river, and a wave pool that simulates breaks for beginner surfers. Trampolines and a bird park will keep the water-phobic entertained. It certainly gives longtime waterpark Waterbom (see p. 69) in Kuta some competition. Admission is free for children measuring under 80cm (31.5 in.) and Rp100,000 for everyone else. The park is open daily 9am to 6pm.

Where to Stay

The main choice of accommodations in Uluwatu is between five-star-uber-luxury hotel or multimillion-dollar villa. One new luxury property to look out for is the **Anantara**, which will debut in early 2012. However, in recent years, many of the rustic surfer accommodations have come of age and make a good alternative for those on a budget.

VERY EXPENSIVE

Alila Villas Uluwatu ★★ This top-of-the-line eco-resort has Green Globe's stamp of approval, meaning that all the materials are sustainable or recycled and the use of water and energy meets stringent requirements. Perched upon a plateau of wild savanna landscape, every villa has a spectacular ocean view and its own pool. Each guest is assigned a personal butler who coordinates with a leisure concierge to customize experiences that meet your interests, schedule, and preferences. It also offers "Alila Journeys," half-day wellness programs that include yoga and meditation

PECATU INDAH development & THE NEW KUTA

Once called Dreamland in Pecatu Indah, this development is now called New Kuta—a strange name and an even stranger place. The original name came from a white-sand beach on the western coast of the Bukit peninsula, a favorite haunt for local and international tourists due to its gorgeous beach, laid-back warungs, and a slice of old Bali beach life, which many (including us) considered paradise. Sadly "Dreamland" has become a nightmare. Several years ago Tommy Suharto, disgraced son of the former Indonesian president, and his rich cronies tried to develop Dreamland into something grander, but the group initially went bankrupt. Today, they're back in the chips, and the New Kuta development is going full steam ahead. The 400-hectare (1,000-acre) project is well underway and will include private residences, luxury hotels, a convention center, theme park, hospital retirement community, and an international school. The area already has a completed golf course overlooking the old Dreamland beach and recently hosted the 2009 Indonesian Open—the first PGA Golf event to be held in Bali. A huge desalination pipe to water the golf course now runs out into the surf, thus changing the breaks, and will eventually change the coastline of the area. New Kuta bills itself as "the most beautiful investment in the world." Some beg to differ.

classes and self-care recommendations, Bali arts and crafts, culinary experiences, and excursions. While staying here, slip into the cliff-top Sunset Cabana for dinner at dusk and simply get inebriated on the sea air and stars.

Jl. Belimbing Sari, Banjar Tambiyak, Desa Pecatu. www.alilahotels.com. ✆ **0361/848-2166.** Fax 0361/848-2188. 85 units. High season US$715 and up; low season US$650 and up. Rates do not include 21% taxes and breakfast. AE, MC, V. **Amenities:** 3 restaurants; babysitting; gym; outdoor pool; spa. *In villa:* A/C, TV/DVD, hair dryer, minibar, Wi-Fi (free).

Banyan Tree Resort & Spa ★★   One of the best new resorts on the island, the Banyan Tree is the perfect escape if you're looking for a romantic vacation situated around a private villa. Each is palatial, outfitted with an elegant living room, dining area, and bedroom with high ceilings. The villas are located on a steep hill serviced by buggies—all come with spacious plunge pools and Jacuzzis, the latter a rare feature on the island. Some also come with breathtaking ocean views. The staff is friendly, helpful, and not too obtrusive. Book a treatment at the luxurious spa. The beach beneath the resort is gorgeous, if a little rocky—walk a few hundred meters to the right to the Karma Kandara for a better, swimmable shore.

Jl. Melasti, Banjar Kelod, Ungasan. www.banyantree.com. ✆ **0361/300-7000.** Fax 0361/300-7777. 71 units. High season prices rise 15%; low season US$445–US$510 standard rooms, US$995–US$4,500 villas. Rates include breakfast. AE, DC, MC, V. **Amenities:** 3 restaurants; bar; infinity pool; gym; children's club; spa. *In room:* A/C; TV; minibar; private infinity pool, Wi-Fi.

Karma Kandara Villas ★   Karma Kandara is one of the more impressive resorts in Bali. The villas are all privately owned, so while you're in residence you feel comfortably at home, albeit not your own. The one- to four-bedroom whitewashed poolside villas sitting above the surf are covered in bougainvillea. Most bedrooms face the sea and have semi-outdoor bathrooms with grandiose stand-alone tubs for two. The plunge pools have dark wooden decks that make a more private alternative to the resort's main pool, but the *pièce de résistance* is **Nammos Beach Club,** accessed by a private "inclinator" down the near sheer cliff face. Sitting on an impossibly picturesque beach with a fertile coral reef just offshore, this club is great for snorkeling and is exclusive to guests, albeit only thanks to its privileged inaccessibility. DJ music spins nightly. Non-resort guests can pay US$25 to use the beach club facilities for the day. A sister resort is the **Karma Jimbaran** (www.karmajimbaran.com) in Jimbaran Bay, though it's not as fabulous as this location.

Jl. Villa Kandara, Br. Wijaya Kusuma, Ungasan. www.karmakandara.com. ✆ **0361/848-2200.** Fax 0361/848-2201. 46 villas. Peak season US$1,120 and up; high season US$990 and up; low season US$865 and up. Rates include breakfast. AE, MC, V. **Amenities:** Restaurant (Di Mare, p. 153); bar; babysitting; bikes; children's club; gym; Jacuzzi; outdoor pool; room service; spa; watersports. *In villa:* A/C, TV/DVD, hair dryer, minibar, MP3 docking station, Wi-Fi.

EXPENSIVE

Semara Luxury Villa Resort Uluwatu   The new Semara gives its next-door neighbor the Karma Kandara a run for its money. The set of eight chicly-designed villas, each with its own style ranging from colonial to modern, straddles the cliffs with panoramic views of the Indian Ocean and features large gardens with large pools. There's access to a private beach, restaurant, and bar via a steep inclinator. Some of the villas' rooms can be rented individually as hotel rooms. The resort also features one of Bali's few grass tennis courts and a helicopter pad.

Jl. Pantai Selatan Gau, Banjar Wjaya Kusuma, Ungasan. www.semarauluwatu.com. ✆ **0361/848-2111.** Fax 0361/848-2308. 7 units. Peak season US$715–US$935 suites, US$2,570–US$5970 villas; high season US$605–US$825 suites, US$1,920–US$4,840 villas; low season US$495–US$715 suites, US$1,470–US$3,740

LUXURY villas IN ULUWATU

Groups are spoiled for choice in this area by entire estates that rent by the night.

The stunning Karang Putih Villa ★★, Jl. Karang Putih 1, Banjar Kutuh Ungasan, Uluwatu (www.elitehavensbali.com; ✆ 0361/731074; 6 bedrooms; peak season US$2,800; high season US$2,200; low season US$1,500; rates include breakfast; AE, MC, V), has a colonial feel with a modern twist, elegantly furnished with Asian antiquities. The villa has its own private beach club, a floodlit grass tennis court, boules court, putting green, and helipad.

From the Sanskrit word for "Seventh Heaven," we get the Khayangan ★★★, Jl. Goa Lempeh, Pecatu, Uluwatu (www.khayanganestate.com; ✆ 0361/895-4733; fax 0361/736705; 6 villas; peak season US$3,500; high season US$3,500; low season US$3,000; AE, MC, V), a private villa above Selonding Beach, with an unobstructed view of the Indian Ocean. This villa's unique design features 11 antique joglo, once the traditional homes of Javanese aristocracy. The villa has two infinity edge pools, a spa, a tennis court, and even lawn croquet.

Sunsets can be seen from the two master bedrooms fronting the ocean in the Karang Kambar Estate ★, Jl. Karang Kembar, Banjar Jabapura, Desa Kutuh, Kuta Selatan, Badung (www.bali-karang kembarestate.com; ✆ 65/9018-1742 in Singapore; 5 bedrooms; peak season US$1,350 and up; high season US$1,250 and up; low season US$1,000 and up; rates include breakfast; AE, MC, V). The villa has a private beach house on the reef, making it an ideal place to go with children when the tide is out because there are some very exotic fish in the tide pools.

The Long House ★★, Jl. Goa Gong, Kompleks Tiara Nusa, Jimbaran (www.thelonghousebali.com; ✆ 0361/780-3046; 6 bedrooms; peak season US$1,650; high season US$1,150; low season US$900; extra bed US$25; rates include breakfast; AE, MC, V), perched just above the village of Goa Gong above Jimbaran, was built to take advantage of a 180-degree view of endless glassy blue Indian Ocean and the volcanoes in the horizon. The villa has a spa, gym, Jacuzzi, and movie theater; there's even an elevator to get to the three stories without lifting a finger . . . well maybe just to push a button.

Villa Bulan Putih ★★★, Jl. Pantai Bingin Labuan Sait, Pecatu (www.villa bulanputih.com; no phone; 7 bedrooms; peak season US$1,500 7-night minimum stay; high season US$1,500 5-night minimum stay; low season US$1,200 3-night minimum stay; AE, MC, V), is all subdued tones and minimalist modern sculpture that create a sense of calm. Nothing distracts from the stunning views beyond the French windows. A big plus is the immaculate lawn for the wee ones to wander and play impromptu ball games.

villas. Minimum 2- to 4-night stays in villas. Rates include breakfast in suites. Rates do not include 20% taxes. MC, V. **Amenities:** Restaurant; beach bar; gym; golf putting green; infinity pool; 2 floodlit tennis courts; spa. *In room:* A/C, TV, MP3 docking stations, Wi-Fi (free).

MODERATE

Mick's Place Mick's Place in Bingin, near Uluwatu, is a surfer's dream come true. During the past 8 years Mick has built six seriously simple Polynesian-influenced round huts on this patch of cliff above Bingin Beach. It's a perfect location for those who want to explore the famous surf breaks nearby, heal their senses at Mick's Yoga Sanctuary, or rejuvenate body and soul at the on-site restaurant. Rooms only have cold water and are mainly candlelit. Mick also offers shopping expeditions and will even provide you with his own driver.

Jl. Pantai Bingin II, Bingin Beach. www.micksplacebali.com. ☏ **0361/847-0858.** 6 units. High season US$90–US$250; low season US$70–US$200. No credit cards. **Amenities:** Restaurant; outdoor pool; room service. *In room:* Fan.

INEXPENSIVE

Mu Uluwatu   These nine thatched bungalows with wooden floors and stone walls overlook both Bingin and Impossibles, yet are within walking distance of Uluwatu and Padang Padang. Comfortable digs come with king-size beds, mosquito nets, and individual *bales* (thatched pavilions). A saltwater pool and Jacuzzi sit on a nice wooden deck with a smashing view. The friendly French management will arrange yoga on-site and sailing nearby; you can also rent mountain bikes.

Jl. Pantai Bingin, Pecatu. www.mu-bali.com. ☏ **0361/895-7442.** 9 units. Peak season US$70–US$180; high season US$60–US$160; low season US$55–US$150. Rates include taxes and breakfast. No credit cards. **Amenities:** Restaurant; bar; bikes; Jacuzzi; saltwater infinity pool; Wi-Fi (free). *In room:* Fan, TV/DVD (in Bintang bungalow only).

Udayana Kingfisher Eco Lodge ★   This is a superb choice for a very alternative holiday. The 30 hectares (74 acres) of bush land, overlooking Jimbaran and Benoa bays with views of Mount Agung, are protected by the University of Udayana as a flora and fauna refuge. All the eco-friendly buildings rely on solar power, while an extensive rainwater storage system keeps the gardens lush and prolific. The rooms are simple (bordering on spartan) with rattan and tropical materials used for the few bits and pieces of furniture. The 22 types of bougainvillea on-site are home to hundreds of butterflies, and make colorful playgrounds for the over 60 species of birds—the bulbul and the kingfisher being the most common sightings. The staff will give you a simple guidebook and loan you a set of binoculars. On Sundays, guests are welcome to join impromptu cricket matches on the lodge's pitch where several of Indonesia's matches have been held. You're likely to meet some interesting and likeminded people on your stay, as we did, when we befriended a Norwegian ornithologist who aided us in our quest for the kingfisher.

Jl. Kampus Universitas Udayana. www.ecolodgesindonesia.com. ☏ **0361/747-4204.** Fax 0361/701098. 15 units. Year-round US$85–US$90. AE, MC, V. **Amenities:** Restaurant; bar; lounge; outdoor pool; room service. *In room:* A/C, fan, Wi-Fi (free).

Where to Eat

The most noteworthy restaurants are in the large hotels and come with large hotel price tags, although a few cafes on Jalan Uluwatu are worth stopping for. Along the many beach breaks are plenty of local warungs that are good for a cold beer or a simple snack. Choose one that looks busy that day.

VERY EXPENSIVE

Il Ristorante & Sangkar ITALIAN/BALINESE   An Italian inspired and locally influenced cuisine distinguishes these two poolside restaurants in the Bulgari. Overlooking a reflection pool, the resort's signature **Il Ristorante ★★** has masterful Italian cuisine mixing the finest Italian ingredients with the islands' organic produce. For more casual, all-day dining, the **Sangkar** combines authentic Balinese dishes—enriched with various regional influences from the Indonesian archipelago—with a selection of international specialties. The homemade cookies are delicious. You can buy the condiments to bring home, making them possibly the most competitively priced goods with a Bulgari label.

Jl. Goa Lempeh, Br. Dinas Kangin, Uluwatu. ✆ **0361/847-1000.** www.bulgarihotels.com. Reservations recommended. Il Ristorante: main courses Rp300,000–Rp470,000; set menu Rp1,000,000. AE, DC, MC, V. Daily 6:30am–10:30pm (Il Ristorante dinner only).

EXPENSIVE

Di Mare ★ MEDITERRANEAN   Acclaimed as one of Bali's most spectacular dining venues and one of the must-see spots, the Di Mare frames the ocean and sky from atop a craggy overhang 85m (280 ft.) above a crystal lagoon. Executive Chef Raymond Saja turns out zestful Mediterranean-meets-Pacific-Rim cuisine accompanied by an exhaustive list of classic and new world wines. The kitchen uses the freshest season-driven local ingredients; fresh oysters are presented with aplomb.

In the Karma Kandara Resort (p. 150), Jl. Villa Kandara, Br. Wijaya Kusuma, Ungasan. ✆ **0361/848-2200.** www.karmakandara.com. Reservations recommended. Main courses Rp90,000–Rp340,000. AE, MC, V. Daily 7–11am and noon–4pm and 6–11pm.

INEXPENSIVE

Sunset Grill ★ 👫 MEXICAN   If the thought of going Latino appeals while in Bali, this is your place. Ten-year-old Sunset Grill, the first-ever restaurant in Uluwatu, is run by Cacho, from Puerto Rico. He and his Balinese wife make killer *chimichangas* (burritos) with fiery Indonesian chilis complemented by pitchers of marvelous margaritas. In the words of Cacho, "We have several rules here and people don't like that. The first is you can't be in a rush, we don't like beautiful, useless garnishes, and we never ever advertise, in fact we try to discourage business, because it gets too crowded. We only have three staff and me and 30 seats." Full meals without alcohol rarely go above US$7 but then meals are rarely without alcohol. Cacho also runs a pizza delivery service called Papi's (same phone number). A word of advice, don't sit in Cacho's chair.

On the beach in Padang Padang. ✆ **081/337406173.** Main courses Rp30,000–Rp65,000. No credit cards. From lunch until Cacho says it's closing.

Yeye's Warung & Gift Shop 👫 INDONESIAN/INTERNATIONAL   Yeye's is not your typical warung. You have plenty of choice, but the seafood salad of fresh local octopus and prawns is a favorite. The grilled mahimahi or snapper is served with a daily selection of fresh vegetables. If you want your fish served the local way, ask for it steamed in banana leaf with sambal. A few good Indian curries and Thai dishes are thrown in for good measure as are pizzas, *jaffles* (toasted sandwiches), burgers, sandwiches, pancakes, and desserts, which change daily. Thursday is a much-loved night for the barbecue of chicken, seafood, sausages, steaks, and kabobs. At night there's often a surf movie playing and it can all feel a bit Beach Blanket Bingo gone Tropo.

Jl. Labuan Sait, Pecatu. ✆ **0361/742-4761.** Main courses Rp27,000–Rp32,000. No credit cards. Noon–midnight. Past the bridge at Padang Padang beach on Jl. Uluwatu; go straight for a few meters.

NUSA DUA

Nusa Dua is a high-end tourist destination. The 300-hectare (740-acre) government-sponsored, self-contained resort is replete with a manicured golf course, swaying palms, white-sand beaches with pristine waters, and security gates at all entry and exit points. Virtually all accommodations here are five-star, and unlike the rest of the Bukit Peninsula with its barren shrub land and limestone cliffs, sandy soil reaches down to a long stretch of immaculate beach, protected by a reef. Coconut trees abound and remind us that before the local government fashioned this resort complex to "minimize the impact of tourism on the Balinese culture," Nusa Dua was once a coconut plantation. Also in contrast to the rest of the island, the roads are bereft of potholes, the streets are empty and litter free, and not surprisingly, it can all seem a bit sterile; it feels a bit like a gated community in Florida.

The immediate vicinity lacks activities. Many tourists seem content with simple R&R and, being only a 30-minute drive from the airport, it's a convenient place to base yourself on a short break.

Essentials

GETTING THERE & GETTING AROUND

Most if not all hotels in Nusa Dua offer an airport pickup service, but you can also find shuttles and cheap taxis at the airport. (Be sure to take only the official blue-and-yellow metered taxis.) *Bemo* from Denpasar go to Nusa Dua by way of Kuta and Jimbaran.

These big resorts make it so comfortable, you won't have to leave the grounds—but even the most starry-eyed honeymooners might want a break from expensive hotel meals. Hotel taxis are rentable at a pricey US$11 per hour; but if you're going out for the day, it can work out to be more convenient and more cost effective to rent a car and driver from the reliable, trusty taxi company **Amertha Dana ★★** (*☎* **0361/735406**).

Cycling (most hotels rent bikes) is a good way to get a feel for the lay of the land. The hotels are set side by side and a beachside boardwalk takes you all the way down the strip. It's about a 5km (3-mile) walk.

[FastFACTS] NUSA DUA

ATMs   There are ATMs at the St. Regis Resort and at the Bali Collection Mall.

Hospital/Clinic   Prima Medika Clinic, in the Grand Hyatt Hotel (p. 156; *☎* **0361/771234**), has general clinic hours from 9am to 9pm and a 24-hour on-call service.

Mail   Most hotels can send letters and postcards. For parcels and any recorded items the only post office in the area is Udayana, Bukit Ungasan, Nusa Dua (*☎* **0361/771202**).

Police   The police office of Bualu/Nusa Dua is located at Jalan Bypass Ngurah Rai (*☎* **0361/772110**).

Where to Stay

There's little difference between many hotels here so it comes down to personal choice and price. It's worth considering the hotel club floors where they serve sunset cocktails, canapés, all-day refreshments, and breakfasts separate from the hotel's main buffet. With alcohol at a premium on the island, this can work out to be a good deal. Many of the hotels have beach frontage and if they don't they usually have their own beach club accessed by golf carts with liveried staff supplying cold water and fresh towels throughout the day.

VERY EXPENSIVE

Amanusa ★★   If you're on a golf vacation and demand the most luxurious digs, the Amanusa will fit the bill. This Aman resort has a magnificent hilltop setting over-looking the **Bali Golf and Country Club** and Nusa Dua's beaches. It comes with quite a price tag, but a visit to Amanusa is an invitation to service that is gracious and intuitive, and to accommodations that are over-the-top luxurious while remaining in harmony with the surroundings. Rooms are crafted in rich redwood with four-poster

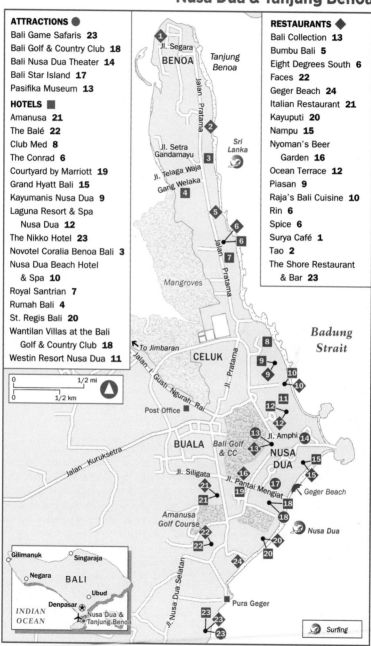

Nusa Dua & Tanjung Benoa

ATTRACTIONS ●
Bali Game Safaris **23**
Bali Golf & Country Club **18**
Bali Nusa Dua Theater **14**
Bali Star Island **17**
Pasifika Museum **13**

HOTELS ■
Amanusa **21**
The Balé **22**
Club Med **8**
The Conrad **6**
Courtyard by Marriott **19**
Grand Hyatt Bali **15**
Kayumanis Nusa Dua **9**
Laguna Resort & Spa
  Nusa Dua **12**
The Nikko Hotel **23**
Novotel Coralia Benoa Bali **3**
Nusa Dua Beach Hotel
  & Spa **10**
Royal Santrian **7**
Rumah Bali **4**
St. Regis Bali **20**
Wantilan Villas at the Bali
  Golf & Country Club **18**
Westin Resort Nusa Dua **11**

RESTAURANTS ◆
Bali Collection **13**
Bumbu Bali **5**
Eight Degrees South **6**
Faces **22**
Geger Beach **24**
Italian Restaurant **21**
Kayuputi **20**
Nampu **15**
Nyoman's Beer
  Garden **16**
Ocean Terrace **12**
Piasan **9**
Raja's Bali Cuisine **10**
Rin **6**
Spice **6**
Surya Café **1**
Tao **2**
The Shore Restaurant
  & Bar **23**

BENOA

*Tanjung
Benoa*

Jl. Segara

Jalan · Pratama

Jl. Setra
Gandamayu

*Sri
Lanka*

Jl. Telaga Waja

Gang Welaka

Jalan · Pratama

Mangroves

To Jimbaran →

CELUK

Jalan · I Gusti Ngurah Rai

Post Office ■

*Badung
Strait*

Jl. Pratama

Jl. Amphi

BUALA

Bali Golf
& CC

**NUSA
DUA**

Jl. Siligata

Jl. Pantai Mengiat

Geger Beach

*Amanusa
Golf Course*

Jl. Nusa Dua Selatan

Jalan · Kuruksetra

Nusa Dua

Pura Geger

0 ____ 1/2 mi
0 ____ 1/2 km

Gilimanuk
Singaraja
Negara
BALI
Ubud
Denpasar
Nusa Dua &
Tanjung Benoa
*INDIAN
OCEAN*

◎ Surfing

8

THE BUKIT PENINSULA | Nusa Dua

beds, sunken tubs, and outdoor and indoor showers. The central 24m (79-ft.) pool is stunning; and in-house dining at the Terrace is an experience in itself, with great views and delicious local cuisine. The beach club, a short drive down the hill, offers a collection of private *bales*. Staff can arrange diversions that range from cycling excursions and island cruises to cooking classes, shopping, and adventure tours.

Bali Golf & Country Club, Nusa Dua. www.amanresorts.com. ☎ **0361/772333.** Fax 0361/772335. 35 units. Year-round US$850–US$1,650. Rates include breakfast. AE, MC, V. **Amenities:** Restaurant (Italian Restaurant, p. 159); babysitting; bikes; gym; 30m outdoor pool; room service; spa; 2 floodlit tennis courts. *In room:* A/C, TV/DVD, hair dryer, minibar, MP3 docking station, Wi-Fi (free).

The Balé ★ *Balé* means "bungalow" in Balinese, but the moniker is rather modest—this is a beautiful collection of villas set on a hill overlooking the ocean. Each villa has its own plunge pool and a day bed in the courtyard. The interiors are elegantly simple, with large bathrooms and outdoor showers. Although not set right on the beach, The Balé has a shuttle that whisks you to its own private beach club in 2 minutes. The resort is popular with yuppies and gay couples. For adults seeking peace, an added bonus is that no children under 15 are allowed.

Jl. Raya Nusa Dua Selatan 76, Nusa Dua. www.thebale.com. ☎ **0361/775111.** Fax 0361/775222. 29 units. High season US$700–US$1,000; low season US$650–US$950. Rates include breakfast. AE, MC, V. No under-15s. **Amenities:** Restaurant (Faces, p. 159); bar; bikes; gym; outdoor pool; spa. *In room:* A/C, TV/DVD, iPod, hair dryer, minibar, Wi-Fi (free).

Kayumanis Nusa Dua If the private-villa-no-children-allowed concept appeals to you but The Balé (above) is too pricey, try the Kayumanis. This is a collection of sophisticated and exclusive adult-orientated villas that lacks the beach facilities offered by the Balé. All the villas feature semi-open bathing facilities complete with outdoor shower recess and a personal pool edged by a sun deck and lounges. A handy feature is a modern kitchenette and a private butler who will make your breakfast in your villa at no extra charge. No two villas are architecturally alike and you can choose between Balinese, Javanese, Oriental, Palembang, primitive, and modern styles.

BTDC Area Nusa Dua. www.kayumanis.com. ☎ **0361/770777.** Fax 0361/770770. 20 villas. Year-round US$554–US$1,159. Rates include breakfast. AE, MC, V. No under-16s. **Amenities:** 2 restaurants, including Piasan (p. 160); Jacuzzi; outdoor pool; room service; spa; tennis court. *In room:* A/C, TV/DVD, hair dryer, kitchen, minibar, MP3 docking station, Wi-Fi.

St. Regis Bali ★★ It would have to take something fairly grand to find a niche in the glut of luxury resorts in Nusa Dua but the "six-star" St. Regis fits the bill. From the private concierge who whisks you through airport immigration and baggage claim to the personal butler assigned to each room or villa, the emphasis at the St. Regis is on service. A number of the villas have private access to a swimmable lagoon, while others sit directly beachfront. Rooms and villas have Balinese and colonial-style furniture and come with private balconies and gardens. The resort also pays special attention to food. Kayuputi offers fine dining while Boneka serves delicious, made-to-order, table-service buffet breakfasts with delicacies including sashimi, oysters, and foie gras. The Gourmand Deli features inventive ice cream flavors.

Kawasan Pariwisata Nusa Dua Lot S6, Nusa Dua. www.stregis.com. ☎ **0361/847-8111.** Fax 0361/847-8099. 124 units. High season US$750 and up; low season US$585 and up. Rates include breakfast. AE, MC, V. **Amenities:** Restaurant (Kayuputi, p. 159); bar; babysitting; bikes; gym; outdoor pool; room service; spa; watersports. *In room:* A/C, TV/DVD, hair dryer, minibar, MP3 docking station, Wi-Fi (free).

EXPENSIVE

Grand Hyatt Bali The self-styled description of being a "Balinese water palace" is a little hard to swallow given there are close to 700 rooms in four very inauthentic, low-rise Balinese-style buildings at this resort. But the grand entrance with views of the immaculate beach and the water features (lagoon pool, outdoor river pool, and water slide) help the cause. Rooms are five-star standard. Ditch the kiddies at Camp Nusa (included in rates; children 3–13) and make a bee-line for the award-winning Kriya spa with its resident nutritionist and ayurvedic treatments.

BTDC Area Nusa Dua. www.bali.grand.hyatt.com. ✆ **0361/771234.** Fax 0361/772038. 630 units. High season US$285 and up; low season US$165 and up; extra charge for kids US$35 Grand room, US$60 Club room. Rates include breakfast. AE, MC, V. **Amenities:** Restaurant (Nampu, p. 159); bar; babysitting; children's club; gym; Jacuzzi; outdoor pool; room service; spa; 3 floodlit tennis courts; watersports; Wi-Fi (US$33/8 hr.). *In room:* A/C, TV, hair dryer, Internet (US$.38/minute) minibar.

Laguna Resort & Spa Nusa Dua ★   Here, they call their type of luxury "indigenous" luxury. Every day features some type of cultural performance and the whole place has a feel of Indonesia's royal roots. The main draws remain the beachfront and the lagoonlike pool accessed directly by ladders from some of the street-level rooms. Large bathrooms are done in marble. Extra special treats include complimentary high tea with tableside dessert service and the midnight massage on offer in a beachfront *bale* after dinner.

Kawasan Pariwisata Nusa Dua Lot N2, Nusa Dua. www.luxurycollection.com/bali. ✆ **0361/771327.** Fax 0361/771326. 271 units. Peak season US$335; high season US$305 and up; low season US$255 and up. Rates may or may not include breakfast. AE, MC, V. **Amenities:** 2 restaurants, including Ocean Terrace (p. 160); bar; babysitting; bikes; gym; Jacuzzi; outdoor pool; room service; spa; tennis court; watersports. *In room:* A/C, TV/DVD, hair dryer, minibar, Wi-Fi (US$14.95/24 hr.).

The Nikko Hotel ☺   The Nikko is unique in Bali, being 15 stories high, making it about 10 stories taller than all other hotels. The normal restriction on buildings being higher than a coconut tree has been supplanted because the hotel is built into the side of a 40-m (131-ft.) cliff. The hotel is protected by dramatic cliffs and coves on either side, giving it its own private beach setting. Rooms with teak floors all have private balconies. An amphitheater features nightly entertainment, including the famous Balinese *kecak* dance. One of the more unique offerings at the Nikko is camel rides on the beach (p. 161)—youngsters will love it. There's also a great children's jungle camp where you can send your little monkeys to rope climb and burn some energy. The pool facilities are superb and include an artificial beach, water volleyball and basketball areas, hot tubs and lap areas, and a water slide.

Jl. Raya Nusa Dua Selatan, Nusa Dua. www.nikkobali.com. ✆ **0361/773377.** Fax 0361/773388. 389 units. Peak season US$320–US$830; high season US$270–US$780; low season US$265 and up. Rates include breakfast. AE, MC, V. **Amenities:** Restaurant (Shore Restaurant and Bar, p. 161); bar; babysitting; children's club; gym; Jacuzzi; 4 outdoor pools; room service; spa; 3 floodlit tennis courts; watersports; Wi-Fi (free in some dining areas). *In room:* A/C, TV/DVD, hair dryer, minibar, Wi-Fi (for a fee).

Wantilan Villas at the Bali Golf & Country Club   These villas are really for golf lovers since they overlook the Bali Golf and Country Club course. Putters will enjoy the immediate accessibility to the course with priority tee times, discounted greens fees, and other guest privileges. Golf widows will enjoy the exclusive access to the private Amanusa Beach Club—a major benefit, as this is by far Bali's best-kept secret and unless you're in residence at the Amanusa it's impossible to use the facilities. Each villa has a private swimming pool and Jacuzzi with a sun deck, and fully equipped kitchen. Each bedroom is freestanding and detached with its own private bathroom. Personal cooks are on stand-by from 7am to 11pm to prepare meals either from the provided menu or according to your fancy.

Bali Golf & Country Club, Nusa Dua. www.wantilangolfvillas.com. ✆ **0361/771791.** Fax 0361/771797. 3 villas. Year-round US$345 standard; US$895 3-bedroom; US$1,195 4-bedroom. Rates include breakfast.

AE, MC, V. **Amenities:** Babysitting; golf course (p. 162); Jacuzzi; outdoor pool. *In villa:* A/C, TV/DVD, hair dryer, Wi-Fi.

Westin Resort Nusa Dua ☺ ⚑

This resort is for those who like to combine a few hours of telecommuting with their vacation. Business travelers will appreciate the Wi-Fi, a club lounge, and rooms with a safe big enough for a laptop. The hotel is also a good choice for families, with little touches for youngsters including a separate check-in area, special buffet counter at breakfast, and, most important, a children's club with complimentary babysitting all day long. With these amenities and rates as low as US$200 for a double during the low season, the Westin is a bargain for families. It's a high-quality version of a cookie-cutter experience—that is, you know what you're going to get: great service, fantastic dining, and beds so comfortable they're branded "Heavenly."

Westin Resort, Nusa Dua. www.westin.com. ✆ **0361/771906.** Fax 0361/771908. 334 units. Year-round US$340 and up. AE, MC, V. **Amenities:** Restaurant; bar; lounge; babysitting; bikes; children's club; gym; outdoor pool; room service; spa; 4 tennis courts; watersports. *In room:* A/C, TV/DVD, hair dryer, minibar, Wi-Fi (US$15/24 hr.).

MODERATE

Club Med ☺ ⚑

Club Med was the first hotel in Nusa Dua but has kept up with constant renovations. And let's face it: You don't come here for the rooms or the food, you come here for your children. On any given day, there are more than 160 youngsters at this resort. All-inclusive packages include all meals, alcohol—excluding champagne and cognac—and activities. The big draw is the children's clubs (for ages 2–17) for different age brackets with age-appropriate activities, so boredom doesn't enter your child's vocabulary. Watersports include canoeing, kayaking, snorkeling, and windsurfing; games include every manner of ball game, archery, and circus games (including the trapeze). Live bands, nightly dinner shows, and baby food on the buffet make nighttime revelry just as hassle-free. Parents can participate in all the activities, as well as enjoy the spa, gym, aqua-gym classes, yoga, a six-hole golf course, and that all-important, all-inclusive bar.

BTDC Area Nusa Dua, Lot 6. www.clubmed.com. ✆ **0361/771521.** Fax 0361/771831. 400 units. Prices per person all-inclusive high season US$293 and up; low season US$260 and up; extra charge for children 2–4 years old US$24–US$48, 5–11 years old US$170. Rates include full board. AE, MC, V. **Amenities:** Restaurant; bar; babysitting; children's club; gym; Jacuzzi; outdoor pool; room service; spa; tennis court; watersports. *In room:* A/C, TV/DVD, hair dryer, minibar, Wi-Fi (for a fee).

Courtyard by Marriott ⚑

Set amid the expensive, shining five-star resorts of Nusa Dua this property fills a much-needed space: a solid resort that's not going to break the bank. This large hotel doesn't offer much in terms of personal service, but the pool is spectacular—it's so large that it has its own island. Rooms are smaller than at neighboring resorts but have everything you need and a number of nice touches, from marble floors to balconies. There's a spa, a gym, and free Wi-Fi, and the public beach is a 5-minute walk away. The Bali Golf and Country Club is next door. Pay an extra US$10 for a poolside room.

Kawasan Parisisata Lot SW1, Nusa Dua. www.marriott.com. ✆ **0361/300-3888.** Fax 0361/300-3999. 250 units. Peak season US$250; high season US$210; low season US$190. Rates include breakfast. MC, V. **Amenities:** Restaurant; lounge; bar; gym; pool; spa; Wi-Fi (free). *In room:* A/C, TV/DVD, fridge, hair dryer, Internet access (for a fee).

Nusa Dua Beach Hotel & Spa ⚑

Architecturally alone in Nusa Dua is this Balinese-styled property featuring sculptures, paintings, and carvings, making it a more sympathetic offering than the other options on this stretch. The mature Balinese gardens—with temples and ponds with gaggles of ducks—make up for the slightly tired interiors. It's about half the price of some of the other hotels and given that they're all on the same stretch of sand, this is great value. There are also nightly performances in the mini-outdoor theater that are good, old-fashioned touristy fun.

Kawasan Pariwisata Nusa Dua Lot N4, Nusa Dua. www.nusaduahotel.com. ✆ **0361/771210.** Fax 0361/ 772617. 383 units. Peak season US$310–US$3,550; high season US$260–US$3,550; low season US$210– US$3,500. Rates include breakfast. AE, MC, V. **Amenities:** Restaurant (Raja's Bali Cuisine, p. 160); bar; lounge; babysitting; bikes; children's club; gym; Jacuzzi; 4 outdoor pools; spa; tennis court; watersports. *In room:* A/C, TV/DVD, hair dryer, minibar, Wi-Fi.

Where to Eat

You'll find limitless restaurants in the hotels. The **Bali Collection** (p. 164) has 36 decent and reasonably priced Indonesian and Western cafes that often have live music and a bit of ambience in the evening—certainly more than you'll find in any mall during the day. Most are open daily for both lunch and dinner, though some spots are open for breakfast for early morning shoppers. Your other bet for reasonable prices and decent Indonesian fare might be to head to **Uluwatu** (p. 145) or **Jimbaran Bay** (p. 133). Unless otherwise noted, restaurants are open daily.

VERY EXPENSIVE

Kayuputi ★★ SEAFOOD   Kayuputi is Bali's chic new place to "do" lunch. Serving chilled and grilled seafood dishes with sharing in mind, the freshest line-caught fish is ideal for the sashimi as a starter; choose from a selection of Sturia and Prunier caviar and seasonal imported oysters. The classy but friendly atmosphere here hits the mark. Outdoor and indoor seating sits just above the beach *bales* and the beautiful people below.

In the St. Regis (p.156), Kawasan Pariwisata Nusa Dua Lot S6, Nusa Dua. ✆ **0361/847-8111.** Fax 0361/ 847-8099. www.stregis.com/bali. Reservations recommended. AE, MC, V. Main courses Rp300,000– Rp720,000; set menu Rp850,000–Rp1,300,000. Daily noon–5:30pm and 6:30–11pm.

EXPENSIVE

Faces ★ INTERNATIONAL   Faces is a destination spot and one of the most relaxing restaurants on the island with its refreshingly uncomplicated cuisine. Poached lobster with wild mushroom sauté, creamy risotto, and truffle essence is a house specialty. A complimentary pickup and drop-off service is provided to guests staying in the Nusa Dua, Tanjung Benoa, and Jimbaran Bay areas.

In the Balé (p. 156), Jl. Raya Nusa Dua Selatan 76, Nusa Dua. ✆ **0361/775111.** Fax 0361/775222. www. thebale.com. Reservations recommended. No children 14 years old and under. Main courses Rp90,000– Rp420,000; set menu US$45. AE, MC, V. 7am–11pm.

Italian Restaurant ★ ITALIAN   As with all things Aman, the Italian Restaurant at Amanusa (p. 154) is just one step ahead. An incredibly generous antipasti table with simply delicious prosciutto and slivers of exquisite salami are a must. Be spoiled with the best bruschetta on Bali. Specialties include the gnocchi with spicy sausage and Napolitano sauce followed by a classic rendition of tiramisu. Book a table in the courtyard overlooking the pool and enjoy the nightly live *rindik* music.

In the Amanusa (p. 154), Bali Golf & Country Club, Nusa Dua. ✆ **0361/772333.** Fax 0361/772335. www. amanresorts.com. Reservations recommended. Main courses Rp300,000–Rp600,000; set menu upon request. AE, MC, V. Daily 7–10pm.

Nampu JAPANESE   With the largest sake and *shochu* beverage selection on the island, this restaurant means business. The collection consists of 14 sakes, served hot or cold, and nine varieties of *sho chu,* made from sweet potatoes. Prices per bottle can be less than an average bottle of wine on Bali, so sip and swig away while sampling the sashimi and sushi. The selection includes tuna, salmon, snapper, kingfish, sea bass, and yellowtail. Other favorites are *kani maki*—deep-fried soft-shell crab rolls with fish eggs—and the *karubi* beef—grilled short ribs with garlic. Nampu also has four teppanyaki tables and a menu of grilled and sautéed dishes to match.

In the Grand Hyatt Bali (p. 156), BTDC Area, Nusa Dua. ☎ 0361/771234. www.bali.grand.hyatt.com. Reservations recommended. Main courses US$17; set menu US$50. AE, MC, V. Daily 6–11pm.

Ocean Terrace ★★ SEAFOOD   This outdoor venue approaches the ideal for a beach restaurant. When the sun goes down and the weather permits, it's hard to beat the ambience. Fine-dining options include 5- to 10- course menus prepared after a personal consultation with the chef. There are a la carte options and fresh seafood choices from the on-site fish tank. Evenings feature live jazz.

The Laguna Resort & Spa Nusa Dua (p. 157), Kawasan Pariwisata Nusa Dua Lot N2, Nusa Dua. ☎ 0361/771327. Fax 0361/771326. www.luxurycollection.com/bali. Reservations recommended. Main courses Rp190,000–Rp980,000; seafood and BBQ buffet Rp495,00. AE, DC, MC, V. Daily 7am–11pm.

Piasan ITALIAN   Balinese Chef Ketut incorporates organic fresh vegetables into many of his dishes at the Piasan. A typical lunch for two may consist of a Caprese salad, followed by homemade fresh angel hair pasta with lobster, tomato, and cream. You can also choose from an assortment of thin-crust Italian-style pizzas. Kayumanis Private Villas doesn't cater to children 15 years old and younger.

In the Kayumanis Nusa Dua (p. 156), BTDC Area. ☎ 0361/770777. Fax 0361/770770. www.kayumanis. com. Reservations recommended. Main courses Rp100,000–Rp300,000. AE, MC, V. Daily 11am–10:30pm.

Raja's Bali Cuisine BALINESE   This beachfront restaurant sits next to the main swimming pool at the Nusa Dua Hotel and Spa. Balinese cuisine is rarely served outside the warungs, so if you aren't feeling adventurous, Raja's is a good place to start. A signature dish is the *bebek betutu,* a whole duck marinated in a secret blend of 16 Balinese spices, wrapped in palm leaves, and slow cooked. Another specialty is *palem sari ulam* (steamed seafood in coconut curry pudding).

In the Nusa Dua Beach Hotel and Spa (p. 158), Kawasan Pariwisata Nusa Dua Lot N4, Nusa Dua. ☎ 0361/771210. www.nusaduahotel.com. Reservations recommended. Main courses Rp140,000–Rp250,000; set menu Rp880,000 for 2. AE, MC, V. Daily 7–10pm.

MODERATE

Geger Beach   This is the main warung on Geger Beach run by the local *banjar* (village community members). It's a decent spot for typical Indonesian fare with beach lounges laid out in front for rent for about Rp5,000 a day. Just beyond the warung, a new resort is going up, so be prepared for a bit of noise. Food is typical good warung grub. Stick with simple requests such as chicken satays and *nasi goreng* (fried rice).

On the beach, next door to St. Regis (p. 156), Nusa Dua. ☎ 0361/746-3117. Main courses Rp10,000–Rp15,000. No credit cards. Daily 8am–8pm.

Nyoman's Beer Garden 🛈 INTERNATIONAL   A curious offering but pleasantly surprising if you want to leave the sterile surrounds of Nusa Dua. International and Balinese cuisine is served by a German chef and if you order a day in advance you're assured fresh lobster, *babi guling* (roast pig) or *bebek betutu* (roast duck). The beer is cold; the company laid-back and convivial. There's nightly live music.

Jl. Pantai Mengiat X. ☎ 0361/775746. Reservations recommended. Main courses Rp15,000–Rp180,000; set menu Rp207,000. AE, MC, V. Daily 10am–midnight.

The Shore Restaurant & Bar ★ SEAFOOD   Designed as a contemporary interpretation of a boat on stilts, this restaurant has three very distinct levels to choose from. The lower deck seating is on the marina overlooking the beachfront; the second level is air-conditioned with full glass panels instead of walls allowing you to enjoy the view; and the top timber deck is an intimate spot for late night cocktails under the stars. The most popular dish is the seafood platter of the catch of the day, Indian Ocean rock lobsters, prawns, squid, tuna loin, and snapper filet. Needless to say, the platter is big enough to share. The surprise favorite is the terrific lasagna. Evenings feature a tapas menu for late-night grazing.

In the Nikko Hotel (p. 157), Jl. Raya Nusa Dua Selatan, Nusa Dua. © **0361/773377.** www.nikkobali.com. Reservations recommended. Main courses Rp150,000–Rp350,000; set menu Rp380,000. AE, DC, MC, V. Daily 9am–5pm and 7–10pm.

Exploring Nusa Dua

With one of the most perfect stretch of **beaches** in Bali, it's hard to leave Nusa Dua. A perfect sunrise/sunset activity is watching the **seaweed farmers** (below) next to **Geger Beach,** which is also the safest place for children to swim. If you're looking for a bit of activity, contact any of the **watersports** companies along the beach. In the bay are glass-bottom boats for snorkeling trips and many places to rent jet skis, sailboats, and catamarans.

Pasifika Museum ★   Located within the boundary of Nusa Dua, this museum displays a collection of Asian and Pacific art with some 300 paintings, including *tapa* bark paintings from Oceania, and 250 objects, including sculptures and tapestries, on permanent display in the 11 pavilions. Be sure to check out the work by Balinese artists Ida Bagus Nyoman Rai and Nyoman Gunarsa.

Bali Collection. © **0361/774935.** www.museum-pasifika.com. Admission Rp70,000 adults; free for children 10 and under. Daily 10am–6pm.

CAMEL RIDES   *Sudan* was the name of the camel that took us for a ride. He was a friendly chap but fairly indifferent to our poking and prodding. We were introduced to him by **Bali Game Safaris** (© **0361/776755;** www.balicamelsafaris.com; US$35 adults, US$20 children 5–12), out of the Nikko Hotel Bali (p. 157). The

---

 THE NUSA DUA seaweed FARMERS

Seaweed farming has long been a source of income to the communities around what's now called Nusa Dua. At the beginning of Nusa Dua's building boom in the 1980s, Suharto's regime decided there was a better use of the land than seaweed farming, and many of the traditional farmers had to leave. Fortunately, the memula bulung (seaweed farmers) have returned to their rightful land and continue their tradition of farming and way of life. Farmers plant and harvest along Geger Beach.

The best time to catch them is at sunrise and they usually plant 1 or 2 days before the full moon. At planting time they carry their boats into the water with huge stacks of seaweed cultivated from deeper water. Indonesia is the second biggest seaweed-producing country in the world and supplies about a quarter of the world's demand for seaweed. What you witness being harvested in Nusa Dua may end up in your cosmetics, medicine, or food stabilizers, but is rarely used with your sushi.

camels will put up with you for about an hour and take you on a giggle-inducing ride down the Nusa Dua beach. Daily trips leave at 9 and 10:30am or at 2 and 3:30pm.

DOLPHIN WATCHING Bali has several dolphin-watching spots, and the best are in Nusa Dua, Tanjung Benoa, and Lovina (p. 258). In Nusa Dua you can go any time of day, whereas you have to go at sunrise or sunset in Lovina. Several tour operators will pick you up and bring you on a glass-bottom boat for a 4-hour tour up-close and personal with these gentle and smart creatures in their own habitat. Any hotel in the area can book these tours, which typically include pickup and drop-off, lunch, dolphin watching, and insurance. Check out **Bali Star Island** (✆ 0361/778076; www.balistarisland.com; US$95 adults, US$55 for children 12 and under, 2 person minimum).

GOLF Bali Golf & Country Club (✆ 0361/771791; www.baligolfandcountry club.com; US$150 and up for 18 holes; special stay and play rates available) is next to the St. Regis Resort. This very good holiday course, once rated among the top five in Asia by *Fortune* magazine, starts at the beach and heads up the hill past the doors of the Amanusa Hotel. Other facilities at the club include an excellent grass driving range and a new golf academy, Acorna Golf Institute, with a resident PGA Professional to give lessons.

SPA Most of the hotels have their own spas but we have two favorites (open daily). Designer Bill Bensley's whimsical approach to the deliciously decadent St. Regis's **Remede Spa ★★★** (p. 156; signature rituals US$121–US$475, massage US$80–US$245, body treatment US$33–US$135; AE, MC, V; daily 8am–11pm) is simply inspired. The overriding theme employs lots of moons and butterflies; the best time to come is at night when the creative lighting makes the butterflies seem as if they're

---

BALINESE dance PERFORMANCES ON THE BUKIT PENINSULA

Below is a list of Balinese dance performances you can attend while staying on the Bukit peninsula. Most are in Nusa Dua and all (except at the temple) include a Balinese buffet. Schedules are always subject to change and so call ahead or ask your hotel or villa concierge about the latest schedule.

Performance	Days	Time	Cost (Rp)
Grand Hyatt Nusa Dua			
Barong	Mon	8pm	388,000
Ramayana	Tues	8pm	388,000
Kecak	Wed & Sat	8pm	388,000
Legong	Thurs	8pm	388,000
Jegog	Fri	8pm	388,000
Balinese Dance Parade	Sun	8pm	388,000
Nusa Dua Beach Hotel			
Legong	Tues	Dinner starts at 7pm; dance at 8pm	350,000
Kecak	Sun	8pm	350,000
Pura Luhur Uluwatu			
Kecak	Daily	6pm	55,000 (no dinner)

ASHES TO ASHES, dust TO DUST: CREMATION

Cremation is the most important ceremony in the Balinese life cycle. It's said to release the soul and so is a time for celebration, not sorrow, and is wonderfully colorful. Cremation is also an extremely costly affair: People begin saving for their cremation in middle age. The average family spends about Rp15 million on the ceremony, about a year's wages, while wealthy families have been known to lavish hundreds of millions of rupiahs. If insufficient money is available, families may have to wait years, sometimes more than a decade, before they can hold a cremation. In this case, bodies are buried and then exhumed after enough money has been saved and collected from the community for the cremation. The cremation is always on an auspicious day chosen by the priest from the local or nearby village, according to the Balinese calendar and the movement of the moon.

A large bamboo tower, its size and shape dictated by the caste of the dead person, is built for the cremation. A wooden life-size bull (for men) or cow (for women) is sometimes carved. On the morning of the cremation, the family of the deceased entertains friends and relatives and then the body is placed inside the bamboo tower. The village kul-kul (wooden gong) is struck and the construction is carried in noisy procession to the cremation ground by the banjar.

Cremation is the most impressive of Balinese ceremonies and usually families don't mind if you watch, although you should bring some money or a nice gift out of respect. One of the best places to see a cremation is in the Jimbaran Bay and Nusa Dua area. The cremation grounds are located in Mumbul in Nusa Dua about 700m (2,300 ft.) after McDonald's on the right-hand side as you come from Kuta. It's best to ask a local at your hotel or villa whether a cremation is happening on the day you want to go.

going to fly away. Each treatment is customized by your own spa concierge. **Laguna Resort & Spa** (p. 157; single treatment US$60–US$145; spa villa for couple, including dinner US$410; AE, MC, V; daily 9am–midnight) offers "midnight massages" on the beach *bales* facing the crashing waves. If the rhythmic movement of your treatment doesn't lull you to sleep, certainly the sea air will.

SURFING At **Sri Lanka** (**best swell:** south; **best size:** the bigger the better; **best winds:** north and northwest, rainy season between Nov–Apr), the immaculate beach carries the polished persona of a private resort beach. The gentle lagoon is fantastic and safe for swimmers and there are all manner of recreational watercraft for rent. On lower tides the reef on the outer side creates and shapes perfect and fast right-hand waves for competent wave-riders.

You reach the **Nusa Dua wave** (**best swell:** south; **best size:** 4–8 ft.; **best winds:** west-northwest) by heading south out of the town and either paddling over or hopping a short boat ride from Geger Beach. For nonsurfers, you can also take a boat and all ages can gain a front-row seat to view the watery battlefield from the safety of the channel. This is one of Bali's heaviest waves, with loads of swell. With a take-off zone as large as an American football field it can be easy to get stuck inside at this heavy right-hander, giving helpless fools lots of time to contemplate their erroneous wave judgment from below the surface in a natural washing machine.

Shopping

The less-than-swanky mall in Nusa Dua, the **Bali Collection** (© **0361/771662;** www.bali-collection.com) has an hourly shuttle that makes the rounds to most of the hotels. The mall sits between the Grand Hyatt Bali to the south and the Melia Bali Sol to the north. The Bali Collection feels like an outdoor mall in a middle-class suburb in America, complete with small restaurants, palm trees, and a tranquil vibe so quiet it's almost desolate. Food outlets include Starbucks, Baskin-Robbins, and, due to the influx of Russians, some Russian fare as well.

Nusa Dua Entertainment & Nightlife

Nusa Dua isn't known for its nightlife but all the hotels have bars for the thirsty. The cream of the crop is the **Nat King Cole Bar** at the St. Regis, which originally made the Bloody Mary famous. The new **Devdan Show** ★(© **0361/770197;** www. devdanshow.com) at the **Bali Nusa Dua Theater** offers traditional Indonesian dance fused with modern contemporary dance, top-notch acrobatics, dazzling costumes, and special effects. It's been equated to Cirque du Soleil. The 90-minute show features dance styles—and dancers—from across the Indonesian archipelago. Shows start at 7pm on Mondays, Wednesdays, Fridays, and Saturdays and cost US$22.50 to US$120.

TANJUNG BENOA

Tanjung Benoa fishing village lies just north of Nusa Dua. The labyrinth of streets makes for a good stroll, certainly more culturally interesting than sterile Nusa Dua. Tanung Benoa is a center for watersports, such as snorkeling, windsurfing, waterskiing, parasailing, and outrigger sailing, thanks to the calm protected lagoon.

For centuries the natural means of communication between this area and the rest of Bali was by boat, as this was easier than the overland route via Jimbaran. Tanjung Benoa, which appears isolated at the tip of the peninsula, was a trading port for Badung and the eastern Bukit, with a world outlook extending right across the archipelago. Its population still bears traces of this mercantile past. Chinese have lived here for centuries and a *Tatu Cina* (shrine) in the local temple bears witness to this presence, as does the Chinese temple located next to the mosque, which is next to the Hindu temple, which is all diagonal to the fish market.

Essentials

GETTING THERE & GETTING AROUND

Tanjung Benoa is 4km (2½ miles) north from Nusa Dua. You can actually walk the beach promenade to Tanjung Benoa from Nusa Dua Beach. **Taxis** from the airport cost about Rp110,000. Tanjung Benoa itself is walkable.

[FastFACTS] TANJUNG BENOA

Hospital/Clinic   Available for drop-ins from 8am to 8pm, with a dentist available by appointment only, is Bali Nusa Dua Emergency Clinic, Jl. Pratama 81, Tanjung Benoa (© **0361/771324**).

Police   A police post is located at Jalan Pratama, at the intersection of the Conrad Hotel and the Nusa Dua Complex in the BTDC area of Nusa Dua.

Exploring Tanjung Benoa

The **Tanjung Benoa harbor** is one of the most placid spots on the island and is perfect for watersports. You can also try the "flying fish," a parasailing-like amusement using an extra-large inflatable kite. The beach is always busy. Be sure to book your watersports ahead of time from June to August as the place can be heaving with locals during the school holidays. There are plenty of operators to choose from but if you're staying in a local hotel, go with the operators they recommend or the services they offer. There'll be little difference in price and you can rest easy that the operators are of a higher standard than those coming off the beach.

For **spa** time, go to the Tanjung Benoa branch of **Jari Menari** on Jl. Pratama 88x (**℃ 0361/778084;** www.jarimenarinusadua.com), the Seminyak-based massage center with its professional, all-male staff for some of the island's best treatments. The yoga-influenced "Connoisseurs Massage" is a bargain at Rp350,000 for 90 minutes. Across the street, the **Jiwa Spa ★★**, in the Conrad (below; single treatment Rp750,000–Rp1,130,000; package Rp1,500,000–Rp1,550,000; AE, MC, V; daily 8am–10pm) offers a more luxurious experience. Take your time and enjoy the private infinity pool and the relaxation lounge as well as the complimentary sauna and steam room. The child-friendly Conrad always keeps the wee ones in mind and so there's a **Jiwa Spa Kids,** where one of the treatments is "back-scratching fun."

Where to Stay

EXPENSIVE

The Conrad ★★ ☺   The most family-friendly of Bali's resorts, the Conrad has over 300m (1,000 ft.) of pristine beach fronting a calm, child-safe lagoon—and a plethora of activities. Friendly, switched-on staffers guide older children and parents in watersports such as kayaking, parasailing, sailing, and wakeboarding; they also run the Kura Kura Kids' Club, where younger ones participate in Balinese arts and crafts, kite-making, and sand-castle-building. The rooms are spacious and contemporary (no delicate antiques to knock over—just clean-lined furniture and comfy couches); each comes with a stuffed toy monkey and rubber bath turtle. There's even a children's hair salon. The rooms have a refreshing contemporary feel with natural linen covers, dark woods, and impressive, original, Indonesian tribal art pieces. The on-site restaurants include the casual Eight Degrees South, and the more refined Spice, for Middle East and Far East cuisine. At East, the lobby bar, the oyster martini is a must; you can then retire to the nearest beach *bale* to star gaze. The Deluxe Lagoon rooms have full ocean views, and you can dive off your terrace into the lagoon.

Jl. Pratama 168, Tanjung Benoa. www.conrad-bali.com. **℃ 0361/778788.** Fax 0361/778780. 360 units. High season US$300–US$648; low season US$230–US$520. Rates include breakfast. AE, MC, V. **Amenities:** 3 restaurants (Eight Degrees South, Spice, and Rin; p. 166, p. 167, and p. 167); bar; babysitting; bikes; children's club; gym; Jacuzzi; outdoor pool; room service; spa; tennis court; watersports; Wi-Fi. *In room:* A/C, TV/DVD, hair dryer, Internet access, minibar.

MODERATE

Novotel Coralia Benoa Bali ★ ☺   This hotel is slightly more upscale than your typical Novotel. The resort straddles the main street: The ocean side is more expensive and has better beach access, while the "garden" side is quiet and secluded. Better still, for the price, are the beach cabanas, which are even bigger suites in semiprivate bungalows (two per pavilion) with outdoor stone tubs. Rooms are big, bright, and airy, decorated in a minimalist Asian style. Lots of activities, including aerobics, soccer, a children's club, and dance and cooking lessons, will keep you on the run if you like. The free shuttle to Nusa Dua is convenient for touring, but it's hard to see that you'd need it. The ocean here is much deeper and better for swimming, too.

Jl. Pratama, Tanjung Benoa. www.novotelbali.com. ✆ **0361/772239.** Fax 0361/772237. 190 units. Year-round US$43–US$210 standard; US$210–US$260 beach cabana. Rates may or may not include breakfast. AE, DC, MC, V. **Amenities:** 2 restaurants; 2 bars; babysitting; children's club; fitness center; 3 outdoor pools; room service; spa; tennis court. *In room:* A/C, satellite TV, fridge, minibar, Wi-Fi (for a fee).

INEXPENSIVE

Rumah Bali ★ 🍴 This bed-and-breakfast is one of the best values in Bali. The bungalows have outdoor kitchens and generous bathrooms (with outdoor shower); deluxe bungalows get their own plunge pool. The people who run this hotel also own **Bumbu Bali** (see below) and they'll send a chef over to cook all your meals if you wish. The peaceful pool is set in a garden, while the beach is just a 5-minute walk away. If you're on a budget, you can stay here and use the beachside pool at the restaurant **Tao** (p. 167) for something close to a five-star experience.

Jl. Pratama, Tanjung Benoa. www.bedandbreakfastbali.com. ✆ **0361/771256.** Fax 0361/771258. 11 units. Year-round US$83–US$103 bungalow, plus US$20 per night high season, plus 21% tax. Rates include breakfast. AE, MC, V. **Amenities:** 2 restaurants; outdoor pool; tennis court. *In room:* A/C, satellite TV, fridge, kitchen, minibar, Wi-Fi (US$3/24 hr.).

VILLAS

Royal Santrian The villas are next door to our favorite spot, the Conrad. It's an excellent location. All white, bright, and brand new, the villas have their own patch of private beach and individual pools. Children under 12 not admitted.

Jl. Pratama, Tangung Benoa. www.theroyalsantrian.com. ✆ **0361/778181.** Fax 0361/776999. 22 units. Peak season US$540–US$740; high season US$490–US$690; low season US$440–US$640. Rates include breakfast. AE, MC, V. **Amenities:** Restaurant; 3 bars; room service; large outdoor pool with Jacuzzi; watersports. *In villa:* A/C, TV, hair dryer, minibar, MP3 docking station, Wi-Fi (free).

Where to Eat

The main street of Tanjung Benoa has plenty of empty cafes that are best avoided.

Bumbu Bali ★★ 🍴 BALINESE At Bumbu Bali you dine in a re-creation of a Balinese village, including a central courtyard. On Wednesdays and Fridays, expect to see local dancers, gamelan players, or the odd *barong* dancer performing between tables. Swiss owner Heinz von Holzen's enthusiasm for Balinese cuisine is so strong that he has even written a book: *Bali Unveiled: The Secrets of Balinese Cuisine*. His food is the real deal and not modified for Western tastes. How can you tell? Good Balinese cuisine is spiced, not spicy. Heinz's sambal is mixed with over 20 spices adding just the right amount of sizzle. Heinz is so insistent on using the freshest ingredients that he has his vegetables harvested overnight in the mountains and brought down to the restaurant each day. A team of four men source just 5kg (11 lbs.) of fish per day for the restaurant. Order the rijsttafel to sample the myriad of goods on offer. For something a bit more conservative, the ultra-rich green papaya soup with seafood is a meal in itself. The restaurant also hosts an excellent cooking school.

Jl. Pratama, Tanjung Benoa. ✆ **0361/771256.** Main courses Rp50,000–Rp175,000. MC, V. Daily 11am–10pm.

Eight Degrees South ★★ BARBECUE Sample delicious barbecue and a variety of salads, pizza, sandwiches, and Asian specialties in an open-air beachside atmosphere. Behind the restaurant is the swimming pool and in front is the wide open expanse of the private beach. Three things to check out: the Bintang beer served in frozen ice mugs; the very fresh lunchtime salad bar; the excellent choice of home-made ice creams.

In the Conrad Bali (p. 165), Jl. Pratama 168, Tanjung Benoa. © **0361/778788.** www.conradhotels.com. Reservations recommended. Main courses Rp175,000–Rp710,000. AE, MC, V. Daily 11am–10:30pm.

Rin ★★ JAPANESE   The menu at Rin is based on experiencing all the known flavors: salty, bitter, savory (or *umami*), sweet, and sour. The traditional flavors and seasonal ingredients of Japanese cuisine are given an eclectic twist. Take, for example, the *Chawan-mushi*, a steamed savory custard blended with foie gras that's silky and smooth yet complex.

In the Conrad Bali (p. 165), Jl. Pratama 168, Tanjung Benoa. © **0361/778788.** www.conradhotels.com. Reservations recommended. Main courses Rp45,000–Rp355,000; set menu Rp300,000–Rp435,000. AE, MC, V. Daily 7am–11pm.

Spice ★ MIDDLE EASTERN   Spice takes advantage of Bali's proximity to the Spice Islands by serving Middle, Near, and Far East cuisine. It also has a tandoori oven. The new man in charge, Chef Richard Miller, also has a few tricks up his sleeve to share and recommends the sub-primal cuts of Wagyu beef with a marbling grade of nine—which translates to "melt in your mouth."

In the Conrad Bali (p. 165), Jl. Pratama 168, Tanjung Benoa. © **0361/778788.** www.conradhotels.com. Reservations recommended. Main courses US$25–US$33; set menu US$70–US$105. AE, MC, V. Daily 7–11pm.

Surya Café ★★ 🍴 SEAFOOD   It doesn't get any more local than this wonderful gem. The quaint eatery serves simple, delicious, fresh seafood made to your specifications. Getting to this joint is half the fun. The Surya is hidden away in a warren of waterfront shacks near the Buddhist monastery and the Chinese temple and a block from the fish market; walk down the alleyway that connects to the side of the house and is bracketed by a billiards hall. To the right, down the alley, you can actually peer into the home of the Chinese proprietress and her Sumbanese husband. The cafe's blue, hand-painted sign has images of smiling lobsters and friendly fish. Enter the restaurant at the end of the *gang* (alley) and to the right you'll see live tanks with all manner of creatures on sale for your supper. The restaurant sits right on the harbor with fishing boats tied to the small pier to the left.

Jl. Segara Lor 21, Tanjung Benoa. © **0361/772016.** Main courses Rp75,000–Rp225,000 per kg. MC, V. Daily 11am–10pm.

Tao ★ 🍴 THAI   Chef Vaewta Chookasem serves up modern Thai food at this stand-alone restaurant across the street from the Ramada. The menu has a few offerings from other Southeast Asian countries as well, but it's best to stick with the Thai. You won't be disappointed. Although they don't like to advertise it, anyone having lunch at Tao is welcome to use the beachfront Ramada pool and facilities for the day. Sunday nights feature live music.

Jl. Pratama 96, Tanjung Benoa. © **0361/772902.** www.taobali.com. Reservations recommended. Main courses Rp62,000–Rp120,000; set menu Rp220,000. AE, MC, V. Daily 10:30am–10:30pm.

UBUD

It appears that each Balinese native
From the womb to the tomb is creative,
And although the results are quite clever,
There is too much artistic endeavor.

–Noel Coward to Charlie Chaplin

Ubud was the cultural, artistic, and spiritual heart of Bali centuries before the tanned, toned, and bejeweled began to sashay through the hallowed haunts of south Bali. Perhaps Ubud's destiny as a point of confluence was sealed in the 8th century by Rsi Markendya, a wandering priest from Java, who (legend has it) found the perfect patch for meditation where the eastern and western branches of the Wos River meet in Campuhan. This holy site is now Guning Lebah temple.

9

Ubud's position as a center of the arts developed under Tjokorde Rai Batur, king from 1850 to 1880, a member of the Satriya family of Sukawati, who themselves had been significant supporters of the arts and culture over the centuries.

Ubud's modern cultural prominence is a result of a fortuitous meeting of one of the scions of the House of Ubud and Walter Spies (see box, p. 169), who came to Denpasar in 1926. At the time, the arts in Bali were undergoing a process of redefinition, because the traditional forms of patronage and funding, namely the rajahs and the temples, were under Dutch colonial rule and were no longer sources of wealth. Survival meant innovation and an important meeting of the minds. Walter Spies came to Ubud on the invitation of Prince Sukawati, and together with friend and fellow artist Rudolf Bonnet, encouraged and financed individual artists in developing new styles that put art and artist ahead of tradition. This is known as the Pita Maha (p. 18).

At about this same time Bali became *the* bohemian destination for glamorous artistic society: Dorothy Lamour, Charlie Chaplin, and Noel Coward loved it; Margaret Mead and her lover Gregory Bateson were married on a ship en route to Bali; and Barbara Hutton fell head-over-heels for Walters Spies, who had a different sort of partner in mind altogether.

By the early 1960s, Ubud had attained fame as a unique artists' community. Enter Arie Smit, the most well-known and longest surviving Western artist in Ubud, whose Young Artists school of painting in Penestanan earned him an enduring place in the history of Balinese art. In the following years the entire artistic region around Ubud flourished, including the enclaves of Campuhan, Penestanan, Sanggingan, Nyuhkuning,

Walter Spies

Russian-born German artist **Walter Spies** is credited with popularizing Ubud and Balinese arts to the western world. After befriending the Ubud royal family on a visit to Bali, he settled in Ubud in the late 1920s. In Ubud, he founded the Pita Maha, an artists' cooperative that helped cultivate local artists. Working with German filmmakers, he helped document Balinese arts in a film called "Island of Demons," which after being shown in the West attracted celebrities such as Charlie

Chaplin, English playwright Noel Coward, and the sociologist Margaret Mead to Ubud. His life wasn't without tragedy; the Dutch colonial government that ruled Bali at the time jailed him for several months for his homosexuality in the late 1930s. During World War II, he met an untimely death after the Dutch government arrested him yet again, for being a German national. While being deported to Ceylon in 1942, Spies died when a Japanese bomb sank the boat carrying him.

Padang Tegal, Pengosekan, and Peliatan. Nearby are the centers of wood carving at Mas and of silverware at Celuk.

Ubud today develops apace with posh luxury hotels and villas, yoga centers, spas—and even a Starbucks (up until a few years ago, a local decree banned foreign chains such as the coffee shop and McDonald's). Bali's swelling tourist numbers—in the form of huge rumbling tour buses that traverse Ubud's narrow streets, and seekers influenced by Elizabeth Gilbert's 2006 book *Eat, Pray, Love*—means that the town is changing quickly, but look outside the bustle of central Ubud, and you'll still find its magic in the nearby temples, arts and crafts outlets, and rice paddies.

ESSENTIALS
Getting There & Getting Around

Many hotels in the area offer a pickup service, and taxis connect from the airport (Rp180,000), about an hour away. Most taxis don't run on meters in Ubud and so make sure that you negotiate before setting off. Most rides from the surrounding resorts into town cost about Rp50,000 each way. *Bemo* (vans that operate as buses) drop you in the center of town, while the tourist shuttles have their own stops, usually on one of the two main drags.

With the encroachment of so many smaller villages into the center of downtown, Ubud is more like an expanding mini-metropolis than a sleepy royal village. Central Ubud is small enough to see on foot and hotels generally provide regular shuttles into town. The main street is **Jalan Raya Ubud,** which runs east to west; **Monkey Forest Road** (Jl. Monkey Forest) runs perpendicular. Jalan Raya Ubud becomes Jalan Raya Campuhan (that is, the "main street" of Campuhan) to the west, which in turn becomes Jalan Raya Sayan. **Minivans** are for rent on every corner for day trips or short jaunts across town. Make sure that they have a meter or you get a fixed price before you set off. **Taxis** are few and far between in Ubud and most have arrived from the south and are looking for a fare to take them back home. **Motorbike** rental costs about Rp50,000 to Rp75,000 for the day. **Bicycles** are available for rent at two or three street-side locations along Monkey Forest Road for about Rp10,000.

Ubud

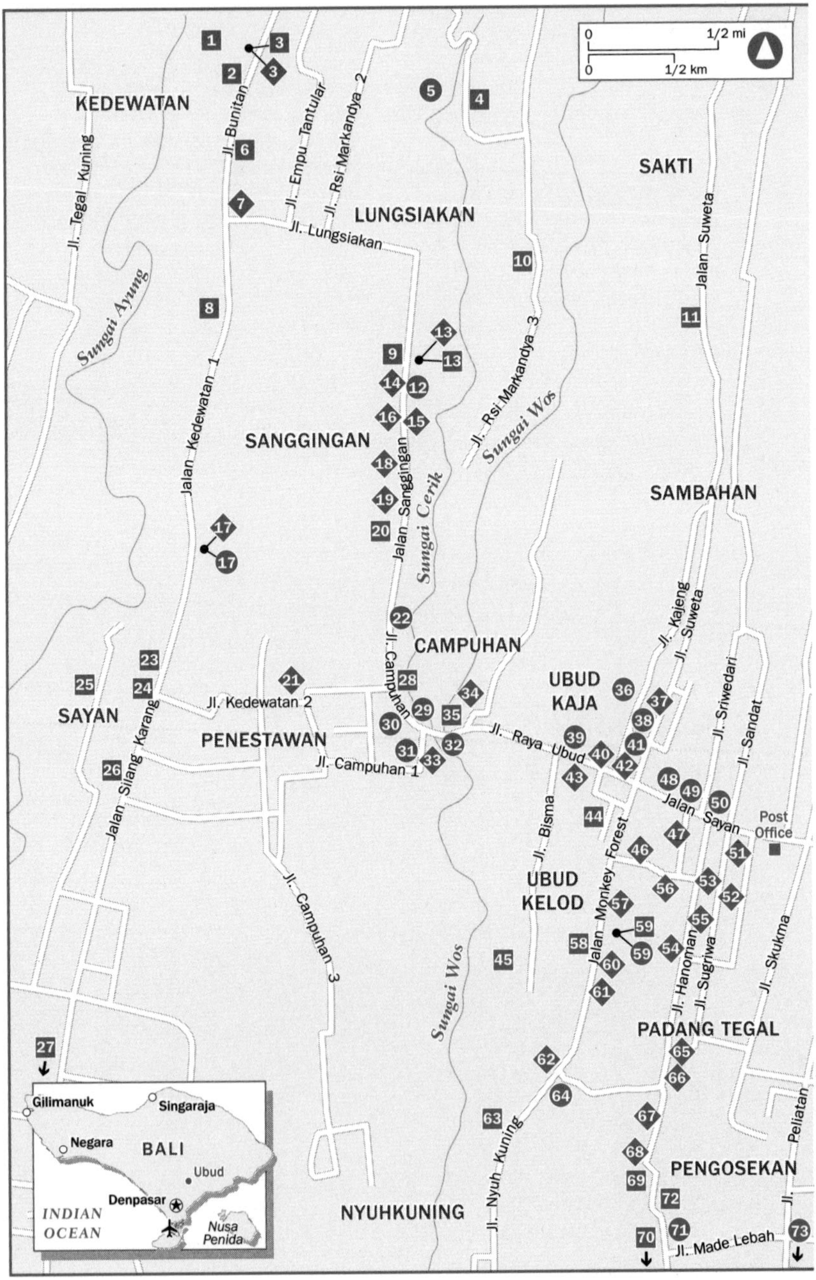

0
1/2 mi
0
1/2 km
KEDEWATAN
LUNGSIAKAN
SAKTI
SANGGINGAN
SAMBAHAN
CAMPUHAN
UBUD KAJA
SAYAN
PENESTAWAN
UBUD KELOD
PADANG TEGAL
PENGOSEKAN
NYUHKUNING
Jl. Bunitan
Jl. Empu Tantular
Jl. Rsi Markandya 2
Jl. Tegal Kuning
Jl. Lungsiakan
Sungai Ayung
Jalan Kedewatan 1
Jl. Rsi Markandya 3
Sungai Wos
Jalan Sanggingan
Sungai Cerik
Jalan Suweta
Jl. Kajeng
Jl. Suweta
Jl. Campuhan
Jl. Kedewatan 2
Jalan Silang Karang
Jl. Campuhan 1
Jl. Raya Ubud
Jl. Sriwedari
Jl. Sandat
Jalan Sayan
Post Office
Jl. Bisma
Jalan Monkey Forest
Jl. Campuhan 3
Jl. Hanoman
Jl. Sugriwa
Jl. Skukma
Jl. Nyuh Kuning
Jl. Peliatan
Jl. Made Lebah
Gilimanuk
Singaraja
Negara
BALI
Ubud
Denpasar
INDIAN OCEAN
Nusa Penida

HOTELS ■

Agung Raka Bungalows **69**
Alam Indah **63**
Alam Sari **4**
Alila Ubud **2**
Amandari **8**
Ananda Cottages **20**
Arma Resort **72**
Bali Spirit Hotel & Spa **70**
Bambu Indah **26**
Casa Luna Honeymoon
   Guesthouse **44**
Chedi Club at Tanah Gajah **79**
COMO Shambhala Estate **3**
Fivelements **27**
Four Seasons Resort at Sayan **24**
Hotel Tjampuhan **28**
Klub Kokos **10**
Komaneka at Monkey Forest **59**
Komaneka Bisma **45**
Komaneka Resort at
   Rasa Sayang **58**
Komaneka Tanggayuda **6**
Maya Ubud Resort & Spa **78**
Samaya Ubud **25**
Sunny Blow Villas Jepun **9**
Taman Bebek Villas **23**
Ubud Hanging Gardens **1**
Uma Ubud **13**
Waka Di Ume **11**
Warwick Ibah Luxury Villas
   & Spa **35**

RESTAURANTS ◆

Bali Buddha **52**
Batan's Waru **46**
Bebek Bengil (Dirty Duck) **66**
Black Beach **53**
Bridges **33**
Cafe Lotus **40**
Cafe Moka **47**
Casa Luna **43**
CasCades Restaurant **77**
Chedi Club Restaurant **79**
Cinta Grill **61**
Clear Café **54**
Coffee & Silver Cafe **62**
Divine Wine Bar
   & Shop **33**
Gaya Restaurant **17**
Glow Restaurant **3**
Ibu Oka **42**
Kafe **55**
Kemiri **13**
Lamak **57**
Minami **14**
Mozaic **19**
Nacho Mama **18**
Nasi Ayam Kedewatan **7**
Naughty Nuri's
   Warung & Grill **16**
Pizza Bagus **68**
River Café **78**
Sari Organic
   (Bodag Maliah) **34**
Siam Sally **65**
TeraZo **37**
The Three Monkeys **60**
Tutmak Warung Kopi **56**
Warung Enak **67**
Warung Lada **51**
Warung Mendez **21**
West End Café **15**

ATTRACTIONS ●

Agung Rai Gallery **75**
Antonio Blanco
   Museum **31**
ARMA Museum of Art **71**
Botanic Garden Ubud **76**
Elephant Safari Park **5**
Gaya Fusion of Senses **17**
Genta Gallery **73**
Goa Gajah
   (Elephant Caves) **80**
Gusti Lempad's Gallery **49**
Han Snel Gallery **36**
Komaneka Fine
   Art Gallery **59**
Murni's Warung **32**
Museum Puri Lukisan **39**
Neka Art Museum **12**
Pura Gunung Lebah **29**
Pura Kebo Edan **81**
Pura Penataran Sasih **83**
Pura Pusering Jagat **82**
Pura Saraswati **41**
Puri Saren Agung
   (Royal Palace) **48**
Rio Helmi Photo Gallery **38**
The Rudana Museum **74**
Sacred Monkey Forest
   Sanctuary **64**
Seniwati Gallery **50**
Sika Contemporary
   Art Gallery **22**
Symon Studios **30**

9

UBUD | Essentials

KUTUH

■ Police Station

Jalan Raya Andong

Jl. Cokorda Gede Rai

Jl. Raya Pejeng Kawan

PELIATAN

76
77
78
78
75

DUKUH

PEJENG

Sungai Petanu

83
82
81

Jalan Raya Pejeng

TEGES

To Mas, Batuan
& Sukawati

Jalan Raya Goa Gajah

74
79
79
80

Jl. Pura

Visitor Information, Tours & Maps

The **information kiosk,** on the south side of Jalan Raya Ubud (② **0361/973285**), near the intersection with Monkey Forest Road, is a good place to start. It has up-to-date listings of dance performances scheduled around town. For other information on good restaurants, shopping, galleries, and museums it's better to check with your villa manager or hotel concierge. Travel agencies are scattered all over town, each offering competitive prices for day trips and shuttles to other tourist areas. We recommend: **HIS Tour & Travel,** Jl. Monkey Forest (② **0361/972621**), **Bintang Tours,** Jl. Raya Ubud, Campuhan (② **0361/975992**), and **Muda Prima Holiday Tours,** Jl. Raya Mawang (② **0361/981465**). A local map called *Pathfinder* is a few years old, but it's the most user-friendly of those available.

[FastFACTS] UBUD

ATMs & Banks ATMs aren't as prevalent as in Seminyak and Kuta, but there are plenty of them around. Ubud has several banks and most exchange cash and travelers checks. Not all banks have ATMs.

Currency Exchange Most hotels and stores exchange money, but the rates are poor. Several money changers are scattered about town; the best is **Central Kuta** (② **0361/ 974381**), on Jalan Raya Ubud in front of Museum Puri Lukisan and between Permata Bank and Animale shop.

Hospitals & Clinics The **Ubud Clinic, Medical, Laboratory Service & Pharmacy** is at Jl. Raya Campuhan 36 (② **0361/974911**). **Ubud Hospital** is at Jl. Dewi Sita (② **0361/974415**). Also you can visit the **Toyo Clinic** (medical and ambulance service), Jl. Pengosekan (② **0361/978078**).

Internet Access Many hotels, cafes, and restaurants offer free Wi-Fi. The cheapest and the fastest Internet cafes are **Netvice Internet,** Jl. Hanoman 35A, Padang Tegal; on Jalan Raya Ubud, **Bali 3000 Internet Café** (② **0361/**

978538) and **Highway Internet Café** (② **0361/ 972107**); and **Fairway Café & Internet,** Jl. Dewi Sita (② **0361/978810**).

Pharmacies Two local pharmacies are: **Ubud Farma,** Jl. Raya Ubud (② **0361/974214**) and **Mua Farma,** Jl. Monkey Forest (② **0361/974674**).

Police Located along Jalan Raya Ubud (② **0361/ 975316**).

Post Office The main post office is at Jalan Jembawan 1. It's open Monday to Thursday 8am to 5pm; Friday 8am to 11am; and Saturday 8am to 1pm.

WHERE TO STAY

Ubud is a rare and precious experience for those seeking something beyond sun, sand, and surf. As central Ubud has become quite congested and touristy, we recommend staying in the lush, terraced rice fields (with beautiful views) over the downtown area; many resorts and guesthouses provide complimentary shuttle service to the center of town and private taxis are fairly inexpensive.

Very Expensive

Amandari ★★ Built within Kedewatan village, the Amandari manages to balance sensitivity and opulence with its unique integration of resort and community. In the 7th century, Hindu priest Rsi Markendea came to this village from Java and founded the sacred temple, Amandari (p. 186) 129 steps below the Amandari. Several times a year village ceremonies require the passage of tall, ritual palanquins and sky-high offerings gracing the heads of the village ladies. The resort itself, laid out like a fanciful Balinese village, is elegant without sacrificing local charm. The plush rooms are in huge, thatch roof stone cottages. Village suites have a ground-level lounge and a cozy upstairs loft bedroom like a rustic tree house. The resort's emerald-green infinity pool mimics the color of the surroundings and blends seamlessly with the green beyond.

Kedewatan-Ubud. www.amanresorts.com. (C) **0361/975333.** Fax 0361/975335. 30 units. Year-round US$850 and up standard; US$3,750 villa. AE, DC, MC, V. **Amenities:** Restaurant; bar; babysitting; bikes; concierge; golf course; health club; Jacuzzi; outdoor pool; room service; spa; tennis court. *In room:* A/C, fridge, hair dryer, minibar, Wi-Fi.

Chedi Club at Tanah Gajah ★★ ☺ The former estate of an Indonesian architect and art collector, this property combines the family's personal art and antique collection with 5 hectares (12 acres) of grounds reminiscent of a grand English estate—albeit entirely Indonesian in design. Shimmering ponds dotted with migrant Java pond herons and Dutch colonial black swans are surrounded by terraced hills of rice paddies tended by generations of Balinese farmers. This is a terrific place for children as there's plenty of room to roam free in a safe environment. Extras include a private butler, evening cocktail hour, private courtyard with plunge pool, and a complimentary bar in your room with crystal decanters of gin, vodka, and whisky. Watch the farmers' daily rituals through the soaring windows of the restaurant.

Jl. Goa Gajah, Tengkulak Kaja, Ubud. www.tanahgajah.com. (C) **0361/975685.** Fax 0361/975686. 20 units. High season US$430 suite, US$700 pool villa, US$990 estate; low season US$360 suite, US$640 pool villa, US$970 estate. Rates include breakfast, afternoon tea, and evening drinks. AE, DC, MC, V. **Amenities:** Restaurant (Chedi Club Restaurant, p. 179); bar; babysitting; bicycles; gym; outdoor pool; room service; spa; tennis court; Wi-Fi. *In room:* A/C, TV/DVD, movie library, stereo or CD, hair dryer, Internet, minibar.

COMO Shambhala Estate ★★★ 📷 If you want a retreat that rejuvenates as it relaxes, look no further than the COMO Shambhala, which calls itself "The Estate," and rightly so. Upon check-in you will be assigned PAs (personal assistants) that look after your complete program. With an ayurvedic doctor, a psychologist, a Pilates instructor, and master yogis from around the globe as well as a knock-out spa restaurant, you're bound to leave feeling better than when you arrived. The property is on the steep, bucolic Ayung River gorge. Private two- and three-bedroom villas share a common living room and pool. New one- and two-bedroom villas have their own private pools. They all have elegant furnishings, oversize and beautifully appointed bathrooms, and balconies that overlook lush jungle.

Desa Melinggih Kelod, Payangan-Gianyar. www.cse.como.bz. (C) **0361/978888.** Fax 0361/978889. 30 units. Year-round US$350 standard, US$850–US$4,300 suite, US$2,050 and up villa; price includes breakfast. AE, MC, V. **Amenities:** 2 restaurants, including Glow Restaurant (p. 181); bar; free airport transfer; babysitting; bikes; concierge; 9 outdoor pools; aqua therapy pool; room service; spa; tennis court. *In room:* A/C, TV/DVD, movie library, stereo or CD, fridge, hair dryer, minibar, Wi-Fi (free).

Fivelements ★ If you're a seeker a la Elizabeth Gilbert and are willing to splurge, this property may just be for you. Focusing on traditional Balinese treatments, raw food, and spiritual arts such as yoga, this boutique property with highly personal service dubs itself a "healing center" rather than a resort. It was built by a friendly Italian-and-American couple who fell in love in Bali and sought out some of the best traditional healers on the island. Luxurious yet rustic rooms, ecologically designed with bamboo walls, are perched right on the banks of a river, and the grounds feature plenty of communal gathering spaces. Even if you're not staying here, it's worth a trip for the excellent massage treatments, which you can follow with a meal on the deck of Sakti, the in-house restaurant.

Br. Baturning, Mambal. www.fivelements.org. ℭ **0361/469206.** Fax 0361/469822. 5 units. Year-round US$475. AE, MC, V. Amenities: restaurant; 2 pools; Wi-Fi; spa/sanctuary. In room: A/C, Wi-Fi.

Four Seasons Resort at Sayan ★   The Four Seasons, on the Ayung River, is incredibly posh, though you needn't feel intimidated. The entrance is a bit extrater-restrial: You cross a long bridge that leads to a lily pond that rests atop the lobby in an immense natural crater of rice terraces. The best rooms are right along the river. Expect Four Season's niceties such as luxurious bathrooms, huge tubs, and plenty of plush towels. The design features natural fabrics and gleaming woods highlighted by precious local art and artifacts. The two-level pool follows the serpentine shape of the river below.

Sayan, Ubud. www.fourseasons.com. ℭ **0361/977577.** Fax 0361/977588. 60 units. Peak season US$600–US$1,050 1-bedroom; US$2,600 2-bedroom; high season US$460–US$950 1-bedroom, US$2,400 2-bed-room; low season US$460–US$850 1-bedroom, US$2,100 2-bedroom; extra person US$100. AE, DC, MC, V. **Amenities:** 2 restaurants; bar; bikes; concierge; health club; outdoor pool; room service; spa. In room: A/C, TV, stereo or CD, fridge, minibar, Wi-Fi.

Expensive

Alila Ubud ★★   The Alila has a beautiful campus with some very mature and elegant gardens as a part of its lovely landscape. Its *pièce de résistance* however is the infinity-edge swimming pool voted one of the "50 Most Spectacular Pools in the World" by *Travel + Leisure* magazine. It's like a cube of water in otherworldly (or at least unlikely) suspension over the spectacular gorge. The rooms could do with an upgrade (there are no bathtubs) but many overlook the stunning northern stretch of the Ayung gorge where the popular rafting trips go by. The self-contained resort is 30 minutes north of central Ubud and offers a regular shuttle service. The riverbank picnics, complete with safari tents and champagne, are a real treat.

Desa Melinggih Kelod, Payangan-Gianyar. www.alilahotels.com. ℭ **0361/975963.** Fax 0361/975968. 64 units. Peak season US$245–US$510; high season US$225–US$470; low season US$185–US$390. AE, MC, V. **Amenities:** Restaurant; bar; airport transfer; babysitting; bikes; concierge; Internet; Jacuzzi; outdoor pool; room service; sauna; spa. In room: A/C, TV, fridge, hair dryer, minibar.

Bambu Indah ★★ 🎒   Savvy travelers with an environmental bent will think they've died and gone to heaven. Bambu Indah's ("Beautiful Bamboo") is the creation of the multitalented team of the Green School (p. 194). The four antique teak *joglo* (Javanese-style bungalows) have the most fantastic view of the Sayan ridge and the Ayung. Just past the swimming pool (that could be mistaken for a natural pond) and the working rice fields is the temple **Pura Dalem Gede Bongkasa.** (The temple isn't easily accessible though because it requires a trek through small back roads. If you make it there, bring your own sarong and sash.) There's no cafe or restaurant on-site but home-cooked organic meals are delivered to your porch at any time of day.

Br. Baung, Sayan-Ubud. www.bambuindah.com. ℭ **0361/977922.** Fax 0361/974404. 11 villas. Peak season US$95–US$295; high season US$90–US$290; low season US$75–US$275. Rates include break-fast. MC, V. **Amenities:** Lounge; babysitting; bikes; outdoor pool; room service; Wi-Fi. In villa: A/C, hair dryer, minibar.

Maya Ubud Resort & Spa   This fine resort is just east of central Ubud. The design makes elegant use of local materials, blended in an immaculate, contemporary style and rooms reflect a refined simplicity, with cool white and yellow tones set against the dark wood of Art Deco furnishings. Floors are river stone and ceilings are thatch. An elevator transports you down the steep valley to the riverside, where the fine spa rooms literally hang over the rushing water. The Maya is self-sufficient, but a shuttle service to town keeps you connected.

Jl. Gunung Sari, Peliatan-Ubud. www.mayaubud.com. ℂ **0361/977888.** Fax 0361/977555. 108 units. High season US$380 standard, US$471 pool villa; low season US$284 standard, US$435 pool villa. AE, DC, MC, V. **Amenities:** 2 restaurants, including River Café (p. 181); bar; airport transfer; bikes; pitch & putt golf; Internet; Jacuzzi; 2 outdoor pools; spa; floodlit tennis court. *In room/villa:* A/C, TV, fridge, hair dryer, minibar.

Samaya Ubud ★★   One of the best new resorts on Bali, the Samaya Ubud offers personal attention, breathtaking views of the surrounding rice paddies, and plush villas next to the Ayung River. Book a riverside room to be lulled to sleep on your *bale* (Japanese pavilion) by the comforting sounds of the rushing water. The bathrooms, decorated with contemporary art and flowers and featuring spacious bathtubs with jets, are some of the most beautiful we've seen. Many of the hotel staff members are ex-employees of the nearby Four Seasons and provide warm, professional service. A luxurious spa offers excellent, reasonably priced treatments, and extras such as afternoon tea and car service to downtown Ubud, both complimentary, make this a stand-out resort.

Sayan, Ubud. http://ubud.thesamayabali.com. ℂ **0361/731149.** Fax 0361/731203. 21 units. High season US$695 1-bedroom, US$1,320 2-bedroom; low season US$595 1-bedroom, US$1,220 2-bedroom. Rates include breakfast. AE, DC, MC, V. **Amenities:** Restaurant; bar; gym; pool; spa; laundry; yoga. *In room:* A/C, TV, DVD, minibar, MP3 docking station, Wi-Fi (free), hairdryer, safe.

Ubud Hanging Gardens ★   If you want to spend the majority of your holiday in the privacy of a luxurious villa, look no further than this resort. Done in traditional Balinese style but with all the modern amenities, each villa comes with its own lagoon-like infinity pool with a stunning view of the surrounding rice paddies. The property is set in a gorge so steep that it's serviced by a tram. The location is rather remote—the resort is set down a winding road and is a 45-minute drive to central Ubud—which is a good or bad thing, depending on your vacation intentions.

Desa Buahan, Ubud. www.ubudhanginggardens.com. ℂ **0361/982700.** Fax 0361/982800. 38 villas. Year-round US$350–US$670. AE, MC, V. **Amenities:** Restaurant; bar; airport transfer; Internet; 2 outdoor pools; spa. *In villa:* A/C, TV, fridge, hair dryer, minibar.

Uma Ubud ★★   A sister resort to the luxurious COMO Shambhala (p. 173), this set of boutique villas is aimed at a hip, young, jet-setting audience who prefer to be close to central Ubud. White gauzy curtains cover the four-poster beds; stand-alone bathtubs are done in black-terrazzo; and some rooms have views of the surrounding rice paddies. Kemiri, the resort's main restaurant, serves lively Asian dishes. The location offers the best of both worlds—you're on a street with some of Ubud's best restaurants and yet the peaceful resort offers beautiful grounds with views of the lush rice paddies beyond.

Jl. Raya Sanggingan, Lungsiakan, Kedewatan, Ubud. www.uma.ubud.como.bz. ℂ **0361/972448.** Fax 0361/975686. 29 units. High season US$275 standard, US$405–US$540 suite; low season US$260 standard, US$375–US$490 suite. AE, MC, V. **Amenities:** Restaurant (Kemiri); bar; babysitting; bikes; concierge; gym; outdoor pool; room service; spa; Wi-Fi (free in public areas). *In room:* A/C, TV/DVD, movie library, hair dryer, minibar.

Waka Di Ume ★   This small boutique-style hotel, nestled among the rice fields of north Ubud, is a relaxing haven for those looking to escape the bustle of town. Distressed woods, alang-alang roofs, natural-colored drapes surrounding the beds, and slate and lime-washed stone filling the pathways, all contribute to an elegant, boho chic. Tuesdays and Thursdays feature special walks through the nearby rice paddies. You would hardly know you were 10 minutes from the center of town.

Jl. Suweta, Br. Sambahan, Ubud. www.wakadiumeubud.com. ✆ **0361/973178.** 178 units. High season US$295–US$446; low season US$260–US$411. AE, DC, MC, V. **Amenities:** Restaurant; cafe; bar; airport transfer (US$35); babysitting; gym; Jacuzzi; outdoor pool; room service; spa; Wi-Fi (for a fee). *In room:* A/C, fan, minibar.

Warwick Ibah Luxury Villas & Spa ★ 🏨 Reminiscent of a European estate but with Balinese design, Ibah is nestled in a dense, 2-hectare (5-acre) garden on the banks of the Campuhan. The property has been hand-crafted with the skill of Tjorkarda Raka Kerthyasa, a mask carver and a member of the Ubud royal family. Each unique villa is filled with antiques and curios from the royal family's private collection. The grottolike pool has lounge areas carved into the stone and walkways and walls covered in verdant vines. The restaurant lacks charm but you can order meals around the pool and complimentary afternoon tea with Balinese cakes is served in an outdoor *bale.*

Warwick Ibah, Jl. Raya Campuhan, Ubud. www.warwickibah.com. ✆ **0361/974466.** Fax 0361/975686. 17 units. High season US$335–US$400 suite, US$495–US$795 villa; low season US$280–US$335 suite, US$280–US$795 villa. AE, DC, MC, V. **Amenities:** Restaurant; bar; babysitting; bicycles; concierge; outdoor pool; room service; spa; Wi-Fi (for a fee). *In room/villa:* A/C, TV/DVD, movie library, stereo or CD, hair dryer, minibar.

Moderate

Arma Resort Culture vultures can feel good about putting their feet up at the Arma Resort as the income generated from the property fuels the owner Agung Rai's other good works, such as the ARMA Museum (p. 188), the dance and drama theater, a public library, and a school. There are terrific dance and music performances here that you should try to see. The resort has a nice pool and a decent restaurant. Some sort of cultural exchange or another is likely to be going on during your stay.

Jl. Raya Pengosekan, Ubud. www.armaresort.com. ✆ **0361/975742.** Fax 0361/975332. 29 units. High season US$145–US$530; low season US$150–US$472. Rates include breakfast. AE, MC, V. **Amenities:** 3 restaurants; cafe; lounge; babysitting; outdoor pool; room service; Wi-Fi. *In room:* A/C, hair dryer, minibar.

Hotel Tjampuhan ★ 🏨 This hotel is a tropical sanctuary with terraces that lead to a beautiful gorge, the Tjampuhan River, and the Gunung Lebah Temple. The hotel was built in 1928 for guests of the prince of Ubud and was chosen by Western artists Walter Spies and Rudolf Bonnet as headquarters for the Pita Maha artists' cooperative. Air-conditioned rooms are larger and have better views than fan rooms. Splurge on a Raja Room (or even Spies's own villa) with verandas overlooking the gorge. There are two pondlike pools, another with cold spring water, and a sunken carved stone grotto in the shape of a mythical beast—one of the more unusual places for a massage.

Jl. Raya Campuhan, Ubud. www.tjampuhan.com. ✆ **0361/975368.** Fax 0316/975137. 67 units. Year-round US$67–US$87 standard with fan; US$90–US$110 standard with A/C; US$164 Walter Spies villa. Rates include breakfast. AE, MC, V. **Amenities:** 2 restaurants; 4 bars; babysitting; 2 outdoor pools and spring bath; spa. *In room:* A/C (in some), fan, fridge, minibar.

Komaneka Resort at Rasa Sayang ★ For those who want to stay right in the fray of Ubud's action, this new resort—part of a chain of Ubud resorts—provides plush suites and luxurious amenities such as an infinity pool that make it stand out on Monkey Forest crowd. The rooms feel a bit like what you'd find at a business hotel (that is, characterless) but they're plush and feature roomy bathrooms with standalone bathtubs. The hotel group also runs a slightly older but similarly modern and chic property across the street, the **Komenka at Monkey Forest,** as well as two more luxurious properties in more rural parts of Ubud. The sister properties are **Komaneka Bisma** (Jl. Bisma; © **0361/971933;** fax 0361/971955; 44 units; high season US$410 suite, US$641 1-bedroom villa, US$825 2-bedroom villa; low season US$346 suite, US$475 1-bedroom villa, US$750 2-bedroom villa; extra bed US$55; rates include breakfast, afternoon tea, and evening drinks) by the Campuhan River valley and **Komaneka Tanggayuda** (© **0361/978123;** fax 0361/973084; 20 units; high season US$405 suite, US$455–US$595 villa; low season US$350 suite, US$400–US$550 villa; extra bed US$55; rates include breakfast, afternoon tea, and evening drinks) in Kedewatan village overlooking the river Oos, 15 minutes by car from Ubud.

Jl. Monkey Forest, Ubud. www.komaneka.com. © **0361/975491.** Fax 0361/971995. 20 units. High season US$313 deluxe, US$372 suite, US$539 villa; low season US$258 deluxe, US$300 suite, US$400 villa; extra bed US$55. AE, DC, MC, V. **Amenities:** Restaurant; outdoor pool; room service; spa. *In room/villa:* A/C, TV/DVD, CD player, fridge, minibar.

Taman Bebek Villas ★★ 🏠 Canadian musicologist Colin McPhee built a Balinese house on the edge of the ridge above the magnificent Ayung River valley in 1944. His house and his life in Bali are celebrated in a marvelous read, *A House in Bali* (1946). The house was a series of thatched huts within a bamboo forest. By 1980, when infamous landscape architect Made Wijaya acquired this land, only the foundations of the houses remained. Made set about re-creating and improving upon the original structures. Today Taman Bebek Villas is still a retreat where painters, writers, dancers, and scholars come for inspiration. Four new Bali Aga Suites surround the pool on the ridge. Our favorite is the Croissant Villa, a mix between Queenslander and the Malaysian styles, with wraparound verandas, spacious garden bathrooms, and colonial Dutch interiors with artworks from Made's personal collection.

Sayan, Ubud. www.tamanbebek.com. © **0361/975385.** Fax 0361/976532. 11 units. High season US$280–US$300 bungalows; low season US$230–US$270; US$450 presidential suite. Rates include breakfast. AE, MC, V. **Amenities:** Cafe; bar; outdoor pool; room service; spa therapy. *In villa:* Fan, kitchenette, minibar.

Inexpensive

Budget choices line Monkey Forest Road and the Jalan Hanoman; better still, turn down any little alley or side street that cuts across them.

Agung Raka Bungalows Just south of central Ubud, these thatched bungalows are arranged around a series of rice paddies and surrounded by a thriving village arts community. Bungalows are basic wood-and-bamboo constructions with rudimentary outdoor bathrooms. Superior bungalows are single occupancy A-frames of teak. Bathrooms are large, modern courtyard facilities that include both a tile tub and a stone-floor shower. The suites are excellent: a dizzying spectacle of stone and marble, big enough for four and great for two.

Pengosekan Village, Ubud. www.agungraka.com. © **0361/975757.** Fax 0361/975546. 19 units. Year-round US$60 standard; US$70–US$150 bungalow. MC, V. **Amenities:** Restaurant; bar; airport transfers; babysitting; massage; outdoor pool; room service; Wi-Fi. *In room:* A/C, TV, minibar.

Alam Indah The Alam Indah overlooks rice fields and is just behind Monkey Forest Road. Rooms are named after the garden inhabitants: lily, lotus, and gardenia, to name a few. Staff are terrific with suggestions on what to do or for local tours. The breakfast is superb, with black rice pudding a must. If you're game, ask the owner Ibu

Wayan and her daughter Metri for cooking classes. Be sure to book a few days in advance for the class.

Nyuhkuning, Ubud. www.alam-indah.com. ⓒ **0361/974629**. 10 units. Year-round US$58–US$110; extra bed US$10. Rates include breakfast. AE, MC, V. **Amenities:** Restaurant; outdoor pool; room service. *In room:* Fan (2 rooms have A/C), TV.

Alam Sari ★ 🏠🐾 ☺   This hotel offers an excellent combination of comfort, social responsibility, setting, and low price—and is a delightful find for families, ecowarriors, and those who want to immerse themselves in Balinese culture. Everything the Alam Sari does is with a thought toward the local economy, ecology, and culture. The hotel almost exclusively employs villagers from neighboring Keliki. Environmentally friendly touches are everywhere, from solar water heaters to the use of recycled paper. Rooms are lovely, with views of the gorge and looming volcano. Traditional music is featured at night.

Keliki, Tromol Pos 03, Tegallalang, Ubud. www.alamsari.com. ⓒ **0361/981420**. Fax 0361/981421. 12 units. Year-round US$60 standard; US$70 suite; US$110–US$250 family unit. Rates include breakfast. AE, MC, V. **Amenities:** Restaurant; bar; babysitting; bikes; exercise room; Wi-Fi. *In room:* A/C, fridge, minibar.

Ananda Cottages ★   Just north of Ubud proper, Ananda Cottages is atmospheric enough for the Balinese experience you're hoping for, and yet situated far enough from the town center to discourage the tourist hordes. The rice fields and thatched cottages of this bungalow campus are almost more "Balinese" than real villages you might visit (where you'll now find TVs instead of shrines, and power machines instead of hand tools). Ananda is also a spiritual place for yoga, and meditation programs run every first and third week of the month; music and dance lessons are available from time to time. The cottages are brick huts with bamboo pavilion roofs. Downstairs rooms are the better choice, with outdoor tubs and patio living rooms. Upstairs rooms have modern bathrooms and small verandas. The small pool is set on an interesting raised rice terrace. The three new deluxe bungalows are very cozy and well worth the outlay.

Campuhan, Ubud. www.anandaubud.com. ⓒ **0361/975376**. Fax 0361/975375. 85 units. Year-round US$70–US$80 standard without A/C; US$95–US$110 standard with A/C; US$125 bungalow; US$250 villa. AE, MC, V. **Amenities:** Restaurant; bar; babysitting; outdoor pool; room service; spa. *In room/villa:* A/C, fan, fridge, minibar.

Bali Spirit Hotel & Spa   Not too far from central Ubud, in the village of Nyuh Kuning, this is a reasonably priced alternative to the really high-end luxury hotels. You get a great setting and comfortable rooms at a good price, without going overboard on the bells, whistles, and fees. Large, well-appointed rooms come with small kitchen nooks and decks, with local fabrics and materials employed throughout. The pool is a cozy perch with lounges overlooking the gorge, and traditional Balinese bathing pools are in the holy river below. Regular shuttles run to town.

Nyuh Kuning Village, Ubud. www.balispirithotel.com. ⓒ **0361/974013**. Fax 0361/974012. 25 units. Year-round US$95–US$135 standard; US$145 villa. Rates include breakfast. AE, MC, V. **Amenities:** Restaurant; bar; bikes; Internet; outdoor pool & children's pool; room service; spa. *In room/villa:* A/C, TV, fridge, hair dryer, minibar.

Casa Luna Honeymoon Guesthouse   This guesthouse has grown popular mostly through word of mouth and attracts an eclectic, artsy crowd. It's not exactly made for a honeymoon as the name suggests, though, because rooms are fairly run-of-the-mill, in traditional Ubud style; but they're clean and pleasant enough—and the location puts you in the middle of the action in central Ubud. The guesthouse is run by writer and restaurateur Janet de Neefe who also owns **Casa Luna Restaurant** (p. 180) and the Honeymoon Bakery, and runs her own cooking classes.

Jl. Bisma, Ubud. www.casalunabali.com. ✆ **0361/977409.** Fax 0361/973282. 30 units. Year-round Rp402,500–Rp690,000. AE, MC, V. **Amenities:** 2 restaurants; bar; airport transfer; Internet; outdoor pool. *In room:* A/C (in some rooms), fan, minibar.

Klub Kokos ☺ This is a good choice for those traveling with children. Even though it's only 2.5km (1½ miles) from town, it seems off the beaten track because of the round-about drive you need to take to reach the resort; hence, there's no roadside traffic. As there are only seven bungalows, guests are personally looked after by their hosts Krishna Sudharsana, a renowned Balinese artist, and his Australian wife, Cathy. The restaurant has simple options for youngsters; there's a games room and a library for young and old. Cathy and Krishna can arrange courses on kite- or hat-making, dancing, or how to make the intricate temple offerings.

Bangkiang Sidem, Ubud. www.klubkokos.com. ✆ **0361/978270.** Fax 0361/978270. 7 units. Year-round US$60 standard; US$70 2-bedroom; US$120 family unit. Rates include breakfast. MC, V. **Amenities:** Restaurant; Internet; saltwater pool; room service. *In room:* Fan.

Sunny Blow Villas Jepun ★ 🍴 That it's owned by the excellent Japanese Minami (p. 181) restaurant next door gives you an indication of the quality of these bungalows. The comfortable units come with outdoor showers and bathtubs. A beautiful garden stretches through the property, and there's a decent-sized pool. The location is also excellent as it's walkable to bustling central Ubud but faraway enough to offer some peace and quiet. Some of Ubud's best restaurants are just steps away.

Jl. Raya Sanggingan, Ubud. www.minami-bali.com. ✆ **0361/977950.** 9 units. Year-round Rp400,000–Rp700,000. Rates include breakfast. MC, V. **Amenities:** Restaurant; Internet; saltwater pool; room service. *In room:* Fan.

WHERE TO EAT

Dining in Ubud has become as global as dining in any other metropolitan city with many international restaurants in the busy town offering a cosmopolitan selection of Indian, Thai, American, French, Japanese, Italian, and anything south or north of the equator. Small warungs or *gerobak* (carts) sell *babi guling* (suckling pig) and other Balinese delicacies. Unless otherwise noted, restaurants are open daily.

Expensive

CasCades Restaurant ★★ ASIAN/FRENCH CasCades serves fine French food with an Asian twist. The produce here is all fresh and local but the fine, high-quality meats are imported. Try the New Zealand Lamb Nori, a dish of lamb loin wrapped in feather-light pastry. There are also delectable plates of pan-seared bass, river prawn, and scallops, and all manner of decadent desserts. In 2008 the restaurant was honored with the Award of Excellence from *Wine Spectator U.S.A.* for its wine list of more than 160 different quality wines from around the world, which is no easy task in Bali. Adjacent to the restaurant is the Viceroy Bar, featuring a stunning, lacquered, long bar looking out over the dramatic river gorge.

In the Viceroy Bali, Jl. Lanyahan, Ubud. ✆ **0361/972111.** www.cascadesbali.com. Reservations recommended. Main courses Rp80,000–Rp1,500,000; set menu Rp450,000–Rp1,500,000. AE, DC, MC, V. Daily 7–10am, noon–3pm, 6–9:30pm.

Chedi Club Restaurant INDONESIAN Seemingly floating among the rice paddies, the restaurant at the Chedi Club offers a harmonious balance of Balinese and

Indonesian cuisine. The glass windows make a picture perfect frame for the working rice farm in view. Much of the produce is sourced on-site from their own private herb and vegetable garden. Take in a dance at the dramatic open-air amphitheater before your dinner (check for times, normally Tues and Sat in the dry season).

In the Chedi Club Tanah Gajah (p. 173), Jl. Goa Gajah, Tengkulak Kaja, Ubud. ✆ **0361/975685.** www. tanahgajah.com. Reservations recommended. Main courses Rp200,000–Rp600,000. AE, MC, V. Daily 7am–10:30pm.

Mozaic ★★★ INTERNATIONAL   Chef Chris Salans's constant upgrades and refinements to food and decor has turned Mozaic into one of Asia's top fine-dining destinations. Salans employs traditional French ingredients and methods but pays respect to his surroundings with Indonesian flavors such as spicy sambal sauce, turmeric, and cardamom. Guests choose from several six-course, constantly changing tasting menus. Highlights from a recent meal include curry butter roasted yabbies (Australian crayfish), with a delectable truffle sauce, and a crispy seared foie gras served with mango puree. The restaurant offers excellent value for money—a meal like this in the West would cost double. You can also sign up for cooking classes here.

Jl. Raya Sanggingan, Ubud. ✆ **0361/975768.** www.mozaic-bali.com. Reservations recommended. Tasting menu Rp650,000–Rp1,200,000. AE, DC, MC, V. Tues–Sun 6–10:30pm.

Moderate

Bridges ★★ ✦ CONTINENTAL   Bridges is one of our top new restaurant picks for Ubud. Dining takes place on an elegant white veranda overlooking a gorge at this wonderful new restaurant, led by an Australian chef. The setting—made romantic by candlelight and jazz music—complements the accessible and delicious dishes, including excellent homemade pine nut and Roquefort cheese gnocchi, and mushroom and feta tortellini. The appetizers—which have an Asian bent with items such as vegetable tempura and rice paper rolls—are equally wellexecuted, as are the desserts. The restaurant is also great value; you can have something close to a fine-dining experience for well under US$100 for two.

Jl. Campuhan (near Museum Antonio Blanco), Ubud. ✆ **0361/970095.** www.bridgesbali.com. Main courses Rp90,000–Rp195,000. AE, MC, V. Daily 11am–midnight.

Casa Luna BALINESE/MEDITERRANEAN   Casa Luna serves Mediterranean and Balinese cuisine in a relaxed tropical atmosphere and is one of the key meeting places for the October Ubud Writers Festival (p. 28), which was founded by the owner, Janet de Neefe. Janet and her Balinese husband also own Bar Luna, and a cooking school (p. 191). The front of the restaurant serves breads and baked goods and an extensive menu includes children's options. There's live jazz twice weekly but times can be sporadic so check ahead.

Jl. Raya Ubud, Ubud. ✆ **0361/977409.** www.casalunabali.com. Reservations recommended. Main courses Rp50,000–Rp95,000. AE, MC, V. Daily 8am–10pm.

Gaya Restaurant ASIAN/MEDITERRANEAN   This open-sided restaurant with cool breezes and stylish decor sits above the Gaya Fusion of Senses gallery (p. 189). Gaya serves Naples-influenced cuisine and all its breads, grissini, and desserts are baked fresh on the premises daily. The seafood linguine and the carbonara are both winners.

Jl. Raya Sayan, Ubud. ✆ **0361/979252.** www.gayafusion.com. Main courses Rp60,000–Rp190,000; set menus Rp225,000–Rp395,000. AE, MC, V. Daily 7am–11pm.

Glow Restaurant ★★ HEALTH FOOD   The spa cuisine is flavored with Balinese and Southeast Asian spices and composed of organic and locally sourced ingredients with plenty of raw fruits and veggies, though meat and fish are also on offer. Sunday brunch is worth the trek even if you aren't a guest at COMO Shambhala. The first thing that strikes you is the sheer variety of dishes, such as gingerbread hot cakes with lemon sauce, and yellowfin tuna *tataki* with radish, black fungus, ponzu, and fried garlic. Our favorite is the roast tomato, leek, and oregano frittata with Gruyère, though the wild baby greens, ocean trout gravlax, poached egg, and saffron comes a close second. The *pièce de résistance* is their raw food lasagna, which has a mighty following. Pretty local girls practice traditional dance to the sounds of a gamelan orchestra nearby under the strict tutelage of Ibu Wayan, a known taskmaster. Some of Glow's dishes are also offered at **Kemiri,** the restaurant at COMO's sister resort, Uma Ubud (see p. 175), located closer to town.

In COMO Shambhala Estate (p. 173), Desa Melinggih Kelod, Payangan-Gianyar. ✆ **0361/978888.** Reservations recommended. Main courses Rp220,000–Rp320,000; dinner Rp240,000–Rp440,000. AE, DC, MC, V. Daily 11:30am–9:30pm.

Lamak ★★ INDONESIAN   This restaurant is dramatically designed by renowned architect and landscape artist Made Wijaya and features a spectacular steel sculpture against striking burgundy-colored walls. Before tucking into the cuisine, make a beeline for the bar with its funky cowhide bar stools and do-rag uniformed bartenders mixing up one of their signature cocktails. Lamak's kitchen offers Balinese, Indonesian, Asian, and international food but don't mistake this for fusion. The chef's dishes retain their flavorful origins through innovative interpretation. The "Small Plate" Crab Meat with young coconut, lime, and fresh mint is artfully arranged between crispy wonton sheets and is as light as it's delicious.

Jl. Monkey Forest, Ubud. ✆ **0361/974668.** www.lamakbali.com. Reservations recommended. Lunch Rp45,000–Rp95,000; dinner Rp45,000–Rp260,000; vegetarian Rp32,000–Rp95,000; set menu Rp315,000. AE, MC, V. Daily 11am–11pm.

Minami ★★★ JAPANESE   This elegant yet unassuming restaurant is one of our favorites on the island. Minami attracts a strong Japanese contingent and those with a more delicate palate. Start with a perfectly presented bento box with grilled fish, miso-flavored grilled beef, Japanese pickles, and shrimp tempura. In the bright and primarily white restaurant and outdoor courtyard area you can dine on high-end Japanese cuisine and then relish that second or third sake on black leather stools at the immaculately carved buffalo horn bar.

Jl. Raya Sanggingan, Ubud. ✆ **0361/970013.** www.minami-bali.com. Reservations recommended. Main courses Rp85,000–Rp115,000; set menu Rp250,000–Rp300,000. MC, V. Daily 11am–11pm.

River Café ★★ INTERNATIONAL   The main reason for dining here is the gorgeous surroundings. It's a long walk to the restaurant down some very steep steps—be prepared because you have to walk back up afterward. Fresh-baked rosemary and oregano flatbread with balsamic and olive oil is a great start to a delicious light lunch, perhaps followed by carrot soup with ginger.

In Maya Ubud Resort & Spa (p. 174), Jl. Gunung Sari, Peliatan-Ubud. ✆ **0361/977888.** www.mayaubud. com. Reservations recommended. Pasta Rp145,000–Rp260,000; pizza Rp150,000. AE, MC, V. Daily 10am–8pm.

TeraZo MEDITERRANEAN   The spacious interior of this hip bistro is simple yet welcoming. The extensive menu has gazpacho as a welcome starter in the tropical heat and light and delicious spring rolls. The eight-layer pie is a delicious pastry crust

CAFES, coffee & TEA

Bali Buddha, Jl. Jembawan 1 (✆ **0361/ 976432;** www.balibuddha.com; main courses Rp18,000–Rp62,000; MC, V; daily 7am–10pm), in front of the post office to the east of town, is a happening little expat spot with a small grocery that sells fresh bread, organic vegetables, healthy snacks, supplements, and natural skincare products. The menu has organic and house-made salad-soup-sandwich standards along with Indonesian dishes, pasta, and burgers. Vegan, vegetarian, and raw dishes are also available. Upstairs is a popular juice bar—a good place to meet long-staying folks or get info off the bulletin board. It's New Age central here, more or less.

Cafe Moka, Jl. Raya Ubud (✆ **0361/ 972881;** main courses Rp35,000–Rp70,000; no credit cards; daily 8am–10pm), is a great place to pump up with some java and baked goods. Good breakfasts, croissants, and baguettes and delicate, delicious French pastries such as eclairs and tarts should get your sugar rush going.

Tutmak Warung Kopi ★, on Jl. Dewi Sita, near Batan's Waru (✆ **0361/ 975754;** main courses Rp30,000–Rp70,000, latte Rp17,000; MC, V; daily 8am–11:30pm), serves the best coffee in town with great desserts, ice creams, sorbets, and a whole range of healthy treats, from salads to light lunches. There's also a good menu for youngsters. It's across from the soccer field and so easy to find and extremely child-friendly.

The **West End Café** ★, Jl. Raya Sanggingan (✆ **0361/978363;** main courses Rp21,000–Rp54,000; AE, MC, V; Mon-Sat 11am–6pm), in the hip Neka Museum neighborhood, is the place for "afternoon tea" complete with scones, homemade strawberry preserves, clotted cream, tea sandwiches, and tarts. It would look right at home on the main street of an English coastal town.

filled with smoked blue marlin, spinach, ricotta, and mushrooms. There are also a host of grilled items, fine pasta, and gourmet Asian-influenced dishes, such as the *nasi kuning* (yellow coconut rice with raisins, cashews, and strips of egg) and the *kue tiaun* (stir-fried rice noodles, chicken, and local greens). A tempting breakfast menu surprises with ricotta blintzes topped with honey and fresh yogurt.

Jl. Suweta, Ubud. ✆ **0361/978941.** www.baligoodfood.com. Reservations recommended. Main courses Rp58,000–Rp175,000. AE, MC, V. Daily 10am–midnight.

Inexpensive

Batan's Waru EUROPEAN/INDONESIAN Tucked away on a pleasant side street, Batan's Waru is particularly atmospheric at night, when the entrance is lit with candles. The ambitious menu has traditional dishes beyond the usual suspects, and plenty of vegetarian options. For an appetizer, try *urap pakis* (wild fern tips with roasted coconut and spices) or *lemper ayam* (chicken dumplings simmered in a banana leaf). The spicy hummus comes with grilled-pepper flatbread and tomato-mint relish. The restaurant also does smoked duck and a *babi guleng* feast, with a day's advance order, and there's a full menu of pasta, sandwiches, and light fare as well. Finish off with a perfect cup of Illy-brand espresso.

Jl. Dewi Sita, Ubud. ✆ **0361/977528.** www.baligoodfood.com. Main courses Rp15,500–Rp43,000. AE, MC, V. Daily 8am–midnight.

Bebek Bengil (Dirty Duck) ★ EUROPEAN/INDONESIAN   The Dirty Duck is the best place to try Ubud's famous dish. First stewed in local spices, then deep-fried, the duck here is delicious and not quite as oily as in other restaurants. Another way to go is the stuffed chicken with shiitake, sprouts, and spinach. The menu also features salads, sandwiches, and veggie options. Book a table toward the back, which looks out onto the paddy fields.

Padang Tegel, Ubud. ⓒ **0361/975489.** www.agungraka.com/bebekbengil. Main courses Rp12,500–Rp35,000. AE, DC, MC, V. Daily 10am–10pm.

Black Beach ★ ITALIAN   This friendly three-level restaurant is creating a bit of a buzz in quiet Ubud with its novelty factor of, you guessed it, black sand. The bar is covered in black sand from the owner's husband's beach village, Sukawati. As Antonella explains, "The only thing Ubud was missing was a beach bar so we wanted to create one." The top-floor terraced restaurant has rooftop views. On the menu are 16 homemade pasta sauces as well as other Italian classics such as lasagna, pizza, and fresh salads.

Jl. Hanoman 5A, Ubud. ⓒ **0361/971353.** Pizza Rp32,000–Rp74,000; pasta Rp23,000–Rp55,000. MC, V. Daily 7am–11pm.

Cafe Lotus INTERNATIONAL/MODERN INDONESIAN   The food here isn't half bad, but the real reason to come to Cafe Lotus is for the chance to dine in the shadow of the **Pura Saraswati temple** (p. 187). The menu features good Western options, pastas and such, with some modified into fiery dishes using hot chilis, olives, and hearts of palm. Try the Balinese Satay Lilit, a mixed-fish kebab with a hint of coconut, served on skewers on a plate the size of a boat. The fresh health drinks are a delight. No beef is served due to the restaurant's proximity to the temple.

Jl. Raya Ubud, Ubud. ⓒ **0361/975660.** www.lotus-restaurants.com/cafe-lotus-ubud. Reservations recommended. Main courses Rp25,000–Rp54,000. AE, MC, V. Daily 8:30am–11pm.

Cinta Grill INTERNATIONAL   Cinta specializes in barbecue ribs, Indonesian grilled chicken, and satay. Other specialties are Asian curries such as Javanese white chicken, South Indian fish, or North Indian chickpea with freshly ground fresh herbs, roots, and spices. There are very good Caesar salads, a first-rate carbonara, and house-made tortellini with a simple classic tomato and basil sauce. Sweet teeth will love the Dutch apple tart and chocolate fudge cake. Mojitos are the favored drink, especially during the two-for-one special from 4 to 7pm, with five tropical flavors to try.

Jl. Monkey Forest, Ubud. ⓒ **0361/975395.** www.baligoodfood.com/cintagrill.asp. Reservations recommended. Pasta Rp52,000–Rp86,000; curries and soups Rp42,000–Rp86,000; grill Rp68,000–Rp135,000. AE, MC, V. Daily 7am–midnight.

Clear Café ★ ORGANIC   This new cafe in the center of Ubud has a beautiful facade and interior, with ornate wooden doors, a bamboo and stone garden, and marble tables. Diners are requested to leave their shoes at the door, creating a cozy atmosphere that's perfect for lunch or a casual dinner. The largely vegetarian menu features healthy salads and pastas along with Southeast Asian and Mexican entrees. The extensive drink list features tonics and elixirs, along with drinks made from almond, soy, and rice milk. This eatery is sure to be a hit with anyone who's embraced the healthy, granola vibe of Ubud.

Jl. Hanoman 8, Padang Tegal Kaje, Ubud. ⓒ **0361/889-4437.** www.clear-cafe-ubud.com. Rp35,000–Rp70,000. No credit cards. Daily 8am–11pm.

Coffee & Silver Cafe EUROPEAN   Tucked away on a side road, this tiny gem literally lights up at night, with a dragon possessing red, shining eyes on top of the roof. The small but good seafood menu changes daily. Indonesian and Balinese dishes are also available. The emphasis here is on fresh ingredients and solid European food. The Dutch owner Carlsten is usually around answering esoteric queries that come his way about life and occasionally about what things you should see in Ubud. An attached shop sells antiques and curios—decorative art from the Dutch colonial era sits among interesting pen and ink drawings and a mix of treasures.

Jl. Sukma 45, Ubud. ✆ **0361/978228.** Main courses Rp42,000–Rp119,000. AE, MC, V. Daily 8:30am–11pm.

Ibu Oka ★★ BALINESE   Tourists and locals flock like ducks to water for the famous grilled suckling pig at Ibu Oka. The fall-off-the-bone *babi guling* is served with garlic string beans and steamed rice. The restaurant is laid out in a traditional family household compound, and diners sit at low tables, shoeless and comfortable. The ambience of clucking chickens and fighting cocks is sure to raise an eyebrow or two but this is a village warung at heart—despite the throngs of tourists who find it.

Jl. Suweta, Ubud. No phone. *Babi guling* Rp25,000. No credit cards. Daily 11am–2pm.

Kafe VEGETARIAN   This is an extremely popular cafe with fantastic vegetarian mains, California-style burritos, coffee, and desserts. Upstairs houses several of the more well-known nongovernment organizations in Ubud so along with vegans it's filled with a very international crowd. There's also a yoga and massage center and a gift shop with crafts from nonprofit organizations. The big noticeboard has all manner of local news, deals, and events.

Jl. Hanuman 44, Ubud. ✆ **0361/970992.** www.balispirit.com. Main courses Rp22,000–Rp65,000. No credit cards. Daily 7:30am–11pm.

Nasi Ayam Kedewatan BALINESE   This place has been around since the mid-1960s. The specialty of the house is "torn fried chicken" (*ayam goreng suir*). Owner Ibu Mangku's sambal is so spicy you might refry that chicken in your mouth if you aren't careful. Enjoy it with plenty of steaming white rice and cold Bintang beer.

Jl. Raya Kedewatan, Ubud. ✆ **0361/974795.** Main courses start at Rp10,000. No credit cards. Daily 9am–6pm.

Naughty Nuri's Warung & Grill ★ INDONESIAN/BARBECUE   Naughty Nuri's has hosted a number of memorable or unmemorable evenings depending upon the number of martinis served. Run by Indonesian Isnuri and her affable New Yorker husband Brian, this watering hole and restaurant is famous for its Indonesian fare and barbecued pork spareribs. The real deal here, however, is the martinis, which celebrity chef Anthony Bourdain claims are the best outside of New York City. Thursday is sashimi night and is packed with local Ubudians. **Nacho Mama** ★★ (✆ **0361/780-4697**; main courses Rp17,000–Rp42,000; no credit cards; daily 11am–10pm) is part of Naughty Nuri's and serves burritos, tacos, and nachos and some excellent margaritas with lots of Bali limes. If Nuri's is crowded, order the ribs at Nacho Mama's down the road.

Jl. Raya Sanggingan, Ubud. ✆ **0361/977547.** Indonesian Rp20,000–Rp35,000; ribs Rp60,000; burgers Rp50,000–Rp52,000. No credit cards. Daily 10am–10pm.

Pizza Bagus ITALIAN   This is the local pizza joint of choice, which also serves good fresh pasta, gelato ice cream, and some of the best espresso in Ubud. Also offers free Wi-Fi.

Jl. Raya Pengosekan, Ubud. © **0361/978520.** www.pizzabagus.com. Main courses Rp23,000–Rp58,000. MC, V. Daily 9am–10:30pm.

Sari Organic (Bodag Maliah) ★ 🎁 ORGANIC   It's somehow reassuring to know that places like Sari Organic exist and that there are people behind them that believe in "making the world a better place"—their exact words. The project supports local farmers, uses organic produce, and spreads virtue because the only way to get here is on foot taking a pleasant 15-minute trek from Jalan Raya Ubud near the aqueduct down a small pathway through the farms and rice fields. When you arrive you'll be pleasantly surprised by this quirky restaurant with 360-degree views of the paddy fields and wildlife. Call to reserve a table as this place is packed and popular.

Subak Sok Wayah, Ubud. © **0361/972087.** Reservations recommended. Main courses Rp45,000–Rp75,000. No credit cards. Daily 8am–8pm.

Siam Sally ★ THAI   The intrepid duo that brought you TeraZo (p. 181) and Cinta Grill (p. 183) has done it again. Good Thai food is all about getting the balance right with a bit of spice and a bit of sweet and sour. Siam Sally does it right, and all in a spectacular setting with enthusiastic service. Live jazz plays several times a week, but call ahead for the ever-changing schedule.

Jl. Raya Pengosekan, Ubud. © **0361/980777.** www.baligoodfood.com. Reservations recommended. Curries Rp46,000–Rp92,000; main courses Rp42,000–Rp118,000. AE, MC, V. Daily 10am–midnight.

The Three Monkeys MEDITERRANEAN   See no evil, hear no evil, eat no evil—or was that speak? The grub on offer at this bohemian cafe is eclectic and delectable. Choose from seafood, pastas, and Asian-Mediterranean dishes. There's no corkage fee for wine and at night a romantic feel pervades, with the glow of bamboo torches lighting the evening's people-watching parade.

Jl. Hanoman, Ubud. © **0361/975554.** Main courses Rp38,000–Rp59,000. MC, V. Daily 7am–11pm.

Warung Enak ★ INDONESIAN   This is a great place if you'd like to get a primer in Indonesian cuisine, set in a whimsical, artful atmosphere that makes it stand out among the other warungs. The Indonesian menu here reads like a tribute to the 200 and more ethnic groups that populate these fabled islands. Here you can discover the rich and intricate use of more than 60 hand-crushed herbs and spices and lesser known nuts and legumes that achieve strong, tangy, and always interesting flavors. Their famous rijsttafel comes with 17 dishes and rice so that you can really taste across the archipelago. The restaurant also offers cooking classes several times a week.

Jl. Raya Pengosekan, Ubud. © **0361/972911.** www.warungenakbali.com. Main courses Rp50,000–Rp82,000; rijsttafel Rp175,000 for 2. AE, MC, V. Daily 11am–11pm.

Warung Lada INDONESIAN   Served in traditional warung style where you point and pick your dishes, the food here is typical warung grub such as chicken, eggplant, tofu and tempeh, vegetables, *nasi goreng* (fried rice), *mie goreng* (fried noodles), and *soto ayam* (an Indonesian yellow soup served with boiled chicken and vegetables). You can leave here with a full stomach for Rp50,000 for two people.

Jl. Raya Hanoman, Ubud. © **0361/972822.** Rice Rp3,000–Rp5,000; fish and meat Rp6,000. No credit cards. Daily 9am–10pm.

Warung Mendez INDONESIAN   The specialty here is goat, which is much healthier for you than other meats due to its low fat content but difficult to cook. The owner Chef Mendez hails from Yogyakarta and uses his old family recipes, which require simmering for hours before marinating in Javanese spice paste. The goat soup, *sup iga kambing,* is made with nutmeg, ginger, cloves, cinnamon, vegetables, and a squeeze of lime. To find this place, go up Penestanan hill and turn up the mountain road opposite the old Beggars Bush in Tjampuhan.

Jl. Penestanan, Ubud. ✆ **0361/973076.** Main courses Rp43,000–Rp47,000. No credit cards. Daily 10am–10pm.

EXPLORING UBUD

Temples

As you explore Ubud and make friends with the locals and expats, you'll hear different stories about the legends and histories of local temples from guides, scholars, and professors alike. There really isn't one correct version here.

Goa Gajah (Elephant Caves)   One of Bali's most visited tourist sites is a grotto of elaborate stone carvings from the 9th century. The main attraction is the impressive entranceway, made of what appears to be menacing creatures and demons. Legend has it that the main protagonist was an elephant and since the carving at the entrance is elephant-like, they're known as the Elephant Caves. The mouth leads into a small underground T-shaped cave measuring about 9m × 9m (30 ft. × 30 ft.) with several small ledges possibly used by priests to meditate on or even sleep. Aside from the small cave the only other thing to see here is the decorative bathing pool. On the far wall of the pool are six, semi-clad, female figures holding urns pouring water. Women bathe on one side and men on the other.

Bedulu Village, Blahbatu. Admission, including sarong rental, Rp6,000 adults & children. Daily 7am–5:30pm.

Pura Gunung Kawi   This temple was made by King Marakata Near as an altar for King Udayana; an inscription dates the temple to A.D. 945. In the Balinese Hindu faith, death consists of three phases. The first is the cremation of the body, the second is setting free the holy spirit from the spiritual body, and the third is seating the holy body in a sacred abode. Temples (*candi*) were built as the spiritual abodes of deceased kings. Here the Dewa Pitara of King Udayana is seated at the Candi Gunung Kawi temple; other altars were built for his descendants. Today the god Vishnu and goddess Sri are worshiped here as farmers and their *subak* (rice irrigation organizations) come to pray for prosperity.

Tampaksiring. Admission Rp6,000 adults & children; video camera Rp5,000; camera Rp3,000. Daily 7am–5pm.

Pura Gunung Lebah   Located at Campuhan, in the gorge just 1.5km (1 mile) west of Ubud, this temple is an easy walk from the Ubud market and makes a very pleasant early morning stroll. Legend has it that in the 8th century the high priest Rsi Markandya, a holy sage who came from Java to build Besakih Temple, was spiritually attracted to the beautiful area, the confluence of two rivers. He stayed, meditated, and built a temple. Ubud was born.

Campuhan. Admission Rp10,000 adults & children; video camera Rp5,000; camera Rp3,000. Daily 7am–5pm.

Pura Kebo Edan   "Crazy buffalo temple" is in the east Ubud suburbs near Goa Gajah and is said to have been built in the 12th century. Although not a fantastic structure, it's famous for the nearly 4-m (12-ft.) statue known as the Giant of Pejeng. Temple history facts are difficult to pin down but it's thought to be about 700 years old. The Giant of Pejeng is famous for his huge penis, and four penises at that. The first theory is that the animal appears in Brahmanism while others say it may represent Bima, a hero of the epic *Mahabharata,* dancing on a dead body in a myth related to the Hindu Shiva god. We like this version as in this story Bima falls in love with a woman and his desire has risen. However Bima's penis is too big for her and she finds another lover; Bima finds them making love one day and he has them killed. It's hard to decipher the moral of the story here.

Bedulu Village. Admission Rp10,000 adults & children. Daily 7am–5pm.

Pura Penataran Sasih   This temple is about 4km (2½ miles) east of the center of Ubud and is best known for the hourglass-shaped drum more than 2m (6½ ft.) long, the largest single-piece cast drum in the world. It's difficult to see because it's in the inner courtyard high up in a pavilion. The drum's geometric patterns are said to resemble patterns from both Irian Jaya and Vietnam. Estimates of its age vary from 1,000 to 2,000 years old; the legend of its origin says that the drum came to earth as a fallen moon, landed in a tree, and shone so brightly that it stopped a band of naughty thieves from going about their mission. Because the moon was bright both day and night, one of the thieves tried to urinate on it to stop it shining. The thief died and the moon dropped to the ground. What is a fact is that this amazing ancient relic represents the bronze age of Southeast Asia.

Pejeng Village. Admission Rp10,000 adults & children. Daily 7am–5pm.

Pura Pusering Jagat   Literally translated as the "Temple of the Navel of the World," this temple is 100m (328 ft.) south from the main road of Pura Penataran Sasih. The point of interest here is the 1-m (3-ft.) high, elaborately carved holy water vessel, whose exterior is sculpted with a detailed relief thought to depict the Hindu myth of "the churning of the sea of milk." There are several versions of this legend, but they all relate the story of the gods and the demons desperately trying to get their hands on the elixir of immortal life. It's good to know that some things haven't changed since the 14th century. As the story goes, under Vishnu's guidance they set about churning this cosmic sea of milk with the aid of a holy mountain as their pestle and the serpentine *naga* as the pulleys. Carved from a single block of sandstone you can still just make out some of the figures including the undulating *naga* ropes and a number of dancing deities supporting them. In a nearby pavilion is another significant icon, the 1-m (3-ft.) high phallic lingam and its female receptacle, the yoni—an important shrine for Balinese infertile couples and newlyweds.

Pejeng. Admission Rp10,000 adults & children. Daily 7am–5pm.

Pura Saraswati   The royal family commissioned this temple and water garden, dedicated to the Hindu goddess of art and learning, at the end of the 19th century. The main shrine is covered in fine carvings and the *bale* houses and giant *barong* masks are interesting. The restaurant **Cafe Lotus** (p. 183) is situated at the front so diners can look out over the grounds.

Jl. Raya Ubud. Free admission. Daily 7am–5pm.

Puri Saren Agung (Royal Palace)   From the late 19th century to the mid-1940s, this was the seat for the local ruler. It's a series of elegant and well-preserved pavilions, many decorated incongruously with colonial-era European furniture. Visitors are welcome to stroll around, though no signs explain what you're looking at. Evening dance performances are held in the courtyard, by far the best and most dramatic setting for these in Ubud. Many members of the royal family still live here and, if you're lucky enough, one might just show you around. There are six very basic rooms to stay in for around US$50 a night but no facilities on the grounds.

Jl. Raya Ubud. 📞 **0361/975057.** Free admission. Daily 7am–5pm.

Tirta Empul ★★★   The word *tirta* (derived from the Sanskrit) means "water" and *empul* is a Balinese word that means "spring." Balinese regard these springs as sacred and people come from miles around to bathe in the waters. The temple has rice fields to the north, the Pakerisan river to the east, a palace built in Sukarno's day used as a Presidential retreat to the west, and craft stalls to the south. The temple dates from 960 b.c. in the period of the Warmadewa Dynasty. Twelve water spouts pour holy water from 12 sacred springs into a long pool; two Olympic-size pools are used for communal bathing. The main temple courtyard contains shrines and pavilions, one for Brahma, Shiva, and Krishna, one for Mt. Batur, and one for Indra (Dewi Indra).

Jl. Raya Penelokan, Tampaksiring. Admission Rp6,000 adults & children. Daily 8am–6pm.

Museums

Antonio Blanco Museum ★★   This museum pays homage to Bali's famous Catalan expat. Born in the Philippines, Blanco arrived here penniless, but eventually befriended the king, married, had children, and lived the life of Riley all his days. He was a favorite at court and the confidant of many powerful people on Bali and in Indonesia. This grand gallery houses a collection of his homespun, baroque pornography that's as much a romp through Blanco's sexual dalliances as anything. Some paintings feature Blanco's raunchy prose poetry. The consummate egomaniacal artist, Blanco envisioned this monument to himself and participated fully in its creation before shuffling off this mortal coil in 1999. The museum grounds are a trip, with Blanco's monkeys and exotic birds still ruling the roost.

Campuhan-Ubud. 📞 **0361/975502.** www.blancomuseum.com. Admission Rp50,000 adults & children. Daily 9am–5pm.

ARMA Museum of Art ★★   A few kilometers south of Ubud, the Agung Rai Museum of Art (the ARMA) is but one branch of the charming Agung Rai's empire, which includes the museum, a commercial art gallery, a Thai restaurant, a cafe, and a resort (p. 176) all within a stone's throw of each other. Agung Rai, one of Bali's foremost art entrepreneurs, began his professional life peddling souvenirs in Kuta, which exposed him to local artists. He began collecting and gained a reputation by backing these artists; with his fine eye he began promoting their work abroad. ARMA opened with proceeds from Agung Rai's commercial art activities and now has about 250 paintings on permanent display. The collection includes traditional Kamasan-style paintings on tree bark, works by Batuan school artists of the '30s and '40s, and works by Walter Spies and Raden Saleh, considered the father of Indonesian paintings. Check out Bangswaan Jawa's oil on canvas dated 1837 of an Indonesian regent couple—the first Indonesian Western style oil painting.

Jl. Pengosekan. 📞 **0361/975742.** www.armamuseum.com. Admission Rp10,000 adults & children. Daily 8am–4pm.

Museum Puri Lukisan ★ 👜   The Museum Puri Lukisan is one of Bali's most historically fascinating fine-art museums. A major renovation has turned this formerly dilapidated display into something nearly on par with the Neka Art Museum (see below). Founded in 1956, the collection was a joint initiative of the prince of Ubud, Tjokorda Gde Agung Sukawati, and his close friend, Rudolf Bonnet, to showcase the ideas and artistic achievements of the Pita Maha artists' cooperative.

Jl. Raya Ubud. ✆ **0361/975136.** www.mpl-ubud.com. Adults Rp10,000; free for children 14 and under accompanied by an adult. Daily 8am–4pm.

Neka Art Museum ★★ This museum of 400 works was founded by former schoolteacher Suteja Neka, a patron of the arts. The first gallery displays works by new and more established Indonesian artists and operates as a commercial art gallery. Other pavilions are thematically organized. Pay special attention to the **Lempad Pavilion** with works on paper by one of Bali's most revered artists, I Gusti Nyoman Lempad, and the **Arie Smit Pavilion,** showcasing 50 works by the Dutch-born artist who was a personal friend of Neka and lived on-site for many years. Don't miss the view of the **Campuhan Gorge** to get a glimpse of what inspires local artists.

Jl. Raya Campuhan, Desa Kedewatan. ✆ **0361/975074.** www.museumneka.com. Adults Rp40,000, free for children 12 and under. Mon–Sat 9am–5pm; Sun noon–5pm.

The Rudana Museum This is the latest addition to Bali's already prolific stable of museums. Nyoman Rudana and his wife seek to promote the richness of Indonesian art to a wider audience as well as provide a cultural education institution for the public. The museum building was designed according to the Balinese philosophy of *Tri Angga* (foot, body, and head) and *Tri Mandala* (inner court, middle court, and outer court). Contemporary paintings here include works by Indonesian artists Made Wianta, Nyoman Gunarsa, and Sri Hadi Suarsono.

Jl. Cok Rai Pudak 44, Peliatan. ✆ **0361/975779.** www.museumrudana.com. Admission Rp100,000. Daily 10am–5pm.

Art Galleries

Don't pass up the free galleries around town, especially on Jalan Raya Sanggingan going north toward the more high-end resorts.

Agung Rai Gallery ★★ Agung Rai chooses his painting based on *taksu,* which is a theory of "honesty between the artist and the viewer. An artist will follow his heart or instinct. A painting that has a certain special magic does not need to be elaborated upon, the painting alone speaks." Anticipate finding some real treasures here.

Jl. Peliatan. ✆ **0361/975449.** www.agungraigallery.com. Free admission. Daily 8am–6pm.

Gaya Fusion of Senses ★★ Gaya has a strong reputation for developing contemporary art on the island. A constant stream of exhibitions show modern art by locals and foreigners in high regard, such as German Peter Dittmar, Swiss Stephan Spicher, New Yorker Pablo Gentile, and Indonesian artists Alfi, Murni, Made Wianta, and Wayan Karja. Performance art, films, and other community activities are held here. The terrace bar and Gaya restaurant (p. 180) serves the goal of "a space that integrates life and art." Every Sunday from 11am to 1pm is a free art program for children of all ages taught by top Indonesian artists who donate their time.

Jl. Raya Sayan. ✆ **0361/979252.** www.gayafusion.com. Free admission. Daily 10am–10pm.

Genta Gallery This gallery, related to The Rudana Museum (see above), has a well-documented collection that originates from mostly Indonesian artists. Each different pavilion displays a vast range of work from landscapes of daily Balinese life or traditional occasions such as *barong* to very contemporary pieces. Visit the workshop to witness the artists actually putting their ideas onto canvas.

Jl. Raya Lodtunduh 1. ✆ **0361/974254.** www.museumrudana.com/gentagallery. Free admission. Daily 9am–5pm.

Gusti Lempad's Gallery ★ Opposite the market is the former home of I Gusti Lempad, which has been in the family for more than a century. The paintings for sale are by his family but his aren't for sale here (the best place to see them is at Museum Puri Lukisan (p. 188) and Neka Art Museum (p. 189)). I Gusti Nyoman Lempad, like his father and children, was a talented painter who died at the remarkable age of 116 in 1978. He originally painted in the *wayang* style, but moved to a more expressive, freer style, painting and drawing in black Chinese ink on paper.

Jl. Raya Ubud. ℂ **0361/975618.** Free admission. Daily 10am–7pm.

Han Snel Gallery ★ 🎁 The small gallery of Dutch artist Han Snel is on Jalan Kajeng, a pleasant side road off Jalan Raya Ubud. Snel painted in a number of styles, but the most notable was geometric figures of Balinese landscapes and people with a slightly cubist bent. Several stunning portraits of Balinese women speak to how he met his wife: She began modeling for him at 13 and married him at 16. Examples of his paintings can be found in the other galleries in Ubud.

In Han Snel Bungalow, Jl. Kajeng. ℂ **0361/975699.** www.hansnelbungalow.com. Free admission. Daily 8am–9pm.

Komaneka Fine Art Gallery This is one of the few galleries in Bali that has ample space to show off large-scale contemporary works. The prerequisite for any foreign artist displayed is *kontemporer,* a strong connection to the island. One of the top-selling artists here is the masterfully superior I Made Djirna who has achieved international recognition. Keen on painting women as archetypes and mothers, Djirna's women are altogether different from that of non-Balinese artists such as Le Mayeur who depicted women as exotic and sexy.

Jl. Monkey Forest. ℂ **0361/976090.** http://gallery.komaneka.com. Free admission. Daily 8am–8pm.

Rio Helmi Photo Gallery ★ Rio Helmi's Gallery in Ubud sells his work that celebrates the region's people and places, contemporary lifestyles, and Mahayana Buddhism. A man on a mission, Rio is quietly accomplishing the goal of photographing most of the indigenous peoples of Indonesia. His photography has been published in the *New York Times* and *Vanity Fair,* and he has also published several books including: *Bali Style, River Gems,* and *Made in Indonesia.*

Jl. Suweta. ℂ **0361/978773.** www.riohelmi.com. Free admission. Daily 9am–9pm.

Seniwati Gallery ★★ 🎁 In traditional Balinese society, activities are divided by gender and, historically, painting and sculpture were male territory. Of course, there have always been women painters but it was difficult for them to be shown and get their deserved recognition. In 1991 British-born Mary Northmore Aziz converted a house into a gallery for female artists. A number of the Balinese artists that she shows have been heavily influenced by one of the recognized "traditional" styles. Ni Made Suciarmi and her niece, Supini, two of Bali's top classical painters, still work on cloth polished with rice flour and grind their own pigments. Ni Wayan Warti works in the tradition of Batuan, creating paintings full of the eerie supernatural quality the Balinese call *tenget,* while Gusti Agung Galuh's paintings show a strong influence from Walter Spies.

Jl. Sriwedari 2B. ℂ **0361/975485.** www.seniwatigallery.com. Free admission. Tues–Sun 9am–5pm.

Sika Contemporary Art Gallery The owner here abhors commercial art, calling it "too sweet like candy." Instead he and his colleagues are keen on multimedia that identify with the spirit of Balinese art and culture in a nontraditional way.

Jl. Raya Campuhan. ℂ **0361/975084.** www.sikagallery.info. Free admission. Daily 9am–5pm.

The **Bali Purnati Center for the Arts**, Jl. Gunung Abang, Banjar Penataran, Negara Batuan (① **0361/294590;** fax 0361/294591; www.balipurnati.com), has interesting cultural exchanges and events that include performing and visual arts, music, and film. The only way to find out what's on is to call up and see if you get lucky. Opportunities to view live performances don't happen often but if they do you might catch a Wadaiko drum troupe from Japan, a stage performance of I La Galigo by renowned theater director Robert Wilson, or the Kronos Quartet. Accommodations (eight units; year-round US$80; AE, MC, V) here are normally reserved for exchange programs and theater groups, but if you're interested in staying just call ahead and see if there's space.

Symon Studios   Symon Studios used to be called the Art Zoo and the first thing you'll notice is the sign outside that says "DANGER ART!" This weird and wonderful gallery has been a Campuhan landmark for over a quarter of a century. The artist Symon hails from America's Midwest, but that doesn't help to explain his art because the primary subject matter of his paintings is beguiling young Balinese men in various stages of undress. You get the picture. His color palate is bright and bold as Symon was influenced by both Arie Smit and Andy Warhol, not necessarily in that order.

Jl. Raya Campuhan. ① **0361/974721.** www.symonstudios.com. Free admission. Daily 8am–8pm.

Cooking Classes

Classes typically include a morning at the local market and an afternoon in the kitchen. One of the most authentic classes you'll find is the one at **Warung Enak** (p. 185), offered on Mondays, Thursdays, and Saturdays. For Rp450,000, you'll visit a traditional food market, learn six dishes, and have a leisurely lunch. **Casa Luna Cooking School,** Jl. Raya Ubud (① **0361/971257;** www.casalunabali.com; Rp300,000–Rp450,000), is run by expat Australian Janet de Neefe and her Balinese husband Ketut Suardana. Classes are held at Janet's Casa Luna Honeymoon Guesthouse (p. 178). Of the resorts, **Ubud Hanging Gardens** (p. 175), **Samaya Ubud** (p. 175), and **Alila Ubud** (p. 174) offer cooking classes.

   Chris Salans, the renowned chef who has made Mozaic (p. 180) one of the finest restaurants in Southeast Asia, shares his prowess with the lucky few who book ahead for his remarkable cooking classes (① **0361/975768;** www.mozaic-bali.com; half-day class US$90, full day US$130, professional class full day US$130; minimum four participants). Students get their own recipe book and apron, and so even if you don't manage to get it right at home, at least you can look the part.

Spas

All the high-end resorts have good spa services and there are some mom-and-pop-type operations that will really surprise your purse strings as well as your body. Today it isn't just flower baths and foot scrubs, you'll also find alternative and independent wellness centers and detox spas. Spas are open daily.

   The Mother Earth of spas, **COMO Shambhala's wellness retreat** (p. 173; single treatment US$80–US$150; AE, DC, MC, V; daily 10am–7pm) has tailor-made programs prescribed after consultation with a team of professionals, including ayurvedic doctors, nutritionists, and psychologists. Colonic hydrotherapy and herbal cleansers are popular here. Your specialists prescribe daily yoga or martial arts, which help balance your *doshas*—Sanskrit for "fault" or "imbalance." Not that you'd have any of those, but just in case, this is your place. Take advantage of the chlorine-free pool, with massage jets. The raw food menu is thankfully as tasty as it is nutritious.

The spa at **Kayumanis,** Sayan (*(C)* **0361/972-7777;** www.kayumanis-spa.com; single treatment US$50–US$85; package US$175–US$268; AE, DC, MC, V; daily 8am–6pm) is all about some serious pampering. A signature is "Sensory Surrender:" A 6-hour treatment that begins with a brief yoga session and refreshing walk followed by a warm tea tree oil body scrub and then a tea tree oil-infused bath, before being wrapped in a concoction of frangipani and coconut. This is followed by a warm volcanic stone massage and then a simultaneous foot massage and facial.

The **Kirana Spa ★**, in the Royal Pita Maha, Kedewatan (*(C)* **0361/976333;** www.kiranaspa.com; 1-hr. treatments US$100, 2 hr. US$180, 3 hr. US$320, half-day US$400, 1-day US$490; AE, DC, MC, V; daily 9am–9pm), is a joint production between Japan's leading cosmetics company Shiseido (the first such spa outside Japan) and Ubud's royal family. The menu has just five polished and perfect treatments. You can have a spa treatment only or combine the spa time with relaxing in the gardens and swimming pool.

The **Mango Tree Spa** at Kupu Kupu Barong (single treatment US$60–US$90, specials US$70–US$125; AE, DC, MC, V; daily 9am–9pm), sits in a mango tree and uses L'Occitane products. You literally have to climb a tree to reach the spa villas but fortunately stairs are provided for the tender footed.

The award-winning spa in the **Maya Ubud Resort ★★★** (p. 174; single treatment US$60–US$75, package US$121–US$175; AE, DC, MC, V; daily 8am–8pm) is suspended down a gravity-defying cliff. Blending effortlessly with the colors of nature, the spa pavilions are made with local materials and include outdoor bathtubs that sit with the waters of the Petanu River.

Spa Alila ★, in Alila Ubud (p. 174; single treatment US$45–US$65, package US$78–US$170; AE, DC, MC, V; daily 9am–9pm), has excellent therapists who warm up with a daily yoga session for themselves to get in the right frame of mind for working on you. The local treatments made from green tea, bamboo, and virgin coconut oil proved so popular that it started to sell them to guests. The Alila Recovery signature massage includes techniques from Thai, Swedish, and Balinese massage.

At **Spa Hati,** Jl. Raya Andong 14 (*(C)* **0361/977578;** www.spahati.com; single treatment Rp70,000–Rp185,000, package Rp530,000; MC, V; daily 9am–9pm), you can feel good as well as do good since all the proceeds go to support the expansion and upkeep of the Bali Hati School for children in the village of Mas. Of the nine treatments on offer, guests can choose from a 60-minute Blissful Journey massage or Rapture, a 90-minute treatment that includes a rejuvenating body scrub and two well-trained masseuses who'll massage away any remnants of jet lag.

The spa at **Four Seasons Resort Sayan ★★★** (p. 174; massage US$55–US$190, body treatment US$55–US$270, package US$145–US$450; AE, DC, MC, V; daily 9am–9pm), universally accepted as one of the best spas in Bali, has a permanent expatriate spa director, which shows how serious they are about pampering. The Suci Dara Ayurvedic experience is delivered with Indian aromatic herbal oils that will have you seeing out of your third eye. Take advantage of the new *watsu* pool and have a "rebirthing experience," which gets to your inner child with skillfully guided water stretches and movements.

Ubud Outdoors

One of the most enjoyable ways of seeing Ubud is **on foot,** making your way through the *gang* (alleyways) that zigzag through town and crossing over into the fields of rice paddies that take you through quaint villages to see farming life first hand.

BIKING Plenty of places in Ubud rent bikes and it's a lovely way to see the surrounding villages. You should expect to pay about US$70 for the day. Many operators offer leisurely guided biking excursions in Ubud and down through the villages below Kintamani. **Bali Adventure Tours** (☎ 0361/721480; www.baliadventuretours. com; US$79 adults, US$52 children; includes transport and lunch) ends its trip at the Elephant Safari Park (p. 194) where you can have a peak at the gentle giants without having to pay extra for entry. **Banyan Tree Cycling Tour,** Jl. Jambangan, Banjar Baung (☎ 081/33798516 or 0361/805-1620; banyanbiketours.com; US$55 adults, US$40 children under 10, US$40 nonrider accompanying a rider; costs include meals, drink, and transport), begins about an hour's drive from central Ubud with breakfast at a restaurant with panoramic views of the mountains and rice fields. The trip is about 25km (16 miles) almost all downhill. At the end, you're treated to a lovely home-cooked meal at the tour leader's home.

Bali Trail Blazers ★ (☎ 0361/842-7181; www.bali-trailblazers.com; day rides US$100 per person with two-person minimum, 2 days US$330, 1 week US$960, bike rental 1 week US$125, bike rental 2 weeks US$200; tours include gear, water bottle, transportation, lunch, snacks and soft drinks; longer trips include hotel, breakfast, and lunch) offers single-track, off-road biking for experienced, adventurous riders. Trips are led by professional Balinese cyclists and follow steep, thin mountain trails and motorbike paths. Guide I Ketut Sukerta is recommended for riders who want to keep a fast pace. Don't sign up if you're not experienced.

RAFTING White-water rafting on the Ayung River, where rapids can range from class II to IV, is one of Bali's most fun and invigorating experiences. Looking up at the dense jungle from the sacred river can be surreal and you'll see traditional villages, temples, and cliffside stone carvings, some of them old. Don't get too distracted, however, because moments later you'll be dropping down white-water rapids holding on for dear life. The two top companies are **Sobek** and **Bali Adventure Tours. Sobek** ★★★, Jl. By Pass Ngurah Rai 100X Simpang Siur Kuta Bali (☎ 0361/768050; www.balisobek.com; US$79 adults, US$52 children 14 and under; includes transportation, insurance, and lunch), puts its boats in just east of where **Bali Adventure Tours** ★★★ (☎ 0361/721480; www.baliadventuretours.com) begins. Some smaller companies offer cheaper rates but, if you go with them, be careful to check their gear ahead of time. All rafters should be provided with helmets and life jackets. The Ayung River runs faster during the November and December rainy season, when trips are sometimes canceled because of high water.

WALKING Meet in front of the Puri Lukisan Museum at 8:30am for the **Bali Nature Herbal Walk** ★ (☎ 081/23816024; www.baliherbalwalk.com; US$18, including herbal tea, refreshing herbal drinks, Balinese cake or tropical fruits). The walk lasts until noon and exposes you to a wide range of native plants and herbs. You'll learn to identify herbs by sight, smell, and taste, and be introduced to plants that are used for first aid, emergencies, and more serious illnesses.

The **Bali Nature Walk** ★, Jl. Dewi Sita (☎ 081/79735914; Rp200,000–Rp300,000 depending on your pickup site), picks you up from your hotel at about 8am. The walk starts about 30 minutes later from Ubud at one of Bali's oldest temples and takes you through lush jungle and into agricultural farmland. On clear days you can see the charming temple Pura Sibi Alit.

It would be sinful to miss out on Victor Mason's famous **bird walk** ★★★ (Tjampuhan; ☏ **0361/975009;** www.balibirdwalk.com; US$33; Tues, Fri–Sun). British-bred Mason leads the pack when it comes to cavorting with the birds and bees of Ubud. His famous walks start at Beggar's Bush (just over the Tjampuhan bridge, opposite the Antonio Blanco museum) at 9am and end at Murni's Warung (p. 198) and include lunch. Count on seeing lots of birdlife including egrets, white-breasted water hens, and the resident Java kingfisher.

Botanic Garden Ubud ★★ 📷   These gardens, spread over 4.9 hectares (12 acres), provide an excellent look at the variety of lush island plant life. Highlights include the orchid greenhouse, a Muslim garden with a symmetrical tiled path, and the fruit tree area. A labyrinth, purportedly the first in Bali, is a surefire hit with youngsters.

Kutuh Kaja. ☏ **0361/780-3904.** www.botanicgardenbali.com. Admission Rp50,000 adults & children. Daily 8am–6pm.

Elephant Safari Park ★★ ☺   The Elephant Safari Park, run by Bali Adventure Tours, is less of a safari and more of an elephant ride. These native Sumatra elephants are well cared for and live in large, lush enclosures. The owners have worked carefully with locals from Taro village, previously one of Bali's most remote and untouched villages, to make sure that they leave little more than elephant tracks. A safari starts with Pachyderm 101, as knowledgeable guides discuss the animals' care and feeding, local ecology, threats to the native population, and preservation efforts. Then, along with a *mahout* (guide), you go on a galumphing trip through the jungle. A fun elephant show is staged daily at 11am, 1pm, and 3:30pm. The park has recently begun

☺ LEARNING TO love THE EARTH

The Ubud **Green School** ★★★, Jl. Raya Sibang Kaja (15 min. south of Ubud; ☏ **0361/469875;** www.green school.org; call to make a tour appointment; entrance by donation), is a spectacle best seen to be believed and could easily be the wave of the future. Visionary John Hardy and his wife, Cynthia, founded this school with the proceeds from their John Hardy jewelry brand. The school has classes from kindergarten to eighth grade with plans to expand through high school and eventually worldwide. Made almost exclusively out of bamboo, the buildings are an architectural marvel. The world's largest bamboo bridge joins the east and west sides of the campus, emblematic of the founders' goals: to connect learning

with creativity; environmental responsibility with scientific knowledge; respect for self with respect for the many cultures represented in and around the school. Take a tour and be inspired.

The school also runs a day and overnight camp called **Green Camp** ★★★. Activities such as coconut-tree climbing, kite making, bug hunting, and chocolate making are designed to challenge children while educating them about nature. Off-site adventures include volcano climbing, white-water rafting, mountain biking, and scuba diving. Ages range from 5 to 16 years and are residential or day programs. Check out **www.greencamp.com** for more information.

offering a night safari that begins at 6pm every night and includes an elephant talent show and a four-course dinner for US$63 (US$42 for children). You can also stay on their grounds at the Elephant Safari Lodge, which offers spacious rooms with views of the park and its elephants.

Jl. Bypass Ngurah Rai, Pesanggaran. 🕿 **0361/721480.** Fax 0361/721481. www.baliadventuretours.com. Reservations recommended. Admission US$16 adults, US$52 with elephant ride; children 12 and under US$8 and US$36 with elephant ride; family rates and Internet rates available. Admission includes transport, buffet lunch, and show. Daily 8am–6pm.

Sacred Monkey Forest Sanctuary ✋ Yes, there *is* a monkey forest at the southern end of Monkey Forest Road. The towering tree clusters here are home to a troop of bad-tempered but photogenic primates that swing from branches, cannonball into pools, and do everything short of putting on suits and paying taxes, all to the general delight of photo-snapping visitors. Signs warn you not to feed the monkeys, even though locals stand under those very signs selling you bananas and nuts for precisely that purpose. Do so if you really must, but don't tease the critters, who are grumpy enough as it is—just hand them the food. Make sure you have no other food on you—they'll smell it. They're also known to snatch at dangling or glittering objects and to gnaw on sandals. There's a small temple in the forest, and the track also leads to Nyuhkuning, a village known for woodcarving.

Jl. Monkey Forest. 🕿 **0361/971304.** www.monkeyforestubud.com. Admission Rp20,000 adults; Rp10,000 children. No credit cards. Daily 8am–6pm.

AROUND UBUD

Away from the beaches and immersed in rice paddies, you might be tempted to think that you're seeing a less commercial Bali, the "real" Bali perhaps (whatever that means). However, this is a major tourist route, a sort of shoppers' and collectors' circuit that can leave even the most voracious shopper satisfied. Just after leaving the bypass and shortly before the Batubulan bus terminal, the center of all public transport, and heading east, you cross into the old kingdom (now the regency) of **Gianyar.** The royal house of Gianyar allied itself with the Dutch against its traditional foes in the rival palaces thus avoiding the fate of the other kingdoms whose royal lines were almost completely decimated in ritual *puputan* (suicides). This allowed them to continue their artistic endeavors and today the majority of the population is somehow

Getting the Real Deal

When in **Batubulan,** make sure that you really are buying a carved stone piece and not a cheaper mass-produced artwork that's molded rather than carved from lava-stone "concrete." Unless you have a trained eye, you may not be able to tell. Always ask and look for lines that are the tell-tale signs of mold work.

Some unscrupulous carvers in **Mas** sell cheaper woods as sandalwood *(cenana),* which is an extremely expensive material mainly from East Timor. The tricks include rubbing oil on the carvings or packing them in sandalwood chips. It's hard to tell the real deal so either go to a trusted source or assume the worst and alter your price accordingly.

involved in handicrafts and arts. Each village en route to Ubud has its own specialized handicraft or art form with roots in royal patronage.

Batubulan   Batubulan is only about 10km (6 miles) northeast of Denpasar. This is stone carving and *barong* dance central—as if children in this village were born with a chisel in their hands and a rhythm in their walk. Performances take place every morning between 9 and 9:30am and last for about an hour. The performances are for tourists but it's a good way to kick off your shopping. This is where you'll find the Ganesha of your dreams and a Buddha for your boudoir. International shipping isn't a problem, if you can't resist the very large-scale pieces.

Batuan   This unique village just south of Ubud has a rich cultural legacy in both painting and the arts. The style of painting, now referred to as *batuan,* originated here in the 1930s and has continued to this day. The method involves first completing a detailed, black-and-white, pen-and-ink drawing and then filling it in with subdued colors. These days, you can catch an occasional cell phone or motorbike popping up in the scene. Batuan is also noted for the ancient *Gambuh* dance, which is still occasionally performed on full moons and other special occasions. The dance form is on the edge of extinction and yet is considered the ancestor of all Balinese dances. If you hear of one happening, catch it if you can.

Celuk ★ 📷   About 5km (3 miles) from Denpasar, the shops and homes of this town are filled to the gills with silver and gold. Long a center for artisans in elaborate gold jewelry for royal households, Celuk now produces jewelry for the international market. Apprentices begin young and by the time they're in their early teens are producing fine ornaments from the precious metals. Almost every family in Celuk now makes or sells gold and silver work. Prices are competitive and quality is similar. Huge tour buses park outside some of the bigger stores, but don't be put off. Go to some of the smaller shops along the back lanes and you'll be duly rewarded. You'll be told that prices are fixed but they aren't, and so bargain. If you're interested in buying a few gold and silver pieces check the gram rate on the Internet beforehand so that you have an idea of a fair price—all gold and silver is weighed and sold by the gram.

Mas ★   Mas is just 6km (3¾ miles) south of Ubud. Woodcarving is one of Bali's most ancient arts and for centuries craftsmen have been chipping away in Mas. The woodcarvers of this old Brahamana village create both artistic sculptures as well as more traditional characters such as deities, masks, or naturalist animals. Wander the back streets to see the families at work.

Sukawati About 5km (3 miles) south from Ubud is the **Sukawati Art Market** open dawn till dusk. Here you can find production of ceremonial umbrellas, *lamak* (the hangings decorated with Chinese coins and little mirrors seen on shrines at festival time), gold-painted *perada* cloth wrapped around shrines, and other ceremonial pieces. Tourists come by the bucket load to stock up on cheap trinkets, fabrics, baskets, and temple decorations. Be prepared to haggle. The colorful, open-air food market here has literally everything under the sun. You can still see the ancient art of puppet making at the market, which is the least touristy thing about the place.

SHOPPING: ISLAND OF THE GOODS

As the artistic and cultural center of Bali, Ubud is a great base from which to source antiques and artifacts, jewelry and silver, textiles, baskets and bamboo, art, and stone- and woodcarvings. While most things in Ubud are within walking distance, it's worth hiring a car if you're going to hit the outer villages described above. Larger shops take credit cards but the smaller ones often are cash only. Credit card transactions normally incur a 3% commission. Most shops open daily by 9am and close by 9pm, though you'll find places that stay open as late as 10pm.

   Jalan Raya Ubud, beginning at about Antonia Blanco's Museum and ending at around the Bamboo Gallery, has several great antiques and artifacts stores, art galleries, as well as the highly recommended Neka Art Museum (p. 189). **Monkey Forest Road** is lined with outlets selling beads, silver jewelry, cotton and casual apparel, paintings, fabrics, handicrafts, faux designer goods, and some tribal arts and antiques.

   The **Ubud Market ★**, southeast corner of Monkey Forest Road and Jalan Raya Ubud, is open daylight hours. Booths sell handicrafts, fans, batik bags, fabrics, baskets, and jewelry. Everything is affordable but be sure to bargain. The big market is held every 3 days or so when women come in from nearby and mountain villages to sell and buy livestock, hardware, fruits, vegetables, and many other goods.

Books

Ganesha Bookshop ★★ 📖 This beloved Ubud institution with Ganesha, the god of knowledge and art, as its moniker, opened in the 1980s. The owners divide their time between Sydney and Ubud and have made this intellectual haven their labor of love. The shop sells secondhand and antiquarian books and a wide variety of out-of-print books on the Indonesian archipelago. Also for sale are CDs, musical instruments, magazines and gift cards, maps, and other gift items. Jl. Raya Ubud. 📞 **0361/970320.** www.ganeshabooksbali.com.

Periplus Bookstore Periplus publishes a huge range of books and its bookshop almost acts as a publishing center. The myriad of English titles covers literature, art, interior decoration, spirituality, cooking, and Bali and Indonesia. Tourists will find maps and the latest imported magazine to devour. Browsing isn't really encouraged as many books are wrapped in cellophane. The good selection of interactive children's books should ease the holidays. Jl. Raya Ubud. 📞 **0361/971803.** www.periplus.co.id.

Furniture & Housewares

Design Unit Here you can find fashionable modern Asian housewares, lamps, furniture, and the like, all very "Elle Decor," with some nifty bric-a-brac such as wooden bowls and boxes. Local designers who export sell many of their goods here. The store is next door to a handy shipping company. Jl. Andong, Ubud. ☎ **0361/980471.**

Horizon Glassworks Ron and his wife, Ann Seivertson, run this glass studio near central Ubud and allow visitors to watch the fascinating glass blowing. Sculptures, vases, paperweights, and bowls are blown by Ron and then enhanced by his wife with swirls, dots, speckles, shards, and threads of color. Prices range from US$100 up to the thousands. Jl. Raya Kengetan. ☎ **0361/780-4014.** www.horizonglassworks.com.

Island Living On the way to Tegallalang, this vast warehouse specializes in made-to-order furniture. If you're short on time, plenty of ready-made items are for sale, such as Java chests, leather bar stools, and dining tables; there are also planters chairs, old wheels, and furniture crafted from roots and driftwood. If you're going to have a piece made for you, bring a photo of what you're looking for and let your imagination run wild. Shipping is easy and service good. Jl. Andong. ☎ **0361/974064.**

Murni's Warung ★ This place is filled to the brim with Indonesian artifacts, antiques, sculptures, masks, memorabilia, and the odd remnant of the Dutch colonial area. Jl. Raya Campuhan. ☎ **0361/975233.** www.murnis.com.

Papadun A mini Aladdin's den on all things Indonesian, Papadun has some authentic pieces mixed in with all the touristy garb. It's a good source for *wayang* puppets, painted masks, and an assortment of other artifacts. Jl. Raya Sanggingan (in front of Indus Restaurant). ☎ **081/338794377.**

Shalimar Shalimar boutique has both antiques and some great home accessories such as beaded table runners and matching napkins. In the antiques department you can expect to find ethnic art pieces, including masks and *wayang* figurines. Jl. Raya Ubud 88. ☎ **0361/977115.** www.shalimarbali.com.

The Shop ★★ The Shop is an elegant and understated approach to antiques, objects, and design. The stunning wares hail from Indonesia, Burma, Thailand, and Laos and each piece is given a letter of provenance listing details of origin, age, and cultural use. Owner Debbie's favorite piece is a reclining Burmese Buddha in alabaster. You can custom-order housewares and have them shipped anywhere in the world. The shop also sells jewelry designed by the owner and renowned American jeweler Carolyn Tyler. Jl. Raya Sayan 52. ☎ **0361/973508.**

Toko East Toko East has slick contemporary home furnishings sourced from some of the premier designers on the island. Browse the tempting treasures such as Majapahit-inspired bronze works, handmade glass and ceramics, bronze garden lamps, and decorative items with sterling silver finishes, lacquered sea shell accessories, and "hyacinth" water lily weavings. Jl. Raya Ubud. ☎ **0361/978306.** www.dekco.com.

Groceries

Bintang Supermarket There were sighs of disbelief when Ubud got its own Bintang supermarket: Such commercialism is kept at bay in this arty colony. Some people, however, are thankful that they can now buy a wide assortment of canned goods and drinks, fruits and vegetables, pastas, sauces, and dry goods. There's also a section for toiletries and other necessities. Jl. Raya Sanggingan 45. ☎ **0361/972972.**

Delta Dewata This excellent local supermarket stocks fresh fruits, vegetables, meats, and fish as well as household electrical items and stationery needs; it also has a decent children's toy court with amazing bargains. Jl. Raya Andong 14. ☎ **0361/973049.**

Take a Jewelry Tour

Visit the **John Hardy workshop ★★★** in Mumbul near Ubud (Banjar Baturning, Mambul, Abiansemal, Badung; ✆ **0361/469888**; www.johnhardy.com; by appointment only) and watch the production of the John Hardy jewelry brand. An organic lunch is followed by a trip to the showroom where jewelry is 50% off retail prices back home. The quality of craftsmanship here is mesmerizing.

Jewelry

Jean-François Fichot ★★★ 🎁 A master craftsman, artisan, and jeweler, Jean-François Fichot was one of the first artists to base his studio in Bali in the '60s. Jean-François does many things but his greatest gift is working with and embellishing found objects: Imagine a 15th-century Roman coin or a crystal Buddha from Tibet or an antique piece of coral from Cuba. Michael Caine and Elle Macpherson like it well enough as do mere mortals. Exquisite beyond belief; go to his showroom even if you aren't looking to buy, and treat it like a museum tour. Jl. Suweta 6. ✆ **0361/972078.** www.jf-f.com.

Seraphim Search the eclectic mix here for interesting small antique objects as well as exclusive designs of gold and silver jewelry with precious and semi-precious gemstones. Jl. Monkey Forest. ✆ **0361/971139.**

Treasures ★ The specialty here is big, distinctive pieces in 22K and 24K gold. Pieces are the result of a collaboration between local goldsmiths and international designers. All the jewelry is individually handmade by Balinese master artisans, making each piece virtually one of a kind. Pieces feature pearl, shell, and semi-precious stones. Credit cards are thankfully accepted. Jl. Raya Ubud. ✆ **0361/976697.** www.dekco.com.

Textiles & Clothing

Ani's Gallery This shop sells batik in a myriad of colors and nontraditional motifs such as flowers, butterflies, toucans, parrots, and exotic island themes including jungles with palm trees. Browse the hand-painted sarongs, kimonos, and caftans and nice selection of men's batik shirts. Tablecloths, napkins, sheets, and bedcovers are also for sale. Jl. Raya Campuhan. ✆ **0361/975431.**

Macan Tidur ★★★ 🎁 You're guaranteed to find a treasure here that you simply can't live without. Susi is a textiles expert specializing in 18th-century textiles and has a collection that covers every part of Indonesia—you can count on reliable quality and authenticity. Bruno is a painter and a tribal art and ancient jewelry expert. Between

The Threads of Life

The handmade, unique textiles at **Threads of Life**, Jl. Kajeng 24 (✆ **0361/972187**; www.threadsoflife.com), are dyed and woven by local women thanks to the support of a nonprofit organization intent on revitalizing and sustaining this traditional Balinese art form. All proceeds support the organization's research, work, and communities.

9

UBUD | Shopping: Island of the Goods

DANCE & cultural PERFORMANCES

Every night in Ubud and the surrounding villages you'll come across several dance, music, and shadow-puppet performances. A *barong* performance at the **Royal Palace** is the best and most stimulating choice; it's a classical dance story about the struggle between good (personified by Barong, a fun-loving creature in the shape of a shaggy lion) and evil (personified through a witch). Even children will like it. Many of the hotels do small evening shows, and so inquire with your concierge.

Listings below followed by *** mean that free transport is provided from the **Ubud Tourist Information** (📞 **0361/973285**) kiosk, on Jalan Raya Ubud near the intersection of Monkey Forest Road. Get tickets and information at Ubud Tourist Information, ticket sellers on the street, or the place of the performances. The price is the same wherever you buy it. Ask your concierge to check with Ubud Tourist Information, as performances are occasionally canceled because of temple ceremonies or bad weather.

Performance	Days	Time	Cost (Rp)
Agung Rai Museum of Art*			
Kecak Dance	Full/New Moons	7pm	100,000 (150,000 including Balinese dinner)
Mepantigan Arts	Thurs	6:30pm	100,000
Barong & Kris Dance	Fri (except Full/New Moons)	6pm	75,000 (135,000 including Balinese dinner)
Wayang Wong	Sat	7pm	75,000 (135,000 including Balinese dinner)
Legong Classic	Sun	7:30pm	75,000 (135,000 including Balinese dinner)
Bale Banjar			
Women Gamelan & Dance Group	Mon & Fri	7:30pm	65,000
Narita Dewi Gamelan & Dance	Tues	7:30pm	75,000
Chandra Wira Buana	Wed	7:30pm	75,000
Balerung Mandera*			
Legong & Barong Dance	Tues & Fri	7:30pm	100,000
Legong Dance	Fri	7:30pm	100,000
Dancers & Musician of Peliatan	Sun	7:30pm	100,000
Bentuyung Village*			
Jegog (Bamboo Gamelan)	Sun & Fri	7pm	80,000
Kertha Accommodation			
Wayang Kulit	Mon & Thurs	8pm	65,000
Lotus Pond Open Stage			
Women Gamelan with Children Dancers	Tues	7:30pm	80,000
Janger Dance	Sun	7:30pm	80,000

Shopping: Island of the Goods

UBUD

Monkey Forest

Wayang Kulit	Tues & Sat	8pm	65,000

Oka Kartini's

Wayang Kulit	Wed, Fri, Sun	8pm	75,000

Padang Tegal

Kecak Fire & Trance Dance	Wed, Sat, Sun	7pm	75,000

Pondok Bamboo

Wayang Kulit	Mon & Thurs	8pm	75,000

Pondok Pekak

Gamelan & Dance	Sun	7:30pm	75,000

Pura Dalem, Taman Kaja

Kecak Ramayana & Fire Dance	Mon & Fri	7:30pm	75,000
Legong Dance	Tues & Sat	7:30pm	65,000
Kecak Fire & Trance Dance	Wed & Sat	7:30pm	75,000
Jegog (Bamboo Gamelan)	Wed	7pm	80,000
Barong & Kris Dance	Thurs	7:30pm	75,000

Pura Desa Kutuh

Spirit of Bali	Tues	7:30pm	75,000
Legong Dance	Thurs	7:30pm	75,000

Pura Padang Kertha

Kecak & Fire Dance	Fri	7pm	75,000

Pura Taman Sari

Kecak Fire & Trance Dance	Thurs	7:30pm	75,000

Puri Agung, Peliatan*

Kecak (Monkey Chant Dance)	Thurs	7:30pm	80,000
Legong Dance	Sat	7:30pm	80,000

Ubud Palace

Legong Dance	Mon & Sat	7:30pm	80,000
Ramayana Ballet	Tues	7:30pm	80,000
Legong & Barong Dance	Wed	7:30pm	80,000
Legong Trance & Paradise Dance	Thurs	7:30pm	80,000
Barong & Rangda Dance	Fri	7pm	80,000
Legong of Mahabarata	Sun	7:30pm	80,000

Ubud Water Palace

Barong & Kris Dance with Children Dancers	Thurs	7:30pm	80,000
Legong Dance	Sat	7:30pm	80,000

Wantilan

Barong & Kris Dance	Mon	7pm	80,000

Yamasari Stage*

Legong Dance	Wed	7:30pm	75,000

the two the gallery is filled to the brim with an extraordinary collection that includes sculpture, ceramics (such as centuries-old Chinese porcelain salvaged from shipwrecks around Indonesia), weapons, Kris handles, baskets, and even some of Bruno's contemporary oil paintings. A nice touch is a small reference library where guests are encouraged to read about purchases they're considering or simply learn more about Indonesian art. Call ahead for an appointment with Susi or Bruno; both are generous with their knowledge. Jl. Monkey Forest. ✆ **081/23665669.** www.macantidur.com.

Wardani Shop   The best place in town for locally made ikat (dyed cotton), *songket* (brocade fabric), and *endek* (woven textile), some more pricey than others. You'll be told "fixed price," but don't believe it. Try and get to about one-third of what's quoted. Jl. Monkey Forest. ✆ **0361/975538.**

UBUD ENTERTAINMENT & NIGHTLIFE

Ubud's nightlife scene is growing, but it's still rather sedate. **Jazz Café,** Jl. Sukma 2, east of Monkey Forest Road (✆ **0361/976594;** www.jazzcafebali.com), has good live jazz. In fact, Monkey Forest Road has lots of little laid-back places that are more than happy to stay open late. Upscale **Lamak** (✆ **0361/974668;** www.lamakbali.com) stays up, but its scene is mostly calm. **Naughty Nuri's** (p. 184) is popular with the local expat crowd and dinners often become long sessions of storytelling and drinking the restaurant's gin-heavy martinis. Next door is **Ozigo** (✆ **081/2367973**) where there's live music, dancing, and nightly DJ entertainment. **Café Exiles,** Jl. Pengosekan (✆ **0361/974812**), caters to a younger crowd and many tourists. Drinks are cheap and, just to the southeast of central Ubud, it gets crowded on weekend nights. For wine and jazz, head to the **Divine Wine Bar & Shop,** Jl. Raya Sanggingan, next to the Tjampuhan River (✆ **0361/970095;** www.bridgesbali.com). From 5 to 7pm daily beers are two-for-one and red and white wines are offered for Rp50,000 per glass. There's a good wine shop with bottles starting at Rp250,000, a steal in Bali.

CENTRAL MOUNTAINS

Ubud is typically as far north as most visitors to Bali ever reach, even though it's still, geographically and culturally, in the south. The older communities in the mountains adhere to strict social customs, some retain their own dialects, and many remain wary of visitors and interlopers. They may pay lip service to supporting tourism and embrace the income that visitors bring, but the residents of the central mountains don't necessarily see the need to adapt to a more visitor-oriented lifestyle.

This region remains important to all Balinese, because the mountains are traditionally thought to be the homes of their gods. Therefore, it's a spiritual center and place of pilgrimage, where temples and their celebrations abound. Water from here is the source of much of the irrigation for rice in the south, which also enhances the revered place in the hearts of the Balinese of these central mountains. As a result, you'll see many temples devoted to the water goddess Dewi Danu.

10

If you want to visit here, you'll need a car, a driver who can translate, a map, some walking shoes, and a plan. And don't forget your sarong.

ESSENTIALS

Getting There

FROM THE NORTH

If you're coming from the north, take the mountain roads via Kubutambuhan for **Kintamani** or via Singaraja for **Bedugul.**

Most hotels and villas in the area can arrange a driver for you if you don't already have one. If you take a driver and wish to stay overnight, your hotel or villa can usually provide, at no extra charge, accommodations for your driver. You should, however, contribute to his food cost. A half- or a full-day rate with a **Blue Bird** taxi may or may not cover fuel costs. Agree beforehand on what expenses (especially fuel) you're responsible for. Pay at the end of your trip; you're more likely to get better service. Although you could use a taxi to get here, privately hired jeeps or SUVs offer a more comfortable experience.

If you have time on your hands, you can catch a **bus** from Kuta, but they don't stop in all the villages and towns. To get to Bedugul and Candikuning you can take a **Perama Tours bus** (© **0361/751551** in Kuta; www.peramatour.com) from Kuta at 10am for Rp60,000 (3 hr.). For Kintamani, the Perama bus leaves at 10am for Rp150,000 (3 hr.). For those who like to travel with a chicken on their lap, a **public bus** leaves Denpasar to Singaraja, stopping in Penelokan and Kintamani for Rp20,000. Alternatively, you can catch a *bemo* (a van serving as a bus) from Batubulan terminal in Denpasar to Kintamani for Rp20,000.

From the South

TO KINTAMANI & LAKE BATUR   Various roads lead from Ubud to Kintamani; the two major ones are either the Sayan Ridge Road or the slightly more scenic road just to the east that takes in the Tirta Empul Temple and Pura Gunung Kawi complex (see below). Both take about 2 hours. The weather noticeably turns at the top, with the village of Penelokan often surrounded in mist.

As the **Sayan Ridge Road** heads north, you'll pass the upmarket COMO Shambhala and Alila hotels, which are worth a stop for a lunch break.

Before you arrive at the place where the Sayan Ridge Road meets the volcano crater's rim, you'll see a sign for **Bayung Gede,** a traditional Balinese hill village. With its neat narrow lanes, ancient shrines, and well-kept, steep-roofed houses, it has retained its old charm and original low-lying construction.

Your other main option is via the road that goes past **Tirta Empul** (p. 188); you'll also pass **Pura Gunung Kawi** (p. 186). Just above the beautiful temple complex of Tirta Empul sits the **Istana,** the old Bali palace of Sukharno, now owned and occupied by his daughter, Megawati Sukarnoputri, also a previous president of the Republic.

TO BEDUGUL   For a wonderfully scenic route without nearly as much of the litter and villa developments that clutter a great deal of Bali, rent a car and driver and head to Papuan from the south: Take the main road via Tabanan and turn north at Antosari. Continue north from Papuan and turn east at Mayong and travel up through the hills via **Munduk.**

Getting Around

It's easy to get to the central mountains, but trying to go from one village to another cross-country is more difficult—as a quick glance at a map will show. For example, once you're in the Batur area, to reach Bedugul, you need to drive to the north coast, along to Singaraja, and then back up the mountain road via Lake Buyan. Traveling from one village to another can be nearly impossible without the assistance of a friendly hotel owner—there are no metered taxis in this region.

DANAU BATUR

The double caldera of **Danau Batur** (Lake Batur) is 14km (8½ miles) across, 6km (4 miles) wide, and no one is quite sure how deep, although it's estimated at slightly

ATTRACTIONS ●

Bali Handara Kosaido **12**
Bedugul Botanical Garden & Bali Tree Top Adventure Park **8**
Kiadan Pelaga Village **7**
Museum Gunungapi Batur **4**
Oka Agro Tourism **5**
Penatahan Hot Springs **21**
Pura Luhur Batukaru **18**
Pura Penulisan **1**
Pura Ulan Danu Bratan **9**
Pura Ulun Danu **2**
Pura Ulun Danu Batur **3**

HOTELS ■

Bali Handara Country Club **12**
Bali Mountain Retreat **19**
Kebun Raya **8**
The Lodge Bedugul **11**
Munduk Moding Plantation **15**
Puri Lumbung Cottages **16**
Saranam Eco Resort **6**
Sarinbuana Eco Lodge **20**

RESTAURANTS ◆

Café Jatiluwih **17**
Café Teras Lempuna **10**
Ngiring Ngewedang Restaurant **14**
Puncak Bagus **13**

10

CENTRAL MOUNTAINS | Danau Batur

A view OF DANAU BATUR & PENELOKAN

A fantastic spectacle greets you as you come over the ridge at Penelokan and gaze down in wonder at the twin caldera of **Lake Batur,** but the town itself may leave you puzzled. "What happened?" you may ask. The further you descend into the crater, the more you'll find poor accommodations and service and unpleasant encounters with hawkers, and you ask yourself again, "What happened?" Surely, this is one of the greatest, most spectacular natural vistas anywhere, with a beautiful lake and magnificent walking trails, and yet the whole experience is enough to turn anyone off. The accommodations are filthy, the food is generally expensive buffet-style catering to bus tours, and many of the trekking expeditions are hugely overpriced. This is a side of Bali that you might wish to give a complete miss,

which is a great shame because nature has created a wonder that you should be able to enjoy. The best way to tackle this area is with an established Bali-wide trekking agency that can take you in, stay with you for the whole day, and then take you back out.

As for **Penelokan** (Rp5,000 to enter the village), it has a magnificent view to Mount Batur and, across the lake, a collection of restaurants and market stalls, and usually far too many people trying to hustle you. The town has various hotels, with the best choice currently the **Batur Lakeview Hotel** (✆ **0366/ 51394;** www.lakeviewbali.com) with eight rooms at US$40 for a superior and US$60 for a deluxe. The hotel is made of carved stone and rooms are basic, but have amazing views over the lake below.

more than 1,500m (4,921 ft.). It was once a mountain with a peak that rose some 3,000m (9,843 ft.) above sea level; now it sits at only 1,717m (5,633 ft.) and is a very active volcano. You can see the plumes of smoke rising from one of the lower spouts. The most recent eruption was in 1999, but the volcano showed its true rage in 1917, destroying the old village of Batur and taking with it some 65,000 souls.

Farming continues on the nutrient-rich sides of the volcano and the lake feeds the neighboring rice-growing regions of Bangli, Buleleng, Gianyar, Klungkung, and Badung. Not surprisingly, the "temple at the head of the lake," **Pura Ulan Danu Batur**, is held in great reverence: Its priest, known as Jero Gede, is considered the island's most powerful.

Don't let the tourist circus of Penelokan discourage you from venturing further: You'll find many more reasons to linger in the crater itself. The view is the main reason to come here; but try to take in the joyous winding road along the lakeshore to Toya Bungkah, Pura Ulan Danu Batur, or even the hot springs (Air Panas). This area is great trekking territory. If you're going to climb Mount Batur, be sure to book your trekking guide before you arrive.

Around the Crater

Museum Gunungapi Batur ★ One place you should stop is the often-overlooked **Volcano Museum,** at the entrance gates of Penelokan. Eager guides explain every aspect. Scale models of the volcanoes replay the various eruptions of different years; wall maps light up, showing you the various active volcanoes in Indonesia (all 129 of them, more than 20% of the active volcanoes in the world!); interactive computers chart the last 26,000 years and the changing phases and shapes of Mount

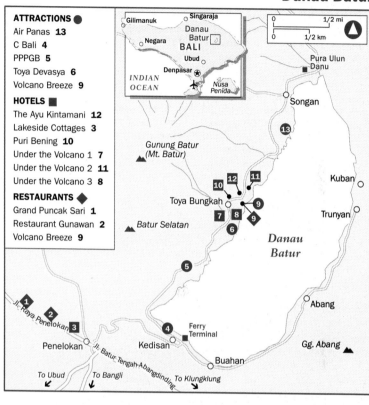

ATTRACTIONS ●
Air Panas **13**
C Bali **4**
PPPGB **5**
Toya Devasya **6**
Volcano Breeze **9**

HOTELS ■
The Ayu Kintamani **12**
Lakeside Cottages **3**
Puri Bening **10**
Under the Volcano 1 **7**
Under the Volcano 2 **11**
Under the Volcano 3 **8**

RESTAURANTS ◆
Grand Puncak Sari **1**
Restaurant Gunawan **2**
Volcano Breeze **9**

Batur. Head upstairs to the viewing deck where various sets of binoculars are trained on the still smoldering crater of Batur or the rather dark and menacing village of Trunyan on the far side of the volcano. Don't forget to tip the guides; they're worth every penny.

Penelokan. ✆ **0366/51152.** www.baturmuseum.info. Admission Rp10,000. Mon–Fri 10am–5pm.

KINTAMANI

The area around here is often referred to as simply Kintamani, though Kintamani itself is the (rather uninspiring) administrative capital; the **local market** (every 3 days) starts at 5am and is over by 10am. The main road passes through the middle of the town.

Pura Penulisan ★   Just beyond Kintamani on the road north is Pura Penulisan, a series of five temples, which rises like a pyramid. It's considered a magical place and is often used for meditation by locals on auspicious nights.

8km (5 miles) north of Kintamani. Admission Rp1,000. Daily 7am–6pm.

Pura Ulun Danu Batur   Just outside Kintamani, on the rim of the crater, is Pura Ulan Danu Batur, Bali's most important temple after Pura Besakih, dedicated to the goddess of the lake, **Ida Bhatari Dewi Danu.** Today's temple is a reconstruction of parts of the old temple rescued from the side of the crater after the 1917 eruption. It has a *meru* (altar) with 11 tiers reflecting its importance—the god of Mount Agung has only nine—and though it's a reconstruction of separate temples, its original form dates to at least the 11th century. Oddly, you can't actually see the lake from inside the temple. Although this is a historically important temple, with a place in the Balinese consciousness, there are other, more attractively situated temples to visit ahead of this one. You'll be charged Rp10,000 by the ladies outside for sarong rental if you forget to bring your own.

Kintamani. Admission including sarong Rp10,000. Daily 7am–5pm.

In the Crater

The two main villages in the crater are **Toya Bungkah** and **Kedisan,** the former having more options in terms of accommodations and restaurants, because of the popularity of the hot springs in the town. If you'd like to stay in the crater, Toya Bungkah should be your preferred choice.

Pura Ulun Danu   Not be confused with Pura Ulun Danu Batur (see above) on the rim of the caldera, this temple is at the head of Lake Batur, in the crater itself. A 20-minute drive beyond Toya Bungkah, this temple, though not particularly large, is revered for its water, the giver of life. The complex is a series of three temples; the one to visit is the farthest one, set majestically into the side of the mountain, beyond Songan, the final village on the shore of the lake. Often before work is done in a given rice field in Bali, a priest and local farmers will travel to Lake Batur and take water from the source, which they sprinkle on their fields. They pour any remaining water into the local irrigation system so that others may benefit. Since the water is viewed as sacred, there's absolutely no swimming around here and you must wear appropriate temple garb to enter.

Admission Rp6,000. Daily 7am–5pm.

TOYA BUNGKAH

If you've made it into the crater itself, you'll pass through this town, either to reach the start of a trek at the head of the lake or for the springs. You'll find a number of trekking agencies and budget accommodations. There are lots of places to stay, and a number of seemingly inhabited houses, but there are precious few people or even the normal signs of village life here—the whole village has the feel of a town where everyone has headed off for the day. The hot springs, **Air Panas** (Rp150,000 including lunch, drink, and towel), can be enjoyed at one of the hotels, such as the **Puri Bening** (p. 211), or at the hot spring and spa resort **Toya Devasya** (✆ **0361/438333**; www.toyadevasya.com; admission for swimming and lunch Rp260,000; no credit cards; daily 9am–7pm). The resort offers a 20-m (66-ft.) swimming pool and several hot spring bathing areas. You don't need to stay here to use the facilities. Various places to stop and have lunch in the town have views across the lake to the far side with the mountains as a backdrop.

KEDISAN

The other village at the base of the crater is Kedisan, which has various options for budget accommodations and also some lovely vegetable gardens and other plants growing down to the edge of the lake. The scenery is charming but there's not a lot going on. Private boats to Trunyan leave from here. **C Bali** runs a small volunteer and clean-up program here (p. 210).

TRUNYAN ⚠

Should you make a trip to Trunyan? We see no reason why you need to take a trip across a lake at an inflated price to see the unpleasant way the people here extort tourists. If you do make the crossing, you'll encounter a Bali Aga village where the main "attraction" is that they lay their dead wrapped in a cotton shroud under an old tree that gives off a scent that negates the stench of rotting corpses.

The trip includes a 20-minute rickety boat ride from Kedisan for upward of Rp1,000,000 round-trip. You'll be escorted to a cemetery and then, as in Michael Jackson's "Thriller" video, people descend on you, insinuating that if you don't give a suitable offering you may not be able to leave. As you leave, more people tug at your arm or surround you in the hope you'll toss more money their way as you bolt for the boat. This is a well-practiced stunt to rip off tourists rather than portray any form of traditional or arcane way of life. Avoid it.

Trekking

The whole crater area, with its staggering views, clear waters, and temperate climate, is ideal for trekking and local tour guides will take you on escorted walks. We say this with an additional caveat: This is about the only area in Bali where you need to keep your wits about you. If you wish to climb Gunung Batur (Mount Batur) you'll come across the motley bunch known as **PPPGB** (previously HPPGB) or the **Association of Mount Batur Trekking Guides** (✆ **0366/52362**). This is the local mountain guide agency and they insist that they have the only government-approved license that allows you to climb Mount Batur. If you wish to climb the mountain, you must use one of their 62 approved guides and pay their rates—even if you arrive with your own professional guide. The rates are commensurate with a monopoly and they don't take kindly to being challenged. Unless you enjoy a degree of intimidation in your negotiations, we advise you not to. They do, however, make great assurances that they're trained and professional.

Also be careful if your tour is to end up anywhere near Trunyan (see above), as you may find yourself being forced to pay a surcharge to get out of there. Be very clear

Along with trekking around and above the lake, you can also go kayaking or canoeing on it. You get a different perspective seeing the crater from the middle of the wide lake. Most trekking agencies also offer canoeing. A recommended agency is **C Bali** ★★ (℃ 0353/ 420541; www.c-bali.com). Its 1-day tour (Rp470,000) includes cycling and canoeing, as well as pickup from hotels and lunch. C Bali has a donation program with Kedisan village: The company accepts small donations of clothing (especially cold-weather clothing) and school supplies to pass on to the villagers and their school. Casual visitors can also participate in C Bali's **Kedisan clean-up** program. If you're interested in long-term volunteering (3 months), C Bali also has a Kedisan residency program.

with your guide before you start that there'll be absolutely no further charges other than those that you've already paid and that there are no boat trips required.

A group of up to four people will pay, collectively, about Rp300,000 for a short trip to the Mount Batur summit for sunrise, a 3-hour walk leaving between 4am and 5am. You should all be given headlamps and flashlights as you'll be starting in darkness. A Mount Batur exploration walk of about 6 to 7 hours will cost up to four of you Rp600,000 or so. A 6-hour summit walk to Mount Abang leaving from the temple at Ulan Danu costs the same, although this one is likely to end near Trunyan and so make sure that you specify that you won't pay a boat charge.

Yet, in spite of it all, the climb is stunningly beautiful. Book with a reputable agency, probably from outside the crater, come for the day, do your trek, and leave.

TREKKING AGENCIES & TOURS Used by many locals who live in Bali, **Gede** (℃ 081/24652455) is a charming man who'll take you on a guided day tour and explain not only the history of the area, but also its flora and fauna. He identifies the local herbs and spices found on the walk and explains their uses. When pressed, he'll even play his flute, which is delightful. He charges US$100 for up to four people for half-day trips. He offers a trip up Mount Batur that ends at—warning!—Trunyan (see above). You'll need to pay a boatman for the round-trip journey. Negotiate beforehand.

If you simply want a local guide who knows the mountains as well as anyone but isn't part of a larger entity (and therefore without insurance), the nice people at **Volcano Breeze** (p. 212; ℃ 0366/51824) cafe will arrange a guide for you. They're honest and have proved reliable in the past. They suggest prices of about Rp300,000 for a group of up to four for a short trip to the summit for sunrise. Note that this is the total price and not per person. They also quote about Rp600,000 for a 6- to 7-hour Mount Batur exploration trek.

Based out of Jakarta but with local representatives, **Pacto** (℃ 0361/288247; www.pactoltd.com) charges US$98 per person, including transport and a guide, for a 10-hr, all-day trek to Mount Batur. They also have trips throughout Bali and other parts of Indonesia.

Clipper (℃ 081/23802675; www.clipperdiscovery.com; sunrise trek including transportation, guide, entrance fee, breakfast, PPPGB, and Clipper guide US$95) will collect you from wherever you are in Bali, take you on a tour with an experienced English-speaking guide, and then return you to your hotel. They're not cheap, but costs include the full day and transportation. They do informative rainforest treks around Mount Batur as well as overnight trips to get to Mount Agung at sunrise.

Owners of the Elephant Park (p. 194), **Bali Adventure Tours** (✆ **0361/721480;** www.baliadventuretours.com), offer white-water rafting, mountain treks, and escorted bike tours around Mount Batur. A 3-hour trek includes lunch and entrance to the elephant park for US$64; a bike tour with the same perks is US$71.

The **Toya Devasya Agency** (✆ **0366/51204;** www.toyadevasya.com) is specifically set up for groups. The packages usually include lunch and a dip in the hot springs (see above). Staff will also take you canoeing, on ridge walks, downhill trekking, and even do an escorted and "policed" trip to Trunyan—which just means they've paid off the village in advance. An escorted trip to Trunyan for two people costs US$136 per person. A Mount Batur sunrise walk is US$47 per person for two people, including lunch and a dip in the hot springs.

Where to Stay

The Ayu Kintamani ★   If you prefer a little luxury at the end of a long day of hiking, this is the place for you. It's the first of its kind for the area—a comfortable luxury resort with villa-style accommodations. The Ayu features romantic villas with hardwood floors and purple accents. Each unit comes with a private pool filled with natural, hot-springs water. The grounds offer good views of Lake Batur.

Jl. Puri Bening, Toya Bungkah, Kintamani. www.theayu.com.✆ **0366/52222.** Fax 0366/51205. 5 units. High season US$285–US$385; low seasonUS$235–US$335. AE, MC, V. **Amenities**: Restaurants; cafe; spa. *In villa*: A/C, hair dryer, minibar, Wi-Fi.

Lakeside Cottages   At the eastern end of Toya Bungkah, this perfectly pleasant but very simple series of rooms caters mainly to trekkers. It's fine, cleanish, and as the name suggests the cottages are on the lake. If you're on a budget and in the area and need a bed, you can do a lot worse. Each room has hot water and terraces to take in the view of the lake. Staff can also arrange trekking or kayaking trips.

Toya Bungkah, Kintamani.✆ **0366/51249.** 10 units. Rp400,000–Rp200,000. No credit cards. **Amenities:** Restaurant; Internet access; small outdoor pool.

Puri Bening   With 29 "deluxe" double rooms and two cottages, this is the largest operation in Kintamani. The whole complex looks to have been carved from a single cement block. It has a very large, hot, spring-fed pool with cold plunge pool—which is about the only thing recommending this place. The poor soul that we met who was staying here was hard-pressed to find any comment about the food, other than, "well, we all have to eat something."

Toya Bungkah, Kintamani. www.indo.com/hotels/puribeninghayato. ✆ **0366/51234.** 30 units. Year-round Rp450,000. No credit cards. **Amenities:** Restaurant; hot spring pool; plunge pool; room service. *In room:* TV.

Under the Volcano 1, 2 & 3   This is a series of separate bungalow-style properties along the same road, all under the same ownership but with different managers. There are a total of 22 rooms of similar decoration set up for trekkers offering budget accommodations and cold-water showers (Volcano 2 has hot water). It's basically clean, but uninspiring.

Toya Bungkah, Kintamani.✆ **0366/51166** for Volcano 1 & 3;✆ **0366/52508** for Volcano 2. 22 units. Year-round Rp100,000. No credit cards. **Amenities:** Restaurant; room service. *In room:* cold water shower.

Where to Eat

KINTAMANI   If there's one shining light in the whole crater, as far as tourism infrastructure is concerned, it's **Volcano Breeze** (✆ **0366/51824;** main courses from Rp15,000; no credit cards; daily 8am–5pm). The fish fresh from the lake is delicious and memorable. On a good day, the friendly staff will play live music and perhaps also try to sell you some local art, likely created by the person selling it. The cafe is on the road down to the side of the lake, next door to Toya Devasya in the middle of Toya Bungkah. Next door is **Under the Volcano** (✆ **0366/51166;** main courses Rp10,000–Rp25,000; no credit cards; daily 7am–8pm) with similar lake-caught fish and other Indonesian offerings.

AROUND PENELOKAN   On the rim of the crater on the road from Penelokan to Kintamani is a series of vast hangarlike restaurants with huge parking lots akin to those at large sporting venues. They cater mainly to bus tourists. They all offer similar, one-stop, buffet-style, all-you-can-eat fare; some do it okay, but the majority rely on paying tour guides to bring in the customers. Most of the large ones can hold up to 600 visitors, and you may find yourself eating with 200 other people. Although the majority of these mass-market restaurants are off-putting, they do have great views.

At the Kintamani end of the crater's rim, **Grand Puncak Sari,** Jl. Raya Penelokan (✆ **0366/51073;** buffet from Rp100,000; no credit cards; daily 8am–5pm), is a perfectly pleasant restaurant that does passable food and offers good views. If you want a more authentic experience, ask for the Balinese lunch (Rp80,000). They make fresh *lawar* (mixed vegetables, coconut, and minced meat) every day, both with and without fresh blood, and many other dishes, which change daily. The Balinese offering is as good as you'll eat on the island, if you can actually find genuine food like this outside of a ceremony.

Close to Penelokan, **Restaurant Gunawan,** Penelokan (✆ **0366/51050;** buffet from Rp85,000; MC, V; daily 8:30am–4:30pm), is one of the better of the larger offerings, seating up to 450 people. They do a pleasant enough Indonesian and Chinese-looking buffet that's popular with Korean and Japanese visitors.

BEDUGUL & DANAU BRATAN, BUYAN & TAMBLINGAN

The area around **Bedugul** village is often referred to as simply Bedugul, though the daily flower, fruit, and vegetable market is in Candikuning.

Although this area has a great variety of attractions, tourism remains aimed at the local rather than the international market and the choice of hotels and restaurants reflects this. Even the five-star golf course has a 1970s' Travelodge feel. Everything appears a bit unloved: It's almost like the whole place was built and then forgotten about. For a truly odd experience, a group of villas on the hillside about three quarters of a kilometer (half a mile) toward Lake Bratan from the golf course looks like a normal resort, but upon closer inspection, you see that no one's there.

Bring your warm clothes. A *bemo* in between stops of Denpasar (Ubung terminal) and Singaraja's Sukasada terminal to this area costs Rp8,000.

A Tour Around the Lakes

Arriving from the south (Ubud or Seminyak), you come through the main road of Candikuning, where you'll see the open-all-day market on your left. Passing this, down the hill, on the left is a great bread shop, **Roti Bedugul,** offering fresh bread around 11am daily. On the right hand side as you drop down is **Danau Bratan** with an overpriced watersports center on the far side, framed majestically by the mountains behind. The town itself has little else to offer other than more shops than you care to count selling exactly the same snacks, drinks, and basic toiletries.

Carry on out of Candikuning, away from Bedugul, along the lake shores and you'll come to one of the most picturesque and photographed of temples, **Pura Ulan Danu Bratan** ★ (western bank of Lake Bratan; Rp10,000; daily 7am–6pm), with its formal gardens and clipped lawns set against the backdrop of the lake. Technically, it's *on* the lake, built on a series of small islands. It was built in reverence to the goddess of the lake and the water she provides. This is a great place to feel the natural calm of the water—just don't swim in it: These are holy waters.

This road then leads onward, past the golf course, to lakes **Buyan** and **Tamblingan.** These were originally one lake until the early part of the 19th century when a landslide created two. The high road above the lake on the road to Munduk is possibly the best place to take in the view. There are a couple of viewing places to stop along the way.

If you're arriving via the scenic Munduk route described on p. 215, you'll see all these sites in reverse order.

Exploring Around & Near the Lakes

Bali Tree Top Adventure Park ★★★ ☺ One of Bali's most popular family attractions, the Bali Tree Top Adventure Park is a safe introduction to zip-lining and rope courses, plus you get up close and personal with the local flora. You're attached at all times by at least one rope, and usually two, to your mountaineer's safety harness, which feels reassuring when you cross between two high-wire points on a swinging obstacle, with 50m (164 ft.) of fresh air between you and the ground. With the four different levels, it's fun and safe for children from 5 years through to adults. Gloves are for sale and worth the investment.

In the Bedugul Botanical Gardens, Candikuning. ✆ **0361/852-0680.** www.balitreetop.com. Admission US$21 adult; US$14 children 11 and under. Daily 8:30am–6pm, last entry before 4:30pm.

Bedugul Botanical Garden (Kebun Raya) ★★ 🎁 This wonderland is set in 160 hectares (395 acres) of landscaped and beautifully tended gardens. Opened in 1959 and currently home to almost 2,000 species of different plants, including some 320 varieties of orchids, it contains plants from the mountain areas of eastern Indonesia, areas such as Tenggara, Sulawesi, Maluku, and even Papua. The institution offers a number of scientific services and facilities in support of plant research and conservation, including a herbarium, an orchid house, seed bank, library, glass houses, nursery, and plant database. Bring a picnic.

Candikuning. ✆ **0368/21273.** www.kebunrayabali.com. Admission Rp7,000 adults; Rp3,500 children 4 and under; Rp4,750 children aged 5–students; Rp6,000 per car. Daily 7am–6pm; some indoor exhibits close earlier.

GOLF The **Bali Handara Kosaido** ★★ (✆ **0362/342-2646;** www.balihandara kosaido.com; in-house guest US$85, walk-in guest US$150; AE, DC, MC, V) is Bali's best-known golf course, and built in 1974 certainly its oldest. At 1,128m (3,700 ft.) above sea level, it's possibly the only golf course in the world in a volcano crater. About a 2-hour scenic drive from the Seminyak/Sanur area, Bali Handara has magnificent mountain scenery with beautiful gardens, surrounded by lush rainforest, and

Kiadan Pelaga Village

The **Jaringan Ekowisata Desa (JED;** © 0361/737447; www.jed.or.id; two to four people US$75 per person, overnight US$105 per person; no credit cards), or Village Ecotourism Network, is devoted to developing sustainable ecotourism and travel in Indonesia. Through its program at Kiadan Pelaga village, you learn about the **coffee-making process,** from how the plantations are managed all the way through to the roasting process, and you meet the actual farmers. They also grow dry rice and if you come at the right time of year, you can take part in the harvest. You can also stay the night in the village. The basic accommodations are genuine, rather than a sanitized reenactment of village life.

views over the surrounding lake. It's fair to say that both the course and the attached accommodations could do with some revitalization, but the course remains challenging and the cooler air alone is a worthy attraction. There's a pro shop and optional golf carts.

TREKKING   You can take an official tour with a trekking agency from the south (see chapter 4), find a local guide through your villa or hotel, or simply take a wander on your own. Plenty of trails offer walks through jungle terrain, up a mountain, or through woodland to the lakes.

You can easily find your own way along the shores of Danau Buyan. Take the turn by the police station in **Pancasari** and follow it along to the end and you come across the start of the trail that wanders along the shores. You'll pass various spots to have a lakeside picnic. For nature lovers, one of the best trekking routes is the challenging 7-hour trek from Lake Tamblingan to Jatiluwih. The trek takes you through dense forests, to the caldera Lubang Nagaloka ("Dragon Hideout"), along an ancient trade path used by traders for centuries, all the way to the southern slopes of Mount Batu-karu, and finally ending at Jatiluwih (p. 217), where you can enjoy the undulating paddy field views.

Where to Stay

Bali Handara Country Club   With 77 rooms and a world-class golf course, this is a stay-and-play in a stunning setting, actually set in the volcano. You need not stay to play but incentive packages almost make it worthwhile. Unfortunately, although the golf course is world class, the same can't be said of the accommodations. The rooms are in hues of cream and brown, and the furniture heavy Indonesian and not very elegant; the place could do with a renovation. Stay here if it's convenient and you're a golf nut who wants to wake up overlooking the course.

Jl. Taya Bedugul, Pancasari. www.balihandarakosaido.com. © **0362/22646.** 77 units. Year-round US$135 course view; US$150 garden view. AE, DC, MC, V. **Amenities:** Restaurant; cafe; bar; gym; tennis court. *In room:* Satellite TV, minibar.

Kebun Raya   You can stay the night in the middle of the Botanic Gardens (see above). This large, pavilion-style house has 14 rooms, all with balconies; rooms are smart if somewhat soulless. However, you wake up in possibly the most beautiful, and certainly the largest, garden in Bali with the chance to explore before everyone else.

In the Bedugul Botanical Garden (p. 213), Bedugul. www.kebunrayabali.com. © **0368/203-3211.** 14 units. Year-round Rp150,000 single; Rp360,000 standard; Rp450,000 deluxe. No credit cards. *In room:* TV.

The Lodge Bedugul   This villa is great fun if you're traveling in a group. Outside is a full-length, wraparound balcony with sweeping views out to Lake Buyan. This place comes with all the toys that you might possibly want for a party weekend away: pool table, hot tub, dartboard, karaoke, and a projector and surround sound. All the bedrooms are en suite. The lodge is near lakeside nature trails.

Bedugul. www.thelodgebedugul.com. (✆ **0361/282730** or **0361/745-1315.** Fax 0361/288923. 5 bedrooms. Year-round US$95 standard; US$325 villa. Rates include breakfast. MC, V (in Sanur office only); no credit cards at lodge. **Amenities:** Lounge; Jacuzzi; room service; spa. *In room:* A/C, TV, minibar.

Where to Eat

There are very few places to choose from when it comes to eating in this area but we did find one gem, on Jalan Raya Denpasar in Bedugul. **Café Teras Lempuna** (✆ **0362/342-9312;** main courses from Rp41,000; no credit cards; daily 7am–10pm) serves a mixture of simple pasta, sandwiches, and oddly, a wide selection of Japanese food. The chicken curry and the ginger pork were extremely tasty, as were most of the Japanese dishes on offer. The simple tomato and mushroom salad with miso dressing was so good we came back for it the following day.

MUNDUK

Munduk is on a ridge, with one side reaching south over rice terraces and the other falling just as steeply away with views to the north coast and the seas beyond. This was the home of many weekend places for the Dutch, who came up from their administrative capital of Singaraja, and in town you can still see the evidence of colonial-era villas. The area is known for coffee as much as for walking. The main road runs right through the village.

A charming **waterfall** is at the top of the village; it takes about 20 minutes to walk down to and possibly 25 to get back up. It's impressive year-round, but even more so in the wet season. Clear signs on the road point the way, about two bends north of Puri Lumbung.

In comparison to some of the other people of the central mountains, the people around Munduk seem more congenial, similar to lowlanders. This might have something to do with the history of Dutch influence, as this village has long been accustomed to the comings and goings of foreigners.

Exploring Munduk

A wonderful trek will take you to the hillside Bali Aga villages of **Pedawa** and **Sidatapa,** where they still make sugar in the traditional way and you can admire their bamboo structures or stroll through clove and coffee plantations. For the more adventurous, head for the 1,860-m (6,102-ft.) peak of **Mount Lesong,** reached in 8 hours. Depending on your route, you may take in the caldera **Lubang Nagaloka,** which translates as "Dragon's Hideout." Or, you can follow your nose, so to speak, and go in search of the famous (or infamous) Luwak coffee, made from beans that have been digested and excreted by the civet. A few plantations in the area produce their own. You'll need to ask around, as there are no guarantees of the animal's cooperation. All hotels and villas in the area can organize the necessary guide to take you around.

If you're staying around here, take a **plantation tour** to get an understanding not just of how the locals grow their individual crops, but also of the interdependence of each farmer on his neighbors, particularly those higher up the irrigation chain. Much of this interdependence is being protected by responsible development and leaders of the local community (for example the owner of Puri Lumbung). Most people that you ask will be happy to share their knowledge with you if they speak English.

Where to Stay

Munduk Moding Plantation ★★ ☺ 📷   On the road from Bedugul to Munduk, take the turn toward Golbek and stay at this gem. This recently opened venture is a collaboration between a local farmer who was trained at the Shangri-la and an international economist. The accommodations are on 5 hectares (12 acres) of coffee plantation and bring much-needed vitality and service to this area. The long view down to the north coast over the pool and terrace at sunset are spectacular, with the mountains of Java in the background. The villas have an open feel and are beautifully set in natural stone with polished hardwood floors, freestanding stone baths, and separate outside showers. The kitchen serves its own organic produce and offers traditional Balinese food.

It will take about 40 energetic minutes to complete a plantation tour, which includes strawberry picking. A guided tour with the knowledgeable manager who, before attending hotel school, farmed his family's land, explores surrounding plantations, the flora and fauna, and the interdependence of the farmers, their crops, and water. With a couple of horses, a tennis court, and children's area, this is a wonderful getaway.

The owners are committed to protecting the area's natural beauty and environmental and cultural heritage and are working with the local population to develop the area, with a sensitivity toward their needs. They also work closely with their like-minded neighbors at Puri Lumbung.

Munduk. www.mundukmodingplantation.com. ✆ **0362/700-5321.** 5 units. Year-round US$145 standard; US$155 grand suite; US$175 villas. AE, MC, V. **Amenities:** Restaurant; spa; tennis court. *In room:* TV/DVD, stereo or CD, hair dryer, minibar, MP3 docking station.

Puri Lumbung Cottages ★★★   The best option in Munduk is this charming bungalow-style hotel. You can choose from 17 bungalows, although more are being added as we go to press. Some are *lumbung* (former rice barn) style on two floors, while others are more traditional villas with each room in a different style or size. All are set in a lovely garden of fruits and spices. The restaurant serves decent enough food, such as chicken in a basket or wok-fried pork for about Rp36,000 each, but don't get too excited.

The main reason to stay here is to learn and explore, but you're also helping support the local community. The owner, Nyoman Bagiarta, was a hotelier who worked for an international hotel chain. He repurchased his grandfather's land and set up this hotel not just as a way to help local people through employment and supporting traditional crafts but also to serve as a template for other hotels owned and run by Balinese. He's well respected locally and is also the founder of the **Tamblang Sacred Springs Conservation Project,** which educates farmers about sustainable agriculture and the preservation of indigenous trees.

Puri Lumbung has daily traditional cooking classes, as well as dance and music classes, guided tours of the nearby coffee plantations, and educational walks that focus on temples, agriculture, or history. Or you can simply sit on your balcony and take in the long view to the north coast—don't miss the sunset.

Munduk. www.purilumbung.com. ℗ **0362/701-2887.** 36 units. Year-round US$85 standard; US$105 cottage; US$120 villa. MC, V. **Amenities:** Restaurant; spa. *In room:* Minibar (in villa only).

Saranam Eco Resort Set on 2 hectares (5 acres) of nature's finest land on the Bedugul road, surrounded by verdant rice paddies, this is a convenient base for exploring the lower mountain region. Ten freestanding bungalows have private terraces. Although the central building is large, the rattan and bamboo furnishings, alang-alang roofs, and garden blend unobtrusively into the hillside and surrounding terrain. The views from the restaurant and most of the rooms are wonderful. Rooms are functional, with a hot water shower and bath. The main restaurant, which serves a huge buffet throughout the day, is a popular stop for busloads of tourists.

Jl. Raya Baturiti, Kecamatan Baturiti. www.saranamresortbali.com. ℗ **0368/21038.** 35 units. Year-round US$85–US$125 standard; US$185 bungalow. Rates include breakfast. MC, V. **Amenities:** Restaurant. *In room:* TV, minibar.

Where to Eat

The inviting **Ngiring Ngewedang Restaurant,** Munduk (℗ **081/23807010;** www. ngiringngewedang.com; main courses Rp35,000–Rp60,000; MC, V; daily 7am–9pm), is perched on the bend above the road with clear views over its own coffee plantation to the Bali lowlands. It has its own small coffee museum, will take you on a tour of the plantation, and conclude with a demonstration of the traditional methods of drying, roasting, and grinding coffee beans. The restaurant sells a variety of coffee and light meals but actually sends its coffee to Singaraja to be processed. On the road at the Munduk end of the lake above Tamblingan, warung **Puncak Bagus,** Jl. Raya Denpasar, Banyuan (℗ **08/283727637;** main courses start at Rp15,000–Rp25,000; no credit cards; daily 8am–9pm), has a spectacular view of the two lakes. They serve a pleasant *nasi campur* (mixed rice) at Rp25,000.

Firefly Suppers ★★★ 📷 Part of Big Tree Organic Farms' offerings is a weekly dinner dubbed the "Firefly Suppers," hosted by the farm's charming owners, Ben and Blair Ripple. They prepare an extravagant menu of their seasonally fresh organic produce. They also work with micro-producers from all over the region, and will talk about their part in helping to educate consumers and producers alike in sustainability. The dinner is served on their farm under a banana-leaf-thatched roof, lit by hundreds of torches. Among some of the locally harvested, sustainable products is sea salt from the beaches of east Bali. The crystals are collected from the brine and then dried in the wind and sun; what's left forms the miniature hollow pyramids of sea salt, which has graced the tables of Donna Karan.

Bedugul area. ℗ **0361/954010.** www.bigtreebali.com. Reservations required; location may change depending on number of reservations. 6-course meal US$50 per person. MC, V. May–Oct only.

GUNUNG BATUKARU

Bali's second highest mountain is, much of the time, mainly overlooked. Batukaru is accessible from Tabanan (p. 269) in the southwest or through a mountain road (the turn off just below Bedugul). The Bedugul road where you turn off at **Pacung** and pass through **Jatiluwih** is one of the most enchanting low roads in Bali. The Jatiluwih area has been designated a UNESCO natural world heritage site. You pass centuries-old rice paddies with a long, unspoiled view, perhaps the most spectacular of all in

Waka Land Cruises ★★

Waka Experience (𝄞 **0361/723629;** www.wakaexperience.com; adults US$93, children ages 5–10 US$47) runs tours of Jatiluwih and its surrounds in a Land Rover. The route traverses rice fields and rainforest and stops off at a traditional farmhouse, a hot spring, and an ancient quarry where the stone is still cut by traditional methods to build temples and shrines all over the island. An Indonesian and Balinese lunch is served in a restaurant in the mountains with your choice of red and white wine and even a cognac.

Bali, to the mountains of Agung and Batur on one side, while skirting the slopes of Batukaru on the other. The ancient terraces stand as they have for hundreds of years.

The water from the natural **Penatahan Hot Springs** (Yeh Panas; about 9km/5½ miles north of Tabanan; Jl. Batukaru, Desa Penatahan; 𝄞 **0361/725489;** admission Rp20,000; daily 8am–6pm) near the bank of the river Yeh Ho contains sulfur, potassium, and sodium, which are thought to have curative properties for skin and some other diseases. Penatahan village has a waterfall and the hot springs come up in the middle of a temple under the big banyan tree. According to the local lore, King Jaya Wikrama suffered from a serious skin disease. Upon the minister's suggestion, the king was taken to a traditional meditation healer who received blessings from the gods that a hot spring should pour from the ground. The healer asked the king to take a bath until he completely recovered. To express his gratefulness, the king then built the temple on that location.

PURA LUHUR BATUKARU This ancient temple is set against the magnificent backdrop of Batukaru mountain, at the very end of the road to the mountain. The enchanting site is often shrouded in mist. You can reach a beautiful water pavilion via a floating platoon connected by hand-pulled ropes. As this is such a remote temple, swathed in outstanding and peaceful beauty, only the most determined fellow travelers will have shared your journey.

Where to Stay

Bali Mountain Retreat ★ 👜 Set on the eastern side of the slopes of Mount Batukaru, and accessed through a long (2-hr.) but rewarding drive from the lowlands, this simple offering has a great view, some nice rooms, and one of the most beautiful yoga or dance studios. The straightforward accommodations are a blend of traditional Balinese and contemporary Asian styles, ranging from well-appointed rooms in a handcrafted teak house to comfortable bungalows. Food is served buffet-style, which is more appropriate for the mass market and, given the size of this operation, seems unnecessary. However, it's a good place to base yourself. Staff will organize and advise on treks, and on a good night some get guitars out.

Batukaru. www.balimountainretreat.com. 𝄞 **08/283602645.** 5 units. High season Rp220,000–Rp980,000; low season Rp200,000–Rp895,000. MC, V. **Amenities:** Restaurant; bar/cafe; room service; spa; Wi-Fi.

Cempaka Belimbing Villas Midway between Sanda and Tabanan, with views of the surrounding rice field and forests beyond, this large property has 16 traditional rooms in individual villas, six with pools. Rooms are large and decently furnished if slightly sparse, but the surrounding countryside and terraced fields are the draw. All rooms are individually sized: Some have bathrooms as big as the bedrooms, others have views on various sides, but all have terraces looking down the gently sloping resort, over the pool, and on to the surrounding tropical countryside.

Br. Suradadi, Belimbing, Pupuan-Tabanan. www.cempakabelimbing.com. ℭ **0361/745-1178.** Fax 0361/745-1179. 16 units. High season US$120–US$160; low season US$100–US$140; extra bed US$15. Rates include breakfast, check Internet for discounted rates. MC, V. **Amenities:** Restaurant; bar; lounge; bikes; Jacuzzi; outdoor pool; room service; spa. *In room:* A/C, fan, TV, minibar.

Sanda Butik Villas ★ 🏨 Just outside Sanda village, on the winding road from Papuan to Tabanan, this hotel makes a great stop-off point for journeys from the north or a relaxing getaway if you're in the warmer south. The rooms are villa-style with polished cement floors and sunrooms with full height glass walls. You almost feel as though you're sitting in the fields. You can enjoy historic Indian curry with chutneys and popadom in the charming colonial pavilion that also doubles as the living room and meeting point for the free cocktail hour—where Ted, an old East African hand, serves his terribly colonial, pink gin cocktails. Settle down in the library and enjoy some great books about Bali. Air-conditioning and hot water are included, but the accommodations include showers only and not baths.

Desa-Sanda, Pupuan-Tabanan. www.sandavillas.com. ℭ **08/283720055.** 7 units. Year-round from US$99. Rates include breakfast. AE, MC, V. **Amenities:** Restaurant; outdoor pool; room service. *In room:* A/C, fan, TV, minifridge.

Sarinbuana Eco Lodge ★ On the slopes of Mount Batukaru, this lodge has stunning mountain views. The bungalows are furnished in a traditional style, with many pieces of furniture made from locally grown bamboo. The three-bedroom family bungalow has lots of carved timber and handpicked furniture. A huge amount of thought and a great deal of love has gone into the development of this beautiful spot.

Sarinbuana specializes in educational workshops with courses on Balinese customs, such as cooking and calligraphy. There are farming workshops on locally grown crops, including coffee and vanilla and in the right season rice planting or harvesting, although the latter is truly backbreaking. The lodge also offers special half-day seminars on sustainability or social and community projects, so you can take your knowledge back home with you. The owners truly practice what they preach here, and what they preach we should all be hearing.

Batukaru, Tabanan. www.baliecolodge.com. ℭ **08/2897006079.** 4 units. High season Rp1,373,000–Rp2,060,000; low season Rp1,248,000–Rp1,872,000. Rates include breakfast. MC, V. **Amenities:** Restaurant; lounge. *In room:* minifridge, hot and cold shower.

Where to Eat

On the main road from Sanda south to Tabanan and at the same turn-off as Cempaka Belimbing, the remote roadside cafe **Belimbing Café (Starfruit Café),** Jl. Raya Belimbing (no phone; main courses Rp25,000; no credit cards; daily 8am–9pm), is owned by the same good folk that own the popular Café Batu Jimbar in Sanur (p. 111). The view is quite spectacular. The extensive menu has many pasta and Indonesian dishes and does them very well. It makes an excellent lunch stop on the way north or south. Look out for the puddings, too.

If you could bottle a view, **Café Jatiluwih,** Jatiluwih (© **0361/815245;** sandwiches and main courses starting at Rp10,000; no credit cards; daily 9am–5pm), would be serving the most exquisite drink in town. It has *soto ayam* (spicy chicken soup) at Rp12,000 and a selection of sandwiches. The whole affair is aimed at the tourist market, but it's worth stopping, having some local coffee, and just taking in the view.

EAST BALI

Dominated by the holy mountain Gunung Agung, east Bali is one of the island's most beautiful and traditional regions. It remains largely unspoiled, with not one factory marring the landscape. Here, vistas of terraced rice fields and bamboo forests take the place of bars, cafes, and trendy shops. Several tourist areas are wound together by the coastal road: inland Sidemen, with its beautiful scenery and lush stepped vistas; Tulamben, Padangbai, and Amed, all known for their great diving and snorkeling; and Candidasa, a long-established, if slightly tired resort area.

The locals are descendants of the Majapahits who first settled and established a court here after their flight from Java. The Regents of Klungkung were the last of the Balinese to hold out against the Dutch in 1908 and a towering monument in Semarapura commemorates the final battle. As you travel through the east, you might notice a rich variety of older customs that have managed to resist modern Javanese influence ever since their initial arrival after the 15th century.

EXPLORING EAST BALI

Essentials

GETTING THERE

The best way to explore the east is by **car** or **motorcycle,** both easily rented throughout Bali. If you don't want to rent a car, you can pick up a **taxi.** Negotiate a price before you leave, though, as this is generally cheaper than letting the meter run.

Bemo (vans that serve as buses) run between Batubulan station and the main towns of Candidasa, Amlapura, and Klungkung. You can also catch a *bemo* from these towns to the smaller villages in the area. Prices range from Rp3,500 up to Rp15,000 and depend on what you negotiate. You're likely to pay more than the locals.

You can also get to Padangbai and Candidasa by **Perama Tours bus** (© **0361/751551;** www.peramatour.com) throughout the day from Kuta, Sanur, Lovina, and Ubud. Check the timetable on the website. You can arrange a drop-off at a hotel for an extra price. Prices range from Rp25,000 to Rp125,000 one-way.

You have two options for getting to the east. With the first, you follow the **coastal road** from Sanur toward Kusamba, and then north toward Amlapura, passing Manggis en route. At Amlapura, the road forks north through Tirta Gangga and round toward Culik. At Culik you can turn left and continue to Tulamben and the north coast or turn right for Amed.

HOTELS ■

Alam Asmara Dive Resort **22**
Alam Batu Beach
   Bungalow Resort **50**
The Alila Resort Manggis **17**
Amankila **15**
Batu Belah **45**
Bayu Cottages Hotel
   & Restaurant **37**
Bloo Lagoon Resort **13**
Blue Moon Villa **35**
Dharma Homestay **12**
The Golden Rock **41**
Good Karma **44**
Life in Amed **36**
Mimpi Resort **46**
Nirarta Centre for
   Living Awareness **6**
Patal Kikian **7**
Pondok Wisata
   Lihat Sawah **5**
Puri Bagus **24**
Puri Sawah Villas **33**
Rama Candidasa **19**
Santai Hotel **42**

Scuba Seraya
   Resort **48**
Seraya Shores **28**
Siddhartha Resort **49**
Tauch Terminal Resort
   & Spa **47**
Villa Asada **18**
Villa Djamrud **32**
Villa Sasoon **23**
Villa Talia Vashti **16**
Villa Tirta Ayu **32**
Watergarden **20**
Wawa Wewe II **39**

RESTAURANTS ◆

Anda Amed Resort **43**
Garpu Restaurant **19**
Komang John Café **35**
Le Warung
   Restaurant **13**
Life in Amed **36**
Omang Omang Café **11**
Sails **38**
Santai **42**
Vincent's **21**

ATTRACTIONS ●

Bali Asli **34**
Budakeling **30**
Bukit Demulih **1**
Charlie's Factory **26**
Klungkung Market **4**
Nyoman Gunarsa
   Museum **3**
Pantai Kecil/
   Bias Tugal **10**
Pelangi Workshop **8**
Pura Besakih
   (Mother Temple) **25**
Pura Goa Lawah **9**
Pura Lempuyang **40**
Pura Silayukti **14**
Puri Agung
   Karangasem **29**
Sadus Tiles **8**
Taman Gili &
   Semararaja Museum **4**
Taman Tirta Gangga **31**
Taman Ujung
   Water Palace **27**
Tihingan **2**

Petang
Kayubihi
Menanga
Penebel
Melinggih
Rendang
Tampaksiring
Manggis
Bangli
Buitan
Bugbug
Sengkidu
15 16 17
18
Candidasa
20
21 23
19 19
22 24
Teluk Amuk
(Amuk Bay)
Gili Mimpang
14
Padangbai
Blue Lagoon
Klungkung
(Semarapura)
12
Gili Tepekong
13
11 13
10
Padangbai Beach
Amuk Bay
Lebih Beach

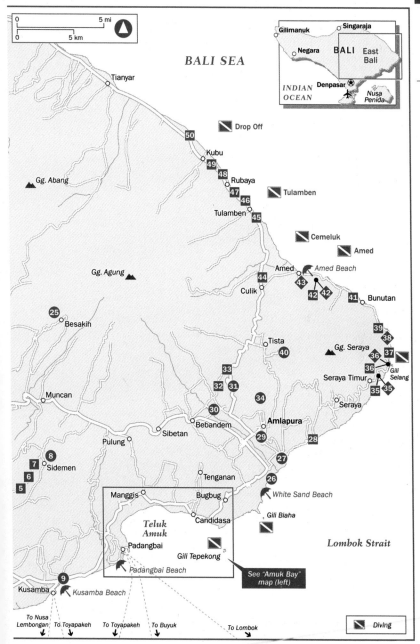

BALI SEA

Tianyar

Gilimanuk · Singaraja

Negara   BALI   East Bali

INDIAN OCEAN   Denpasar ✈

Nusa Penida

◼ Drop Off

50

Kubu

49

48 ◼ Rubaya

47

46 ◼ Tulamben

Tulamben 45

Gg. Abang

◼ Cemeluk

◼ Amed

Gg. Agung

Amed   ☂ Amed Beach

44   43

Culik   42 42   41 ◦ Bunutan

25
◦ Besakih

39
38

Tista   Gg. Seraya ▲   37 ◼

40   36 37

36

Seraya Timur   Gili Selang

33   35 35

Muncan   32 31

34

30   Seraya

Bebandem   Amlapura

Pulung   Sibetan   29   28

8   27

7 ◦ Sidemen   Tenganan   26

6   Manggis ◦   Bugbug ◦   White Sand Beach

5   Candidasa ◦   Gili Biaha ◼

Teluk Amuk

Padangbai   Lombok Strait

Gili Tepekong ◼

Padangbai Beach

See "Amuk Bay" map (left)

9

Kusamba ◦   Kusamba Beach

To Nusa Lembongan   To Toyapakeh   To Toyapakeh   To Buyuk   To Lombok

◼ Diving

0   5 mi
0   5 km

This delightful road round the coast ends up back at Amlapura. The roads are good, if narrow, and you get a chance to see how the villagers go about their daily lives. One stop of note in Seraya is the small, open-air, hand-weaving showroom of **Threads of Life ★★★**, a nonprofit organization working to revitalize local weaving. Take a private tour to learn about the weaving and dying processes.

The second option, mostly used by visitors coming **from Ubud,** is, upon leaving Ubud, to head toward Gianyar, and then north to Bangli and east to Rendang. Not far from Rendang is the turn to Pura Besakih (p. 231), or keep trucking on toward Amlapura traveling through Sibetan, home of *salak* (the snake fruit, p. 227).

Another **scenic route** worth mentioning is the road from Semarapura (Klungkung) via Sidemen and Iseh. The endless paddy field views are breathtaking.

GETTING AROUND

East Bali tends to have no authorized metered taxis, although some *bemo* operators are happy to drive you where you need to go. Be sure to have the phone number of your destination in case the driver isn't familiar with it.

VISITOR INFORMATION

A **tourist office** (Taman Kerta Gosa; ✆ **0366/21448,** but don't count on anyone answering; Mon–Fri 8am–2pm) is in Semarapura in the Semararaja Museum of Taman Kerta Gosa (p. 225). However, like all tourist offices in Bali, it isn't set up to give you independent advice, but rather sell you commission-based tours. The tourist information in **Amlapura,** Jl. Diponegoro (✆ **0363/21196,** again, don't count on anyone answering; Mon–Fri, erratic hours), covers the whole area of Karangasem and does have a host of useful information as well as a useful website (**www.karangasem tourism.com**) with dates for major ceremonies. The staff are helpful and able to give good information on what to see and do in the area. A similar little publication called *Agung* is available in area hotels and restaurants.

[FastFACTS] EAST BALI

ATMs   East Bali has few options for getting cash. Although money changers are available in Candidasa, Padangbai, and Amed, ATMs are a rarity. Two ATMs are in Klungkung on the main street near the market; Padangbai has an ATM beside Hotel Madya, in front of the ferry terminal; Bangli has one ATM in the BRI bank on Jalan Kutai; your last chance is in Amlapura, outside the Hardy's supermarket. A couple of hotels may offer an ATM service with a surcharge. Always carry small change as most locals can't change large denominations (a Rp100,000 note is the equivalent of over a week's wages).

Credit Cards   Not many places in the east take credit cards so ensure you have enough cash before heading here. Most dive resorts are able to process credit cards but may charge you 2.5% to 3% surcharge.

Food   Most towns sell snacks and basics such as pasta but you'll not find much Western food on sale in the area.

Toiletries   Shampoos and some sun creams are available in small shops. There are no tampons for sale north of Seminyak or east of Ubud.

Wine & Alcohol   Beer is readily available in most warungs and shops in the area, but wines and spirits can be in short supply. If you're traveling east, bring your own.

KLUNGKUNG (SEMARAPURA)

Klungkung is the original name of the capital of the Gelgel Regency, which changed its name in 1992 to Semarapura in tribute to the Semarapura "Palace of the God of Love." Klungkung was considered to be the most important of all the regencies from the 17th century until the regency finally ceded to the Dutch in 1908. The royal family was descended from the emperors of the Majaphit. In 1710, Dewa Agung Jambe I, the regent of Klungkung, built Taman Gili, the royal palace. By the end of the 18th century Kerta Gosa, the so-called Halls of Justice, often referred to somewhat ambitiously as Bali's Sistine Chapel, was erected in the middle of an artificial lake. Though the Dutch made use of the Court, in 1908 they destroyed most of the rest of the palace after their bloody victory against Dewa Agung Jambe II. The fight on April 18, 1908, proceeded until the death of the last of the combatants, which included women and children. The king and many of his followers chose *puputan* (ritual mass suicide) rather than face defeat and disgrace. The end of the battle marked the fall of the last of the Balinese kingdoms. A monument opposite Taman Gili commemorates this last stand.

Exploring Klungkung & the Nearby Villages

Villagers from the nearby hills head to the city's market every 3 days, and make it a huge social event. The sprawling **Klungkung Market** has hundreds of traditional stalls selling hand-woven fabrics, religious paraphernalia, including the long-handled Balinese ceremonial umbrellas, and lots of glittering mirrored items for the home or family shrines. A couple of stalls sell artifacts and some antiques. Be sure to haggle. For more shopping, the main street has three antiques shops that occasionally have old textiles worth a peek. Other curiosities are mixed together with real antiques and always worth a rummage. As ever, beware of sophisticated copies.

Located 3km (2 miles) west from Klungkung, **Tihingan ★** village is a center for makers of gamelans and other traditional musical instruments. The process requires strong workers and specialist pitchers to ensure the right tone is achieved. The quality gongs from Tihingan have a global renown. A few showrooms on the main street have tradesmen at work, typically out first thing in the morning when it's cool. Although some of the showrooms will sell you gamelans, expect to pay a few million rupiah.

A small side road off the main Klungkung road will take you to the fishing and salt-making village of **Kusamba,** where the beach is lined with colorful fishing boats, salt-making huts, and rows of shallow troughs. The work of raking and sprinkling the sand with water before the filtration process starts before dawn. Sea water is carried from the ocean and poured into specially dug ponds. Once the water has evaporated, the salty residue is placed in shallow troughs, made from split palm trees, and more sea water is added. Further evaporation and purification yields fully formed, pyramid-shaped salt crystals. Some chefs consider Balinese salt to be some of the finest in the world. Buy some to help support the hard-working farmers and their families.

Taman Gili & Semararaja Museum The Taman Gili, "Island Garden," in the center of Klungkung contains three important elements: Kerta Gosa, Bale Kambang, and the Semararaja Museum. Though the whole complex is sadly deteriorated due to neglect, it's still very much worth a look.

DINING & breaking RECORDS IN KARANGSEM REGENCY

A *megibung* ("people eating communally") is a unique traditional meal of the Karangsem regency associated with weddings, cremations, or temple ceremonies—or anything that involves a meeting of the community.

Participants are divided into groups called *sela*, which consist of eight people of the same gender, sitting cross-legged around a large, woven rattan plate known as a *nare*, heaped with piles of rice. At the edge are piles of vegetables, maybe steamed *kangkung*, and *urap*, a vegetable salad of long green beans and grated coconut. Servings of pork satay, sometimes grilled pork, and a curry are dispensed by helpers and everyone tucks in—all eating with their right hand. The table can't start to eat until eight people are seated.

If a *pedanda* (high priest) is in attendance, he eats alone, off his own plate known as a *dulang*. His meal consists of rice, vegetables, and duck rather than pork—unless he's a vegetarian. Duck symbolizes wisdom.

In 1996, 19,768 people participated in the *Guinness World Records*' largest communal eating event, consisting of 2,452 *selas* and 152 *wanci* (special tables for the high priest). Participants came from all over the Karangsem regency to help break the previous record.

Although it has undergone many restorations, one of the best examples of *wayang* painting in Bali is on the ceiling of the **Kerta Gosa.** The panels of gods and demons are arranged in nine layers. The first and lowest level depicts the five tales of Tantri, the Indonesian version of a *Thousand and One Nights*. The next two levels illustrate episodes of the story of Bhima Swarga who ventures into the underworld to redeem his parents' souls. During his time in hell, he battles with demons and witnesses the gruesome torture of the sinful. The fourth row depicts Garuda's search for the elixir of life; the fifth is the Balinese astrological calendar; the next three panels show the climax of the story with Bhima's visit to heaven and the rewards from the high god. The epic tale ends, gloriously, in enlightenment and justice. Kerta Gosa was considered the supreme court of Bali, where the rajah would meet with his advisors to discuss the law and human affairs. Those on trial could look up at the reliefs on the ceiling and see the moral story of Bhima Swarga and the dreadful punishments and depictions of hell and then look further and see the panels of heaven and find consolation.

The **Bale Kambang ★★** is surrounded by ponds, and features another richly painted ceiling of the traditional Kamasan style. This building was originally the royal guards' headquarters and used for royal tooth-filing ceremonies, conducted as a rite of passage for teenagers, where several front teeth are filed into sharp points. The extensively restored ceilings have decorative paintings of Balinese astrology, the story of Pan and Men Brayut and their 18 mischievous children, and the adventures of the Sutasona, the Balinese role model for nonaggressive strength and a legendary Buddhist hero who was able to turn arrows and spears, hurled at him from the gods, into flowers.

The **Semararaja Museum** has various archaeological objects, traditional artifacts, ceramics, painting, and furniture on show.

Jl. Untung Suropati 3. ✆ **0366/21448.** Admission Rp12,000. Daily 8am–6pm.

Nyoman Gunarsa Museum This museum was built to honor the famous and powerful king Dalam Waturenggong who protected Bali from Muslim influences. It's home to a large collection of classical and contemporary Balinese artwork and work of the founder, Dr. Nyoman Gunarsa. A selection of masks, puppets, ceramics, and stone carvings dates from the 17th to 19th century. The entrance is behind the Trimurti statue and is surrounded by policemen statues.

Jl. Petigaan Banda 1. ✆ **0366/22256.** Admission Rp25,000. Mon–Sat 9am–5pm.

Pura Goa Lawah About 2km (1¼ miles) east of Kusamba, and popularly known as the Bat Cave, this is one of the nine *kahyangan jagat* (directional temples) on Bali, which protect the island from evil spirits. Pura Goa Lawah is revered as a sacred site for Brahma, the Hindu god of creation. The dark interior is filled with a seething mass of bats that makes the walls of the cave appear to be alive. Sea water here is thought to be blessed and is brought to the mother temple of Besakih. Legend has it that a tunnel extends from the cave up to Besakih some 30km (19 miles) away, though it has yet to be discovered. The temple is one of *sad kahyangan* (six great temples of Bali) and the cave is a favored site of *nyekah* (deification of a deceased family member's soul) pilgrimage. The best time to visit is during *odalan,* the temple birthday (June 1), when pilgrims flock to be blessed.

Rp4,000. Parking Rp1,000. Daily 8am–5pm.

Where to Stay & Eat

Klungkung doesn't have enough draw to merit staying overnight. Base yourself nearby in Ubud or Manggis instead. If you do, however, find yourself in the city roaming for something to eat, the best place to aim for is the **market** (see above), just behind a row of shops to the east of Taman Gosa. A selection of stalls cooks up basic Indonesian fare. In the evening, the **Pasar Senggol** (night market in the same location; 5pm–midnight) has Indonesian cuisine and some Chinese-influenced offerings. It's loud and chaotic and really quite fun.

THE SIDEMEN VALLEY ★★

One of Bali's most scenic areas, where exceptionally beautiful verdant rice terraces tumble down hills to deep valleys, the Sidemen makes a great side trip from Ubud or a stop off on the way to Amed (p. 244). Sidemen is also known for its traditional

What to Eat in Sibetan

Sibetan is the home of *salak* (snake fruit), an applelike fruit covered with what looks like snakeskin. If you happen to be driving by Sibetan late at night or very early in the morning, stop by Sibetan market, which sells some of the best *babi guling* (roast suckling pig) around. The trading's all finished by 6am.

You can buy traditional cement tiles from **Sadus Tiles** (☎ 08/5237064151; www.sadustiles.com). A Dutch woman and her Balinese husband create beautiful, handcrafted cement tiles that are redolent of Dutch colonial Java. They make both traditional patterns as well as more modern designs using recently introduced Dutch compounds. Just watching the process is fascinating and they'll welcome you to the factory whether you buy or not.

weaving. *Songket*, a ceremonial cloth for weddings that's richly decorated with gold or silver thread, is one of the best known and several weaving shops along the main road sometimes offer weaving demonstrations. Look for the signs outside the shops or ask your driver who'll be sure to know.

The road from Semarapura to Duda through Sidemen and Iseh, with breathtaking paddy field views among some of the most stunning in Bali, is a great way to approach Pura Besakih (p. 231). Both Walter Spies and Theo Maier resided in the countryside near Iseh to seek peace and inspiration—and to escape overcrowded Ubud.

Exploring Sidemen Valley

CYCLING ★★ 📷 The Sidemen valley offers some of the best cycling in Bali as the roads aren't as busy as others. Most hotels in the area offer free use of their mountain bikes; otherwise specialist tour agents can organize trips that include rental of bike and helmets, refreshments, lunch, and insurance.

A good cycling trip begins in the heart of snake-fruit country, **Selat,** and takes you through Iseh, a small mountain village down to **Sidemen.** You'll cycle through valleys of uninterrupted rice terrace views, see plantations bearing a variety of crops, pass fighting cocks in baskets, and experience the daily life of the Balinese. The trip is mostly downhill and should take about 2 hours.

TREKKING Most tour operators from the south can arrange a half- or full-day trek through the Sidemen valley. If you're staying in the area, your hotel will help you with hiring a local guide; expect to pay about Rp25,000 to Rp35,000 an hour.

Some well-trodden footpaths meander through the rice fields. With plenty of intoxicating views, crags and rivers to cross, and a smattering of temples, this is a rambler's paradise. With or without a guide, you're never too far from a road so don't worry about getting lost. Besides, you might stumble on a small village where most Balinese will welcome you with open arms and point you in the right direction.

WHITE-WATER RAFTING An exhilarating outing on the Telega Waja river begins in Muncan and takes you through 14km (9 miles) of terraced rice fields, lush tropical jungle, cascading waterfalls, and steep canyons of clean, natural spring water. Classified as a class IV river (class III being the easiest), this adventure is suitable for children as young as 6. Book through **Sobek ★★★** (☎ 0361/768050; www.bali sobek.com; adult US$79, children ages 7–15 US$52; includes transfers, refreshments, lunch, and insurance).

PELANGI WORKSHOP ★★ 🎁 Stop at the Pelangi Workshop (no phone; Jl. Soka 67; daily 8am–5pm) in Sidemen village where you can see up to 40 people working on foot looms. The workshop produces some of the finest ikat, *endek,* and *songket* fabrics and textiles in Bali which are exported all over the world, as well as to other Balinese shops. Opposite the workshop is a small store producing some traditional Lontar painting.

Where to Stay & Eat

Nirarta Centre for Living Awareness ★   This tiny resort of six Balinese villas has magnificent views of the surrounding rice fields and mountains. Stunning scenery and organic food make this retreat a favorite for groups and health seekers. Founded by psychologist Peter Wrycza and his wife Ida Ayu, who comes from a family of Balinese healers, the center follows a mix of spiritual disciplines and philosophies. Activities include meditation, meeting with high priests, trekking, and yoga.

Banjar Tabola, Sidemen. www.awareness-bali.com. ℂ **0366/530-0636.** 11 units. Year-round US$50–US$64. AE, MC, V. **Amenities:** Restaurant. *In room:* Hot shower, tea and coffee.

Patal Kikian ★   At the top of a steep hill, not far from the center of Sidemen, is this enchanting homestay offering basic accommodations. Each bungalow has a terrace perfect for enjoying the rice field views below. There's even a small pool, for those brave enough for the cold. Ida Ayu Mas Andayani, who runs this family business, is always on hand to share stories and show you her photo album with the likes of David Bowie and Mick Jagger. She can also arrange trips to the local weavers or a trek. Supper under the stars is served on your own terrace.

Sidemen. ℂ **0366/23005.** Year-round US$81–US$88. No credit cards. **Amenities:** Outdoor pool; room service. *In room:* Fan.

Pondok Wisata Lihat Sawah   This charming family-run guesthouse is surrounded by paddy fields with breathtaking views. They also offer workshops on *songket* weaving and can arrange hikes through the local countryside. The rooms have traditional matting for the walls, four-poster beds, and an assortment of antique-style furniture. The owners also have three private villas. The restaurant serves up a basic selection of Thai, European, and Indonesian food.

Br. Tebola, Sidemen. www.lihatsawah.com. ℂ **0366/530-0516.** 12 units. High season US$35–US$55; low season US$30–US$50. No credit cards. **Amenities:** Restaurant; bicycles; concierge; room service. *In room:* Fan, minibar.

BANGLI & GUNUNG AGUNG

Visiting Bangli, in the center of a panoramic rice-growing area, makes a great alternative route through the east. The mountain town has a famous temple that was founded as early as the 12th century, if not before, and the beautiful Pura Kehen is one of Bali's best. Market days (every 3 days) are always colorful, when inhabitants from the hills come to town to sell their wares, trade, and catch up on local gossip.

[Fast FACTS] BANGLI

Hospital   The hospital is on Jalan Kusumayudha, just down the road from the post office.

Mail   The **post office** is at Jalan Kusumayudha 18.

Police   The police are on Jalan Nusntara, on the road to Penelokan.

Visitor Information   The **Sasana Budaya Arts Centre** on Jalan Sriwijaya (ℂ **0366/91537**) has a tourist center (Mon–Fri 8am–3pm).

Exploring Bangli

Bukit Demulih, literally the "hill of no return," is about 3km (2 miles), about an hour's walk, west of Bangli. At the top of the hill is a small, picturesque temple and stunning views over central Bali. En route, you'll find a small, holy waterfall, located in a bamboo setting. Take a guide from your hotel.

The town, the old capital of the regency, is dominated by the *puri* (palaces). The Bangli court established its independence from Klungkung in the 19th century and played an influential role in Balinese politics through to the post-independence era. Eight royal households are spread around the main crossroads. The most prominent is the **Puri Denpasar,** the palace of the last rajah of Bangli, who died 30 years ago. His descendants have restored much of the palace, and there's now a small hotel in the pavilions run by the rajah's grandson. The **royal ancestral temple** lies just to the north of the crossroads, on the western side. Huge ceremonies are held here, attended by all descendants of the royal house, including many who live in other parts of Indonesia.

Pura Dalem Penunggekan   The Temple of the Dead is a pleasant stroll away from the town center. The exterior walls depict the graphic fate of souls in heaven and hell as witnessed by Bhima (p. 226) while trying to retrieve the souls of his parents from hell. One panel details the lurid fate of adulterers while another portrays sinners as monkeys.

Jl. Merdeka. No phone. Admission Rp5,000. Daily 7am–5pm.

Pura Kehen   The Temple of the Hearth, or the Temple of Fire, the state temple of the old kingdom, is one of Bali's most beautiful temples and stands at the northeastern boundary of town, seemingly in the middle of the forest. Three copper stelae testify to its antiquity and importance. The earliest one, written in Sanskrit, seems to date to the 9th century and mentions the deity Hyang Api, the god of fire. The second is in old Balinese, and the third is in old Javanese, the latter mentioning Hyang Kehen (the same deity from the 9th century inscriptions) and indicating eight villages around Bangli that worship the deity.

The temple was constructed on eight terraces, after the manner of ancient animistic sanctuaries that are built into the southern slope of a hill, much like Pura Besakih (see below). A flight of 38 stairs adorned with *wayang* statues leads to the main entrance, where a frightening *kala makara* demon guardian is carved on the gateway. The outer courtyard has a huge, old banyan tree with a *kul kul* drum inside, as well as a flat stone for offerings. The walls are inlaid with Chinese porcelain—a common feature of ancient temples and palaces. The temple has 43 altars, including one 11-roofed *meru* (altar) to Hyang Api. Several are dedicated to the ancestors of *sudra* commoner clans such as the Ratu Pasek and Pande—which means that worshipers from all over Bali come to pray here, especially on its *odalan* (Mar 3). The huge Padmasana throne in the northeastern-most corner has beautiful carvings at the back.

Jl. Sriwijaya. No phone. Admission Rp6,000. Daily 6am–6pm.

The Sasana Budaya Art Center   The Bangli area has various types of ritual *baris,* dances typical of the mountain regions, such as the *baris jojor* (eight men in a line with spears), *baris presi* or *tamiang* (eight men in a circle with leather shields), and *baris dadap* (men in pairs with bat-shaped curled shields made from holy *dadap*

Organized tours are the best way to visit the temple as on-site guides can be intrusive and off-putting. Many visitors are appalled by the treatment they receive from guides and touts outside the entrance. Our advice is to arrange a visit to the temple with an organized tour agent. This way, you should avoid being harassed by touts. If you do go on your own, you'll be approached by guides, who can be very persistent, looking to offer their services. You don't need to use a guide to view the temple. If you wish to hire an on-site guide, make sure that you agree to a price beforehand: Rp20,000 to Rp30,000 should be enough.

wood). The dances are performed especially at *odalans*. This arts center is one of the largest in Bali and occasionally hosts dance performances—though it's not always open. Get information on show times from the tourist information office in the same building.

Jl. Sriwijaya. Inquire at on-site tourist information center (Mon–Fri 8am–3pm) for performance times.

On the Slope of Gunung Agung

Pura Besakih (Mother Temple) ★★ 📷 Bali's largest and holiest temple, Pura Besakih, is alternatively known as the "Mother Temple" and translates literally as the Temple of Spiritual Happiness. It's named after the dragon god believed to inhabit the mountain and is said to be the only temple where a Hindu of any caste can worship. The temple consists of between 28 and 35 separate structures depending how you count them, and although the precise origins of Pura Besakih remain unclear, the stone bases of Pura Penetaran Agung date back at least 2,000 years. This site has been used as a Hindu place of worship since at least the late 13th century, when the first Javanese conquerors settled on Bali.

Pura Besakih is about 1,000m (3,300 ft.) above sea level. Steps ascend through split gates to the main courtyard where the Trinity shrines are wrapped in cloth and decorated with flower offerings. There are a number of temples but many of their inner courtyards are closed to visitors. Eighteen separate sanctuaries belonging to different regencies and caste groups surround the main temples dedicated to Shiva, Brahma, and Vishnu. To the Balinese, visiting the temple sanctuaries is a special pilgrimage.

The mountaintop setting gives Pura Besakih an almost mystical quality, even more so if you get there for sunrise. Try to reach the temple before 9am, as after this time many tourist buses start to arrive and it can get very busy. Further, given its popularity, it also attracts the more voracious of the local touts who can make the experience a distinctly unspiritual one.

Admission Rp10,000. Daily 7am–6pm. Visitors must wear sarong and sash to enter, both of which can be purchased or rented at the entrance.

Gunung Agung

Gunung Agung, Bali's highest and, for this reason, holiest mountain, reaches just over 3,100m (10,170 ft.) and is usually at least partly obscured by cloud and mist. To the

Balinese, Bali is the entire world, and Gunung Agung is the world's most sacred point. They believe that Mount Agung is a replica of Mount Meru, the central axis of the universe. And so, half way up, they built Pura Besakih, the Mother Temple (see above). At some stage in their life, all Balinese must make a pilgrimage up the mountain, the closest point to heaven and where the gods live when they visit mother earth. However Mount Agung, although not a technically difficult climb, is one of Bali's biggest trekking challenges and shouldn't be taken lightly and not without a guide (see below for guide recommendations). Start well before dawn, armed with a strong flashlight, water, food, warm and waterproof clothing, and sensible shoes or boots. The best time for a climb is during the dry season of April through October. However as a holy mountain, climbing isn't permitted when major religious events are held at the temple at Besakih, which is most of April. Check exact dates, as they operate on the Balinese calendar.

CLIMBING GUNUNG AGUNG

The shortest and most popular route up Mount Agung is from Selat or Muncan, which involves the least walking, due to serviceable roads from either town that lead to the Pura Pasar Agung (Agung Market Temple). From this temple, the climb takes between 2 and 4 hours depending on your level of fitness. Leave by 3am at the latest if you want to get there for sunrise. The other route starts from Pura Besakih and the climb is longer and more challenging, and only really suitable for the physically fit. From Besakih you have the option of either attacking the climb in one hit of between 5 and 6 hours or doing it with an overnight camp. Most prefer to start around 10 or 11pm arriving at the summit in time to enjoy the sunrise—rain, mist, and other climbers permitting.

At the summit on a clear morning you enjoy a 360-degree view over the Lombok Strait to Mount Rinjani and verdant Bali. Be prepared for adverse weather conditions as storms develop quickly. There are no shops along the route.

Guides are available in Besakih. We recommend: **Gung Bawa Trekking** (© 08/123878168), a reliable guide who has been trekking this mountain for years; **M&G Trekking** (© 0363/41464) in Candidasa who can offer alternative routes; or **Ketut Uriada** (© 08/123646426), based in Muncan, who's very knowledgeable about the area.

Where to Stay & Eat

Bangli has a couple of places to stay with very basic accommodations. **Artha Sastra Inn,** Jl. Merdeka 5 (no phone; year-round Rp35,000–Rp50,000; cold water showers), is opposite the *bemo* terminal and close to the market in an old palace (the building was once the royal place of Bangli), though the grandeur is somewhat faded. The nine rooms vary enormously, and so look at a few before you commit to staying.

The **Bangli Inn,** Jl. Rambutan (© 0366/91419; year-round Rp150,000; cold water only; no shower, breakfast included), is the more conventional, with clean rooms built around a small courtyard.

For food during the day, the bus terminal has several stalls while the road beside the terminal transforms into a small **night market** *(pasar malam)* come sundown with the full range of satays, soups, and rice and noodle dishes. **Depot Murni,** Jl. Merdeka 18, just south of the town center, is a typical, local warung with the usual rice and noodle offerings at inexpensive prices.

PADANGBAI

Fifteen minutes south of Candidasa is the little fishing village of Padangbai, with a beach aglow with the colors of wooden *prahu* boats. Simple fish restaurants and dive shops line the main road, while behind the village are dozens of small homestays and simple eateries. Just to the north is the perfect little Bloo Lagoon Beach.

Essentials

GETTING THERE & GETTING AROUND

Padangbai is the main port for the ferries to Lombok (p. 291), Nusa Penida (p. 129), and the Gili Islands (p. 324). If you do decide to **rent a car** in the area, expect to pay between Rp200,000 and Rp300,000 a day. Motorbike rental will cost around Rp100,000 a day. **Perama Tours** (© 0363/41419; www.peramatour.com) offers a wide variety of **bus routes** to and from Padangbai and all round Bali. The company has offices near the jetty (daily 7am–7pm). You can catch a *bemo* serving Candidasa, Amlapura, and Semarapura from the car park at the port entrance. If you're looking to travel south to Kuta, most **taxis** offer a fixed price of around Rp300,000.

Not-So-Valuable Visitor Information

Although they look official, the tourist information offices in Padangbai are basically commercial enterprises looking to sell you their tours or services.

[FastFACTS] PADANGBAI

Mail   A **post office** is located opposite the ferry terminal, on the right hand side near to Depot Dona.

Toiletries   **Titi Shop** on the main Denpasar road near the ferry terminal sells toiletries and basic food requirements.

Exploring Padangbai

Commanding a high headland at the northern end of Padangbai, **Pura Silayukti** (free admission; daily 24 hr.) is one of Bali's oldest temples. It was founded by the great Javanese Hindu sage Empu Kuturan who arrived here in the 11th century. He subsequently built a retreat on the hillside overlooking the bay, which was later to become Pura Silayukti. As one of the oldest temples, there's very little of architectural interest left to look at. The caves beneath are more interesting.

FISHING   Local fishermen will take you out fishing. Expect to pay between Rp100,000 and Rp200,000 for half a day. Fishermen only fish late at night till first thing in the morning or late afternoon until sunset. Bloo Lagoon Resort (see below) can arrange trips with its own fishing boat and is happy to cook up any catch.

SCUBA DIVING   Amuk Bay—with Padangbai to the south and Candidasa to the north—has some of Bali's best diving. This is also Bali's premier location for sharks—but fear not, as they're mainly reef sharks with some tiger sharks, and there have been no attacks reported in recent memory.

The **Bloo Lagoon,** just north of Padangbai, is the only site suitable for beginners, with its gentle white sand slope. Plus, it's a treasure-trove of marine life that includes reef sharks, rhinopias, cuttlefish, leaf scorpion fish, frogfish, lionfish, nudis, and a huge area of stag horn coral. Excellent night diving will expose you to cat sharks, Spanish dancers, crustaceans, basket stars, and hunting cephalopods.

Mimpang is an area with three rock pinnacles that break the surface and which, at the southern, deeper end (known as Shark Point), offers a spectacular wall with profuse corals, fish, and the opportunity to see pelagics.

The breathtaking **Tepekong,** a 300-m (984-ft.) long rock, is for experienced divers only due to the steep walls, cold water, and strong currents. In Tepekong's famous canyon, with its swirling waters and dramatic, craggy walls, are huge schools of sweet-lips, maybe Mola mola (ocean sunfish), white-tip reef sharks, and turtles.

Gili Biaha ★★★, a little to the north, offers some of Bali's most stunning diving. A vast number and a great diversity of fish, sharks, and frequent pelagic visitors live against a backdrop of chiseled black walls with beautiful, healthy corals and often superb visibility. Diving here is best at slack, high tide.

The currents at Mimpang, Tepekong, and Biaha require care and respect: Not only can a gentle current become a torrential river within a matter of minutes, but also both up and down currents are quite common at these sites.

Having recently been awarded the GoEco operator status, **Geko Dive ★★**, Jl. Silayukti (© **0363/41516;** www.gekodive.com), is now one of only eight dive operators in Bali to merit this award. Established in 1997, and catering to both beginners and professionals, it offers a full range of PADI certification courses, dive assistance, and dive-and-accommodations packages. Expect to pay between US$70 and US$120 for two dives with lunch, dive computer, and local transfers.

Waterworx, Jl. Silayukti (© **0363/41220** or 08/11375889; www.waterworxbali. com) offers diving and snorkeling in the area and around Nusa Penida. TheSSI-registered dive school has a great team that provides courses in English, French, and German. It offers courses for both PADI and SSI and free local pickup. Two dives, including equipment and drinks, cost between US$75 and US$90.

If you're in Seminyak and you want to dive in Padangbai, contact **AquaMarine Diving ★★★**, Jl. Raya Petitenget 2A (© **0361/473-8020;** fax 0361/4738021; www.aquamarinediving.com; US$115, 2 person minimum, transport and lunch).

SNORKELING   Padangbai has some of the best snorkeling in the east including some great places for children to enjoy themselves without the strong currents that besiege most of Bali. Local warungs along the beaches rent out snorkel gear. One of the safest spots to snorkel is in front of the **main beach.** However, this beach can get quite crowded so you may wish to head for **Pantai Kecil,** otherwise known as Bias Tugal, to the west of the village. There are a few warungs here where you can have a simple meal and get a traditional massage. At least one new development is currently under construction up on the hill but don't let it put you off. **Bloo Lagoon ★** (see "Scuba Diving" above) is also another, near-perfect small bay with some great snorkeling.

Where to Stay

Most homestays are on Jalan Silayukti or in the village. Prices range from Rp40,000 (yes, only US$4) up to about Rp100,000 a night. One in particular is the **Dharma Homestay,** Jl. Silayukti (© **0363/41394;** Rp100,000–Rp150,000), close to the beach. The best rooms are on the top floor with stunning views over the village.

Bloo Lagoon Resort ★   This is the best place to stay in the area. Sitting on top of a hill with panoramic views, the resort consists of self-contained villas surrounding a central pool and dining area overlooking the perfect, yet small, Bloo Lagoon Beach. The resort has an eco-friendly approach and strives to integrate energy-saving technologies; it composts, grows its own food, and recycles water. The amphitheater occasionally hosts Balinese and Western performances. **Spa Biroo** overlooks the sea at the top of the hill and offers a selection of treatments from manicures and pedicures and aromatherapy massages using high-quality essential oils, to the Shama-Shama massage, a four-hand treatment.

Jl. Silayukti, Padangbai. www.bloolagoon.com. © **0363/41211.** Fax 0363/41099. 23 units. High season US$128 1-bedroom, US$178 2-bedroom, US$196 3-bedroom; low season US$108 1-bedroom, US$158 2-bedroom, US$176 3-bedroom. Discount available when booking online. AE, MC, V. **Amenities:** Restaurant (see below); babysitting; concierge; children's club; outdoor pool; room service; spa; watersports. In room: A/C, fan.

Where to Eat

The small **Le Warung Restaurant** ★, in the Bloo Lagoon (main courses Rp25,000–Rp50,000; AE, MC, V; daily 7:30am–10pm), uses organic produce from its garden. The chef serves simple, tasty salads, soups, and pastas with homemade sauces. Indonesian food and well-made curries are also available. Fresh juices, cappuccinos, and teas are available all day. Nine years ago, **Omang Omang Café** ★, Jl. Silayukti (© **08/123638052;** www.omangcafe.com; main courses Rp35,000–Rp75,000; no credit cards; daily 10am–11pm), was the first restaurant to open in Padangbai and it's still the best place. It cooks up a selection of wholesome, organic Western and Asian fusion dishes at reasonable prices. The barbecue is by far the most popular choice, with memorable spareribs marinated in a secret sauce. The best option on the Asian menu is the chicken with cashews, though the puddings and homemade ice creams steal the show (Rp12,000 a scoop). On Monday nights, enjoy the live jazz/blues band from 7 till 10pm.

MANGGIS

Some of the best quality hotels on the east coast are around Manggis. In fact, the proximity to Candidasa makes Manggis a good alternative to staying in that resort; hiking, cycling, and the lovely Sidemen valley are only a short drive away.

What to Do in Manggis

LEARN TO COOK   Learn Balinese basics at the Alila Resort (p. 237). This **cooking class** ★★ (www.alilahotels.com/manggis; US$85 for half-day, US$95 seafood school, other specialty packages available; peak season incurs additional surcharge; daily) offers visitors a hands-on introduction to Balinese and Indonesian cooking. By the end all students make, among other things, their own perfect wok-cooked *nasi goreng* (fried rice).

Rent a *jukung* (local fishing boat) from the Alila hotel and hook your own fish. Once back on land you'll learn to cook a variety of tasty seafood dishes, which include a local fish and prawn curry or fish wrapped in banana leaves.

GET A MASSAGE   At the **Alila spa** (www.alilahotels.com/manggis; single treatment US$30–US$80, packages US$25–US$125; AE, MC, V; daily 9am–9pm), the

Plenty of festivals take place within Tenganan and the surrounding villages: the region celebrates over 200 ceremonies annually. Go to **www.karangasem tourism.com** for details; dates vary year to year. The following two events happen during **Usaba Samah,** a month-long festival held during the fifth month of the Balinese calendar (May or June).

Maling-Malingan Some cultures imprison thieves for their crimes; others use harsh punishment such as amputation. In Tenganan, they have *maling-malingan.*

Preparations start early in the morning with the village elders hanging pieces of meat and bones from the ceiling of the *Bale Agung* (great pavilion). At 9am, two young boys steal the meat and are chased by the community through the village. The thieves are dragged back to the *Bale Agung* to face their punishment: They're dressed in banana leaves, necklaces, and bracelets of meat and bones, and their faces and bodies are painted white and red. Once they're made up, the thieves are paraded around the village. The moral of the story is that anyone who steals isn't welcome in the village.

Mekare Kare The symbolic *Mekare Kare* is a warrior dance between two men, armed with two pieces of thorny Pandanus leaves and a *tamiang,* a shield of plaited rattan. There's no jury, just a select group of men (called *tukang belas*) who supervise the fight. Both warriors agree not to hit the face of their opponent, and although there's no punishment for breaking the agreement, most men endeavor not to, for fear of losing their reputation and social prestige. The duel has no time limit and the *tukang belas* only stop the fight when they see any sign of anger on the competitors' faces. This is not a real game because there are no winners or losers. Instead, the emphasis is on the dancing techniques.

The whole event ends with a performance of the *abwang* dance by the bachelors and maidens of village of Subak Daha. At the end of the *Mekare Kare* is a *megibung,* a communal eating ritual, where the dancers/fighters eat together in the *wantilan* (public hall). The meal is intended to wash away any bad feeling produced by the fight.

Balinese traditional beauty recipes use local ingredients, such as indigenous plants, fruits, herbs, and spices. The virgin coconut oil is sourced from the local villages. A signature treatment, the "Decleor Relax with frankincense resin," is superb for jet lag and costs a reasonable US$80 for 2 hours.

VISIT TENGANAN VILLAGE About 3km (2 miles) inland from the main road just south of Candidasa, is a traditional village inhabited by the Bali Aga people, Bali's original inhabitants who have lived here since well before the arrival of the Javanese. Their culture is thought to date back to just before the Majapahit Empire (1294–1478). They don't fraternize outside of their walled community and work and live in a communal society. Don't be fooled by their basic living conditions, however, the community owns a number of paddy fields that are leased to farmers from nearby villages. With rice prices at an all-time high, Tenganan villagers are among the wealthiest on Bali.

Tenganan is also well known for its double ikat weaving better known as *kamben gringsing*—one of only three or four places in the world that still retain this skill. (You can also find this art form practiced in Japan and Gujarat in India). Excellent samples can fetch up to several thousand dollars; most heirloom pieces aren't for sale at any price. Just outside the walled village are a number of small shops selling a fabulous array of hand- and machine-woven textiles and baskets. Visitors are welcome to enter the village on payment of a small donation. The best time to visit is mid-year when very traditional pre-Hindu festivities keep the village busy for weeks on end.

Where to Stay & Eat

The Alila Resort Manggis ★★   The Alila Resort is one of the best places to stay in the area. On a former coconut plantation by the sea, the resort's acres of sweeping green lawns are anchored by a huge swimming pool. Blocks of well-designed rooms stand back at the side. This hotel has so many activities and excursions, you barely need to leave, unless it's with one of the well-informed guides. The beach itself is mainly pebble but don't let that put you off. The food is knock-out and afternoon tea on the lawn is a great pleasure. The restaurant **Sea Salt ★** (reservations recommended; main courses US$25, set menus start US$70; daily 7am–10:30pm) is set in a traditional Balinese pavilion. The Australian chef uses organic food, mostly from the resort's own garden, and local ingredients to create fresh, modern interpretations of Balinese cuisine: Take, for example, the Balinese risotto, or the seared salmon with local sea salt and fragrant pounded *tabieun*—an indigenous sweet, slightly numbing long pepper. A highlight is the exotic ice creams, such as cardamom, Bali coffee, and ginger flower. The resort occasionally hosts live Balinese performances.

Buitan, Manggis. www.alilahotels.com. ℂ **0363/41011.** Fax 0363/41015. 55 units. Peak season US$280–US$650; high season US$260–US$600; low season US$210–US$500; discounted rates on Internet. AE, MC, V. **Amenities:** Restaurant; babysitting; concierge; outdoor pool; room service; spa; watersports. *In room:* A/C, TV, hair dryer, minibar.

Amankila ★★   If you want to splurge in Bali on one Aman resort—a name synonymous with exclusivity and wealth—make it the Amankila. This romantic, very private resort is nestled on a huge hillside with luxurious villas linked by raised walkways, all enjoying spectacular views of the Indian Ocean and Nusa Penida. The spacious rooms are designer-luxurious with four-poster beds, extravagant fixtures and fittings, cushioned window seats, and private terraces. Bathrooms are ballroom size, some with sunken tubs. Certain villas come with their own private pool; the huge main pool cascades down three levels. Not surprisingly, Amankila has one of the only good beaches in the vicinity. The beach club has a nearly 45-m (148-ft.) pool, day beds, and a beautiful restaurant. The **Beach Club** (reservations recommended; main courses US$15–US$23, set menu US$110–US$150; daily 11am–10:30pm) has an extensive lunch menu of salads, sandwiches, pizza, fish and chips, and one of the best burgers on the island.

Jl. Raya Manggis, Manggis. www.amankila.com. ℂ **0363/41333.** 33 units. Year-round US$850 and up standard; US$1,650 and up suite. AE, DC, MC, V. **Amenities:** 3 restaurants; bar; babysitting; bicycles; concierge; gym; outdoor pool; room service; spa; watersports. *In room:* A/C, hair dryer, minibar, MP3 docking station, Wi-Fi.

Puri Bagus ★★   Puri Bagus is a short ride from the town center and a good compromise between Candidasa's ultraluxe options and the budget stops. Pretty and romantic, this hotel is the best in its class. Set on land jutting into the ocean, with steps leading right down to the beach, the good-size bungalows are airy and light, thanks to many large windows. Cool, outdoor bathrooms have hand-held showers. The pool has a deep section for scuba practice, or turning somersaults, and a shallow area for youngsters. Dance programs and movies are offered at night, plus there's a full range of free daily activities and good dining seaside.

Manggis. www.manggis.puribagus.net. © **0363/41304.** Fax 0363/41290. 26 units. High season US$140 superior villa, US$625 6-room villa; low season US$120 superior villa, US$600 6-room villa. AE, DC, MC, V. **Amenities:** 2 restaurants; 2 bars; bicycles; concierge; outdoor pool; room service; nearby tennis court; watersports. *In villa:* A/C, fridge, minibar.

Villa Asada ★★ Part of a group of seven villas designed by Popo Danes, the famous, locally trained Balinese architect, this four-bedroom villa, 10 minutes from Candidasa, overlooks Amuk Bay. Muted cream furnishings complement the large floor-to-ceiling glass windows and doors. With open-air sitting areas, the villa enjoys the cool breeze from the ocean.

Manggis, Candidasa. www.villaasada.com. © **0361/731074.** Fax 0361/736391. Peak season US$695; high season US$645; low season US$595. AE, MC, V. Rates include breakfast. **Amenities:** Bar; outdoor pool; spa therapy; Wi-Fi. *In villa:* A/C, hair dryer.

CANDIDASA

Candidasa was once the main tourist resort in the area and the last large resort before Amed. It now serves mainly as a center for scuba diving and snorkeling. The town itself is laid out along the seashore, although the golden sand beach that people once flocked to has been destroyed. Local developers blew up the reef to provide building materials for hotels for the tourists who came to visit the golden sand beaches . . . and without the protective reef, the beach went away. That's a fairly clear definition of irony. The beach is now a combination of sand, pebbles, or groynes (concrete buttresses), which have been installed in an attempt to reclaim some of the golden sand. It's impassible at high tide.

The main road passes through the town and accommodations and restaurants are laid out along either side, although the best of both aren't necessarily on the seaward side. You can tell that Candidasa was popular at one point and although the area is trying to reclaim some of its former glory, it will take years for the beach to recover—if indeed it does. At this point, Candidasa does make a good base to explore this scenic and interesting region, given its central location.

Essentials
GETTING THERE & GETTING AROUND
Hotels outside the town, such as the **Alila** and **Amankila** (see above), offer regular shuttles into town. Most hotels offer airport pickup for a fee and most restaurants and dive shops provide free pickup and drop-off. Motorbike rental and *bemo* are also available. **Safari** (© **0363/41707**), on the main road, is a reliable and friendly tourist agency with a selection of cars, jeeps, and motorbikes.

[FastFACTS] CANDIDASA

Hospital The Candidasa **clinic,** on Jalan Raya Candidasa, can provide for basic medical needs.

Internet Access If your hotel has no Internet, a few shops on the main street do. **Happy's** (☎ **0363/41019**) may have slow service, but charges are low—about Rp10,000 per hour.

Mail The **Asri Shop,** on the main street, offers postal services.

Police The **police station** is on the main road at the junction to the Rama Candidasa Hotel.

Exploring Candidasa

Although Candidasa itself doesn't offer any decent snorkeling or diving, the sights of Padangbai and the islands of Gili Tepekong, Gili Mimpang, and Gili Biaha are only a 10-minute boat ride away. Otherwise, the diving at Amed and Tulamben is a short drive away. For **trekking,** there are plenty of paddy field walks around Candidasa, on the slopes of Mount Agung. If you're staying in the area, ask your hotel or villa to organize a trek with a local guide.

BEACHES The imaginatively named **White Sand Beach** ★★ is one of Bali's most beautiful beaches. But please, don't tell anyone about this place. It's a secret! The entrance to the beach road is well hidden between Candidasa and Amlapura. A kilometer or so after the hamlet of Bug Bug in the village of Peraci, a very small sign denotes **Pantai Pasir Putih.** Then a kilometer or two down a rickety track (although the road is improving), through some lush countryside of small villages and beautiful temples, brings you to a stand where you buy a ticket for Rp5,000. Nearly a kilometer of white sand is unmarred by hotels, though umbrellas and loungers are waiting for you. The waters are clear blue and the coconut palms provide shade. At the southern end, a line of fishing outriggers (*jukung*) prove that this is still a working beach, but it's left to the tourists for the best part of the day. The fancy hotels on the east coast make special outings here for their guests, complete with rather unnecessary picnic lunches and icy cold drinks. About a dozen simple thatched warungs offer visitors cold drinks, beer, and either freshly caught fish or river prawns, barbecued on coconut husk fires served with rice and vegetables or maybe a salad.

CHARLIE'S FACTORY ★★ Long-term American resident, surfer Charlie Wayan Jaya (**www.islandmystk.com**), has created his own little organic empire within a coconut grove. Known in Japanese guide books as "Soapaman Charlie," with the nearby local "secret" surf break now "Soapaman Point," Charlie is becoming something of a tourist attraction in his own right. His bamboo factory creates fragrant organic soaps, virgin coconut oils, cocoa butter, and creams. His palm sugar syrup gives ice cream and pancakes a whole new meaning. Follow the road from Candidasa to Amlapura. About 7km (4 miles) later turn off at the sign to Jasri. Follow the bumpy road to Jasri beach, where you'll see the factory, a large bamboo pyramid.

MASSAGE & SPA The secluded dive destination **Alam Asmara Resort** (see below) is for people who want to get away from the crowds and prefer a quiet place to indulge in diving. After your time in the water, head for the spa for a traditional massage using techniques from both Bali and Java (body massage Rp250,000– Rp350,000, scrub treatment Rp450,000–Rp800,000, ocean detox Rp350,000– Rp600,000; AE, DC, MC, V; daily 9am–9pm).

At the **Jaya Spa** at the Puri Bagus Candidasa (see below), the Royal Balinese treatment attempts to balance body, mind, and soul and leaves you totally relaxed (single treatment Rp275,000–Rp350,000, package Rp550,000; AE, MC, V; daily 9am–9pm).

SPEAR FISHING If you love catching big fish such as mackerel and tuna, try your hand at spear fishing. Mr. Toron, a Balinese fisherman (contact him through **Bali Dives,** Denpasar; ✆ **0361/412981** or 08/123813994; www.balidives.com; US$250 per person including boat from Sanur, US$175 per person including car to Candidasa, but not boat), is a qualified spear fisher. He knows the water around Candidasa so well that he guarantees that you find some fish—the question is whether or not you can spear them. Lunch will be a barbecue of your own freshly caught fish on one of the nearby beaches (remind his staff about the barbecue before you go, as they have a tendency of forgetting small details). All transfers, lunch, drinks, boat, and guide costs are included.

Where to Stay
EXPENSIVE
Villa Talia Vashti ★ The three-bedroom Villa, on its own white sand beach with spectacular ocean views, is about as upmarket as it gets in this part of town.

Jl. Raya Candidasa. www.taliavashti.com. ✆ **08/11147350.** 3 units. Peak season US$400; low season US$250. Rates include breakfast. MC, V. **Amenities:** Pool bar; babysitting; Jacuzzi; infinity pool; room service. *In villa:* A/C, TV/DVD, Wi-Fi (free).

Villa Sasoon The villa is hidden in a quiet part of Candidasa. Each villa has three pavilions surrounding its own private pool. Private kitchens allow guests to cook for themselves or for the on-call chef to come in and create special meals.

Jl. Puri Bagus. www.villasasoon.com. ✆ **0363/41511.** Fax 0363/41911. 5 units. High season US$300 2-bedroom, US$250 1-bedroom, low season US$260 2-bedroom, US$200 1-bedroom. Rates include breakfast. MC, V. **Amenities:** Room service. *In villa:* A/C, TV/DVD, fully equipped kitchen, Wi-Fi (free).

MODERATE
Alam Asmara Dive Resort This bungalow-style dive resort has an on-site dive shop. The darkish rooms are nicely furnished with outdoor bathrooms. The small pool and restaurant patio look out to the sea. This is one of the best options on the sleepy Candidasa strip. Guests receive a complimentary 50-minute massage upon arrival.

Jl. Raya Candidasa, Candidasa. www.alamasmara.com. ✆ **0363/41929.** Fax 0363/42101. 12 units. Year-round US$115. MC, V. **Amenities:** Restaurant; bar; airport transfers; concierge; outdoor pool; room service; spa. *In room:* A/C, TV, hair dryer, minibar.

Rama Candidasa This large, beachfront resort set in a tropical garden is a bit large for this area, but its amenities and activities make it a good choice. The large pool has plenty of sea-facing loungers and *bales*. Each of the pleasantly decorated rooms comes with an ocean view or veranda and Balinese antique-styled furniture and white linen. Of the activities on offer here, choose from Balinese dance lessons, cooking classes, trekking, or yoga. If that seems too hectic, check yourself into the hotel's spa and enjoy one of the amazing acupressure massages.

Jl. Raya Sengkidu, Karangasem. www.ramacandidasahotel.com. ✆ **0363/41974.** Fax 0363/41975. 72 units. Peak season US$140–US$195; high season US$120–US$175; low season US$100–US$155; extra bed US$30. AE, MC, V. **Amenities:** Restaurant (see below); bar; outdoor pool; spa; watersports; Wi-Fi. *In room:* A/C, TV/DVD, minibar.

Watergarden ★★ The simple thatched bungalows of the Watergarden may not be spectacular, but they're plenty comfortable. Each has a wide veranda overlooking the lily ponds that give the hotel its name. The best and most private rooms are at the back and have their own charming water features. In-house dining at the Watergarden Café is some of the best in town. The place has a laid-back feel that draws lots of return guests and attracts many expat locals.

Jl. Raya Candidasa, Candidasa. www.watergardenhotel.com. © **0363/41540.** Fax 0363/41164. 14 units. High season US$128–US$148 standard, US$320 villa; low season US$120–US$135, US$300 villa. AE, MC, V. **Amenities:** Restaurant; bar; airport transfer; small outdoor pool. *In room:* A/C (in some), TV, minibar, Wi-Fi.

Where to Eat

Vincent's (© **0363/41368;** www.vincentsbali.com; main courses Rp50,000–Rp120,000; MC, V; daily 10:30am–10:30pm), on the main road almost opposite the lotus lagoon, on the inland side, serves Indonesian and Western food alongside an extensive wine list and good cocktails. The large street-facing lounge area has an inviting ambience. The rear garden is great on hot summer nights.

The menu at **Garpu Restaurant,** in the Rama Candidasa Resort & Spa (see above, reservations recommended; main courses US$15–US$30, set menu US$15–US$30; AE, DC, MC, V; daily 7am–11pm), has mainly Mediterranean and Balinese delights. Spaghetti marinara is served with an abundance of shellfish in a rich tomato sauce. You'll be tempted at dessert by the pudding or perhaps simply by the cocktail list. There's a live Balinese performance every Saturday night.

AMLAPURA

The sprawling town of Amlapura doesn't have a lot to interest the tourist, although it does have a bustling marketplace. The main attractions are the three palaces, faded remnants of what was once Bali's richest and most powerful kingdom.

Essentials
GETTING THERE
The best way to get here is by car and driver but there are plenty of *bemo* and **public buses** from Batubulan bus station in Denpasar to Singaraja, stopping at Padangbai, Candidasa, and Gianyar en route. The bus station for Singaraja and Tirta Gangga is on the corner of Jalan Sudirman and Jalan Untung Surapati. These cost between Rp10,000 and Rp15,000 one-way. Allow about 3 hours to get here from Denpasar.

[FastFACTS] AMLAPURA

Food **Hardy's,** on Jalan Diponegoro, although a large supermarket, doesn't have the same assortment of Western foods as in other Hardy's stores in the south. There's no alcohol (including no beer) on sale.

Hospital The city **hospital** is on Jalan Ngurah Rai.

Mail The **post office** is on Jalan Gatot Subroto.

Pharmacy An **apotek** is on Jalan Ngurah Rai 47.

Exploring Amlapura

The neighboring villages of **Asak, Bungaya, Subagan,** and **Timbrah,** on the road to Amlapura coming from the south, are traditional villages resembling the archaic Bali Aga village of Tenganan (p. 236). Although not as interesting as Tenganan, they're worth a visit especially during festival time. Watch out in June or July for the exquisite *rejang* dance performed by unmarried girls, and the *abung*, preformed by unmarried men.

West of Amlapura is **Budakeling,** known for its Buddhist Brahmin priests, whose lineage dates back to the 15th century. It's also known for the inscribers of Sanskrit *lontar* manuscripts and traditional silver and gold artisans. This is a good place to look at the work of the silversmiths who are less pushy than those in Celuk (near Ubud).

The stunning scenery around Budakeling is worthy of an early morning trek. From the Lempuyang hills, you can enjoy the sights of the misty village hamlets, lush green hills, and the cool bamboo forests as the sun rises. Climb the Puncak Sari hill and get a bird's-eye view of Budakeling from the top. Bring a guide from your hotel.

Puri Agung Karangasem These charming palaces display a mix of European and Balinese architecture, and a wealth of mythological creatures and figures. You can easily observe the colonial influence with its all faded grandeur. Parts of the eclectic architecture are decorated with carved *wayang* figures and others with Dutch finery. You'll see portraits of royal personages, including the last Rajah Anak Agung Gede Putu, whose mesmerizing eyes make it easy to believe he was the proud husband of nine wives and father to countless children. The rajahs certainly knew how to live well. Some members of the royal family still live here.

Jl. Teuku Umar. No phone. Admission Rp10,000. Daily 8am–6pm.

Pura Lempuyang This is one of Bali's *sad kahyangan* (six temples of the heavens). On the slopes of the often misty Gunung Lempuyang, it sits at the top of 1,700 steps that wind their way through lavish jungle. As you ascend, the temperature drops. Views are generally awe inspiring; early morning is the best time to visit. The faithful visit Lempuyang to ask for blessings, solve domestic problems, cure sickness, or even gain power. The major festival in Lempuyang is held every 6 months on the Thursday after Galungan (every 210 days). During the rainy season the mountain is at its most majestic, but the stone steps can be slippery.

The signposted road to Lempuyang heads off from the main road 3 kilometers past Tirta Gangga. No phone. Admission by donation. Daily 24 hr.

Taman Tirta Gangga Tirta Gangga, "holy water of the Ganges," was built in 1948 by the same rajah as the Taman Ujung (see below) with more opulence and certainly more success. It's believed that after a tour of the Palace of Versailles, near Paris, I Gusti Bagus Jelantik was so inspired by the architecture and fountains that he decided to build a second water palace. He wanted this one to be greater and more ornate than Taman Ujung. Sadly both water palaces were damaged by the 1963 eruption of Gunung Agung. But you can still enjoy the swimming pools and ornamental ponds where the last rajah bathed. The cool spring waters make it a pleasant place to linger for a few hours—though never on a Sunday, when it fills with local Balinese coming to relax or to flirt with their intendeds.

The area surrounding Tirta Gangga has acres of emerald *sawah* (rice) glittering on perfectly formed terraces making for some great trekking. If you're staying locally, request your hotel or villa to hook you up with a local guide. Otherwise, ask the ticket office at Tirta Gangga if they can find you a guide. Expect to pay about Rp100,000 for a 4-hour trek for two people.

Tirta Gangga. No phone. Admission adult Rp5,000. Daily 6am–6pm.

Taman Ujung Water Palace   Known as Taman Soekasada Ujung by the Balinese, this was once a private retreat of I Gusti Bagus Jelantik, Karangasem's last rajah. The Taman Ujung Water Palace was built in 1919 and almost destroyed when Gunung Agung erupted in 1963. The palace was further damaged by the earthquake of 1979. Much of it was (less than sympathetically) renovated in 2004, but you can still see the remnants of the main pool and admire the views from higher up the hill.

Taman Ujung is sometimes the venue for upscale dinners when flickering candlelight and lavish table settings lend it a softer and more romantic atmosphere. There are also classic Balinese dance performances and occasionally ceremonies.

Jl. Diponegoro. ✆ **0363/21383.** Admission adults Rp10,000. Daily 8am–6pm.

Where to Stay

Although the palaces are worth a look, there's nothing in the way of suitable accommodations in the center of Amalpura. The nearest can be found near Tirta Gangga, about 7km from Amlapura.

The one-bedroom **Villa Tirta Ayu** (Beautiful Spring) and two-bedroom **Villa Djamrud** (Emerald), Tirta Gangga Water Palace Villas, Desa Tirta Gangga, Amlapura (**www.tirtagangga-villas.com**; ✆ 0363/21383; fax 0363/21383; Tirta Ayu year-round US$350–US$400; Djamrud year-round US$120–US$250; rates include breakfast; payment online), overlook the beautiful Water Palace.

Stay the night on top of a hill in the **Puri Sawah Villas,** Tirta Gangga, Karangasem (✆ **0363/21847;** four units; high season Rp300,000–Rp250,000, low season Rp250,000–Rp200,000; rates include breakfast; no credit cards), a fairly basic but pleasant place with beautiful views of the surrounding paddy fields.

Seraya Shores ★   About 6km (3¾ miles) from Amlapura, just past the Ujung Water Palace, is the cozy resort of Seraya Shores. In an old coconut plantation, the resort looks over a delightful stretch of black sand shore. The **restaurant** is the best value spot in the area—another luxury. The "no menu" policy allows Chef Sasa to offer only the freshest ingredients: local market produce, organic vegetables, fresh caught fish, and sometimes lobster and fresh river prawns in an Indo-Euro fusion. The well-trained staff members are proud of their English skills taught by the boss, Amanda. She also organizes dive trips and picnics to **Pantai Pasir Putih** (p. 239) and a fabulous drive to Amed and back through Tirta Gangga.

Dusun Merajan, Seraya Barat. www.serayashores.com. ✆ **08/1338416572.** 7 units. High season US$80–US$165; low season US$65–US$150; extra bed US$10. No credit cards. **Amenities:** Restaurant; bar; babysitting; outdoor pool. *In room:* Fan.

Where to Eat

The pickings in Amlapura have been slim, up until Australian chef Penny Williams recently opened the cooking school and restaurant **Bali Asli ★** (Jl. Raya Gelumpang; ✆ **08/2897030098**; www.baliasli.com.au; market tour and class daily 9am–1pm Rp800,000; includes free transport from Candidasa; cash only). Passionate and devoted to Balinese and Indonesian cooking, Williams is a former chef of Alila Manggis and taught classes there for several years. Her new establishment offers not only lessons in the kitchen but also off-the-beaten-track excursions such as planting rice in the paddies and fishing in a *junkung.* Bali Asli is also open for breakfast, lunch, and afternoon tea, serving a delicious array of Balinese dishes that are tempered down in spice for international visitors.

AMED

Amed is the generic name given to a string of villages that line the coast on Bali's northeast corner. The main north-south road roller-coasters through the fishing hamlets of Amed, Jemeluk, Bunutan, Bangli, and Lipah and on to Banyuning and Aas, before reaching Seraya and back to Amlapura. Along the way, it passes magnificent landscapes of lofty mountains and curving bays of crystal tourmaline waters. The pebble beaches are lined with *jukung,* brightly painted fishing outriggers. Each morning around 7am, a spectacular sight awaits early risers, as the fishing *jukung* return, sometimes laden with catches of baby mackerel.

Amed remained a backwater for many years, the home of hill farmers, salt makers, and fishermen. The lack of development became its greatest asset, however, because it has retained the charm and ambience of old Bali known to only a lucky few. Now the secret is out and small luxury hotels and villas are appearing with increasing regularity.

Amed enjoys a Mediterranean climate with two very distinct seasons. Several months of the year are green and misty, whereas the other months have no rain at all and the dry vegetation turns to gold.

Getting There

If you're coming from the south, it's easy to rent a car and driver for a drop-off or to escort you for several days. From the airport to Amed costs around Rp350,000. You can also easily rent a motorbike or car and driver in Amed: although there are no car agencies, drivers with cars available for day trips are easy to find.

Exploring Amed

You can enjoy numerous scenic and very hilly walks around Amed, which is especially beautiful during the rainy season (Nov–Apr) when the temperature is cooler and the hills are green and misty—a sight difficult to imagine during the hot, dry months. A local guide from your hotel is all you need to take you into the hills.

BIKING TO PANTAI PASIR PUTIH   You can bike from Amed to Pantai Pasir Putih (p. 239). A car takes guests from their hotel to one of several starting points off the main road; it's a mainly downhill ride to the beach that follows back roads through luscious rural areas, rarely visited by Westerners. The trip takes about 2 hours before arriving at the beach. Cars transport guests back to their hotel. For information and bookings call **Ketut Surya** (© **08/5238231850**) or **Komang Bajing** (© **08/ 124667752**).

SCUBA DIVING & SNORKELING   Amed is one of Bali's top dive areas and the small bays provide many good snorkeling locations with shallow waters and few currents. Snorkeling gear is available through the dive operators. One of the best dive companies is **Euro Dive,** Lipah (© **0363/23605;** fax 0363/23605), with PADI certified guides specializing in the dive sites in and around Amed as well as Tulamben, just 20 minutes away. If you're in south Bali and you want to take a diving excursion to this part of the island, contact **AquaMarine Diving,** Jl. Raya Petitenget 2A, Seminyak (© **0361/473-8020;** fax 0361/738021; www.aquamarinediving.com; US$85).

Although the marine life here is superb, some coral bleaching occurred in 1998 thanks to El Niño, and although the reef is recovering, we can't yet tell when it will reach its former glory. Conditions here, from shore or boat, are easy, with good visibility.

Amed Reef, with many different kinds of sponges and gorgonians, is home to everything from lobsters, shrimp, and goby sets to blue-spotted rays and schools of barracuda. White-tip reef sharks, Napoleon wrasse, big trevally, and large schools of bannerfish, snapper, and fusilier can be found at **Amed Wall.** The deep slope after the wall is rich in invertebrates with crinoids and commensals. **Lipah Bay,** a small black sand bay, is home to a 20-m (66-ft.) steel freighter wreck encrusted with sponges, gorgonians, and coral bushes and inhabited by clouds of anthias, and parrotfish and angelfish. The deeper slope is dotted with sea fans. **Gili Selang** on Bali's eastern point can, like all exposed sites, have ripping currents and is therefore a site for experienced divers only. You may encounter white-tip reef sharks, Napoleon wrasse, turtles, and dolphins, along with low-lying, healthy corals with many moray eels, schools of fish, nudis, and pygmy seahorses. **Amed Ghost Bay** is good for muck-diving: Mimic octopus and Wonderpus, frogfishes, Ornate and Robust ghost-pipefish, stonefish—we're never sure quite what we'll find here.

Where to Stay

Despite its size, the **Bayu Cottages Hotel & Restaurant,** Jl. Raya Pantai Amed, Lipah (www.bayucottages.com; ✆ **0363/23495;** 6 units; high season US$50, low season US$42; MC, V), has plenty of facilities. Looking over the beach in Lipah, the boutique hotel has a pleasant saltwater pool and an open-air, sea-view restaurant. Rooms have hot water, air-conditioning, and satellite TV.

The **Santai Hotel,** Bunutan, Amed (www.santaibali.com; ✆ **0363/23487;** fax 0363/23585; 10 units; high season US$77–US$125, low season US$70–US$115; additional person US$12, children 11 and under US$6; rates include breakfast; MC, V), is a small older resort squeezed in by the beach with a big tropical garden, a good restaurant (see below), and a large swimming pool.

Blue Moon Villa ★　British-owned, and run by the ever-efficient Komang John, this small resort commands views across the bays. The rooms have big beds and filmy mosquito nets. Hot and cold water is readily available. The airy, open dining room is surrounded with gardens, though some prefer to use the *bales* with low tables and cushions. The menu has daily specials, offering plenty of fresh fish and an eclectic mix of Indonesian and Western dishes.

Selang Beach, Amed. www.bluemoonvilla.com. ✆ **0363/21428.** 9 units. Year-round US$77–US$99 standard; US$120–US$246 suite; US$585 villa; under-12s US$14. MC, V. **Amenities:** Restaurant; bar; babysitting; bicycles; 2 outdoor pools; room service; spa therapy; watersports. *In room:* A/C, minibar.

The Golden Rock　On a rocky knoll overlooking the sea in Aas, this lovely place is a specialized detox and cleansing retreat. Guests can check in for 4, 7, or 10 days and spend time cleansing and healing their mind, body, and spirit. The Rock offers yoga and *tai chi* as well as a range of interesting, sophisticated equipment designed to help guests regain their equilibrium.

Aas. www.theretreatbali.com. ✆ **08/2897008592.** 4 units. Year-round 4-day €755 single, €635 shared; 7-day €1,220 single, €1,035 shared; 10-day €1,250 single, €1,050 shared. **Amenities:** Restaurant; outdoor pool; sauna and infrared sauna. *In room:* A/C, TV.

Good Karma As a stylish, tropical paradise of bamboo huts, this rustic place is very popular with many guests who return year after year. Each of the 15 rooms look straight on to the beach, and being fan-cooled and having only cold-water showers doesn't seem to deter the guests' enthusiasm. The rooms farthest from the main building are the most private and popular. The small restaurant offers local and European dishes and some Japanese. The seafood fried rice is worth a visit.

Jl. Culik, Amed. No phone. 18 units. Year-round US$15–US$30. No credit cards. Rates include breakfast. **Amenities:** Restaurant. *In room:* Fan.

Life in Amed This villa resort on the beach toward the southern end of the Amed strip of villages at Lean has good, if basic, facilities. Some offer both upstairs and downstairs bedrooms, making them ideal for families. The cozy, open dining area has some of the best food in Amed. The two beach bungalows require advance booking.

Lean. www.lifebali.com. ✆ **0363/23152.** 11 units. High season US$93–US$150, low season US$70–US$128. AE, MC, V. **Amenities:** Restaurant; babysitting; Internet; outdoor pool; room service; spa; watersports. *In room:* A/C, TV/DVD, hair dryer, minibar, movie library.

Wawa Wewe II Cheap and cheerful, this resort is popular with French and American tourists as well as local expats. It's often fully booked, especially during July and August. Some of the rooms look out to the sea and many have an upper mezzanine floor. Open-air bathrooms have hot and cold water. The Buddha-shaped pool is the focus of activity. The friendly staff is eager to help and can find you a motorbike to rent or may even offer to accompany you to a local village ceremony or take you sightseeing.

Lipah. ✆ **0363/23522.** 10 units. High season US$46–US$116; low season US$35–US$70. Rates include breakfast. No credit cards. **Amenities:** Restaurant; outdoor pool. *In room:* A/C, fan.

Where to Eat

The **Anda Amed Resort** (reservations recommended; sandwiches and wraps US$4–US$5, main courses US$4–US$8; MC, V; daily 7am–10pm) dining room looks out to sea and has a Mediterranean-inspired menu together with lots of local favorites. The white gazpacho and salads are particularly good.

The restaurant at Blue Moon Villa, **Komang John Café ★** (see above; reservations recommended; main courses US$5–US$10, set menu US$6–US$8; MC, V; daily 7:30am–10:30pm) attracts plenty of outside guests and has a fresh and eclectic menu. The seared fresh tuna salad is exceptional as is the chocolate pudding cake. It has a good bar with cocktails, spirits, and wines. Most nights you'll catch Komang John and friends in the midst of a good old fashioned guitar jam session.

The tiny dining area of the **Life in Amed** (see above; main courses start at US$4; AE, MC, V; daily 7am–11pm) offers some of the best food in the area. The arugula salad with toasted pine nuts, feta cheese, and beetroot is especially good. Live Balinese traditional music and dances can be arranged upon request.

Arguably Amed's best restaurant, **Sails,** Jl. Raya Lean, Lean (✆ **0363/22006;** reservations recommended during high season; main courses US$6–US$13; no credit cards; daily 11am–10pm), has fresh fish, New Zealand lamb chops, steak, very good mashed potatoes, and well-prepared local dishes.

The **Santai,** Bunutan (✆ **0363/23487;** www.santaibali.com; reservations recommended; main courses US$11–US$19; MC, V; daily 7am–11pm, last order 9pm), is a long-established, small resort in Jemeluk and one of the few places that has a foreign chef—from Norway no less. The menu features local grilled fish and Indonesian dishes. You can also enjoy good espresso coffee and an impressive bar selection and wine list.

TULAMBEN

This small village on the northeast coast has become a center for divers. Its *raison d'être* is the wreck of the *Liberty*, a U.S. Army supply ship that was attacked by a Japanese submarine during World War II. The dive is an easy walk-in off the beach about 25m (82 ft.) from the shore. Its deepest point is about 30m (98 ft.) and the shallowest about 5m (16 ft.). It's suitable for all levels of certification and experience.

Essentials

GETTING THERE & GETTING AROUND   Some people stay in town or drive from Amed or Kuta. Infrequent public minibuses to Singaraja and Amlapura are available but because the area is now focused more on tourism, these services tend to be unreliable. Rent a car and driver either on the street or through your hotel.

FAST FACTS   As yet, Tulamben has no ATMs, banks, money changers, Internet cafes, emergency services, or basically anything at all. The hotels and homestays usually provide shuttle services or arrange transport and sometimes Internet access.

Scuba Diving

Most resorts in Tulamben and on the northeast coast run their own boats and PADI operations. The best dives are early morning or night dives during the full moon.

Being on Bali's northeast coast, Tulamben Bay receives very plankton-rich waters from the Indonesian Throughflow (the major ocean current that moves from the Pacific to the Indian Ocean). Coupled with the different physical environments found in the area, this means the bay contains a stunningly diverse underwater ecosystem.

The 120-m (394-ft.) U.S. Army Transport **Liberty shipwreck ★★** lies 20m (66 ft.) offshore and offers an extraordinary density of marine life, including a huge school of big-eyed trevally, bumphead parrotfish, leaf scorpionfish, and pygmy seahorses. If you go night-diving, look out for the flashlightfish, Spanish dancers, and cephalopods.

Both the **Coral Garden** (which runs eastward from the *Liberty* shipwreck) and the upper area of the **Wall/Drop-off** (at the eastern end of the bay) provide wonderful shallow dives where you're limited by air supply rather than bottom time, and yield an incredible variety of marine life from Thecacera nudis to boxer crabs to frogfish and ribbon eels in all stages of development. Deeper on the Wall/Drop-off are reef sharks, sponges, and gorgonian fans (one of 3m/10 ft. diameter), and occasional sightings of whale sharks and Mola mola.

 Avoid the Underwater Crowds

Because many PADI companies are now organizing day trips to Tulamben from the south, the dive sites are overcrowded after 11am. To avoid the crowds, plan to stay overnight and dive early in the morning or late in the afternoon.

Another Shipwreck

Both divers and snorkelers will find the **Japanese shipwreck** off Banyuning worth a visit. It's possible to wobble in from the rocky beach or rent a local fishing boat and enter the water that way. Under the trees on the beach, a small warung serves cold drinks, beer, juice, and decent local food. You can rent snorkeling gear from your hotel or from the outfitters on the beach in front of the shipwreck.

Slightly north of Tulamben is **Kubu,** where conditions always seem to be calm. Here you'll also sight plentiful gorgonians, bommies with beautiful soft corals, and scores of nudis. Five minutes eastward by outrigger, **Batu Kelebit** is where you're most likely to see pelagics including—on rare occasions—dolphins. Farther east, **Batu Niti** has the area's most pristine corals.

Due to the beach entry, Tulamben is also great for **snorkeling** and for the 1-day introduction to diving offered by some dive companies (although you need booties and open-heeled fins, not full-foot fins for walking on the rocky beach).

Contact **Scuba Seraya Dive,** 5 minutes south of Tulamben Bay in the Scuba Seraya Resort (p. 249; ☎ **0361/282594;** fax 0361/282594; www.scubaseraya.com; one shore dive US$28, 2 boat dives US$78 and up). If you're coming from the south, contact **AquaMarine Diving ★★★**, Jl. Raya Petitenget 2A, Seminyak (☎ **0361/ 473-8020;** fax 0361/738021; www.aquamarinediving.com; US$115 in Tulamben, US$100 and up outside Tulamben per person, 2 diver minimum).

Where to Stay & Eat

Many more divers and tourists are coming to the northeast coast, and so warungs and would-be restaurants are springing up along the main road, but the quality and selection on offer isn't convincing. Most guests dine in their hotels.

Alam Batu Beach Bungalow Resort   Favored mainly by German guests, the Alam Batu has a dining area built onto a rocky promontory, pleasant gardens, and a pool. The four air-conditioned and six fan bungalows are rather dingy but have airy open bathrooms. The garden spa offers a small selection of treatments. Evening meals are communal buffets with Balinese and European dishes for Rp150,000.

Jl. Batu Pemasuh, Batu Ringgit, Kubu. www.alambatu.de. ☎ **0363/23324.** 12 units. High season US$112–US$123; boat show season (Jan–Mar) US$100–US$112. MC, V. **Amenities:** Restaurant; lounge; Internet; outdoor pool; spa; watersports. In room: A/C (in some), fan, minibar.

Batu Belah ★ 🛏   At the eastern end of the village, Batu Belah is a tiny but pristine homestay with a lovely pool and restaurant, built into the rocks above the sea.

Sekar Karang, Tulamben. www.eastbaliresort.com. ☎ **08/179755214.** 4 units. Year-round US$88. Rates include breakfast. No credit cards. **Amenities:** Restaurant; outdoor pool. In room: A/C, fan, TV, fridge.

Mimpi Resort   This was the first resort in the area and caters mostly to German divers. The beachfront restaurant and pool area are surrounded by bougainvillea. The Ocean View rooms are the best option but rates are rather expensive for the accommodations offered.

Tulamben. www.mimpi.com. ℂ **0362/94497.** 54 units. High season US$146–US$225; low season US$121–US$200. AE, MC, V. **Amenities:** Restaurant; bar; babysitting; bicycles; concierge; Internet; outdoor pool; room service; spa; watersports. *In room:* A/C, TV (in some), hair dryer, minibar.

Scuba Seraya Resort ★ This lovely small resort with a peaceful stretch of beachfront is preferred by many world-famous underwater photographers. The eight air-conditioned cottages and four private villas (each with kitchenette, outside tub, and cushioned outside sitting area) overlooking the ocean, are built in spacious, well-tended gardens. The restaurant serves a good choice of simple, tasty international and local food all day. On-site is one of the area's best scuba-diving shops.

Tulamben. www.scubaseraya.com. ℂ **0361/282594.** Fax 0361/282594. 12 units. High season €85 standard, €165 villa; low season €70 standard, €150 villa (rates set in euros). MC, V. **Amenities:** Restaurant; outdoor pool; room service; spa; watersports. *In room:* A/C, hair dryer, kitchenette.

Siddhartha Resort A little farther to the west, this brand-new resort is definitely the best resort on the northeast coast. With 30 tastefully decorated rooms in three different price ranges and two oceanfront "dream villas," there's something to suit every budget. The resort has a 1,500 sq. m (16,145 sq. ft.) spa and a state-of-the-art PADI diving school. The restaurant serves international and Balinese dishes.

Kubu, Karangasem. www.siddhartha-bali.com. ℂ **0363/23034.** Fax 0363/23035 32 units. Year-round €42–€150 (rates set in euros). Rates include breakfast. V, MC. **Amenities:** Gym; outdoor pool; room service; spa. *In room:* A/C, fan, TV/DVD (in some), minibar, pool (in villas).

Tauch Terminal Resort & Spa This is a budget beachfront resort with bungalows and air-conditioned rooms, pool, bar, restaurant, shop, and spa. Permanently booked solid, this isn't a resort for anyone who likes privacy but a must for those who prefer safety in numbers and spend most of their holiday underwater.

Banjar Kubu Village. www.tulamben.com. ℂ **0361/774504.** Fax 0361/778473. 20 units. Year-round €85–€135 (rates set in euros). AE, MC, V. **Amenities:** Restaurant; bar; babysitting; concierge; outdoor pool; room service; spa; Wi-Fi. *In room:* A/C, hair dryer, minibar.

NORTH BALI

For most visitors to Bali, the north is the world on the other side of the mountains. It's the wild and open side of Bali that has been the least touched by recent tourism. The majority of tourism here is contained, mercifully, to the flatlands west of Lovina. Although it's a backwater nowadays, the regency of Buleleng is central to Bali's colonial history and hosted the old capital, the port of Singaraja, the major trading post for the Dutch, Chinese, and Arabs, and the disembarkation point for generations of visitors.

Getting There & Getting Around

There's virtually no taxi service in the north. *Bemo* (vans used as buses) use Singaraja as a hub, but aren't useful for getting to small, secluded villages. Visitors rely on rented cars and drivers.

You have several options for approaching north Bali. From the **south,** the obvious route is to take the main road from Denpasar, pass Lake Bratan, toward Singaraja. The road passes through hillside terraces of vegetables and fruits climbing to about 1,200m (3,937 ft.). The **east** route approaches via Tulamben or past Mount Batur. The last route, by the **west,** tends to be congested with larger vehicles ferrying workers on their way around Bali or back to Java. However if you turn off the main western road at Antosari, this takes you through the foothills of Mount Batukaru, through stunning picturesque paddy fields up through Pupuan, best known for its coffee and clove plantations.

TEMBOK, SEMBIRENTENG & TEJAKULA

Coming from the east and leaving Amed behind, the scenery changes dramatically between Kubu and Tembok. The dark lava stone and cactus landscape gives way to lush fruit plantations and steep hills with waterfalls. On your drive, visit the unusual pillared horse baths in the center of **Tejakula,** a village famous throughout Bali for silver crafts, unique dance performances, and *wayang wong* mask dances.

Exploring Near Tembok, Sembirenteng & Tejakula

Set on the hillside overlooking the ocean, **Puri Bagus Ponjok Batu,** Jl. Raya Singaraja, Tejakula (© **0362/21430;** www.bagus-agro.com; set menu US$25; cooking classes US$35; treks US$40–$55), is a farm of 5 hectares (12 acres) that organizes simple, tasty Indonesian set lunches served in a gazebo. Cooking classes can be arranged with 2 days notice

Bebali Weaving in Pacung

Supported by donations and with a great deal of dedication, **Nyoman Sarmika** of Surya Indigo keeps the ancient tradition of *bebali* weaving on back-strap looms alive. Using natural dyes, these simple but beautiful cloths, which are said to have magical properties, have been used for rites of passage in Bali for generations. Visit his small shop (📞 **081/ 23626535**) on the main road in Pacung (Tejakula, Buleleng, 20km/12 miles east of Singaraja) and chat with him about the area, too.

and you can also undertake treks from Sembiran up to the farm, through palm plantations and over lava rock slopes. Stopping en route you can see how coconut oil is made and *arak* (a rice-based alcoholic brew) produced.

This part of Bali is home to some of the oldest **Bali Aga villages,** settlements that weren't influenced by the customs brought to Bali from the Javanese courts. Some of these settlements were originally ancient trading posts with India, China, and beyond as long ago as the 1st century A.D.

LES   This small village in the hills has one of the highest waterfalls in Bali, a 30-m (98-ft.) cascade with a cool bathing pool called **Yeh Mampeh.** Just follow the sign to Les on the road after Tejakula and dip your toes in the cool pool.

PURA PONDOK BATU   This imposing temple has recently been renovated in true north Bali style. Rebuilt entirely out of the dark, austere, lava stone readily available in the north on a promontory overlooking the Bali Sea, this is one of the important temples founded by Danghyang Nirartha, the priest who came from Java in the 16th century. It's said that he performed miracles on this site.

SEMBIRAN & JULAH   From Pacung, take the steep, winding road up to **Sembiran,** an ancient Bali Aga village with lovely sea views. Ancient traditions—religious, social, and architectural—are kept alive here and most of the village temples are built with round megalithic stones. Enjoy a coffee with the locals or go to one of the small village warungs. People here speak their own dialect of Balinese, and the entry and exit signs wishing you "Welcome" and "Goodbye" are in Balinese rather than the usual Indonesian. The nearby village of **Julah** is one of Bali's oldest. Look out for the giant *kemit* tree, where corpses were laid out in ancient times. There's also a large Pura Dalem (Temple of the Dead) of black local stone at the foot of the village.

Where to Stay & Eat
VERY EXPENSIVE

Spa Village Resort ★   This heavenly beachside spa resort, a member of Small Luxury Hotels of the World, oozes peacefulness and calm. Its individually tailored "discovery paths" are dedicated to healing, rejuvenation, wellness, and spirituality, all with Balinese origins or using traditional techniques. Weekly programs incorporate specific dietary regimens and even training in traditional Balinese massage. All dietary needs are catered to and an extensive healthy and locally sourced menu is available.

Jl. Singaraja-Amlapura 100, Desa Tembok, Tejakula-Buleleng. www.spavillage.com. 📞 **+65/68362455** in Malaysia. Fax 0321/487397. 31 units. Year-round US$265–US$385 standard; US$385–US$505 suite; US$455–US$575 villa. Rates include breakfast. AE, DC, MC, V. **Amenities:** Restaurant; bar; airport transfer; bikes; concierge; gym; outdoor pool; room service; spa; watersports; Wi-Fi (in lobby). *In room/villa:* A/C, TV/DVD (villa only), hair dryer, minibar, MP3 docking station.

North Bali

BALI SEA

Banyuwedang · Pondok Sari Beach · Pemuteran · Pejarakan · Banyupoh · Musi · Sanggalangit · Gerokgak · Celukan Bawang · Pengulon · Seririt · Banjar · Busungbui · Pangkungparuk · Gg. Sanglang · Gg. Musi · Gg. Patas

North Bali — Gilimanuk · Singaraja · Negara · BALI · Ubud · Denpasar · INDIAN OCEAN · Nusa Penida

ATTRACTIONS ●	Pura Agung Pulaki **5**	Puri Kanginan Palace **20**
Atlas North Bali Pearls **5**	Pura Beji **24**	Reef Seen Aquatics &
Banjar Air Panas **8**	Pura Dalem **25**	Turtle Hatchery **3**
Biorock Project **1**	Pura Kerta Kawat **6**	Sawan **28**
Buddhist Wihara temple **9**	Pura Maduwe Karang **30**	Sudaji **27**
Dutch bridge **22**	Pura Melanting **6**	Suwug **26**
Gedong Kirtya & Puri Kawan **18**	Pura Pabean **5**	**HOTELS** ■
Jagaraga **29**	Pura Pondok Batu **33**	Adi Assri Resort **4**
Klenteng Ling Gwan Kiong	Pura Puncak Manik **6**	Alam Anda **35**
Chinese Temple **21**	Pura Tirta **5**	Amertha Bali Villas **4**
Old Harbour **22**	Puri Bagus Ponjok Batu **32**	Bali Taman Resort & Spa **16**

MODERATE

Alam Anda ★ ◆   This long-established, Mediterranean-style dive resort has over 400m (1,312 ft.) of beachfront and is simple luxury at its finest. Guests choose between comfortable bungalows with open bathrooms and sea or garden views, or one of the two new beachfront villas with private pools. The restaurant is patrolled by two pet ducks that come running when popcorn is served. A garden spa offers inexpensive Ayurvedic treatments, which in town would be triple the price. This resort has no delusions of grandeur, is good value for your money, and on the whole quite charming. British hostess Kim is a font of local knowledge. The hotel is often full and so book ahead.

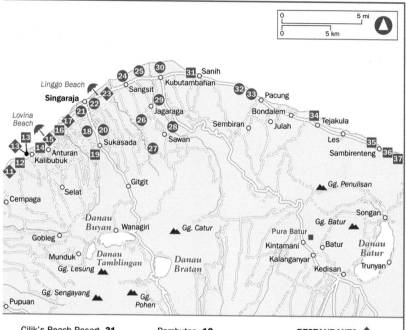

Cilik's Beach Resort **31**
Damai **13**
Gaia Oasis & Abasan
  Hillside Retreats **34**
Jubawa Homestay **4**
Matahari Beach Resort **4**
Poinciana Resort **36**
Pondok Sari **2**
Puri Bagus Lovina **16**
Puri Bali **14**
Puri Ganesha Villas **4**

Rambutan **12**
Rare Angon Homestay **4**
Reef Seen **3**
Rini **14**
Royal Residence Rangdu **10**
Shanti Hotel & Restaurant **19**
Spa Village Resort **37**
Sunari Resort **14**
Taman Sari Bali Cottages **1**
Taman Selini **4**
Zen Resort Bali **7**

RESTAURANTS ◆
Cosy Resto **17**
Damai **13**
Devosi **23**
Jasmine
  Kitchen **11**
Kwizien **17**
Ranggon
  Sunset **17**
Sea Breeze **11**
Warung Bambu **15**

Sembirenteng, Buleleng. www.alamanda.net. ✆ **081/24656485.** 29 units. Year-round US$40 standard; US$85–US$88 villa, all prices per person. Rates include taxes and buffet breakfast. AE, V. **Amenities:** Restaurant; bar; outdoor pool; room service; spa; watersports; Wi-Fi. *In room/villa:* A/C, hair dryer, minibar.

Poinciana Resort   This is a small resort run by a Balinese woman who spent 25 years in Australia. Simply decorated bedrooms are in several traditional Balinese buildings in a garden setting or beachfront. The restaurant offers a choice of inexpensive Indonesian and Western food; choose the specialty catch of the day. The resort offers guests complimentary use of their kayaks and can arrange fishing trips. For those wishing to take things even easier, a beachside *bale* (thatched pavilion) is available for massages and other simple spa treatments.

Jl. Amlapura Tejakula Tembok. www.poincianaresortbali.com. *C* **081/23859951.** 9 villas. Year-round US$76–US$180. Rates include taxes and breakfast. No credit cards. **Amenities:** Restaurant; airport transfer; outdoor pool; room service; Wi-Fi (for a fee). *In room:* A/C.

INEXPENSIVE

Gaia Oasis & Abasan Hillside Retreats   This yoga retreat combines two separate resorts, one on the beach and one in the hills. Both are eco-friendly and run as nonprofit organizations. Seminars and healing programs are presented here by an assortment of experts. Restaurants at both resorts offer a buffet of seafood and vegetarian dishes. Smoking and alcohol are frowned upon.

Dusun Tegal Sumaga, Tejakula. www.gaia-oasis.com. *C* **081/23853350.** Fax 0362/28428. 30 units. Year-round US$75 doubles, US$54 single. MC, V. **Amenities:** Restaurant; babysitting; room service. *In room:* Fan, hot shower, Wi-Fi.

AIR SANIH & SURROUNDING VILLAGES

Going east from Tembok, the uneven road winds through Air Sanih, a small village famous for a natural cold-water spring with public pools. Entry is around Rp3,000; the springs are open 7am to 7pm.

Exploring Near Air Sanih

This lush area just to the east of Singaraja produces the best rice in Bali. Given the importance of rice in Balinese culture, some of the most highly decorated temples are dedicated to the irrigation and rice goddess, Dewi Sri. Bring a picnic. Sarongs and sashes can be borrowed at the gates for a small donation for temple upkeep.

PURA MADUWE KARANG   In Kubutambahan, this is one of the largest temples in north Bali and is dedicated to protecting the crops that grow on land without irrigation. The reliefs show scenes from the Ramayana epic and daily Balinese life, together with the most photographed temple carving in Bali—a foreigner on a bicycle wearing shorts from the Dutch era, largely believed to portray the first foreign artist, W. O. J. Nieuwenkamp, who traveled around the area on his bike in 1904. The back wheel is in the form of a lotus flower.

PURA BEJI   Eight kilometers (5 miles) before Singaraja, look for the sign on the right for Pura Beji temple in **Sangsit,** again dedicated to Dewi Sri. Dating back to the 15th century, this unusual sandstone temple has intricate and unusual carvings reminiscent of South America. The temple sponsors have left carved portraits on the back of the main portal. You can rest under venerable frangipani trees before taking a short walk through the rice fields to the Pura Dalem, temple of the dead.

PURA DALEM   This temple is dedicated to Siwa and the souls of the dead with erotic carvings reflecting a Balinese heaven and hell. The carvings of this famous temple just outside the village also show how their peaceful village life was abruptly changed forever by the Dutch colonialists bringing guns and terror and, later, cars and planes—heaven is the representation of the island before the colonists arrived.

Back on the main road from the temple, look for the turn south toward **Jagaraga,** the site of the last battle fought by 16,000 Balinese soldiers led by Gusti Jelantik against 3,000 well-armed Dutch troops in 1849. Nowadays, there's nothing to see.

Continue along the road into the mountains to visit the foundries of the few remaining traditional gamelan and gong makers in the village of **Sawan.** Ask the locals how to get to the nearby traditional villages of **Sudaji,** to see the marketplace with huge ancient trees, and **Suwug,** to sit at the warung in the main square built into the roots of a huge banyan tree.

Where to Stay & Eat

Cilik's Beach Resort This very private property has several individually designed bungalows and one *lumbung* (traditional rice barn) set in extensive and beautiful beachfront gardens. The authentic Indonesian buildings are made of timber from Kilimantan, marble from Java, red bricks from southern Bali, and bamboo from the mountains. Each bungalow is filled with a collection of antique furniture giving them a charming, homey feel. A selection of fresh, local food is cooked to order.

Air Sanih, Singaraja. www.ciliksbeachgarden.com. © **0362/26561.** Fax 0362/26561. 4 units. Year-round US$140–US$225 Villa East; US$126–US$183 Villa West; US$99–US$141 Oktagonal; US$70–US$98 *lumbung*. No credit cards. **Amenities:** Restaurant; babysitting; Internet access; room service; watersports and boat rental. *In villa:* Stereo/CD, hair dryer.

SINGARAJA

Singaraja, the capital of Bali's largest regency, Buleleng, is the second most important town on the island and has a rich cultural and social history. With more than 100,000 inhabitants, this now quiet town was the important center of regional government under the Dutch for hundreds of years. Cut off by the mountains, the north developed independently from the south. It took the Dutch years of fighting before they eventually vanquished the south and finished the main Singaraja to Denpasar road. All that remains of the colonial splendor are some tree-lined boulevards and, sadly, very few of the beautiful villas.

The original kingdom of Buleleng, which reached as far as Blambangan in East Java in the 17th century, was founded by the royal family of Singaraja. The direct descendants and their families still live in the palaces today, although not quite in the same style.

Essentials

GETTING THERE & GETTING AROUND

If you're coming by car from the **east,** take the coast road. From the **southeast,** drive through Kintamani and past the Batur volcano. The main road from the **west** passes through two tourist extremes, the quiet and peaceful fishing village of Pemuteran (p. 263) and the rather run-down, budget-travel location of Lovina (p. 257). From the **south,** the winding road from the market town of Bedugul goes past the famous but overly touristy Git Git Waterfall before dropping down to the coast.

Three bus stations here have *bemo* and bus services to the rest of the island and a service to Java. The station on the eastern side of Singaraja, **Penarukan Terminal,** Jl. Surapati, serves east Bali (Amlapura, Kintamani, Gianyar) and ends in Batubulan Terminal, Denpasar, 3 hours later. **Banyuasri Terminal,** Jl. Jend Sudiman, on the western side of Singaraja, serves the western destinations of Lovina, Permuteran, and Gilimanuk (2 hr.). This service continues over to Java ending in Yogyakarta, 21 hours later. **Sukasada Terminal,** Jl. Mayor Metra, in the south, serves Gigit, Bedugal, and ends in Ubung Terminal, Denpasar (3 hr.). Prices range from Rp10,000 to Yeh Sanih up to Rp30,000 to Denpasar.

Taxis aren't available here. You can rent cars and drivers on the street or through the hotels in Lovina.

[FastFACTS] SINGARAJA

ATMs/Banks   Banks are open daily from 8am to 3pm. All the main Indonesian banks have a branch in Singaraja. **Bank Mandiri,** Jl. A. Yani 60 (☏ **0362/25333**), on the main street is easy to find.

Hospitals   The hospitals are **Kerta Husada,** Jl. A. Yani (☏ **0362/26277**) and the **Singaraja Public hospital Rumah Sakit Umum,** Jl. Ngurah Rai (☏ **0362/22573**).

Mail   The **post office** is on Jalan Gajah Mada 150 (☏ **0362/21788**).

Pharmacies   **Pharmacies,** open daily from 8am until 7 or 10pm, are on Jalan A. Yani and in the Kerta Husada.

Police   The **police station** is on Jalan Pramuka (☏ **0362/241510**).

Visitor Information   The **tourism office** is on Jalan Veteran 23 (☏ **0362/28170;** Mon–Fri 8am–5:30pm, Sat 8am–noon). It provides a pamphlet on the Buleleng Regency and a Singaraja map.

Exploring Singaraja

Coming in from the east and passing the **Dutch bridge** and the **Old Harbour,** it's difficult to imagine just how important this port was in the centuries of Dutch colonialism. Just along from the large, freedom-fighter monument between the bridge and the harbor, the recently renovated **Klenteng Ling Gwan Kiong Chinese Temple ★** is well worth a visit. All the white-painted rows of shops in this old part of town were built in the early 1900s and have delicately carved Art Deco friezes.

PURI KAWAN & PURI KANGINAN PALACE ★   Follow the tree-lined Jalan Ngurah Rai—with a few remaining colonial villas on each side—south toward the statue of the winged lion symbol of Buleleng. Turn left to find Jalan Veteran 20 and the famous **Gedong Kirtya ★** (free admission; Mon–Thurs 7:30am–3:30pm, Fri 7am–12:30pm, weekends and public holidays closed). This library has more than 3,000 ancient texts written in Javanese *kawi* and old Balinese script, inscribed on *lontar* palm leaves. Founded by the Dutch, in what must have been a state of guilty conscience, the library opened in 1928. The other collection of *prasasti* inscriptions on bronze are the oldest examples of writing on the island. The library is part of the old Puri Kawan and Puri Agung palace complex. Just across the road, peer through the imposing gates of the **Puri Kanginan Palace.** Sometimes you can get lucky and you're invited in to have a look and see what life must have been like for royalty in centuries gone by.

Shopping

Both **Pasar Banyuasri** (just off Jl. A. Yani near the imposing statue of a farmer with his bullocks) and **Pasar Anyar** (off Jl. Diponogoro) sell everything from fresh fish to sarongs. The **gold shops** on Jalan Sawo, off Jalan Diponogoro, sell good value jewelry appealing to Westerners. **Hardy's** supermarket, at the north end of Jalan

Ngurah Rai, is good for a small selection of everything from imported Western food to cosmetics.

Berdikari ★, Jl. Dewi Sartika 42 (☏ **0362/22217;** daily 7am–7pm), is one of the best shops for hand-woven ikat in Indonesia and home to the only silk weavers on the island. Visitors can see the fascinating dyeing and weaving process from start to finish. Presidents and politicians come here to buy ikat for formal wear and their photographs line the walls. The expensive fabrics can also be woven to order. Prices are fixed and credit cards aren't accepted.

Where to Stay·& Eat

The handful of hotels in town caters purely to Indonesian business travelers. Although in the past it was impossible to get a decent meal in Singaraja, some little restaurants are opening up at last. **Devosi,** on Jalan A. Yani, is an airy warung over-looking rice fields on the main road to the west. Also on the beach to the west, a group of small restaurants have sprung up on Jalan Pantai Penimbangan Barat, such as **Cosy Resto** and **Ranggon Sunset,** with fresh grilled seafood and simple rice and noodle dishes at reasonable prices.

Shanti Hotel & Restaurant 🎁   Ten minutes south of Singaraja, high up in the green hills of Sambangan, this hotel and restaurant offers easy, interesting treks through beautiful scenery to nearby villages and waterfalls. In the traditional Balinese kitchen, visitors can see how coffee and coconut oil are processed by hand. The shady restaurant has an extensive menu that uses fresh local produce and creates gourmet experiences for pennies. Stay overnight in one of the two pristine rice-barn villas to really get the most out of this very special experience.

Sambangan, Singaraja. www.shanti-northbali.com. ☏ **0362/700-1331.** Fax 0362/23120. 2 units. Year-round US$70. Rates include breakfast. MC, V. **Amenities:** Restaurant; bar; room service; spa therapy. *In villa:* Fan, TV/DVD.

LOVINA

In the 1960s, five small villages were fused into one under the collective name of Lovina or "Love Indonesia," by the Rajah of Singaraja. Because he thought that the area had great potential for tourism, he published many articles in the foreign press that led to Lovina becoming a new and popular destination for the hippie crowd.

To the west of Singaraja, this long stretch of flat, black, sandy beach is good for swimming, snorkeling, and dolphin- and local-fishermen-watching, and is now a favorite haunt for backpackers and northern European retirees on low budgets. Some of the locals are doing what they can to smarten Lovina up a bit, but it's perhaps a little past its sell-by date; furthermore, it has become notorious as a red-light district in recent years. But, if cheap, cheerful, and low-key is your thing, this may be the place.

A sad part of the area's history is that it has historically quarried for coral and overfished. The coral used to be burned to make building lime for mortar—a crying shame. Happily, as an unexpected and recent side effect of tourism, the coral is now protected and the local fishermen have much better respect for how to fish the sea without destroying their own source of livelihood.

Don't Chase the Dolphins of Lovina

Everyone in Lovina will try to sell you an early morning dolphin trip. Because of the number of people involved, these trips should now be rechristened dolphin "chasing" rather than dolphin "watching," with up to 30 loud boats involved in the hunt. Consequently, actual sightings are becoming increasingly rare and most of the dolphins have wisely moved to other locations. Expect to pay around Rp50,000 per person for a 2-hour trip.

Another annoyance involving dolphins can be found at the somewhat commercial **Melka Hotel.** Here you pay US$50 for a 20-minute swim with large dolphins kept in rather small pools. Some guests (especially young women) are scared when the dolphins become overly friendly. There have been tales of physical and even sexual abuse by the male dolphins on unsuspecting tourists. As this is entirely out of character for the normally sweet and docile dolphin clan, one might assume that this is retribution for their wretched conditions.

Essentials

GETTING THERE & GETTING AROUND

Public *bemo* come here from Singaraja, the south, and Gilimanuk in the west, stopping all along the main road. Hop on and hold on.

Pak Komang (📞 081/338365761) and his group of transportation friends are reliable, speak reasonable English, and are happy to organize a car and driver for tours or to take you anywhere on the island. **Perama Tours** (📞 0362/41161) has two offices in Lovina (one in the Perama Hotel) and charges reasonable rates for getting around the island. **Motorbikes** can be rented all over town at your own risk for around Rp50,000 per day. Remember, drive with caution. Like Singaraja, no **taxis** are available: only private transport with cars and drivers.

[FastFACTS] LOVINA

ATMs/Banks   Lovina has two **ATMs** on the corner of the main road and Jalan Pantai Bina Ria but no banks.

Internet Access   Several Internet cafes are dotted around the village. The most reliable is **Spice Link,** Jl. Pantai Binaria (📞 0362/41509; daily 8am–11pm).

Mail   The **post office** is on the main road, about a 5-minute drive from the village center. Open Monday to Thursday 8am to 3pm, Friday until noon, and Saturday until 1pm.

Pharmacy   Coming from Singaraja, just after the traffic lights on the left hand side, is a small **pharmacy** and a general practitioner's office with a doctor on 24-hour call.

Police   The new **Tourist Police** office is just outside the Sunari Resort (p. 262).

Visitor Information   A **tourist information** office (📞 0362/25141) is on the main road in the center of the village and is open Monday to Thursday and Saturday 7am to 5:30pm, and Friday until 1pm.

Exploring Lovina

The main draw of Lovina is the clear, calm water and its black-sand beaches. Sadly, the coral reef here isn't in pristine condition due to bleaching and the dynamite fishing of a past era. However, snorkelers still have plenty to see and beginning divers can use this location for introductory dives. Night diving is also very popular.

Spice Dive, Kaliasem and Jl. Binaria (© **0362/41512;** www.balispicedive.com), a PADI certified dive school, is a good place to learn to scuba dive. Although Lovina isn't suitable for accomplished divers, trips can be organized to Menjangan Island or Tulamben (about 2 hr. away).

Sailing, fishing, and **spear fishing** can be done at **Kubu Lalang** hotel, Jl. Singaraja Tukadmungga (© **0362/42207**). Fix your prices before you head out. Expect to pay about Rp70,000 per hour for fishing and about Rp100,000 per hour for other activities. You can also pay the fishermen to take you snorkeling (about Rp30,000 per hour). Most fishermen are part of a local village association, which allows them to use their fishing boat to ferry tourists around. As a result, prices are generally fixed.

The other big draw of Lovina is dolphin-watching (see above).

SPAS   Local black sand is added to your massage oil at the **Damai** (p. 262; © **0362/ 41008;** www.damai.com; massages Rp450,000–Rp950,000, water healing Rp1,000,000 for one person; AE, MC, V; daily 8am–8pm), making for a terrific scrub. Private spa pavilions can be booked for Ayurvedic massages at about Rp650,000 for an hour and the ultimate six-hand massage is around Rp950,000 for an hour. A less expensive spa is **Agung's,** Jl. Damai (© **0362/42018;** full body massage Rp150,000, facial Rp150,000–Rp175,000; no credit cards; daily 11am–7pm), but in comparison to the Damai, is a little gloomy.

Shopping

The artist **Made Ariana** (© **081/338459153**) has made quite a name for himself, so make an appointment to visit his studio if you're interested in Balinese expressionism. **Biyu Nasak Gallery** (© **081/338030275**), on the main road in the center of the village, has a primitive "ancient" art collection. **Bakery Lovina** (© **0362/42225;** daily 7am–9:30pm), on the main road, sells expensive but freshly baked bread and cakes, together with wine, alcohol, and a range of imported deli products.

West of Lovina

BANJAR & AIR PANAS   The **Buddhist Wihara temple,** in the hills behind Banjar village, is home to Bali's only Buddhist monk and is a colorful mix of Balinese and more traditional Buddhist architecture. Admission is free but a donation is expected.

The holy hot springs or **Air Panas** in Banjar village are very popular with the locals. The three, hot-spring bathing pools, set in well-maintained gardens, have clean changing rooms and are open to the public daily from 8am until 6pm. If you want to take a dip in the slightly sulfurous waters, get here in the early morning and bring your own towel. A small **restaurant** overlooking the pools serves local dishes at reasonable prices and has some simple **rooms** with beautiful garden views.

SERIRIT   All roads from Singaraja to Java and the west or to Denpasar and the south pass through **Seririt**. This small town has two banks with ATMs, a chemist, and a much-understocked Hardy's supermarket. The only local color, so to speak, is a group of Balinese ladies selling flowers for temple offerings.

Just after Seririt on the road to Gilimanuk, is the **Zen Resort Bali,** Jl. Pantai Uma Anyar (**www.zenresortbali.com**; ℂ **0362/93578;** fax 0362/93579; 14 units; year-round US$119–US$148; MC, V), a peaceful place with simple but colorful rooms and a large swimming pool. Rates include Ayurvedic, meditation, or pranayama retreats as well as special workshops available on request.

CELUKAN BAWANG   This is the most important port in north Bali although not particularly attractive. The docks are only worth a peek if fishermen from other parts of Indonesia with their beautifully painted wooden boats happen to be visiting. The morning is the best time to find them.

GEROKGAK   Just before entering this village, look for a sign on the left to the *objek wisata alam bendungan* or reservoir. This is a peaceful place to walk or take a picnic and chances are you'll be completely alone.

PENYABANGAN   Follow the sign for **Atlas North Bali Pearls** (ℂ **081/ 23877012;** daily 9am–6pm) down a dirt road toward the beach. Call the company beforehand to book one of its interesting introductory tours. After seeing how incredibly complicated the cultivation process is, you'll never look at a pearl the same way again. The little cafe-cum-showroom serves very good coffee and offers the chance to buy a lovely local pearl or two at relatively competitive prices.

BANYUPOH   This little village is famous for two things: grapes and temples. There's no real growing season here, and so don't be surprised to see a vineyard full of grapes ready for harvest next to a plot that just has new shoots.

PURA AGUNG PULAKI   This has been an important place for ancestor and spirit worship since prehistoric times. The first story based on historical fact dates from the 16th century when the priest **Dang Hyang Nirartha** (1460–1550) came from Java with his family, bringing with him a purer form of Hinduism. He found a holy spring at Pulaki. The temple has since become one of Bali's nine most important directional temples and is also home to hordes of holy monkeys. The new temple, carved out of the mountainside, was completed in 1984 and has heavy, black lava stone buildings and ornate carvings. Visit the temple at full moon to see the colorful throngs of worshipers who come from all over Bali to pray for fortune and prosperity. A good Balinese Hindu has to pray at Pura Agung Pulaki at least once every year. Foreigners are allowed into the temple if they wear a sarong and a sash and pay a small donation.

PURA KERTA KAWAT   Entering Banyupoh village, watch for a sign on the left to Pura Kerta Kawat, down a small road lined with vineyards. Balinese people believe that praying here increases prosperity.

PURA MELANTING   Just along the main road is the sign for Pura Melanting, an awe-inspiring temple hidden in the forest and reached by a flight of wide stone steps. It's frequented by a steady stream of worshipers who believe that praying here increases prosperity and good fortune. In 1997, the simple temple buildings were destroyed by a forest fire. Sadly, it has since been rebuilt in the overly ornate neo-Balinese temple style reminiscent of Chinese temples, with no expense spared and no surface devoid of carving. Still, this is a wonderful place for meditation.

PURA PABEAN   On the beach across the road from Pulaki, two huge megaliths from earlier times disappeared into the sand in the 13th century and were only redis-covered and re-erected in 1997 in their original position. Ida Bagus Tugur, an archi-tect with no formal training, began to build a new temple on the hill behind the megaliths in 1987, using spiritual inspiration and instructions from old *lontar* palm leaf books. During excavations for the foundations, skeletons and gold jewelry were found, proving that the site could have been linked to the necropolis in Gilimanuk and other prehistoric sites in the area.

PURA PUNCAK MANIK   This is a small temple built around a sacred spring high up in the hills behind Pura Melanting. You have to climb hundreds of steps, but those hardy enough to reach the top are rewarded by magnificent views.

PURA TIRTA   This small, recently renovated temple is famed for the spring that provides the holy water for many temple ceremonies.

Where to Stay

You'll find a huge selection of small backpacker hotels along the main and side roads leading down to the beach throughout the Lovina villages. These cheap accommoda-tions have seasonal rates. If you're on a budget, it pays to shop around and compare prices. Two of the cheapest places in the center of town, close to the beach, are **Rini** and **Puri Bali** on Jalan Marwar, and offer a choice of fan or air-conditioned rooms with cold or hot water, swimming pool, and a small restaurant. When staff members say that rooms have hot water, check it out yourself: "Hot" to them may mean "tepid" to you.

EXPENSIVE

Damai ★   High up in the hills with lovely views of the Bali Sea, Damai is the best place to stay out of town. Set in beautiful gardens, the older rooms are very pleasant but have no privacy. Bathrooms are small but each room has a Jacuzzi in the walled garden outside. The brand-new, Singaporean-style villas have infinity plunge pools with lovely views. The interiors are rather cool with black walls and European furni-ture— somewhat incongruous with the surroundings. The **spa** offers an extensive range of treatments and one of only a few six-hand massages on the island—and you thought four was excessive. Don't miss the large Japanese-style breakfast.

Jl. Damai, Kayu Putih, Singaraja. www.damai.com. ✆ **0362/41008.** 13 villas. High season US$259–US$1,670; low season US$234–US$930; extra bed US$90. Rates include breakfast. AE, DC, MC, V. **Amenities:** Restaurant (Damai, see below); babysitting; outdoor pool; room service; spa; Wi-Fi. *In room:* A/C, TV/DVD, hair dryer, minibar.

Puri Bagus Lovina   The first hotel west of Singaraja is this well-run family hotel. Villas are set far apart from each other in lovely gardens leading to the beach. The restaurant next to the double-level pool has an extensive menu. Popular romantic dinners cost US$75 and include a bottle of local wine.

Jl. Raya Seririt Gilimanuk, Desa Pemuteran, Buleleng. www.bagus-discovery.com. ✆ **0362/21430.** Fax 0362/22627. 40 villas. High season US$200–US$390; low season US$185–US$375. AE, DC, MC, V. **Amenities:** Restaurant; bar; babysitting; children's club; outdoor pool; room service; spa; watersports; Wi-Fi (for a fee). *In villa:* A/C, hair dryer, minibar.

MODERATE

Bali Taman Resort & Spa   Built in 1989, this low-end resort and spa was one of the first hotels in the area and although the rooms are clean, the decor has kept its late 1980s feel. Credit cards are accepted, which in these parts is a plus.

Jl. Raya Lovina, Lovina. www.balitamanlovina.com. ✆ **0362/41126.** 30 units. Year-round US$50–US$110. MC, V. **Amenities:** Restaurant; bar; lounge; Internet (for a fee); outdoor pool; room service; spa; tennis court. *In room:* A/C, TV, stereo or CD, hair dryer, minibar.

Rambutan ☺   This is a long-standing, popular, family-run child-friendly resort. The children's playground even has a tree house. Two freeform pools make up for not being directly on the beach and you can rest easy while the children run around safely in the garden. The rooms are very simple, with rattan furniture, carved wooden doors, and tile floors. Restaurant prices are in U.S. dollars and include all the usual international and Indonesian favorites. The owners are avid supporters of the Singaraja Orphanage and are happy to take guests there who might like to help.

Jl. Rambutan, Lovina. www.rambutan.org. ✆ **0362/41388.** Fax 0362/41621. 28 units. High season US$35–US$110 rooms, US$125–US$230 villas; low season US$28–US$95 rooms, US$110–US$200 villas. MC, V. **Amenities:** Restaurant; Internet (for a fee); 2 outdoor pools; room service. *In room:* A/C, fan, TV, DVD (in villa), kitchenette (in villa), minibar.

Royal Residence Rangdu 🍴☺   These traditional villas sleep between 4 and 10 and are set in lush green hills, for a bargain price that lures Europeans to this all-inclusive resort. Meals are served to your villa three times a day, or half-board is also available. The location is a bit isolated, but it's a good choice if you're looking for a private place to recharge your batteries. The resort pilots its own boat off the coast for dolphin-watching excursions.

Jl. Muntig, Desa Rangdu, Beleleng. www.royalresidencerangdu.com. ✆ **0362/94783.** Fax +31847454928 in the Netherlands. 7 units. 95€–650€. MC, V. *In villa:* butler service; pool; radio; Internet (added charge).

Sunari Resort   With over 80 rooms and villas, this is the largest hotel in Lovina. Set on the beach, it has a 24-hour **restaurant** serving local, Chinese, and European fare. The rooms can be a bit gloomy, but the gardens and pool are very pleasant.

Lovina Beach. www.sunari.com. ✆ **0362/41775.** Fax 0362/41659. 83 units. All year round US$130–US$150; extra bed US$30. MC, V. **Amenities:** Restaurant; gym; outdoor pool; room service; Wi-Fi (for a fee). *In room:* A/C, TV, minibar.

Where to Eat
EXPENSIVE

Damai ★★ 🍴 BALINESE   Meals here are expensive but worth every rupiah. The six-course tasting menu changes every evening and offers traditional Balinese dishes with Scandinavian touches; the interesting a la carte menu offers such delicacies as tuna *tataki* (seared tuna) and mahimahi on cauliflower puree with almonds. Although the food tends to be a little overplated, it's cooked to perfection. An eight-course Champagne Brunch on Sundays (11am–2pm) is good value at Rp245,000 (children 11 and under Rp155,000). Every night includes a Balinese performance and live music.

In the Damai (see above), Jl. Damai, Kayu Putih, Singaraja. ✆ **0362/41008.** www.damai.com. Main courses Rp195,000–Rp235,000; set menu Rp360,000. AE, DC, MC, V. Daily 7am–11pm.

MODERATE

Jasmine Kitchen THAI/CAFE   This little restaurant serves the usual Thai favorites and wonderfully wicked cakes baked daily. Fresh prawns in chili sauce are an excellent choice. The wine list is small with local "Wine of the Gods" on offer.

Gang Binaria, Kalibuk-Lovina. © **0362/41565.** Main courses Rp25,000–Rp68,000. No credit cards. Daily 9am–10pm.

Kwizien INTERNATIONAL   This popular restaurant was taken over by a Dutch couple in 2007 and was subsequently revamped and fitted with air-conditioning. The menu features imported steaks (Rp90,000–Rp125,000 for a T-bone) and local food with rather strange dishes such as meatballs in blueberry sauce.

Jl. Raya Singaraja, Seririt-Kaliasem. © **0362/42031.** www.balikwizien.com. Main courses Rp25,000–Rp90,000. MC, V. Daily 5pm–midnight.

Sea Breeze INDONESIAN/INTERNATIONAL   At the end of Jalan Pantai Binaria next to the Lovina dolphin statue, is this favorite hang-out for locals and a perfect spot for sunset drinks. Good breakfasts are also served. A live band plays a few nights a week.

Jl. Pantai Binaria. © **0362/41138.** Main courses Rp45,000–Rp100,000. No credit cards. Daily 8am–11pm.

INEXPENSIVE

Warung Bambu BALINESE   On the side road to Puri Bagus, this bamboo cafe serves the best Balinese food in the area. Apart from the rijsttafel for Rp115,000 and their surprise menu for Rp175,000 per person, none of their tasty dishes is over Rp50,000. Cooking classes for a minimum of two persons have to be booked 1 day in advance and cost Rp300,000 per person. Only local wines are served. Balinese dance performances take place on Wednesday and Sunday nights.

Jl. Puri Bagus Pemaron. © **0362/31455.** Main courses Rp30,000–Rp50,000. Special meals, *betutu dolong* (steamed duck), and Balinese Night Rp300,000, 2-person minimum, order 1 day in advance. MC, V. Daily 11:30am–10pm.

Lovina Entertainment & Nightlife

Most of the nightlife in Lovina takes place in the little bars and restaurants that have an evening happy hour. The lone club on the main road to the east of the village is impossible to miss: It's a huge concrete eyesore, the pyramid-shaped **Volcano Club.** The disco is open from 9pm until late Wednesday to Saturday. Regular Balinese dance performances and other cultural events are organized by the **Lovina Culture Foundation** (© **0362/41293**): Ring for information on performances in town.

PEMUTERAN

When a small group of pioneer investors bought land in Pemuteran in the mid-1980s, they vowed to adhere to the ideals of gentle tourism and to create a hideaway for discerning visitors. Its position 3 to 4 hours drive from the south means that this peaceful fishing village has been more carefully developed than similar places in Bali.

When guests have made the trip once, they tend to return. There's no nightlife, no ATMs, no hawkers on the beach, no jet skis—just a large bay, good for swimming, and a handful of small resorts each with their own restaurant and some with PADI dive centers. Everyone's goal here is to offer visitors a peaceful respite and some of the best snorkeling and diving in this part of Indonesia.

Essentials

GETTING THERE & GETTING AROUND

Public *bemo* buses are available along the main road from dawn to dusk, or "express" buses between Singaraja and Gilimanuk are also available. **Puri Ganesha** (see below) offers transfers by Harley-Davidson bike with a "jockey" and a car for the luggage.

If you're traveling from the south or airport before 3pm, the quickest scenic drive over the central mountains takes around 3½ hours. After 3pm, when the rush hour begins, be prepared to spend longer in the car. Transfers from Ubud take between 2½ and 3 hours; from Amed and Candidasa, around 4 hours.

Taxis as such aren't available, but there is a **Village Drivers Association** (✆ 081/337903234), although its rates are higher than finding someone direct.

[FastFACTS] PEMUTERAN

Doctors   The small **Pemuteran Clinic** (✆ 081/915678011) has a doctor on call 24 hours who will also come to your hotel. If there's something really serious, call experienced, English-speaking **Dr. Handra** (✆ 081/23605733) who will come from Singaraja. He accepts credit cards—and charges European prices.

Internet Access   Because this is such a rural area, **telephones** and **Internet connections,** even those using satellites, tend to be erratic. There are no Internet cafes but most of the hotels do have an Internet service for their guests, albeit not necessarily on all day.

Pemuteran Outdoors

The excellent dive school **Reef Seen Aquatics,** in the Reef Seen resort (see below; ✆ 0362/93001; www.reefseenbali.com), predominately caters to certified divers. However, they can also arrange introductory dive courses when given notice. For snorkeling, pay a local villager at one of the smaller dive concessions for Rp200,000 per day to take you to reefs in and around Pemuteran.

The fantastic **Biorock Project ★★**, in front of Taman Sari hotel, is a perfect place for children to enjoy snorkeling. The waters in Permuteran are usually calm and visibility is clear. You can also start or end the day with a boat ride. Enjoy the sun rising or setting and you may even catch a glimpse of a whale or dolphin—but no promises. Pony rides are available along the beach. Reef Seen can organize all these activities.

The **Turtle hatchery** project based at Reef Seen educates the local community about not killing turtles or stealing their eggs. The hatchery helps raise awareness of the need for conservation while enabling the birth and growth of different species of turtles: Olive Ridley, Green, and Hawksbill. When the turtles are mature and healthy enough, they're released back into the sea. Sponsor and release your own turtle when you visit—the money all goes to a good cause.

PEMUTERAN'S biorock PROJECT

By the late 1990s, a combination of coral bleaching and dynamite fishing had decimated the reefs at Pemuteran. This made for a bleak outlook for the local residents, who relied on fishing for their own consumption and as a draw for marine tourists, divers, and snorkelers.

However, in June 2000, the Taman Sari Resort donated US$12,000 to start the **Karang Lestari Proyek** (Coral Protection Project). This project uses low-voltage electricity to promote and accelerate coral growth on metal frames. Taman Sari Resort supplies the electricity and further funding is supplied by private donations.

The technology comes from the **Global Coral Reef Alliance** (GCRA; www.globalcoral.org) in the United States. The basic principle is that when electrodes are immersed in seawater, limestone is created, making a strong base on which corals readily grow, sometimes five times faster than normal.

This process generates a high pH level in the water, in which corals flourish, therefore more energy can be used to reproduce and build. These corals are also more resistant to environmental stress and it's believed that they will also withstand future seasonal temperature rises (the cause of coral bleaching).

The Karang Lestari Proyek, at 2.4 hectares (6 acres), is the world's largest coral-reclamation project. At present, over 40 metal frames of various shapes and sizes at depths of 5 to 10m (16–33 ft.) have a variety of hard corals growing on them, in various stages of development. Despite the fact that this is a young project, the area makes an interesting and educational day's diving.

The project is fully supported by the people of Pemuteran village. In order to restore the fish population, everyone has agreed to observe the site as a no-fishing area. They've also agreed to stop dynamite and cyanide fishing.

Where to Stay & Eat
VERY EXPENSIVE

Puri Ganesha Villas ★★★ 🎁   At the far opposite end of Pemuteran Bay is one of our favorite places to visit that was voted World's Best Beach Hideaway by *Travel + Leisure* magazine. Egyptologist, designer, and food connoisseur Diana von Cranach runs this beautiful spot as though she's entertaining house guests, not paying clients. The long list of celebrity repeat guests is too secretive to mention. Each beautiful freestanding one- to three-bedroom villa has its own private, 12-m (39-ft.) pool. The style is Barbados-beach-house-meets-classic-Bali, with antiques and wooden floors. Many people make the journey from the south just to stay here. To top it all, Diana runs an amazing kitchen specializing in raw and living food, and alongside the daily changing menu she also offers a raw food-healing program and cooking classes.

Desa Pemuteran, Gerokgak. www.puriganesha.com. ✆ **0362/94766.** Fax 0362/93433. 4 villas. Year-round US$550–US$725. AE, MC, V. **Amenities:** Restaurant; babysitting; Internet; room service; spa. *In villa:* A/C, kitchenette, minibar, outdoor pool.

EXPENSIVE

Matahari Beach Resort ★★   This peaceful, rather ornate resort with an Olympic-size pool is set in beautiful gardens. Each of the spacious, traditionally furnished

A few kilometers to the west is the small village of Goris, with a tidy and interesting daily market. The highlight here is the famous *babi guling* (suckling pig). Queues of locals wait for the pig to be delivered every morning around 7:30am to **Bali Re**, a warung at the front of the market. It's so good that even Hermès-bag-toting tourists from Pemuteran have been spotted licking their fingers here. A portion costs around Rp15,000. Get there early, because once it runs out for the day, that's it.

rooms has a marble bathroom and garden shower but the private terraces can be a little gloomy. The resort is a Relais & Châteaux member, and so expect excellent, formal dining in the restaurant with prices to match. Balinese music and dance performances are held regularly. The huge spa has an interesting range of treatments and a special pavilion for tea ceremonies. Outside guests are welcome at the spa, but book well in advance.

Jl. Raya Seririt Gilimanuk, Desa Pemuteran, Buleleng. www.matahari-beach-resort.com. ✆ **0362/92312.** Fax 0362/92313. 32 units. Year-round US$205–US$514. Rates include breakfast. AE, DC, MC, V. **Amenities:** 2 restaurants; bar; bikes; concierge; gym; outdoor pool; room service; spa; tennis court; watersports; Wi-Fi (for a fee). *In room:* A/C, movie library, hair dryer, minibar.

MODERATE

Amertha Bali Villas   On the main road is this collection of modern, southern Bali-style one-, two-, and three-bedroom villas with private pools and a little beachfront restaurant. The villas are managed by Taman Sari Bali Cottages (see below), just along the road. Stay in a villa near the beach because those closer to the road can be noisy.

Dusun Pemuteran, Gerokgak-Buleleng. www.balitamansari.com. ✆ **0362/94831.** Fax 0362/93264. 15 units. High season US$99–US$415; low season US$84–US$400. MC, V. **Amenities:** Restaurant; 2 outdoor pools; room service; spa; tennis court; Wi-Fi (for a fee). *In villa:* A/C, TV/DVD, hair dryer, kitchenette, minibar.

Pondok Sari   Next to Taman Selini (see below), this hotel has 30 standard rooms, four deluxe bungalows, and a villa set in tropical gardens. The beachfront restaurant serves adequate international and local fare.

Jl. Raya Seririt Gilimanuk, Pemuteran. www.pondoksari.com. ✆ **0362/92337.** Fax 0362/94738. 35 units. High season US$69–US$260; low season US$62–US$239. MC, V. **Amenities:** Restaurant; bar; lounge; outdoor pool; room service; spa. *In room:* A/C, hair dryer.

Taman Sari Bali Cottages ★   At the west end of the village, this hotel is a favorite with expats and tour groups as much for the charming cottages and easy rates as for the garden, ambience, and laid-back nature. Make sure to reserve early during school holidays. Rooms and villas are scattered throughout a large garden facing the sea. A small swimming pool with bar is next to the restaurant. Spa treatments are on offer.

Dusun Pemuteran, Gerokgak-Buleleng. www.balitamansari.com. ✆ **0361/742-1165.** 12 units. High season US$58–US$362; low season US$55–US$350. MC, V. **Amenities:** Restaurant; bar; babysitting; outdoor pool; room service; spa; watersports; Wi-Fi (for a fee). *In room:* A/C, TV/DVD, hair dryer, kitchenette (villa only), minibar.

Taman Selini On the main road in the center of the village, the Taman Selini has 11 Balinese-style bungalows with terraces facing the garden and a large swimming pool. The bar has an outside lounging area by the beach opposite the popular restaurant that serves very good Greek meze as well as Indonesian and international favorites.

Jl. Raya Seririt Gilimanuk, Pemuteran. www.tamanselini.com. © **0362/94746.** 12 units. Year-round US$120–US$250; extra bed US$10. MC, V. **Amenities:** Restaurant; outdoor pool; room service; Wi-Fi (for a fee). *In room:* A/C, hair dryer.

INEXPENSIVE

Many inexpensive lodgings are on Jalan Raya Gilimanuk. One is the **Jubawa Homestay** (© **0362/94745;** 23 units; year-round Rp250,000–Rp350,000; no credit cards; includes breakfast and 1 hour Internet per day), just after Matahari Beach Resort, which has 12 clean rooms, most of them with air-conditioning and hot water. Noise from the nearby road can be annoying. The little restaurant serves frugal Balinese and Thai food. The **Rare Angon Homestay** (© **0362/94747;** year-round Rp250,000–Rp350,000; MC, V), near the entrance to Taman Sari, has three clean air-conditioned rooms and a small restaurant that sometimes serves fresh grilled fish.

You can't miss the sign for **Adi Assri Resort** (www.adiassri.com; © **0362/94838;** fax 0362/94838; 64 units; high season US$65–US$310; low season US$55–US$300; extra bed US$15; rates include breakfast; MC, V) on the main road after Jubawa on the beach side. This new resort has bright, airy rooms although they're a bit stark, and the layout and full glass front offers little privacy. The pool area and restaurant are near the beach and spa treatments are available.

Reef Seen (www.reefseenbali.com; © **0362/93001;** year-round Rp500,000; MC, V) is down a dirt track just after Amertha Bali Villas (see above). The five pleasant rooms have garden bathrooms, air-conditioning, and hot water. Chris Brown has been in Pemuteran for many years and he had the original PADI dive school in the area. He also initiated the original reef and turtle saving projects (p. 264). Village children learn and practice Balinese dancing here and their performances are magical.

WEST BALI

West Bali is best defined as the area west of Tabanan on the southern coast of Bali and the **West Bali National Park** (**Taman Nasional Bali Barat**). If you're visiting Bali for 5 days or more, a journey west is a great escape from "downtown" Bali because this area sees very few international visitors. Traveling west requires planning for at least 1 overnight stay with a car and driver.

This 71km (44 mile) strip of volcanic sand coast is home to the Malay-speaking Bugis and Balinese Christians. Most of the population of west Bali are rice farmers, fishermen, or plantation workers and are increasingly Muslim due to the area's proximity to Java. The coastal towns of west Bali were settled by Bugis Javanese seafarers during the 17th century, who established a trading center in **Negara.**

ESSENTIALS
Getting There & Getting Around

The west is serviced by one main road that stretches from Tabanan to the port village of Gilimanuk, the transit point for ferries to Java. Although the only misrouting possible would take you north to Singaraja or Lovina, it's not advisable to self-drive; instead, take a car and driver. If you're planning an extended stay here, most hotels offer car or motorbike rentals or complimentary use of a car; many will also have bicycles available for guests. Driving from Denpasar to Gilimanuk takes 4 hours. Seaside and mountain villages are never more than 10km (6 miles) off the main road.

[FastFACTS] WEST BALI

Banks   Most banks here exchange cash and travelers checks. Major banks are in Tabanan and Negara.

Clinics & Hospitals   In Tabanan, head to **Dharma Kerti Clinic,** Jl. Manik 14 (✆ **0361/811424**), or **Gelgel Hospital,** Jl. Mawar (✆ **0361/811444**). In Negara, try **Negara Public Hospital,** Jl. Gelar (✆ **0365/41006**), and **Kerta Yasa Clinic,** Jl. Ngurah Rai 143 (✆ **0365/41248**).

Police   Police are stationed at Jalan Pahlawan in Tabanan (✆ **0361/811210**), Jalan Raya Melaya, in Melaya (✆ **0365/41302**), and Jalan Tanah Lot (✆ **0361/812399**) and Jalan Pekarangan Baturiti in Tabanan (✆ **0361/93347**).

TABANAN

Tabanan encompasses a broad range of landscapes from the lofty peaks in the north, including **Mount Batukaru** (p. 217) and part of Mount Bratan with its dramatic volcanic lake, to the verdant rice plains in the south. Beautiful black sand beaches between Pasut and Klatingdukuh are being developed for tourism, but apart from the busy seaside temple of **Tanah Lot** this isn't an overly visited area.

The main highway from Java passes through the gently sloping southern part of Tabanan along the coast, making it a commercial center. Tabanan is known for its dancers and gamelan musicians and was home to the famous pre-World War II dancer I Mario who perfected the kebyar dance. Tabanan is also home to one of Bali's last royal families who maintain and live in a palace (see "Puri Anyar Kerambitan (Royal Palace at Kerambitan)" below).

Going west to Tabanan is simply a matter of following the signs from Denpasar and Seminyak—only one east to west road runs along Bali's southern coast.

Exploring In & Around Tabanan

Kediri is south of Tabanan and has one of the busiest cattle markets in Bali, **Pasar Hewan.** There's not much to see unless you're in the market for livestock, but it's a small detour on the way farther south to the pottery town of **Pejaten,** famous for its lovely pottery and terra-cotta tiles with figures of gods, goddesses, and *wayang* (shadow puppet) heroes. Also on sale are glazed Chinese ceramics. The prices are unbelievably cheap.

The **Margarana Monument,** 2km (1¼ miles) west of Marga (to the north of Tabanan), commemorates the **November 20, 1946 battle** against Dutch forces who sought to regain Bali as a colony after the departure of the Japanese. From here, one of the great figures in Balinese history, Gusti Ngurah Rai, led a band of independence fighters. Inside is a shrine in honor of Ngurah Rai and the words of his final letter ending in "Freedom or death."

On Bali's western coastline at Tanah Lot, 20 minutes drive north from Seminyak, the Greg Norman-designed championship golf course **Nirwana Bali Golf Club ★★★** (in the Pan Pacific Nirwana Golf Spa & Resort, see below; Mon–Fri US$165, Sat & Sun US$175) is acknowledged as one of the world's best; both *Asian Golf Monthly* and *Golf Digest* have voted it the number one course in Indonesia. International competitions are staged here and the caddies are some of the best on the island. Golf carts with a caddy are compulsory and a drink service is provided. Lessons are available with the resident PGA professionals.

Mandala Mathika Subak (Subak Rice Museum) This museum dedicated to rice cultivation in Bali features dioramas of typical rice field irrigation systems from A.D. 600 that feed the beautiful rice terraces adorning Bali's volcanic slopes. Well-versed guides explain how rice terraces are constructed, planted, and harvested using the rudimentary wooden tools on display. You'll never look at a bowl of rice in quite the same way again.

Jl. Raya Kediri. ✆ **0361/810315.** Admission Rp5,000. Daily 8am–5pm.

Pura Taman Ayun East of Tabanan, this huge elegant state temple is surrounded by a moat. Built in 1634 and renovated in 1937, it was the main temple of the

Mengwi kingdom until 1891. The flowing fountain and lovingly tended grounds are sometimes used as a background for Balinese royal feasts. Notice the *meru* (altar) dedicated to the god of fertility or "shrine of Ulun Suwi" on the east side of the main complex. The grounds house a total of 50 shrines and pavilions.

Jl. I Gusti Ngurah Rai. ✆ **0361/235600.** Admission Rp4,100. Daily 8am–6pm.

Pura Tanah Lot ★ Located along the east-west road in Beraban village on a rock that's only accessible at low tide, this temple is one of the most popular and important sea temples on Bali. Sunset is the preferred time to visit and is thus teeming with tourists. You have to wade through a row of commercial shops and cafes before you arrive at the temple itself, while aggressive touts try to sell you all manner of things. After all that, non-Balinese visitors aren't allowed inside the actual temple. If you do want to visit, it's best to come before lunch during the day—after all, you can catch the spectacular sunsets all over the southern coast and don't need to come here for that.

All the sea temples were constructed to be in sight of each other and form a chain along the coast. From Pura Tanah Lot, look to the cliff top of Uluwatu in the distance to the south, and to the other side to the west toward Perancak near Negara.

> ### To Go or Not to Go?
>
> An old superstition says that it's bad luck if you visit Pura Tanah Lot with your betrothed before marriage and it will cause you to break up before your nuptials.

Pura Tanah Lot is associated with the Majapahit priest Nirartha, who refashioned Balinese Hinduism in the 16th century. It remains an important prayer site and is where followers of the faith pray for the success of their crops and generally anything else associated with agriculture. Farmers in rural areas make pilgrimages to the temple to seek blessings that will safeguard their livelihood, while urban-dwelling Hindus often visit Tanah Lot in family groups to meditate and seek spiritual guidance.

A number of black sea snakes are hidden among the rocks and crevices surrounding Tanah Lot. Although these snakes are tame, be cautious and refrain from unnecessarily aggravating them or wandering off unaccompanied. These snakes are believed to be the guardians of the temple and protect the entire area from unseen evil forces—don't let them think you're one of them. Although poisonous, they're not deadly; if bitten, seek medical treatment immediately.

Beraban. Admission Rp3,300. ATM on site. Daily 7am–4:30pm.

Puri Anyar Kerambitan (Royal Palace at Kerambitan) ★★ 🎁 To the west of Tabanan is the 17th-century Puri Anyar Kerambitan. Its royal family represents Bali in its current progressive form, with roots in Balinese history dating from the 13th century. The family enjoyed great prosperity until the law of Land Reform in 1961 restricted ownership of land to 5 hectares (12 acres) per family. The family estate of then around 300 hectares (741 acres) was taken and redistributed. Under these new circumstances, it became a challenge to maintain the palace, its grounds, and many temples.

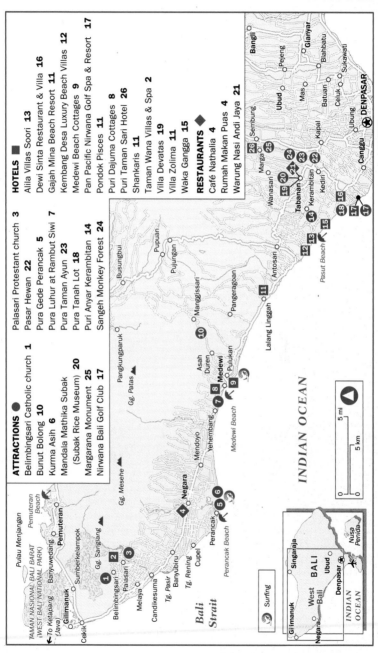

ATTRACTIONS ●
Belimbingsari Catholic church **1**
Bunut Bolong **10**
Kurma Asih **6**
Mandala Mathika Subak
(Subak Rice Museum) **20**
Margarana Monument **25**
Nirwana Bali Golf Club **17**
Palasari Protestant church **3**
Pasar Hewan **22**
Pura Gede Perancak **5**
Pura Luhur at Rambut Siwi **7**
Pura Taman Ayun **23**
Pura Tanah Lot **18**
Puri Anyar Kerambitan **14**
Sangeh Monkey Forest **24**

HOTELS ■
Alila Villas Soori **13**
Dewi Sinta Restaurant & Villa **16**
Gajah Mina Beach Resort **11**
Kembang Desa Luxury Beach Villas **12**
Medewi Beach Cottages **9**
Pan Pacific Nirwana Golf Spa & Resort **17**
Pondok Pisces **11**
Puri Dajuma Cottages **8**
Puri Taman Sari Hotel **26**
Shankaris **11**
Taman Wana Villas & Spa **2**
Villa Devatas **19**
Villa Zolima **11**
Waka Gangga **15**

RESTAURANTS ◆
Café Nathalia **4**
Rumah Makan Puas **4**
Warung Nasi Andi Jaya **21**

The present (seventh-generation royal family) King Anak Agung Ngurah Oka Sila-gunadha (Bapak Oka as he prefers to be known) had a vision to "share this gift of the ancestors" with the world and he opened the palace to visits in 1967. Feasts have been presented here for Mick Jagger, David Bowie, and Supertramp, Prime Minister Fukuda of Japan, and ministers and ambassadors from all over the world. A drama ritual named *Tektekan,* created by Bapak Oka for royal performances, is sometimes staged under the control of priests: Daggers seemingly penetrate the flesh of men in trances portraying the fight between good and evil called *Rwa Binedha.* If you book ahead, enticing Balinese feasts can be arranged for you, too. You can also stay in one of the palace rooms, simple but filled with antiques. Call well ahead of your intended stay or tour.

Desa Baturiti, Tabanan. ©/fax **0361/812774.** www.balipurikerambitan.web.id. Reservations required. AE, DC, MC, V. Open only for pre-ordered dinner and events.

Sangeh Monkey Forest   Spend a morning north of Tabanan (or a 30-minute ride from Denpasar) on 7 hectares (17 acres) of land surrounding the 17th-century **Pura Bukit Sari** temple, set within groves of nutmeg trees. The majority of the monkeys here are macaques, ranging from babies to larger 10-kg (22-lbs.) adults. Keep a firm grip on your jewelry, glasses, and toupee as the mischievous residents are adept at snatching any object that isn't tied down and will laugh in your face while they're at it.

Jl. Imam Bonjol. © **0361/235600.** Admission Rp20,000. 24 hr.

Taman Kupu Kupu (Bali Butterfly Park)   Billed as the largest butterfly park in Asia, this preserve is best seen in the early morning when the butterflies arise and take flight. The park promotes the study, breeding, and preservation of more than 300 species of butterflies found in Indonesia and is home to the rare birdwing butterfly. If your children are budding entomologists this is a great opportunity to further their interests. It's 7km (4 miles) north of Tabanan on the way to Penebel.

Jl. Batukaru, Sandan Wanasari. © **0361/814282.** www.balibutterflypark.co.cc (in Indonesian). Admission Rp30,000. Daily 8am–5pm; last entry 4pm.

Where to Stay
EXPENSIVE

Alila Villas Soori ★★★   Despite being in western Bali, this new villa resort is within a 1-hour drive from the restaurant and bar scene of Seminyak. And being in such remoteness is certainly worthwhile, with pristine Art-Deco villas set on a black-sand beach framed by palm trees. The units come with plenty of indoor and outdoor lounging spaces, not to mention a plunge pool that snakes around your room, a spacious bathtub, and an Apple TV unit stocked with movies and music. A beautiful restaurant serving modern "comfort food" by former Jean-Georges chef Ashton Hall, and a large pool, yoga classes, horse riding, and even Segway tours give you plenty of recreational options, although you might never leave the comfort of your superb villa.

Banjar Dukuh, Desa Kelating, Kerambitan, Tabanan. www.alilahotels.com. © **0361/894-6388.** Fax 0361/8946377. 44 units. Year-round US$600 beach villa; US$650 rice terrace villa; US$750 ocean villa; US$1,200–US$1,500 1- to 4-bedroom villas; US$10,000 10-bedroom residence. Rates may or may not include breakfast and taxes. AE, MC, V. **Amenities:** 2 restaurants; infinity pool; spa; bikes; massage. *In room:* A/C, TV, hair dryer, fridge, minibar, MP3 docking station, Wi-Fi (free).

Pan Pacific Nirwana Golf Spa & Resort ★ This is the place to go if you're looking for a fairway to heaven. The luxurious rooms in this five-star resort sit in lush landscaped gardens and rice terraces surrounding the massive swimming pools. Rooms offer spectacular ocean views and villas have plunge pools and butler service. Sunset dinners with views of the Tanah Lot are a highlight—and possibly one of the best ways to see the temple. The golf course (see above) has spectacular ocean views, rice fields as bunkers, and four sets of tees. There's a clubhouse, shops, a driving range, spa, and massage and drink service. The Nautilus Pizzeria and Pub is great for snooker, darts, karaoke, or cheering on your team at a sporting event with a cold draft in hand.

Jl. Raya Tanah Lot, Tabanan. www.panpacific.com/bali. ☎ **0361/815900.** Fax 0361/815901. 278 units. High season US$180–US$650; low season US$150–US$620. AE, DC, MC, V. **Amenities:** 4 restaurants; 2 bars; babysitting; bikes; children's club; concierge; golf course; gym; Internet (for a fee); Jacuzzi; outdoor pool; room service; spa; tennis court. *In room/villa:* A/C, TV/DVD, movie library, stereo or CD, hair dryer, minibar.

Villa Devatas ★ This majestic villa is low-key luxury. The stunning five-bedroom estate is set in immaculate tropical gardens with a river and rainforest at the property edge. Facilities include a pool with Jacuzzi, an air-conditioned game and media room, a spa, and an air-conditioned gym. Bathrooms are spacious with indoor and outdoor showers, fluffy towels, and Bulgari amenities.

Jl. Raya Tabanan, Cepaka. www.bali-villadevatas.com. ☎ **081/353021188.** 1 unit (5 bedroom). Peak season US$1,250 and up; high season US$800–US$1,200; low season US$650–US$1,100; extra guest US$50. Rates include breakfast, and exclude taxes. AE, MC, V. **Amenities:** Bar; babysitting; gym; Jacuzzi; 2 outdoor pools; room service; spa; Wi-Fi (US$5/24 hr.). *In villa:* A/C, fan, TV/DVD, movie library, minibar.

MODERATE

Kembang Desa Luxury Beach Villas About 30 minutes north of Tanah Lot, these four luxury villas are spread over 3 hectares (7 acres) of land with the feeling of a grand estate overlooking rice fields on one side and beach views on the other. The light, whitewashed wooden villas are tastefully decorated. The pool has special fiber-optic lighting that re-creates a "stars in the sky" effect.

Jl. Pantai Klecung, Tabanan. www.balikembangdesavillas.com. ☎ **0361/742-3964.** 4 units. High season US$550–US$1,750 low season US$490–US$1500. Rates exclude taxes. No credit cards. **Amenities:** Restaurant; bikes; outdoor pool; room service; spa. *In villa:* A/C, TV/DVD, movie library, stereo or CD, hair dryer, minibar, MP3 docking station, Wi-Fi (free).

Waka Gangga ★ ☺ 👜 Despite the simplicity of this resort—no TVs—you'll be spoiled by a soul-pampering spa, cozy canopy beds, and amazing views. The formula here is about reviving the spiritual self with the natural energy of the Indian Ocean and mountains. Activities include horse rides on the beach and to Pura Tanah Lot; catamaran sailing; bicycling around local villages; and Land Cruiser tours. The pool and restaurant are on Yeh Gangga beach. The individual lanais are charming and atmospheric with king-size beds, sunken bathtubs, and a garden shower. All the lanais have views, but go for one of the northernmost ones because they edge the lovely rice paddies that you can soak in from your deck. Children will have plenty of room to run around, cots are free, and babysitting is available.

Yeh Gangga, Tabanan. www.wakagangga.com. ☎ **0361/484085.** 10 units. Year-round US$230 US$470. Breakfast included in villa only. Rates include taxes. AE, DC, MC, V. **Amenities:** Restaurant; bar; outdoor pool; room service; spa. *In room:* A/C, fan, fridge, hair dryer, minibar.

INEXPENSIVE

Dewi Sinta Restaurant & Villa   Near the ticket office to Tanah Lot is this mid-range hotel with 27 comfortable and modern rooms dotted along a descending terrace. The open hall is a popular stage for cultural dances (such as the *kecak* or *legong*) performed for large tourist groups. You might be lucky enough to catch one during your stay.

Pura Tanah Lot, Tabanan. www.indo.com/hotels/dewisinta. (C) **0361/812933.** 27 units. High season US$26–US$48; low season US$18–US$40. Rates include breakfast and taxes. MC, V. **Amenities:** Restaurant; bikes; outdoor pool; room service. *In room:* A/C, TV, minibar.

Puri Taman Sari Hotel   Near the Margarana monument, in coconut groves and rice fields, this traditional Balinese compound is owned by a member of the royal family of Mengwi. It offers classes in cooking, dance, and gamelan. Bikes are also available and there are some nice walks in the area.

Umabian, Desa Peken, Kecamatan Marga. www.balitamansari.com. (C) **0361/742-1165.** 16 units. High season US$70–US$115; low season US$55–US$100. Breakfast extra. Rates include taxes. MC, V. **Amenities:** Restaurant; bikes; outdoor pool; room service. *In room/villa:* A/C, TV, Wi-Fi (in rooms only).

Where to Eat

Aside from the restaurants in the hotels, on the main road in the heart of Tabanan town is **Warung Nasi Andi Jaya** where there's a painted sign of a pig on the outside but no signage with the name. Just ask anyone where it is. It serves delicious, freshly roasted pork all day long at around Rp15,000 to Rp25,000 per dish. Several other warungs are also along the main road; a night market is on the south side of town.

TABANAN TO NEGARA

Following the coast to Negara to the far west are nice views but little tourist development except for the surf colonies at **Balian** and **Medewi.** Go northward from **Antosari** and you'll pass waterfalls at **Pujungan,** south of Pupuan: It's a walk of a couple of kilometers to two falls, one 50m (164 ft.) in height. This road takes you through rice paddies and spice trees and descends into coffee plantations to **Pupuan.** The other alternative is to drive north via **Pulukan** to Pupuan. This steep and scenic road also goes through spice-growing areas and then at about 10km (6 miles) before **Manggissari,** the winding road leads you through a **Bunut Bolong,** a huge ficus tree with a tunnel in it.

Because points west of Tanah Lot are infrequently visited by tourists, accommodations and dining are sparse and not up to the standards of the more developed areas of Bali. You will, however, encounter dozens of inexpensive homestays and basic bungalows for backpackers and surfers. We've selected accommodations with five or more rooms or cottages that offer ocean or mountain vistas. Bring snacks and picnic supplies.

Balian

This beach that is known for sharks is past Tabanan, 1½ hours west of Denpasar. Don't turn left at the first surfboard sign coming into town—it leads to the beach and nowhere else; carry on and take a left up the hill after crossing the bridge. This brings you to the hillside offering views to assess the waves and numerous homestays and warungs. The classic **Balian wave** (**best season:** dry Apr–Oct; **best swell:**

south-southwest; **best size:** 3–5 ft.; **best winds:** east-northeast) is a left to the north of the river mouth, but the right off the other side can get good too. Just watch out coming in on this side on lower tides as the shore break can be surprisingly heavy. Crowds can be pretty thin up this way.

WHERE TO STAY & EAT

Gajah Mina Beach Resort ★   Located near Lalang Linggah village, this cozy little resort overlooking a white sand beach is an affordable getaway for both singles and families. The stone cottages have local antiques and comfortable furniture hand-selected by the owner. The restaurant caters to the primarily European clientele and offers a mix of simple Thai and Indonesian fare and a limited but well selected wine list. The best feature is the tourist-free beach. The famous surf break at Balian is a 10-minute walk from the resort. Natural caves and ancient stone carvings offer romantic walks on cliff tops, headlands, coconut groves, and deserted beaches nearby. The resort also serves as a yoga retreat and prepares *jamu* (healing Indonesian concoctions from local plants) and vegetarian meals.

Suraberata, Lalang Linggah, Selemadeg, Tabanan. www.gajahminaresort.com. ✆ **081/23811630** or 081/934355633**.** Fax 0361/731174. 11 units. High season US$120–US$240; low season US$110–US$220. Rates exclude 21% taxes. MC, V. **Amenities:** Restaurant; airport transfer; babysitting; bikes; outdoor pool; room service; spa; watersports, Wi-Fi. *In room:* A/C, TV, minibar.

Pondok Pisces ★   The owners of this resort, who run arguably the friendliest resort in the Balian beach area, live on the property and the staff reflects the hospitality of the owners. The eclectic mix of bungalows with beach and river views are each decorated with individual flavor. There's no air-conditioning, but ocean breezes and fans are all that's needed for comfort. The restaurant serves respectable European and local fare.

Balian Beach, Banjar Pengasahan, Lalang Linggah. www.pondokpiscesbali.com. ✆ **0361/780-1735.** 5 units. High season Rp560,000–Rp990,000; low season Rp510,000–Rp900,000. Rates include breakfast and taxes. AE, MC, V. **Amenities:** Restaurant; cafe; babysitting; room service. *In room:* Fan, TV/DVD, movie library, fridge.

Shankaris   Located on Suraberata beach, about 2 hours from the airport, Shankaris, formerly the Sacred River Retreat, caters to wellness Sybarites interested in yoga, health food, and spiritual studies. The resort has well-appointed, single- and two-story villas, a vegetarian restaurant, yoga retreat, and pool overlooking the beach. Perfect for the New Age crowd, it hosts equinox solstice celebrations, drumming circles, crystal healing, and moon rituals. The Ganesha waterfall cave is a special treat for those interested in communing with the happiest of all Hindu deities.

Jl. Denpasar, Gilimanuk, Subrata, Selamadeg Barat. www.shankarisbaliretreat.com. ✆ **0361/814993.** Fax 0361/814992. 13 units. Year-round US$48–US$72. MC, V. **Amenities:** Restaurant; cafe; lounge; outdoor pool; room service; Wi-Fi (for a fee). *In room:* A/C, TV.

Villa Zolima ★★ ☺   It's a 5-minute drive to Balian surfer beach and 10 minutes to Soka beach with its fishermen, fresh lobster, and fish from these luxurious yet understated villas. The modern tropical structures have infinity pools looking over rice fields and the ocean. Children will be in heaven in large expansive playing fields, on the trampoline, and in the adorable Swiss Family Robinson-style tree house complete with child-size furniture. The helpful villa manager greets you on arrival and a chef cooks for you and handles the grocery shopping. Most fruit and veg come from the on-site organic garden. And, it's only an hour's drive from Seminyak.

Joged Bumbung: The Local Gamelan Music & Dance

Northwest Bali is known for gamelan *Joged Bumbung* ★★, played on about 15 bamboo instruments that produce mellow, haunting, soothing tones and vibrations that can be felt by the body as much as by the ears. Some of the bamboo instruments are so large that musicians sit on them and play them with large mallets. The best ensemble to watch is the **Jegog Mebarung** where two or more orchestras try to out-perform one another.

Lalang Linggah. www.villazolima.com. ✆ **0361/759668.** 4 bedrooms. Peak season US$1,000; high season US$800; low season US$600. Rates include car with driver, breakfast, afternoon tea, and first lunch or dinner, and taxes. MC, V. **Amenities:** Airport transfer (free), babysitting; outdoor pool; room service; spa therapy; Wi-Fi (free). *In room:* A/C, fan.

Medewi

After a 2½-hour drive from Kuta, a long way from the main Bali surf hub, look for the sign to **Pantai Medewi** (**best season:** dry Apr–Oct; **best swell:** south; **best size:** 4–6 ft.; **best winds:** light winds only), with its old school Bali surfing environment. Its "fatter" left waves and rippable walls are preferred by long-boarders. Barrels are rare. Bring reef-boots as the rocks are sharp, the entrance to the break is difficult, and there's an abundance of sea urchins. This area is for serious surfers and not great for swimming. Go early before the winds pick up or venture out with a calm forecast in hand. Medewi is rarely crowded because few choose to make the drive. If you like surfing uncrowded waves with friendly locals and visitors, Medewi might just be your place on the Island of the Gods.

Pura Luhur at Rambut Siwi This is another 16th-century temple related to the history of Nirartha. Rambut Siwi means "worship of the hair." Legend has it that Nirartha gifted a lock of his hair that's stored in one of the three enclosures. The stunning cliff overlooks a long, wide stretch of beach and is between the villages of Air Satang and Yeh Embang, at the end of a 300-m (100-ft.) long side road. Look for the sign at the turn-off near the warungs.

Rp2,000 sarong rental, Rp10,000 recommended donation. Daily 7am–5pm.

WHERE TO STAY & EAT

Medewi Beach Cottages These cottages are ideal for surfers looking for high and long rolling waves and are lovely for those looking for serenity in rugged mountainous surrounds. The spacious cottages come with all the bells and whistles, a large and attractive pool area, and a bar and restaurant.

Pantai Medewi. www.medewibeachcottages.com. ✆ **0361/852521.** 20 units. High season US$87–US$114; low season US$75–US$102. AE, MC, V. **Amenities:** Restaurant; bar; airport transfers; outdoor pool; room service. *In room:* A/C, TV, fridge.

Puri Dajuma Cottages ★ Travelers headed to Gilimanuk will enjoy an overnight here, the halfway point. You'll be perfectly situated to explore both coastal Bali and the rarely visited mountain villages of Asah Duren and Manggissari, where cloves and *kopi* (coffee) are the staple crops. The spacious, comfortable cottages (all with ocean views) are a 2km (1¼ miles) walk from Medewi beach. The resort is family friendly, with a wading pool for the youngest of the bunch. The restaurant serves simple European and local dishes and a wide selection of vegetables and fruit organically grown in its own gardens.

Pekutatan, Negara. www.dajuma.com. ✆ **0365/43955.** 18 units. Year-round US$165–US$276. MC, V. **Amenities:** Restaurant; bar; bikes; Jacuzzi; outdoor pool and wading pool; room service; spa. *In room:* A/C, TV, hair dryer, minibar.

NEGARA & AROUND

Negara is a quiet district capital that comes to life during the famous **bull races (Makpung)** in early August. Until recently, buffalo were simply a means of transportation but now they pull decorated mini-carriages in races in and around Perancak (see below). The race developed in the 1930s. The jockeys dress in traditional clothing with vests, scarves, and krises (swords). Carts are decorated in full regalia and the bulls pull them around the 2km (1¼-mile) course. Teams are divided by the river, Ljo Gading, that divides the two townships; team names are Timur (East) and Barat (West). In the Magembeng, an affiliated race for the female cows, cows can run 100m (328 ft.) in 9 seconds, with their cow bell (*gembeng*) ringing. However, style and elegance count as much as their speed.

Watch bull race practice every Sunday morning on the black sand beach Delod Berawan, which used to be home to hunted crocodiles. (Curiously enough, it's said that this sand cures rheumatism.) Mendoyo, to the north, hosts some of the best races on Bali. Get race dates from the **Bali Tourism Board** in Denpasar (✆ **0361/ 223602**). Like all things in Bali, take the start times with a grain of sand.

While in Negara, visit with the local **palm sugar farmer** in his small farm in Palasari to observe how this buttery brown sweet is harvested and processed. He also grows and processes cacao fruit that's dried, ground, and shipped to chocolate manufacturers. Book this tour through the Taman Wana resort (see below). Simply tip the staff from Taman Wana who will help you find the farm. Give a donation to the farmer—he'll be pleasantly surprised.

A few banks, ATMs, a post office, hospital, police station, petrol station, and Hardy's supermarket make this a good place to stop for supplies.

Exploring Negara

PERANCAK   Nirartha arrived here in 1546 where a limestone temple, **Pura Gede Perancak,** was built in commemoration. Bull races take place at **Taman Wisata Perancak** park (✆ **0365/42173**) with occasional runs for prearranged tour groups.

In Perancak village, you can visit the community-run turtle conservation program, **Kurma Asih** or **Turtle Lovers Group** (Rp25,000). It aims to save the overhunted turtles. Join the effort and "adopt a nest." See if you can set a baby turtle free and share the joy as he takes his first stroke in the water. Nearby are beautiful Madurese-style fishing boats in Perancak Bay.

LOLOAN TIMUR   Small traditional *jukung* and sampans sail quietly up the river toward this unique Bali village south of Negara, home to a Muslim Bugis community that preserves 300-year-old traditions. Most are descendants of sailors from Sulawesi who used to be pirates and settled here at the end of the 17th century. A large mosque is in the center and Bugis-style stilt houses are in the area.

BELIMBINGSARI & PALASARI ★★   The Dutch exiled Christians to the far west in 1939 after attempting to convert the local Hindus and causing religious unrest in east Bali. Visit the **Catholic** (in Belimbingsari) and **Protestant** (in Palasari) **churches** that are monuments to Balinese, Hindu, and European design and ornamentation. The local pastors will happily show you the churches and various building projects in progress. Their Christian practice has a distinct Balinese Hindu influence.

Cekik & Gilimanuk

Cekik, on the far west coast near to Gilimanuk, is, known as the entrance to Bali's only national park, **Taman Nasional Bali Barat (West Bali National Park).** People who want to start an early trek in the park have limited options in places to stay. Try the **Hotel Lestari** (✆ 0365/61504) for between Rp150,000 and Rp350,000 or **Hotel Sari** (✆ 0365/61264) for Rp150,000.

On the way to Gilimanuk, visit the **Jayaprana Grave.** It may be a hot hike up but the views are stunning. The grave is revered by the Balinese, who remember the sad outcome of a typical 17th-century love story here (king covets beautiful woman who loves the king's adopted son; king has son killed; beautiful woman commits suicide).

In the 1960s, archaeological excavations nearby revealed the oldest evidence of human life on Bali with figures ranging, depending on your sources, from about 3,000 to 4,000 years old. Bronze jewelry, axes, pottery, and funerary offerings are on display at the **Museum Situs Purbakala Gilimanuk** (✆ 0365/61328; admission Rp5,000 donation; Mon–Fri 8am–4pm), 500m (1,640 ft.) south of the ferry port, and it's well worth spending the money to visit. Gilimanuk is the main port for the 24-hour ferry service to Banyuwangi in East Java. No Balinese would pass through Gilimanuk without enjoying the explosive *ayam betutu* chicken dish served at the famous **Mem Tempe** warung at the top of the steps behind the little bus terminal.

Where to Stay

Taman Wana Villas & Spa ★★ 🎒   Tucked away in the hills of Palasari, 30km (19 miles) from Bali's west coast, this luxury resort caters to visitors primarily from Europe seeking a total escape. The resort sits atop a hillside overlooking the Palasari reservoir, rice terraces, and in the distance the Java Sea. The comfortable rooms are well appointed. The restaurant has a limited menu but serves vegetables and fruits from the resort's organic gardens. Start the day hiking and biking through the nearby Palasari and Belimbingsari villages in the early morning. Staff members are happy to show you around, or you can take the golf carts on a guided tour.

Jl. Taman Wana, Palasari, Negara. www.bali-tamanwana-villas.com. ✆ **0365/470-2208.** Fax 0365/470-2209. 27 units. Peak season US$185–US$360 standard, US$1,035 suite; high season US$170–US$345 standard, US$1,020 suite; low season US$150–US$325 standard, US$1,000 suite; extra bed US$35. DC, MC, V. **Amenities:** Restaurant; bar; babysitting; bikes; Jacuzzi; outdoor pool; room service; spa. *In room:* A/C, TV/DVD, movie library, hair dryer, minibar.

Where to Eat

As you move along the south coast to the west the local fare becomes spicier. If you like your goat satay dipped in five-alarm chili you'll love eating along the southern coast. In Negara, the tidy little **Café Nathalia,** Jl. Ngurah Rai 107 (✆ **0365/41161;** main courses Rp45,000–Rp90,000; MC, V; daily 11am–10pm), in the Wira Prada Hotel, is best known for its spicy Chinese food but also has some of the best *nasi* *goreng* (fried rice) and fried Indonesian noodle dishes on the southern coast. Follow your meal with a cup of high-octane local coffee. **Rumah Makan Puas**, Jl. Ngurah Rai 60 (*©* **0365/41618;** main courses Rp40,000–Rp80,000; no credit cards; daily 11am–10pm), just 100m (328 ft.), from the Wira Prada hotel, is best known for its twice-cooked spicy chicken—surprisingly tender given that it's grilled and then fried.

TAMAN NASIONAL BALI BARAT (WEST BALI NATIONAL PARK) ★

The Taman Nasional Bali Barat (West Bali National Park) is teeming with wildlife unseen in east Bali. This is your chance to see a Varanus salvator monitor lizard devouring violet crabs or a long-tailed macaque making off with your hat and sunglasses. The only indigenous animal you won't see is the Balinese tiger—hunted to extinction in the 1930s. Its smaller cousin, the clouded leopard, still roams these forests.

West Bali National Park comprises 770 sq. km (300 sq. miles) of forest, 1,000m (3,300 ft.) of pristine beach, and outlying islands with some of the best diving and snorkeling in Indonesia. The park is surrounded by privately owned plantations and forests, which provide a buffer zone for the park's 200-plus animal species to wander and forage freely. Within the park's boundaries are savanna, monsoon forest, arid volcanic slopes, coral islands, and mangrove swamps. The volcanic peak **Gunung Patas** dominates the park at an elevation of 1,412m (4,632 ft.).

The park is well known as the last refuge of one of the rarest birds on earth, the Bali starling. Unfortunately, the only way to see this endangered bird is in captivity where they're being bred and released. If you're a birder, take the 2-hour walk along the beautiful **Tegal Bunder trail** to see a variety of local species such as kingfishers, sunbirds, hornbills, orioles, and the ever-present yellow vented bul-bul. Birding is best done in the early morning between 6 and 8am. Bring binoculars. You'll see a variety of monkeys, including the ubiquitous long-tailed macaque and the beautiful ebony langur. Several deer species, such as barking deer and large red stags, inhabit the park and the surrounding area. Visit the **Bali Starling Pre-Release Centre** (Rp50,000; daily 8am–3pm). Here the Bali myna or jalak putih birds are being raised and saved from extinction in the wild, though there are many in captivity around the world. Ask for directions at the park office in Labuan Lalang.

Menjangan Island ★★ has what are possibly Bali's best dive sites. The waters are calm and clear except in January and February when the sea is rough and windblown. The coral reef walls off Menjangan teem with angelfish, anthias, butterfly fish, and gobies. Swimming with green turtles is a highlight—your guide will know where to find them. Qualified dive shops attached to the resorts in Pemuteran (p. 263) can outfit and transport you to your chosen dive destination. Snorkeling is particularly rewarding in and around Menjangan as the waters are clear and the currents gentle.

An extremely untidy harbor is the starting point for boats to Menjangan. If you're not going through a local dive operator or hotel, expect to pay around Rp330,000 for the boat plus an extra Rp150,000 per person to cover park and guide fees for the island, insurance, and snorkel gear. Pleasant and knowledgeable English-speaking guides will be happy to take you on a day snorkeling trip to the island or to see other less frequented parts of the park. If you're not interested in water activities other than

For viewing wildlife in the park, have your guide take you to a water hole where a variety of local wildlife gathers in the early evenings to take their fill before retiring.

to cool off, just pack a picnic, towels, lots of sun cream, hats, and take the boat to Menjangan anyway. Explore the island, swim, and visit **Pura Gili Kancana,** one of Bali's oldest and most revered temples.

FISHING   One of the locals can take you out for a combined fishing and snorkeling trip to the offshore reefs. Bring sun block and a picnic with plenty of beverages packed in ice. These narrow dugouts provide an invigorating downwind sail if the winds are above 5 knots. Cost is typically Rp200,000 to Rp250,000 per day. Arrange boats at the Labuan Lalang park office.

HORSEBACK RIDING   Contact The Menjangan (see below) for riding in and around the park. The cost for 1½ hours of riding is US$30, including a guide.

SCUBA DIVING & SNORKELING   A number of qualified dive centers are along the beach at Pemuteran (p. 263), the best being Kuta-based **Archipelago Dive Sarana** (℃/fax **0361/287666**) and Nusa Dua-based **Yos Diving** (℃ **0361/773774;** fax 0361/775439; www.yosdive.com). Two island dives cost US$150, including lunch.

    Menjangan Island, part of West Bali National Park, was Bali's first internationally known diving location. Famous for wall-diving with easy conditions, Menjangan is 30 minutes from mainland Bali and offers warm waters, white sand, and visibility that can reach 50m (164 ft.) plus. Between 1997 and 1998, Menjangan's reef flats not only suffered from a population explosion of the coral-eating crown of thorns starfish, but also from coral bleaching as a result of El Niño; the walls, however, were unaffected. These walls start at 10m (33 ft.) and descend to 26 to 60m (85–197 ft.); they're full of nooks and crannies, overhangs, and crevasses, and covered with Bali's highest concentration of gorgonian fans as well as soft corals and sponges. The fish life is prolific and you may see turtles. Although you can occasionally see whale sharks, there are only rare sightings of pelagics around Menjangan as the island is protected from the cold ocean currents. Various dive sites circle the island: the main three are **Garden Eel Point, Pos Two,** and **Anker Wreck,** which lies at 35 to 50m (115–164 ft.), though the calm conditions and good visibility can make it easy to forget that this is a deep dive.

    Secret Bay (aka Gilimanuk Bay) was Bali's first and so best-known **muck dive.** At 2km (1¼ miles) wide, 3 to 12m (10–39 ft.) deep, this is the only bay off the narrow Bali Strait (currents reach 7 knots) and acts as a large catch tank for many larval and juvenile fish and rare marine species. The water is cold and the fish fat and healthy. You can see unusual nudis, Banggai cardinalfish, gobies, Ambon scorpionfish, filefish, puffers, dragonets, seahorse and pipefish, juvenile Batavia batfish, and many other organisms. Elsewhere juveniles hide to avoid predators, but here in Gilimanuk there are very few large fish, leaving the juveniles with no need to hide. The bottom is fine sand with patches of algae and sea grass, some branches, and coconuts (housing for many octopi). Night-diving yields Bobbit worms, cephalopods, wandering crustaceans, and frequent surprises.

Taman Nasional Bali Barat & Gilimanuk

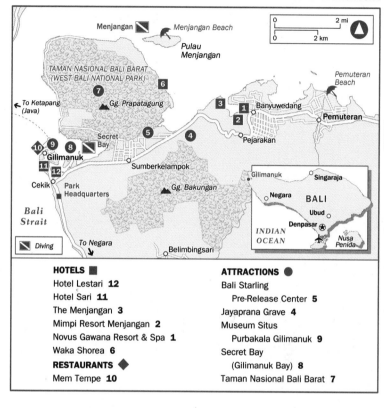

HOTELS ■
Hotel Lestari **12**
Hotel Sari **11**
The Menjangan **3**
Mimpi Resort Menjangan **2**
Novus Gawana Resort & Spa **1**
Waka Shorea **6**

RESTAURANTS ◆
Mem Tempe **10**

ATTRACTIONS ●
Bali Starling
  Pre-Release Center **5**
Jayaprana Grave **4**
Museum Situs
  Purbakala Gilimanuk **9**
Secret Bay
  (Gilimanuk Bay) **8**
Taman Nasional Bali Barat **7**

TREKKING   It's not possible to enter and explore the park alone. You can choose from 2-, 4-, or 7-hour treks through the park. The bird walk normally takes 2 hours. The 4-hour trek is a leisurely passage through the foothills and the 7-hour trek is a rigorous hike to the slopes of Mount Klatakan. During the dry season it's possible to obtain an overnight camping permit. Bring mosquito repellant and netting for your overnight stay. All tours must be guided by locals who charge the following:

2-hour trek: Rp150,000 for one to two persons; Rp250,000 for three to five people.
4-hour trek: Rp200,000 for one or two persons; Rp300,000 for three to five people.
7-hour trek: Rp400,000 for one or two persons; Rp500,000 for three to five people.
Overnight camping guiding fees range from Rp800,000 to Rp1,175,000 for four people.

Guides can be booked at the park center in Cekik near Gilimanuk but there's more chance of finding someone who speaks English at the Labuan Lalang harbor office. Discuss and arrange a trek personally with one of the guides the day before. Because of the heat, try to start early in the morning.

Where to Stay & Eat

Although it's possible to dive or snorkel at Menjangan Island on a day trip from south Bali, because it's 3½ hours by road plus a short boat ride, it's much better to stay overnight.

The Menjangan ★★ 🎁 📷 This nature-lover's paradise and well-kept secret inside the National Park is a favorite among the local expat community due to its remote location on "the other side of Bali." The resort sits among 362 hectares (895 acres) of forest and has a beach that looks onto the Menjangan Island. Stay in the forested area at Monsoon Lodge—where the rooms were recently renovated with modern furniture—or in one of the new sleek beachfront villas. The resort has a stable of 30 horses from Australia, a yacht for day cruises, and indigenous wildlife including deer, wild boar, and amazing bird life. Take a day and nighttime safari in an open-air jeep. Dine on Indonesian or Western fare at the amazing five-story **Bali Tower Bankirai Restaurant ★★★** constructed from 28-m (92-ft.) long logs from Kalimantan.

In West Bali National Park. Jl. Raya Gilimanuk-Singaraja, Km 17, Desa Pejarakan-Buleleng. www.menjangan resort.com. ✆ **0362/94700.** Fax 0362/94708. 23 units. High season US$190–US$290 standard, US$650 villa; low season US$150–US$200 standard, US$550 villa. Rates include breakfast. MC, V. **Amenities:** Restaurant; cafe; bar; bikes; Jacuzzi; outdoor pool; room service; spa; watersports; Wi-Fi (free). *In room/villa:* A/C, fan, TV/DVD, hair dryer, minibar.

Mimpi Resort Menjangen ★ This resort makes a great base for diving, muck diving, and snorkeling excursions in the west due to its on-site PADI dive center. There's a large swimming pool in the gardens and there are also hot spring pools. The standard rooms are simple but the large, more expensive villas have private gardens and plunge pools. Some of the villas have an outside bathtub that can be filled with sulfurous water directly from the nearby hot springs.

Banyuwedang. www.mimpi.com. ✆ **0362/94497.** Fax 0362/94498. 54 units. High season US$145 standard, US$265 villa; low season US$120 standard, US$240 villa. AE, MC, V. **Amenities:** Restaurant; bar; babysitting; bikes; concierge; Internet (for a fee); outdoor pool; room service; spa; watersports. *In room/villa:* A/C, TV, hair dryer; minibar.

Novus Gawana Resort & Spa Just next door to Mimpi, the rooms here are *lumbung* (traditional rice barn) style and the bedrooms, built into the roof, are reached by a wooden staircase. The swimming pool and restaurant overlook the mangrove bay and the national park beyond. This resort also has its own PADI dive facilities.

Banyuwedang. www.novusgawana.com. ✆ **0362/94598.** Fax 0362/94598. 16 villas. High season US$267–US$349; low season US$243–US$324. Rates exclude taxes and breakfast. MC, V. **Amenities:** Restaurant; bar; outdoor pool; room service; spa; Wi-Fi (for a fee). *In room:* A/C, fan, stereo or CD, hair dryer, minibar.

Waka Shorea ★ In the West Bali National Park just across from Menjangan Island and a short 20-minute boat ride away from Labuan Lalang harbor, this outpost of the Waka chain is set on a private peninsula on the white coral beach. Most of the rustic rooms are very pleasant and nothing if not relaxing.

Jl. Raya Seririt Km 15, Gilimanuk. www.wakaexperience.com. ✆ **0362/94499.** Fax 0362/94666. 16 units. Year-round US$185–US$285. AE, MC, V. **Amenities:** Restaurant; bar; babysitting; Internet (for a fee); outdoor pool; room service. *In room:* A/C, fan.

LOMBOK

A traditional local saying goes "You can see Bali in Lombok, but you can't see Lombok in Bali!" Lombok is ignored by Bali, but Lombok doesn't ignore Bali; and there are beautiful views of Bali's Mount Agung from Lombok. Bali and Lombok are often called "sister islands," in which case Lombok is the shy and beautiful younger sister, often overshadowed by her glamorous older sibling. Lombok is often referred to as the "Bali, 20 years ago" and certainly many of the features that make Bali so appealing to visitors also exist on Lombok, and yet the island is also a unique and fascinating destination in its own right.

Lombok has a rich and diverse culture, which blends the traditions of the indigenous Sasak people with Balinese Hindu and Arabic influences, to name a few. Many of Lombok's traits and customs are similar to those of Java and Bali, yet its people retain traditions and beliefs unique to the island, particularly in language, cultural performances, celebrations, and the arts. Village life is based on the mainstays of farming and traditional handicraft production. The Sasak people are friendly and relatively unaffected by tourism, with a warm tradition of hospitality to visitors.

At around 5,300 sq. km (2,046 sq. miles), Lombok is only slightly smaller than Bali. The pace on Lombok is unhurried and the atmosphere laid-back; the beaches are uncrowded and tourism enclaves aren't marred by high-density development. Although the island has good infrastructure, tourism development only started in the 1990s and it has had a slow, steady growth rather than a gold-rush expansion since then.

The new airport that opened in 2011 is going to alter dramatically the fortunes of southern Lombok—traditionally the island's poorer region. It has heralded a new development spurt as real-estate speculators have flooded in. Plans are underway to develop a stretch of pristine beach in Lombok's south into a complex of international five-star resorts, similar to the Nusa Dua development in Bali, and the whole of the south is set to undergo a huge building boom. Don't expect the Lombok you see today to be the same one you'll see a decade from now.

LOMBOK IN DEPTH
A Brief History of Lombok

The indigenous Sasak people of Lombok are descendents of a Malay race who have inhabited Lombok for at least 2,000 years. As part of the Indonesian archipelago, Java has influenced Lombok to varying degrees,

BEST LOMBOK experiences

Climbing Gunung Rinjani Demanding, frustrating, yet hugely rewarding, the climb up Mount Rinjani is a highlight of any visit to Lombok. If a climb up a 3,726-m (12,224-ft.) high volcano is too daunting, treks through the lush forests of the Rinjani National Park have their own rewards. See p. 317.

Heading to the Gili Islands Needing no introduction, the famous islands of Gili Air, Gili Meno, and Gili Trawangan—collectively known as the Gilis—are the only destination for many travelers to Lombok. Three archetypal coral islands, surrounded by white sands, palm trees, and clear turquoise waters also have no cars, and hence no traffic or pollution. See chapter 15.

Sunning & Surfing in the Southwest & South Coasts Few places in Indonesia have such a stunningly beautiful vista as the south coast of Lombok. This is where the island meets the Indian Ocean, and its endless rhythms have carved a series of magnificent beaches, bays, peninsulas, cliffs, and inlets into the shoreline. The climate lends itself to days wandering uncrowded beaches, sunbathing on the white sands, and swimming in calm bays. For the adventurous, the south coast is also the surfing mecca of this part of Indonesia. See p. 305 and 308.

Relaxing in Senggigi Although Senggigi, the main beach resort in the west of the island, makes the perfect base for exploring the rest of Lombok, it's easy to just choose one of the beautiful resort hotels and spend your days here instead. The beaches are gorgeous, the resort luxurious. See p. 298.

Catching a Local Festival Lombok's population is a mixture of Sasak Muslims, Balinese Hindus, Chinese Buddhists, and more; festivals and special events are held most any time of the

conquering and incorporating the island into the Majapahit Empire in the 14th century. Today's Sasak aristocracy still claims Javanese ancestry.

The Balinese colonized Lombok in the 18th century, ruling the island for 150 years until 1894. The influence of Bali has always centered in the west, where Balinese still constitute at least 10% of the population. The last king of Lombok reigned over western Lombok during the mid-1800s and oversaw the construction of an impressive number of temples. He also restricted the land rights of the Sasak aristocracy, introduced an inflexible taxation system, and demanded forced labor of Sasak peasantry. The Sasak revolted several times in the 19th century, with Islam the unifying factor among the armies scattered and isolated across the island.

Sasak leaders approached the Dutch for help in overthrowing the Balinese in the early 1890s. The Dutch, mistakenly believing that Lombok was rich in tin, obliged and the Sasak War broke out in 1894. The Balinese were soundly defeated and many of their temples and palaces were destroyed.

Over the centuries, Lombok has been populated by migrants from Java and other Indonesian islands, particularly Bugis shipbuilders and seafarers from Sulawesi. As part of the historical Spice Islands, Arab traders, Chinese, and Dutch all made their homes in Lombok and thus the island has become a melting pot of religions, cultures, beliefs, and ceremonies.

The majority of the population today practices a moderate form of Islam, which is still changing and evolving with the impact of modernization and education. Most year. Don't miss the **Bau Nyale Festival** (p. 310) in February or March. In July, the **Senggigi Festival** is a wonderful whirl of color, culture, and sound. In October, **Perang Topat** (p. 295) at Lingsar Temple is a fascinating ritual and hilarious local fun. Catch a *gendang beleq* performance—unique to Lombok (p. 286); watch elegant Sasak *tari* dancing, with colorful and dramatic costumes; or ask a local to take you to see a traditional *nyongkolan* wedding procession in the villages, with the beautifully dressed bride and groom parading down the street accompanied by dancing crowds and the weirdly hypnotic, wailing *kecimol* (p. 286) music.

Buying Local Handicrafts Quite a few of the crafts for sale on Bali come from the villages of Lombok and so those you see here are a fraction of the price on Bali. Lombok **pottery** is exported throughout the world. Distinctive designs in terra cotta and earthenware are hand-thrown in the small villages, such as Masbagik, Penujak, and Banyumulek, by successive generations of potters.

Wood carving is a Lombok specialty, particularly furniture and ornamental objects carved into intricate designs with mother-of-pearl inlay, called *cukli.* The markets and villages around **Sayang Sayang** in west Lombok, just to the east of the old airport, have a wide selection of these hand-carved items. Purchase magnificent sea trunks with beaten brass hinges and hasps, ornately carved wooden screens and room dividers, or highly polished decorative bowls and ornaments—all for bargain prices. See p. 312.

Escaping to the Cool Highlands If the tropical heat is wearing you down, escape to the cool mountain retreat of the **Sembalun** valley. High on the northeast shoulder of Mount Rinjani, Sembalun is steeped in history and mass tourism is still a distant thought. See p. 318.

Sasak Muslims observe Islamic religious practices, such as prayer five times a day and fasting during the month of Ramadan. There are two main groups among the Sasak: **Waktu Lima,** meaning "five times" (the number of times worshipers pray per day) are Sunni Muslims, and **Waktu Telu,** "three times," are nominal Muslims who combine Islamic observances with a mosaic of Hinduism, animism, and ancestor worship. Other religions, particularly Hinduism and Buddhism, peacefully coexist alongside the Muslim population.

Art, Architecture & Music

Lombok is famous for its highly collectible and distinctive hand-thrown **pottery.** Huge pots, cooking and dining implements, and ornamental pottery are crafted in the villages of Banyumeluk, Penujak, and Masbagik. Other interesting crafts include hand-carved wooden furniture, ornaments, sculpture, and finely woven cloth called ikat. *Osap,* a more rustic form of *songket* textile, is spun with cotton and is still common in many villages and available throughout the Sasak areas of the island. Old pieces can command thousands of dollars although most can be yours for the price of lunch.

Examples of **Dutch colonial architecture** are still evident around the old port in Ampenan and in the administrative buildings that line the main road through Mataram. You can still see a few examples of old **Sasak architecture,** the traditional houses of the time before the advent of the Dutch, in the north around Bayan; in the

The *Rudat*

Try to catch a *rudat* performance while you're on Lombok. *Rudat* combines theater and military skill, with performers dressed in uniforms, wielding guns, and re-enacting their Dutch colonial military training, often with humorous, tongue-in-cheek overtones. There are no regular scheduled performances unless you arrive during the Senggigi Festival in July. Otherwise, inquire at your hotel or tour office for current cultural festivals and performances.

south particularly in the villages of Rambitan and Sade; and in the small villages on the northeast coast. Traditionally, houses were very small and not very high, with a sweeping thatched roof of alang-alang grass. The floors are made from dried cow dung, compressed and polished over the years. New layers of cow dung are added when the flooring wears down and the smell disappears fairly quickly. Two-story *lumbung* (former rice huts) on pillars usually have woven bamboo walls and thatched alang-alang roofs. *Lumbung* have a distinctive shape to the roof, which curves down from the apex and then flattens out at the eaves, like a bonnet.

Gendang beleq ("big drums") is the distinctive music of Lombok and forms an important part of island culture. Join in almost any major event or cultural performance in Lombok and you'll see a band of colorfully dressed dancers carrying huge drums across their bodies, filling the air with an irresistible beat. These drums are actually a variant of the *kendang* drum that traditionally accompanies gamelan orchestras throughout Indonesia. The barrel-shaped drum produces a deep bass tone and a characteristic high-pitched slap. The *gendang beleq* used in Lombok are distinctive because of their huge size—usually around 1.5m (5 ft.) in length and 50cm (20 in.) in diameter. Drummers train for years to master the drumming and maneuvering of the size and weight of the drums in skilful and graceful performance.

Kecimol music, also found on Lombok, is similar and often accompanies marriage processions through the streets of the villages. A vibrant combination of performers includes drums, gamelan, keyboard, and flutes dancing along with someone on a megaphone mounted on a small carriage. This raucous fusion moves to an almost military marching beat. The keys are played in an Arabic style, with wailing flutes lending Eastern tones to the mix. The whole ensemble is accompanied by a vocalist singing love songs. It's an unmistakable sound, played at high volume, announcing the parade to all the villages and homes it passes along the way.

Eating & Drinking in Lombok

Lombok means "chili" in Sasak, so it's no surprise that traditional Sasak food is often fiery hot. Lombok is a melting pot of cultures and this is reflected in the styles of food available, ranging from Dutch-influenced breads and the pancake or crepe-like *martabaks* to authentic Chinese cuisine, spicy Padang food from Sumatra, and traditional Indonesian fare.

Sate pusut is a delicious local satay, with meats, spices, and coconut pressed onto flat skewers and grilled. **Satay tanjung** is a tasty specialty from the Tanjung in north Lombok, but also found in the cities, featuring fresh fish and spices wrapped on skewers and grilled. **Lemper** are small parcels of sticky rice filled with shredded chicken or beef and spices, wrapped in coconut leaves. **Lontong** are small conical-shaped cakes of rice that have been wrapped in leaves and steamed.

Lombok is famed for its specialty chicken dish **ayam taliwang** (small, free-range village chicken), though it originates from the neighboring island of Sumbawa. A whole *ayam kampung* is grilled over coconut husks and served with sambal. *Pelecing ayam* is grilled chicken broken into pieces, added to the spicy and piquant sauce, and slowly simmered, turning the marinade into a delicious red coating.

Being a Muslim island, pork isn't readily available except in the tourist areas and at Chinese restaurants, and lamb is rare. Goat *(kambing)* however, is very popular. A whole, young goat cooked on a spit is the meat of choice for celebrations, parties, and festive occasions, especially the Islamic festivals of Idul Adha and Eid-ul-Fitr. Beef is also freely available on Lombok and a staple in Lombok diets (unlike their Hindu cousins in Bali). **Beef rendang** is simmered for hours in coconut milk and spices.

Large tuna, snapper, Spanish mackerel, barracuda, and a huge variety of shellfish are found in the seas off Lombok. **Ikan** (fish) are generally served whole and baked, fried, or more often, grilled on outdoor barbecues over a fire of charcoal and coconut husks. Local **cumi cumi** (squid) and **udang** (prawns) are cooked in fiery sambal, braised in oyster sauce, or deep fried.

Particularly popular in Lombok are **pelecing kangkung** and **pecel,** sold from *kaki lima* and warungs everywhere. *Pelecing kangkung* is locally grown *kangkung* (a type of leafy water spinach) boiled and served with fresh bean sprouts and topped with a fiery red chili and tomato sauce. *Pecel* is a variant that combines *kangkung,* cabbage, and other vegetables, fresh bean sprouts, and sometimes tomato with spicy peanut sauce and prawn crackers. **Lalapan** is a plate of fresh cabbage, snake beans, and cucumber served with spicy sambal. **Beberuk** (or *beberuq*) is a typical Sasak side dish of finely diced snake beans and small, round eggplant (aubergine), with tomato, chili, shallots, lime, and spices. **Ares** is a unique dish made from the inner stem of the banana tree and mixed with coconut milk and spices. **Olah-olah** is made from the heart of banana tree flower mixed with coconut cream, mild spices, and finely chopped snake beans. **Rujak** is unripe fruit such as mango or papaya, mixed with ripe apple, guava, or pineapple, coated in a hot and sweet and sour sauce of sweet soy, palm sugar, and chilies.

Despite being a Muslim island, alcohol is readily available in all the tourism areas.

GETTING THERE & GETTING AROUND

Getting There By Air

The new **Lombok International Airport** (**LOP**), also known as **Bandara Internasional Lombok**, which opened in 2011, is located in Praya in Central Lombok. It replaces the Mataram Airport near Lombok's capital. It makes destinations in southern Lombok such as Kuta—long off the tourist map—more accessible, while making the tourist hub of Senggigi and northern Lombok slightly less convenient by

Lombok

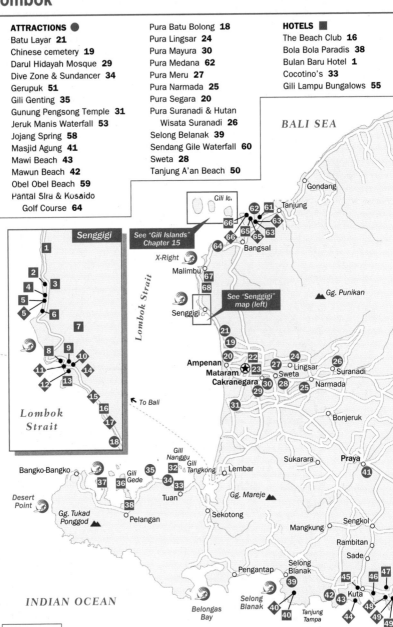

ATTRACTIONS ●
Batu Layar **21**
Chinese cemetery **19**
Darul Hidayah Mosque **29**
Dive Zone & Sundancer **34**
Gerupuk **51**
Gili Genting **35**
Gunung Pengsong Temple **31**
Jeruk Manis Waterfall **53**
Jojang Spring **58**
Masjid Agung **41**
Mawi Beach **43**
Mawun Beach **42**
Obel Obel Beach **59**
Pantal Sira & Kosaido
  Golf Course **64**

Pura Batu Bolong **18**
Pura Lingsar **24**
Pura Mayura **30**
Pura Medana **62**
Pura Meru **27**
Pura Narmada **25**
Pura Segara **20**
Pura Suranadi & Hutan
  Wisata Suranadi **26**
Selong Belanak **39**
Sendang Gile Waterfall **60**
Sweta **28**
Tanjung A'an Beach **50**

HOTELS ■
The Beach Club **16**
Bola Bola Paradis **38**
Bulan Baru Hotel **1**
Cocotino's **33**
Gili Lampu Bungalows **55**

BALI SEA

Gondang

Gili Is.

See "Gili Islands"
Chapter 15

Tanjung

62 61
66   63
65 63
64   65
          Bangsal

X-Right

Malimbu
67
68

See "Senggigi"
map (left)

Senggigi

Gg. Punikan

21
19
20 22 27 24
Ampenan   23 Lingsar   26
Mataram   Sweta   Suranadi
Cakranegara 30 28 25 Narmada
              29
31

Bonjeruk

Senggigi

1
2
4 3
5
5 6
  7
8 9
    10
11   14
12 13
  15
    16
    17
      18

↖ *To Bali*

Lombok
Strait

Gili
Nanggu
Gili 32 *Gili Tangkong*
Gede 35
Bangko-Bangko   34   Lembar
        37 36 33
Desert   Tuan   *Gg. Mareje*
Point   38
  Gg. Tukad   Pelangan   Sekotong
  Ponggod

Sukarara
Praya
41

Mangkung   Sengkol

Rambitan
Sade

Pengantap   Selong
            Blanak   45 46 47
INDIAN OCEAN   39   Kuta
            Selong   42 43
Belongas Blanak 40 *Tanjung* 44 48
Bay   40   *Tampa*   49 49

[🏄] Surfing

Gili Nanggu Cottages **32**
Hati Suci Homestay **54**
Heaven on the Planet **52**
Holiday Resort **4**
Hotel Lombok Raya **22**
Hotel Tugu Lombok **66**

Jeeva Klui Resort **67**
Kuta Paradise **47**
Lembah Rinjani **56**
Lombok Garden Hotel **23**
Lombok Lodge **61**
Matahari Inn **45**

Medana Resort **63**
Novotel Lombok
  Resort **49**
The Oberoi **65**
Pearl Beach Resort **37**
The Puncak **68**
Puri Bunga Beach
  Cottages **9**
Puri Mas Boutique
  Resort & Spa **6**
Puri Mas Kerandangan
  Resort **7**
Qunci Villas **5**
Santosa Villas & Resort **3**
Secret Island Resort **36**
Sempiak Villas **40**
Senggigi Beach Hotel &
  Pool Villa Club **13**
Sheraton Senggigi
  Beach Resort **8**
Tastura Hotel **46**
Via Vacare **36**
Windy Beach Resort **2**

RESTAURANTS ◆
Ashtari **48**
Asmara Restaurant **10**
Bumbu Café **12**
Café Alberto **15**
De Quake Restaurant **11**
Kokok Pletok **66**
Laut Biru Café **40**
Lumbung Restaurant &
  Sunbird Café **65**
Medana Resort **63**
Pondok & Senaru
  Restaurant **57**
Qunci Villas **5**
Square Restaurant **14**
Vue **49**
Warung Bule **44**
Warung Menega **17**

plane. The airport will handle all domestic and international flights and is expected to expand the flight options to Lombok significantly.

Airline offices on Lombok are, as of press time, still located in Mataram, though they'll likely move to Praya by publication: **Batavia Air,** Jl. Pejanggik 88 (✆ **0370/648998**); **Garuda Indonesia,** Jl. Panca Usaha 11 (✆ **0370/638259**); **Indonesia Air Transport (IAT),** Jl. Adi Sucipto (www.indonesia-air.com); **Lion Air,** Jl. Sriwijaya 81 (✆ **0370/629111**); and **Silk Air,** Jl. Panca Usaha 11 (✆ **0370/628254**). In Cakranegara, there's **Merpati Nusantara Airlines,** Jl. Pejanggik 69 (✆ **0370/636745**).

FROM BALI   Lombok is only 25 minutes by air from Bali. Payment online is difficult though, and so buy tickets direct from the airline counters at the domestic airports or through local travel agents in both Bali and Lombok. Many seats can't be held for longer than a few hours so make sure you have time to spare. An alternative to booking direct is to get your hotel or tour operator to book transfers for you; the costs involved aren't much more than the flight tickets.

Bali to Lombok airfares are approximately Rp385,000 to Rp450,000, depending on the season. A **Domestic Departure Tax** of Rp25,000 from Denpasar and Rp100,000 from **Lombok International Airport** is applicable to all travelers and is paid when you check in to your flight.

Garuda Airlines (✆ **08/041807807,** at the Bali airport ✆ 0370/649999; www.garuda-indonesia.com) flies a comfortable 737 jet every evening to facilitate international arrivals and departures.

Lion Air (✆ **08/041778899,** on Bali ✆ 0361/765183; www.lionair.co.id) flies three times daily.

Merpati Airlines (on Lombok ✆ **0370/621111,** at the Lombok airport ✆ 0370/633637, on Bali ✆ 0361/235358; www.merpati.co.id) flies five times daily.

Trans Nusa Air (on Lombok ✆ **0370/616-2428** or 0370/616433, on Bali ✆ 0361/760218; www.transnusa.co.id) and **Trigana Air** (on Lombok ✆ **0370/646839,** on Bali ✆ 0361/760218; www.trigana-air.com) operate three flights daily.

FROM ELSEWHERE IN INDONESIA   Daily direct flights from Jakarta to Lombok are usually timed to connect with European flights. Lombok is easily accessible from Jakarta, Bali, Jogyakarta, and Surabaya and is an important connection for travel to the eastern islands, in particular Sumbawa, Komodo, and Flores.

Garuda Indonesia (see above) has direct flights between Lombok and Jakarta twice daily. **Lion Air** (✆ **0370/663444;** www.lionair.co.id) has daily flights between Lombok, Jakarta, and Surabaya. **Merpati Airlines** (see above) has flights between Lombok, Bali, Jakarta, Surabaya, Bandung, Sumbawa, Flores, Kupang, and many other Indonesian destinations. **Trans Nusa Air** (✆ **0370/616428** or 0370/616433; www.transnusa.co.id) flies between Lombok and Sumbawa four times a week. **Batavia Air** (✆ **0370/648998**; www.batavia-air.co.id) has daily flights between Lombok, Surabaya, and Jakarta.

FROM OUTSIDE INDONESIA   The new **Lombok International Airport** handles an increasing number of international flights. Currently **Silk Air** (a subsidiary of Singapore Airlines; ✆ **0370/62825,** 0370/628254, 0370/628256; www.silkair.com) flies direct between Lombok and Singapore, three times a week. **Garuda Airlines** (see above) flies between Kuala Lumpur in Malaysia and Lombok via Jakarta. **Merpati Airlines** (see above) has daily flights between Lombok and Kuala Lumpur, Malaysia, with a short stopover in Surabaya.

Getting There By Sea

Padangbai Harbour provides the sea link between Bali and Lombok. **Lembar Harbour,** on Lombok, is approximately 1 hour south of Senggigi. Public ferries depart every hour from 12:35am to 4:55am, and then at 7:55, 8:15, 9:50am. The crossing takes approximately 4 to 5 hours and costs Rp36,000. Get to your boat a half-hour before departure. Night ferries run at 9:20, 10:25, and 11:30pm.

Perama Tours (Main office: Jl. Legian 39, Kuta, Bali; © **0361/751875** or 0361/751875; www.peramatour.com) offers a complete transfer package, which includes pickup from destinations throughout Bali and Lombok, bus transfer to the local harbor, ferry ticket, and transfer from the harbor to your destination, on either island. Depending on weather and number of bookings, the company may use its private boat transfer direct to the Gilis (chapter 15) and then on to Senggigi; otherwise it's the public ferry. Travel time is approximately 8 hours. The return leg from the Gilis leaves at 7am and from Senggigi at 9am. Times and prices are as follows from: Lovina, 9am, Rp450,000; Kuta, 10am, Rp350,000; Sanur, 10:15am, Rp350,000; Ubud, 11am, Rp350,000; Candidasa, 12:30pm, Rp325,000; Padangbai, 1:30pm, Rp300,000.

THE FAST BOATS Gili Cat ★(© **0361/271680;** www.gilicat.com) is the most reputable fast-boat service between Bali and Lombok. Its fleet includes the new Gili Cat Enterprise; the boat departs daily from Gili Trawangan at 9am, stops on Lombok (at the Teluk Kodek pier, just north of Senggigi) at 9:10am before arriving at Padangbai on Bali at 10:30am. The boat leaves Padangbai on Bali at 11:30am daily and arrives in Gili Trawangan and Lombok at 12:40pm and 1pm, respectively. In the high season, a second round-trip journey originating on Gili Trawangan is completed in the afternoons. The service also includes free transfers between Padangbai, Ubud, Kuta, and Sanur on Bali. Journey time is around 1 hour; tickets are listed as costing Rp660,000 one-way and Rp1,200,000 round-trip on the website, though if you book directly at its offices, you'll only pay Rp550,000 one-way; Rp1,100,000 round-trip. If your trip happens to be cancelled due to bad weather, the company refunds your money back on the spot.

Blue Water Express (BWS; © **0361/895082** or 081/338418988 after hours; www.bwsbali.com) provides transfers between Bali and Gili Trawangan, stopping at Teluk Kode on Lombok. BWS operates two boats, with 25- and 15-passenger capacities, departing from Benoa Harbour, Bali (20 minutes from Kuta) daily at 8am, arriving in Lombok at 10am; and from Gili Trawangan at 11am. BWS leaves Lombok at 11:30am, arriving in Bali at 1:30pm. Fares include air-conditioned hotel transfers in Bali. Tickets cost Rp690,000 one-way; Rp1,300,000 round-trip. Price is the same regardless of where you disembark.

Island Getaway (on Bali © **0361/751570**; on Lombok © **08/7864322515**; www.island-getaway.com) also provides a fast-boat service from Bali's Benoa Harbour (20 minutes away from Kuta) daily at 8am to Teluk Kode and Gili Trawangan.

Getting Around

Airport taxis (dark blue) service incoming flights; a taxi counter is in the arrivals hall at the airport, with fares to various destinations around Lombok displayed. Light blue **Blue Bird Taxis** (© **0370/627000**) service most destinations in Lombok and are easily flagged down on the roadside. All taxis in Lombok automatically use their meters and fares are low, so there's no need to haggle prices (unlike in Bali). Guide and driver **Andra** ★★ (© **081/915768015**; based in Sengkol) speaks English well

📎 **Newspapers & Websites for Lombok**

The **Lombok Guide** (www.thelombok guide.com), the island's English-language newspaper, is published every 2 weeks and is an invaluable resource.

Other useful sites include **www. lombok-network.com** and **www.goto lombok.com.**

and can organize trips and transfers. An 8-hour tour around the island including petrol is Rp450,000. Ask for the Toyota Avanza as other cars in his fleet are less comfortable.

Bemo (vans operating as small public minibuses) also ply the routes from city to city, and from Ampenan to Senggigi on the west coast. Smaller private *bemo* (with open backs and bench seating) are available for charter, but you need good negotiating skills, and so it's far easier (and often more economical) to use taxis or rent a car.

Rent a car from: **Lombok Car Rentals** (✆ 0370/660-9477; www.lombokcar rentals.com; daily US$15–US$40); **Lombok Car Hire** (✆ 081/8362905; daily US$20–US$35); and **Lombok Hotel and Travel** (✆ 0370/665-0238; www. lombokhotelandtravel.com; daily Rp350,000–Rp500,000).

Daily motorbike rentals are available from **Lombok Komodo** (✆ 0370/692225; www.lombokkomodo.com; Rp35,000–Rp75,000).

[Fast FACTS] LOMBOK

ATMs & Banks In Mataram, banks are at Jalan Pejanggik 2 and Jalan Langko; in Cakranegara, you'll find banks along Jalan Pejanggik. Two banks are located on Jalan Raya Senggigi in Senggigi. ATMs are in Mataram, Senggigi, and Praya, but you're best advised to bring cash.

Currency Exchange Most hotels and stores will exchange money, but rates are poor. Try the exchange offices at Jalan Raya Senggigi Km 13 (✆ 0370/692247) and Jalan Raya Senggigi Km 10 (✆ 0370/693693) instead.

Hospitals & Clinics In Mataram, the options are **Mataram General Hospital,** Jl. Pejanggik 6 (✆ 0370/622254); **Santo Antonius**

Hospital, Jl. Koperasi 16 (✆ 0370/636767); **Army Hospital,** Jl. HOS Cokroaminoto 7 (✆ 0370/640149); Siti Hajar Islamic Hospital, Jl. Catur Warga (✆ 0370/623498); and **Klinik Risa Husada,** Jl. Pejanggik 115 (✆ 0370/625559). In Senggigi, try the **Senggigi Medical Clinic,** in Senggigi Beach Hotel (p. 300; ✆ 0370/693856).

Internet Access Many cafes in Senggigi and Kuta offer free Wi-Fi; for Internet cafes in Mataram, try: **Elian Internet,** Mataram Mall; **Wartel,** Jl. Pejanggik; **Telkom,** Jl. Pendidikan 23 (✆ 0370/633333; 24 hr.). In Senggigi, try **Planet Internet** (✆ 0370/693920), **Superstar Internet,** or **Millennium Internet**

(✆ 0370/693860; 24 hr.), all on Jalan Raya Senggigi.

Pharmacies In Mataram, **Kimia Farma,** Jl. IGK Jelantik Gosa (✆ 0370/624845); **Airlangga Farmasi,** Jl. Airlangga 25A (✆ 0370/634221); **Masyarakat Farmasi,** Jl. AA Gde Ngurah (✆ 0370/633547); **Kemala Hikmah Pharmacy,** Jl. Langko 64 (✆ 0370/646322).

Police The main police are at Jalan Langko 77, Mataram (✆ 0370/632733), with another office at Jalan Raya Senggigi (✆ 0370/693267) in Senggigi.

Post Office Lombok's main post office is at Jalan Sriwijaya 37, Mataram (✆ 0370/632645;

Mon–Thurs 8am–5pm, Fri till 11am, Sat till 1pm). Other offices are at Jalan Langko, Mataram (✆ 0370/631642; Mon–Thurs 8am–4:30pm, Fri till 11am, Sat till 1pm); Jalan Raya Senggigi (Mon–Sat 8am–6pm); and in Segara Anak Cottages, south Lombok (✆ 0370/654846).

Tourist Offices & Visitor Information In Mataram: the **West Lombok Tourist Office** is located at Jalan Suprato 20 (✆ 0370/621658; Mon–Thurs 7:30am–2pm, Fri till 11am, Sat 8am–1pm) and the **West Nusa Tenggara Tourist Office** is at Jalan Singosari 2 (✆ 0370/634800; Mon–Thurs 8am–2pm, Fri till 11am, Sat till 12:30pm). In Senggigi call ✆ 0370/632733. The tourist information center on Mount Rinjani is open daily 6am to 6pm.

WEST LOMBOK

West Lombok is the most developed area of the island for tourism. Just as in Bali, tourists in Lombok generally don't stay in the cities and instead head straight for the beaches. **Senggigi** (p. 298) is the main beach resort approximately 20 minutes drive from the airport. The west interior is lush with agricultural lands and mountains sheltering small picturesque towns and villages. On the coast, the wide **Lombok Strait** separates Lombok from Bali and forms a series of picturesque bays and beaches. This region has a long history of Hindu settlement and traces of the old empires are still visible in the large Hindu population, temples, and traditional ceremonies.

Getting There & Getting Around

From the airport, you can pick up a dark blue airport **taxi** from the arrivals terminal. From the airport to the city center costs around Rp120,000 and takes about 1 hour.

Blue Bird taxis ply the route between Senggigi and the cities, and around Senggigi, and can be rented for most destinations around the island. Yellow public *bemo* connect the cities of Ampenan, Mataram, and Cakra. Fares are around Rp5,000. To explore the cities, **rent a car and driver** rather than using taxis.

The Cities

The three main cities of Lombok—Ampenan, Mataram, and Cakranegara—were clearly defined in the past, but as populations have grown the three have melded together to create what is, for Lombok, an urban sprawl.

Ampenan was originally Lombok's main seaport. With its numerous cheap hotels, old buildings, plentiful *cidomo* (horse carts), gold and pearl shops, and its Arab quarter, Ampenan is a colorful town to explore in its own right. The remains of the port are at the end of the road to the west, at the intersection of the five roads of central Ampenan. This area becomes a market at night, filled with warungs and *kaki lima* (food carts) for cheap, tasty food and local flavor. Cultural shows, such as *gandrung* dance or the shadow puppet play *wayang sasak,* take place here on special holidays. Some Dutch colonial architecture is still visible toward the beach. Ampenan has a reasonably large Arab and Chinese population and you'll see an interesting Buddhist temple on the road to the old port. **Kebun Roek,** near the traffic lights in Ampenan on the road from the airport, is the site of the local market. Every day traders set up stalls selling fresh produce from around the island, local snacks, live chickens, and fresh fish in the afternoon when the fishing boats come in.

SPECIALIZED LOMBOK tours

Sunda Trails (*C* **0370/647390;** www.sundatrails.com) offers off-the-beaten-track tours to remote villages. Run by the enthusiastic Anita, with many years of experience traveling throughout Lombok and the nearby islands, Sunda works closely with local communities and is ideal for those with an interest in different cultures. Tours can be tailor-made for individuals or groups. Ready-made tours range from trips around Lombok and the islands to the east, tours to Mount Rinjani, trekking and trips to Komodo Island to see the Komodo dragons, and trips based on specific cultural festivals or events.

To see Lombok up close and personal, book a tour through **Lombok Biking Tours** (*C* **0370/692164**). These safe and professional cycle tours are designed for all levels of fitness, from easy rides near Senggigi to challenging trips through hills and over winding roads. Friendly and experienced local guides accompany your trip on well-maintained bicycles and mountain bikes. Tours include the services of a local guide, bottled water, and snacks, plus private transport to wherever your trip begins and ends. The company's shop is located on the main street in Senggigi (next to Bumbu Café).

Mataram starts about 3km (2 miles) to the east of Ampenan, and is the administrative center for Lombok and Sumbawa. Numerous government offices, banks, mosques, and churches line the main street. The public hospital (Rumah Sakit Umum), the main post office, and Mataram University are all here. The cultural center **Taman Budaya** (*C* 0370/622428), on Jalan Majapahit, regularly presents traditional music and dance. You can often visit during rehearsals.

Cakranegara (often abbreviated to Cakra) to the east of Mataram, is Lombok's main shopping area. The main road is lined with electronics and textile shops, bookstores, sporting goods stores, and other small businesses. The only shopping mall in Lombok is just past the monument on the main road from Mataram to Cakra. The upstairs food court has cheap local meals.

The main road continues farther east to **Sweta** (almost a city in its own right) and the **Bertais Bus Terminal,** serving destinations in east Lombok and where it's possible to arrange transport to neighboring Sumbawa and to the islands of Flores and Komodo. The main road is wide and in good condition, and is the main route across Lombok to the east coast.

EXPLORING THE CITIES & NEARBY TEMPLES

While in Mataram, visit the excellent **Museum Negeri ★★** (Jl. Panji Tilar Negara 6 *C* 0370/632159, admission Rp20,000; Tues, Wed, and Thurs 8am–2pm; Fri 8am–11am; Sat 8am–12:30pm; Sun 8am–2pm). The only official museum in Lombok, this small but complete collection offers a good overview of Lombok's history, geology, ecology, and ethnography, with sections about everything from local volcanoes to weddings, and local resistance against Dutch colonial rule after World War II. The collection has good English explanations.

Local temples are open daily, 10am to 5pm; admission (and occasional eel feeding) is by donation. **Pura Meru,** on Jalan Selaparang in Cakranegara, was built in 1720 by Balinese Prince Anak Agung Made Karang and is the largest temple on Lombok. The interior enclosure has 33 shrines as well as the three multitiered *meru* (mountain altars) representing the Hindu trinity. This important temple for the Balinese hosts an annual Pujawali festival, held over 5 days during the full moon in September or October, the biggest Hindu event on Lombok.

Pura Mayura, just across the street from Pura Meru, was built in 1744 as the court temple of the last Balinese kings in Lombok. A *bale kambang* (floating pavilion) in a large artificial lake is used as a meeting place. Today the palace gardens are a playground for children. The temple sits behind the sedate water gardens.

The temple of **Gunung Pengsong,** on Jalan Gajah Mada south of Mataram, resides on a hilltop with vistas of rice fields, the sea, and Gunung Rinjani. Populated by monkeys, this is the hill the Balinese aimed for in the mythic account of their initial arrival in western Lombok. In March or April, a buffalo is sacrificed here to ensure a rich harvest. The Bersih Desa, or "village purification" festival, held every year at harvest time, finds the area spruced up to honor the rice goddess, Dewi Sri.

Pura Lingsar, Desa Lingsar, Narmada, is sacred not only to Lombok's Hindu community, but also for local Waktu Lima and Waktu Telu Muslim followers. Built around 1714, Pura Lingsar was originally dedicated to the prevailing animist beliefs of the time, and some of the original animist statues remain today. This is the only temple on Lombok where all the religions—Hindu, Buddhist, Christian, and Muslim—come together to pray for prosperity, fertility, rain, health, and general success. **Perang Topat** festival is held here annually usually in December and features a ritualized war with rice cakes, which also serve as an offering to the Gods. Lingsar has spring-fed pools within the temple grounds and is home to large freshwater eels. Visitors are welcome to accompany a temple priest to feed them hard-boiled eggs, purchased at nearby stands.

Pura Narmada, around 10km (6 miles) east of Cakranegara in Narmada, was created around 1805 as a replica of Gunung Rinjani and Segara Anak, the lake within Rinjani's crater. The gardens at Narmada are beautifully maintained and surround the pools and lake. Check for performances of traditional dances on special occasions. Some of the other pools at Narmada are available for swimming (modest attire, please) and are popular with the locals.

Pura Suranadi, a complex of three temples a few kilometers north of Narmada in Suranadi, is the oldest and holiest of the Balinese temples in Lombok, founded by the 16th-century Javanese priest, Danghyang Nirartha. Underground streams bubble up into restored baths, used for ritual bathing. Suranadi is regarded as the place to obtain the proper holy water for Hindu cremations. Huge sacred eels live in the pools and streams here, and can sometimes be lured out with an offering of boiled eggs (purchased at a nearby stall). To see a sacred eel is considered very lucky; conversely, it's taboo to eat the eels or to contaminate their water.

Beyond Suranadi, on the main road before the temple, is **Hutan Wisata Suranadi** (Rp4,000; daily 8am–5:30pm), literally the "Suranadi Tourist Forest."

When on Lombok. . .

Be respectful of the Muslim culture, which tends to be more conservative than the Hindu culture. This might mean not drinking alcohol in public, outdoor spaces. Women are also advised not to wear bikinis in towns and villages; carry a sarong to wrap up in public.

Stroll through the botanical garden with labeled specimens and observe birds, monkeys, and butterflies.

WHERE TO STAY

Hotel Lombok Raya   This faded but functional property offers decent accommodations at the center of Mataram. The rooms are somewhat musty and rundown but provide bathtubs, TVs with English programming, and balconies. The Mataram Mall is a 5-minute walk away.

Jl. Panca Usaha 11, Mataram. www.lombokrayahotel.com. © **0370/632305.** Fax 0370/636478. 135 units. Year-round Rp419,000–Rp519,000. Rates exclude breakfast and taxes. AE, DC, MC, V. **Amenities:** Restaurant; gym; pool; spa. In room: A/C, TV; minibar.

Lombok Garden Hotel ★   It's rare to find such a pleasant property in the center of Mataram. The sprawling grounds of this resort contain an older section of bungalows and a newly built, tall complex of luxury rooms surrounding a long pool with new, lounge-worthy patio furniture. It caters largely to an Indonesian clientele.

Jl. Bung Karno 7, Mataram. © **0370/636015.** Fax 0370/636219. 103 units. Year-round Rp460,000–Rp730,000. MC, V. **Amenities:** Restaurant; coffee shop; pool; Internet. In room: A/C, TV; minibar.

WHERE TO EAT

In the Mataram Mall, try **Delicio Restaurant** (daily 9am–9pm) for Chinese and international meals, coffee, and delicious Western cakes. **Oceanic Café** is great for salads and dim sum and **Elements** in the new wing serves fresh juices and coffee. Across the road from the Mall is **Pizza Hut.**

At night, **Jalan Pejanggik** (the main street of Mataram) comes alive with many covered stalls set up along the road. Seating is basic, at plastic chairs and tables. *Ayam taliwang,* Lombok's chicken specialty, is served at many of the stalls here, together with barbecued fish and seafood, satays, and a wide range of the local fast food. Prices fall in the Rp10,000 to Rp25,000 range.

Seafood Nikmat SEAFOOD   Nikmat is equally popular with locals and visitors. Ignore the less-than-glamorous surroundings and enjoy some of the best seafood in Lombok. Chef William trained in Australia and uses a combination of traditional

---

ISLAND OF 1,000 MOSQUES

Whereas Bali is a majority-Hindu island, in Lombok 90% of the citizens are Muslim, and tourists can visit hundreds of mosques. Lombok is called the "Island of 1,000 Mosques" and dozens of new ones are constantly being built across the island. Most mosques welcome visitors but require appropriate dress. Men should wear trousers and collared shirts. Women should cover their heads and wear long sleeve shirts and cover their ankles with long skirts or trousers. The busiest day is Friday, the Muslim holy day.

One of the biggest mosques in Lombok is **Masjid Agung**, Jl. Mq. Sapian in Praya. Started in 1982, it's still under construction and from the outside looks only mildly impressive. The inside prayer hall, however, is big enough to hold hundreds of people, has marbled floors and pillars, and large balconies. Women pray at back of the room.

Darul Hidayah Mosque, Jl. Dasan Calan, in Cakranegara, just outside of Mataram, is one of the island's prettier mosques, with tall minarets and peaked domes.

All the way up the western coast of Lombok you'll find beaches full of traditional fishing boats called *jukung*. Hitch a ride over to the Gilis (chapter 15) for some snorkeling and lunch. The trip should take up to an hour each way but ask beforehand as it depends on the wind and currents. These boats do have motors so don't worry too much if you find yourself in the middle of the ocean without any wind. Book a day in advance if possible. Expect to pay about Rp250,000 for a half-day for four people.

cooking and Asian-fusion styles. Live lobsters swimming in the tank, fresh crabs and prawns on ice, and a selection of the best fish from the daily markets keep customers coming to Nikmat. Highly recommended is the fresh crab in piquant Padang sauce—a huge, delicious meal for two.

Jl. Panca Usaha 1, Cakranegara. ✆ **0360/634330.** Main courses Rp10,000–Rp13,500. No credit cards. Daily 11am–11pm.

SHOPPING
Mataram Mall, Jl. Pejangik, Cakranegara (daily 9am–9pm), is Lombok's only real mall. **Hero Supermarket,** at street level, is useful for some Western goods, food, and toiletries. The **Drugstore** next door has imported toiletries, nutritional supplements, and medicines. McDonald's and KFC have outlets too.

Many of Lombok's **weaving** and **basketry** industries are located near Cakranegara. Turn left at the central traffic lights and look for the market on the right near the bridge. The baskets in particular are sold in Bali at many times the Lombok price. Farther east, near the Bertais bus terminal, the next large town east of Cakra (sometimes referred to as Sweta) has a huge daily market, with all kinds of goods on sale from foodstuffs, to clothing, to exotic birds, handicrafts, and more.

The West Coast
The main road along the west coast starts at Ampenan and winds its way parallel to the beaches. Orientation and travel is easy. Heading north from Ampenan is **Pura Segara,** a Balinese sea-temple. The **Chinese cemetery,** on the main road just out of Ampenan, has interesting graves painted in bright colors with Chinese decorations.

Batu Layar, on the hill a couple of kilometers before Senggigi, has an important ancestral grave (*makam*) where Muslims picnic and pray for health and success. Lombok has many *makam,* typically the graves of important religious leaders that have become shrines. The graveyard and the nearby beach are very popular during Muslim holidays, particularly Eid-ul-Fitr (Lebaran) and at Lebaran Topat.

Nearby **Pura Batu Bolong** (literally meaning "rock with a hole") is an interesting Hindu temple on a cliff facing Bali across the Lombok Strait. Built on a large rocky outcrop with a hole at the base, it's said that virgins were once sacrificed to the sea from the seatlike rock at the outermost point. Colorful Hindu ceremonies are held here every month at the dark and full moons, and at Hindu festival times. Admission and compulsory temple sash are by donation. Come here to watch the sunset, with fantastic vistas across to Gunung Agung on Bali.

The **beaches** of the west coast are large, sweeping bays of clean turquoise water, white sands, and coconut groves.

SENGGIGI

Nowhere near as large or busy as its Bali counterparts, Senggigi is the main tourism center on Lombok and, apart from the Gili Islands, the most developed tourism area. Senggigi is a great base for exploring the rest of Lombok, with day trips within a few hours' drive of town.

Getting There

Senggigi is about a 1-hour drive from Lombok International Airport. Rent a dark blue airport **taxi** from the arrivals terminal at the airport (around Rp150,000). From Lembar Harbour, either charter a **bemo** or catch a Blue Bird taxi. It's possible to join with other travelers in sharing the cost of chartering a *bemo*. From other destinations, taxis are the easiest form of transport.

Orientation

Senggigi Beach is the large bay that forms the center of Senggigi, with the main road running parallel to the beach and large resorts occupying the space between. The main road in Senggigi is lined with small shops, tour agencies, restaurants, bars, and nightclubs. The town has a couple of supermarkets, one BNI bank, numerous ATMs and money changers, and a post office.

Tourism development runs north along the coastal road for about 10km (6 miles). About 2km (3 miles) north is **Kerandangan Valley,** with a popular beach and some nice hotels. Past that is **Mangsit** with boutique-style hotels positioned along breathtaking bays. Farthest north is **Lendang Luar,** with two hotels—Bulan Baru (p. 301) and Ebano R & R—perched on the long stretch of pristine beach.

Mainly deserted, white-sand beaches, flanked by coconut groves, and untouched by hotel development, continue all the way north along the main coastal road. **Malimbu** and **Nipah** are two picturesque bays good for snorkeling, swimming, and getting away from it all, less than a half-hour from Senggigi.

Teluk Nara and **Teluk Kodek** are on a large bay that forms a natural harbor, about 25km (15 miles) north of Senggigi. All the main dive operators have boats here, which transfer guests to the Gili Islands, as an alternative to nearby Bangsal Harbour. **Bangsal Harbour** (p. 314) is reached by turning left at the crossroads in Pemenang; it's easy to catch the public ferries (actually large outrigger boats) out to the Gilis, or to charter boats for island hopping from here.

Where to Stay

EXPENSIVE

Jeeva Klui Resort ★🏖 If you're looking for Seminyak-style villa accommodations but only want to pay half the price, this is a great new option to consider, particularly for a honeymoon. The one- and two-story bungalows, built in a traditional style, have five-star amenities such as flat-screen televisions and sleek bathrooms. Request one that fronts the beach for extraordinary sunset views. The private, secluded beach also offers snorkeling, and complimentary afternoon tea is served. The resort plans to open a unique tent-style property in East Lombok in 2012.

Jl. Klui Raya 1, Klui Beach, Senggigi. www.jeevaklui.com. ℂ **0370/693035** or 8/2150000800. Fax 0370/693036. High season US$181–US$197, US$345 4-person villa; low season US$130–US$138, US$242 4-person villa. Rates include breakfast and exclude taxes. MC, V. **Amenities:** Restaurant; pool; spa. *In villa:* A/C, TV; DVD player; hair dryer, Wi-Fi (free).

Sheraton Senggigi Beach Resort ★   In central Senggigi with [...] of beachfront, the Sheraton also has a large swimming pool with [...] fantastic waterslide for children. Within the grounds are two priva[te] walls right on the beachfront. Each 2-bedroom villa has its own c[...] private pool. Ultra-luxurious furnishings and every conceivable c[...] class of their own, with a price tag to match.

Senggigi Beach. www.sheraton.com/senggigi. ☎ **0370/693333.** 154 units. Peak season US$155–US$235 standard, US$695 villa; high season US$145–US$305 standard, US$685 villa; low season US$125–US$200 standard, US$655 villa; extra bed US$35. Rates include breakfast. AE, MC, V. **Amenities:** 2 restaurants; pool bar; fitness center; outdoor pool; spa; 2 floodlit tennis courts; watersports; Wi-Fi (free in lobby). *In room/villa:* A/C, TV, hair dryer, minibar.

MODERATE

Holiday Resort ☺ ✎   Formerly part of the Holiday Inn chain, but always of a superior standard, the Holiday Resort sits on its own stretch of beach in Mangsit. Comfortable rooms and chalets look out over the ocean or the lush gardens. The freeform pool overlooks the beach and has a Jacuzzi. Across the road from the main resort are the self-contained apartments. With two bedrooms, a living and dining room, and fully equipped kitchenette, these are ideal for long-term guests and families.

Senggigi Beach, Mangsit. www.holidayresort-lombok.com. ☎ **0370/693444.** 189 units. Peak season US$87–US$134; high season US$70–US$117; low season US$70–US$117; extra bed US$20. AE, MC, V. **Amenities:** 2 restaurants; lounge/bar; children's club; fitness center; Jacuzzi; outdoor pool; spa. *In room:* A/C, hair dryer, minibar.

Puri Mas Boutique Resort & Spa   Puri Mas has two boutique properties: one on the beachfront at Mangsit and the other set in pretty gardens in the Kerandangan Valley. Both have charming rooms and private villas, furnished with antiques and col-lectibles, set in lovely beachfront gardens. In Mangsit, the one-bedroom luxury villas are set within walled gardens with fantastic pools separating the bedrooms from the main living areas; the open-air garden bathrooms are delightful.

The **Puri Mas Kerandangan Resort,** Jl. Wisata Alam, Desa Kerandangan (3 units; high season US$100; low season US$95; AE, MC, V) has private Balinese-style villas set alongside a pool in beautiful gardens with lotus ponds and romantic *bales*. All rooms come with their own verandas and the furnishings are rather ornate with lots of carved wood typical of the Lombok style.

Jl. Raya Mangsit Beach, Senggigi. www.purimas-lombok.com. ☎ **0370/693831** (for both resorts). 26 units. High season US$95 standard, US$154 suite, US$299 villa; low season US$72 standard, US$121 suite, US$276 villa. AE, MC, V. **Amenities:** Restaurant; bar; babysitting; bikes; concierge; outdoor pool; room service; spa. *In room/villa:* A/C, hair dryer, minibar, Wi-Fi (free).

The Puncak ★   The digs here could take the award for the world's most panoramic view for a bed-and-breakfast. Suspended on a steep hill 200m (600 ft.) above the ocean, this modern, five-room villa, decked out with wood floors and eco-friendly lighting, has gorgeous sunset views of the Lombok Strait. The Belgian owner lives upstairs and is on call at all hours of the day. The grounds are tight but offer a round-the-clock restaurant and a beautiful lap pool suspended on the edge of the cliff. Each room can be booked individually. The high-up location might make it difficult to leave the property, and so it's more worthy of your consideration if you plan on spending your holiday chilling out.

.ır 13, Senggigi. www.guestroom-lombok.com. ℂ **08/2111139595.** 5 units. High season 120€; ...eason 100€. Rates include breakfast and taxes. Rates quoted in euros. Payments only through ...pal or cash. **Amenities:** Restaurant; pool. *In room*: A/C, TV.

Qunci Villas ★★ 📖 The extremely popular Qunci Villas incorporates two fabulous boutique properties on the beachfront in Mangsit, within around 100m of each other. The stylish rooms and private villas with personal plunge pools feature minimalist architecture and elegant furnishings. The newer **Qunci Pool Villas** have a stunning infinity pool on the beachfront, with a wooden deck and sumptuous lounging platforms with big padded cushions. The Zen harmony of the buildings and the decorations uses natural tones and clean classic lines, and combines wood, stone, and flowing landscaping so that nothing grates on the nerves. A smooth teak tree trunk is casually parked on the lawn as a garden seat; a slab of slate masquerades as a table top; and a huge, hollowed-out boulder creates a unique bathtub.

Jl. Raya Mangsit, Senggigi. www.quncivillas.com. ℂ **0370/693800.** 47 units. High season US$110 garden view, US$135 ocean view, US$135–US$320 pool villa; low season US$85 garden view, US$110 ocean view, US$110–US$295 pool villa. Rates exclude taxes. MC, V. **Amenities:** 2 restaurants; 2 bars; spa. *In villa*: A/C, hair dryer; minibar, Wi-Fi (free).

Santosa Villas & Resort ★ ☺ This resort stretches between Senggigi Beach and the center of town. A recent renovation transformed the old hotel into a stunning resort with fountains, lotus and koi ponds, and a range of accommodations from comfortable standard rooms to spacious suites. The magnificent, lagoon-style pool with arched bridges and swim-up bar commands fantastic views over the bay. Four private villas hide behind high sandstone walls, with wooden decks, garden seating, and private pools. The spacious bedrooms open onto a large and luxurious marble bathroom, with sunken bathtub and separate rain showers.

Jl. Raya Senggigi Km 8, Senggigi. www.santosavillasresort.com. ℂ **0370/693090.** 191 units. Year-round US$60 standard, US$350 villa; extra bed US$25. AE, MC, V. **Amenities:** 2 restaurants; lounge; outdoor pool; spa; 2 tennis courts. *In room/villa*: A/C, TV, hair dryer, minibar.

Senggigi Beach Hotel & Pool Villa Club ☺ This resort occupies the entire peninsula that juts out into Senggigi Bay and faces two separate beachfronts. The hotel has a full range of activities and facilities and is good value for families. Choose from a range of different styles of rooms, from standard to bungalows, though the ocean view bungalows are the nicest. Within the grounds of the hotel, but separated from the main resort, is the **Pool Villa Club**—16 luxury villas with separate reception, entrance, and restaurant that surround a canal-style swimming pool. Local sandstone, marble, coconut wood, and ethnic decorations create a delightful ambience, while all fittings and facilities are modern. The four-person Jacuzzi on a sandstone deck beside the pool has angled doors for privacy, or can be opened up to enjoy the views.

Jl. Pantaai Senggigi, Mataram. www.senggigibeachhotel.com. ℂ **0370/693210.** 166 units. High season US$125 standard, US$275 villa; low season US$100 standard, US$250 villa; extra bed US$25. Rates include breakfast and taxes. AE, DC, MC, V. **Amenities:** 3 restaurants; children's club; Jacuzzi; outdoor pool; spa; 2 tennis courts; Wi-Fi (US$2/hr.). *In room/villa*: A/C, TV, hair dryer, minibar.

INEXPENSIVE

The Beach Club 📖 This delightful little place, on the beach just before Senggigi and next to Café Alberto (p. 303), is popular with Lombok expats and tourists. The club has lounging *bales* and tables on the beach, a backpacker's cottage, and three beautiful timber bungalows with thatched roofs nestled in a beachfront garden. In the center of the pretty tropical garden is a gorgeous swimming pool, with an elevated deck and comfortable sun loungers to take in the ocean views.

Jl. Raya Batu Bolong, Senggigi. www.thebeachclublombok.com. ✆ **0370/693637** or 081/805243380. 6 units. Year-round Rp220,000–Rp550,000. Rates include breakfast and taxes. AE, DC, MC, V. **Amenities:** Cafe; restaurant; bar; outdoor pool; Wi-Fi. *In room/villa:* A/C, TV/DVD, movie library, minibar.

Bulan Baru Hotel (the New Moon) ⚱ Located 1km (half a mile) north of Windy Beach, the Bulan Baru is nestled in a pretty valley opposite a long peaceful stretch of beach. The rooms are spacious and comfortable and feature open-air garden bathrooms. The central pool has swim-up bar service. Bulan Baru is 7km (4 miles) north of Senggigi—close enough to enjoy all the facilities of the tourist resort, but far enough away to have a sense of village living.

Jl. Raya Senggigi, Setangi. ✆ **0370/693785.** 12 units. Year-round Rp250,000; extra bed Rp50,000. No credit cards. **Amenities:** Restaurant; bar; Internet; outdoor pool. *In room:* A/C, minibar.

Puri Bunga Beach Cottages On a terraced hillside overlooking Senggigi Beach, opposite the Pasar Seni (Art Market), this was one of the first hotels in Senggigi. Choose from budget to midrange cottages. Interiors are simply decorated and rather basic, but all have private terraces with fantastic views of the stunning sunsets.

Jl. Raya Mangsit Beach, Senggigi. www.puribungalombok.com. ✆ **0370/693013.** 46 units. High season Rp600,000–Rp1,500,000; low season Rp400,000–Rp1,000,000. Rates exclude taxes. AE, MC, V. **Amenities:** Restaurant; bar; babysitting; bicycles; concierge; outdoor pool; room service; watersports. *In room:* A/C, TV, hair dryer, minibar, Wi-Fi.

Windy Beach Resort For travelers less concerned with plush surroundings and more concerned with unwinding in a beautiful natural environment, Windy Beach is the perfect choice along this stretch. This rustic and charming property on its own beachfront in north Mangsit offers basic but comfortable rooms; the deluxe bungalows are more spacious. Walk along the peaceful, white-sand beach, relax and read in beachside *bales,* or lay by the beachfront pool to watch the stunning sunsets.

Jl. Raya Mangsit Beach, Senggigi. www.windybeach.com. ✆ **0370/693191.** 16 units. High season US$62–US$72; low season US$50–US$60; extra bed adult US$10, children 11 and below US$5. Rates include breakfast and taxes. No credit cards. **Amenities:** Restaurant; outdoor pool. *In room:* A/C, hair dryer, minibar.

Where to Eat

Look out for theme dinners and traditional **dinner shows** at the hotels. Shows usually feature traditional music, theater, and dance presentations by local performers and are accompanied by a reasonably priced buffet dinner. The Sheraton, Santosa, Holiday Resort, and Qunci Villas often host cultural dinner dances.

You can find domestic and imported groceries at the **Deli Senggigi** (Jl. Raya Senggigi; ✆ **0370/693841**). For good coffee and decent baked bread, head to the Swiss-owned **Café Lombi** (Senggigi Square; ✆ **081/8365790;** www.cafelombi. com), which promises foam in your cappuccino or your money back.

EXPENSIVE

Qunci Villas ★★ ⛫ INTERNATIONAL For the ultimate in romance, book the Romantic Dinner for Two at Qunci Villas (p. 300). An intimate *bale* on the beach is draped with flowing curtains, and decorated with glowing candles and fresh flowers. The scrumptious meal includes king prawn salad, soup, and a platter of assorted seafood—lobster, crab, fish, prawns, clams—accompanied by rice and water spinach.

Dessert is a homemade lemon tart with berry coulis. A bottle of white or red wine is included in the very reasonable price of Rp250,000 per couple.

Jl. Raya Mangsit, Senggigi. © **0370/693800.** www.quncivillas.com. Main course Rp58,000–Rp150,000. MC, V. Daily 7am–10pm.

MODERATE

Square Restaurant ★★ 🏢 INTERNATIONAL   Square is indisputably the fine dining choice in town. Executive Chef Wayan Budiana has been involved in the Bali restaurant scene for many years, most notably at the hugely successful Mozaic (p. 180), before moving to Lombok. The restaurant has a temperature-controlled wine cellar and one of the best-stocked bars in Lombok. Imported wines, Cuban cigars, beautifully presented meals, efficient and friendly service, and top-quality produce are all hallmarks of dining here. Foie gras has almost become the restaurant's signature dish, pan-seared and served with apple chutney and tamarind. Or try the beef tenderloin, with mashed potato and broccoli au gratin.

Jl. Raya Senggigi, Senggigi. © **0370/664-4888.** www.squarelombok.com. Lunch Rp45,000–Rp70,000; dinner Rp60,000–Rp150,000; set menu Rp275,000. AE, MC, V. Daily 11am–11pm.

Warung Menega 🏢 BARBECUE/SEAFOOD   Slightly out of town, to the south near the Bintang Hotel, this is a similar seafood barbecue experience to those in Jimbaran on Bali. Warung Menega serves fresh local seafood barbecues every day for lunch and dinner. Tables are set up on the sand, with the waves only a few paces away. Wonderfully fresh snapper, barramundi, grouper, and other fish are barbecued and served whole, with rice, water spinach, and a selection of dipping sauces. Guests select fish, lobster, prawns, squid, and local clams displayed on ice near the barbecue; price is determined by weight. The local clams, topped with a piquant barbecue sauce and then lightly grilled, are seriously delicious and only Rp60,000 per kilo (2.2 lbs.).

Jl. Raya Senggigi 6, Senggigi. © **0370/663-4422.** www.menega.com. Seafood per kg: crab Rp100,000; lobster Rp350,000–Rp550,000; fish Rp75,000–Rp60,000. No credit cards. Daily noon–11pm.

INEXPENSIVE

Asmara Restaurant ☺ 🥄 GERMAN/INDONESIAN/SASAK   This place has deservedly been one of Senggigi's most popular restaurants for many years. On the main street, just up from the Art Market, the restaurant offers street-side or elegant indoor dining. There's also a separate bar, billiards room, library, and PlayStation for youngsters. Children also have a special menu, with sensible prices and serving sizes. The restaurant offers a good selection of local Sasak and Indonesian dishes, together with German specialties and international food. Organically grown herbs, homemade breads and yogurt, and fresh local produce set this restaurant apart from the rest. Try the locally produced pineapple wine—a dry, white wine with a subtle pineapple finish and a kick. It's the Lombok version of grappa. Special dishes of seasonal fare are available every week, and a great-value, three-course lunch is available every day for just Rp45,000. Every Friday night is "Stammtisch," a German tradition of "open table" (buffet), where anyone is welcome to join the table of expats and residents enjoying the good food and live music.

Jl. Raya Senggigi, Senggigi. © **0370/693619.** www.asmara-group.com. Set lunch Rp55,000; Indonesian Rp35,000–Rp60,000; Western Rp60,000–Rp175,000. MC, V. Daily 8am–midnight.

Bumbu Café THAI   The pad Thai and the curries taste a little more Indonesian than Thai, but given the slim pickings, it's not a bad choice for lunch or a casual dinner.

This streetside cafe, located in the heart of Senggigi, is a favorite of Lombok expats. Fresh juices and continental dishes are also on the menu.

Jl. Raya Senggigi, Senggigi. ☏ **081/805237126.** Lunch Rp40,000–Rp60,000; dinner Rp50,000–Rp100,000. No credit cards. Daily 11am–11pm.

Café Alberto ★ ☺ ITALIAN/SEAFOOD On the beach, just at the south entrance to Senggigi, is one of the best Italian restaurants in Lombok. Café Alberto also has an open lounge area, a pool, and a poolside bar overlooking the ocean. Guests are invited to spend their day by the beach, swimming in the pool, lounging on the comfortable banquettes, taking advantage of the free Wi-Fi, as well as enjoying the great food. Fresh seafood barbecues, authentic pastas, bruschetta, and wood-fired pizzas are Café Alberto's best dishes. Don't forget to try the homemade limoncello.

Jl. Raya Senggigi, Senggigi. ☏ **0370/693039** or 0370/693313. www.cafealbertolombok.com. Indonesian Rp20,000–Rp55,000; pasta Rp48,000–Rp55,000; seafood Rp70,000–Rp80,000. MC, V. Daily 9am–midnight.

De Quake Restaurant ★ 📍 SEAFOOD This delightful find sits on the beach-front in the Pasar Seni (Art Market). Enjoy the best strawberry margaritas in town while lazing on the cushions and watching the magnificent Senggigi sunset. The superbly fresh seafood dishes include a scallop and cucumber salad for Rp38,000, or a seafood basket for two with lobster, king prawns, squid, fish, crab, clams served with steamed rice, and water spinach for Rp635,000.

Art Market, Senggigi. ☏ **0370/693694.** www.dequake.com. Main courses Rp45,000–Rp55,000. MC, V. Daily 10am–11pm.

Senggigi Outdoors

Senggigi Reef, off the point near the Senggigi Beach Hotel, has good coral for snorkeling and, in the right conditions, some decent surf breaks. You can rent **snorkel** gear from the beachside stalls. You can also rent **canoes** from the beach on the weekends and during peak tourism times. Local **outrigger boats** (*prahu*) are lined up on the beach between the Santosa Resort and the Art Market and can be chartered for trips along the coast or out to the Gili Islands. The cost is between Rp300,000 and Rp450,000, depending on the number of passengers and number of islands on your itinerary. North of Senggigi, most beaches are deserted and you can easily find your own exclusive beach for the day.

The **Senggigi wave** (**best season:** dry, Apr–Oct; **best swell:** west/southwest; **best size:** 3–5 ft.; **best winds:** southeast) is in front of the Senggigi Beach Hotel. This great right and left beach break can produce long rides when the swell is up. The wave is best on mid- to high tides and is only a short paddle from the beach. The crowds here are generally light and the peaceful serenity of surfing these white-sand beaches with very few surfers can be just the ticket for those wary of the growing Bali crowds.

Shopping

The **Pasar Seni** (Art Market; Jl. Raya Senggigi; daily 9am–9pm) is just south of the Sheraton between the main road and Senggigi Bay, and can also be reached by the beach. The market sells handicrafts and souvenirs from around Lombok, as well as T-shirts, sarongs, and clothing. You'll also find some more upmarket shops, such as **Exotic Style,** the **Little Shop,** and **Treasure Chest,** which all sell a selection of gifts, homewares, jewelry, and resort wear.

Most shops are along **Jalan Raya Senggigi** and are open daily 9am to 9pm. **Ciokolata Boutique,** next door to Senggigi Jaya Supermarket, sells a great range of designer resort and street wear. The boutique also has a small but lovely collection of expensive and exquisite Autore pearls, grown in Lombok.

Bayan, next to Restoran Taman, has a huge selection of Lombok handicrafts ranging from hand-carved wooden furniture, oil paintings, light shades and lamps, ceramics, and housewares at ridiculously low prices.

In the far right corner of Senggigi Plaza is **House of Pearls,** with beautiful fresh- and saltwater pearls and jewelry.

Spas

Although Lombok doesn't have the same range of options as Bali, there are a couple of good spas in the Senggigi area. For some of the best value treatments here, head to **Royal Spa** (Jl. Raya Senggigi, next to the Santosa Villas and Resort; ✆ 0370/686-6577) for inexpensive body massages (Rp85,000 for 60 minutes; Rp110,000 for 90 minutes) and foot reflexology (Rp65,000 for 60 minutes; Rp80,000 for 90 minutes). The **Puri Mas Resort** (p. 299) offers pampering in a more luxurious environment with reasonable prices.

Senggigi Entertainment & Nightlife

The hugely popular **Happy Café ★** (✆ 0370/693984; daily noon till late), on the corner of the main street and Senggigi Plaza, has live music nightly. Popular with expats, locals, and tourists, Happy Café has a laid-back, friendly atmosphere and a good selection of drinks, snacks, and main meals. Most people come for the music and the fun after 9pm.

Marina Café, Jl. Raya Senggigi (✆ 0370/693136; www.marinasenggigi.com; daily 7pm till late), is the busiest and most popular nightspot in town. Dining is available in the courtyard downstairs, and snacks are served from the bars on both levels. Marina regularly showcases top bands and DJs from around Indonesia. The regular house band plays covers of top-40 hits.

The **Sahara Club,** in Senggigi Plaza (✆ 0370/619-4143; daily 6pm till late; cover Fri and Sat Rp20,000), is regularly packed with locals, particularly the young and trendy set from Mataram. This Egyptian-themed club has live bands, floor shows, and top Indonesian DJs.

The beer garden at the **Asmara** restaurant (p. 302) is a popular watering hole for Lombok expats.

THE SOUTHWEST COAST & ISLANDS ★★

South of Lembar Harbour, the main port on West Lombok, the southwest coast is one of the most spectacular areas on the island and remains relatively undeveloped. Thirteen pristine, largely uninhabited islands lie just off the coast with excellent diving and snorkeling. This is a destination that has yet to be discovered—join in on the secret and you'll be rewarded with an amazing, off-the-beaten-track experience. A few of the islands have simple accommodations for travelers. No doubt this is the Gilis (chapter 15) of the future, and so come before the masses hear about it.

Exploring the Southwest Coast & Islands

The drive itself to this stretch of coast is a worthwhile trip, as the road meanders through villages where life is untouched by tourism. Along the roadside you'll see locals building and repairing boats, laying out handmade bricks to dry in the sun, working in the fields, and sometimes guiding primitive wooden plows harnessed to huge water buffalo as they prepare the fields for planting. Take your time exploring and don't be afraid to wander down some of the small dirt roads toward the beaches—often deserted paradises. The local people are delightfully friendly and children often call "hello" whenever they see you.

Heading south past Lembar Harbour, toward **Sekotong** on the left side of the road, is a sealed road leading up the hill. The steep climb results in a magnificent **panorama** across the fields, and stretches out across the clear waters, the white coastline, and the many small dot islands. A bit farther along the main road is **Taun,** a peaceful village on a wide, placid bay. Three lovely islands—Gili Nanggu, Gili Tangkong, and Gili Sudat—are easily accessible by local outrigger boats from here. A small sign in the nearby village will direct you to the local boat rental area, where you can arrange boat trips at reasonable rates.

Before you reach the local marine culture complex (Balai Budaya Laut), you'll find a small dirt road leading off toward **Gili Genting,** a small hill in the ocean just off the point. At high tide it's separated from the mainland by a shallow stretch of water and at low tide it's possible to walk out to explore the island. The rock formations are ancient lava flows carved into tunnels and caves by the sea and providing sheltered nooks and crannies of shade—a perfect setting for a picnic lunch.

Continue south and across the road on the beachfront is **Dive Zone** (✆ 081/339544998; www.divezone-lombok.com; excursion to Sekotong or Kuta US$52–US$110, to Belongas US$58–US$145), the only dive facility in this part of Lombok. Dive Zone's local experts have pioneered the development of previously unknown dive sites in this area. They also offer island-hopping tours to explore the many islands around Sekotong and farther south. A long jetty stretches over the sea at the Dive Zone site (one of the **Sundancer** facilities, a high-end resort that's been under construction for years), with coral and fish clearly visible in the clear water below.

At the next intersection is a signpost for Labuhan Poh and Pelangan, the site of **Bola Bola Paradis** (see below).

The largest of the islands here is **Gili Gede,** appropriately meaning "Big Island." The island is easily accessed by boat from the village of Tembowong. Local boat owners charge between Rp100,000 and Rp150,000, depending on the number of passengers. Gili Gede, **Gili Nanggu,** and **Gili Asahan** are among the few in the

LOMBOK'S (& THE WORLD'S?) greatest WAVE

Desert Point (**best season:** dry Apr–Oct; **best swell:** west/southwest; **best size:** 4–8 ft.; **best winds:** southeast), voted by Australian surf magazine *Tracks* as the world's greatest wave, is located near a tiny fishing village called **Bangko Bangko** on the mountainous southwest tip of Lombok. As getting there is a real mission overland due to poor road conditions, instead many surfers prefer to surf this from the regular charter boats departing Bali's Benoa Harbour on week-long "surfaris." The more intrepid and hardy adventurer can stay at the small, basic homestays that have recently sprung up in the area and wait for the notoriously fickle wave to come alive. When it does turn on, it's not unknown for helicopters to drop a load of pro surfers on the spot for the day's action. Crowds can get big, especially if the place is firing. Tricky currents separate those who should be out there from those who shouldn't, but on its prime days there are enough perfect waves to please the masses. Look out for the crowds of local youngsters riding pieces of wood on the calmer days.

area that have accommodations. The surfing mecca of **Bangko Bangko** is on the far southwest tip of Lombok. Although the road deteriorates after Labuhan Poh, it's still passable for most vehicles in the dry season. The drive to the point is dotted with tiny villages, making it a worthwhile trip even for nonsurfers.

Where to Stay & Eat

Accommodations in the area are found on the mainland or on several of the southwest Gilis (Gili Gede, Nanggu, and Asahan). The islands are the place to go if you want to be completely unplugged from modern life (that is, no air-conditioning, televisions, or fresh running water), while mainland accommodations offer more amenities.

ON THE MAINLAND

Bola Bola Paradis 🏨   This peaceful hotel in Pelangan is one of the few places to stay in the southwest. Funky designed rooms and comfortable lounging platforms on the terraces are set on lawns leading to the beach. Comfortable rooms are also in the main building, and have private terraces facing the beach. The restaurant can arrange fresh fish and seafood dinners. The hotel organizes snorkeling and boat trips.

Pelangan. www.bolabolaparadis.com. ✆ **081/75787355.** 11 units. Year-round Rp325,000 standard, Rp350,000 superior, Rp440,000 luxury. Rates exclude breakfast. No credit cards. **Amenities:** Restaurant; bar; room service. *In room:* Fan, minibar.

Cocotino's ☺   One of the few professionally run resorts in the area, this new property offers semi-detached bungalow accommodations on a secluded beach within spitting distance of several of the southwest Gilis. Built-in day beds in the rooms make it a good choice for couples traveling with a small child and the spacious villas are perfect for bigger families. The resort offers an on-site diving and snorkeling center.

Dusun Pandanan, Desa Sekontong Barat, Kecamatan Sekotong, Kabupaten Lombok Barat. www. cocotinos-sekotong.com. ✆ **081/933136089.** 20 units. High season US$150; low season US$73. Rates include breakfast and exclude taxes. MC, V. **Amenities**: Restaurant; bar; airport transfer; spa; Wi-Fi. *In room:* A/C, TV, hair dryer.

Sempiak Villas & Laut Biru Café ★ 🍴 On the road between Sekatong and Kuta are these three gorgeous new villas on a stunning, white-sand beach—and they're a bargain. Each of the villas is uniquely designed and features vaulted ceilings and wood-paneled walls. The cafe, housed in a *lumbung*, offers excellent dishes including butter chicken and delectable desserts; it's open only during daytime hours. Lombok's terrible roads make it difficult to get to the villas and the cafe (and once you get there it's quite isolated), but it's certainly worth the effort.

Selong Belanak Lombok. www.sempiakvillas.com. ℂ **08/2144303337.** 5 units. Rp630,000–Rp1,260,000. Rates exclude taxes. AE, MC, V. **Amenities:** Restaurant; outdoor pool; DVD library. *In room:* Internet access, minibar, MP3 docking station.

ON THE ISLANDS

Gili Nanggu Cottages 🛍 This places offers the only accommodations and restaurant on Gili Nanggu. *Lumbung* bungalows are right on the beach. Basic but comfortable, the bungalows have a bathroom and hammocks downstairs and bedrooms upstairs. Farther back are cottages with air-conditioning and hot water. The carpeted floors are incongruous, but the cottages are comfortable if you intend to stay for a few days. The restaurant serves fresh seafood, although prices are higher than usual. Cold beer and drinks, and a good snack menu, are available during the day.

Gili Nanggu. www.gilinanggu.com. ℂ **0370/623783.** 17 units. Year-round US$30–US$44 standard. Rates include taxes. No credit cards. **Amenities:** Restaurant. *In room:* A/C (in some), fan.

Pearl Beach Resort ★★ 🛍 🍴 This is one of our favorite places to stay in all Lombok—it strikes just the right balance between comfort and that "deserted tropical island" feel. It offers the only accommodations on the island of Gili Asahan. Run by a friendly Lombok native and owned by a German, the resort offers modern bungalows with outdoor bathrooms, hot water, and electricity via a generator in the evenings. Each bungalow has a porch with a day bed on a swing for lounging, and a small restaurant offers complimentary free-flow tea and coffee. Excellent snorkeling featuring pristine reefs is accessible just off the shore. The resort plans to have an in-house dive center ready by early 2012.

Gili Asahan. www.pearlbeach-resort.com. ℂ **081/907247696.** 6 units. Year-round Rp570,000. Rates include breakfast. V. **Amenities:** Restaurant; bar; snorkeling. *In room:* Fan.

Secret Island Resort These accommodations on Gili Gede are nothing fancy, but are adequate and a perfect base for exploring the surrounding islands. Choose from a range of eclectic rooms, with cottages facing the beach and a hillside villa overlooking the ocean. The resort has its own speedboat with experienced captain for fishing charters and offers snorkeling and island-hopping tours. They also offer transfers from Bali and Senggigi (and other locations by arrangement), making getting to the island easy. With no roads and very little development, a few days here offers travelers the chance to relax and recharge on a true deserted island.

SW. 12 Gilis; Sekotong, Gili Gede. www.secretislandresort.com. ℂ **081/803762001.** 12 units. High season Rp240,000 standard, Rp780,000 villa, Rp480,000 reef bungalow; low season Rp200,000 standard, Rp650,000 villa; Rp400,000 reef bungalow. Rates include breakfast. No credit cards. **Amenities:** Restaurant; bar; babysitting; bikes; watersports. *In room:* Fan, Internet (for a fee).

Via Vacare 🛍 This Dutch-run property offers rustic bungalows that "challenge" their guests to unplug from modern life. The rooms are basic but comfortable; candles and oil lamps stand-in for electric lamps in the evenings and water is carried by the bucket. Even cheaper backpacker accommodations are offered in open-air pavilions facing the beach. The Dutch owner, Jet, offers daily yoga classes and guests are invited to help cook meals in the kitchen. Good diving and snorkeling are just a short boat ride away.

Gili Gede. www.viavacare.com. ☎ **081/934374793.** 4 units. Rp250,000–Rp400,000 bungalow; Rp75,000 budget accommodations. Rates exclude breakfast. No credit cards. **Amenities:** Restaurant; library; yoga. *In room*: Fan.

KUTA & THE SOUTH COAST ★★

In an island nation with a seemingly infinite sublime coastline, the south coast of Lombok surely rates among the best. **Kuta** is the south coast's main village and center of tourism development, and is the hub for exploring the southern beaches. Around 60km (37 miles) south of Mataram and about 1½ hour's drive from Senggigi, Kuta (sometimes spelled Kute) makes for a wonderful day trip from other points in Lombok, or as an alternative holiday destination in its own right. Kuta is a small haven of hotels, homestays, backpacker hostels, and simple restaurants catering mainly to surfers. The small-scale development evokes Bali in the 1980s. Kuta and the surrounding beaches have gained an international reputation as some of the best surfing destinations in southeast Asia. Although the beaches are stunning, also be prepared for a rustic atmosphere in Kuta catering to backpackers, hippies, and surfers. With the new airport just having opened, though, Kuta is getting set to take off in a more developed fashion, and may someday become similar to the better-known Kuta in Bali.

Getting There & Getting Around

From the cities, head south along the main road to Praya, passing through small villages along the way. Public transport is infrequent; **rent a car** or motorbike, or car with a driver for a day trip. The new Lombok International Airport is accessible by taxi in 30 minutes while the village is around 1½ hours from Senggigi.

Exploring the South Coast

As you drive to the south, the landscape becomes much drier away from the mountains and wide fields of crops become the norm. On reaching the south coast the landscape opens up to reveal a long coastline with some of the most sublime beaches and views in Indonesia.

On the east side of the road, just before Kuta, is **Rambitan,** a village with clusters of low, thatch-roofed homes with cow dung floors of the traditional Sasak style, as well as thatched *lumbung*. On the west side of the road is **Sade,** a hilltop village with one of the oldest mosques in Lombok, **Mesjid Kuno.** Both villages are interesting examples of traditional Sasak architecture and communal living in compounds, where life continues as it has for centuries. Residents act as guides for a small fee, encourage walks through either of these villages, and are happy to share a glimpse of their lifestyles with visitors. A small donation is requested at both sites.

Around 4km (2½ miles) east of Kuta is **Tanjung A'an ★★★**, a beautiful, white-sand bay flanked by lava rocks perfect for swimming. Farther east is **Gerupuk,** well known as a top surf location.

To the west of Kuta are a series of beautiful beaches and bays hidden behind headlands and rolling hills, providing peaceful and secluded spots for picnics and swimming. **Mawun Beach** is around 30 minutes drive to the west and is a picturesque bay

SURFING ON LOMBOK'S southern PENINSULA: EKAS BAY

The south coast is where the gentle Lombok waters meet the Indian Ocean, forming great swells and surf breaks. It's easy to rent a board and a surf guide to learn to surf or access the more challenging surf breaks in the area.

Ekas Bay (Teluk Ekas; **best season:** dry Apr–Oct; **best swell:** west/southwest; **best size:** 3–5 ft.; **best winds:** southeast) on Gili Melayu, Lombok's islandlike southern peninsula, is home to a variety of breaks. "Outside Ekas" is a powerful left-hander to satisfy the most power-hungry chargers; "Inside Ekas" has a much mellower wave breaking both left and right. Those not wanting an extreme challenge can surf the left-hander, with its great conditions for beginners. Ekas is never crowded as the surf charter boats rarely pass these waters and it's often only surfed by guests at **Heaven on the Planet** (www.heavenontheplanet.co.nz; ℂ 081/23705393 or 081/23751103; minimum 2-night stay; rates per night all-inclusive for twin share: high season AU$130 for more than 10 nights, AU$150 less than 10 nights; low season AU$110 for more than 5 nights, AU$130 less than 5 nights; no credit cards). The owners of Heaven on the Planet recently opened **Ocean Heaven** 1km (half a mile) away, which offers similarly off-the-beaten track accommodations on a pristine beach.

with a nice, white-sand beach and calm waves, perfect for swimming. **Mawi,** just west, has good right- and left-hand barrels for surfing when the swell is large enough. Farther west are picturesque **Selong Belanak** and many more scenic bays and beaches, largely deserted, although the road deteriorates rapidly and the going can be rough. Use an experienced local guide with a good vehicle.

Just to the east of the main Kuta area, the beach in front of the Novotel (p. 310) is sometimes referred to as **Mandalika,** named after legendary Princess Mandalika. See the box, "Bau Nyale Festival."

Where to Stay

Kuta Paradise   This is one of the better budget accommodations in Kuta, though that's not saying a whole lot given the options. Newly built, the bungalows lack any character, but they're clean and provide some basic amenities. The location puts you across the street from the beach, and it's at the edge of Kuta's development, on the way to the Novotel so more peace is offered here than at some of the more centrally located accommodations. There's a decent lap pool at the center of the property and an open-air restaurant serves international dishes.

Jl. Pariwisata Pantai, Kuta Pujut, Lombok. www.kutaparadise.webstarts.com. ℂ **08/7864311153.** 6 units. High season Rp600,000; low season Rp450,000. Rates include breakfast. No credit cards. **Amenities:** Restaurant; pool. *In room:* A/C, TV, DVD player.

Matahari Inn   In town rather than on the beach, the Matahari is one of the original hotels in Kuta and still offers good value, budget accommodations. The standard rooms, basic but reasonable, are set in pretty gardens with a swimming pool. The six villas are better quality, built in Sasak style with a thatched roof, and decorated with traditional, inlaid wood furniture. The spacious garden bathrooms have bathtubs and modern fittings. A good restaurant on-site serves international "tourist food" and a selection of local dishes.

BAU NYALE festival

This festival (Feb or Mar) commemorates the legend of the Putri (Princess) Mandalika, who was so beautiful and adored that, when she was of marriageable age, every prince in Lombok sought her as his bride. Legend says that when she couldn't choose between the suitors and fighting broke out between the rivals, rather than throw the kingdom into chaos, she ended her life by leaping into the sea, saying, "Kuta," or "Wait for me here," in the local Sasak language.

When she disappeared into the waves, hundreds of *nyale* (sea worms) floated to the surface. Local *dukun* (priests) announced that the worms were the Princess's hair, or that her body had been transformed into the worms. Thus, every year in February or March, when the conditions are right for spawning and the *nyale* worms return to the site, locals remember the Mandalika legend.

Tens of thousands (some say up to 100,000) of revelers attend the all-night celebrations of the Bau Nyale festival. A full program of cultural performances takes place on the beachfront, the highlight being an enchanting reenactment of the Princess Mandalika legend. Young people from the villages who are normally kept separated are permitted to flirt and strut. It's also the time to compete with improvised *pantun* poetry, a ritualized form of competing in rhyming couplets.

Early in the morning, around 3am, the first worms spawn and the crowd rushes into the water to catch them, amid much laughter and excitement. Associated with fertility, the sea worms are cooked and eaten for good luck and prosperity. As part of the fertility rituals, they're ground up and placed in irrigation channels to help ensure bountiful crops.

Jl. Raya Pantai, Kuta, Lombok. www.indo.com/hotels/matahari. ☎ **0370/655000.** 4 units. Year-round US$26–US$79. Rates include breakfast. No credit cards. **Amenities:** Restaurant; outdoor pool. *In room:* A/C, fan.

Novotel Lombok Resort ★★ ☺   This is the only truly comfortable place to stay in Kuta and is quite an anomaly for the area. The Novotel sits on the pristine white sands of Mandalika Beach, just east of Kuta. The resort is built in the traditional Sasak style and blends beautifully with its surroundings through the use of natural woods, stone, and earth tones. The Pool Villas are top of the range, with lovely gardens, private swimming pools, and lounging *bales*. The spacious rooms are decorated in ethnic style and have gorgeous natural bathrooms. The resort itself offers so many activities and facilities that it's almost easy never to step out to explore the coast. Every day features complimentary classes for guests in subjects such as Bahasa Indonesian, pottery making, weaving, woodcarving, and more, all taught by talented locals. A range of activities is geared to children. Other options include aqua aerobics, beach volleyball, archery, diving, and snorkeling for the active; plus, the glorious body treatments offered by Vous Spa for the less energetic. Kafe Chilli sits under a high thatched roof on the beachfront and offers informal dining and live entertainment every night. The resort's stylishly designed, fine-dining restaurant Empat Ikan (dinner only) specializes in seafood.

Mandalika Resort Pantai Putri Nyale, Pujut Lombok Tengah, Mataram. www.novotellombok.com. ☎ **0370/653333.** 101 units. High season US$120–US$465; low season US$89–US$438. Rates may or may not include breakfast. AE, MC, V. **Amenities:** 2 restaurants; children's club; 4 outdoor pools including children's pool; spa. *In room/villa:* A/C, TV, hair dryer, minibar, Wi-Fi (for a fee).

Tastura Hotel   On the main road opposite Kuta Beach, the Tastura has a lagoon pool, restaurant, shop, and convention hall. These midrange accommodations are in a great location for exploring the area and a magnificent beach is across the road.

Jl. Raya Pantai, Kuta, Lombok. www.hoteltastura.com. ✆ **0370/655540.** 25 units. High season US$45–US$85; low season US$35–US$75. Rates include breakfast and exclude taxes. AE, MC, V. **Amenities:** Restaurant; outdoor pool; room service. *In room:* A/C, TV, minibar.

Where to Eat

Ashtari ★ 🏠 INTERNATIONAL   On the main road out of town to the west, about 2km (1¼ miles) from central Kuta, Ashtari is set high on a hill with sublime views over Kuta and the southern beaches. Open only for breakfast and lunch, visitors love the homemade vegetarian meals and laid-back ambience. The emphasis is on fresh, organic, and natural local ingredients. Fresh juices, herbal teas, smoothies, and other delicious and healthy beverages are also available. Try a freshly baked baguette with goat's cheese, sun-dried tomatoes, and avocado, washed down with a divine rose-hip tea. There's a good selection of magazines and board games. A suspended balcony begs you to reach for your camera.

Kuta, Lombok. ✆ **081/75787502.** ashtarionlombok@gmail.com. Main courses Rp30,000–Rp150,000. No credit cards. Daily 7am–6pm.

Vue SEAFOOD   The service at this Novotel (see above) restaurant is impeccable though the food is only average. But if you're looking for a romantic setting and a fine-dining atmosphere, this may be your only choice unless you're willing to make the haul to Senggigi. While the lobster spring roll and Caesar salad appetizers are perfectly fine, we found the seafood and the pastas to be overcooked. Perhaps the owners could lure back the chef from Warung Bule (see below).

In the Novotel, Pantai Putri Nyale, Kuta, Lombok. ✆ **0370/653333.** www.novotellombok.com. Main courses Rp100,000–Rp200,000. AE, DC, MC, V. Daily noon–10pm.

Warung Bule ★★ 🍴 SEAFOOD/INTERNATIONAL   This unassuming little eatery offers impressive "modernist cuisine" by the charming local chef Hamiri who used to work at the Novotel down the street and once cooked at an international conference attended by American President Barack Obama. Warm orange walls line the airy dining room with a view of the beach. The menu features good cocktails, freshly caught lobster and king prawns, and international dishes such as Singaporean chili crab and fish'n'chips – all at a fraction of the price you'd pay at a hotel.

Jl. Raya Pantai Kuta, Lombok. ✆ **081/917996256.** Main courses Rp30,000–Rp300,000. No credit cards. Daily 1–10pm.

Kuta Entertainment & Nightlife

Most of Kuta's late night activities happen on hammocks strung in front of hotels, but a crop of new bars and cafes have become popular watering holes. **Gecko's Lounge 'N' Bar**, Jl. Raya Pariwisata (✆ **081/7362971**), has live bands on Wednesday and Saturday nights and serves pizzas cooked in a wood-fired oven. Next door, **The Spot** and **Café 7** are also popular. Both offer a wide range of drinks, provide free Wi-Fi, and show sports and movies. Streets in Kuta are dark at night and petty crime is sometimes a problem. Travel with friends or by hotel cars after dark.

CENTRAL LOMBOK

Lombok is divided into four governmental regions: west, central, east, and the recently created north Lombok regency. The south of the island, except for those areas bordering the west and east coasts, is therefore classified as "central Lombok." The central area, mainly on the southern slopes of the Gunung Rinjani mountain range, is cooler and more lush than the south thanks to abundant rainfall in the wet season and protection by forests and jungle throughout the rest of the year.

Getting There & Getting Around

The main road that runs through the cities continues east across the entire island, providing easy access to the central and eastern regions. **Public buses** and *bemo* run from Bertais bus terminal near Sweta, but for exploring the area properly and the small villages off the main road, private transport is essential. Alternatively, the interesting villages of the area can be explored on day trips from Senggigi or Kuta.

Exploring & Shopping: Central Lombok

A drive through this area takes you through numerous villages specializing in traditional crafts.

About a half-hour drive southeast of Cakranegara, the town of **Praya** is the hub of the south and seat of the Central Lombok governmental administration. This is the home of the **Saturday market,** central to many of the area's handicraft villages.

Five kilometers (3 miles) to the west of Praya is the weaving village of **Sukarara,** where ikat and traditional cloth is made and sold. Weavers work outside many of the shops, using antiquated back strap looms. Some of the larger pieces can take several months to weave and collectors from around the world visit this village to purchase the blankets, sarongs, and cloth.

The Thursday market is farther south at **Sengkol; Beleka,** about 10km (6 miles) east of Praya, is the site of a Wednesday market. Both local markets sell food and vegetables, live chickens and fish, as well as some locally produced household goods.

Families of **Loyok,** a small dusty village on the road to Tetebatu, make traditional woven products, using rattan, grasses, and bamboo. The good-quality baskets, boxes, mats, and other weaving are often sent to Bali, where they fetch much higher prices. Prices here are cheap but, as anywhere in Indonesia, bargain anyway. Visit the shops and the family compounds out back, where several generations of the same family sit around, chatting and weaving.

On the main road east across the island, around 50km (31 miles) from the cities, a signposted road leads north to **Tetebatu,** on the southern slopes of Gunung Rinjani. This area is wet and misty during rainy season, cool and lush during the dry. A nice waterfall called **Jeruk Manis** ★ is about an hour's walk to the north of

Tetebatu, through a monkey-filled forest. The scenery is lovely and the falls are worth seeing, but it's best to take a local guide with you, as there have been problems with theft in the past. Guides can be organized at any of the homestays listed below.

Near Lendang Nangka is **Jojang Spring,** with great vistas and a forest inhabited by black monkeys. In August, Sasak boxing takes place in the village.

Heading farther east on the main road, a turnoff at Lenek leads to the small village of **Pringgasela.** This area is a major center for ikat and traditional fabrics produced by hand on old-fashioned looms. Visit the small houses and shops here to purchase the distinctive, traditionally woven, colorful fabrics.

Where to Stay & Eat

Accommodations and places to eat in the area are scarce. What few exist are usually basic homestays and backpacker accommodations that can be booked on arrival, and basic warungs and roadside stalls.

Wisma Soedjono (www.wismasoedjono.com; ℂ **081/8279774;** year-round Rp175,000–Rp250,000; no credit cards), in Tetebatu, is set high on the hillside with views of the countryside, and is the most popular hotel and restaurant in the area. The Dutch colonial-style hotel, one of the original hotels in the area and family owned, has a range of fan-cooled rooms and a pool. The more expensive rooms have hot water. The restaurant (Rp15,000–Rp30,000) serves Indonesian and Sasak food, with some Western-style snacks.

Also in Tetebatu, **Hakiki** (no phone; high season Rp250,000–Rp400,000, low season Rp200,000–Rp350,000; no credit cards) is a lovely place to get away from it all. Set in rice fields at the end of Waterfall Street, the lovely bungalows with fans have terraces overlooking rice fields and mountains. There's also a good restaurant.

Another option in Tetebatu is **Green Orry** (ℂ **0376/22782;** high season Rp300,000–Rp400,000, low season Rp250,000–Rp350,000; no credit cards) with thatched-roof, fan-cooled rooms and bungalows. The better rooms are nicely decorated, very clean and comfortable. The good restaurant serves Indonesian and Western food at reasonable prices and the hotel can arrange guides and tours in the area, as well as tickets with Perama Tours to Bali and other destinations.

NORTH LOMBOK

Dominated by the purple peaks of the Rinjani mountain range and the majesty of Lombok's famous volcano, Gunung Rinjani, the north of the island offers stunning landscapes and long curves of deserted beaches. Jungles and rainforest with towering plantations of mahogany and teak provide ample opportunity for trekking and eco-tourism. North Lombok is generally undeveloped and allows travelers to get a sense of the history and traditional roots of the island. Don't expect tourist markets or restaurants and bars catering to Westerners.

Getting There & Getting Around

North Lombok is reached by two main roads, both in good condition and offering different scenic routes. The **coastal road** that runs from Ampenan all the way up the west coast to the north of the island provides stunning views of the many beautiful bays and beaches of the west coast, as well as vistas over the Gili Islands and Bali.

The **Pusuk Pass,** a winding mountain road that starts in **Gunungsari** and runs through the mountains inland, terminates at **Pemenang** in the north. The pass provides wonderful views of valleys and gorges, with rivers running through the tropical forests and small villages among the trees. Families of gray monkeys live in the jungle and come down to the road to beg for food from passing motorists.

A *bemo* runs from Gunungsari through the Pusuk Pass up to the north coast (about 30 min.; Rp5,000). *Bemo* also run regularly between Ampenan and Senggigi, and less frequently from Senggigi to Bangsal and Pemenang. The best way to see the north is by rented car or motorbike, or with a car and driver.

Bangsal is at the crossroads where the main coastal road meets the Pusuk Pass Road, with Jalan Raya (main street) continuing north all the way around the island to the east coast. The road to the west only runs about 1km (around half a mile) to **Bangsal Harbour,** the main point of departure to the Gili Islands (chapter 15).

Exploring North Lombok

Use a local guide, who can lead you through the jungle to waterfalls or point out places of interest, when exploring the trails of north Lombok. Negotiate a fee beforehand.

Bangsal is a pretty village with a large Balinese Hindu population, surrounded by rice fields, temples, and close to the ocean and the mountains. The village has a few small homestays, particularly on the road to the harbor, and makes a good base for exploring the north. The harbor, however, is renowned for the annoying touts and sellers who try to force travelers to charter boats and buy goods before going to the Gili Islands.

Farther north, a small, signposted road branches off from the main road to **Pantai Sira,** a beautiful, white-sand beach with good snorkeling on the offshore coral reef. This is also the site for the world-class **Kosaido Golf Course** (book via email at lombokkosaido@baligolfclubs.com; US$65–US$85 greens fee and caddy).

On the tip of the next peninsula north is a small temple, **Pura Medana,** an ancient Hindu site with wonderful sunset views and a peaceful atmosphere.

Tanjung, 5km (3 miles) north of Bangsal, is a large village with numerous warungs and shops, and one of the few public telephone offices (where you can make phone calls) in the north. Tanjung has an interesting daily **cattle market** for cows, goats, and horses.

Gondang, farther up the coast, is a small town near a good beach. **Tiu Pupus Waterfall** is a 20-minute walk beyond the end of a poorly marked, rocky road. The falls flow into a deep pool with nice swimming. The trek through the traditional Sasak village of **Kerurak** makes the effort worthwhile. Another half-hour trek from Tiu Pupus leads to **Kerta Gangga Waterfalls ★**, with three beautiful waterfalls set in the jungle.

The dusty, traditional village of **Segenter,** on the road to Anyar, provides a glimpse into the harsh reality of life on the island's dry side. The 300 villagers in this northern interior village eke out a basic living raising corn and beans, yet they welcome visitors with a smile and proudly share their simple life with tours through the village.

Bayan, farther north, is renowned as the root of early Islam on Lombok and maintains old dance and poetic traditions, such as *kemidi rudat,* a theater performance based on the *Thousand and One Nights.* One of the oldest and most important Waktu Telu (p. 285) mosques is in Bayan, and important sacred sites from Lombok's ancient past are located nearby.

The road from Bayan leads to **Senaru,** the gateway to the **Rinjani National Park.** The pretty village in lovely scenery has fantastic views of the volcanic mountains. The **Sendang Gile waterfalls ★★** at Senaru are among Lombok's most spectacular,

A Waterfall & Jungle Trek

You can engage the services of guides from the **Pondok Senaru & Restaurant** (p. 318) near the car park at Senaru for the less-than-a-hour trek through the jungle to the lovely **Tiu Kelep** waterfall. First, pay the modest admission fee at the gate (around Rp20,000) to **Sendang Gile Waterfall,** good for swimming.

Negotiate an additional fee of around Rp50,000 for a guide to take you through the forest to Tiu Kelep. Climb the rocks to the hidden cave behind the falls and follow the local legend that says for every pass behind the waterfall, you take 1 year off your age.

even after descending the 200-plus vertical steps to stand below them. The water cascades in a steep, vertical drop down the hillside into a rocky stream below.

Where to Stay

Hotel Tugu Lombok ★★★
This is a destination, rather than simply a place to stay, and is unlike any other hotel on Lombok. This luxurious resort is perched on a pristine beach neighboring the Kosaido Golf Course. Tugu Lombok features hundreds of original artworks and antiques collected as a loving testament to the long forgotten, original cultures of Lombok and Java. The Bhagavad Gita suites are highly recommended for those seeking luxury in a style reminiscent of the Indonesian royalty of yesteryear. Antique furnishings, soaring ceilings, and luxurious appointments are housed in private 400-sq.-m (4,305-sq.-ft.) villas with personal plunge pools. Air-conditioning, glowing candles, and perfumed air greets the tired traveler. The modern bathrooms open into a private garden with a rain-shower. A gigantic boulder, hollowed in the center, forms a bathtub to be filled with warm water and scented flowers.

Sire Beach, Sigar Penjalin, Tanjung. www.tuguhotels.com. (C) **0370/612-0111.** 19 units. High season US$215 standard, US$265 suite, US$450 villa; low season US$175 standard, US$225 suite, US$410 villa. AE, MC, V. **Amenities:** Restaurant; bar; babysitting; bikes; gym; outdoor pool; room service; spa; watersports. In room/villa: A/C, TV/DVD, movie library, stereo or CD, hair dryer, Internet (for a fee), minibar, MP3 docking station.

Lombok Lodge ★
Although this new boutique property is just next door to the Oberoi (see below) and has even poached a chef from its neighbor, don't expect it to have the same feel. Where the Oberoi is traditional, the Lombok Lodge is sleek and modern. Design aficionados will appreciate the minimalist architecture with straight, geometric lines and beige walls. The rooms are swanky and modern, all overlooking a long infinity pool and the ocean, and feature amenities such as Hermes bath products, Bose sound systems, and iPods. The beach here isn't as nice as the Oberoi's, but the property offers day trips to the nearby Gili Islands. As expected from an Oberoi chef, the food is quite good but service is slow.

Jl. Oberoi, Tanjung, Lombok. www.thelomboklodge.com. (C) **0370/662-2926.** 9 units. High season US$431–US$490; low season US$375–US$425. Rates include breakfast. AE, MC, V. **Amenities:** Restaurant; bikes; 25m infinity pool; spa. In room: A/C, TV, DVD player, minibar, MP3 player, Wi-Fi (free).

Medana Resort
On the road to the Oberoi, overlooking palm groves and the ocean, this small resort is not as expensive or opulent as others in the area. Medana has spacious and comfortable bungalows set on terraced banks leading to a magnificent swimming pool. Each bungalow has canopied beds, teak furnishings, and garden bathrooms with sunken bathtubs, and private terraces overlooking the palms and the

glorious sunsets across the Gilis, Bali, and beyond. The resort also has its own glass-bottom boat and traditional sailing outrigger for exploring the brilliant reefs and the Gili Islands.

Jl. Medana, Tanjung. www.medanaresort.com. ✆ **0370/612-8000.** 6 units. Year-round US$115–US$142; extra person US$25. Rates include breakfast and taxes. MC, V. **Amenities:** Restaurant; bar; outdoor pool; room service; watersports. *In room:* A/C, TV, hair dryer, minibar.

The Oberoi ★★   Like most Oberoi resorts around the world, the Lombok version is a haven for those seeking the ultimate in luxury and service. Located on the tip of the Medana peninsula, not far from the Kosaido Golf Course, the Oberoi has one of the most sublime beaches in the area, with views of the Gili Islands. The heart of the resort is the huge, three-tiered infinity pool that seems to float out over the ocean. Most of the villas have private, walled courtyards and swimming pools. The rooms are luxurious with huge beds, spacious living areas, and all the comforts one would expect of a world-class resort. The garden bathtub is big enough for two, and is lined with scented oils and softly glowing candles. The other 30 luxury pavilions share the resort facilities, with cozy lounging and relaxing areas dotted around the pool and beachfront. The spa is renowned for its lavish body treatments, and an H2O Dive Center is on the beachfront.

Medana Beach, Tanjun. www.oberoihotels.com. ✆ **0370/613-8444.** 50 units. High season US$396–US$446 standard, US$570–US$1,077 villa; low season US$360–US$405 standard, US$520–US$1,075 villa. Rates exclude breakfast. AE, DC, MC, V. **Amenities:** 2 restaurants; bar; babysitting; bikes; concierge; gym; outdoor pool; room service; spa; tennis; watersports. *In room/villa:* A/C, TV/DVD, movie library, stereo or CD, hair dryer, Internet (for a fee), minibar, MP3 docking station.

Where to Eat

Apart from warungs and local eating houses, dining in north Lombok is limited to the upmarket resort hotels in the area; however, none are far from each other and it's easy to stay at one resort and dine at any of the others nearby.

You can enjoy fine dining at the Oberoi (above) at both the **Lumbung Restaurant ★★** and the **Sunbird Café ★** (AE, DC, MC, V; daily 6:30am–11pm). Continental and Asian-fusion cuisine is available at both, with the emphasis on fresh seafood. Start with seared sea scallops on soba noodles with shiitake, roasted sesame, and soy (say that five times fast!) for Rp160,000. For a main course, try Indian curry chicken with basmati rice, Indian pickles, and chutney at Rp195,000, or Australian lamb with sun-dried tomato and gnocchi for Rp385,000. Expat guests from Bali and the Gilis often hop over by speedboat to the beachfront Sunbird Café to dine on Asian tapas (Rp75,000–Rp130,000) and sip imported wines.

The **Kokok Pletok ★★** (a la carte US$5–US$10, set menu US$18; AE, DC, MC, V; daily 7am–11pm) in Hotel Tugu (p. 315) is a magnificent venue surrounded by statues of the rice Goddess Dewi. Breakfast includes bacon and eggs, eggs Benedict, muesli, fresh fruits, homemade yogurt, and traditional Indonesian breakfasts such as *bubur ayam* and *nasi goreng* (fried rice). The resort also offers a range of theme dinners (main courses Rp110,000–Rp215,000; set menu Rp315,000–Rp360,000), where guests are served authentic Indonesian dishes by waiters dressed in period costumes.

Medana Resort (p. 315) is a good alternative for those staying at the Oberoi, Tugu, and other resorts at Pantai Sire with lower prices than the others. The restaurant (main courses Rp45,000–Rp60,000; MC, V; daily 8am–10pm) offers a range of Indonesian specialties, fresh seafood, and Western dishes. Try the special rijsttafel, a huge feast with dessert for two people at Rp325,000.

Climbing Rinjani: Lombok's Sacred Volcano

Located on the north of the island, **Gunung Rinjani** ★★★ soars 3,726m (12,224 ft.) above sea level and is the second-highest **volcano** in Indonesia. Visitors from around the world come to Lombok to climb Gunung Rinjani to its crater lake or demanding summit. It's considered a "Home of the Gods" and the mountain is a pilgrimage site for prayer; pilgrims bathe in the pools and hot springs, which are said to have healing powers.

The 4-km (2½-mile) wide caldera near the top of the volcano is filled by a beautiful, crescent-shaped lake, **Danau Segara Anak** (Child of the Sea Lake). The 230m (755 ft.) deep lake contains plentiful fish and provides habitat for birds and other wildlife. A smaller volcanic cone, **Gunung Baru Jari,** was formed a mere couple of hundred years ago and juts from the crater's interior at the edge of the lake. Caves, waterfalls, and hot springs nestle around the volcano, most importantly **Aik Kalak** on the northeast of the crater, where the volcanically heated waters are said to cure illnesses and skin diseases. The **Rinjani National Park** (admission Rp150,000) is the nature reserve of 41,330 hectares (102,129 acres) surrounding the volcano.

Treks can be made from either the park's northern gateway at **Senaru** or its western edge at **Sembalun Lawang.** Most popular is a 3-day, 2-night route starting at Sembalun village and returning via Senaru. The first day's hike begins around 8:30am and covers around 12 km (7 miles) in roughly 7 hours of rainforest walking. After camping on the rim of Gunung Rinjani, hikers reach the summit the next morning (often in time to see the sunrise) and then descend to the lake, where they soak in a hot spring. Camp is made back at another section of the crater rim. The third day's descent covers some 8 km (5 miles) in time for transfers back to hotels.

A shorter, two-day, one-night climb from Senaru, where a number of trekking centers can organize trips, reaches the crater rim but not the summit. Companies in both Senaru and Sembalun Lawang can organize these treks, and shorter options, and offer basic homestays.

One of the most popular companies is the **Rinjani Trek Management Board** (RTMB; ✆ **0370/641124** or 081/1390047; www.lombokrinjanitrek.org). Originally set up and sponsored by the New Zealand government, it forms a partnership between the Rinjani National Park, the tourism industry, and the local community. Cooperatives are at Rinjani Trek Centre (RTC) in Senaru and the Rinjani Information Centre (RIC) in Sembalun Lawang (p. 321). Under the guidance of the RTMB, each center is run by a stakeholders' committee who look after roster systems for guides and porters, village tours, trail maintenance, and handicraft sales. Revenue from trekking and entry fees is used for conservation, training, and management of the Rinjani Trek, thus ensuring sustainability of this natural resource for the future. In 2004 the Rinjani Trek won the World Legacy Award for Destination Stewardship. Rinjani National Park is currently being considered for Geopark status and World Natural Heritage status by UNESCO.

Guides and porters at the trek centers have many years' experience on the mountain and in Rinjani National Park, together with a vested interest in safe and eco-friendly trekking, and are therefore a recommended choice. Two-day treks are US$200. Three-day treks are US$310. Both include the entrance fee, gear, meals including alcoholic beverages, porters, and return transport.

A cheaper yet still reputable company is the **Rinjani Trekking Club,** Senggigi Km 8 (✆ **081/75730415;** www.info2lombok.com). The 3-day route described above costs US$190; for 2 days, it's US$150. Prices include guides, porters, equipment,

TIPS FOR trekking GUNUNG RINJANI

- Always use a reputable trekking business and check that it has facilities to cope with emergencies.
- Never wander away on your own, even if you're an experienced climber. A number of deaths and injuries have occurred on the mountain. Loose shale and unstable surfaces are hazards.
- Use good quality, comfortable shoes and take a walking stick to help with the inclines.
- Make sure that you have a warm jacket and enough clothes because it's cold on the mountain.

- Check that your trekking company is supplying sleeping bags and blankets.
- Don't try to save money by trekking on your own or using unauthorized guides. Licensed guides have identification, and are experienced to handle your trek and the conditions on the mountain.
- Don't take passports or carry valuables that aren't essential to your trek.
- Please respect this natural wonder. Don't litter or leave anything on the mountain, except your footprints.

meals (excluding alcohol), entrance fees, and transfers to and from hotels. Groups leave daily and single travelers or small parties might have to travel together.

Trekking on the volcano isn't for everyone. A certain level of fitness is needed and climbing to the summit is particularly strenuous. Altitudes of over 2,700m (8,858 ft.) are reached in all these treks and, even on the equator, nighttime temperatures can be very cold, with strong winds and occasional rain. When climbing, use only authorized guides and reputable trekking businesses. Take as few valuables as possible and make sure the guides carry first-aid equipment.

The best time to climb Gunung Rinjani is during the dry season from around April to October, and ideally in July and August when sunny days and cooler temperatures allow the most comfortable climbing and provide the clearest views. Few guides take guests during the rainy season from December until March and early spring and late autumn are also sometimes wet.

WHERE TO STAY & EAT

Lembah Rinjani ★, Sembalun Lawang (✆ **081/805720243** or 0370/692179; year-round Rp275,000; no credit cards), is a charming and rustic mountain retreat at the foot of the Rinjani volcano. Rooms are basic, but very clean and comfortable, with private terraces and astounding views of the mountain, which seems to rise up immediately in front of you. The air here is clear and cold, rising up in mists when you breathe. At its restaurant, try the local curries, tasty soups, and stir-fries—all great for warming up. A house specialty is the *serbat* (a traditional Javanese drink), made with fresh cinnamon, nutmeg, ginger, and other ground spices. The staff is very knowledgeable about the area and many of them serve as guides and porters for climbing the mountain. Ask for one of them to show you around or guide you on a short mountain trek. The view from the small mountain just out of town is incredible and you can see a Hindu temple halfway up.

The **Pondok Senaru & Restaurant,** Rinjani National Park, Senaru (✆ **0370/ 692179;** main courses Rp10,000–Rp25,000; no credit cards; daily 8am–9pm), presents a good value on a small hillside next to the public parking area in Senaru, at the entrance to the Rinjani National Park. Stop here for a cool drink when visiting the waterfalls (p. 314) and enjoy the fine views from the garden *bales* over the rice terraces and jungle-covered foothills. The restaurant serves sandwiches and Indonesian meals for lunch and dinner. Basic accommodations are also available (Rp300,000– Rp600,000; no credit cards).

EAST LOMBOK

The east of the island is the least visited and developed, although large towns here support a thriving local population. Many of the villages in eastern Lombok are strongly Islamic. Travelers have reported harassment in the past, although most of the people are merely curious and eager to welcome visitors to their homes. You'll likely be curious too. Without the tourism infrastructure, you get a close-up look at the lifestyles and culture of the Sasak people.

Most people come here to catch a ferry to neighboring **Sumbawa,** en route to the islands of **Komodo** and **Flores** (see p. 322).

Getting There & Getting Around

East Lombok extends from Masbagik, on the main east-west road, across the island and encompasses the eastern slopes of the Rinjani mountain range down to the peninsula on the southeast corner of Lombok.

Public buses regularly travel the route across the island to **Kayangan,** the main port on the east coast. For exploring outside of these parameters, you'll need private transport. Rent a car or motorbike in Senggigi, the cities, or Kuta; alternatively, you could rent a car and driver to guide you around, but be prepared to pay the costs of accommodations and meals for the driver.

Exploring East Lombok

The beauty of the people in this area is that, if you're stuck, they'll always offer you a meal and a place to stay, in the true tradition of Sasak hospitality. Cross the island on the main road that links east to west. **Bonjeruk,** before the pottery village of Masbagik, is a village of numerous *dalang* (puppeteers) and many of the puppets for the shadow play *wayang sasak* are made here. Before you reach the coast, turn right at the road to **Selong,** the capital city and business hub of east Lombok. The atmosphere is reminiscent of a large town in the 1950s, with wide, tree-lined streets and old Dutch colonial architecture.

From Selong, return to the main road, heading toward Pringgabaya and turn left at the signpost to **Sapit,** a small village on the southern slopes (though seemingly at the top) of the Rinjani mountain range, where there's one of the few hotels in the area (the Hati Suci Homestay, p. 322). The steep road winds through mountain villages, interspersed with pretty fields of crops and patches of jungle. Low clouds gather on the mountains and the air is cool; the view is breathtaking, with villages and fields stretched in the distance, and the rainforest extending up the peaks behind.

It's easy to continue up over the mountain and down to the main villages of Sembalun Lawang and Sembalun Bumbung (see below) on the other side. From there, the road winds down the mountain and meets up with the main coastal road in north Lombok. An alternative and challenging route is to return to the main road and travel to the east coast from there on the main road that circumnavigates the island north.

The main east-west road intersects the coastal road at **Labuhan Lombok.** This is the main port in East Lombok, serving the shipping route from the eastern islands.

The port proper is called Kayangan. Gorgeous, **panoramic views** can be had from the hills before the harbor. Labuhan Lombok is a bustling town with plenty of warungs and eateries to refuel. A small hotel is close to the center of town, on the road out to Kayangan, for those wishing to stay, and the public ferry between Lombok and Sumbawa operates nonstop daily.

Following the main coastal road, heading north from Labuhan Lombok, the road winds past fields of tobacco and corn, with occasional glimpses of the Alas Strait, the sea separating Lombok from Sumbawa. The coastline of Sumbawa Island looms surprisingly close. At the small town of **Transat** there's a sign for Gili Lampu Bungalows (p. 322), with a dirt road leading down to the restaurant and beach.

The east is also home to the daily **Tanjung Luar Fish Market.** Arrive by 7am to see dozens of varieties of fish unloaded from boats and laid out on concrete floors, where the bargaining begins. On most days, visitors can see sharks and large manta rays among the catch of smaller fish. The fish odor can be strong, so bring a handkerchief to cover your nose. Or escape into the tamer, still colorful, vegetable market that abuts the fish stalls. Most of the bigger fish are sold early and the market winds down around 10am.

Labuhan Pandan is a small town on the northeast coast with shops and small warungs. The road north from Labuhan Pandan is in good condition and provides sublime views of the ocean. Small, white-sand-fringed islands are visible farther out in the bright blue water, while the green bulk of Sumbawa Island fills the horizon.

Farther north, the road winds up into the hills and the coastline drops away as it passes through small towns baking in the hot sun; sleepy houses are surrounded by fields of dry crops and browning grass. In one, an arched entrance to the soccer field proudly announces its creation in 1945—and it looks like the place, and pace, probably hasn't changed much since then.

The hills grow steeper and then become mountains, as the road journeys up onto the eastern slopes of the awesome Rinjani mountain range. To the left is the towering volcano, with fold after fold of mountain range swathed in green jungle.

The two huge islands of **Gili Sulat** and **Gili Lawang** stretch for miles along the coast. Both are uninhabited because fresh water is scarce, but they have great potential for ecotourism with their intact ecosystems, ample fishing, wetlands, mangroves, and superb snorkeling and diving. Currently, the only way to visit is to organize a trip with a local fishing boat. Inquire among the fishermen on the beaches and arrange a trip with transport back at the end of the day, for around Rp350,000.

The road gradually meanders back to hug the coast on the north face of the island, passing many small bays with deserted beaches. **Obel Obel** is a long, black-sand beach popular with locals for picnics and swimming. Small groups of children play in the calm waters while adults enjoy the shade of the trees that line the beachfront.

 The East Coast Islands

These islands (*gilis*), unlike the famous Gili Islands (see chapter 15) of northwest Lombok, are uninhabited and relatively unexplored. It's impossible to count all the islands, as many small coral atolls rise just above sea level, but there are at least eight.

The staff at Gili Lampu Bungalows (p. 322) can organize day trips and snorkeling out to **Gili Lampu**, reached by a small outrigger boat in about 20 minutes. Boat charters can also go to any of the other islands off this section of coast.

Leaving the coast, the road climbs into the mountains again and becomes tough going, with large sections broken by flooding and large potholes. In one section you'll see what was obviously a major riverbed at one time, but has since collapsed as a result of some recent disaster and filled with rock and debris. A new roadway and recently constructed bridge ride over the top of the shambles, allowing access to the remnants of the original road farther on.

In **Sambelia** district, not far from the main town of Bayan (p. 314), the road gives way completely to a landscape strewn with huge rocks and boulders, tossed into piles and swept into drifts as if some insane giant had thrown marbles across the valley floor. This is the result of the floods and landslide that struck this area in January 2006. Heavy rains almost every monsoon season do some damage to these roads and whenever a new section is built, within a few years it's potholed and parts are washed out by flooding. A makeshift side track leads around the wreckage and the road continues along to the north coast. Branching off the main coastal road at **Kali Putih,** a smaller road runs inland through the mountains with wonderful scenery of dense forests and huge old trees, opening up to valley vistas and towering mountain ranges.

Sembalun Bumbung and neighbor **Sembalun Lawang** are in a high, cool valley on the slopes of Gunung Rinjani, surrounded by lush fields and valleys. Both villages are alternative points to Senaru for climbing Mount Rinjani and there are a number of tour agencies that organize treks in the region, as well as several small homestays. **Rinjani Trek Management Board** (RTMB; © 0370/641124; www.lombokrinjanitrek.org; p. 317) operates the Rinjani Information Centre (RIC) in Sembalun Lawang. **Lembah Rinjani** (p. 318) is a small homestay at the base of Rinjani volcano. Farther on, the steep, rough road through the mountains eventually leads to Sapit (p. 319).

Where to Stay & Eat

Accommodations are very scarce in this part of the island. The **Jeeva Klui Resort** in Senggigi (p. 298) is slated to open a new resort on this part of the island by 2012, consisting of luxury tents, which will be the most comfortable accommodations in the area. Otherwise, be prepared to rough it a little, although the following places are clean and comfortable.

Only a few years ago these mountainous Indonesian islands fringed with miles of pristine coral reef were visited only by the truly intrepid. But an improving tourist infrastructure and some of the world's best dive sites, as well as rainforest trekking and picture-perfect traditional villages, are attracting a growing stream of adventure seekers and nature lovers. The number of visitors to **Komodo National Park**—the region's star attraction—increased by almost a third in 2010, though still only to 45,000.

Labuan Bajo, a small fishing community in northwestern Flores, is the jumping-off point for most trips to the two islands. Coral on the north coast was damaged during recent hurricanes but the protected **Maumere Bay** provides good day dive trips. Whales, dolphins, and whale sharks are sometimes seen.

Most divers book spots on live-aboard boats that cruise the coast of Komodo, a string of bays and tiny islets declared a UNESCO World Heritage Site in 1986. Given a few days, divers are practically guaranteed sightings of sharks, manta rays, and giant schools of bright tropical fish. Many seasoned divers proclaim it to be one of the world's healthiest underwater environments. And because the government limits the annual number of visitors to 60,000, it's likely to stay that way.

Most of the local dive shops are based in Labuan Bajo. **Dive Komodo** (📞 0385/41862; www.divekomodo.com) is recommended for both day and live-aboard trips. **Seven Seas** (📞 0361/473-5742; www.thesevenseas.net) is also good for longer live-aboard journeys. Several operations in Bali and Lombok also organize trips. **Dive Around Bali** (📞 081/237549845; www.divearoundbali.com) works with Flores-based companies. **Gili Divers** on Gili Trawangan (📞 081/23755037; www.gilidivers.com) runs week-long, live-aboard trips.

Any of these companies can help book trips on land as well, including trips to see the eponymous **Komodo dragons,** lizards that can grow as long as 3m (10 ft.).

The top Flores hike is around three lakes on the cone of Mount Kelimutu: Mineral deposits make each a different color. Trips leave from Maumere, a city with a small airport near the center of Flores.

The **Gili Lampu Bungalows** (there's no direct contact to the Gili Lampu Bungalows itself and so contact its agent Lombok Eco Logdes, Jl. Sungai Meninting 18, Ireng, Ampenan, Lombok; www.lombok-ecolodge.com; 📞 0370/692225; no credit cards) are on the main coastal road heading north from Labuhan: Look for the small town of Transat and turn right at the sign for Gili Lampu Bungalows. The six bungalows, made from coconut and woven bamboo, are basic, clean, and comfortable. The largest has two bedrooms, a fan, and a Western toilet with cold water shower. At between Rp50,000 and Rp90,000, including breakfast, they're a bargain. The beach is only about 30m (100 ft.) away from the restaurant.

Perched in the forest, almost at the top of the mountain, the **Hati Suci Homestay,** Sapit (www.hatisuci.tk or www.desa-sapit.com; 📞 081/8545655 or 0370/636545; fax:0370/624695; year-round US$135–US$150; no credit cards) has rooms and bungalows on terraced slopes with wonderful views down the mountain. The rooms are very basic and the electricity supply is erratic, but there's a small restaurant and the friendly owner organizes trips to the nearby hot springs, and guides trekkers up Mount Rinjani.

THE GILI ISLANDS

The Gili Islands: Where travelers go for a few days and wind up staying a month. Situated off the northwest coast of Lombok, these three mini tropical barefoot heavens have crystal-clear aquamarine seas, perfect white-sand beaches, and coral reefs with drop-offs and ledges for spying turtles, manta rays, and myriad forms of aquatic life. Once considered simply a budget destination for backpackers on a side trip from Bali, the Gilis are now a popular destination in their own right and have come of age in recent years.

The quietest is the middle island, **Gili Meno.** Life unwinds at a relaxed pace and service and accommodations are suitably in line. One step slightly up the development chain is **Gili Air,** with a greater variety of restaurants, guesthouses, and villas. This is also a real working island with a permanent local population with an income outside of tourism. **Gili Trawangan,** or simply **Gili T**, is at the other extreme and is best known as a party island, but it's no longer a one-trick pony. In recent years the addition of luxury villas with private pools, air-conditioning, freshwater showers, and 24-hour electricity has enticed the return of travelers who came here many years ago, but now feel comfortable visiting with their spouse and children. That's not to say the original magic has gone, but rather that partying is no longer the sole reason to come here.

One of the Gilis' biggest draws is scuba diving. With year-round water temperatures of about 28°C (82°F), the islands are one of the world's best places for viewing turtles and, from December to April, manta rays. Between them, the three islands feature at least 18 accepted dive spots. The currents are strong and drift diving is the norm. Although the big dive schools with swimming pool training facilities are based on Gili T, the other islands sit marginally closer to the dive sites. It doesn't really matter which island you choose for convenience to the sites.

Each of the Gilis is completely free of cars and motorcycles with the only transportation being *cidomo* (horse-drawn carriages) and bicycles. However, be ever vigilant of the miniature horses trotting up behind you—there's only so much room on the boardwalks that circle each island.

15

GETTING TO, BETWEEN & AROUND THE GILIS

The Gilis are easily accessible from Bali by boat or plane, both forms of transport taking approximately 2 hours door to door. From Lombok, it's just a hop, skip, and a boat ride away.

Most tourists prefer to arrange private transfer services through the hotels or villas at which they're staying on the Gilis. This will include pickup, meeting and greeting service, and being escorted to your suite door.

By Air

The Gilis don't have an airport and sea planes have yet to catch on. You'll have to fly first to Mataram, Lombok, and then take a boat. For information on getting to Lombok by air, see p. 287.

On arrival in Mataram, if you haven't organized private transportation, purchase a ticket from the taxi office to either **Bangsal** (the public harbor) or **Teluk Nare** or **Teluk Kodek** (both private harbors). The journey takes approximately 40 minutes; cost is about Rp120,000 each way. The taxi can take you on the Monkey Forest route or the coastal route (p. 291), so you can get in a touch of sightseeing on your way. Either route takes the same amount of time and the same amount of money—although the coastal route is prettier.

By Boat

The trip takes you across **Wallace's Line,** a deep-water boundary running from Australia to Borneo. To the east live Asian and Australasian flora and fauna, and to the west Asiatic. Chances are you'll see dolphins and a whole array of bird life, which seem also to observe the boundary.

PUBLIC BOAT FROM BANGSAL PUBLIC HARBOR, LOMBOK Taxis must finish their journey at the port gate which, for reasons best known to the *cidomo* drivers, is 600m (2,000 ft.) from the actual port. You can either walk this remaining distance or take the ever-present *cidomo* (horse-drawn carriage), which at an average of Rp30,000 per single journey is hardly going to break the bank. Once at the harbor, buy a boat ticket from the office; don't be tempted to buy a ticket from anyone else, no matter how enticing the deal may sound. Prices from the ticket office are fixed.

Boat Costs (Rp) to:	Air	Meno	Trawangan
Public	8,000	9,000	10,000
Charter (up to 12)	155,000	170,000	185,000

Boats run daily 8am to 4:30pm; the journey takes approximately 40 minutes but can take longer depending on the weather.

Bangsal has a small shop selling snacks and toiletries. You can buy supplies here or wait until you arrive on the islands. All the islands now have their own basic stores.

FAST BOAT FROM BALI A number of direct, fast-boat services are now available from Bali to Gili T. No boat service is available to Gili Meno because it's too shallow; **Island Getaway** (see below) offers a service to Gili Air at no extra cost.

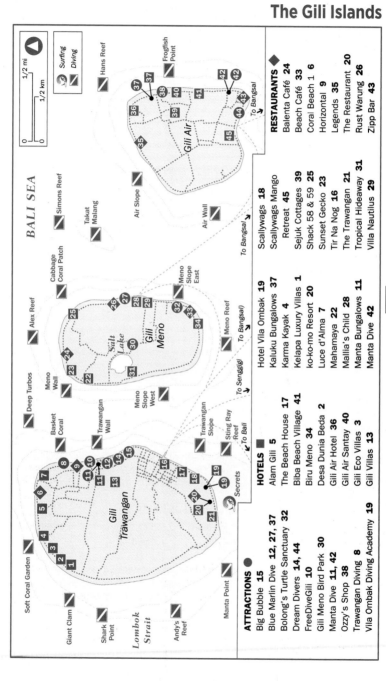

The Gili Islands

BALI SEA

Lombok Strait

Surfing

Diving

1/2 mi
1/2 km

Soft Coral Garden
Giant Clam
Shark Point
Andy's Reef
Manta Point

Deep Turbos
Basket Coral
Trawangan Wall
Trawangan Slope
Sting Ray Reef
Secrets
To Bali

Meno Wall
Meno Slope West
To Senggigi
Salt Lake
Gili Meno
Meno Slope East
Meno Reef
To Bangsal
Cabbage Coral Patch
Alex Reef
Simons Reef
Takat Malang

Gili Trawangan

Gili Air
Air Slope
Air Wall
To Bangsal

Hans Reef
Frogfish Point

ATTRACTIONS
Big Bubble **15**
Blue Marlin Dive **12, 27, 37**
Bolong's Turtle Sanctuary **32**
Dream Divers **14, 44**
FreeDiveGili **10**
Gili Meno Bird Park **30**
Manta Dive **11, 42**
Ozzy's Shop **38**
Trawangan Diving **8**
Vila Ombak Diving Academy **19**

HOTELS
Alam Gili **5**
The Beach House **17**
Biba Beach Village **41**
Biru Meno **34**
Desa Dunia Beda **2**
Gili Air Hotel **36**
Gili Air Santay **40**
Gili Eco Villas **3**
Gili Villas **13**

Hotel Vila Ombak **19**
Kaluku Bungalows **37**
Karma Kayak **4**
Kelapa Luxury Villas **1**
ko-ko-mo Resort **20**
Luce d'Alma **7**
Mahamaya **22**
Mallia's Child **28**
Manta Bungalows **11**
Manta Dive **42**

Scallywags **18**
Scallywags Mango Retreat **45**
Sejuk Cottages **39**
Shack 58 & 59 **25**
Sunset Gecko **23**
Tir Na Nog **16**
The Trawangan **21**
Tropical Hideaway **31**
Villa Nautilus **29**

RESTAURANTS
Balenta Café **24**
Beach Café **33**
Coral Beach 1 **6**
Horizontal **9**
Legends **35**
The Restaurant **20**
Rust Warung **26**
Zipp Bar **43**

If you're staying in Kuta, Seminyak, and Sanur, one of the most established options is **Blue Water Express** (© **0361/895-1082;** 081/338418988 after hours; www.bwsbali.com), which departs Bali International Marina in Benoa Harbour daily at 8am and Gili T at 11am. Journey time is 2 to 2½ hours; tickets cost Rp690,000 one-way; Rp1,300,000 round-trip. For those staying near Ubud, Candidasa, or the east coast, it's quicker to depart from **Padangbai,** about 2 hours from Seminyak. Check the weather forecast before you book as the journey is far more pleasant on calm seas.

Gili Cat ★ (© **0361/271680;** www.gilicat.com) is the most reputable fast boat between Bali and the Gili Islands. Its fleet includes the new Gili Cat Enterprise; the boat departs daily from Gili T at 9am, stops on Lombok (at the Teluk Kodek pier, just north of Senggigi) at 9:10am before arriving at Padangbai on Bali at 10:30am. The boat leaves Padangbai on Bali at 11:30am daily and arrives in Gili T at 1pm. In the high season, a second round-trip journey originating on Gili T is completed in the afternoons. The service also includes free transfers between Padangbai, Ubud, Kuta, and Sanur on Bali. Journey time is around 2 hours; tickets are listed as costing Rp660,000 one-way, Rp1,200,000 round-trip on their website, though if you book directly at its offices, you only pay Rp550,000 one-way, Rp1,100,000 round-trip. If your trip is canceled due to bad weather, your money is refunded back on the spot.

Island Getaway (© **0361/753241;** www.gili-paradise.com) boats depart Benoa Harbour daily at 8am; and from Gili T at 10:30am. The trip takes 2 to 2½ hours; tickets are Rp660,000 one-way; Rp1,200,000 round-trip.

SHUTTLE BUS & BOAT FROM BALI If you have time or a tight budget, you may wish to experience how the locals travel. Catch the **public ferry** (capacity 100) from Padangbai. The **Perama Tours** (main office: Legian 39, Kuta; © **0361/751551** or 0361/751875; www.peramatour.com) shuttle bus and boat service runs daily from several points on Bali by bus to Padangbai, and then direct to Gili T on the slow boat. The service takes around 8 hours. Although the boat looks like it lists heavily, it has looked this way for a long time. Times and prices are from: Kuta, 6am, Rp450,000; Sanur, 7am, Rp520,000; Ubud, 7am, Rp450,000; Padangbai, 11am, Rp450,000.

The return leg from Gili T leaves at 7am and 9am from Senggigi.

Getting between the Gili Islands

Although they're very close, it's not particularly easy to get between the islands. Tourist **boats** shuttle between the islands, running a circuit starting in Air, going on to Meno, and then to Gili T and back to Meno, and finally Air, twice daily. The boats leave pretty much on time, with timetables at each ferry point, and give you a chance to take in an island for the day at little cost. The fixed fares are: Air to Meno Rp17,000; Air to Gili T Rp19,500; Gili T to Meno Rp19,000. Boat times are posted in the station office. It's a good idea to check the times a day ahead of your planned trip.

To **charter** your own boat, you need to negotiate with one of the omnipresent boatmen. The boatmen are businessmen too and the cost will vary depending on how wealthy they think you are—prices are steep, around Rp200,000 one-way. Have some sympathy though: Petrol isn't cheap, the engines are expensive to run, and they aren't guaranteed a return trip. Negotiate, but be fair.

Getting Around the Gili islands

Once on each island, the only mode of transport is nonmotorized. You can use a *cidomo*, rent a bicycle, or just walk. What's the rush, anyway? Expect to pay between Rp20,000 and Rp30,000 for a *cidomo* for a short trip, and multiples thereof if you make stops along the way. **Bikes** can be rented throughout the islands. They aren't cheap and only a few come with chains and locks. You'll be likely to leave your bike outside a restaurant only to return and find it missing. Due to the size of the islands, if you walk along the road you may well find it parked outside another bar. Thankfully most shop owners are understanding and no deposit is taken because no bikes leave their home island.

[FastFACTS] THE GILI ISLANDS

ATMs There are several ATMs on the main strip on Gili T though as yet Gili Meno and Gili Air don't have ATMs. Bring cash.

Business Hours Most restaurants on the islands are open for breakfast, lunch, and dinner, but exact times are nebulous. During high season, restaurants open early and close late due to the influx of customers; in the low season, opening and closing times depend on whether owners think customers are nearby and so opening times aren't guaranteed. Therefore, we haven't listed opening and closing times for most restaurants.

Credit Cards You'll have the most luck trying to pay with a credit card at some of the bigger resorts, private villas, and dive schools on Gili T (with a 3–5% surcharge). Unless otherwise noted, accommodations and restaurants don't accept credit cards.

Doctors All the islands have a nurse available who can treat basic first-aid conditions. For more serious conditions, a doctor's surgery is available 24 hours on Gili T behind the Vila Ombak hotel (p. 329).

Electricity Each of the Gilis suffers from a shortage of electricity. Sometimes the local electric company cuts the supply, and so you can find yourself walking and dining under the stars. Most accommodations and restaurants on Gili Meno and Gili Air don't have backup generators, but many of the bigger resorts on Gili T do.

Etiquette The majority of Gili Islanders are Muslim, so please have respect and display as little nudity as you can. Don't sunbathe topless. Bikinis should be limited to the beach only.

Internet Access There are enough Internet cafes and shops that offer Internet access on the islands but they're all painfully slow. Expect to pay about Rp500 a minute. Some villas and premises on Gili T now offer free Wi-Fi.

Police There are no police on any of the islands, which partly accounts for the relaxed vibe. Any thefts, harassments, or complaints can be made to the island **Kepala Desa** (Head of the Village). They take crime very seriously and will go to extreme lengths to ensure the issue is cleared up, generally taking matters into their own hands. Most of the people associated with the Kepala Desa don't speak English, so always take someone from your hotel or villa with you and give them a contribution of thanks for their efforts. For insurance purposes you may need to visit the nearest police station in Mataram, Lombok.

Post Office There are no post offices on any of the islands. However, you can buy stamps from **William's Bookshop** on Gili T. Some hotels will post letters if you ask.

Seasons High season is July, August, Christmas, New Year, and Nyepi (Balinese New Year, typically either Mar or Apr). Book months in advance as accommodations, though plentiful on Gili T, fill quickly and some people find themselves camping on the beach (although many are there possibly because they couldn't find their way home). During low season, things are decidedly quieter. Though most accommodations' prices are open to negotiation any time of the year, you'll have more success during the low season. Rainy season falls between November and April, but with less rain than Bali and Lombok it's still worth a visit during these times.

Shopping Various small kiosks sell drinks, snacks, basic food, toiletries, and suntan lotion on all three islands. Prices are considerably higher than the mainland. A few stalls and shops make and sell souvenirs items, but you're best off doing your souvenir shopping on the larger islands.

Travel Agents **Perama Tours** has offices on all the islands and can arrange transportation back to Lombok and Bali. It can also arrange a selection of tours to the nearby islands.

Water The Gilis don't have freshwater. Don't drink water from the tap. Bottled water is widely available; make sure the bottles are sealed.

GILI TRAWANGAN

Gili T has moved on from being the backpacker, mushroom-addled, hedonistic discount paradise of yesterday. "A pity," the old hands might say. Although Gili T has cast off its grungy origins—it's the only island of the three where fresh well water and air-conditioning are the norm, and new developments are opening almost weekly with levels of service previously unheard of—it's not quite on the jet-set radar yet, though it won't be long.

Many people are drawn by the still-famous party nights (Gili T is packed with bars that are never more than a few minutes away from most hotels), whereas others come for the lack of traffic. You can cycle the island in an hour and a half; the clean, white-sand beaches are endless; and the social options the same.

Gili T is now a serious tourist destination with coffee shops, a doctor's surgery, pool bars, pizza, sushi, boutique hotels, and luxury villas. In the last 10 years, or even just 2, Gili T has come a long way. And though the hardcore traveler may have moved on, the essence of island life remains. It's calm, safe, and a beautiful place to hang out.

The **port** is on the east coast. Most small boats moor just north of the port on the beach. Expect to get your feet wet. **Perama Tours** is also located just north of the jetty and can assist with transportation needs and trips to outlying islands on one of its boats.

[FastFACTS] GILI TRAWANGAN

ATM/Banks Several ATMs line the main strip of Gili T, near the jetty. You can get **cash advances** on Gili T, but expect to pay a hefty charge of at least 7% to 10%.

Hospital/Clinic A 24-hour, English-speaking emergency **clinic** is well signposted just behind Vila Ombak Hotel; a nurse is available daily 8am to 6pm for basic first aid.

Internet Access Various places offer **Internet** access and most of the top-end villas and restaurants have Internet or even Wi-Fi. It can be very slow though.

Water Gili T has **no fresh water,** it's mostly well water. None of the tap water, even piped into high-end hotels, is potable.

Where to Stay

Most accommodations are on the east and north coasts alongside the best swimming and snorkeling. Places here are just off the main drag. Book ahead if you're traveling in July, August, and around Christmas and New Year, when hotels can get booked up months in advance. When booking, one consideration to be aware of is the sound from the mosque near the jetty, where the morning call to prayer starts at 5am.

A few offerings dot the west coast, but as the water is shallow and the beaches full of remnants of dead coral, there's little swimming to be done here. The roads are covered in many places, especially on the western and northern coast, in soft sand that makes it difficult for both *cidomo* and bikes. You may have to get off both at times.

Head for the north for peace and quiet. The strip of town is only a 10-minute cart ride away. Don't forget to take the driver's telephone number if you want a late return. Most *cidomo* stop running around 11pm but if you arrange ahead you'll find someone to give you a lift. Failing that, it's no more than a lovely 30-minute stroll. Take a torch—or let the stars guide you.

EXPENSIVE

Gili Villas ★ One of the latest villa complexes to hit the island, these luxurious two-bedroom villas (they can be offered as one-bedrooms depending on the season and availability) have every modern convenience you'll need. When fed up with the noise and chaos of the town strip, you can chill out in your own peaceful, secluded environment. Breakfast can either be served in your villa or at **Coco's** (p. 332) in the front, which is under the same ownership.

www.gilivillasindonesia.com. © **081/23755721.** 4 villas. Peak season US$225–US$275; high season US$195–US$245; low season US$145–US$195. Rates include breakfast, and exclude taxes. MC, V. **Amenities:** Airport transfers (on request); babysitting; bikes; pool. *In villa:* A/C, fan, TV/DVD, MP3 docking station & Wi-Fi on request.

Hotel Vila Ombak ★ This is a perennial favorite with expats from Bali over for the weekend. The resort is far larger than you'd notice, with 61 rooms of varying size and quality. The traditional *lumbung* (rice-barn) huts have terraces, hammocks, and some have balconies. The quality of the food has been suspect in the past but don't let this put you off. The management is currently updating and adding new bungalows and a seafront terrace. The resort recently opened a second location, **Hotel Vila Ombak Sunset,** on the western side of the island with slightly higher rates. The modern bungalows are quite comfortable, if a little bland. The grounds offer one of the island's biggest swimming pools and sunsets are spectacular, but the remote location makes it difficult to come and go freely to the busier side of the island.

www.hotelombak.com. © **0370/614-2336.** 61 units. Rp1,400,000–Rp2,200,000 standard; Rp1,900,000–Rp4,800,000 cottage. High season Rp350,000 surcharge. Discounts available online. AE, MC, V. **Amenities:** 2 restaurants; bar; 3-level outdoor pool with Jacuzzi; room service; spa; Wi-Fi. *In room/cottage:* A/C, satellite TV, minibar.

Kelapa Luxury Villas ★★ If you want the best that Gili T has to offer, this is one to consider. This luxury set of villas stands out from the crowd with their uber-design—and so does their price tag. Let the in-house chef cook up a fantasy of dishes or self-cater in your kitchen. There's talk of a tennis court and a helipad. Truly, Gili T has come a long way.

www.kelapavillas.com. ✆ **081/933147723.** 10 villas. US$170–US$185 1-bedroom; US$260–US$315 2-bedroom; US$375–US$390 3-bedroom; US$625 4-bedroom. High-season surcharge US$40 per night. Rates include taxes. AE, MC, V. **Amenities:** Bikes; outdoor pool; tennis court; room service. *In villa:* A/C, satellite TV/DVD, kitchen, Wi-Fi.

ko-ko-mo Resort ★★   The Gilis, long known for their sleepy beachside bungalows and no frills villas, are going upmarket. The ko-ko-mo villas will be the first "five star" development on Gili T, featuring one-, two-, and three-bedroom villas and a fine-dining restaurant. Husband and wife team Matthew and Di Somerton use traditional Balinese design and Javanese furniture in what they call "elegant tropical." On their dedicated patch of beach are large king-size beach beds for two, just the ticket for a lazy day with a loved one.

www.kokomogilit.com. ✆ **0370/613-4920.** 9 villas. Year-round Rp1,500,000 1-bedroom; Rp2,500,000–Rp3,000,000 2-bedroom; Rp4,200,000 3-bedroom. Rates exclude taxes. AE, MC, V. **Amenities:** Restaurant (the Restaurant, p. 332); outdoor pool. *In villa:* A/C, satellite TV, DVD/CD, minibar, Wi-Fi.

MODERATE

The Beach House ★   A Gili T institution, the Beach House was one of the first luxurious villa complexes on the island. Due to its success and popularity, it's usually fully booked well in advance. Choose from studio rooms and tree houses (Indonesian stilt houses), bungalows, and the four-bedroom villa. All the units are set back from the main strip in a tropical garden with palm trees and frangipani. Each is simply decorated with modern furniture. The pool overlooks the main drag making it ideal for people-watching. If you'd prefer to hide out, several villas have private pools.

www.beachhousegilit.com. ✆ **0370/642352.** 32 units. Year-round Rp400,000 Tree House; Rp450,000 studio; Rp550,000 standard bungalow; Rp850,000 pool bungalow; Rp2,500,000 2-bed villa; Rp4,000,000 4-bed villa. Rates include breakfast and exclude taxes. AE, MC, V. **Amenities:** Restaurant; bar; outdoor pool; room service. *In room:* A/C, TV/DVD, kitchen (in villas).

Desa Dunia Beda ★★   Located on the quiet northern side of the island, but not too far away from the action, this collection of traditional Javanese bungalows is one of the classiest options on the island. The bungalows, some of which come with air-conditioning, feature four-poster beds, rustic wooden walls, and antique furnishings. Prime snorkeling is accessible right in front of the resort, though the entry is a little rocky (wear booties). A gorgeous lap pool graces the front of the property. A great choice if you're on a romantic vacation and don't want to stay in the fray, yet want accessible dining options.

www.desaduniabeda.com. ✆ **0370/614-1575.** Fax 0370/614-1585. 12 units. Year-round US$135. MC, V. **Amenities:** Restaurant; pool; Wi-Fi; library. *In room:* A/C (in some), fan, minibar.

Gili Eco Villas   The eco name is for real, because all the electricity here is harnessed from either solar panels or wind—and they're completely off the grid. Air-conditioning, although in every room, costs extra and the owners encourage you to go without it. The profit from the air-conditioning supplement is donated to Gili Eco Trust or one of the Biorock projects in front of the resort. Even the water from the villas is recycled. And although the green credentials are impressive in themselves, the owners still manage to deliver a stunning resort of antique Javanese *joglo* houses with charming furnishings of reclaimed wood.

www.gilecovillas.com. ✆ **0361/847-6419** or 0370/636057. 7 villas. High season US$145–US$165 1-bedroom, US$200–US$230 2-bedroom; low season US$95–US$115 1-bedroom, US$150–US$180 2-bedroom. Rates include breakfast and exclude taxes. AE, MC, V. **Amenities:** Babysitting; massage; outdoor pool; port transfers, Wi-Fi (free by pool). *In villa:* A/C (additional cost), DVD, kitchen.

Luce d'Alma   Although this place is billed as the only four-star hotel on the island, many other hotels offer similar levels of comfort. However, the 16 air-conditioned rooms here have modern furnishings and, unusual for Gili T, their own bathtub. The hotel itself has a large swimming pool, Jacuzzi, gym, and spa.

www.lucedalmaresort.com. ✆ **0370/614-6877.** 16 units. Year-round US$90–US$150. MC, V. **Amenities:** Restaurant; babysitting; bikes; gym; Jacuzzi; outdoor pool; sauna; spa; Wi-Fi (free). *In room:* A/C, TV/DVD, hair dryer, minibar.

Scallywags ★ 🍴   Located behind the WAG club, Scallywags is stylish on first glance, so you know what to expect from the rooms. The 10 bungalows have a modern Asian style mixed with a colonial feel. Each has its own small garden with lounge furniture. The large rooms themselves have modern features such as flatscreen TVs, solar-heated water, and Internet. Each room has been soundproofed and made eco-friendly with solar paneling. The swimming pool area includes a large *beruga* (gazebo) at one end and a pool bar on the other. Scallywags also has its own speedboat, the *Jackie O,* which guests can use for water-skiing or other watersports. Even if you're not staying here, the restaurant is worthy of your attention.

www.scallywagsresort.com. ✆ **0370/648792.** Year-round US$85–US$135. Rates include breakfast and taxes. MC, V. **Amenities:** Restaurant (Scallywags, p. 333); bar; outdoor pool; room service; watersports; Wi-Fi (free in restaurant & lounge). *In bungalow:* TV, hair dryer, Internet access, minibar.

The Trawangan ★   Opened by an Australian pro-surfer, this new cozy property offers more than the typical surfer's digs: The modern rooms and villas feature contemporary art, small private terraces, and pleasant outdoor bathrooms. The property feels a little crowded, but it boasts a decent location right at the southern edge of the island's main tourist strip. A beachside bar with tree-house tables and horse sculptures made out of driftwood keep things interesting.

www.thetrawangan.com. ✆ **0370/664-7066.** Fax 0370/647741. Year-round Rp800,000 single room, Rp2,500,000 2-bedroom villa, Rp3,500,000 4-bedroom villa. **Amenities:** Restaurant; bar; pool. *In room/villa:* AC, fan, TV/DVD, hair dryer, Internet, minibar.

INEXPENSIVE

Alam Gili   Located on the quieter northern shore, this tranquil and traditional, beachfront, Indonesian-styled resort features eight spacious bungalows in a stunning tropical garden and is part of the larger family-run Alam Group. If you really want to spoil yourself, take the huge, two-story "Fish Suite" with its ornate wood carvings, sea view, and air-conditioning. The beach out front has great snorkeling.

www.alamindahbali.com. ✆ **0370/613-0466.** 8 units. Year-round US$55–US$75 standard; US$95 Fish Suite. Rates include breakfast and exclude taxes. MC, V. **Amenities:** Restaurant; outdoor pool. *In room/bungalow:* Fan (A/C in Fish Suite).

Karma Kayak   Grace and Astrid from Holland have set up six bungalows on the quiet northern coast far from the madding crowd. Each bungalow is simply decorated in its own individual style with ikat fabric. This idyllic setting is perfect for those wishing to escape the loud music and party scene. The lounging area on the beach is adorned with *beruga* and sun loungers. It's the perfect place on the island to chill out, enjoy sangria, and tuck into some great tapas.

www.karmakayak.com. ✆ **081/805593710.** 6 units. Year-round Rp350,000–Rp600,000. Rates include breakfast and taxes. No credit cards. **Amenities:** Restaurant (Karma Kayak, p. 333). *In bungalow:* A/C (in some).

Manta Bungalows These *lumbung* bungalows are affiliated with the dive school **Manta Dive** (p. 337), one of the most respected dive schools on the island, and are situated right behind the school. The hotel has recently completed eight new bungalows to complement the existing six, and added a new swimming pool with child-friendly area.

www.manta-dive.com. © **0370/643649.** 14 units. Year-round US$50–US$75. MC, V. **Amenities:** Restaurant; bar; outdoor pool. *In bungalow:* A/C, minibar.

Tir Na Nog Surprisingly, this lively Irish bar has very good accommodations, set back on the other side of the road so that you're no more troubled by noise and revelers than at any other place in the middle of town. The 11 bungalows are clean and comfortable with fresh, hot water and air-conditioning; for those on a budget there are also 10 standard rooms. The owners of the bar also own the franchise **Ryoshi** sushi restaurant next door.

www.tirnanogbar.com. © **0370/639463.** 21 units. Year-round from Rp300,000. Rates include taxes. MC, V. **Amenities:** Restaurant; bar; airport transfer; babysitting; bikes; freshwater pool; Wi-Fi. *In room/ bungalow:* A/C, kitchen.

Where to Eat
MODERATE

The Restaurant ★★ AUSTRALIAN Australian chef Matthew, the co-owner of ko-ko-mo Resort (see above) has a long history of working both in Sydney and Bali. His new venture is this upmarket restaurant, serving the finest local and imported meat and seafood. Expect to see beef carpaccio with black truffle oil and game terrine with sweet mango jam and pickled onion on the appetizers list. If that isn't enough to whet your appetite, the main courses include quail stuffed with rice and mushrooms and lobster pasta. With an impressive wine list to match, and a piano playing in the background, this will certainly be a revelation to anyone returning after a few years away from Gili T.

In the ko-ko-mo Resort (p. 330). © **0370/642352.** www.kokomogilit.com. Main courses Rp65,000–Rp270,000. MC, V. Daily 7am–10pm.

INEXPENSIVE

Don't discount the **Beach House** (p. 330; Rp20,000–Rp60,000; MC, V; daily 7am–10pm)—Gili T's original barbecue and salad bar is still going strong. The **Coco** cafe (no phone; Rp15,000–Rp25,000; MC, V; daily 7am–6pm), the only Illy coffee shop on the island, serves baguettes, homemade cakes, milkshakes, and fresh fruit juices. It's right on the main drag. The lovely hand-painted wall at **Gili Deli** (© 081/23764443; Rp30,000–Rp35,000; daily 7am–6pm) conjures up images of a cafe that you'd expect to see in the hip area of a big city. This great little place serves up salads, wraps, and baguettes along with local coffees. The established local fish restaurant **Juku** (no phone; Rp25,000–Rp50,000; daily 7am–10pm) is popular with the expat community for its reasonably priced grilled fish. The well-known, Bali-based chain **Wrap a Snapper** (© 0370/612-4217; Rp27,000–Rp61,000; daily 7am–11pm) serves up the best fish and chips on Gili T.

Coral Beach 1 🏕 PIZZA The best pizzas on the island come busting hot, straight from a wood-burning oven at Coral Beach 1. The five *bales* stretched by the sea are an ideal place to lounge away the day with some of the best snorkeling on the island. If you don't manage to get one of the *bales,* deck chairs are on offer where you can dangle your feet directly in the water and feast away.

No phone. Main courses Rp20,000–Rp45,000. Daily 7am–10pm.

Gili Trawangan

THE GILI ISLANDS

Horizontal ★ BAR/WESTERN   This bar and restaurant sits on a beach littered with sun loungers in front of one of the best snorkeling areas. The options are endless to curb any munchies: Will it be pizza from the wood-burning oven or a hearty burger? Or perhaps simple nibbles such as Thai cakes, Vietnamese rice rolls, or a fresh and tasty salad? After dark, it's cocktail hour—sip on margaritas until it's time for zeds.

✆ **0370/613-9248.** www.thegiliislands.com. Rp60,000–Rp90,000. MC, V. Daily 8am–midnight.

Karma Kayak 🎁 TAPAS   Enjoy sunset views while tucking into the house specialties here: authentic Spanish tapas, such as *boquorones fritas* (fried anchovies), prawns, and Spanish tortilla. The chicken satays are some of the best on the island. In the evening, a barbecue features marinated meat or fish.

In the Karma Kayak (p. 331). *✆* **081/805593710.** Tapas Rp16,000–Rp30,000. AE, MC, V. Daily 7am–9:30pm.

Kiki Nova WARUNG   This local warung makes one of the best *nasi campur* (mixed rice) on the island. Different every day, the dish is a selection of vegetables, fried meat, and shrimp, and usually a curry. Go before 2pm, otherwise you may find it all gone.

No phone. *Nasi campur.* Rp20,000. Daily 7am–5pm.

Persona INDIAN   Curries are the order of the day here. The kitchen serves up a freshly made Indian cuisine of the usual tandoori delights with naan bread. Chicken tandoori, *daal,* and *tikka masala* are all delicious. Once you've dined, lie back on one of the mattresses on the beach and enjoy a hookah.

✆ **0370/660-7233.** Main courses Rp25,000–Rp50,000. MC, V. Daily noon–10:30pm.

Scallywags ★ BARBECUE/WESTERN   From the folks that brought you the Beach House (p. 330) next door, this is a new favorite on the island, serving wraps, paninis, salads, and many non-Asian options. In the evening, the place is alive with revelers feasting on barbecue fresh fish, prawns, and meat, and choosing from the salad bar and plenty of freshly made pastas. Situated right on the shore front, on the busy southern stretch, you'll get plenty of atmosphere, value, and fresh organic food. Don't forget to try the Caipirosca cocktail.

In Scallywags Resort (p. 331). *✆* **0370/614-8792.** www.scallywagsresort.com. Main courses Rp20,000–Rp70,000. MC, V. Daily 7am–10pm.

Exploring Gili Trawangan

BOATING   Most villas can rent you a glass-bottom boat or will recommend a man to call. Otherwise, it's easy to arrange this through various outlets on the island. The boat people rent out their boats for a full-day or half-day to one or all the islands. The trip usually entails stopping at a few snorkeling spots as well as one of the other islands for lunch. For a full day, don't pay more than Rp450,000 for a trip to Gili Meno and the nearby area, and Rp600,000 for all three islands.

CYCLING   Rent a bike from many of the shops along the main strip. A rental store next to Coco Cafe (p. 332) rents bikes from Rp25,000 a day. Don't pay more than Rp50,000 a day, although you may well hear offers higher than this. A perfect way to spend an early morning or a late afternoon is a cycle round the island. One road hugs the coast, but much of it on the south and north sides are soft sand, which make for tough going at times. Plenty of other roads crisscross the center of the island passing local houses and through small villages while keeping under the shelter of the coconut palms. A trip around the island should take an hour or two depending on your route. Take a map as there are plenty of dead-end tracks. But the island is so small, you're never too far from a friendly face to show you the way home.

BIKING & SNORKELING TOUR: GILI TRAWANGAN

START:	**Desa Dunia Beda Resort.**
FINISH:	**Amandalu Bar.**
TIME:	**Approximately 5 hours.**
BEST TIMES:	**Morning is better for calmer snorkeling waters; afternoon is better for sunset views.**

There are few places as pleasant for biking and snorkeling in Bali and Lombok than Gili T. Without vehicles on the island, the only danger and annoyances of biking are perhaps being side-swiped by the occasional donkey cart or getting your tires stuck in the fine, white sand. By exploring the island on bicycle, you can also easily reach the best snorkeling spots within just a few hours. If you decide to cycle around the entire island without stopping it will take approximately one hour; the western side of the island is a little more difficult to traverse on wheels as the cement path is replaced by sand. **Bikes** can be rented at most hotels for around Rp50,000 and **snorkels** can be rented at beachside stands for Rp30,000 to Rp50,000 per day. And although the bicycling is easy, we recommend that you're an experienced snorkeler to complete this tour.

Begin at the Desa Dunia Resort, on the north side of the island:

1 Desa Dunia Resort

The resort (one of our favorites on the island) features *joglo* bungalows that are worth a look for their traditional Javanese architecture, which keep the interiors cool through special air vents and water storage units. Afterwards, plunge into the crystal blue waters in front of the resort for some of the best snorkeling on the island—you'll see decent reefs and great varieties of fish, including cuttlefish and manta rays. It's a good idea to have booties on your feet, as the entry into the water is a little rocky.

Bike clockwise several hundred meters (yards) to:

2 Coral Beach II

This little pizzeria features beachside pavilions on stilts that are perfect for lounging and a coffee, along with a decent wood-fired pie.

Bike clockwise a few doors down to:

3 Villa Almarik

In front of this resort is some of the most popular snorkeling on the island—the current will allow you to drift south; don't go farther than the jetty, which sees a lot of boat traffic. On your drift, you'll probably see a couple of friendly turtles (one swam right alongside us for several minutes), along with plenty of bannerfish and parrotfish. A non-profit group has also placed several art installations in the shape of various marine life underwater to encourage coral growth.

Biking & Snorkeling Tour: Gili Trawangan

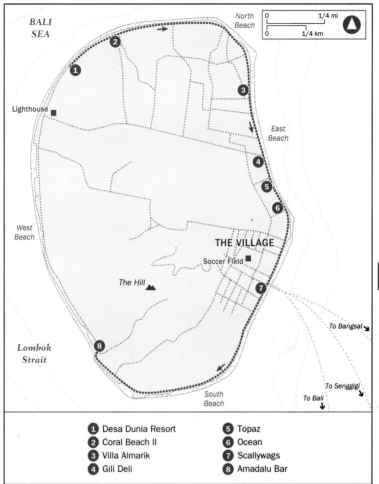

BALI SEA

North Beach

0 | 1/4 mi
0 | 1/4 km

① Desa Dunia Resort
② Coral Beach II

③ Villa Almarik

Lighthouse ■

East Beach

④

⑤

⑥

West Beach

THE VILLAGE

Soccer Field ■

The Hill ▲

⑦

To Bangsal

Lombok Strait

⑧

To Senggigi

To Bali

South Beach

① Desa Dunia Resort
② Coral Beach II
③ Villa Almarik
④ Gili Deli
⑤ Topaz
⑥ Ocean
⑦ Scallywags
⑧ Amadalu Bar

After your snorkel, walk to the jetty and cross the street to:

4 Gili Deli

Take in a refreshing fruit juice or iced tea at this urban-hip eatery; it's a central hub for travelers so you'll likely meet a few kindred snorkelers and bikers. Take a stroll down the back alleys behind the Deli, where you'll find a mosque and a kindergarten.

Return to Villa Almarik to retrieve your bicycle and continue clockwise to:

5 Topaz

Browse the racks at this hip little shop selling dresses, bikinis, and silver jewelry.

Hop on your bicycle and continue clockwise to:

6 Ocean

Stop at this second little shop for funky jewelry and mementos to take back home.

Hop on your bicycle and continue clockwise to:

7 Scallywags

This popular beachfront bar and restaurant offers a nice, relaxing patch of sand to laze about on and sample its menu of barbecue fish and meats, along with an array of cocktails.

Continue along the main path for about 1km (½ mile). Along the way, the development of Gili T peters out, allowing you to cycle through the natural setting on the south side of the island. The path bends north after a certain point; keep your eyes out for:

8 Amadalu Bar

This little shack is a great place to take in one of Gili T's perfect sunsets—and the beers are only Rp20,000.

THE FIVE BEST dive SPOTS ON THE GILIS

Deep Turbos: Advanced divers
Location: East of Gili T
This site has spectacular topography. At 30m (98 ft.), it has a sandy bottom between large sea mounds. You'll find a good variety of corals, huge sea fans, and plenty of overhangs and cracks to explore. Garden eels cover the sandy bottom and barracuda, leopard sharks, and giant rays can also be seen here.

Hans Reef: All levels
Location: Northeast of Gili Air
Famous for its muck diving, this site provides an opportunity to view some of the smaller, stranger creatures found in these parts. Frog fish, leaf scorpion fish, sea horses, black spotted morays, spearers, pipe fish, and many types of shrimp and other macro life are here.

Shark Point: All levels
Location: Northside Gili T
This is probably the most popular site off Gili T and excellent for viewing larger marine life. It's a vast open area with a flat, sandy bottom and a series of ridges that fall away into deeper water and progressively deeper canyons parallel to the shore. Advanced divers can find reef sharks in the canyons. Everyone can see cuttlefish, stingrays, and tons of turtles in the shallows. In the past, this has been a favored hang-out for huge bump-head parrot fish.

Simons Reef: Advanced divers
Location: Northeast of Gili Meno
This great deep dive offers a variety of corals not seen at many of the other sites. At 30m (98 ft.) it has a sandy bottom between large sea mounds, which rise some 20m (66 ft.) from the sea bed. Sand bar formations here are similar to sand dunes in a desert.

Sunset Point (A.K.A. Manta Point): All levels
Location: Southside Gili T
This gently sloping reef has a variety of hard and soft corals interspersed with bombies and large table corals that provide shelter for fish. With rarely any current, it's an excellent site to get close up to reef sharks, stingrays, cuttlefish, and octopus. At the right time of the year (Dec–Mar), as the name suggests, you may well see a passing manta ray.

Learning to Free Dive

FreeDiveGili offers a rare opportunity to learn to free dive. An experienced Scuba Schools International (www.divessi.com) instructor will teach you all the techniques required to enable you to dive longer and deeper. Located near the swimming beach on Gili T (℃ 08/5857187170; www.freedivegili.com), the 2-day introductory course costs Rp2,100,000. Run by British free diving champion Michael Board, divers learn breathing methods that allow most people to hold their breath for 2 minutes and reach depths of up to 20m (66 ft.).

DIVING ★★★   The Gili Islands may be a bit sleepy on land, but they come alive under water. With some 3,500 individual species living in the reefs and seas of Indonesia, compared with only around 1,500 species off the Great Barrier Reef, you're rarely disappointed. Some 25% of the world's reefs are in Indonesia and the Gilis offer some of the best sites with the richest diversity. Diving here offers you clear, visible, and mainly safe waters.

The area has also become globally regarded as one of the premier **turtle-viewing** spots (both hawksbill and Olive Ridley), with year-round water temperatures of 28°C (82°F). Other fish and marine life you're likely to see include black- and white-tip reef sharks, cuttlefish, moray eels, angel fish, ghost pipefish, pink leafed scorpion fish, blue ringed octopus, and, from December to March, manta rays.

Because it attracts so many divers (with ten PADI-certified dive shops on Gili T alone) much of the coral near shore has been damaged, giving south Lombok a slight edge on undersea color. But with some 18 accepted dive sites, many suitable for beginners, and so many professional, internationally credited dive schools, diving options are available for all abilities and the Gilis are probably the best place in Indonesia for dive courses ranging from first certifications to instructor-level classes. All the PADI dive schools on the Gilis charge the same amounts. Prices for a single dive typically start at Rp370,000; you'll pay Rp590,000 for an introductory scuba course; it's Rp3,400,000 for a PADI open-water certificate, which takes 3 or 4 days, and Rp2,700,000 for an advanced open-diver certification. You'll encounter many other non-professional, non-accredited dive schools on the islands. Use only the PADI-certified ones.

A few recommended dive shops are: **Blue Marlin Dive** (℃ 0370/613-2424; www.bluemarlindive.com); **Dream Divers** (℃ 0370/634496; www.dreamdivers.com); **Big Bubble** (℃ 0370/625020; www.bigbubblediving.com); **Manta Dive** (℃ 0370/643649; www.manta-dive.com); **Vila Ombak Diving Academy** (℃ 0370/614-2336; www.hotelombak.com); **Trawangan Diving** (℃ 0370/614-9220; www.trawangandive.com); and **Gili Divers** (℃ 081/23755037; www.gilidivers.com).

In recent years, increasingly destructive and more concentrated fishing practices, coupled with the increase in pollution that tourism brings, has led to reef damage. The use of heavy anchors has been addressed to some extent with the introduction of mooring buoys, and mercifully, fishing techniques involving dynamite or cyanide have, with the financial support of the **Gili Eco Trust** (www.giliecotrust.com), now been banned. Concern about the destruction of the reef and the need to protect the marine life and the islands' microcosm led to the creation of the Gili Eco Trust in 2001. All seven of the dive centers on the Gilis participate and anyone wishing to dive around these islands needs to pay a one-time fixed fee of Rp40,000, which goes to the trust to help pay for beach cleaning, recycling, education, and reef conservation. The Trust is expanding its programs to cover education and awareness initiatives as well as projects that help the local community develop more sustainable practices.

One of the major projects of the Trust has been **Biorock ★★**. The Biorock is an artificial structure pumped with a small electrical current which, over time, allows the development and regeneration of a coral reef system. Currently 33 reef modules are in operation and the work to date has shown remarkable results.

HORSEBACK RIDING Stud's Horse Riding Adventures (✆ 081/75746079) offers beach rides and treks around the island through the coconut plantations. Most of the horses are actually ponies but there are some of the bigger boys. Take a memorable sunset ride followed by a swim in the sea.

KAYAKING Astrid, a former kayaking medalist, will take you out on a half-day kayaking expedition via **Karma Kayak** (p. 331; Rp300,000 per person). Lunch is a picnic on the beach of Gili Meno, en route. Trips are subject to the weather and the currents on the day.

SNORKELING ★★ The best snorkeling on the island, with plenty of varieties of coral, is the **north coast** where you're virtually guaranteed to see turtles. Another popular spot is off the **east coast.** Start at the northeasterly spot and be carried south by the currents, which can be very strong. Ask the dive schools for any advice on currents. You can rent snorkeling kits from plenty of places on the island. Expect to pay between Rp30,000 to Rp50,000 a day.

SURFING At the southern end of the island is a fast right-handed break, better known as **Secrets.** This break is best tackled at high tide with a southwest or south swell. The wave can get big in shallow waters and is best left to the experts.

WATERSPORTS The **Beach House, Scallywags,** and **Kelapa Luxury Villas** (see "Where to Stay," above) can all arrange banana boats, donuts, and water-skiing. (Children never seem to tire of the banana boat.) It's not cheap though: Expect to pay Rp700,000 for an hour and Rp400,000 for half an hour.

Gili Trawangan Entertainment & Nightlife

Gili T certainly lives up to its time-honored, party-island reputation. For such a small island, and no matter the season, there's ample opportunity at plenty of bars and nightspots to let your hair down every night of the week. During high season, the

Don't Get Burned on Gili T (or Anywhere in Indonesia)

Along with Gili T's reputation as a party destination, it unfortunately also has a reputation for the availability of drugs, particularly ecstasy and cannabis. Things quieted down considerably after an undercover police crackdown in 2008. Although the reputation of the island remains, the liberal drugs policy of turning a blind eye has gone for good. You may, however, still be approached. The penalty for possession of even one seed is a minimum 4 years in prison, and for dealing the penalty is a life sentence or death. **Avoid** contact and association with drugs and dealers **at all costs.**

place is packed with revelers. If you think you're sneaky for coming here during low season, you've got another think coming: The party seems undeterred even through the low season. Popular full-moon parties feature DJs from Bali and Europe. Rotating party nights have historic followings, although with the island's popularity, more than one venue is now popular on any given night.

Monday: Blue Marlin. Located above the dive school, the dance floor comes alive to the sounds of throbbing trance and tribal tunes.

Tuesday: Beach House. With many tables facing the beach, a mirror ball, and disco music (really), it's a relaxed place for drinks and dancing.

Wednesday: Tir Na Nog. Or simply, "the Irish Bar," you don't need to ask for directions to this place in the evening—just follow the crowd. If you're enjoying your time on Gili T, you'll end up here at some point. If you're not enjoying your time on Gili T, this may be just the pick-me-up, with dancing on the bar a nightly sport, great music, and a lively crowd **Thursday: Blue Beach Bar.** In front of the Hotel Ombak, this is a Gili T establishment of long-standing. Live bands play every night, except Sunday, and are generally good. Happy hour prices attract crowds.

Friday: Rudy's. An institution on Gili T, this is one of the island's original bars and it still has heaps of appeal today. Locally owned and operated, it's the place to meet people from all over the world, rubbing shoulders with expats and locals while downing the legendary magic (as in magic mushroom, legal in Indonesia) cocktails. Rudy's is a lively place any night of the week, but it's a traditional Friday-night spot.

Any night: Sama Sama. This bar has gained heaps of popularity because of the great live music and impromptu jam sessions. Some of the best reggae music can be heard here, not only from the band but from the lively musical crowd.

GILI AIR

Gili Air, "Island of Water," is the nearest island to Lombok and popular with guests on the mainland who visit for the day. This is also the most populated of the three Gilis, with just over 1,000 local inhabitants, descendants of Bugis, Mandar, and Sulawesi. The majority of accommodations here are locally owned and managed with only a few foreign-owned properties (unlike on Gili T).

The **public boat harbor Koperasi,** bang in the middle of the south coast, is open daily 8am to 5:30pm; look at the timetable on the wall for public boats.

[FastFACTS] GILI AIR

ATMs   There are none on the island as of the time of going to press.

Bicycles   You can rent bicycles at Ozzy's (p. 342).

Hospital/Clinic   The village clinic is behind the harbor; ask for directions. At the time of writing, a nurse was on call from 8am to 6pm, but there's no way to know that this is always the case.

Internet Access   Ozzy's Shop (p. 342), Gili Air Hotel (below), and Gecko Cafe, behind the Perama Tours office, offer Internet access.

Where to Stay

The majority of lodgings are on the north and east coasts near the best snorkeling. Gili Air is still quite primitive when it comes to running water and most accommodations still offer only saltwater showers.

Biba Beach Village ★   This villa hotel and restaurant has been lovingly built by Italian owners Claudio and Sabrina, making it one of the more charming places to stay on the island—if you can get a room. The interior has been carefully furnished in a traditional Indonesian style that effortlessly mixes with the modern amenities. Each bungalow has a king-size bed and a single bed. All the rooms have terraces, with chairs and tables overlooking the garden and out over the sea.

The restaurant sits directly on the beach. Dinner is served in *buruga* (open-sided, thatched platforms on stilts) adorned in colorful fabrics. Claudio takes great pride in his food and the Italian menu offers a selection of freshly made pastas, *fritto misto* (fried, mixed seafood), and gnocchi. The fresh ravioli dishes (Rp35,000) change daily. A specialty is the hand-stuffed mushroom ravioli served with a simple butter sauce. The spaghetti with fresh, homemade tomato sauce is as good as it gets, and perhaps even better considering the location. The mouthwatering bruschetta is worth the visit alone.

www.bibabeach.com. ✆ **081/917274648.** 3 units. High season Rp650,000 standard, Rp800,000 superior; low season Rp300,000 standard, Rp500,000 superior. Rates include breakfast and taxes. Cash only. **Amenities:** Restaurant. *In room/bungalow:* A/C (superior), fan (standard).

Gili Air Hotel   This hotel's 29 chalets are all arranged around a garden, with direct sea views from about a dozen units. Rooms are simple; the more basic have fans and a shower room although the luxury suites offer TVs, air-conditioning, and fridge. All rooms have saltwater showers, which are only so refreshing, but freshwater is planned for the future. Nowadays the resort is looking somewhat out of date, but it has the most magnificent views from the half-dozen beachfront *bales*. Thanks to the Italian owners, the food here is good and very popular with Italian tourists. Choose from an extensive Italian menu featuring pasta, with some Indonesian favorites thrown in for good measure, or a nightly seafood and meat barbecue. During high season, the restaurant serves up crab or lobster live from the aquarium. Prices are steep for this island, but don't be afraid to try to negotiate a better price during the low season.

www.hotelgiliair.com. ✆ **0370/662-1448** or 0370/643580. 29 units. High season US$75–US$164; low season US$53–US$145. Rates include breakfast and taxes. MC, V. **Amenities:** Restaurant; bar; Internet access; saltwater pool. *In room:* A/C (in some), TV (in some), minibar.

Gili Air Santay 🏨 This is a great budget choice and as such gets very busy in the summer. Traditional Sulawesi bungalows are spread out in a tropical garden, about a 100-m (330-ft.) stroll to the beach. All the fan-cooled bungalows have a large balcony with hammock, and are a perfect place to laze the day away. Book well ahead if you want to stay in the high season. The beachside restaurant Santay serves delicious, authentic Thai food as well as traditional Sasak and European foods. If you've overdone barbecue fish and had enough local fodder, this is the place to head for.

www.giliair-santay.com. ✆ **081/803758695.** 10 units. High season Rp280,000 standard, Rp350,000–Rp650,000 bungalow; low season Rp150,000 standard, Rp220,000–Rp400,000 bungalow. Rates include breakfast and taxes. Cash only. **Amenities:** Restaurant. *In room/bungalow:* Fan.

Kaluku Bungalows These seven traditional-styled *lumbung* bungalows, all with sea views, are next door to the Blue Marlin Dive (p. 337). Dive and stay options are available. Otherwise make use of the swimming pool, one of a few on the island, and the restaurant. Accommodations have small terraces in front, double beds with luxury linens, and modern, outdoor shower rooms.

www.kalukubungalow.com. ✆ **0370/636421.** 7 units. High season Rp750,000, low season Rp400,000. MC, V. Rates include breakfast. **Amenities:** Restaurant; bar; outdoor pool. *In room/bungalow:* A/C, TV, minibar.

Manta Dive Part of a popular chain based on Gili T, these recently built *lumbung*-style bungalows with balconies are constructed around a pool with sea views. Rooms are basic with modern amenities. Some great bars and restaurants are right in front of the dive school. This place offers competitive stay and dive packages.

www.manta-dive.com. ✆ **0370/629366** or 081/353050462**.** 11 units. Year-round Rp400,000–Rp600,000. MC, V. **Amenities:** Outdoor pool. *In bungalow:* A/C, minibar.

Scallywags Mango Retreat ★ Scallywags on Gili T is well-known for its fantastic value accommodations and restaurant and this recent new branch will likely become a big hit as well. Comfortable rooms with flatscreen television, modern furnishings, and contemporary art open up onto a lagoon-like swimming pool that meanders between mango trees, hence the name.

www.scallywagsresort.com. ✆ **0370/6145301.** High season US$135; low season US$85. AE, MC, V. **Amenities:** Restaurant; Wi-Fi in restaurant. *In room:* A/C, TV, Internet.

Sejuk Cottages 🏨 Set back from the beach, nestled in a former coconut plantation, these Sasak-style bungalows of various shapes and sizes are uniquely designed using Lombok wood with alang-alang roofing. The best units are the luxury bungalows with upstairs terraces. Each bungalow is named after an Indonesian plant or flower, most of which can be found in the beautifully manicured gardens. Most bungalows have two double beds making these perfect for families and small groups. The only downside is that the hotel doesn't have a restaurant of its own, but with so much on offer nearby, it's only so much of a drawback.

www.sejukcottages.com. ✆ **0370/636461** or 081/339535387. 11 units. Year-round Rp280,000–Rp450,000 standard without A/C; Rp480,000–Rp800,000 superior with A/C; Rp600,000 bungalow. MC, V. Rates include breakfast and taxes. **Amenities:** Bar; pool. *In room/bungalow:* A/C (in some), fan, TV (in some), fridge.

Where to Eat

Most restaurants on the island offer a similar menu and with few exceptions, the quality is the same. It's a mixture of Indonesian with basic Western food, and plenty of Italian options thrown in. Try and order your food before you're hungry as the pace of service can be pretty relaxed.

One new standout that defies expectations is **Scallywag's Organic Beach Club** at Scallywags (see above), a Gili T institution. It offers freshly grilled seafood and steaks, sandwiches, and fajitas. Dining takes place on folding tables directly on the beach and it's perfect for either a casual lunch or a romantic beachside dinner.

The **Santay** at the Gili Air Santay (see above) for Thai, and **Biba** ★ at Biba Beach Village (see above) for Italian, are also two excellent choices.

Most of the restaurants listed below are nothing more than open-air beach shacks. Almost none of them have phone numbers or credit-card machines.

The **Green Café** serves a selection of sandwiches, pasta, and some delicious Sasak home cooking for Rp15,000 to Rp25,000. **Munchies** (Rp10,000–Rp25,000) is popular with travelers for its reasonably priced, fresh fish barbecues. It also serves local curries. Prices for fresh fish are agreed upon when you choose. **Tami's** (Rp20,000–Rp40,000) serves a variety of local cuisines mostly to day visitors from the Oberoi Hotel on Lombok. The dish to try is the delicious grilled chicken, but the rest of the menu isn't much different from others on the island—and it's slightly more expensive.

The **Wiwin Café** (Rp25,000–Rp30,000) gets packed in the evening thanks to its large selection of fresh fish. The fish is weighed in front of you and you agree upon a price. Also on the menu is local and European food and some pretty good Indian curries. The bar has a large selection of local and Western booze. The attached bookshop has a good selection of secondhand books.

Zipp Bar (Rp35,000–Rp50,000) is an ideal place to pass the day. Lounge on one of the sun beds and sip cocktails until you doze. Jump in the water and enjoy some of the best snorkeling on the island. Try a pizza from a wood-burning oven. A range of pastas, burgers, local food, and sandwiches are also available. Watch out though, you may be charged from the more expensive "tourist" menu. Same food, different prices; ask for the local menu. If you're looking for some late-night drinking, this is the place to head. Either look out for, or watch out for, the crowd-pleasing, full-moon parties.

Exploring Gili Air

Snorkeling and diving are the main focus on Gili Air. For **surfers,** one right-hand break is mostly frequented by locals rather than tourists who prefer the better known breaks at Gili T. The break is located on the southwest coast.

The best place to enjoy **snorkeling** on Gili Air is to start on the east coast at the top of the island and drift down with the currents. If you haven't brought your own gear you can rent it from plenty of beach bars and hotels. Expect to pay about Rp30,000 for mask and fins per day. If you'd prefer to explore farther offshore, rent a glass-bottom boat. Owners offer a day rate rather than charging by the hour so make the most of it and spend a day cruising round all three islands stopping for a well-deserved lunch before heading back at sunset. Expect to pay about Rp80,000 per person (four-person minimum) from **Ozzy's Shop** (© **0370/622179;** daily 8am–9pm).

For **diving,** three established groups operating on the island are **Blue Marlin Dive** (see p. 337), **Dream Divers** (see p. 337), and **Manta Dive** (see p. 337). All have their headquarters on Gili T. Costs are fixed across all islands so there's no haggling. You can, however, save slightly by booking online.

Cycling on Gili Air is not for those looking for a leisurely spin round the island. There are lots of areas where you'll need to dismount and push. This is best done early evening or first thing in the morning when it's slightly cooler. Expect to take about an hour to an hour and a half to circumnavigate the island. A day's rental from Ozzy's Shop costs Rp30,000.

Gili Air Entertainment & Nightlife

As with the other Gilis, Air is famous for its full-moon parties. DJs from Bali and overseas fly in to mix tunes for revelers. The best places are **Zipp Bar** (see above) and **Legends,** a reggae joint in the north with a great beachfront tree house to fall out of.

GILI MENO

Gili Meno, the middle of the three islands, is the smallest and quietest with few permanent inhabitants and thus retains the most original charm. Most accommodations and food options are on the eastern coast, near some of the best snorkeling. However, a few secluded snorkel spots on the north coast are worth the trek. You'll also see the best sunsets here, with Mount Agung in the distance.

The **harbor** is on the east coast. The **Perama Tours** boat ticket office (𝄐 **0370/ 632824**) is in Kontiki Meno on the southeast coast.

[FastFACTS] GILI MENO

ATM/Bank   Gili Meno has no ATM and very few places accept credit cards.
Hospital/Clinic   A clinic in the center of the island is managed by a nurse and open daily.
Internet Access   There's a small *wartel* (phone shop) for Internet at the harbor.

Where to Stay

Book well in advance because accommodations are limited and in high demand; some places like Shack 58 & 59 are booked solid for months.

Biru Meno   At this quiet out-of-the-way place on the southernmost tip of the island, the only sound you'll hear is the water lapping on the coral beach. The rooms are decorated with natural matting and bamboo furniture although the gardens have been creatively decorated using locally sourced implements and an abundance of flowers. Swags of coral adorn the place giving it a mystical feel in the evening. The restaurant has great pizzas from its wood-fired oven and grilled fish and curries.

www.birumeno.com. 𝄐 **081/339758968.** 8 units. High season US$30–US$40; low season US$60–US$70. Rates include breakfast and taxes. **Amenities:** Restaurant. *In room:* Fan.

Mahamaya   This brand-new eco-friendly boutique beachfront resort contains the most upscale accommodations on quiet Gili Meno. The project of a British brother-and-sister pair, the resort offers ultra-modern villas with secluded terraces next to one of the island's best snorkeling spots, Turtle Point. The resort offers lessons in guitar, cooking, painting, and jewelry design, along with the usual watersports offerings of most hotels.

www.mahamaya.co. ✆ **0370/637616.** 22 units. Year-round Rooms from US$150; villas from US$210. Rates include breakfast, and taxes. **Amenities:** Restaurant; bar; freshwater pool; watersports; Wi-Fi (free). *In room/villa:* A/C, fan.

Mallia's Child   Situated right on the beach, these basic, clean bungalows are a little overpriced for what they offer, but are in a handy location if you're looking to relax in the center of the island action. It's a great place to watch the world go by, but not much else. The attached restaurant has a wood-burning pizza oven and serves all the usual Indonesian and basic Western foods. The evenings feature a good barbecue.

www.malliaschild.com. ✆ **0370/622007.** 8 units. Year-round US$25–US$35 standard; US$50–US$70 family room. **Amenities:** Restaurant. *In room:* Fan.

Shack 58 & 59 ★ 👜   Shack 58 is a delightful villa with the ocean just meters away and a perfect honeymooners' choice. The simply furnished bedroom has both a double bed and a single bed. A further *bale* and gazebos on the seafront are perfect for watching the sunrise and Mount Rinjani in the background. Shack 59 is set inland and is a one-room cottage with a gazebo on the waterfront. You'll be well looked after by husband and wife team Hengkie and Nirah who serve up a barbecue under the stars.

www.shack58.com. No phone. 2 villas. Year-round 65€ Shack 58; 45€ Shack 59. Rates include breakfast and exclude taxes. Payment available via PayPal. *In room:* A/C, fan, TV/DVD, fridge (Shack 59).

Sunset Gecko ★ 👜   This eco-friendly, Japanese-owned place is situated on a fantastic spot on the island's northeast coast. Its isolated position means you get a front seat to the island's most stunning sunsets. The small A-frame rooms and two-bedroom wooden house are simply furnished and adorned with ikat fabrics. Don't be put off by the communal bathrooms, because they're clean and beautifully designed with environmentally friendly soap.

www.thesunsetgecko.com. ✆ **081/3535667743.** 13 units. Year-round Rp70,000–Rp200,000 standard; Rp450,000–Rp500,000 4-person rooms, Rp1,000,000 8-person big hut. Rates exclude taxes. Credit card info missing. **Amenities:** Restaurant. *In room:* Fan.

Tropical Hideaway 🤿   Recently opened by the owner of one of the Gilis' better known dive shops, Blue Marlin, the comfortable bungalows offer luxuries such as air-conditioning that most other accommodations on the island don't have—and prices are competitive. The hotel also offers good-value dive-and-stay packages, making it a good option if you're an adventurous underwater explorer.

www.tropicalhideawaysresort.com. ✆ **0370/704-4603.** 10 units. Peak season Rp650,000; high season Rp550,000; low season Rp425,000. Rates exclude taxes. MC, V. **Amenities:** Restaurant; bar; pool; Wi-Fi. *In room:* A/C, minibar.

Villa Nautilus ★   This place is ideal for those who aren't quite ready to leave behind the modern world. Each of the five stone villas has a bed almost large enough to get lost in; a plush living area with floor-to-ceiling windows; air-conditioning; and a balcony with sun loungers facing the sea. One villa can be turned into a family villa. These are the most luxurious accommodations you'll find on the island with a price tag to match, but well worth it. The in-house **Bibi's Cafe** has a selection of Indonesian cuisine and wood-fired pizzas for Rp20,000 to Rp30,000.

www.villanautilus.com. ② **0370/642-1431.** 5 villas. High season US$99, peak season US$86, low season US$76; extra person US$20. Children 1 and under stay free in parent's room. Rates include breakfast and exclude taxes. MC, V. **Amenities:** Restaurant. *In room:* A/C, fan.

Where to Eat

As on Gili Air, most of the island restaurants don't take credit cards. When ordering, always check whether the fish is fresh or frozen. Most places offer frozen fish during the day and a fresh fish barbecue in the evening. Various restaurants serve pizzas from their own wood-burning ovens. **BiBi's Cafe,** part of Villa Nautilus (see above), is also a good choice for pizza and Indonesian food.

Located on the northeast of the island, **Balenta Café** (② **081/933122903;** Rp20,000–Rp50,000) is ideal for day-trippers from Gili T. The kitchen offers a daily catch served to your order or as a delicious fish satay. Stop by in advance to tell them if you're hoping to visit for lunch or dinner and would like fresh fish—that way you're guaranteed it. The restaurant also has a **turtle hatchery** with a breeding program.

Beach Café (Rp25,000) is a simple idyllic beach bar serving a mean curry and the usual local offerings. After supper, lie beside the fire lit on the beach in the softest sand and enjoy star gazing.

Situated bang in the middle of the main drag, visit **Rust Warung** (② **081/ 805241600;** Rp15,000–Rp50,000) in the evening for one of the island's best seafood barbecues. You can often enjoy listening to someone strumming on a guitar.

Exploring Gili Meno

Snorkeling and **diving** ★★★ are the main attractions here. Good snorkeling is along the northwest coast, near Balenta Café. You should see lots of **sea turtles** to the north of Balenta. The other good place is off the east coast near Amber House and Shack 58. Beware of strong currents at both of these locations. Snorkeling gear is available for rent (around Rp20,000 per day, negotiate for longer) at numerous shops and restaurants around the island.

At the time of writing there's only one dive shop on Gili Meno: **Blue Marlin Dive** (② **0370/639980;** www.bluemarlindive.com). Being based in Meno means that you're slightly nearer to more of the dive sites, but apart from that there are no benefits. Prices are fixed throughout the Gilis (p. 337).

One of the nicest things to do is to take a **stroll around the island.** A few guides will show you the way, if you don't fancy getting lost on the maze of dirt tracks that crisscross the island. On the way to the charming saltwater lake in the middle of the island, you pass through small villages, coconut plantations, and fields of peanuts and maize. If you're here during the dry season (May–Oct), look out for the salt mining.

In the center of the island is **Gili Meno Bird Park** (no phone; Rp50,000; 9am–dusk), with over 300 species of birds on show, including parrots, flamingos, pelicans, eagles, and pheasants from around the world. The park has deteriorated over the years and could do with some love and attention.

Situated on the southeast coast is the small **Bolong's Turtle Sanctuary** (no phone; www.gilimenoturtles.com; by donation; 9am–dusk) with a breeding program for 500 turtles. Once the green and loggerhead turtles reach a suitable age and size they're released back into the wild.

16

PLANNING YOUR TRIP TO BALI

GETTING THERE

By Plane

Denpasar Airport, aka **Ngurah Rai International Airport** (**DPS;** ℂ **0361/751011;** www.baliairport.com) is 13km (8 miles) southwest of Denpasar, Bali. For airport information and connection to airline reservations counters, call ℂ **0361/751011,** ext. 1454. When you leave Bali, you pay an airport departure tax of Rp150,000 at immigration.

Most visitors from the U.S. and Canada fly here via Taipei on **China Airlines,** Bangkok on **Thai Airways,** Jakarta on **Garuda Indonesia,** Singapore on **Singapore Airlines,** Tokyo on **Japan Airlines,** Hong Kong on **Cathay Pacific,** or Seoul on **Korean Air.**

Cathay Pacific via Hong Kong serves Bali from the U.K. and Europe; tickets can be purchased from **British Airways, Singapore Airlines,** or **Air France.** Flights from Australia and New Zealand can be booked through **Qantas.** To find out which airlines travel to Bali.

For specific details on getting to and around **Lombok,** see p. 287.

GETTING INTO TOWN FROM THE AIRPORT

Public transportation is nonexistent from the airport. Many private drivers may approach you upon your arrival; ignore them and head straight to the official taxi counter, located outside the arrival hall on the right. The official taxis charge fixed fares for destinations around the island; prices range from Rp60,000–Rp135,000 for south Bali destinations, Rp195,000 for Ubud, and Rp335,000 for East Bali. Pre-pay the attendant and show your driver the receipt. Many hotels and resorts arrange complimentary airport transfers— check with your hotel. Local and international rental car agencies have booths at the airport, though this option isn't recommended. See p. 347.

 N 200,000?

GETTING AROUND

Bali is made up of three main roads that circumnavigate the island and hundreds of smaller roads that traverse the countryside. It takes approximately 3 hours to travel the length and breadth of Bali. Road conditions on the main roads are generally good but can be heavily populated with slow trucks. The conditions of the minor roads are generally determined by the weather. During the rainy season, road conditions fall foul of torrential rain and heavy traffic leaves the roads covered in potholes and debris.

Although there's an extensive public transport system for locals, journeys tend to be very long and don't take in smaller destinations. Most visitors opt for private cars and drivers.

By Private Car & Driver

The best way of seeing the sights of Bali is by renting a car and a driver. It gives you the freedom to explore the backwater of this picturesque country. Plenty of car-rental agencies on Bali offer day services or weekly rentals; your hotel or villa may have its own cars and drivers available for you as well. Having a driver takes away the stress of having to navigate the small roads around the island; they can also help with any translations as once you leave the main areas very few people speak any English.

Drivers on overnight stays will find their own suitable accommodations at very little cost to you. You'll be expected to pay the driver's food and accommodations but the cost of the vehicle, insurance, and petrol should be included in the price. Expect to pay about Rp350,000 to Rp450,000 a day, open to negotiation.

Before renting a car and driver make sure that they have all the relevant paperwork and insurance in place and agree on all costs ahead of the rental period. Also make sure that they have a good command of English and are knowledgeable about the island.

By Rental Car

A word of warning about rental cars: Any foreigners involved in even minor traffic violations or accidents may be vulnerable to exploitation, and thus this option isn't recommended. However, rental cars are easy to procure on the island. To rent a car you're supposed to have an International Driving License or a locally issued tourist driving license together with a copy of your passport. However, most rental businesses will rent you a car with a copy of your home national driver's license.

If your car rental agency requires one, one-month licenses are issued on the spot for Rp150,000 at the **Foreign License Service,** Jl. Gunung Sanghiang, Denpasar (© **0361/422323**). You'll also need to show a copy of your passport and your home national driver's license.

Before you drive away in your car, ensure that it has all its registration documentation (Surat Tanda Nomor Kendaraan Bermotor or **STNK,** vehicle registration certificate) and copies of any insurance policies.

You must be vigilant at all times when driving in Bali. The Balinese rarely stop to check for on-coming traffic, which can often cause drivers to slam on their breaks or

---

⚠ Driving Infringements

Always ensure that you have the car documentation with you as well as your international driver's license. The police carry out regular spot checks and you'll be fined for any infringements. Not wearing a seatbelt while driving or as a passenger, or not wearing a helmet on a motorcycle is also an infringement. Stay calm during all dealings with the police, don't argue with them, and don't offer them a bribe. They're less interested in whether you've committed a traffic violation and more in what you have in your wallet. A standard fine should be Rp50,000 but police will try to get as much money as they can from you. Don't flash a full wallet of cash, as you might not see it again.

swerve to avoid a collision. At night, many motorcycles and cyclists rarely have lights on and street lighting is limited. Traffic lights aren't always observed. Accidents are common.

Vehicles are left-hand drive. The national speed limit is 70kph (43mph) but you won't find many areas in which to do this.

Expect to pay between US$18 to US$45 a day for vehicle rental, though the bigger agencies charge a lot more. Prices will either be in rupiah or U.S. dollars. The cheapest form of transport is a Suzuki jeep, which should cost about US$18 a day; a Toyota Kijang should cost about US$22 a day; a top of the range limousine-style Suzuki costs US$45. These prices should include some insurance but always check what insurance you're getting before agreeing to a price.

International chains on the island include: **Avis,** Jl. Danau Tamblingan, Sanur (© **1800/656545** or **0361/282635**; www.avis.com), and **Hertz,** Ngurah Rai airport (© **0361/768375;** www.hertz.com). Local companies include: **Bali Car Hire** (© **081/23871684** or 0361/411499; www.balicarhire.com), also in Denpasar, a reliable company with a good variety of cars available; and **CV Amertha Dana,** Legian (© **0361/888-8890;** www.amerthadana.com), which doesn't have new cars but the rates are good and service very attentive, and it rents motorcycles.

By Motorcycle

The easiest, cheapest, and fastest way to get around Bali is by motorcycle. However it's also the most dangerous with daily accidents and weekly motorcycle deaths.

Plenty of companies on the streets will rent you a motorcycle if you have a home or local driver's license. It should cost you about Rp50,000 a day for a basic 110 to 125CC scooter, less if you're renting long term. Surfer racks should be available at no extra cost.

Always check the motorcycle first to make sure that everything is working: brakes, indicators, and wheels. Also ensure that you have the right insurance and vehicle registration documents, which you need to carry with you at all times. All motorcyclists must wear helmets and these should be supplied at the time of rental for no extra charge. Ensure the helmet fits properly. If you can't find one that fits, buy one.

TIPS ON HOTELS

Bali accommodations range from bungalows that cost Rp40,000 (yes, US$4) to luxury villas at US$1,000 a night. Budget accommodations are generally quoted in rupiah (Rp) while mid-range and luxury accommodations are quoted in US dollars. An increasingly popular trend for families and groups is to rent a villa, which can go from US$100 up to US$5,000 per night and are usually served by a retinue of staff. At the lower end, and for a more local experience, are *losmen* (traditional homestays, a corruption of the Dutch word "logement") or rustic bungalows. In the better homestays, expect a clean and simple room with a double or two single beds. They usually don't have air-conditioning but will have a fan. Better places will have an attached bathroom with a cold-water shower, Western toilet, and hand basin. The lower budget places sometimes have a squat toilet and *mandi* (a bucket of water to splash over your body).

Many villas and bungalows have open-air bathrooms, often set in a lush garden. They're definitely a very Balinese experience, but may also shelter little uninvited insect guests and are best avoided if you have low tolerance for critters.

Booking a vacation to Bali and Lombok—particularly for Americans, Brits, and Europeans making the long-haul flight—is never easy. Here are a few tips to take the stress out of your planning, and to make sure you get the most for your money:

- **Decide what kind of holiday you want before you book your room.** If you're going on a romantic honeymoon, you might want to splurge on a fancy resort since you'll be craving plenty of alone time with your loved one. If you're planning to do a lot of touring around the island, book something more cost-friendly, since you'll be spending a lot of time outside your hotel or resort. It's never a pleasant feeling when you spend a lot on your accommodations and end up feeling beholden to the resort, rather than touring your destination.

- **Know what to expect.** Many hotels offer complimentary transfers to the airport, free Wi-Fi, and daily breakfast included in the room rate. Make sure the hotel you book provides all the above.

- **Bargain hard.** Some hotels offer free nights, if you book more than two or three. If the hotel won't budge on the room rate, ask them to throw in extras such as free massages, dinners, and excursions.

- **Don't go during high or peak season.** Rates double during the summer and around Christmas and New Year.

- **Visit www.agoda.com.** This new, burgeoning, Asia hotel website has some of the most competitive rates on accommodations in Bali and Lombok.

Use it as a baseline for bargaining directly with the hotel.

- **Know your taxes.** Hotels charge a 21% tax, on top of the room rate. Remember to figure that into your final bill before you put down a deposit.

- **Book a cheaper hotel next to a beach club or a fancy resort.** Beach clubs such as **Cocoon** in Kuta, and **Ku De Ta** and **Potato Head** in Seminyak, offer beachfront dining and swimming pools to the public. Many top-end resorts, including the **W Resort** in Seminyak, the **Ayana** in Jimbaran Bay, and **Karma Kandara** at Uluwatu, allow visitors to use their pools or beaches if they pay a fee or dine in their restaurants. Find out what the policy is of your intended resort—and then look next door.

- **Consider a villa.** If traveling with a larger group or a family, villas are often a cost-efficient option. Not only are rates often cheaper when you break it down per room (and many come with the luxuries of a five-star hotel), but villas often have in-house chefs that charge you only for the cost of groceries for your meals. But one drawback is that many villas require a minimum-stay length, restricting your movement around the island, especially given Bali's terrible traffic congestion.

- **Go to Lombok.** Lombok offers the same quality of accommodations for half the price, more peace and quiet, and better beaches and diving than Bali. Flights to Lombok are frequent, inexpensive (around US$50 each way), and short (less than 30 minutes).

Bali's resorts and fine Western hotels cost a fraction of what luxury accommodations would cost elsewhere. Promotional and Internet rates are available at all hotels in Bali and Lombok. You're most likely to pay the published rack rates that are listed in this guide in high and peak seasons. Especially in the off season, it pays to shop around; you can show up at the front desk of even the largest hotels and ask for the best rate.

Almost all hotels charge a 21% tax (10% government tax and 11% service) on top of the quoted rates. Some hotels tack on a charge in peak and high seasons—the 2 or 3 weeks around Christmas and New Year, plus the months of July and August. Some establishments might charge only 17% tax and some only the 10% government tax with no service added. Check when you're booking.

Villas

Bali is becoming increasingly famous for its **private villas** complete with staff. Indonesia's low labor costs—at one-third the already low levels of Thailand—result in single villas employing teams from 5 to over 30 people.

If you're traveling for longer than a week and plan on staying in one place for more than a few days, we recommend the villa option. You'll have more space and privacy for your money. It's also an attractive option for families and groups traveling together.

Some villas and hotels are decadently over the top. We're talking private spas and helipads—you know, the necessities. Almost all stand-alone villas come with pools, gardens, and a full-time fleet of staff that usually includes a round-the-clock cook, housekeeper, gardener, and babysitter. Other standard features include air-conditioning, kitchens, stereo systems, satellite televisions, and IDD telephones. Most include an airport pickup and transfer; some have same-day laundry service, grocery shopping and restaurant delivery services, car and motorbike rentals, and catering. All villa compounds offer 24-hour reception and security. None of the villa complexes are beachfront but all are close to the action.

Not every place sold as a "villa" actually fits the bill. Prices vary widely: Some operators claim to go as low as US$30 a night (which usually just means a stand-alone hut on hotel grounds), but realistically you're looking at upward of US$200 a night for a decent location and a private pool. At the top of the range, nightly rents can easily go north of US$1,000 a night. The general rule "you get what you pay for" applies.

Most villas will have breakfast or a light snack ready for you on arrival. You then order your meals from a menu and they buy the groceries for you. Private villas normally have a higher quality of food, presentation, and service, but are much more expensive. Most stand-alone villas will buy your groceries, prepare your meals, and charge between 10% and 30% in addition to the grocery bills. As a general rule, the more expensive the villa the higher the additional expense on meals, but there are exceptions. Do the math first.

Look carefully at who's running the villa (the owner? local company? Western company? local staff who answer to an overseas owner?) and who you're renting through (directly from the owner? a management company? an established villa agent? someone who just opened a month ago after his friend told him how easy it was?). Each has its pros and cons. If an agency is running things, see whether it's been reviewed in the foreign press.

Ask how long the villa has been taking commercial guests. Villas normally take a year or so to get to the best service levels. Also, in the first 6 to 12 months of operation great villas may offer introductory prices below market rates to spread awareness of their new offerings.

RENTAL AGENTS

Elite Havens, Jl. Raya Semer, Banjar Semer, Kerobokan (*C* **0361/731074;** fax 0361/736391; www.elitehavens.com), is the leading luxury villa agency in Bali.

Bali Villa Worldwide (BVW), Jl. Laksmana 3B, Oberoi-Seminyak (© **0361/ 732013;** fax 0361/736705; www.balivillaworldwide.com), manages a selection of top-notch properties available for rent all round Bali.

BaliOn, Pantai Seseh, Canggu (© **0361/848-3038;** www.balion.com), is a family-run agency with a broad selection of budget to luxury options on the island.

Bali Tropical Villas, Jl. Raya Seminyak, Gang Lalu 7, Seminyak (© **0361/ 732083;** fax 0361/732083; www.bali-tropical-villas.com), has been run by Anita Lococo for over 15 years. There's nothing she doesn't know about most properties on the island; she has even written books on the subject.

Bali Experience, Jl. Banjar Anyar Kaja 89, Kerobokan (© **0361/844-5934;** fax 0361/847-5160; www.bali-experience.com), has an easy-to-navigate website that makes choosing even harder as there are so many wonderful properties.

MONEY & COSTS

THE VALUE OF INDONESIAN RUPIAH VS. OTHER POPULAR CURRENCIES

Rupiah	Aus$	Can$	Euro €	NZ$	UK£	US$
10,000	A$1.12	C$1.15	0.81€	NZ$1.41	£0.71	US$1.17

Frommer's lists prices in the local currency, except where notified. The currency conversions quoted above were correct at press time. However, rates fluctuate, so before departing consult a currency exchange website such as www.oanda.com/currency/converter to check up-to-the-minute rates.

The unit of currency in Indonesia is the **rupiah,** from the Sanskrit word for wrought silver, "rupya." Coins come in denominations of Rp25, 50, 100, and 500. Notes are Rp1,000, 2,000, 5,000, 10,000, 20,000, 50,000, and 100,000; the largest denomination is worth about US$10 (£5.90). The rate of exchange is relatively stable. At press time, the average was about **Rp10,000 to US$1.17.**

Cash is king in Bali and Lombok. Wherever you go you'll need to have low denominations of cash to pay for parking, entrance to museums, tips, or taxi rides, or to buy knickknacks. Although Rp100,000 bills are useful for high-priced items, smaller shops and taxis don't carry large amounts of change. There seems to be an expectation that the customer should provide appropriate change, rather than the other way round.

More expensive hotels and resorts and certain businesses geared towards tourists charge in U.S. dollars while inexpensive accommodations, restaurants, and other businesses charge in Indonesian rupiah. We've listed prices accordingly.

The maximum amount of currency that you can bring into Bali is US$10,000 in cash.

ATMs

ATMs are everywhere in south Bali. You can make withdrawals with credit cards and some debit cards on the Maestro and Cirrus networks. Most ATMs dispense money in multiples of Rp50,000, though a few machines dispense Rp100,000 notes. All ATMs are clearly marked with which denominations they pay out.

GETTING YOUR MONEY'S worth WHEN CHANGING CURRENCY

Although there are good, honest money changers, there are also many unscrupulous vendors. Here are a few tips when using money changers:

o Make sure you do your own calculations. Don't rely on the staff: Some calculators can be tampered with.

o Check to see whether there's a commission fee. Be cautious—you may have a good rate of exchange but have to pay a hefty commission rate. If the commission is low, ensure that you're getting a good exchange rate.

o Count the money yourself. Better still, count it twice. Don't pass it back to the staff to recount as you may find a few notes missing after leaving the shop.

o The money changers should give you a receipt. If they don't, insist.

o Be aware of counterfeit bills. If a note doesn't feel right, ask for another one. Don't accept any damaged currency.

o Be sure to count zeros on a note. Rp10,000 is roughly equivalent to US$1 and Rp100,000 is US$10.

Some banks allow maximum withdrawals of Rp1,250,000 at one time but will allow up to three withdrawals in a day. Others allow Rp3,000,000 at one time with a maximum of Rp6,000,000 withdrawal in a day. The best ATM is **Permata Bank,** where you can withdraw Rp3,000,000 in Rp100,000 notes up to a maximum of two withdrawals. These ATMs are in the **Circle K** on Jalan Laksmana in Seminyak, on Jalan Legian near the turning to Jalan Double Six in Kuta, Jalan Tamblingan in Sanur, and Jalan Raya Ubud in Ubud. Other good banks include Bank Central Asia (BCA), Bank Lippo, Bank Mandiri, Bank Negara Indonesia (BNI), and Permata Bank. Outside the main tourist areas you won't find many ATMs. On Lombok you'll find ATMs in Mataram, Senggigi, and Praya.

Withdrawal charges depend on your bank in your country. Cash advances on credit cards are treated as loans and accrue interest daily. You'll be charged a transaction fee, too. Withdrawals made with debit cards should only be charged a transaction fee: Inquire at your bank for rates. Sometimes it's better to pay for things on a credit card directly rather than paying in hard cash.

Credit Cards

All high-end hotels, shops, restaurants, and nightclubs accept credit cards. Visa and MasterCard are the most commonly accepted cards but some do take American Express and Diners Club. Merchants may charge a 3% to 5% surcharge for credit transactions. Payments are usually in rupiah but some companies have been known to charge in U.S. dollars, particularly large hotel chains. If this is the case, ask them to clarify what exchange rate they're using as you may be better off paying in cash.

Foreign Exchange

Most major currency can be exchanged in banks, hotels, and authorized money changers in the main tourist areas. Rates depend on the currency and the denominations you're holding. U.S. dollars are the preferred currency but euros and sterling are also popular. U.S. bills issued before 2006 receive a lower rate than newer ones. Sometimes any old, folded, or damaged notes won't be accepted due to the high risk of the note being forged.

Money changers generally offer the best rates and are the most convenient. Daily opening times vary from 9am until 10pm. Double-check your money before leaving as there are money-changing scams, especially in the Kuta (on Bali) area. State-sponsored **Wartel Telecommunications Service** offices are the best. Banks generally offer the next favored rate but going into a bank is time-consuming and often exhausting. Hotels offer the lowest rate of exchange. Cashing traveler's checks requires a passport.

HEALTH

Taking simple precautions such as getting vaccinated, using mosquito nets and insect repellents, and watching what you eat and drink can greatly reduce the risk of exposure to a number of diseases that thrive in the tropical climate.

Consult your doctor before leaving. Besides the routine vaccinations recommended in your own country, you may need to get the following vaccinations at least 4 to 6 weeks before your trip to allow time for your vaccines to take effect: hepatitis A and B, typhoid, and tetanus-diphtheria.

Swine Flu

Numerous cases of **swine flu** in Bali were reported in 2009. In the event of another outbreak, the Balinese Health Department, proficient in dealing with matters of epidemics, works with the Denpasar Airport Health Office. Any planes that now arrive in Bali from countries confirmed to be infected with the H1N1 virus will be sequestered briefly at a remote aircraft parking area where the plane and its passengers are sprayed with disinfectant. Passengers will then disembark and be subjected to thermal scanners to determine if any have an elevated body temperature which, if discovered, would earn a more thorough medical examination by the airport's H1N1 containment team. Although this sounds like a lengthy procedure, it's all undertaken very quickly and without much delay.

Bug Bites & Other Wildlife Concerns

Dengue fever is a viral infection that typically causes flulike symptoms, including fever, muscle aches, joint pains, headaches, nausea, and vomiting, often followed by a rash. It's transmitted by Aedes mosquitoes, which bite during the daytime, especially in the morning and late afternoon.

Malaria is another common disease transmitted by Anopheles mosquitoes, which are most active after sundown. Malaria is common in Lombok and easterns part of Indonesia, but not in Bali. You're recommended to take malaria prophylaxis. Purchase your antimalarial drugs before travel as some of the recommended antimalarial drugs aren't always available over the counter. Discuss with your doctor at least 3 to 4 weeks before traveling because some of the malaria prophylaxis need to be taken 2 weeks before entering the malaria area.

A few cases of **rabies** have recently occurred in Bali and the local government has been actively vaccinating dogs to help control the disease. Although there's no official recommendation by the government for humans to get the rabies vaccine, it may be worthwhile for those spending a lot of time in rural areas, working in veterinarian positions, or anyone who may come into contact with bats and monkeys. If you do get bitten or scratched by a monkey or bat during your travel, you must go directly to the hospital and take vaccination procedures against rabies.

Dietary Red Flags

You can't drink the water from the taps on Bali and Lombok, but bottled water is cheap and readily available. Just about every hotel will supply you with a couple of bottles or a jug of boiled water—to be extra cautious, use it to brush your teeth as well. The ice in Bali is generally okay to use as the production is government controlled. Stay clear of ice in nontourist areas where it could be locally produced.

One of the most common illnesses that affects travelers is **diarrhea,** which usually occurs with a sudden change in diet. Infectious agents are the primary cause and people traveling from developed countries to developing countries experience rapid and dramatic change in the type of organisms in their gastrointestinal tract. To prevent traveler's diarrhea, avoid foods or beverages from street vendors and small warungs that look questionable (the presence of other tourists and locals eating is always a good sign), and avoid raw or undercooked meats and seafood. Keep yourself hydrated. Any electrolytes solution or tablets will help hydrate you and assist with maintaining the right balance of minerals in your body. For more serious cases, antibiotics can be prescribed at any pharmacy.

Some travelers will also be diagnosed with a stomach bug that we like to call **Bali Belly,** more akin to an acute case of gastroenteritis, which can be caused by a bacterial or parasitic infection. It's usually passed on by the fecal-oral route. Symptoms include abdominal pain, nausea, vomiting, and diarrhea. The illness can last a few days or a few weeks and can leave the victim bedridden and too ill to move. Consult a doctor immediately.

Sun Exposure

The equatorial sun can burn your skin faster than you think even on cloudy days. In July, the climate feels cooler due to the cool breezes but this is the time when most are unaware of the dangers of the sun. Limit exposure or liberally apply a high factor sunscreen. The sun is at its strongest between 11am and 2pm. Always keep hydrated. **Pocari Sweat** and other similar rehydrating drinks are sold everywhere but water remains the number-one priority.

What to Do If You Get Sick Away from Home

We list hospital and emergency numbers in the "Fast Facts" sections throughout this book. Plenty of English-speaking doctors are available on Bali; the better qualified doctors can be found in the more touristy areas of Bali and Lombok. If you do need a doctor, ask your hotel or villa concierge first, because they're likely to have one on call.

Apotek, Indonesian pharmacies, can be found on most busy streets in Bali and Lombok. They stock some Western brands but mostly local medicine. **Kimia Farma** is a Japanese pharmacy chain that stocks well-known medicinal brands and toiletries. It also has a doctor on-site who can prescribe antibiotics for less serious illnesses.

If you suffer from a chronic illness, consult your doctor before departure. Pack prescription medications in the original containers with pharmacy labels in carry-on luggage, otherwise they may not make it through airport security. Carry a copy of your prescription form and any other paperwork detailing what the drugs are for and who they've been prescribed to.

[FastFACTS]

Area Codes   The country code for Indonesia is **+62** while the area code for Bali telephones is **036.** Cell phone prefixes usually begin with **081.**

Business Hours   Most places keep daily "daylight hours," which on the equator pretty much means 9am to 6pm (or a little later).

Car Rental   See "Getting Around: By Car," earlier in this chapter.

Cell Phones   Although most cell phones have the technology to work overseas, the cost of using your home phone is prohibitively expensive. The best way to use a cell phone in Indonesia is to bring an unlocked GSM phone with you and insert a local SIM card purchased from one of the thousand *wartels* (phone shops) on the islands. Expect to pay around Rp50,000 for your SIM card; top-up credit can be purchased from around Rp1,000,000. Bali generally has good network coverage. In the mountains you may find patches where there's limited network coverage but you're never far from a phone line that works. In Lombok, phones are available in the cities and all tourist areas, and all cell phones work in these areas, too. In some of the more remote areas, particularly close to mountains, signals can fail. Alternatively, international calls can be made cheaply through **Skype** (www.skype.com) or any voice-over Internet protocol services.

Crime   See "Safety," later in this section.

Customs   Customs allows you to bring in, duty free, 200 cigarettes, 50 cigars, or 100g (3.53 oz) of tobacco; cameras and film; 1l (2.11 pints) of alcohol; and perfume clearly intended for personal use. Forbidden are guns, weapons, narcotics, pornography (leave it at home if you're unsure how it's defined), televisions, fresh fruit, Chinese medicine, and printed matter with Chinese characters. Plants might also be confiscated. On arrival at the airport all bags are screened for alcohol. Anyone caught carrying alcohol over their duty-free allowance will find it either confiscated or have to pay a high penalty. Rates aren't fixed and can be negotiated!

Disabled Travelers   With hilly terrain, bumpy (and sometimes nonexistent) sidewalks, and few public wheelchair ramps, Bali poses challenges for disabled travelers. However, Bali makes up for it to some extent with caring people and a willingness to help. A number of international resorts including the Bali Grand Hyatt, the Westin Resort, the Ayana, and the Le Méridien Golf Resort (all listed in the appropriate "Where to Stay" sections of chapters) have wheelchair access for guests. Two, well-established companies can arrange all your travel needs, suitable accommodations, and any equipment rental. They also have a full-service bus with a lift facility. Special caretakers can be arranged through these websites at a cost of approximately US$20 a day. Contact **Bali Access Travel,** Jl. Danau Tamblingan 31, Sanur (✆ **0361/851-9902;** www.baliaccesstravel.com), or **Bali Mobility and Tours,** Jl. Danau Tamblingan 54, Sanur (✆ **0361/281780;** www.bali mobility.com). **Bali International Diving Professionals** (✆ **0361/285065;** www.bidp-balidiving.com), based in Sanur, is an experienced, **International Association for Handicapped Divers** (IAHD; www.iahd.org) qualified dive team, and has specially modified boats to assist with divers with disabilities.

Doctors   Many international hotels have doctors on call; Bali also boasts two international hospitals. See "Hospitals," below.

Drinking Laws   You won't find alcohol in halal restaurants catering to Muslims, but there are no restrictions elsewhere. The legal drinking age is 17, but the police rarely enforce this law.

Driving Rules   See "Getting Around," earlier in this chapter.

Drug Laws Although you might be offered marijuana at every turn, Indonesia officially takes drug offenses very seriously. American and Australian forces have teamed up with Indonesian police to fight drugs, along with terrorism, and penalties for mere possession include long jail sentences and large fines.

Electricity Currents are usually 220 to 240 volts (50 AC). Plugs are the European-style, two-pin plugs.

Embassies & Consulates **Australia:** Jl. Tantular 32, Renon, Denpasar (① **0361/ 241118;** Mon–Fri 8am–noon and 12:30–4pm). The Australian consulate also assists nationals of **Canada** and **New Zealand. U.K.:** Tirtra Nadi 20, Sanur (① **0361/270601;** Mon–Thurs 8:30am–12:30pm, Fri 11:30am–6:30pm). **U.S.A.:** Jl. Hayam Wuruk 310, Denpasar (① **0361/ 233605;** Mon–Fri 8am–4:30pm).

Emergencies Bali has a new emergency response center that coordinates all governmental bureaus and services: dial ① **112.** Otherwise, you can call the national numbers: ① **110** for the police, ① **118** for an ambulance, ① **113** in case of fire, and ① **111/115-151** for search and rescue. The Red Cross can be reached at ① **26465.** (You must dial the local area code if you're using a cell phone.) The Indonesian Red Cross is at Jalan Imam Bonjol, Km 3, Denpasar (① **0361/480282**), on Bali, and at Jalan Bung Karno 29, Mataram (① **0370/623885**), on Lombok.

Family Travel Bali is an ideal family destination—the whole family, whether you have very young children or older children, will find something to suit their tastes in Bali. Lombok less so, because it doesn't offer the same variety of activities and is much less developed than Bali. Hotels and restaurants are well equipped for children and babies. Nearly all hotels have cots and high chairs and if a restaurant doesn't have a children's menu it's generally happy to make something simple for them to eat. Babysitting is easy to organize both night and day and reasonably priced. Some of the larger hotels have specialist children's clubs with designated children check-in. Generally, youngsters up to the age of 12 are allowed to share a hotel room for free, though some hotels charge a nominal fee. Many attractions offer family packages at great discounts. Children under 4 are usual free but not always, especially at water parks or animal parks. Most supermarkets stock baby food and toiletries, albeit for a very expensive price because most is imported from the West. There's no need to bring strollers as there are very few places to use one. To locate accommodations, restaurants, and attractions that are particularly child-friendly, refer to the "Kids" icon throughout this guide.

Gasoline/Petrol Please see "Getting Around: By Car," earlier in this chapter.

Health Please see the earlier "Health" section.

Hospitals The two best hospitals equipped for foreigners are in Kuta. The **Bali International Medical Centre (BIMC),** Jl. Bypass Ngurah Rai 100X (① **0361/761263**), is open daily from 8am to midnight; you can request them to send a medical person to your hotel. Another option in Kuta is the **International SOS Bali,** Jl. Bypass Ngurah Rai (① **0361/710505**).

Insurance We highly recommend that you have an insurance policy in place before arriving in Bali and Lombok. Make sure that it covers medical expenses. Although the hospitals in Bali are good, there are some services that they can't supply—in these cases, you may be evacuated to Singapore for further medical attention. Some policies don't cover "dangerous activities," which can include surfing, scuba diving, bungy jumping, horseback riding, and some watersports. For information on traveler's insurance, trip cancellation insurance, and medical insurance while traveling, please visit **www.frommers. com/planning/**.

Internet & Wi-Fi Wi-Fi access is increasingly common in Bali. Restaurants, cafes, and even convenience stores in the south often provide complimentary Internet. Increasingly hotels and resorts are doing likewise, though some properties still charge. Around Bali, Internet cafes charge between Rp10,000 and Rp30,000 an hour. You'll find it more difficult to use the Internet outside of south Bali and Ubud. In some remote locations, there may be no Internet or computers at all.

Language English is used widely across the tourist areas in Bali and Lombok, so much so that you barely need to learn a word of Bahasa, the official language of Indonesia, to get around. Most locals, though, don't speak English; see chapter 17 for some useful phrases.

Legal Aid Contact your consulate if you find yourself in legal trouble. See "Embassies & Consulates" above.

LGBT Travelers The Balinese are Hindu, unlike the rest of Indonesia, which is predominately Muslim. In Bali you'll find a relatively rich gay scene although not one that's openly flaunted. Although homosexuality is accepted, any public display of romance, whether straight or gay, is frowned upon. The Indonesian legal age of consent for straight and gay sex is 16. Bali is a gay-friendly place, and it's unlikely that gays will encounter any problems while on holiday, especially in the touristy areas of the south. Gay travelers should spend time in Seminyak, with its open gay scene and plenty of gay-owned and gay-friendly accommodations, bars, and nightclubs. There's also a gay cruising area north of Petitenget beach. For up-to-date information on the best places to stay and Bali's gay scene, check out the following websites: www.bali-rainbows.com; www.utopia-asia.com; www.rainbowtourism.com; www.balifriendlyhotels.com; and www.baligayguide.com. Lombok, a Muslim island, frowns upon homosexuality and you'll find it difficult to find suitable accommodations and accepting people. The only exception is the Gili Islands, where there's a slightly more laid-back attitude.

Mail Your hotel can send mail for you, or you can go to the post office in Denpasar, at Jalan Raya Puputan Renon (℡ **0361/223566**). Other branches are in Kuta, at Jalan Raya Kuta (℡ **0361/754012**), Ubud, and Sanur. For big items, packing and shipping services are in all major tourist areas, but the cost can be exorbitant. The Lombok main post office is at Jalan Sriwijaya, Mataram (℡ **0370/632645**).

Medical Requirements No inoculations or vaccinations are compulsory for entry into Indonesia, but please see the earlier section "Health."

Mobile Phones See "Cell Phones," earlier in this section.

Newspapers & Magazines The *Yak* (covering Seminyak) and the *Bud* (covering Ubud) are the best entertainment and listing magazines on Bali. For Indonesian news, pick up a copy of the *Jakarta Post* or the *Bali Times*.

Packing Bring your swimming suit, sunscreen, and sunglasses of course. But beyond that, a few warm layers are recommended for evenings and visits to inland areas. Certain nightclubs and restaurants have a "smart casual" dress code but most establishments are tolerant of beachwear. An umbrella is also a good idea. For more helpful information on packing for your trip, download our convenient Travel Tools app for your mobile device. Go to www.frommers.com/go/mobile/ and click on the Travel Tools icon.

Passports All non-Indonesians need passports to enter Bali.

○ **Australia** **Australian Passport Information Service** (℡ **131-232**, or visit www.passports. gov.au).

○ **Canada** **Passport Office,** Department of Foreign Affairs and International Trade, Ottawa, ON K1A 0G3 (℡ **800/567-6868;** www.ppt.gc.ca).

- **Ireland   Passport Office,** Setanta Centre, Molesworth Street, Dublin 2 (✆ **01/671-1633;** www.foreignaffairs.gov.ie).

- **New Zealand   Passport Office,** Department of Internal Affairs, 47 Boulcott Street, Wellington, 6011 (✆ **0800/225-050** in New Zealand or 04/474-8100; www.passports.govt.nz).

- **United Kingdom**   Visit your nearest passport office, major post office, or travel agency or contact the **Identity and Passport Service (IPS),** 89 Eccleston Square, London, SW1V 1PN (✆ **0300/222-0000;** www.ips.gov.uk).

- **United States**   To find your regional passport office, check the U.S. State Department website (travel.state.gov/passport) or call the **National Passport Information Center** (✆ **877/487-2778**) for automated information.

Petrol   Please see "Getting Around: By Car," earlier in this chapter.

Police   Dial ✆ **110** for the police. Also see "Emergencies" above.

Safety   Although Bali is one of the safest places to travel in Asia, there's no denying that **traffic** plays the most serious threat to a visitor's life. Sidewalks are constantly abused by cars and motorbikes who see them as quick routes when traffic is at a standstill; at night beware the many gaps in the pavements that have been known to catch the compos and non-compos mentis alike. Drivers think nothing of driving at high speeds through villages and towns, overtaking on bends, braking hard or swerving to avoid chickens, dogs, and potholes. If you feel uncomfortable, ask your driver to slow down, and then ask again. Many drivers think that all visitors to the island like them to drive fast and will therefore show their appreciation for this at the end of the day. Your safety is more important.

With regards to riding a motorcycle, always wear a helmet and be vigilant at all times especially at night when dogs prowl the streets, children cycle their bikes without headlights, and locals walk and gather in nonlit areas. Most riders on the island learn to ride a motorbike at an early age—you'll see some as young as 9 or 10 ferrying their younger brethren—and they don't have to sit for any road test examinations.

The basic rule you need to keep in mind is that as a foreigner the accident is always your fault. The thinking is that if you hadn't been here, the accident wouldn't have happened. Take our advice and book a driver.

If you're staying rurally, the local *banjar* (village council) will take pride in the low crime rate and very often take matters into its own hands if members find any impropriety among their own. Only after they've had their time with the perpetrator, do they call the police.

Although much of Indonesia still relies on graft or backhanders for the smooth conduct of business, crime itself remains low and especially so in the tourist world. However do take the usual safety precautions you would anywhere. Violent crime is rare, pickpockets are not. Exercise considerable caution by using a money belt, particularly in crowded tourist areas, and being careful not to flash large wads of cash. Most hotels or villas will provide you with a safety box; use it. If nothing else, make sure your suitcase has a good lock on it.

Given the world we live in, and notwithstanding the lack of crime, there's still much emphasis on security and you'll encounter standard—if sometimes only rudimentary—security checks at most hotels and restaurants. Don't be alarmed, they search everyone and will usually also want to have a peek in the front and back of your car. Take the slight intrusion in your stride; it's for everyone's benefit.

If you have an issue, contact your consulate (p. 356).

Senior Travel Bali is a perfectly good choice for senior travel, but many attractions don't offer senior discounts. Seniors may want to choose quieter locations such as Jimbaran Bay, Ubud, and East Bali.

Smoking Most restaurants, hotel lobbies, and bars have banned smoking, while Bali legislators are moving to ban smoking on beaches too. Check with your hotel concierge for the latest info.

Solo Travelers Single travelers will find Seminyak and Kuta, with an assortment of nightlife and bars, the most attractive areas on Bali.

Student Travel Check out **STA Travel** (*℃* **800/781-4040** in the U.S; www.statravel. com; and *℃* **0800/819-9339** in the U.K.; www.statravel.co.uk) for the best advice, cheap flights, and accommodations for Bali and Lombok.

Taxes Some hotels and restaurants factor government taxes (10%) into their quoted prices, but most of them put it as an additional charge. Bali has no value-added tax (VAT).

Telephones **To place a call from your home country to Bali:** Dial the international access code (011 in the U.S. and Canada, 0011 in Australia, 0170 in New Zealand, 00 in the U.K.), plus Indonesia's country code **(62),** the city or local area code (**361** for Kuta/Seminyak, Jimbaran, Nusa Dua, Sanur, and Ubud; **362** for Lovina; **363** for Candidasa; **370** for Lombok and the Gilis), and the six-digit phone number (for example, 011 62 362 000000). **Cell phone numbers** don't have a city or local area code, and begin with an 08 followed by a long string of numbers. Dial Indonesia's country code **(62)** followed by the number.

To place a call within Indonesia: You must use the area code if calling between states. For calls within the country, area codes are all preceded by a **0** (for instance, **0361** for Kuta/Seminyak, Jimbaran, Nusa Dua, Sanur, and Ubud, **0363** for Candidasa, **0370** for Lombok, and so on). Dial the city or area code preceded by a **0,** and then the local number (for example, 0362/000000). For cell phones, add a 0 to the number.

To make a landline call to a local landline phone, don't include the local code (that is, dial 1234567 not 0361/1234567).

To place a direct international call from Indonesia: Dial the international access code **(00),** plus the country code, the area or city code, and the number (for example, to call the U.S., you'd dial 00 1 000/000-0000). International country codes are: Australia, **61**; Canada, **1**; New Zealand, **64**; U.K., **44**; U.S., **1**.

To reach the international operator: *℃* **102**.

Time Bali and Lombok are 8 hours ahead of Greenwich Mean Time (G.M.T.), except during daylight saving time, which isn't observed. That's 13 hours ahead of Eastern Standard Time (E.S.T.) in the U.S. For help with time, translations, and more, download our convenient Travel Tools app for your mobile device. Go to www.frommers.com/go/mobile/ and click on the Travel Tools icon.

Tipping Tips are always welcome but not expected. Generally larger more upmarket restaurants and hotels add between 15% and 21% to the bill to cover 10% government tax and allow something for service. As most waiters, masseurs, guides, or taxi drivers earn under Rp100,000 a day and work long hours, an appreciative tip for their hard work is always a nice thing to do. When staying at a villa, if no service has been added, allow between 5% and 10% of the total bill to be split between the staff. Make sure they're all aware, even the gardeners, as some villa managers will pocket the full amount themselves. For longer stays, a discretionary amount is acceptable. Round up taxi bills to the nearest thousand. For help with tip calculations, currency conversions, and more, download our convenient Travel Tools app for your mobile device. Go to www.frommers.com/go/mobile/ and click on the Travel Tools icon.

Toilets   Western-style toilets with seats are becoming more common than the Asian squat variety, though cheap *losmen* (homestays) and some less touristy public places still have the latter. Always carry toilet paper with you, or you might have to use your hand (the left is customary) and the dip bucket.

VAT   See "Taxes" earlier in this section.

Visas   Procedures in Bali, Lombok, and Indonesia can change without given notice. For up-to-date information, contact the nearest Indonesian embassy or consulate in your country. For a list, go to **www.indonesia.go.id**.

Visitors from the Australia, Canada, New Zealand, United Kingdom, United States, and most of Europe can get **Visas on Arrival (VOA)** through Ngurah Rai International Airport or the seaports of Padangbai and Benoa in Bali and Selaparang Airport in Lombok. For stays of up to 30 days, the charge is US$25 payable by credit card and most major currencies. For stays of longer than 30 days, a tourist or business visa must be arranged before arrival.

Your passport must be valid for at least 6 months from the date of your arrival, and must also have at least two blank pages. Overstays are charged US$20 per day for up to 60 days. Overstay violations are liable to 5 years imprisonment or a fine of Rp25 million.

The Indonesian Embassy in **Australia** is at 8 Darwin Ave., Yarralumla, ACT 2600 (✆ **612/62508600;** www.kbri-canberra.org.au); in **New Zealand** at 70 Glen Rd., Kelburn, Wellington, New Zealand (✆ **475/8697-9899;** www.indonesianembassy.org.nz); in the **U.K.** at 38 Grosvenor Square, London W1K 2HW (✆ **020/7499-7661;** www.indonesian embassy.org.uk); in the **U.S.** at 2020 Massachusetts Ave. NW, Washington D.C. 20036 (✆ **202/775-5200;** www.embassyofindonesia.org).

Visitor Information   Browse the **Bali Tourism Board** website at www.balitourism board.org. You can get other Bali travel information at the **Bali Government Tourism Office,** Jl. S. Parman, Renon (✆ **0361/222387;** Mon–Thurs 7am–2pm, Fri 7–11am, Sat 7am–12:30pm), and at the **Department of Tourism, Post, and Telecommunications,** Jl. Raya Puputan, Niti Mandala (✆ **0361/225649;** Mon–Thurs 7am–3pm, Fri till noon). Tourist offices on Lombok can be found at: Jl. Suprato 20 (✆ **0370/621658;** Mon–Thurs 7:30am–2pm, Fri till 11am, Sat 8am–1pm) and Jl. Singosari 2 (✆ **0370/634800;** Mon–Thurs 8am–2pm, Fri till 11am, Sat till 12:30pm) in Mataram; and in Senggigi (✆ **0370/632733**). You can find a list of Frommer's travel apps at www.frommers.com/go/mobile/.

Water   Avoid tap water in Bali and Lombok unless properly boiled. Bottled water is available everywhere, and restaurants in tourist areas seem to use it as a matter of course, but you should always ask to be sure.

Wi-Fi   See "Internet & Wi-Fi," earlier in this section.

Women Travelers   For the female traveler, Bali is a safe island to discover on your own or in a group. On the whole, Balinese men are fairly benign to the appearance of Western women, however we're seeing an increase in visitors from neighboring countries who've come to work on the building sites and in the fields that think nothing of wolf-whistling, cat-calling, and making lewd propositions. Most of them are harmless but you should be vigilant when walking around at night in areas where these men hang out. The only people to be wary of are the **Kuta cowboys,** men who prey on women looking to establish a relationship. For them, this is an opportunity to obtain some much-needed funds and have some fun at someone else's expense.

While traveling around the island, dress appropriately so as not to offend. Although tight shorts and bare shoulders are acceptable on the beaches, they're frowned upon in the more rural areas.

For those traveling to Lombok, as long as you're respectful of the Muslim culture and dress appropriately you shouldn't be bothered.

Bali and Lombok are generally safe and single travelers face no real threat or dangers. That said, don't throw common sense out of the window. Women on their own, in particular, should still be careful especially when out alone in the evening. Both men and women should beware of nightclubs: There have been a few cases of people having their drinks spiked. Never leave your drink unguarded or with a stranger.

BASIC INDONESIAN

17

The national language of Indonesia is Bahasa, but English is spoken widely where travelers to Bali congregate. On Lombok, English is less prevalent. Over 350 different dialects are spoken throughout the Indonesian archipelago but Bahasa, the national language, is spoken by over 65% of the population. Learning simple greetings and phrases will make your visit to Bali more enjoyable for both you and the locals who take an interest in where you come from, what you do for a living, and where you're staying.

The indigenous language to Bali is "Basa Bali," spoken in the home by all Balinese natives. Basa has high, intermediate, and low versions used depending on caste and age of the person being addressed. To avoid the caste intricacies of Basa Bali, most of the local people on the island speak Bahasa outside the home.

BASIC GRAMMAR

Bahasa is easily spoken by nonnative speakers because it's nontonal and written using the Roman alphabet. There are no plurals, genders, or tenses, making it easier to pick up than some other languages. The few basic rules in grammar include the following:

To indicate past tense, place the word sudah before the verb.

To indicate the future tense, place the word akan before the verb.

To form a plural, repeat the word. For example, ayam for chicken, ayam-ayam for chickens.

ESSENTIAL WORDS & PHRASES

GREETINGS

English	Bahasa Indonesian
Hello	**Halo**
Welcome	**Selamat dating**
Goodbye (See you later)	**Sampai jumpa**

English	Bahasa Indonesian
Good morning	**Selamat pagi**
. . . afternoon	**Selamat sore**
. . . evening	**Selamat malam**
. . . night	**Selamat tidur**
Goodbye (Person addressed is leaving)	**Selamat jalan/Dadah**
See you soon	**Sampai ketemu lagi**

USEFUL PHRASES

English	Bahasa Indonesian
Hello, how are you?	**Halo, apa kabar?**
My name is. . .	**Nama saya. . .**
I would like. . .	**Saya mau. . .**
Where is. . . ?	**Dimana. . ?**
the airport	**bandara**
the harbor	**pelabuhan**
the boat	**kapal**
a hotel	**hotel**
the beach	**pantai**
When is. . . ?	**Kapan. . .**
breakfast	**sarapan/makan pagi**
lunch	**makan siang**
dinner	**makan malam**
the performance	**pertunjukan**
How much is that?	**Berapa harganya?**
What time is it?	**Jam berapa sekarang?**
Do you speak English?	**Apakah anda bisa berbahasa Inggris?**
I don't speak Indonesian	**Saya tidak bisa berbahasa Indonesia**
Sorry, but I don't understand	**Maaf, tapi saya tidak mengerti**
Yes	**Ya**
No	**Tidak**
Not yet	**Belum**
Maybe	**Mungkin**
Please	**Tolong**
Excuse me (To draw the attention of a person.)	**Permisi**
Thank you	**Terima kasih**
I'm sorry	**Maaf**
Don't mention it ("No problem")	**Tidak apa-apa**
You're welcome	**Kembali**
Entrance	**Jalan masuk**
Exit	**Jalan keluar**
Toilet/Bathroom	**Kamar mandi**
Men	**Pria**
Women	**Wanita**

EMERGENCIES

English	Bahasa Indonesian
I'm from. . .	**Saya dari Negara. . .**
Help me	**Tolong**
I'm lost	**Saya kesasar**
I'm hurt/sick	**Saya sakit**
Call an ambulance	**Panggillah ambulans**
Call a doctor	**Panggillah Dokter**
I'd like to call this number	**Saya mau telepon nomor ini**
Hospital	**Rumah Sakit**
Police	**Polisi**
Fire	**Kebakaran**
Pharmacy	**Apotek**
Accident	**Kecelakaan**
Emergency	**Darurat**
Please take me to. . .	**Tolong antar saya ke. . .**
I'm allergic to. . .	**Saya alergi. . .**
Where are the toilets?	**Dimana kamar kecil?**
Leave me alone	**Jangan ganggu saya**

NUMBERS

0	**Nol**
1	**Satu**
2	**Dua**
3	**Tiga**
4	**Empat**
5	**Lima**
6	**Enam**
7	**Tujuh**
8	**Delapan**
9	**Sembilan**
10	**Sepuluh**
11	**Sebelas**
12	**Dua belas**
13	**Tiga belas**
14	**Empat belas**
15	**Lima belas**
16	**Enam belas**
17	**Tujuh belas**
18	**Delapan belas**
19	**Sembilan belas**
20	**Dua puluh**
21	**Dua puluh satu**

English	Bahasa Indonesian
22	Dua puluh dua
30	**Tiga puluh**
40	**Empat puluh**
50	**Lima puluh**
60	**Enam puluh**
70	**Tujuh puluh**
80	**Delapan puluh**
90	**Sembilan puluh**
100	**Seratus**
1,000	**Seribu**
10,000	**Sepuluh ribu**
100,000	**Seratus ribu**
1,000,000	**Satu juta**

MONTHS

January	**Januari**
February	**Februari**
March	**Maret**
April	**April**
May	**Mei**
June	**Juni**
July	**Juli**
August	**Agustus**
September	**September**
October	**Oktober**
November	**November**
December	**Desember**

DAYS

Monday	**Senin**
Tuesday	**Selasa**
Wednesday	**Rabu**
Thursday	**Kamis**
Friday	**Jum-at**
Saturday	**Sabtu**
Sunday	**Minggu**

TIME

What time is it?	**Jam berapa sekarang?**
Today	**Hari ini**
Tomorrow	**Besok**
Yesterday	**Kemarin**

English	Bahasa Indonesian
Next week	**Minggu depan**
Next time	**Kapan-kapan**
Hour (o'clock)	**Jam**
Day	**Hari**
Week	**Minggu**
Month	**Bulan**
Year	**Tahun**

TRAVEL & SIGHTSEEING

English	Bahasa Indonesian
Please take me to. . .	**Tolong antar saya ke. . .**
How long is the trip?	**Berapa lama perjalanan?**
How do I get to. . .	**Bagaimana cara saya ke. . .**
Go right	**Belok kanan**
Go left	**Belok kiri**
Go straight	**Jalan terus**
At the corner	**Di sudut**
Next to. . .	**Di samping. . .**
Behind...	**Di belakang...**
In front of. . .	**Di depan. . .**
Opposite	**Di seberang**
Near to. . .	**Dekat dengan. . .**
Far from. . .	**Jauh dari. . .**
Here	**Disini**
There	**Disana**
South	**Selatan**
North	**Utara**
East	**Timur**
West	**Barat**
Stop	**Berhenti**
I am staying at. . .	**Saya tinggal di. . .**

AT THE TABLE

English	Bahasa Indonesian
Restaurant	**Restoran**
What are the house specialties?	**Apa yang special disini?**
May I see a menu?	**Boleh saya lihat menu?**
I'm a vegetarian.	**Saya vegetarian.**
Please don't make the food too spicy.	**Jangan dibikin terlalu pedas.**
I'd like the . . .	**Saya mau. . .**
Waiter	**Mas/Mbak**
May I have the bill?	**Saya mau bayar?**
Keep the change	**Simpan saja kembaliannya**
Enjoy your meal/Bon appétit	**Selamat makan**

Index

See also Accommodations and Restaurant indexes, below.

General Index

Accommodations